MAHOMMEDAN LAW

CONTAINING

THE LAW RELATING TO SUCCESSION AND STATUS

COMPILED FROM

AUTHORITIES IN THE ORIGINAL ARABIC

BY

SYED AMEER ALI, P.C., C.I.E., LL.D., M.A.

BARRISTER-AT-LAW

MEMBER OF THE JUDICIAL COMMITTEE OF HIS MAJESTY'S PRIVY COUNCIL

SEVENTH EDITION

BY

RAJA SAID AKBAR KHAN,

Vol. II

KITAB BHAVAN

NEW DELHI-110002

First Published in India 1986
Reprinted ---- 2008

Published by
Nusrat Ali Nasri for Kitab Bhavan
1214, Kalan Mahal, Darya Ganj, New Delhi-110002.

Printed at : Lahooti Fine Art Press 1711, Sui Walan
New Delhi-110002 Tel.: 23286349

PREFACE TO THE SEVENTH EDITION

This is the seventh edition of the monumental work of the late Syed Amir Ali on Muhammadan Law. The last edition was published in 1965 which was received by the legal circles with great approbation. Since the publication of the last edition quite a number of cases have been decided by our courts on the subject in hand and these are being given as an addenda in this edition.

It is hoped that the profession will welcome this edition also.

RAJA SAID AKBAR KHAN

20th October, 1976.

PREFACE TO THE FIFTH EDITION

In the preface to the Fourth Edition of this work I ventured to refer to the necessity on the part of Judicial Officers and Lawyers practising in the Courts of Justice for a study of the Mahommedan Law, especially the principles relating to succession and status. The necessity is so obvious that I hardly think I should repeat my suggestion. How often unacquaintance with the rules leads to miscarriage of justice is illustrated by the cases which I have referred to in this work.

The admirable work of Mr. Mayne greatly helped the study of Hindu Law. A study of Hindu Law, however, is not attended with the same difficulty which a Judge experiences in the case of the Musulman Law. The Mitakshara exercises undisputed authority in Upper India; the Mithila school is recognised only in a part of Northern India; whilst the Mayukha is dominant in the Maharashtra country and the expositions of the Smriti Chundrika are undisputed in Southern India.

The Mahommedan Law, on the other hand, is divided into five schools; the Shiahs and the Sunnis differ fundamentally in their rules and principles of exegesis; the four Sunni schools, although agreeing in the principles, differ in their expositions. These differences add to the difficulty of understanding the governing rules. I venture to hope that I have succeeded in presenting the Law dealt with in this volume in as clear a light as possible.

AMEER ALI.

July, 1928.

PREFACE TO THE FIRST EDITION

To those not born and bred within the pale of Islam, the study of the Musulman Law is usually attended with great difficulties. The works which at present exist in the English language are few in number; and though France has been more prolific in this respect, the valuable contributions of the Moslems to the Science of Jurisprudence and Law are, for the most part, wrapped in the intricate folds of a language as difficult to acquire as it is copious in its diction.

In India, even among educated Moslems, a knowledge of the Musulman Law, if not actually obsolete, has become extremely rare. Few cultivate it as a science, or study it analytically as a branch of comparative law. Those who apply themselves to its study are satisfied with a barren and unprofitable acquaintance with the simple rules of inheritance. This is the consequence of the policy inaugurated by Lord William Bentinck. Prior to his time, the Musulmans occupied the foremost position among the people of India. The cultivation of their law and their literature was encouraged by successive British Governors; their traditions were respected, and they themselves were treated with a certain amount of consideration due to the former rulers of the land. All this changed under Lord William Bentinck's administration, and the Indian Mahommedans were relegated into the cold shade of neglect. Their institutions gradually died out, and the old race of *Moulvis* and *Muftis*, who had shed a lustre on the reigns of the Marquis of Wellesley and the Marquis of Hastings, became extinct. Whilst the French in Algeria were endeavouring to give a new impetus to the cultivation of Moslem Law and literature by subventions and Government assistance, and whilst they were utilising the indigenous institutions with the object of improving the condition of their subjects, the British in India allowed the study of every branch of Mahommedan learning to fall into decay. The mischief which has resulted from this mistaken policy can hardly be overrated. Owing to an imperfect knowledge of Musulman Jurisprudence, of Musulman manners, customs and usages, it is not infrequent, even now, to find cases decided by the highest Law Courts against the principles of the Mahommedan Law. It is not surprising, therefore, to learn that every miscarriage of justice adds to the long roll of indictment which the popular mind has framed against British rule in India. Latterly a desire, no doubt, has been evinced by some of the Local Governments—notably by the Governments of Bengal and of Madras—to repair to some extent the evils caused by the neglect of half a century. Nothing tangible, however, has yet been achieved towards securing efficient administration of justice in Mahommedan cases.

Owing to the broad divergences existing between the various legal schools, no branch of the Mahommedan Law is perhaps more difficult to master than that relating to personal *status*.

The treatise which I now place in the hands of the public is intended to obviate partially those difficulties, and supply in some measure the want of a compendious work on the Mahommedan Personal Law. I have embodied in it the substance of a series of discourses delivered by me in several sessions as Lecturer on Mahommedan Law at the Presidency College of Calcutta. To this I have added a synoptical sketch of the Sunni and the Shiah Law of Inheritance.

I have endeavoured in the following passage to deal with the subject from a comparative and analytical point of view. How far I have succeeded, I leave to the public to judge.

I venture, however, to hope that, as this treatise is entirely *sui generis* and tentative in its character and scope, a generous reception will be accorded to it, in spite of defects which it must necessarily contain.

In order that this volume should be useful to the practical lawyer as well as to the student, I have carefully verified the legal *dicta* and scrupulously given my references.

Before mentioning the original authorities I have consulted, a few remarks on the works already in existence in the European languages will not, I think, be without interest to the reader.

Macnaghten's *Principles and Precedents of the Mahommedan Law*, Hamilton's translation of the Persian version of the *Hedaya*, Baillie's *Digest*, Shama Churn Sircar's *Lectures*, and Mr. Rumsey's *Law of Inheritance* are the only works in the English language which require any specific mention. Until recently, Macnaghten's work was regarded as the greatest authority on Musulman Law, though latterly it has fallen much in the estimation of lawyers and Judges. I venture, however, to think that, in spite of many defects and frequent inaccuracies, Macnaghten's Synopsis of the Hanafi and the Shiah Law may safely be regarded as the most useful elementary treatise for students preparing for public examinations.

Hamilton's translation of the *Hedaya* is of great practical value to those who can discriminate between the doctrines of the various Sunni schools. The difficulty, however, which lawyers frequently have in finding out in the *Hedaya* the principles actually in force among the Hanafis, detracts much from its usefulness.

Mr. Baillie's *Digests* are a free paraphrase of portions of the *Fatawai 'Alamgiri* and the *Shara'ya-ul-Islam*. They are works of great merit, and afford considerable assistance to all engaged in the study of Mahommedan Law. In spite of Mr. Baillie's great erudition, inaccuracies are to be found, to one of which prominent attention was directed in the case of *Mst. Asloo*.[1]

The usefulness of these *Digests* would have been greatly enhanced, if Mr. Baillie had thought it worth his while to give in every case, as he has done in some instances, the references to the authorities he was paraphrasing or translating. This omission has been, to some extent, supplied by Babu Shama Churn Sircar, whose lectures in other respects are, in the main, transcriptions of Baillie's *Digests*. His introductions are of great value to all lawyers anxious to study scientifically Musulman Jurisprudence.

Mr. Rumsey's treatise is an extremely valuable and comprehensive work on the Hanafi Law of Inheritance.

The French works on Musulman Law and Musulman Jurisprudence throw into shade anything existing in the English language. D'Ohsson's *Tableaux Generale de l'Empire Ottoman*, published under the patronage of the King of Sweden in 1778, will always remain a magnificent monument of Western genius and industry. It contains by far the most complete and correct summary of the Hanafi Law, civil, criminal, political and moral, in force in the Ottoman Empire.

Besides D'Ohsson's grand work, Perron, Sautayra, Querry, Sice, Lasalle, de Menerville, Du Caurroy, Vincent, and various others have enriched the French language with valuable contributions on Mahommedan Law. All these authorities

---

1 20 Weekly Reporter, p. 297.

have proved of great value to me in preparing the present treatise.

The historical portion of my Introduction is founded on the *al-Kamil* of Ibn-ul-Athir and the judicial on Imam Fakhruddin Razi's *al-Mahsul* (المحصول),[1] the *Kukkadamat* of Ibn-Khaldun,[2] the *Millal-wan-nihal* of Shahrastani,[3] and D'Ohssons *Tableaux Generale*.

The principles of the Shiah Law have been derived from the *Shara'ya-ul-Islam*, the *Mafatih*, the *Irshad-ul-Allamah*, and the *Jam'a-ush-Shittat*. This last work is a valuable digest of Shiah cases, and the *dicta* contained therein have an authority equal to those of the *Fatawai 'Alamgiri* among the Hanafis. Besides the above I have also consulted the *Nail-ul-Maram*, the *Jam'a-i-'Abbasi*, the *Mabsut* and the *Tahrir-ul-Ahkam*. For Shiah traditions I have referred to the *Bihar-ul-Anwar*.

For the Hanafi Law, I have consulted the two *Fatawas*, the *Kanz-ud-Dakaik* (Persian translation), the *Hedaya* (English and Persian translations), the *Fusul-ul-Imadia*, the *Inaya*, the *Kifaya*, the *Durr-ul-Mukhtar*, the *Radd-ul-Muhtar*, Ibrahim Halebi, &c.

For the Shaf'ei and Maliki Law, the *Kitab-ul-Anwar*, the *al-Muharrar*, the *Ikhtilaf-ul-A'immah*, Perron's translation of Sidi Khalil Sautayra, &c.

In addition to those already mentioned, I have referred to a number of other works, all of which are specifically mentioned in the notes.

Whilst acknowledging the various authorities to whom I have been greatly indebted, I desire in this place to convey my thanks to Dr. Rost and Mr. A. G. Macpherson, Legal Adviser to the Secretary of State for India, for allowing me the unrestricted use of the India Office Oriental and Law Libraries.

The importance at this moment of the study of the Personal Law of the Mahommedans cannot, I think, be overrated.

Belonging myself to the little known, though not unimportant, philosophical and legal school of the M'utazilas, and thus occupying a vantage ground of observation as regards the general progress of ideas among other sections of the Musulmans in India,

---

1 India Office Copy, A. b., p. 319.

2 Du Slane's Translation, *Prolegomene d' Ibn-Khaldoun.*

3 Curetone's Edition.

I cannot but observe the movement which has been going on for sometime among them. The advancement of culture, and the development and growth of new ideas, have begun to exercise the same influence on them as on other races and peoples. The young generation is tending unconsciously towards the M'utazilite doctrines, whilst the old, if Shiahs, become Usulis, and if Sunnis, Puritans of the Wahabi type.

It must not be supposed, however, that this movement results from the weakening of the Islamic faith. It originates more from the desire to revert to the pristine purity of Islam, and to cast off the excrescences which have marred its glory in later times. The progress of thought is chiefly evidenced by the views which the great majority of Moslems now entertain respecting the institutions of polygamy, slavery, and the facility of divorce without the sanction of the Kazi. Whatever may have been the necessity for polygamy in the earliest stages of society, in modern times it can only be regarded as an unmitigated and unendurable evil. Owing to the growth of these views and a better appreciation of the spirit of the Koran, the Moslems of India generally look upon polygamy as opposed to the Islamic precepts.

To me it appears that great changes are imminent in the social institutions and the personal laws of the Indian Musulmans. How they will be achieved, whether by a general Synod of Moslem doctors or by the direct action of the Legislature, it is impossible to say.

In view of this imperceptible current of ideas, imperceptible perhaps to outsiders, but not to those who live within the bosom of Islam, it is particularly necessary that those who hold in their hands the destiny of India should pay attention to the laws of the only homogeneous people in that country.

Should this treatise prove useful in extending a more general knowledge of the Personal Law of the Mahommedans, I shall consider myself amply repaid for the time I have devoted to this, my holiday task.

AMEER ALI.

REFORM CLUB,
20th December, 1880.

ADDENDA

Case-law which has developed after the publication of last edition (1965) is being given as an addenda.

Page 19

Foot Note (1) See also P L D 1961 Lah. 1036, P L D 1961 Lah. 431, P L D 1963 Lah. 141 (F. B.), P L D 1965 S C 104.

Page 22

Foot Note (1) See also A I R 1928 Oudh 568 (570), where it has been held that Family arrangement cannot be stated by mere conduct. There must be a *bona fide* dispute, the settlement of which can be termed family arrangement.

A I R 1932 P C 158 (161). In a compromise of conflicting claims, family arrangement was arrived at, whereby the widow agreed to take whatever her claim was not absolutely but subject to certain condition. The compromise being a family arrangement was binding on the parties.

Page 23

Foot Note (3) Add : It must be noted that according to the latest Legislation in Pakistan, Custom is no longer the law of the land. It is merely of historical value as a relic of the past.

Foot Note (4) Add : Custom is no longer the rule of decision in matters of succession or alienation of a Muslim.

Foot Note (5) Add : The above-noted Privy Council decision is no longer law in Pakistan.

Page 29

Foot Note (1) See also P L D 1971 S C 366.

Page 30

Foot Note (1) But now see section 4 of the Family Laws Ordinance VIII of 1961, page 531, whereby law of representation has been introduced in the case of male and female lineal descendants of the propositus.

Page 134

Foot Note (2) See also A I R 1938 Lah. 462, A I R 1949 Cal. 436, P L D 1972 Kar. 653.

Page 161

Foot Note (3) See also P L D 1968 Lah. 1216, P L D 1969 Dacca 47.

Page 173

Foot Note (1) See also 1969 D L C 613.

Page 180

Foot Note (1) See also A I R 1932 P C 25, P L D 1968 Lah. 587, 1968 S C M R 335.

Page 190

Foot Note (1) See also P L D 1970 Lah. 503 (513).

Page 191

Foot Note (1) See also P L D 1970 Lah. 503 (513).
Foot Note (3) See also 1969 D L C 613.

Page 221

Foot Note (4) See P L D 1969 Dacca 47 ; P L D 1970 Azad J & K 9 at page 12, P L D 1970 Lah. 475. A Hanafi minor girl given in marriage by her father or grandfather even if the marriage has been consummated with consent before attainment of puberty (16) or force before the age of 18 retains her option of repudiation of marriage.

Page 225

Foot Notes (1) & (2) See also P L D 1964 Lah. 382, P L D 1970 Lah. 1, P L D 1972 Pesh. 1 (10). Father is competent to get the custody of the minor children after the mother ceases to be entitled to custody, 1975 S C M R 305 where wife on account of illtreatment by the husband is compelled to go to the house of her parents taking alongwith her male children above the age of 7, she can't be deprived of such custody at the instance of the delinquent husband.

P L D 1966 Azad J & K 1, Welfare of the minor is the decisive factor in case of custody of a minor but ordinarily welfare of the minor lies in the minor being allowed to remain in the custody of the parent whom the personal law entrusts with custody.

P L D 1965 Lah. 695. There is no Qur'anic or traditional text on the right of Hizanat. In the light of the conflicting views expressed in various textbooks of Muslim Law on the subject, the courts keeping in view the welfare of the minor are competent to come to their own conclusions.

Therefore minor son and daughter remaining in custody of the mother for 9 years and reared and brought up by her without any support from the father, held that the welfare of the minor lay in allowing the minors to remain in custody of the mother.

P L D 1970 Kar. 619, P L D 1969 Lah. 166. Mother to retain the custody of minor daughter till the attainment of puberty.

Page 229

Foot Notes (3) & (4) See P L D 1965 Lah. 695, P L D 1963 Kar. 465, P L D 1967 Lah. 333. Divorced mother entitled to retain custody of minor daughter till puberty provided she does not marry minors *ghair mahram*. Anyhow the loss of qualification is not absolute and she will still remain Hazina if there is no person better entitled to custody.

P L D 1969 Lah. 166. Custody of a minor married girl is to remain with the mother till she attains puberty and cannot be given to the husband of the minor girl.

Page 241

Foot Note (1) See P L D 1968 Lah. 587. Marriage described as an act of Ibadat, its objects are Sakun (peace of mind), Muwaddat (mutual love) etc.

Page 244

Foot Note (1) See P L D 1968 Lah. 1216, P L D 1969 Dacca 47. Proposal and aoceptance must be uttered by contracting parties to the marriage personally or through his or her vakil in the presence and within the hearing of the witnesses.

Page 246

Foot Note (2) In Pakistan age of majority for purposes of marriage of a girl has been fixed at 16 years. See Dissolution of Muslim Marriages Act in the Appendix.

Page 254

Foot Note (1) See also 1969 D L C 613, where it has been held that acknowledgment of a person as son raises a strong presumption of a valid marriage between the acknowledger and the mother of the acknowledgee.

Page 255

Foot Note (6) See also P L D 1968 Lah. 1216, P L D 1969 Dacca 47.

Page 292

Foot Note (1) See al so P L D 1970 Lah. 503 (513).

Foot Note (3) See also 1969 D L C 613.

Page 294

Foot Note (2) P L D 1968 Lah. 587, 1968 S C M R 335. Held marriage with a fifth in the presence of four wives is irregular but the child of such union is legitimate.

Page 333

Foot Note (1) See also P L D 1969 Dacca 47, P L D 1970 Azad J & K 1 (12), P L D 1970 Lah. 457. Girl given in marriage by father or other guardian while below 16 has option of repudiating the marriage between 16 and 18 even if the marriage has been consummated before 16.

Page 366

Foot Note (1) See also P L D 1967 Azad J & K 32. Wife refusing to live with the husband without a just cause, not entitled to maintenance nor to dissolution of marriage on account of non-maintenance under such circumstances.

P L D 1966 Lah. 763 Husband duty bound to maintain his wife. Past maintenance can also be decreed from the date of accrual of cause of action.

P L D 1971 Lah. 151. Widowed mother of a minor son entitled to claim past maintenance for period of Hizanat from the grandfather of the minor boy.

Foot Note (3) See also P L D 1967 Azad J & K 32.

Page 372

Foot Note (4) See also P L D 1967 Lah. 1104 (1109). An agreement of the husband with the wife allowing her to live separately if he takes a second wife is not opposed to public policy under Muslim Law. In such a case the husband would not be entitled to a decree for restitution of conjugal rights.

Page 373

See also P L D 1967 Lah. 1104 (1109). Held a husband had entered into an agreement that wife would be entitled to separate maintenance in case he marries a second wife would not be entitled to decree for restitution of conjugal rights after he has married second wife.

Page 391

Foot Note (2) See also P L D 1972 Pesh. 37.

Page 394

Foot Note (1) See also P L D 1967 Pesh. 328, P L D 1969 S C 194. The principle of Asumat presupposes two agreements with regard to dower by agreement in private for a real amount and the other agreement in public for the glorification of the family Asumat precedes the marriage. But dower fixed by a registered deed cannot be challenged.

Page 400

Foot Note (1) See 1968 D L C 143. Payment of prompt dower is condition precedent to the decree for restitution of conjugal rights even if the marriage has been consummated.

1970 D L C 276. Non-payment of prompt dower good ground for refusing to the husband decree for restitution of conjugal rights.

Page 411

Foot Note (1) See also 1970 D L C 560. Dower is a debt owed by the husband to the wife.

1970 D L C 260. Written statement of the wife in matrimonial proceedings that that she demanded the dower debt which has not been paid should be treated as demand for prompt dower.

A I R 1927 All. 319. Possession of widow after husband's death shall be presumed to be as lien for payment of dower debt.

A I R 1927 All. 268. Execution of deed stipulating payment of dower on demand and securing its payment by mortgage of immovable property. Such execution converts the dower debt into mortgage debt.

Page 416

Foot Note (1) See also 1970 D L C 560.

Page 434

Foot Note (3) See also P L D 1967 S C 97 where Khula' has been described as "a charter granted to wife".

Page 436

Foot Note (3) See also P L D 1962 S C 55, P L D 1965 Kar. 185. Held under Shia law Talak must be orally pronounced in the presence of the wife and two witnesses in the set form of Arabic words.

Page 453

Foot Note (2) See P L D 1974 S C 22.

Page 459

Foot Note (1) See also P L D 1970 Lah. 1, where it was held that Khula' is not the same thing as Talak and a wife who has obtained a Khula' from her husband can remarry the same husband without undergoing an intervening marriage.

Page 466

Foot Note (6) The recent trends in Pakistan are that the husband is not the sole arbiter in case of Khula'. See P L D 1975 Azad J & K 27. Held that even under Hanafi Law, the power of a Judge to grant Khula' is not dependant on the consent of the husband.

P L D 1975 Lah. 766. One of the conditions for the grant of a Khula' is that if the wife has obtained on marriage some tangible returnable property from the husband, she should be made to return it, in case the husband does not forego the same and asks for its return.

But if during the trial he makes no demand it would be presumed that he conferred no benefits or he would not seek the return thereof.

P L D 1975 Lah. 241. Wife entitled to Khula' if she satisfies the conscience of the court that it would be forcing her into a hateful union. Wife to return the benefits received if the husband so demands or insists upon it.

P L D 1968 Lah. 411. Khula' cannot be granted on the ground of wife's self-confessed adultery. Khula' would not be granted on the ground for which wife is exclusively responsible. If the husband is responsible for the rift marriage may be dissolved. If the husband is not blamable nor does the blame lie on the wife but unbridgeable gulf of differences exists, the marriage may be dissolved.

P L D 1963 Dacca 602, P L D 1969 B J 5, P L D 1967 S. C. 97, P L D 1972 Kar. 40. Wife entitled to Khula' as of right if she can prove circumstances which show that keeping the marriage intact would be forcing her into a hateful union. P L D 1971 S C 192 (192—196). In a suit for dissolution of marriage on the ground of habitual cruelty, misappropriation of property ; non-maintenance, a new plea of Khula' if allowed by the High Court is grossly improper.

Page 475

Foot Note (3) See also P L D 1964 S C 456.

Page 484

Foot Note (1) See also P L D 1963 Dacca 602. Husband's accusation of wife's intimacy or love with another, is not accepted as a ground of *Lian*.

CONTENTS

		PAGES
TABLE OF CASES CITED	... ...	v—xxii
TECHNICAL TERMS EXPLAINED	... ...	xxiii—xxv
INTRODUCTION	... ...	1—14

PART I

The Law Relating to Succession

CHAPTER I—GENERAL OBSERVATIONS

Section I—Applicability of the Mahommedan Law ...	15—19
Section II—Change of Sect—Effect—Limitations on the disposing powers of a Mahommedan — Joint-Family Custom	20—29
Section III—Principles of Differentiation between Heirs and Non-Heirs	29—34
Section IV—Funeral Charges—Devolution of the Right of Inheritance	35—42
Section V—Ancient Arab Customs—The Reforms of Mohammed	42—44

CHAPTER II—HANAFI LAW OF SUCCESSION

Section I—Classification of Heirs	44—48
Section II—*'Asabah* (Agnates) or "Residuaries" ...	48—53
Section III—Uterine Relations or "Distant Kindred"...	53—63
Section IV—The Doctrine of *Wala*	63—66
Section V—The Doctrine of Return or *Radd* ...	66—68
Section VI—Double Inheritance or Vested Interests ...	68-69
Section VII—The Doctrine of Increase or *Aul* ...	69-70
Section VIII—Posthumous Children, etc.	70-71
Section IX—Miscellaneous Examples	71—80

CHAPTER III—CAUSES OF EXCLUSION FROM INHERITANCE

Section I—Partial Exclusion	80-81
Section II—Total Exclusion	81—85

CHAPTER IV

The *Mafkud* or Missing Person	86—89

PAGES

CHAPTER V

Maliki and Shaf'ei Rules of Succession ... 89—93

CHAPTER VI—SHIAH LAW OF SUCCESSION

Section I—Classification of Heirs ... ... 94—98
Section II—Consanguineous Relations ... 98—102
Section III—*Miras-ul-ansab* ... ... 102—106
Section IV—The Succession of Heirs of the Second Class ... ... 106—109
Section V—The Succession of Relations of the Third Class ... ... 109—111
Section VI—Rules relating to the Succession of Husbands and Wives (*Ahkam-ul-Azwaj*) ... 111—114
Section VII—Causes of Absolute Exclusion from Inheritance (*Mawanah-ul-Irs*) ... ... 114—118
Section VIII—Relative Exclusion الحجب (*al-hajab*) ... 118—120
Section IX—General Rules of Succession ... 120—122

CHAPTER VII

The Khojahs and Cutchi Memons ... ... 123—131

CHAPTER VIII

The Bait-ul-Mal 132-133

PART II

The Law Relating to Status

CHAPTER I

The Conflict of Law ... ... 134—169

CHAPTER II—THE STATUS OF LEGITIMACY

Section I—Sunni Doctrines ... ... 169—185
Section II—Shiah Doctrines ... ... 185—189
Section III—Presumption of Legitimacy ... 189—195

CHAPTER III—THE DOCTRINE OF ACKNOWLEDGMENT

Section I—Acknowledgment of Paternity ... 195—200
Section II—Acknowledgment of other Relationship ... 200—209

CHAPTER IV—THE *Wilayet-ul-ijbar*, THE *Patria Potestas*

The Right of Guardianship for Marriage ... 209—222

PAGES

CHAPTER V

The Custody of Children (*Al-Hizanat*) ... 222—240

CHAPTER VI—THE STATUS OF MARRIAGE

Section I—General Observations ... ... 241—247
Section II—The Legal Disability to Marriage (*Asbab-ut-Tahrim*) ... ... 247—255
Section III—The Form of Marriage ... ... 255—263
Section IV—Consent 263-264
Section V—Guardianship for Purposes of Marriage ... 264—271
Section VI—Express or Implied Consent ... 271—276
Section VII—Testimony ... ... 276—283
Section VIII—Conditions of Marriage ... ... 283—288
Section IX—Valid Retirement (*Khilwat-us-Sahih*) ... 288—291
Section X—Proof of Marriage ... ... 291—293

CHAPTER VII—ILLEGAL AND INVALID MARRIAGES—OPTION OF PUBERTY—CAUSES FOR WHICH MARRIAGE MAY BE CANCELLED—EFFECT OF CHANGE OF RELIGION ON THE STATUS OF MARRIAGE

Section I—Illegal and Invalid Marriages ... 293—315
Section II—Further Principles Relating to Invalid Marriages ... ... 315—320
Section III—Invalid Marriages (*continued*) ... 320—326
Section IV—*Al-Kafat*, or Equality in Marriage ... 326—331
Section V—The Option of Puberty (*Khyar-ul-Bulugh*) ... 331—340
Section VI—Causes for which a Marriage may be cancelled ... ... 340—344

CHAPTER VIII

Effect of Change of Religion on the Status of Marriage 344—353

CHAPTER IX

Marriage under the Shiah Law ... ... 354—357

CHAPTER X

Temporary Marriages ... ... 358—363

CHAPTER XI—RIGHTS AND DUTIES OF THE MARRIED PARTIES

Section I—Maintenance—Absent Husband ... 364—380
Section II—Conjugal Domicile and Restitution of Conjugal Rights ... ... 380—384

PAGES

Section III—Maintenance of Children, Parents and other Relations ... ... 384—390

CHAPTER XII—*Mahr* OR DOWER—PROMPT AND DEFERRED DOWER—WIDOW'S LIEN FOR DOWER

Section I—General Observations ... ... 390—397
Section II—Prompt and Deferred Dower ... 397—416
Section III—Refusal of Conjugal Rights ... 416—422
Section IV—Miscellaneous Principles Concerning Dower ... ... 422—431

CHAPTER XIII—DISSOLUTION OF THE MARRIAGE CONTRACT—PRE-ISLAMIC INSTITUTIONS—*Talak*—DIFFERENCE AMONG THE SCHOOLS

Section I—General Observations ... ... 431—434
Section II—*Talak* ... ... 434—438
Section III—Capacity for *Talak* ... ... 438—453
Section IV—*Talak-ul-Mariz* (Repudiation by the Sick) 453—458
Section V—Miscellaneous Principles ... ... 458—466

CHAPTER XIV

Khula and *Mubarat* ... ... 466—477

CHAPTER XV—DISSOLUTION OF THE STATUS OF MARRIAGE BY A DECREE OF THE JUDGE—FOR WHAT CAUSES—*L'aan*—DIFFERENCE AMONG THE SCHOOLS

Section I—Cruelty, Ill-treatment and Desertion ... 477—483
Section II—*L'aan* ... ... 484—487
Section III—The Legal Consequences resulting from the Proceeding by Imprecation 487-488
Section IV—*Talak-ul-Innin*—Impotency as a Cause of Divorce ... ... 488—492

CHAPTER XVI

The Status of Infancy—Personal Emancipation—Emancipation of Property—Indian Act IX of 1875 493—496

CHAPTER XVII

Guardianship or Tutelage—Its Object and Scope under the Mahommedan Law—The Father the Primary Guardian—Testamentary Guardians—Indian Act IX of 1880 ... ... 496—508
Appendices ... ... 509—555
Index ... ... 557—572

TABLE OF CASES CITED

PAGE

A

A *v.* B 366, 491
Abasi *v.* Dunne 229, 232
Abbas Naskar *v.* Chairman District Board 40
Abbasi Begum *v.* Rajrup Koer 507
Abdool Adood *v.* Mohammud Makmi 26
Abdool Futteh Moulvie *v.* Zebunnissa Khatun ... 380
Abdool Razak *v.* Agha Mahomed Jaffer Bindanim 19, 181, 196
Abdul *v.* Hussenbi 381
Abdul Ali Ismailji and his wife Husanbi, *In re* ... 381, 436
Abdul Aziz *v.* *Mst.* Bashiran 487
Abdul Bari *v.* Nasir Ahmad 30
Abdul Cadur Haji Mahomed *v.* Turner 128
Abdul Ghani *v.* Aziz-ul-Huq 350, 352
Abdul Hossain Khan *v.* Bibi Sona Deva ... 23, 27
Abdul Hussain *v.* Ghulam Hussain 33
Abdul Kadir *v.* Salima 383, 390, 420, 421
Abdul Karim *v.* Amina Bibi 383
Abdul Karim *v.* *Mst.* Fazilat-oon-nissa ... 403
Abdul Karim *v.* *Mst.* Muniran 505
Abdul Khader *v.* Azeema Bi 451
Abdul Khader *v.* Chidambaram Chattiyar ... 26, 508
Abdul Latif Khan *v.* Niaz Ahmed ... 273
Abdul Majid Khan *v.* Krishnamachariar 37, 40
Abdul Razzaq *v.* Agha Mohammad ... 19, 192, 197
Abdul Rehman Kutty *v.* Aisha Beevi 178, 185
Abdus Sattar *v.* *Mst.* Agida Bibi 409
Abdul Serang *v.* Putee Bibi 45
Abdul Wahab Khan *v.* Mushtaq Ahmed ... 409, 411, 412
Abdul Wahid Khan *v.* *Mst.* Nuran Bibi 33
Abdullah *v.* Shams-ul-Haq 412
Abdur Rahman *v.* Inayat Bibi 394
Abdus Samad *v.* Alimuddin 412
Abraham *v.* Abraham 18, 24 127,
Achina Bibee *v.* Ajeejunnissa Bibee 25, 26
Achiruddin Ahmed *v.* Sakina Bewa 34

PAGE

Aga Mahomed Jaffer Bindanim *v*. Koolsoom Beebee ... 113, 379
Ahmad Ali *v*. Sabha Khatun 457
Ahmad Qasim *v*. Khatun Bibi ... 378, 445, 446, 451
Ahmed Hussain *v*. *Mst*. Khadija 409, 410
Ahsanullah *v*. Najabat Ali 192, 200
Aisha Bibi *v*. Subodh Chakravarty 346
Aishan Bibi *v*. Sain 366
Akbarally *v*. Muhammadally 19
Akimullah Khan *v*. Abadi Begum 508
Alauddin *v*. Farkhanda Akhtar 340
Ali Bakhsh *v*. Allah Dad 412
Ali Bakhsh Khan *v*. Kaeem Bibee 407
Ali Hussain *v*. Sajuda Begum 113
Ali Muhammad Khan *v*. Azizullah Khan 412
Alimunnessa Khatoon *v*. Hasan Ali 28
Allah Diwaya *v*. Kammon Mai 339
Allisaheb *v*. Shesho Gobind Kul Karni 40
Amanatunnissa *v*. Bashirunnissa... 409
Amar Ilahi *v*. *Mst*. Rashida Akhtar ... 226, 229, 230, 235
Ameer Ammal *v*. Lankara Narayan Chetty 413
Ameerunnissa, *In the matter of* 229
Ameerunnissa *v*. Moradunnissa 413
Amin Beg *v*. Saman 350
Amir Dulhin *v*. Baijnath Sing 40
Amir Hassan Khan *v*. Mohammad Nazir Hussain ... 412
Amiruddin *v*. Khatun Bibi 435, 437
Amjad Khan *v*. Ashraf Khan 34
A. M. Muhammad Ibrahim *v*. Ma Ma 394
Anis Begum *v*. Mohammad Istifa Wali Khan ... 421
Anjumanara Begum *v*. Nawab Arif Kadir 34
Ansar Ahmad *v*. Samidan 230, 235
Ardhanari Mudaliar *v*. Abdul Rahiman 505
Asa Beevi *v*. Karuppan 31
Asgur Ali *v*. Munaffat Ali 263
Asha *v*. Kadir Ibrahim Rowther 446, 449
Ashabai v. Tyeb Haji Rahimutalla 27, 128
Ashraf Ali *v*. Assad Ali 450
Ashrufooddowla Ahmad Hossain Khan *v*. Hyder Hossain Khan 179, 191, 192, 196, 200
Asirunnessa Khatun *v*. Buzloo Meah 384
Asloo *v*. Umdatoonnissa 113
Assamathennessa Bibee *v*. Roy Luchmeeput Singh ... 37

PAGE

Atchley *v.* Spriggs 172
Ayat-un-nissa *v.* Karam Ali 450, 457
Aylsford Peerage, the 172
Azeemun *v.* Asgar Ali 412
Azima Bibi *v.* Munshi Shamalanand 19
Azimunnissa Begum *v.* Clement Dale 15, 16
Aziz *v.* *Mst*. Naro 457
Aziz Bano *v.* Muhammad 221, 333
Azizullah Khan *v.* Ahmadullah Khan 411, 412
Azizunnissa Khatoon *v.* Karimunnissa Khatoon 181, 301
Azmat Ali Khan *v.* Lalli Begum 196, 199
Azmatullah *v.* Imtiaz Begum 378, 451

B

Bachchoo *v.* Bismillah 444
Bachman *v.* Bachman 39
Bachun *v.* Hamid Hussain 409
Badal Aurat *v.* The Queen-Empress 267, 336
Badarunnissa Bibee *v.* Mafiatulla 449
Badruddin *v.* Aisha Begum 369
Badrunnissa *v.* Mafittala 457, 482
Bafatun *v.* Bilaiti Khanum 19, 65, 66, 85, 113
Bai Baiba *v.* Bai Daguba 42
Bai Baiji *v.* Bai Santok 27
Bai Hansa *v.* Abdulla Mustaffa 421
Bai Jina *v.* Kharwa Jina 383
Bai Machhbai *v.* Bai Hirbai 196
Bai Saroobai *v.* Hussain Somji 34
Baindail *v.* Baindail 159
Baker *v.* Baker 438
Baker Hussain Khan *v.* Shurfunnissa Begum ... 190, 191
Bakhshan *v.* Dolhin 504
Bakshi Kishen Prasad *v.* Thakur Das 253
Balak Ram *v.* Inayat Begum 40
Balqis Fatima *v.* Najmul Ikram Qureshi ... 434, 451, 469
Bano Begum *v.* Mir Aun Ali 394
Basha *v.* Muthan 506
Basir Ali *v.* Hafiz 394
Bashir Ahmad *v.* Zubaida 397
Bayabai *v.* Ismail Ahmad 388
Bayspoole *v.* Collins 422
Bazayet Hossein *v.* Dooli Chand 41

PAGE

Bedar Bukht v. Mirza Khurrum Bukht 401
Beedhun Bibee v. Fuzaloollah 230
Beeju Bi v. Syed Murtuja 409, 412
Behram Khan v. Akhtar Begum 339
Begum v. Faiz Bakhsh 263
Begum Zohra Majid v. Mohammad Ishfaqul Majid ... 480
Bethell v. Hillyard 144, 145
Bhagwan Bakhsh v. Drigbijai 19
Bhagwant Singh v. Kallu 83
Bhaiya Sher Bahadur v. Bhaiya Ganga Bakhsh Singh ... 19, 158
Bhawal v. Bajnath Partap Narain 504
Bholanath v. Maqbulunnissa 41
Bhoocha v. Elahi Bux 225, 230, 235
Bhutnath Dey v. Ahmed Hossain 505
Bibi Ahmed-un-nissa v. Ali Akbar Khan 256, 257
Bibi Amu v. Asiat 180, 190
Bibi Rehana Khatun v. Iqtidaruddin Hasan ... 401, 405
Biland Sahai v. Begum Noor 36
Birtwhistle v. Vardill 138, 166, 167
Bosville v. Attorney-General 170
Boyes v. Bedale 168, 169
Breadalbane Case 164
Brinkley v. Attorney-General 144
Brooks v. Brooks 140
Bukhsh Ally v. Ameerun Bibee 451
Bulund Khan v. Janee 415
Bussunteram Marwary v. Kamaluddin 41
Buzuloor Raheem v. Shumsunnissa 382, 383
Buzul-ul-Raheem v. Luteefutoonnissa 468

C

Campbell v. Campbell 193
Campbell v. Delaney 41
Cassumbhoy Ahmedbhoy v. Ahmedbhoy Hubibhoy ... 130
Chandra Bindo Kunda v. Sh. Allah Bux 421
Chan pir v. Fakar Shah 397, 429
Charan v. C. Mathur 385
Chetti v. Chetti 140
Chidrambaran Chettiyar v. Ma Wyein 83
Chuki Bibi v. Shamsunnissa Begum 411
Clarke v. Clarke 273
Collector of Muradabad v. Harbans Singh 394

PAGE

Collis *v.* Hector 142
Cooverbai Nasarwanji *v.* Hyat Bi 411, 412
Copis *v.* Middleton 422

D

Dallumal *v.* Hari Das 36, 37
Dalrymple *v.* Dalrymple 166
Daulan *v.* Dossa 338
Davalava *v.* Bhimaji Dhond 40
Daya Muhammad The (Advocate-General *ex relation*) *v.* Muhammad Husen Huseni (otherwise called Aga Khan) 123
De Thoren *v.* Attorney-General 164
Dhan Bibee v. Lalon Bibee 195, 200
Dinsab Kasimsab *v.* Muhammad Hussain 388
Don's Estate, *Re* 138
Dular Koer *v.* Dwarkanath Misser 383

E

Eidan *v.* Mazhar Hossain 401, 419

F

Fahiman *v.* Bulaqi 409
Faizullah Khan *v.* Abdul Jabbar 36
Fakhruddin *v.* Abdul Hosain 508
Farooq Leivers *v.* Adelaide Bridget Mary 134, 345
Fateh Din *v.* Gurmukh Singh 508
Fatesangji Jaswantsangji *v.* Harisangji Fatesangji ... 27
Fatima Benti Hafedah *v.* Administrator General Zanzibar 193, 197, 296
Fatima Bibee *v.* Ahmad Buksh 465
Fatima Bibi *v.* Noor Mohammad 381
Fatima Bibi *v.* Sadruddin 401
Fazeelun Bibee *v.* Omda Bibee 197
Fazilat-unnissa *v.* Kamarunnissa 196, 200
Fazl Karim *v.* Haji Moolla Buksh 13
Fazlur Rahman *v.* *Mst.* Aisha 435, 437
Fenton *v.* Livingstone 166
Feroze Din *v.* Nawab Khan ... 192, 197, 199
Fulchand *v.* Nasib Ali Chowdhry ... 448, 449, 451
Furzund Hossain *v.* Tanu Bibee 436
Fuseehun *v.* Kajo 228, 230, 235

PAGE

G

Gangadhar *v.* Rachappa 195
Genu Meah *v.* Begummah Bibi 382
Ghasiti *v.* Juggu 28
Ghasiti *v.* Umraojan 28
Ghaus *v.* *Mst.* Faiji 350
Ghazanfarali *v.* Kaniz Fatima 195
Ghufoorun Bibi *v.* Musutkedeh 412
Ghulam Ali *v.* Saghir-un-nissa 415
Ghulam Fatima *v.* Muhammad Bashir 388
Ghulam Mohyuddin *v.* Khizar Hussain 452
Ghulam Muhammad *v.* Emperor 337
Ghulam Sakina *v.* Falek Sher 333, 341
Ghulam Sakina *v.* Umar Bakhsh ... 434, 435, 466
Gobardhan Das *v.* Jassodamoni Dassi 347
Gohar Begum *v.* Suggi 238
Golden *v.* Gillian 422
Goldsmid *v.* Bromer 154, 155, 160
Goodman *v.* Goodman 168
Goodman's Trusts, *Re* 165
Gujjadhur Proshad *v.* Abdoollah 45
Gul Khan *v.* *Mst.* Karam Nishan 84
Gul Muhammad *v.* *Mst.* Wazir 215
Gurney *v.* Gurney 170

H

Habiba *v.* Siwa Kyan 40, 41
Habib-ur-Rahman Chowdhury *v.* Altaf Ali Chowdhury 175, 178, 190, 192, 199, 200
Hadi Ali *v.* Akbar Ali 413
Hakim Khan *v.* Gul Khan 16, 23, 25
H. A. Lucas *v.* Theodoras Lucas 141
Hamid Ali *v.* Imtiazan 436, 449
Hamid Hussain *v.* Kubra Begum ... 382
Hamidulla *v.* Faizunnissa 449, 457
Hamidullah Khan *v.* Najjo 415
Hamir Singh *v.* Zakia 39, 505
Hamira Bibi *v.* Zubaida Bibi ... 391, 395, 410
Hamira Bibi *v.* Zubaida Bibi 415
Hancock (f. c. Peaty) *v.* Peaty 246
Harrod *v.* Harrod 263
Hasan Ali *v.* Mehdi Hussain 505

PAGE

Hasan Ali v. Nazo 33
Hasan Kutty v. Jainaba 264
Hasnumiyya v. Halimunnissa ... 407, 409, 429
Hassarat Bibi v. Golam Jaffar 464
Hayat-un-nissa v. Muhammad Ali Khan 18, 20, 36
Henry Imlach v. Zuhoorunnisa 499
Herbert v. Herbert 140
Himmat Bahadoor v. Sahebzadi Begum 206
Hirbaee v. Gorbai 27, 127, 128
Hirbaee v. Sonabai 27, 124, 127
Hirbai v. Hiraji 504
Hosseinooddeen Chowdhry v. Tajunnissa Khatoon ... 416
Hurmoot-ool-nissa Begum v. Allahdia Khan ... 31
Husaini Begum v. Muhammed 382
Husaini Begum v. Rustam Ali Khan 383
Husaini Begum v. Zia-ul-nissa Begum 505
Hussain v. Rahim Khan 412
Hussain Khan v. Sirdar Khan 400
Hussey Hunt v. Bozelli 141
Hyde v. Hyde and Wodmansee 149, 152, 156, 157, 160

I

Ibrahim v. Syed Bibi 436
Ibrahim Abubakar v. Tekchand 36
Ibrahim Moola v. Inayet-ur-Rahman ... 439, 443
Idu v. Amiran 229
Ihsan Hasan Khan v. Panna Lal 191
Imam Ali v. Arfatunnissa 381, 450
Imambandi v. Mutsaddi ... 192, 200, 500, 504, 505, 508, 510
Imamdin v. Aman Bibi 350
Imdad Ali v. Ghulam Jilani 89
Imdad Hossein v. Hosseini Baksh 415
Imperial Bank of Gaya v. Bibi Sayeedan 408
Imtiaz Begum v. Abdul Karim 409
Inayat Begum v. Maryum 34
In re Abdul Ali Ismailji and his wife Husanbi ... 381, 436
In re Bozelli's Settlements, Hussey-Hunt v. Bozelli ... 141
In re Haji Ismail Haji Abdullah 129
In re Isso 227
In re Johnson 422
In re Kasam Pirbhai and his wife Hirbai 451

PAGE

In re Knox 141
In re Raja Sahib 445
In re Taplin 163
I L R 36 All. 280 (1914) 508
In the matter of Ameerunnissa 229
In the matter of Khatija Bibi ... 236, 283, 368
In the matter of Mahin Bibi 215, 236
In the matter of Tayheb Ally 225
In the matter of the application of Zaynab Bibi ... 116
In the matter of the Petition of Luddon Sahiba ... 380
In the matter of the Petition of Najibunnissa ... 199
In the matter of the Petition of Ram Kumari ... 346
Iqbal Begum *v. Mst.* Syed Begum 19
Ismail Ahmed Peepadi *v.* Momin Bibi 184, 195
Itwari *v.* Sm. Asghari 382, 383

J

Jafri Begum *v.* Amir Muhammad Khan 36, 37
Jahan Khan *v.* Mandley 499
Jahuren Bibi *v.* Soleman Khan ... 390, 397, 409, 410, 423, 429
Jainan *v.* Rullia 264
Jaker Ali Chowdhry *v.* Raj Chunder Sen 25
Jammya *v.* Diwan 16, 27
Janbi Bibi *v.* Abbas Ali 412
Janee Khanum *v.* Amatool Fatima 410
Jaun Bibee *v.* Sheikh Munshee Beparee ... 419, 451, 487
Jeswant Singjee Ubby Singjee *v.* Jet Singjee Ubby Singjee 175
Jhanda *v.* Hussain Bibi 378
Jiand Khan *v.* The Province of Sind 193
Jogu Bibi *v.* Mesel Shaikh 256
Johnson *v.* Johnson's Administrator 151
Jones falsely called Robinson *v.* Robinson 154
Jwala Buksh *v.* Dharam Singh ... 23, 25, 127
Jynaj Begum *v.* Umrav Begum 407, 429

K

Kali Dutt Jha *v.* Abdool Ali 505, 506
Kaloo Shaikh *v.* Gureeboolah 214, 215
Kamar Kadir *v.* Bibi Luddan 363
Kanchan Modi *v.* Baijnath Singh 42
Kannasami Chetty v. Rahimat Ammal 505
Karim Bakhsh *v. Mst.* Mukabuar 307
Kariyadan *v.* Kayal Beeran 385

PAGE
Kasam Pirbhai and his wife Hirbai, *In re* ... 451
Kent *v.* Burgess 141
Kanward *v.* Kenward 140, 141
Keolapati *v.* Amar Krishna 85
Kevan *v.* Crawford 422
Khair Din *v.* Muhammad Hussain 29
Khajah Hidayat Oollah *v.* Rai Jan Khanum 40, 175, 190, 196, 292
Khajurunnissa *v.* Roushan Jehan 20, 175
Khajurunnissa *v.* Saifullah Khan 415
Khambata *v.* Khambata 18
Khanum Jan *v.* Jan Bibi 31
Kharag Narain *v.* Hamida Khatoon ... 505
Khatija Bi *v.* Umar Sahib ... 481, 487, 488
Khatija Bibi *In the matter of* 236, 283, 368
Khijarannissa *v.* Risannissa 415
Khurshet Bibi *v.* Keso Venayek 40
Khushal Singh *v.* Jaimal 200
Khushi Muhammed *v.* Mohammed-un-nissa 229, 230, 231
Khwajeha Solehman Quadir (*Sic*) *v.* Nawab Sir Salimullah Bahadur 34
King *v.* Inhabitants of Brampton 164
Kishwar Khan *v.* Jewan Khan 40
Knox, *In re* 141
Korban *v.* King-Emperor 237, 283
Kulsumbi *v.* Abdul Kadir 273
Kumarunnissa Bibi *v.* Hussaini Bibi 397
Kundan *v.* Aisha Begum 227
Kunhi *v.* Moidin 421
Kunhi Mamod *v.* Kunhi Moidin 32

L

Lacon *v.* Higgins 141
Lakhmi Narain *v.* Saadat Ali 40
Lalan Bi *v.* Muhammad Ashfaq ... 437, 445, 446
Lardli Begum *v.* Mahomed Amir Khan ... 225
Latafat Hussain *v.* Hidayat Hussain 32
Lavtour *v.* Teesdale 141
Lindo *v.* Belisario 154
Lucas *v.* Lucas 141
Luddon Sahiba *In the matter of the petition of* ... 380

PAGE

M

Macdogall v. Chitnuvis 140
Mafizuddin Mandel v. Rahiman Bibi 337
Mahadev Lal v. Bibi Muniran 405
Maharana Shri Fatesingji v. Harisingji Fatesingji ... 27
Mahatala Bibee v. Ahmed Haleemoozzaman ... 193, 292
Maher v. Maher 160
Mahin Bibi, *In the matter of* ... 215, 236
Mahomed Arshad Chowdhry v. Sajida Banu ... 113
Mahomed Wajid v. Tayyaban 41
Mahommed Rowther v. Ibrahim Rowther 23
Mahommed Sidick v. Ahmed Abdul Haji Abdul Satar ... 27, 130
Mairaj Fatima v. Abdul Wahid 89
Maitheen Bivi Umma v. Ithappiri Verkey ... 34
Majid Mian v. Bibi Sahib ... 410, 411, 412
Ma Khatoon v. Ma Mya 190
Mallac v. Mallac 141
Ma Mi v. Kallandar Ammal 444, 449, 451
Mangat Rai v. Sakina Begum 401
Manigir v. Amargoba 40
Manihar Bibi v. Rakha Singh 405
Maraim-un-Nissa Begum v. Imdadee Begum ... 400
Mardan Saheb v. Rajak Saheb 197
Marfat Ali Mirja v. Jabedannissa ... 457
Marshal v. Marshal and St. Clair 141
Mashal Singh v. Ahmad Hussain 411
Masit-un-Nissa v. Pathani 196, 200
Matadin v. Sheikh Ahmed Ali 505, 508
Maung Kyi v. Ma Shaw Baw 256
Mauraj Mource v. Sh. Mohd. Hashim 41
Mazhar Ali v. Budh Singh 39, 89
Meher Ali v. Amani 399
Mebarally v. Shakerkhanoobai 381, 382
Metar Sen Singh v. Maqbul Hasan Khan 83
Middleton v. Pollock 422
Mir Ali Hussain v. Sajuda Begum 113
Mir Azmat Ali v. Mahmud-ul-Nissa 384
Mir Mahar Ali v. Amani 85, 399
Mir Sarwar Jan v. Fakhr-ud-din Md. Chowdhry ... 508
Mirabivi v. Vellayanna 27, 131
Mirkha v. Bhagirthebai 40
Mirwahed Ali v. Rashid Beg 410

PAGE

Mirza Bedar Bukht *v.* Mirza Khurrum Bukht ... 402
Mirza Sulleman Kadar *v.* Nawab Mehdi Begum Surreya Bahu 393
Mofazzal Hossain *v.* Basid Sheikh 507
Mohabbat Ali Khan *v.* Mohammad Ibrahim Khan ... 190, 192
Mohabuth Ally *v.* Mymonissa 449
Mohamed Umar Khan *v.* Muhammad Niazuddin Khan 196
Mohamed Wajid *v.* Tayyuban 41
Mohammad *v.* Ghulam 20
Mohammad Abdur Rahman *v.* Muhammad Ibadul Ghani 504, 506
Mohammud Afak *v.* Ekram Ali 26
Mohammed Ali v. Ghulam Fatima ... 366
Mohammed Arshad Chowdhry *v.* Sajida Banu 65, 66, 113
Mohammad Bakhsh *v.* Crown 337
Mohammad Haji *v.* Kalimabi 380
Mohammed Ibrahim *v.* Ghulam Ahmed ... 18
Mohammad Irfan *v.* *Mst.* Mahando ... 437, 439, 448
Mohammed Ishaq *v.* *Mst.* Sairan Bibi 445
Mohammad Rahimullah, *In re* 378
Mohammed Sadiq *v.* Fakhar Jehan 430
Mohammed Shoaib *v.* Zaib Jehan 409, 412
Mohammad Yasin *v.* Mumtaz Begum 450
Moharram Ali *v.* Aisha Khatoon 457
Moolla Casim *v.* Moola Abdur Rahim 30
Moonshee Bazul-ul-Raheem *v.* Luteefutoonnissa 383, 468, 470
Morris *v.* Davies 163
Mst. Aisha *v.* Barkat Ali 232
Mst. Amina Bibi *v.* Muhammad ... 397
Mst. Amtul Rasul *v.* Karim Bakhsh ... 415
Mst. Bakht Bibi *v.* Qaim Din ... 381
Mst. Bashiran Bi *v.* Abdul Wahab 421
Mst. Beeby Bachun *v.* Sheik Hamid Hussain ... 409, 410
Mst. Bhawan *v.* Gaman 383
Mst. Bibi *v.* *Mst.* Bibi 232
Mst. Bibi Maqbulunnissa *v.* *Mst.* Bibi Umatunnissa ... 412
Mst. Bukshan *v.* *Mst.* Doolhin ... 504
Mst. Fakhre Jehan *v.* Muhammad 487
Mst. Fatima Bibi *v.* Lal Din 390, 397, 423
Mst. Fuseehun *v.* *Mst.* Kajo 230
Mst. Ghulam Kubra Bibi *v.* Mnhammad Shafi ... 256, 257
Mst. Haji *v.* Palio 337

PAGE

Mst. Husnoo *v.* *Mst.* Wahedunnissa 190, 191
Mst. Izhar Fatima Bibi *v.* *Mst.* Ansar Bibi ... 409
Mst. Jamil-un-nissa *v.* Sheikh Muhammad Zia ... 19
Mst. Kaniza *v.* Hasen 294, 301
Mst. Khatijan *v.* Abdullah 366
Mst. Maimuna Begum *v.* Shafaat Ullah 401
Mst. Maina Bibi *v.* Chaudri Vakil Ahmad 409, 410, 411, 412
Mst. Mariam *v.* Qadir Bakhsh 378
Mst. Muhammadi *v.* Jamiluddin 369
Mst. Nasiban Bibi *v.* *Mst.* Iqbal Begum 397, 429
Mst. Nawabunnissa *v.* *Mst.* Fuzloonnissa 194
Mst. Pukhraj Begum *v.* Hidayat Ali 415
Mst. Rahim Bibi *v.* Chirgh Din 179
Mst. Rahim Jan *v.* Muhammad 421
Mst. Rasulan *v.* Mirza Naimullah Beg 420
Mst. Sahib *v.* Rafiuddin 421
Mst. Sakina Begum *v.* *Mst.* Shahr Bano 40
Mst. Subhanbi *v.* *Mst.* Umraobi ... 34
Mst. Subhani, *re.* 113
Mst. Sughra Begum *v.* Muhammad Din 386
Mst. Umatul Mehdi *v.* *Mst.* Kulsoom 410
Mst. Wahid-un-Nissa *v.* *Mst.* Shubrattun 41
Mubarak-un-Nissa *v.* Mansab Hassan Khan ... 408
Muhaidin Tharagnar *v.* Saimmba Amonal 388
Muhammad *v.* Mujeeb-un-nissa 227
Muhammad Allahdad Khan *v.* Muhammad Ismail Khan 178, 196, 198
Muhammad Awais *v.* Harsahai 36, 37
Muhammad Azam Khan *v.* Akhtar-un-nissa ... 439, 445
Muhammad Azmat Ali Khan *v.* Ladli Begum ... 196, 199
Muhammad Bashir *v.* Ghulam Fatima ... 226, 227, 229, 235
Muhammad Ibrahim *v.* Ma Ma 394, 427
Muhammad Ibrahim bin Muhammad Sayat Parkar *v.* Ghulam Ahmed bin Muhammad Sayad Roghe and another 18, 20, 213
Muhammad Ishak *v.* Sheikh Akramul Huk ... 408
Muhammad Ismail Khan *v.* Fidayatunnissa ... 175
Muhammad Kamil *v.* Imtiaz Fatima ... 32, 52
Muhammad Karimullah Khan *v.* Amani Begum ... 409
Muhammad Sadiq *v.* Mohammad Hasan ... 191, 194, 196
Muhammad Shafiqullah Khan *v.* Nuhullah Khan ... 190
Muhammad Shamsuddin *v.* Noor Jehan 388

PAGE

Muhammad Subhanullah *v. Mst.* Saghirunnissa ... 401
Muhammad Sultan Begum *v.* Sirajuddin Ahmad ... 427, 428
Muhammad Taqi Ahmad *v.* Farmoodi Begum ... 401, 415
Muhammad Yakub Hussain *v.* Inayet Jan ... 408
Muhammad Zaman *v.* Naima Sultana 256, 403
Muhammad Zubair *v. Mst.* Bibi Sahidan 409, 412
Mulka Jehan Sahiba *v.* Mahommed Uskuree Khan ... 339
Mulkah Do Alum Nawab Tajdar Bahoo *v.* Mirza Jehan Kadr 393
Mulkan Bibi *v.* Muhammed Wazir Khan 382
Mulleeka v. Jumeela 415
Mushaf Hussain Shah *v.* Hamida Begum 388
Musthan Saheb *v.* Assam Bibi 402
Muttyjan *v.* Ahmed Ali 39
Muzaffar Ali Khan *v.* Parbati 113, 413, 507
Muzhar Ali *v.* Budh Singh 39

N

Najibunnissa, *In the matter of the petition of* ... 199
Najmunissa *v.* Sirajuddin ... 369, 418, 421
Narsingh Das *v.* Najmoodin Hussein 41
Nasiruddin Shah *v.* Amtul Mughni Begum 390, 400, 401, 402, 405, 407
Nasrat Husain *v.* Hamidan 18, 419, 420
Nawab Bibi *v.* Mohammed Dost 421
Nawab Mirza Mohammad Sadiq Ali Khan *v.* Nawab Fakhar Jehan Begum 35
Nawab-unnissa *v.* Fuzuloonissa 194, 292
Nawasi Begum *v.* Dilafroz 415
Nawzish Ali Khan *v.* Ali Raja Khan 34
Niboyet *v.* Niboyet 160
Nizamuddin *v.* Anandi 508
Noor Jehan *v.* Eugene Tischence 347
Noronarain Roy *v.* Neemaeechand Neogy 85
Nujmooddeen Ahmed *v.* Beebee Hosseinee ... 396
Nur Ali *v.* Malka Sultana 19
Nur Begum *v. Mst.* Begum 227
Nur Kadir *v.* Zuleikha Bibi 236, 283
Nurrunnessa *v.* Khaja Muhammad 407, 429
Nuruddin Ahmad *v.* Masuda Khanum 418, 419
Nuzeerun *v.* Ameeruddeen 40

PAGE

O

Ogden *v.* Ogden 169
Omda Bibee *v.* Jonab Ali 197, 200
Omdat-oon-nissa *v.* Mirza Asad Ali 392, 403

P

Pakrichi *v.* Kanhacha 387
Patchett *v.* Holgate 172
Pathummabi *v.* Vitil Ummachabi 40
Piers *v.* Piers 163
Pir Mohammad *v.* The State of Madhya Pradesh ... 337
Pirthipal Singh *v.* Hussaini Jan 41
Plowes *v.* Bossey 175, 291
Poonoo Bibi *v.* Fyez Baksh 287, 449

Q

Qamar Din *v.* *Mst.* Aishabibi 32
Qasim Hussain *v.* Kaniz 407

R

Rafiqa Begum *v.* Aisha Begum 194
Rahilan *v.* Sanaullah 417
Rahiman Bibi *v.* Mahboob Bibi 294, 301
Rahimatbai *v.* Hirbai 27, 128
Raj Bahadur *v.* Bishen Dayal 18
Raja Sahib, *In re* 445
Ram Chander Chuckerbutty *v.* Brojonath Mazumdar ... 507
Ramachandrayya *v.* Abdul Qadir 505
Ramcharan Lal *v.* *Mst.* Hanifa Khatun 41
Ram Churn Sanyal *v.* Anukul Chandra Acharjiya ... 507
Ramdayal *v.* Munna Lal 421
Ramija Bibi *v.* Sharifa Bibi 412
Ram Kumari, *In the matter of the petition of* ... 346
Ram Prasad *v.* Bibi Khadijtul Kubra 412, 415
Ramzan Ali *v.* Asghari Begum 409
Ranee Khajoorunnissa *v.* *Mst.* Roushan Jehan ... 20
Rashid *v.* Sherbano 465
Rashid Ahmad *v.* Anisa Khatun
190, 378, 435, 436, 437, 439, 441, 444, 449, 451, 459
Rasul Bakhsh *v.* *Mst.* Bhalan 445
Razia Begum *v.* Sabebzadi Anwar Begum 172

PAGE

Re. Bischoff Shein 165
Re. De. Wilton 140
Re. Don's Estate 138, 166, 167, 168
Re. Goodman's Trusts 165
Re. Green Nayes 141
Re. Herrel Angeline *v.* Dick 138
Re. Khatija Bibi 236, 283, 368
Re. Paine 140
Re. Sinclay 172
Re. Ullee, the Nawab Nazim of Bengal's infants ... 155
Re. Wilson's Trusts 168
Relumal Kewalmal *v.* Hazur Bakhsh 505
Re. Wright's Trust 168
Rex *v.* Hammerssnilk 160
Rex *v.* Stourton 172
Reza Hossein *v.* Ifatoonissa 409
Risk *v.* Risk 154
Rook Begum *v.* Walagawhur Shah 194
Roshanbai *v.* Suleman 194
Rukiyya Begum *v.* Radha Kishen 397, 429
Rup Lal Chowdhury *v.* Latu Lal Chowdhry ... 25
Russ *v.* Russ 160
Russel *v.* A. G. 163
Russell *v.* Russell 172
Ruttan *v.* Domee Khan 504

S

Sabur Bibi *v.* Ismail 409
Sadakat Hossain *v.* Mahomed Yusuf 196, 199
Sadiq Hussain Khan *v.* Hashim Ali Khan ... 178, 192, 200
Sadiya Begum *v.* Atta Ullah 457
Saña Begum *v.* Zaheer Hasan 382
Sahebzadee Begum *v.* Mirza Himmat Bahadur 85, 118, 188
Sahib Jan *v.* Ansaruddin 415
Sainuddin *v.* Latif-un-nissa Bibi 450
Salim-un-nissa *v.* Saadat 225
Salveson (or Von Lorang) *v.* Austrian Property
Administrator 141
Samir Sheikh *v.* Aijan Bewa 34
Sampatia Bibi *v.* Mir Mahboob Ali 410
Sara Bai *v.* Rabia Bai 436, 445, 446, 465
Sardar Bibi *v.* Muhammad Bakhsh 19, 20

	Page
Sardar Muhammad *v. Mst.* Maryam Bibi	350
Sastry Velaider Aronegary *v.* Sembecoutty Vaigalie	163
Satgunj *v.* Rahmat Dil	480
Sayeeda Khanum *v.* Muhammad Sami	449, 466
Scott *v.* Sebright	273
Shafiullah *v.* Emperor	337
Shah Abdul Ilyas *v.* Ulfat Bibi	380
Shah Bano *v.* Iftikhar Muhammad Khan	407, 416
Shahzada Begum *v.* Abdul Hamid	279
Shamshad Ali Shah *v.* Hasan Shah	465
Shamsunnissa *v.* Ashrafunnissa	246
Shankar Das *v.* Mehbub Jan	415
Shaw *v.* Attorney-General	160
Shaw *v.* Gould	161, 167, 168
Sheikh Abdool Shukoor *v.* Raheem-unnissa ...	419
Sheikh Abdur Rahman *v.* Sheikh Wali Muhammad ...	412
Sheikh Muhammad Rowther *v.* Aisha Bibi ...	402
Sherif Saib *v.* Usanbibi	450
Sherwood *v.* Ray	209
Shivji Hassan *v.* Datu Mavji Khoja	128
Sibt Ahmad *v.* Amina Khatun	213
Sibt Muhammad *v.* Muhammad	179
Simonin (f. c.) Mallac *v.* Mallac	141
Sirinivasan *v.* Sirinivasan	159
Sitaram *v.* Amir Begum	505
Skinner *v.* Skinner	347
Skottowe *v.* Young	138, 168
Soorma Khatoon *v.* Altafunnissa Khatoon ...	416
Sottomayor *v.* De Barros	160, 161
Spwack *v.* Spwack	163
Suddertonessa *v.* Majada Khatun	23
Sugra Bibee *v.* Masuma Bibi	392, 394
Suldhana *v.* Suldhana	141
Suleman *v.* Abdul Shakoor	40
Suleman Sahib *v.* Kadir Ibrahim ...	31
Sultan Begum *v.* Serajuddin Ahmed	394, 400
Sultan Khan Mangal Khan *v.* Gullu	237
Sumsuddin Goolam Husein *v.* Abdul Hussein Kalimuddin	31
Sundari Letani *v.* Petambari Letani	347
Sundramal *v.* Ameenal	83
Surmust Khan *v.* Kadirdad Khan	16, 27
Syad Mir Ujmuddin Khan *v.* Zia-ul-Nissa Begam ...	65

PAGE

Syed Ali Nawaz Gardezi *v.* Lt.-Col. Muhammad Yousaf 8, 134, 141, 161, 252
Syed Bazayet Hossein *v.* Dooli Chand 41
Syed Rashid Ahmed *v.* *Mst.* Anisa Khatoon 19, 439, 441, , 444, 449, 451, 459
Syedun *v.* Velayet Ali Khan 504

T

Tahir-un-nissa *v.* Nawab Hasan 409
Taj Bi *v.* Maula Khan 294, 301
Tajbi *v.* Nattar Sharif 403
Taliamand *v.* Muhammad Din ... 181, 294, 301
Tamina Khatoon *v.* Gohar Jan 227
Taplin, *In re* 163
Tasaduq Hussain *v.* Tasaduq Hussain 162
Taufikunissa *v.* Ghulam Kamber 401, 402
Tayheb Ally, *In the matter of* 225
Thattoli *v.* Kunhammad 504, 506
The Advocate-General *v.* Mohammed Hossen Hosseni otherwise called Agha Khan 123
The Aylesford Peerage 172
The King *v.* the Inhabitants of Brampton 164
Thoren *v.* Attorney-General 164
Toonanjan *v.* Mehndee Begum 113
Tyebhoy Essofalle Thingna *v.* Collector of Allahabad ... 194

U

Ufzool Begum *v.* Ladlee Begum 415
Ullee, *Re.* the Nawab Nazim of Bengal's Infants 155
Umardaraz Ali Khan *v.* Wilayat Ali Khan ... 113
Umda Begum *v.* Muhammadi 401, 406
Umed Ally *v.* Safihan 410
Umra Khan *v.* Sultana 388

V

Vadake Viti Ismal *v.* Odakel Beyakuth Umah ... 451
Vaithilinga Odayar *v.* Ayyathorai Odayar 83
Venkatachalam Pillai *v.* Sethu Ram 508
Virbhadrappa *v.* Shekabai 40
Vulanda *v.* Crown 337

W

Waheedun *v.* Wasee Hossain 197
Wahedun-nessa *v.* Shubratun 39, 408

PAGE

Waj Bibi *v.* Azmat Ali 448
Wajeh-oon-Nissa Khanum *v.* Mirza Hassan Ali ... 116, 392
Wajid Ali *v.* Jaffar Hussain 437
Wajid Ali Khan *v.* Sakhawat Ali Khan 421
Warrender *v.* Warrender 149
Wazeer Ali *v.* Karim Ali 368
Wilayat Hussain *v.* Allah Rakhi 419
Wilson *v.* Wilson 159
Wilson's Trusts, *Re.* 168
Wise *v.* Sundolonnissa 292
Wood *v.* Dixie 422
Woomatul Fatima Begum *v.* Mariamunnissa Khanum ... 410, 415
Wortham's case 245
Wright's Trusts, *Re.* 168

Y

Yasin Khan *v.* Mohammad Yar Khan 41
Yeajuddin *v.* Rup Manjari Dasi 504
Yusuf Ali *v.* Collector of Tippera 16

Z

Zafar Hussain *v.* Ummatur Rahman 481, 488
Zahooran *v.* Mirza Naimullah Beg 420
Zakera Begum *v.* Sakina Begum 394
Zamin Ali *v.* Aziz-un-Nissa 190, 409
Zohoorooddeen Sirdar *v.* Baharoollah Sirdar ... 16
Zubair Ahmad *v.* Jai Nandan Prasad 412
Zubardust Khan *v.* His Wife 350
Zubeda Begum *v.* Wazir Muhammad 333
Zynab Bibi, *In the matter of the application of* ... 84, 116

TECHNICAL TERMS EXPLAINED

	Page
'Aariyét	... 261
'Adl	... 510
Ahkam-ul-Azwaj	... 111
Akar	500, 513
Akhbari	... 8
'Akil	439, 467
Al-Hajab	... 118
Al-Hawaíj-ul-aslia	... 242
Al-Kafat	... 326
Al-kiswat	... 501
Amanat	... 370
'Amr-ba-yed	... 455
Asabah-be-nafsihi	49, 89, 256
Asabat-un-Nasabiye	... 48
Asabat-us-Sababiye	... 48
Ashraf	... 431
As-Sum'at	... 426
At-t'aam	... 501
Aul	...69, 93
Ayyam-i-Jahilyét	... 1
Bai-mukasa	... 406
Bait-ul-Mal	... 132
Baligh	439, 467
Batil	250, 294, 301, 312
Bulughiyet	210, 493
Daf'a-ul-'aar	... 484
Dain	... 370
Dar-ul-Harab	135, 266
Dar-ul-Islam	135, 345
Diat	...63, 81
Du'a-Kunut	... 509
Dukhul	304, 308, 349
Farr	... 463
Fasid	250, 294, 301
Fasik-ul-mutah-hattik	265, 325
Faskh	... 374
Fazuli	283, 340, 514
Firash	171, 342
Ghair-mahram	230, 366
Ghair-Mamunah	... 231
Ghair-marsumah	... 445
Ghair-mukallid	... 13
Ghibat-ul-munkatta	... 219
Ghurur	... 183
Hadd	262, 290
Hadd-ul-kazf	... 484
Hajj	269, 356
Haram	... 300
Hakim-ush shar'a	... 154
Harbi	253, 499
Hazanat	222, 223
Hazina	222, 229
Hizanat	222, 223
Hurriyet	... 246
'Iddat	70, 290, 310, 317
Iflas	... 373
Ihram	... 255
Ihsan	290, 302
Ihtiat	371, 491
Ijara	... 261
Ijma'a-ul-Ummat	... 6
Ijtihad	... 374
Ikrah	321, 439
Imamate	... 3
Ikhtiar	... 455
Ikrar	... 196
Ila	... 478
'Innin	... 490
Jabr	... 209
Jadd-ul-Fasid	... 265
Jahaz	430, 492
Juzam	... 342
Kabinnameh	259, 288
Kafil	... 370
Karabat	... 99

	Page
Kasd	... 467
Katl	... 114
Kharaj	132, 503
Khilwat-us-sahih	288, 290
Khyar-ul-Bulugh	331, 495
Khyar-ul-Itk	... 331
Kitabia	143, 345
Kiyas	... 6
Kufr	81, 114, 238, 281
Kufu	266, 268
L'aan	... 484
Lakit	... 238
Mafkud-ul-khabar	86, 93
Mahjur	... 221
Mahkama	... 288
Mahram	... 230
Mahr-nameh	256, 288
Mahr-ul-misl	... 262
Mahr-ul-Mu'ajjal	... 399
Mahr-ul-muwajjal	... 400
Majbub	... 490
Majhul-un-nasab	... 265
Majoosia	... 223
Mamn'u	... 433
Manf'at	... 399
Mariz	... 355
Marsumah	... 445
Marz-ul-mout	... 470
Mashiat	455, 457
Mata	... 514
Mawanah-ul-Irs	... 114
Miras-ul-ansab	... 102
Mooltakit	... 513
Muataddah	201, 299, 300, 304
Mubah	... 433
Muddat	... 286
Muhrim	255, 356, 490
Muhsan	... 290
Muhsina	... 485

	Page
Muhtasib	... 473
Mujtahid	... 7
Mukaddam	... 500
Mukhtar	... 457
Muraf'a	... 489
Murahik	... 459
Murtedd	... 348
Mushuz	... 478
Mustamin	... 347
Musaheret	... 299
Musharraka	... 492
Mushrikin	... 251
Mutabanna	... 196
Muzaribat	... 370
Nafkah	303, 364, 367
Nasab	94, 187, 329
Nikah-ul-fasid	... 301
Nikah-ul-mutaa	... 284
Nikah-ul-muwakkat	... 284
Nikah-ush-shigar	285, 286
Nushuz	370, 377, 478
Radd	... 66
Raj'at	452, 458
Rikkiyèt	... 114
Risalat	... 81
Rushd	... 493
Sabab	94, 95
Safiha	157, 211
Saham-bi'l-karabah	... 99
Saibba	264, 271
Saghir	157, 245, 332
Shadi	... 257
Sharai	257, 258
Sarir	157, 245
Sheikh-ul-kabir	... 242
Shubh	182, 297, 299
Shubhat-ul-akd	182, 298, 299
Shubhat-ul-milk	... 297
Shubh-Ishtibah	... 297

	Page
Shurut	... 481
Sigha	... 259
Sukua	... 510
Tadlis	... 343
Tafrik	... 459
Tafwiz	449, 455
Tahrim-un-nasab	... 248
Talak-ul-bain	... 436
Talak-ul-bida'at	... 435
Talak-ul-innin	... 488
Talak-ul-mariz	... 453
Talak-ur-raj'ai	452, 458
Talak-us-sunnat	434, 435
Tamkin-i-Kamil	... 365
T'asib	... 94
'Urfi	257, 258
Usuli	... 8
Wahdaniet	... 81
Wala	... 63
Walad-ul-mulainah	... 189
Walad-uz-zina	52, 243, 296
Wala-ul-itq	95, 96
Wala-ul-mawalat	... 65
Wala-z-zamin-il-jarirah	95, 96
Wali-ul-akrab	220, 268, 269
Wasi	... 267
Wilayet-ul-Ijbar	209, 265
Yeteem Saghir	... 513
Zamin-ul-jarirah	... 95
Zav-il-Arham	45, 53, 94
Zav-il-Furuz	... 45
Zimmi	253, 499
Zina	295, 297, 356
Zowjiyet	... 95
Zu-farz	98, 99
Zu-karabat	... 99

INTRODUCTION

Position of Mahommedan Jurisprudence.

THE Jurisprudence of the Moslems occupies a pre-eminent position among the various systems which have, at different times, been in force among different communities. Considering the circumstances under which it originated, the difficulties it had to contend with, and the backward condition of the people among whom it attained its development, it may be regarded as one of the grandest monuments of the human intellect. The legislation of Mohammed has, accordingly, a special significance for philosophic observers whom the study of the progress of mankind, as evidenced in the laws of society, attracts and interests. The resemblance, which the Islamic regulations bear to pre-Mahommedan institutions in some of their essential features, deserves careful consideration, as it serves to show the points of contact between the old conditions of society, stigmatised by the Musulmans as the Ayyam-i-Jahilyet ("the days of ignorance") and the reformed system. This resemblance has induced some critics to charge Mohammed with plagiarism. It seems to me, however, that the charge is founded upon an erroneous conception of Arab society as it existed in those days. At the time when Mohammed promulgated his laws, the Jews were, probably, the only people inhabiting the Arabian peninsula who possessed organic institutions; they formed in the midst of the pagan Arabs, strong communities governed by their own special code. The intimate connection which from time immemorial existed between the Arabs and the Jews, joined to the belief that they were both descended from a common stock, had tended to engraft many Jewish ideas upon Arab manners and customs. In the relations of domestic life especially the influence of the Jews was most strongly marked. The Prophet, in his efforts to introduce a purer Faith and a healthier organisation among his people, did not so entirely overlook the exigencies of society and the requirements of human growth as to denounce all existing institutions, the inevitable result of which would have been to reduce everything to chaos. His constructive mind perceived in them the germs of development, and accordingly he allowed them a place in his system, with such modifications and alterations as would bring those institutions into harmony with a progressive condition of society. But there can be little doubt that he regarded them as temporary in their character, for he unquestionably looked forward to a time when customs and usages consistent with a limited culture, and rules framed for primitive circumstances would disappear with the widening of the social horizon, or would become modified to suit the needs of national and individual progress.[1]

---

1 See The Spirit of Islam, Ed. 1923.

Whilst the similarity of the personal laws of the Mahommedans to the Hebraic domestic regulations can be satisfactorily explained by the presence of the Jews in the midst of the Arabs, the resemblance which certain features of the Musulman Law bear to Roman Jurisprudence does not admit of so easy a solution. Ibn-Khaldun explains it as the effect of Byzantine learning on Saracenic thought. The Abbaside sovereigns were, no doubt, surrounded by men versed in Greek and Roman literature and science. It is not unlikely that the influence of these scholars and philosophers extended to the jealous circle of the legists. It is also possible that the remains of Byzantine learning in Syria and Egypt may have affected the juridical conceptions of the men who, in the second and third centuries of the Musulman era, built up the Sunni system of law. The principles of the Law of Pre-emption, with its fine distinctions regarding servitudes, coparcenary, etc., give rise to an impression that, though the foundations of the law were laid in Hijaz, the finishing touches were given in places where foreign conceptions had grown up round purely Saracenic ideas. The position, therefore, of the Musulman legal system seems to be this, that whilst the major portion of its rules regarding domestic institutions bears the closest analogy to Hebraic laws, the principles which regulate the dispositions of property have little in common with the Hebraic system, but offer a strong resemblance, in certain instances, to Roman Jurisprudence.

The Musulman legists trace almost all the principles to the Koran. It is regarded, in fact, to contain the fundamental prescriptions which regulate the various relations of life; the religious, civil, and criminal laws which provide for the constitution and continuance of the body politic; and even the germs of political rules and social economy. The absence in the Koran of a systematic arrangement is explained by the circumstance that the Code was gradually built up during the lifetime of the Prophet. The moral principles and the legal rules, which make up the work, were enunciated, not simultaneously as a completed code of laws, but in accordance with the exigencies of the moment and the requirements of each special case.

The Koran.

The Koran, however, was never intended to form a complete code of laws. Its silence on many points, legal as well as doctrinal, is supplemented by the oral precepts delivered from time to time by the Prophet, and by a reference to the daily mode of his life as handed down to posterity by his immediate followers. The unhappy religious schism which has, until now,[1] divided the Mahommedan world into the two great sects of the Shiahs and the Sunnis, owes its origin chiefly to the relative value attached to the various traditions, according to the source from which they are received. Very shortly after the decease of the Arabian Lawgiver, it became habitual with some of those who had during

1 Within recent years, chiefly owing to the general attitude of Christendom towards Moslem nations, a better state of feeling is growing up between the two sects.

his lifetime been intimately associated with him, but who had never lost their inimical feelings towards his family, to throw into the background all the traditional sayings of the Founder which appeared to support the rightful title of his son-in-law to the Caliphate. In later times, under the Ommeyades and the succeeding dynasty, traditions were often manufactured to support their respective claims to the headship of Islam. These reputed sayings are accordingly rejected by the partisans of the *Ahl-i-Bait*.[1] Abu Bakr, who was elected to the Caliphate immediately after the decease of the Prophet, had directed that the traditional sayings should be collected and embodied in an authoritative work before they had faded from the memory of men; but he did not survive to see it completed. The first collection did not appear until the reign of Osman, the third Caliph.

The Imamate.

The question of the *Imamate*, the spiritual headship of the Musulman Commonwealth, forms the most distinctive feature of difference between the Sunnis and the Shiahs, and gives a characteristic complexion to the juridical doctrines of the two schools. The Shiahs repudiate entirely the authority of the *Jamaat* (or the universality of the people) to elect a spiritual chief who should supersede the rightful claims of persons indicated by the Founder of the Faith ; whilst the Sunnis regard the decisions of the assemblies, however obtained, as of oecumenical importance. The question came up for discussion and settlement immediately on the decease of the Prophet, when it became necessary to elect a Caliph or successor to the Prophet to assume the leadership of Islam. The Hashimites, the kinsmen of Mohammed, maintained that the office belonged by right to 'Ali,[2] as one who had been pointed out by the Prophet as his successor. The other Koreishites, who were traditionally hostile to the Bani Hashim, insisted upon proceeding by election. But the moment was critical, for Islam was yet in its infancy and at the mercy of hostile forces bent on its destruction. To keep alive the Faith and maintain intact the structure raised by the Prophet, the speedy choice of a vicegerent was of vital importance. Whilst the Banu Hashim were engaged in the obsequies of Mohammed, Abu Bakr who, by virtue of his age and position at Mecca held a high place in the estimation of the Arabs, was elected to the office of Caliph by the votes of the Koreish.

The Caliph 'Omar.

Abu Bakr died in the third year of his Caliphate, and was succeeded by 'Omar (*Ibn-ul-Khattab*). Under this great man the conquest of Syria, Egypt and Persia was achieved by the Moslems. Upon his decease the Caliphate was offered to 'Ali on the conditions that he should govern in accordance with the precedents established by the two former Caliphs. 'Ali

1 The Ahl-i-Bait, "People of the House of Mohammed".

2 The son-in-law and cousin of the Prophet. He married Mohammed's daughter, Fatima, from whom the descendants of the Prophet take their name of Bani Fatima (the Fatimides).

declined to accept the office on those terms, declaring that in all cases respecting which he found no positive law or decision of the Prophet, he would rely upon his own judgment. This notable declaration forms another point of difference between the Shiahs and the Sunnis. The Caliphate was then offered to 'Osman,[1] who consented to the terms imposed by the electoral body. The legal divergence between the Sunni and the Shiah schools dates virtually from this epoch. The willingness of 'Osman to follow implicitly the precedents established by Abu Bakr and 'Omar, without any question as to their applicability to the ever-varying exigencies of human life, impressed a distinctive character upon the Sunni doctrines. Both Abu Bakr and 'Omar had, during their Caliphates, deferred to 'Ali's exposition of the law, and judgments were invariably given according to his interpretation of the traditions. 'Osman seems to have set a different example. This well-intentioned but weak chief, governed entirely by his secretary and kinsman, Merwan, afterwards a Caliph himself, was killed, after a short and troubled reign, by the revolted Egyptian soldiery led by Mohammed, the son of Abu Bakr. Upon his death 'Ali was elected to the Caliphate. His accession was the signal for two fierce revolts on the part of the opposite faction. The one headed by 'Ayesha, the daughter of Abu Bakr, was suppressed without much difficulty; the other was more successful. 'Osman had, during his lifetime, appointed one of his kinsmen, M'uawiyah, the son of Abu Sufian, to the governorship of Syria. This ambitious chief perceived in the murder of 'Osman an opportunity for his own aggrandisement; and the insurrection raised by him proved, indirectly, the cause of the many disasters which have befallen Islam. Defeated in several consecutive battles, he appealed to arbitration, which was agreed to by 'Ali with the object of avoiding further bloodshed. Abu Musa al-'Ash'ary was appointed an arbitrator on behalf of the House of Mohammed, and 'Amr-ibn-ul-'Aas on behalf of M'uawiyah. 'Amr[2] persuaded Abu Musa that, with the view of healing the wounds which the differences between 'Ali and M'uawiyah had inflicted on the Moslem world, it was necessary to set aside both chiefs and elect another Caliph. Abu Musa agreed to the suggestion, and on the people assembling to hear the verdict of the arbitrators, he pronounced the deposition of both M'uawiyah and 'Ali. He was followed by 'Amr-ibn-ul-'Aas, who declared that he agreed with Abu Musa in deposing 'Ali, but that he confirmed M'uawiyah in his office. The boldness of the artifice, and the shamelessness with which it was carried into effect, struck with dismay all those who had seen in the arbitration a means for preventing further bloodshed in Islam. This proceeding of 'Amr-ibn-ul-'Aas exasperated the Fatimides and both parties separated vowing undying hatred towards each other. 'Ali was shortly after assassinated whilst engaged in prayers[3] in a mosque at Kufa. His assassination enabled M'uawiyah to consolidate his power both in Syria and Hijaz.[4]

1 'Osman was the son of 'Affan, the son of Ab-ul-'Aas, the son of 'Ommeyya.

2 The 'Amr who conquered Egypt.

3 11 Safar A. H. 37—28 July A C 657.

4 See Short History of the Saracens.

The rise of the sects.

Until the accession of this chief to the office of the Caliphate, which the stern virtues of the early Caliphs had sanctified and adorned, no distinctive appellation was assigned to or assumed by either party. The partisans of 'Ali were known simply as the Bani Hashim. Under M'uawiyah, the followers of the House of Mohammed began to call themselves *Shiahs* or "adherents" and their enemies *Nawasib*, rebels, or *Khawarij* (insurgents or deserters). The Fatimides adopted green, the colour of the Prophet, as the symbol of their cause; the Banu 'Ommeyya, on the other hand, assumed white for their standard. Up to this time the divergence between the two factions was chiefly political and dynastic. Under the Abbasides, who overthrew the dynasty of 'Ommeyya, the faction which advocated the principle of election in preference to hereditary succession, adopted the name of *Ahl-us-Sunnat wa'l Jama'at* ("People of the Traditions and the Assembly"). Their doctrinal and legal differences began now to assume the type and proportions they retain at the present moment.[1] The Shiahs reject not only the decisions of the oecumenical Councils, but also all traditions not handed down by 'Ali or his immediate descendants—those who had seen the Prophet and held familiar intercourse with him.

The Shiah doctrines.

According to the Shiah doctrines, the oral precepts of the Prophet are in their nature supplementary to the Koranic ordinances, and their binding effect depends on the degree of harmony existing between them and the laws of the Koran. Thus, those traditions which seem to be in conflict with the positive directions in the text are considered to be apocryphal. The process of elimination is conducted upon certain recognised principles founded upon logical rules and definite data. These rules have acquired a distinctive type among the M'utazilas, who have eliminated from "the holy traditions" such alleged sayings of the Prophet as appeared incompatible and out of harmony with his developed teachings as explained and illustrated by the philosophers and jurists of his family.

The Sunni doctrines.

The Sunnis, on the other hand, base their doctrines on the entirety of the traditions. They regard the concordant decisions of the successive Caliphs and of the general body of jurists (*Ijm'a-ul-Ummat*) as supplementing the Koranic rules and regulations, and as almost equal in authority to them.

Sources of Mahommedan Law—Sunni doctrines.

According to the Sunni doctrines, the sources of the Mahommedan Law are invariable in their order and limited in their number. With reference to these fundamental bases of jurisprudence, as they are called, there is little or no divergence

1 See, however, The Spirit of Islam where I have given a fuller account of the origin of the two sects, Ed. 1923; and Short History of the Saracens

among the several branches of the Sunni school, though they differ much in their mode of interpretation and exposition of the laws. (1) The Koran ; (2) the *Hadis* or *Sunnat* (traditions handed down from the Prophet); (3) the *Ijma'a-ul-Ummat* (concordance among the followers); and (4) *Kiyas* (the exercise of private judgment based on analogy), constitute the bases upon which Sunni jurisprudence is essentially founded. The *Hadis* (pl. *Ahadis*) embraces (*a*) all the words, counsels, and oral laws of the Prophet (*Kawl*) ; (*b*) his actions, his works, and daily practices (*F'yl*); (*c*) and his silence (*Takrir*), implying a tacit approbation on his part of any individual act committed by his disciples. The rules deduced from these subsidiary sources vary considerably in respect of the degree of authority which is attached to them. If the rules, or traditional precepts, are of public and universal notoriety (*Ahadis-al-mutwatireh*), they are regarded as absolutely authentic and decisive. If the traditions, though known publicly by a great majority of people, do not possess the character of universal notoriety, they are designated as *Ahadis-al-mashhura*, and stand second in rank to the *Ahadis-al-mutwatireh*; whilst the *Akhbar-i-wahid* which depend for their authenticity upon the authority of isolated individuals, have little or no value attached to them. Thus, every tradition purporting to be handed down by the contemporaries and companions of the Prophet, regardless of their actual relationship to him, is considered to be authentic and genuine, provided certain arbitrary conditions framed with the view of testing the value of personal testimony are complied with.

Ijma'a-ul-Ummat implies general concordance. Under this collective name are included all the apostolic laws, the explanations, glosses, and decisions of the leading disciples of the Prophet, especially of the first four Caliphs[1] (the *Khulafai-Rashidin*), on theological, civil, and criminal matters.

Kiyas, the exercise of private judgment, forms the principal point of difference among the four sub-divisions of the Sunni school of jurisprudence.

The Shiahs do not admit the genuineness of any tradition not received from the *Ahl-i-Bait* ("the People of the House"), consisting of 'Ali and Fatima and their descendants or adherents, and repudiate entirely the validity of all decisions not passed by their own spiritual leaders and Imams. In the application of private or analytical judgment and in drawing conclusions from the ancient precedents they also differ widely from the Sunnis.

Effect of the Shiah persecutions.

The persecutions to which the Shiahs were, from time to time, subjected, and the mysterious disappearance of their last Imam, have induced among them the belief that though *ghaib* (absent) he is yet alive and that he will soon make his appearance to lead them to victory. Partly in consequence of this belief, and partly as a result of the repression from which they have invariably suffered, the Shiahs have entirely dissociated the secular

1 Abu Bakr, 'Omar, 'Osman and 'Ali.

from the spiritual power. In Shiah countries the Church and the State are distinctly separate from each other. Though a Shiah sovereign bows to the authority of the *Mujtahids* (expounders of the law), he submits to them not so much as spiritual chiefs, but rather as counsellors whose views ought to be adopted in secular matters, as the reflex, probably of the opinions of the Invisible Leader or Imam. Until the Saffavian Sovereigns[1] made the Shiah creed the State religion of Persia, it was the religion of a persecuted and hated sect.

The effect of this separation of the spiritual from the temporal power is most clearly marked in the doctrine of Escheats. According to the Shiahs, there is no escheat to the *Bait-ul-Mal* (the public treasury). The idea of a *Bait-ul-Mal* is "abhorrent" to the Shiah creed.[2] All escheats, which occur only in cases where the deceased leaves no possible heir, go to the spiritual Imam, and in his absence (*ghibat*) to his representative (the *Mujtahid*), who distributes the proceeds among the poor of the intestate's native city.

Sub-sections of the Shiahs.

The Shiahs are divided into several sub-sections. For example, the *Isna 'Asharias* or *Imamias* (the followers of the twelve Imams)[3], the *Isma'ilias* (the followers of Isma'il, one of the sons of

---

1 Shah Isma'il Sufi was the founder of this dynasty in the sixteenth century of the Christian era; hence the name of the dynasty.

2 Jam'a-ush-Shittat, Book on Inheritance.

3 Different branches of the 'Alides or Fatimides have ruled under the different denominations of Ameer, Imam, Sharif, and Caliph, in different parts of the Musalman world, such as the Banu Ukhaydur, the Banu Musa, the Banu Kitadah at Mecca, the Banu Taba-Taba in Northern Yemen, the Banu Ziyad in Southern Yemen, the Banu Idris in Morocco, the Banu Fatima (Fatimides) in Africa and Egypt. The order in which the Shiahs recognize the Imams is as follows:—

(*i*) 'Ali, (Murtaza, the Chosen) (A H 35, A C 656).

(*ii*) Hasan, (Mujtaba, the Elect) (A H 40, A C 660).

(*iii*) Husain, (Shahid-i-Kerbela, the Martyr of Kerbela) (A H 50, A C 670).

(*iv*) 'Ali, (Zain-ul-'abidin, the Ornament of the Pious) (A H 60, A C 679).

(*v*) Mahommed, (al-Bakir, the Profound) (A H 94, A C 712).

(*vi*) J'afar, (as-Sadik, the Trusty) (A H 117, A C 734).

(*vii*) Musa, (al-Kazim, the Patient) (A H 148, A C 765).

(*viii*) 'Ali ibn-Musa, (ar-Riza, the Acceptable) (A H 183, A C 799).

(*ix*) Mohammed, (at-Taki, the Pious) (A H 203, A C 818).

(*x*) 'Ali, (an-Naki, the Pure) (A H 220, A C 835).

(*xi*) Hasan, (al-'Askari, of al-'Askar) (A H 254, A C 868).

(*xii*) Mohammed, (al-Mahdy, the Guide) (A H 260, A C 873).

This last Imam, according to the Shiah belief, disappeared at a very tender age, in a grotto at Surramun-Raa (Sirmanrey or Samara). He is believed to be still alive and they look forward with earnest anticipation to his re-appearance to re-establish the universal Caliphate and to restore the purity of the human race. The Sunnis believe that he is not born yet, and that he will appear towards the close of the world with Jesus Christ. These two different views have two different bearings on the law, as is shown in the text; see Short History of the Saracens.

J'afar as-Sadik, the sixth Imam), the *Zaidias*, the *Batinias* (the allegorists), etc. They differ from each other not so much on the interpretation of the law as on doctrinal points.

The M'utazilas.

The school of the M'utazilas, regarded by Shahristani and others as an offshoot from the Shiah branch, differs from the parent stock in essential particulars. The rise of this independent school forms one of the most interesting features in the history of Islam. It originated in the secession of Wasil bin 'Ata, a contemporary of Abu Hanifa, from the doctrines taught by Imam Hasan al-Basri (of Basra).

Hasan was educated in the school of the early Fatimide philosophers, and the liberality of his views was in remarkable contrast to that of his age. Wasil imbibed knowledge at the same source, but he separated from Hasan on the question of free will and predestination, and founded a school of his own. His disciples have, from the fact of his secession, assumed the designation of M'utazilas or *Ahl-ul-'Itizal* (Separatists or Dissenters). Wasil soon formulated the principles which constituted the basis of his difference from the other existing schools. His impulsiveness often led him to overstep the limits of moderation in his antagonism to intellectual tyranny; yet the general rationalism which distinguished his system of philosophy and jurisprudence from every other, attracted the most advanced and cultured minds to his side. Imam Zamakhshari (the author of the *Kashshaf*, the most notable commentary on the Koran), Abu'l Hasan 'Ali al-Mas'udi, "Imam—historian and doctor,"[1] Mirkhond and Khondemir, the authors respectively of the *Rouzat-us-Safa* and *Habib-us-Siyar*, were all M'utazilas. There can be no doubt that the moderate M'utazilas represented the views of 'Ali and the most liberal and learned of his early descendants, for the doctrines of the Fatimides bear a strong analogy to those of the school founded by Wasil and reformed by Zamakhshari.[2]

The Akhbaris and the Usulis.

The Indian[3] Shiahs are chiefly *Isna-A'sharias* or *Imamias*. These are divided into two sub-sections, the *Akhbari* and the *Usuli*, who form, so to speak, separate schools of law. The *Akhbaris* adhere to certain principles of interpretation laid down by the *Mujtahids* or "expounders of law", and are guided entirely by their exposition. The *Usulis*, on the other hand, deny entirely the influence of authority in matters of opinion, unless such authority should be in harmony with the dictates of reason and judgment. They accept only such traditions as are found to be genuine upon a most critical exegesis, and allow the exercise of private judgment in the application and interpretation of legal principles.[4] They are, in this respect, in accord with the principal Sunni school; and

1 Ibn-Khallikan.

2 Compare the 1st Khutba of the Nahj-ul-Balaghat, the chapter on Free Will in the Bihar-ul-Anwar, and other Shiah traditions.

3 Now Indo-Pakistan Sub-Continent.

4 Syed Ali Nawaz Gardezi *v.* Mohammad Yousaf P L D 1963 S C 51.

in their acceptance of the doctrine of evolution, they approach most closely the M'utazilas.

Isma'ilias, Khojahs and Borahs.

The *Isma'ilia* branch of the Shiahs, which professed esoteric doctrines, had a peculiar origin. About the beginning of the eleventh century it split into two sections, the western and the eastern, who owned allegiance to different Grand Priors. In the Bombay Presidency, there are large numbers of *Isma'ilias.* They are divided into two sections called respectively Borahs and Khojahs. Both communities appear to have been converted from Hinduism to Islam in the early part of the thirteenth century by *Isma'ili* missionaries called *Da'is.*[1] The Khojahs belong to the eastern sub-division of *Isma'ilias* and are the followers of Hasan Sabah, "the Old Man of the Mountain." His representative resides at Bombay and still holds spiritual sway over them.[2] On questions of inheritance the Khojahs are governed chiefly by Hindu customs. Although many of them have for years past tried to place themselves under the law of the religion they profess, the British Indian Courts have allowed them so far no escape from the bondage they had accepted on their original conversion. In the highlands of Gilgit and Hunza[3] also there are large numbers of *Isma'ilias* of the eastern branch, who are subject to the Musulman Law. The Borahs, on the other hand, belong to the western sub-division and their *Da'i-ud-D'awat* or Grand Prior, lives in Yemen. They are divided into two groups, *viz., Sulaimani* and *Daudi,* and are for the most governed by the general principles of the Mahommedan Law. In certain parts of Gujerat, however, there are Sunni Borahs, who were originally Hindu Rajputs and have retained Hindu customs.[4]

Memons.

The Memons of Bombay and Cutch, a cognate community to the Borahs and Khojahs, follow the Hanafi or Shafei doctrines, but, like the Khojahs, on questions of succession are subject to customs, more or less Hindu in origin, which I shall discuss in its proper place.[5]

The Shiah school of Law.

The Shiah school of Law was founded by the apostolical Imam J'afar as-Sadik, the sixth Imam of the House of Mohammed

---

1 One who invites, a missionary; see The Spirit of Islam, Ed. 1923.

2 See Short History of the Saracens.

3 These two hilly tracts are now included in the State of Azad Kashmir.

4 See post, p. 27.

5 By virtue of section 2 of the Muslim Personal Law (Shariat) Application Act, 1937, custom is no longer the rule of decision in the matter of succession to Muslims of any sect except in matters relating to succession to agricultural land and to religious endowments to which the Act is not applicable. In West Pakistan, however, the West Pakistan Muslim Personal Law (Shariat) Application Act, 1962, notwithstanding any custom or usage, makes the Shariat Law applicable to all matters regarding succession etc. in cases where the parties are Muslims.

in the second century of the Hejira and is historically anterior in date to that of the Sunnis. It represents the reforms introduced by the Arabian Prophet in the customary rules relating to inheritance prevalent among the ancient Arabs. As in the old Roman Law the devolution of property among them was governed by the rule of agnacy. Neither women nor persons connected to the deceased through them had any right of succession. Agnatic relations or persons connected through males were alone recognised as entitled to take a share in his inheritance. The rule was founded in the very essence of primitive society which depended for its existence on the united strength of a band of males subject to one head. Thus it was that whilst adopted sons and even slaves had rights, the children of daughters and sisters had no place in the customary rules which regulated succession; for the women passed out of the family on their marriage, and their children were subject to a different head. The *patria potestas*, it will be seen later, was as noticeable a feature of the pre-Islamic Arabian customs as of the Roman Law, and its vestiges are strongly marked in that branch of the Mahommedan Law which relates to the rights of the father over his non-adult children.

The rule of agnacy.

In the Koran there are specific provisions for the succession of daughters and sisters. The Shiahs have carried these rules to their logical conclusion and have cut out from their system the artificial doctrine of agnacy. The Sunni Law, however, still retains largely the old rule.

The reason for its perpetuation in the Sunni system has a peculiar and interesting history. When the Abbasides succeeded in overthrowing the 'Ommeyades, they found it necessary to legitimatise their title to the Caliphate, for the eyes of the Moslem world were still turned to the descendants of the Prophet as the rightful heirs to his temporal and spiritual heritage—and in effecting this they found their chief support in the doctrine of agnacy. They claimed that as descendants of the Prophet's uncle, 'Abbas, they were his "agnates" and as such had a better title than the descendants of his daughter Fatima.[1] And this was the keystone of the fabric built up by the ablest monarch of the House of 'Abbas, Mansur, the real founder of the Sunni church.

The rule of agnacy has thus remained, chiefly from dynastic reasons, a part of the Sunni system. In early times it was as strongly enforced as under the old Romans. If a person died without leaving any "agnatic" relation but a daughter's or sister's child, his property did not go to the latter but escheated to the Caliph. In 896 A. C. the Caliph M'utazid b'Illah abolished this cruel rule; and laid down that in the absence of sharers and "agnates" (*'Asabah*), the "uterine relations" should succeed.[2] And this has remained the law ever since.

---

1 They ignored entirely the title of 'Ali, the cousin of the Prophet. Ali being a cousin of the Prophet could not according to the agnatic theory succeed in the presence of the Prophets' uncle 'Abbas.

2 See Short History of the Saracens.

Abu Hanifa.

The founder of the first distinctive Sunni school was Abu Hanifa.[1] This great jurist was born in the year 80 of the Hejira during the reign of 'Abdul Malik ibn-Merwan. He was educated in the Shiah school of law, and received his first instructions in jurisprudence from Imam J'afar as-Sadik and heard traditions from Abu 'Abdulla ibn-ul-Mubarak and Hamid bin-Sulaiman. Abu Hanifa often quotes the great Shiah Imam as his authority. On his return to his native city of Kufa, though he continued to remain a zealous and consistent partisan of the House of 'Ali, he seceded from the Shiah school of law and founded a system of his own, diverging completely on many important points from the doctrines of the Shiahs; and yet so close is the resemblance between his exposition of the law and their views, that there is no reason for doubt as to the source from which he derived his original inspiration. The latitude which he allows to private judgment in the interpretation of the law seems to be unquestionably a reflex of the opinions of the Fatimide doctors.

A proper comprehension of the teachings of Abu Hanifa is of considerable assistance in illustrating and understanding the legal doctrines of the Shiahs. The Imam 'Azim or the great Imam as Abu Hanifa was commonly styled, died in the year A. H. 150. The school which he founded goes by the name of *Hanafi* and its tenets are in force among the majority of the Indian Musulmans—among the Afghans, Turkomans, almost all Central Asian Mahommedans, the Turks, and the Egyptians. His school owns by far the largest number of followers. Abu Hanifa's teachings were amplified by his disciples, Abu Yusuf and Mohammed, who have, in the estimation of many Sunnis, almost overshadowed the fame of their great master. When the disciples differ from the Imam, their opinions are generally adopted in preference to those of the master. When the disciples differ among themselves, it is open to the Musulman judge to accept and give effect to the exposition most consistent with the requirements of justice and the circumstances of the times.[2]

On some questions, however, the opinion of one is regarded by consensus as of greater weight than of the other. And where there is no general agreement with regard to a particular exposition, in some localities the views of Abu Yusuf are accepted, in others those of Mohammed.

The founder of the second school of law among the Sunnis was (Abu 'Abdullah) Malik ibn Ans, whose tenets are in force in Northern Africa, especially in Morocco and Algeria. He died in the year A. H. 179 during the reign of Harun ar-Rashid.[3]

1 Abu Hanifa an-Noman ibn-Sabit (A C 699-769).

2 See Sir W. Jones' Works, Vol. III, p. 510.

3 His greatest legacy to his followers is known by the name of Muwatta, which treats of the oral dicta of the Prophet.

Shaf'ei

Shaf'ei[1] was the founder of the third school. He was born at Ghizah in Syria, in the same year in which Abu Hanifa died. He died in Egypt in the year A. H. 204 (A. C. 819) during the Caliphate of al-Mamun. He was a contemporary of the Shiah Imam 'Ali ibn-Musa ar-Riza. Shaf'ei's doctrines are generally followed among the Musulmans of the Malabar Coast and Ceylon, in Northern Africa, partially in Egypt, in Southern Arabia, and the Malayan Peninsula. In recent years his doctrines have made great progress in India and his followers are found among all ranks of Mahommedan society.

Ibn Hanbal.

The fourth school was originated by Ahmed ibn Hanbal.[2] He flourished during the reigns of al-Mamun and his successor, M'utassim b'Illah. These two Caliphs were M'utazilas. Ibn Hanbal's extreme fanaticism, and the persistency with which he tried to inflame the bigotry of the masses against the sovereigns, brought him into trouble with the rulers. He died in the odour of great sanctity in the year A. H. 241. Ibn Hanbal and his patristicism are responsible for the ill-success of Mamun in introducing the M'utazila doctrines throughout the empire, and for the frequent outbursts of persecution which deluged the Mahommedan world with the blood of Moslems.

The followers of Ahmed ibn Hanbal called the Hanbalis, though few in number, are found chiefly in Hazramaut (Hadramaut) and 'Oman.

Abu Hanifa, Maliḳ, Shaf'ei and Ibn Hanbal are the founders of the four orthodox schools among the Sunnis (the *Mazahib-ul-arb'a*). Their doctrines are essentially the same as regards the fundamental dogmas (*usul*), though they differ from each other in the application of private judgment and in the interpretation and exposition of the Koran.

Shaf'ei, Malik, and Ibn Hanbal almost entirely exclude the exercise of private judgment in the exposition of legal principles. They are wholly governed by the force of precedents. They do not admit the validity of a recourse to analogical deductions, or of such an interpretation of the law whereby its spirit is adapted to the special circumstances of any particular case. Their followers are accordingly designated *Ahl-ul-hadis* (traditionists *par excellence*).[3]

The exercise of private judgment, consecrated by the Prophet and adhered to strictly by his immediate descendants, had induced the development of a liberal spirit among the Fatimides; and this had its legitimate influence on the mind of Abu Hanifa. The value which he and his disciples attached to the exercise of Kiyas

1 Abu 'Abdullah Mohammed ibn Idris ash-Shaf'ei'.

2 Abu 'Abdullah Ahmad ash-Shaibani al-Marwari ibn-Hanbal (shortly Ahmad ibn-Hanbal).

3 Shahristani; Ibn Khaldun.

is proved by a series of passages given in the *Fatawai Alamgiri.*[1] The followers of Abu Hanifa are styled *Ahl-ur-Rai wa'l Kiyas* ("people of judgment and reason").

The Ghairmukallid.

Within recent years a new sect has sprung up among the Sunnis of India, the members of which call themselves *ghair-mukallidin* or *non-conformists.* Their opponents sometimes designate them *Wahabis,* which is neither correct nor just. The *ghair-mukallid,* as his name implies, does not conform to any particular sect, but approaches most closely the Shaf'eis in doctrinal matters. Like them he pronounces during prayers the word *amin* in a loud voice (which is technically called *amin-b'il-jahr*), and makes the ceremonial gesture of raising the hands *above* the ears at a particular point of the service, which is called *raf'a-eddain.* These have been held to be "merely minor matters of difference not affecting the essentials of the service."[2] Apart from doctrinal differences a *ghair-mukallid* is generally subject to the Hanafi school of law.

A Sunni Mahommedan belonging to any of these sects may validly perform his devotions under the leadership of a member of another sect.[3]

Position of women in Islam.

The reforms instituted by Mohammed effected a vast and marked improvement in the position of women. Both among the Arabs and the Jews who inhabited the peninsula of Arabia the condition of women was extremely degraded. The Hebrew maiden, even in her father's house, stood in the position of a servant;[4] her father could sell her if a minor. He, and after his death his son, disposed of her at their will and pleasure. The daughter inherited nothing except in the extremest case.[5] Among the pagan Arabs, a woman was considered a mere chattel, she formed an integral part of the estate of her husband or her father; and the widows of a man descended to his son or sons by right of inheritance, as any other portion of his patrimony.

The status of women in Islam.

Under the Islamic laws, as will be shown in detail hereafter, a woman occupies a superior legal position to that of her English sister. As long as she is unmarried, she remains under the parental roof, and until she attains her majority, she is, to some extent, under the control of the father or his representatives. As soon, however, as she is of age, the law vests in her all the rights

1 In page 383 of the third volume occurs a passage taken from the Muhit, which is worth quoting. It says: "If the concurrent opinion of the Apostolic Companions should not be forthcoming, but there should be a concordance among their tab'iun, the Kazi should follow the principles observed by the latter; should there be, however, a difference among the Tabi'un, the Judge should compare their arguments and adopt the judgment he deems preferable". Other passages of like import are contained in the same volume, which place the doctrines of the Hanafite school in the clearest light possible. Tabi'un are the immediate disciples of the Companions.

2 Fazl Karim *v.* Haji Mowla Bukhsh (1891) L R 18, I A 59; s. c. I L 18 Cal. 448.

3 *Ibid.*

4 Numbers xxx, 17.

5 Dollinger, The Gentile and the Jew, Vol. II, p. 341.

which belong to her as an independent human being. She is entitled to share in the inheritance of her parents along with her brothers, and though the proportion is different, the distinction is founded on a just comprehension of the relative circumstances of brother and sister. On her marriage she does not lose her individuality. She does not cease to be a separate member of society, and her existence does not "merge" in that of her husband. No doctrine of "coverture" is recognised; and her property remains hers in her individual right. She can sue her debtors in the open Courts, without the necessity of joining a next friend or under cover of her husband's name. She continues to exercise, after she has passed from her father's house into her husband's home, all the rights which the law gives to men. All the privileges which belong to her as woman and a wife are secured to her not by the courtesies that "come and go", but by the actual text in the book of law. She can alienate or devise her property without asking the leave of her husband. She can act as an administratrix or executrix, or be appointed a *Mutwallieh* (governor of a charitable endowment).

A Moslem marriage.

A Moslem marriage is a civil act, needing no *mullah*, requiring no sacred rite. The contract of marriage gives the man no power over the woman's person beyond what the law defines, and none whatever upon her goods and property.

A Musulman wife.

A Musulman wife retains in her husband's household all the rights which the law vests in her as a responsible member of society. She can be sued as a *femme sole*. She can receive property without the intervention of trustees. She has a distinct lien upon her husband's estate for her ante-nuptial settlement. Her rights as a mother do not depend for their recognition upon the idiosyncracies of individual judges. She can enter into binding contracts with her husband, and proceed against him in law if necessary. Her earnings acquired by her individual exertions cannot be wasted by a prodigal husband, nor can she be ill-treated with impunity by one who is brutal.

An introduction to a treatise on the Personal Law of the Mahommedans will not be complete unless attention is briefly drawn to the disqualifications which exclude individuals from the enjoyment of certain civil rights. These disqualifications are primarily political in their nature.

Difference of religion, or what would be called in Musulman legal treatises "infidelity" implied in early times unqualified hostility to the Commonwealth of Islam, and apostasy was tantamount to treason. Accordingly, all sects agree in excluding the non-Moslem, as well as the person who has abjured the Musulman faith, from the right of succession to the inheritance of Musulman relations on the ground that by so doing they keep out hostile and treasonable elements from the Mahommedan body politic.

The Indian Act XXI of 1850 has removed the impediment to succession which the Musulman Law imposed on the person who abjured Islam.

PART I
THE LAW RELATING TO SUCCESSION

CHAPTER I
GENERAL OBSERVATIONS

SECTION I
APPLICABILITY OF THE MAHOMMEDAN LAW

THE introduction of Musulman Law into India[1] is co-eval with the establishment of Mahommedan rule in the country but it made no change in the enjoyment by the Hindu inhabitants of their religion, laws, or ancient usages and institutions. At the present moment nearly seventy[2] millions of the population profess the religion of Islam, and the followers of the Arabian Prophet are to be found in every part of the Indian[1] continent. As the devolution of property among Mahommedans, wherever located, and all matters relating to status and dispositions made by them are governed by their personal law, it is important to have some idea of the exact applicability of the Mahommedan Civil Law and of the rules under which it was administered in British India.[3]

[4]21 Geo. III C. 70, s. 17.

The British Government at the commencement of its ascendancy assured to the people by a solemn Act of Parliament the full enjoyment of their laws and customs. Section 17, 21 Geo. III, c. 70, enacted that in all suits and actions before the Supreme Court of Judicature at Fort William in Bengal, inheritance and succession to lands, rents and goods, and all matters of contract and dealing between party and party shall be determined in the case of Mahommedans by the laws and usages of the Mahommedans, and in the case of Hindus by the laws and usages of the Hindus, and where only one of the parties was a Hindu or a Mahommedan "by the laws and usages of the defendant."

Section 13, 37 Geo. III, c. 142, made a similar provision in respect of the Supreme Courts of Madras and Bombay. The present High Courts of Judicature in the several Presidencies, which, in the exercise of their Ordinary Original Civil Jurisdiction, have succeeded to the powers of the old Supreme Courts, are subject to the same rules.[5]

---

1 Now Indo-Pakistan sub-continent.

2 This number has by now gone almost doubled and is estimated at one hundred and thirty millions.

3 It continued to be administered in the Indo-Pakistan sub-continent with the changes brought about after the Independence.

4 Now this discussion is merely of historical interest.

5 The provisions in the Charters of the Supreme Courts guaranteeing the administration of Hindu and Mahommedan law have formed the subject of judicial decision in the case of H. H. Azimunnissa Begum *v.* Clement Dale (1871) 6 Mad. H. Court Rep., 455.

[1]Reg. IV of 1793, s. 15.

For the Mofussil, or the area outside the Ordinary Original Civil Jurisdiction of the Supreme Court of Fort William, section 15 of Regulation IV of 1793 provided that "in all suits regarding succession, inheritance, marriage and caste, and all religious usages and institutions, the Mahommedan Laws with respect to Mahommedans are to be considered as the general rules by which the judges are to form their decision".

Similar laws were enacted soon after for the Mofussil of Madras and Bombay.

[1]Act XII of 1887, s. 37.

The law now in force regulating the powers and jurisdiction of the Civil Courts in Bengal, the North-Western Provinces and Assam is Act XII of 1887. Section 37, subsection (1), enacts that in the matters specified therein, the Muhammedan or Hindu Law "shall form the rule of decision, except in so far as such law has by legislative enactment been altered or abolished"

Subsection (2) declares that "in cases not provided for by subsection (1)[2] or any other law for the time being, the Court shall act according to justice, equity and good conscience."

Subsection (1) is by no means exhaustive. To give one example, it makes no mention of "gifts" or voluntary donations as one of the subjects in which the Hindu or Mahommedan Law, as the case may be, should furnish the rule of decision. The Courts, therefore, have proceeded on the principle that it was not the intention of the Legislature to confine the application of the Hindu or Mahommedan Law to the subjects specifically mentioned; and that the law of the parties should, under the rule of "justice, equity and good conscience" be applied to other matters, unless such law is opposed to any substantive enactment. Thus, it has been held that it is in conformity with equity and good conscience, that all questions relating to gifts should be governed by the Mahommedan Law.[3] It has also been held that the Mahommedan Law applies not only to the parties to a transaction but extends to persons although of different creeds, deriving title from one or other of them.[4]

In section 37, Act XII of 1887, there is no reservation in favour of customs *dehors* the general Mahommedan Law. Nor did the older Acts, which it has replaced, contain any provision in that behalf. The Courts in the Bengal Presidency have accordingly not given effect to customs in variation of that law.[5]

---

1 Now this discussion is merely of historical interest.

2 "Succession, inheritance, marriage, caste, or any religious usage or institution." The subjects are the same as in s. 15, Reg. IV of 1793.

3 Zohorooddeen Sircar *v.* Baharoolla Sirdar (1864) Gap No. W R 185; Yusuf Ali *v.* Collector of Tippera (1882) I L R 9 Cal. 138.

4 H. H. Azimunnissa Begum *v.* Clement Dale, supra.

5 Surmust Khan *v.* Kadirdad Khan (1866) Agra (N.-W. P.), C F B R Ed., 1867, 39 [Judgment of the Full Bench based on Reg. IV of 1793, s. 15 and Reg. III of 1803, s. 16 (1)]; Hakim Khan *v.* Gul Khan (1882) I L 8 Cal. 826; s c. 10 Cal. L R 603; Jammya *v.* Diwan (1900) I L 23 All. 20.

[1]In the Bombay Regulation IV of 1827,[2] the Punjab Laws Act (IV of 1872) relating to the jurisdiction of the Punjab Civil Courts, the Madras Courts Act (III of 1873), the Central Provinces Act (XX of 1875), the Burmah Courts Act (XI of 1887), and the Oude Act (XVIII of 1876), the Legislature **has** expressly provided that subject to certain conditions, customs prevailing among "any body or class of persons" should form the rule of decision by the Court.[3]

It will be noticed that in all these Acts the Legislature expressly declares that, in the absence of any specific provision for any particular case, the Courts shall decide according to "justice, equity and good conscience".

---

1 Now this discussion is merely of historical interest.

2 Repealed by Act XIV of 1869.

3 S. 26 of Reg. IV of 1827 provides as follows:—"The law to be observed in the trial of suits shall be Acts of Parliament and Regulations of Government applicable to the case; in the absence of such Acts and Regulations the usage of the country in which the suit arose, if none such appears, the law of the defendant; and in the absence of specific law and usage, justice, equity and good conscience alone." The importance that has been attached to custom in the Bombay decisions is due to the special provisions of this Regulation.

S. 5 of Act IV of 1872 provides—"In questions regarding inheritance, special property of females, betrothal, marriage, dower, adoption, guardianship, minority, bastardy, family relations, wills, legacies, gifts, partition or any religious usage or institution, the rule of decision shall be—

S. 1. Any custom of any body or class of persons which is not contrary to justice, equity and good conscience and has not been declared to be void by any competent authority.

S. 2. The Mahommedan Law, in cases where the parties are Mahommedans . . . . except in so far as such law has been altered or abolished by legislative enactment or is opposed to the provisions of this Act or has been modified by any such customs as is referred to in the preceding clause of this section."

S. 6 declares that "in cases not otherwise specially provided for the Judges shall decide according to justice, equity and good conscience."

S. 5 of Act XX of 1875 provides that "in questions regarding inheritance, special property of females, betrothal, marriage, dower, adoption, guardianship, minority, bastardy, family relations, wills, legacies, gifts, partition, or any religious usage or institution, the rule of decision shall be the Mahommedan Law in cases where the parties are Mahommedans . . . . . . except in so far as it is opposed to the provisions of this Code, provided that when among any class or body of persons or among the members of any family any custom prevails which is inconsistent with the law applicable between such persons under this section and, which, if not inconsistent with such law, would have been given effect to as legally binding, such custom shall, notwithstanding anything therein contained be given effect to."

S. 6 declares that "in cases not provided for by s. 5, or any other law for the time being in force, the Courts shall act according to justice, equity and good conscience."

Note:—The above provisions of different enactments now stand repealed by section 6 of the Muslim Personal Law (Shariat) Application Act, 1937 (XXVI of 1937). The effect of the Act of 1937 is to abolish custom in all questions (save questions relating to agricultural land.) In West Pakistan, however, the West Pakistan Muslim Personal Law (Shariat) Application Act (V of 1962) as amended by the West Pakistan Ordinance XXXIX of 1963 abolishes custom in all matters of succession etc,

Mahommedan Law applies to all Moslems.

The Mahommedan Law applies to all Musulmans whether they are so by birth or by conversion.[1] In this connection it is necessary to bear in mind the distinction between *Islam* and *Iman* (faith). Any person who professes the religion of Islam, in other words, accepts the unity of God and the prophetic character of Mohammed is a Moslem and is subject to the Musulman Law. So long as the individual pronounces the *Kalma* of *Tauhid*[2] the *Credo* of Islam, it is not necessary for him or her to observe any of the rites and ceremonies, or to believe in particular doctrines which imply *Iman* or belief. This distinction has often been lost sight of by British Indian Courts which have, in dealing with Mahommedan cases, assumed the position and function of Courts of Conscience.[3]

The observance of rites and ceremonies, apart from the religious aspect, is useful only as pieces of testimony regarding the communion to which a person belongs and the school of law to which he or she is consequently subject.

A *sui juris* Mahommedan male or female, can at any time go over from one sect to another.[4] No formality is required for that purpose. A slight variation in the performance of prayers, the addition of a sentence in "the Confession of Faith"[5] effectuates the change.

Sunnis and Shiahs can intermarry.

Sunnis and Shiahs may validly intermarry without any change of sect or communion. And a woman of the Sunni sect married to a Shiah husband is entitled to the privileges secured to her married position by the law of her sect.[6] The performance by her of ceremonies usually observed in Shiah families on the anniversary of the martyrdom of Husain[7] would be no evidence

---

1 See the remarks of Lord Kingsdown in Abraham *v.* Abraham (1863) 9 Moo. I A 195. *See also* Khambata *v.* Khambata (1935) 59 Bom. 278.

2 *i.e.*, Confession of Unity.

3 In case of Raj Bahadur *v.* Bishen Dayal (1882) I L 4 All. 343, the learned Judges were in error, it is respectfully submitted, in holding that "in determining whether parties are Hindus or Mahommedans within the meaning of s. 24 of Act VI of 1871 [now replaced by s. 37 of Act XII of 1887], we must apply its terms strictly, and confine their operation to those who may properly be regarded as orthodox believers in the one religion or the other." This is wholly wrong.

4 Muhammad Ibrahim *v.* Ghulam Ahmed (1864) 1 Bom. H C R 236; Hayat-un-nissa *v.* Muhammad Ali Khan (1890) L R 17 I A 73; s c, I L 12 All. 290.

5 The Kalma-i-Shahadat is in these words: "I bear witness that there is no God but God: and I bear witness that Mohammed is the Prophet of God." To which the Shiah adds "and I bear witness that 'Ali is the Commander of the Faithful, Imam of the pious and successor of the Prophet".

6 Nasrat Husain *v.* Hamidan (1882) I L 4 All. 205; Hayat-un-nissa *v.* Muhammad Ali Khan, *supra*.

7 In the month of Muhurram.

of a change of sect. That can be effectuated only by her offering her prayers (*namaz*) according to the Shiah ritual or by pronouncing the Shiah "Confession of Faith"

In one case the Calcutta High Court has laid down very broadly that "the great majority of Mahommedans in this country being Sunnis the presumption will be that the parties to a suit or proceeding are Sunnis unless it is shown that they belong to the Shiah sect."[1] This *dictum* must be accepted with reservation. In some parts of the country the Shiahs preponderate in numbers; it would be difficult in those districts to make any such presumption.[2] It is submitted that in every proceeding involving a question of Mahommedan Law, the Court should require the parties to state to which school of law they are subject, and in case of difference to adduce evidence in support of their respective allegations, and then decide by what law the question at issue is to be determined.

Presumption in favour of a Moslem child.

When either of the parents is a Moslem, the Musalman Law presumes the child to be a Moslem (until it is able to make a choice, in other words, attains majority),[3] and the right to its succession is regulated by the laws of Islam, and of the school or sect to which the parent conforms.

Moslems inherit from each other though they may belong to different sects, but *the succession is regulated by the rules of the school to which the deceased belonged or conformed during his life-time.*

---

1 Bafatun *v.* Bilaiti Khanum (1903) I L 30 Cal. 683, 686; *See also* Iqbal Begum v. Mst. Syed Begum A I R 1933 Lah. 802 : 140 I C 829: Akbarally *v.* Mohammedally A I R 1932 Bom. 356: 138 I C 810; Syed Rashid Ahmed *v.* Mst. Anisa Khatoon A I R 1932 P C 25; Mst. Jamil-un-nissa *v.* Sheikh Mohammed Zia A I R 1937 All. 547; Sardar Bibi *v.* Muhammad Bakhsh P L D 1954 Lah. 480.

2 As most Shias of Indo-Pakistan sub-continent are Athna 'Asharias, the presumption is that a Shia is governed by Athna 'Asharia exposition of the law: Akbarally *v.* Mohammedally A I R 1932 Bom. 356; (1932) Bom. L R 655. Isma'ilis, however, are not necessarily governed by Shia Law of succession : Nur Ali and another *v.* Malka Sultana and others P L D 1961 Lah. 431.

3 Such a person shall be presumed to remain a Muslim until he renounces his religion: Bhagwan Bakhsh *v.* Drigbijai (1931) I L R 6 Luck. 487; A I R 1931 Oudh 301. The mere adoption of some Hindu forms of worship does not amount to such renunciation: Azima Bibi *v.* Munshi Shamalanand I L R 40 Cal. 378. In order to be deemed to be a Muslim it is not necessary that the person concerned should observe any particular rites or ceremonies, or be an orthodox believer, for no Court can test or guage the sincerity of religious belief: Abdul Razzaq *v.* Agha Mohammad (1894) 21 A 56: 64 I L R 11 Cal. 666.

The presumption, however, may be rebutted by general conduct and surrounding circumstances. Thus, if an illegitimate son of a Muslim woman from a Hindu husband is brought up as a Hindu, and is married according to Hindu rites to a Hindu girl, he will be deemed to be a Hindu though his mother was a Muslim: Bhaiya Sher Bahadur *v.* Bhaiya Ganga Bakhsh Singh (1914) 41 I A 1; I L R 36 All. 101.

SECTION II

CHANGE OF SECT—EFFECT

LIMITATIONS ON THE DISPOSING POWERS OF A MAHOMMEDAN—JOINT-FAMILY CUSTOM

Change of Sect—Effect.

In the Islamic system, the different schools and sub-schools are so intimately connected with the different persuasions, sects or communions to which they appertain, that when a person belonging to one communion or sect or sub-sect goes over to another, his status and the dispositions made by him, as well as the succession to his inheritance, are thenceforward governed by the rules of the school to which he now belongs. For example, a Shiah on adopting the Sunni persuasion would subject himself to the Sunni Law. So a Hanafi becoming a Shaf'eite, or an Akhbari becoming an Usuli would be governed by the Shaf'ei or Usuli principles as the case may be, and *vice versa.* From this point of view it may be said that the entire Musalman Law is a personal law.[1]

Distinction between the Shiahs and the Sunnis.

One great outward distinction between the Shiahs and the Sunnis is, that whilst the former pray with their hands held straight down by their side, the latter offer their prayers, with hands folded in front.[2] Between the Hanafis and the Shaf'eis, it consists in the former pronouncing the word *amin* (amen) in a low voice in their prayers, whilst the latter pronounce it loudly.[3]

No distinction between ancestral and self-acquired property.

In the Mahommedan Law there is no distinction between ancestral and self-acquired property. The owner for the time being has absolute dominion over all property in his possession whether he has acquired it himself, or whether it has devolved upon him by inheritance. He can sell or dispose of it in any way he likes, provided operation is given to it during his lifetime. It is only with regard to dispositions intended to take effect after the donor's death or made *in extremis* that his power of disposition is limited by the right of his heirs. He cannot by a testamentary disposition reduce or enlarge the shares of those who by law are entitled to inherit.

Ranee Khajoorunnissa v. Mst. Roushan Jehan.

This principle was recognised by the Privy Council in the case of *Ranee Khajoorunnissa* v. *Mussamat Roushan Jehan,*[4] though it was laid down rather too broadly, the consequence of which has

---

1 Mohammad *v.* Ghulam (1864) 1 B H C 236; Hayat-un-nissa *v.* Mohammad (1890) 12 All. 290 : 17 I A 73.

2 Another method of distinguishing a Shia from a Sunni is that the former does not believe in a Pir. A disciple of a Pir cannot be a Shia: Hayat-un-Nissa *v.* Mohammed Ali Khan I L R 12 All. 290 (P C); Sardar Bibi *v.* Muhammad Bakhsh P L D 1954 Lah. 480 (490).

3 Amin-bi'l-Jahr.

4 (1876) L R 3 I A 291.

been to give rise to considerable misapprehension regarding the general policy of the Mahommedan Law. In that case, it appeared that one Rajah Deedar Hosain, who died in 1841 possessed of large zemindaries and leaving a number of heirs, had executed, prior to his death, two instruments, one purporting to be a deed of gift in respect of certain properties, the other a will in respect of the residue of his estate in favour of his eldest son, Enayet Hosain, under which the latter took possession of the entire estate of his father. The latter instrument ran as follows :—

"I divide the remaining two-thirds now under my possession, uninterfered and unconcerned by any one else, into three portions. One portion to be laid out as the executor may think proper for the testator's welfare, hereafter by charity and pilgrimage, and keep up the family usage, namely, the expenses of the mosque and *tazeadaree* of the sacred martyrs, and for the comfort of the travellers, the surplus amount to be appropriated by himself, the executor. From the other two-thirds after paying off all the debts of my creditors, giving allowances as per shares to the executor himself, and my sons, daughters, and wives, the right-holders, and salary-holders, that is, friends and servants, repairs of houses and court expenses, etc., including other necessaries as below detailed without diminution and increase ; he shall keep every one by his good conduct and affection contented and satisfied." Upon a suit by one of the other heirs of Deedar Hosain two principal questions came up for decision before the Privy Council, (*a*) the validity of the gift, and (*b*) that of the will. On these two points their Lordships expressed themselves in the following terms :—

"The policy of the Mahommedan Law appears to be to prevent a testator interfering by will with the course of the devolution of property according to law among his heirs, although he may give a specified portion, as much as a third, to a stranger. But it also appears that a holder of property may, to a certain extent, defeat the policy of the law by giving in his lifetime the whole or any part of his property to one of his sons, provided he complies with certain forms. It is incumbent, however, upon those who seek to set up a proceeding of this sort, to shew very clearly that the forms of the Mahommedan Law, whereby its policy is defeated, have been complied with. There is no question of the execution by Raja Deedar Hosain of this deed giving one-third to his son Enayet on the 10th of November 1839. The deed was either—to use English expressions—a deed of gift simply, or a deed of gift for a consideration.

Gift without consideration.

"If it was simply a deed of gift without consideration, it was invalid unless accompanied by a delivery of the thing given, as far as that thing is capable of delivery, or, in other words, by what is termed in the books a seisin on the part of the donee. In their Lordships' judgment there was no delivery of this kind. Even assuming that although the estate was under attachment, a sufficient seisin in it remained to the donor which he could impart to the donee, still it appears by the evidence of Mr. Perry, which is treated as trustworthy on both sides, that in point of fact Rajah

Deedar Hosain remained in receipt of the rents and profits of the property until his death. Therefore, if the deed were a mere deed of gift there was not that delivery of possession which was necessary to give it effect by Mahommedan Law. A question which was touched upon, though not much argued, *viz.*, whether the doctrine of Mahommedan Law relating to 'confusion of gifts' applied, appears not to arise, as there was no delivery of possession.

"But it was contended that this was a deed of gift for a consideration, and therefore that the delivery of possession was not necessary. It was, however, conceded that in order to make the deed valid in this view of the case, two conditions at all events must concur, *viz.*, on actual payment of the consideration on the part of the donee, and a *bona fide* intention on the part of the donor to divest himself *in praesenti* of the property, and to confer it upon the donee. Undoubtedly, the adequacy of the consideration is not the question. A consideration may be perfectly valid which is wholly inadequate in amount when compared with the thing given. Some of the cases have gone so far as to say that even a gift of a ring may be a sufficient consideration ; but whatever its amount, it must be actually and *bona fide* paid."

Family arrangements valid under the Musulman Law.

It is submitted that the view expressed with regard to the will does not appear to be in accord with the Mahommedan Law. Under the Shiah Law to which the parties were subject, Deedar Hosain had an incontestable right to leave by will *one-third* for the purposes described by him, and to leave by way of remuneration to the executor the balance of the income after the performance of the religious ceremonies. But the opinion regarding the will was probably influenced by the result of the conclusions arrived at in respect of the gift which, if no consideration had passed and transmutation of possession in some shape had not been effected, would no doubt be bad. But this decision must be confined to the special facts of that case, for it in no way affects the general provisions of the Mahommedan Law by which the proprietor of an estate may, during his lifetime, with the consent express or implied, of the members of his family, make an arrangement by which one of such members should become the manager and head of the family, the others retaining an interest in the usufruct in proportion to their respective shares. Such a family arrangement is no evasion of the Mahommedan Law, nor is it opposed to its rules. It will be binding upon the members of the family.[1]

Intestacy : the general rule.

The restriction referred to on the testamentary powers of a Musulman, which is not without analogy in some of the Western systems, leads to the consequence that in respect of the major portion of the estate and effects of the *propositus* the distribution takes place as if he had died intestate.

---

1 See L R 50 I A 84.

So far as succession is concerned, there is no distinction between real and personal property, except in the case of a childless widow *under the Shiah Law.*[1]

Custom dehors the Mahommedan Law not recognised.

Mahommedan Law *per se* does not admit the validity of any alien custom which is contrary to, or in conflict with, its prescriptions.[2] In some parts of the country, however, customs are found to exist which are not in conformity with the general Mahommedan Law. In these parts, the Courts under their constitution have to give effect to customs unless they are opposed to "justice, equity and good conscience", or to any express enactment of the Legislature. At the same time it is not easy to determine the limit within which recognised customs should have effect given to them. The tendency of the British Indian Courts has been to enlarge as much as possible those limits. These decisions of the Indian Courts have been largely controlled or cut down by recent rulings of the Judicial Committee.[3]

Hindu customs in Mahommedan families.

Where Mahommedan families have adopted Hindu customs or Hindu families converted to Islam have adhered to old customs, they have frequently done so subject to such modifications as they considered desirable. A Judge, therefore, is not bound nor would he be justified as a matter of law, to apply to a Mahommedan family all the rules and presumptions which have been held to apply to a joint Hindu family.[4]

Jowala Buksh v. Dharam Singh.

In this connection the observations of their Lordships of the Judicial Committee in the case of *Jowala Buksh* v. *Dharam Singh*[5] with respect to the law governing succession among Hindu families converted to Islam possess great importance. Their Lordships said as follows :—

"The case has hitherto been treated upon the assumption, which the plaintiffs seem to have made part of their case, that this family, though converted to Mahommedanism, is to be taken as still conforming to the Hindoo laws and usages ; and that, consequently, the questions of title raised in this cause are to be governed by Hindoo Law. Their Lordships, however, are far from admitting the correctness of that assumption.

---

1 See post, Chap. VII.

2 Hakim Khan *v.* Gul Khan (1882) I L 8 Cal. 826.

3 See Abdul Hossain Khan *v.* Bibi Sona Deva (1917) L R 45, I A 101; Mahommed Rowther *v.* Ibrahim Rowther (1822) L R 49, I A 119.

4 Suddurtonnissa *v.* Majada Khatun (1878) I L 3 Cal. 694; s. c. 2 Cal. L R 308.

5 (1866) 10 Moo. I A 511, 536.

Abraham v. Abraham.

This case is distinguishable from that of *Abraham* v. *Abraham.*[1] There the parties were Native Christians, not having, as such, any law of inheritance defined by Statute ; and in the absence of one, this Committee applied the law by which as the evidence proved, the particular family intended to be governed. But the written law of India has prescribed broadly that in questions of succession and inheritance the Hindoo Law is to be applied to Hindoos, and the Mahommedan Law to Mahommedans; and in the judgment delivered by Lord Kingsdown, in *Abraham* v. *Abraham*, p. 239, it is said, that "this rule must be understood to refer to Hindoos and Mahommedans, not by birth merely, but by religion also."

"The two cases in W. H. Macnaghten's 'Principles of Hindu Law', Vol. II, pp. 131, 132, which deal with the case of converts from the Hindu to the Mahommedan faith, and rule that the heirs according to Hindu Law will take all the property which the deceased had at the time of his conversion, are also authorities for the proposition that the devolution of his subsequently acquired property is to be governed by the Mahommedan Law. Here there is nothing to show conclusively when or how the property was acquired by the great ancestor. There was no conflict, as in the cases just referred to, between Hindus and Mahommedans touching the succession to him."

"Whatever he had is admitted to have passed to his descendants, of whom all, like himself, were Mahommedans ; and it seems to be contrary to principle that, as between them, the succession should be governed by any but Mahommedan Law. Whether it is competent for a family converted from the Hindu to the Mahommedan faith to retain for several generations Hindu usages and customs, and by virtue of that retention to set up for itself a special and customary law of inheritance, is a question which, so far as their Lordships are aware, has never been decided. It is not absolutely necessary for the determination of this appeal to decide that question in the negative, and their Lordships abstain from doing so. They must, however, observe, that to control the general law, if, indeed, the Mahommedan Law admits of such control, much stronger proof of special usage would be required than has been given in this case."

The Indian Law Courts have, to a certain extent, regarded the old customs retained by families converted from Hinduism to Islam as inflexible admitting of no alteration or variation. In dealing, however, with the maintenance of old usages by people converted from one faith to another, especially Islam, it is desirable to bear in mind the following passage from the judgment of the Judicial Committee in *Abraham* v. *Abraham.*[2]

1 (1863) 9 Moo. I A 195.

2 *Ibid.*

"Customs and usages as to dealing with property, unless their continuance be enjoined by law, as they are adopted voluntarily, so they may be changed, or lost by desuetude. It was well observed by Mr. Melvill, that custom implies continuance. If a family of converts retain the customs in part of their unconverted predecessors, is that election of theirs invariable and inflexible? Can neither they nor their descendants change things in their very nature variable, as dependant on the changeful inclinations, feelings, and obligations of successive generations of men?

"If the spirit of an adopted religion improves those who become converts to it, and they reject, from conscience, customs to which their first converted ancestors adhered, must the abandoned usages be treated by a sort of *fictio juris* as still the enduring customs of the family? If it be not so as to things which belong to the jurisdiction of conscience, is it so as to things of convenience or interest? Surely, in things indifferent in themselves, the Tribunals which have a discretion and have no positive *lex fori* imposed on them should rather proceed on what actually exists than on what has existed, and in forming their own presumptions have regard rather to a man's own way of life than to that of his predecessors. Though race and blood are independent of volition, usage is not."[1]

The dictum of the High Court in the case of *Rup Lal Chowdhury* v. *Latu Lal Chowdhury*[2] that the Hindu Law is applicable to Hindu converts to Islam is absolutely without authority and has been dissented from in *Hakim Khan* v. *Gul Khan*.[3]

No presumption of Jointness.

Among the Mahommedans there is no presumption of jointness.[4] When the members of a Mahommedan family live in commensality, they do not necessarily form a "joint family" in the sense in which that expression is used with regard to Hindus ; and, in Mahommedan Law there is not, as there is in Hindu Law, any presumption that the acquisitions of the several members are made for the benefit of the family.[5]

In some parts of India, however, Mahommedan families have adopted the Hindu joint family system. In many instances Hindu families converted to Islam have adhered to the custom and continued to live jointly. In such cases the legal rights of the parties have been held to be subject to the same principles as are applicable to members of a Hindu joint family.[6] *The onus of*

---

1 Now this discussion is merely of historical interest. By virtue of section 2 of the Shariat Application Act, 1937 and section 2 of the West Pakistan Muslim Personal Law (Shariat) Application Act, 1962 (V of 1962), every convert to Islam is *ipso facto* governed by Muslim Law.

2 (1878) 3 Cal. L R 97.

3 *Supra.*

4 *Ibid.* Jowala Buksh *v.* Dharam Singh, *supra*; Abraham *v.* Abraham, *supra*; and Jaker Ali Chowdhry *v.* Rajchunder Sen (1882) I L 8 Cal. 831, note.

5 Hakim Khan *v.* Gul Khan, *supra.*

6 Achina Bibee *v.* Ajeejoonnissa Bibee (1869) 11 W R 45.

establishing the custom as always existing in the family is strictly on the party alleging it.

The mere fact of members of a Mahommedan family living in commensality and holding their properties jointly is not sufficient to raise the presumptions which, under the Hindu Law, arise from *de facto* jointness.[1]

In *Abdul Khader* v. *Chidambaram Chattiyar*[2] it was found that three Mahommedan brothers lived together and traded jointly until the death of one of them, Mowla Ally. After his death, the surviving brothers carried on the old business jointly not only for themselves but for the children of Mowla Ally, who lived under the protection of one of them. This person purported to act as their guardian. For the purposes of this business, the two brothers executed a promissory note for Rs. 5,000 in favour of the plaintiff in that suit. In an action brought on the promissory note in which the infants were also made parties, the Subordinate Judge made a decree against all the defendants including the minors. On appeal to the High Court on behalf of the minors the learned Judges expressed themselves thus:—

"The Subordinate Judge does not tell us upon what principle of law he has based the liability of the appellants. If he has proceeded on the law governing the joint family tenure of property among the Hindus as he would seem to have done, he has clearly fallen into an error. Such a system of holding property is not recognised by the Mahommedan Law, and the principle on which that system is founded cannot be applied to the determination of questions relating to the tenure and devolution of property among Mahommedans. No doubt it would be otherwise in the case of a family which may be proved to have adopted by custom having the force of law the joint family mode of holding property ; but no such custom is alleged in the present case. Under the Mahommedan Law a co-owner is presumed in the absence of an express contract to the contrary to hold his property in severalty whether that property represents a share in, tangible, movable or immovable property, chose in action, or a trading concern."

Joint acquisition.

But where members of a Mahommedan family are living joint, and it is found that they are jointly in enjoyment of their shares in the properties which have descended to them from a common ancestor, the managing member cannot claim an exclusive right to those properties, or assert that the rights of the other members have become barred under the Statute of Limitation.[3] Acquisitions made by the managing member with *joint* funds,

1 Abdool Adood *v.* Mohammad Makmil (1884) I L 10 Cal. 562; *See also* the case of Mohammud Afak *v.* Ekram Ali (1871) 14 W R 374.

2 (1908) I L 32 Mad. 276.

3 Achina Bibee *v.* Ajeejoonnissa Bibee (1869) 11 W R 45.

and kept *jointly*, without any differentiation, would be for the benefit of the family. But where it does not appear that the acquisitions were made with *joint* funds, in other words, with money belonging to all the members, or where the property from the time of its acquisition is kept distinctly apart from the joint properties, the other members would have no right therein.

When a family converted from Hinduism has professed the Mahommedan religion for successive generations ; and a claim to succession is put forward by a female which is opposed on the ground of usage, the Courts of Justice are bound to dispose of the case under the Mahommedan Law and cannot recognise a plea of usage opposed to that law.[1]

In another case the Madras High Court held that, when a custom is put forward for excluding females from succession, it must be shown that it was consciously accepted as having the force of law, and fulfils all the requirements by which a valid custom is established.[2]

Khojas and Memons.

Where large sections of people converted from Hinduism to the Mahommedan Faith have continued to be governed by the Hindu Law of Inheritance, the converse proposition has been maintained. For example, the Bombay High Court, following the decision in the well-known *Khojas and Memons' case*[3] in the Supreme Court of Bombay, has held, in the case of these two communities, that in the absence of satisfactory proof of custom differing from the Hindu Law, the Courts will apply to them the Hindu Law of Inheritance and Succession.[4]

The same principle has been applied to the Sunni Borahs of the Dhanduka Taluka in Gujerat and the Molisalam Girasias in the Broach District, both of whom were originally Hindu Rajputs and were converted to Islam several centuries ago.[5]

Reg. XI of 1793.

These enunciations appear to me to conflict largely with the prescriptions of the Mahommedan Law which, whilst recognising

---

1 See Abdul Hossain Khan *v.* Sona Bibi Deva, supra; also Surmust Khan *v.* Kadırdad Khan (1867) 1 Agra (N.-W. P.) F B R 39, Ed. 1874 29; Jammya *v.* Diwan (1900) I L 23 All. 20.

According to the Muslim Personal Law (Shariat) Application Act, 1937 and the West Pakistan Muslim Personal Law (Shariat) Application Act (V of 1962), Muslim Law will apply, notwithstanding any custom or usage to the contrary. The custom should be deemed to be abrogated.

2 Mirabivi *v.* Vellayanna (1885) I L 8 Mad. 464.

3 Hirbae *v.* Sonabai (1847) Perry's Oriental Cases 110.

4 Hirbae *v.* Gorbai (1875) 12 Bom. H C R 294; Rahimatba'i *v.* Hirbai (1877) I L 3 Bom. 34; Ashabai *v.* Haji Tyeb (1882) I L 9 Bom. 115; Mahommed Sidik *v.* Haji Ahmed Haji Abdul Satar (1885) I L 10 Bom. 1.

5 Bai Baiji *v.* Bai Santok (1894) I L 20 Bom. 53; Maharana Shri Fatesangji Jaswantsangji *v.* Harisangji (1894) I L 20 Bom. 181.

customs springing up in Musulman families that do not transgress rules of public morality, does not admit the validity of alien customs inconsistent with its own positive directions. For example, the members of a Musulman family may choose to hold their properties in a state of jointness, or to let the eldest male member take the entire inheritance of the last owner. If the custom is observed for a long time without demur by any member, it becomes a part of the family law as a *rasm-wa-riwaj-i-Khandan*. Regulation XI of 1793 effected a great change in these family customs, but it does not affect their validity from the standpoint of the Musulman Law. It is a different thing, however, to declare that because Hindus converted to Islam observe for a time some of their old customs or remain, from ignorance or inclination subject to their old laws, such customs or laws, although in conflict with the rules of their religion, should for ever form part of their family law, and they should never be able to release themselves from the bondage of the ancient institutions.

Immoral customs.

But whilst the Musulman Law recognises the validity of usages not opposed to public morality, claims of inheritance based on alleged customs which are immoral in their tendency and are reprobated or prohibited in the Mahommedan system, are not valid.[1]

In the case of *Alimunessa Khatoon* v. *Hassan Ali*,[2] the Calcutta High Court held that, even when certain Mahommedans have been living jointly, and expenses have been incurred for the benefit of any particular member, the burden of such expenses will not be thrown on the other members of the joint family. In that case it appeared that the plaintiff and defendant, brother and sister were living joint in food and estate till 1872, when they separated. At the time of separation they entered into an agreement to the following effect :—

"If claims relating to the joint estate are brought on the ground that they are debts due on account of the time we were joint and living in commensality, then I, *A*, and I, *B*, will pay such claims, according to what is just in equal shares. If either of us do not pay and one of us shall pay the share of the other, then the person who has paid shall recover from the other the amount he has paid for the other."

After the separation a decree was obtained against the brother for the price of certain clothes supplied to him for his marriage which took place while they were joint, and he having paid the amount of this decree sued the sister for one-half of the amount so paid. It was held that, as the debt was not incurred in a matter necessary to the existence of the family, but for the individual benefit of the brother, and that as in a Mahommedan

1 Ghasiti *v.* Umrao Jan (1885) I L 21 Cal. 149; Ghasiti *v.* Jaggu (1893) L R 20 I A 193.

2 (1881) 8 Cal. L R 378.

family the individual benefited, and not the family, is liable for the expenses incurred for the benefit of any particular member, he alone was liable for the debt.[1]

SECTION III

PRINCIPLES OF DIFFERENTIATION BETWEEN HEIRS AND NON-HEIRS

Inheriting and non-inheriting relations.

Both the Sunnis and the Shiahs are generally agreed on the principle by which the individuals who are entitled to inheritance in the estate of the deceased can be distinguished from those who have no right.

For example, a Musulman, upon his death, may leave behind him a numerous body of relations. In the absence of certain determinate rules, it would be extremely difficult to distinguish between the *inheriting* and the *non-inheriting* relations. In order to obviate this difficulty and to render it easy to distinguish between the two classes, it is recognised, as a general rule that when a deceased Musulman leaves behind him two relations, one of whom is connected with him *through the other*, the former shall not succeed whilst the intermediate person is alive. For example, if a person on his death leaves behind him a son and that son's son, this latter will not succeed to his grandfather's estate while his father is alive.

But this rule is subject to one exception. *The mother does not exclude brothers and sisters, either full or uterine from succession.*

Another rule, which is also framed with the object of discovering the heirs of a deceased individual, is that *the nearer in degree excludes the more remote.* This rule, though really covered by the former, is recognised by both schools, but there is great divergence as to the mode of its application in consequence of the difference in the classification of heirs. For example, the Sunnis group the heirs under two heads, *viz.*, *agnates* and *cognates* ; the *agnates* and *cognates* are again respectively sub-divided into descendants, ascendants and collaterals. The object of this division and sub-division is to indicate the order of succession, and the rule applies to each class of heirs, but not to the heirs of the different classes. For instance, a son will take in preference to a son's son, both being in the first class of heirs ; but a son's son will take the residue in preference to the father, although the latter is nearer than the former, because the father is included in the second class of heirs.

---

1 In Pakistan custom is completely dead except in the matter of the right of alienation of those owners of property who got it by means of succession under customary law. Such persons shall continue to be governed by customary law of alienation and their powers of alienation can be still challenged by those who are to succeed after their death or the termination of their limited interest under custom. Khair Din *v.* Mohammed Hussain P L D 1961 S C (Pak.) 468 and the rulings cited therein.

Shiah rules—Rules of differentiation.

Similarly, the Shiahs divide the heirs into three classes, but without the distinction between *agnates* and *cognates*. Each of these classes is sub-divided into two branches; the above rule applies to the heirs of the different classes, but not to heirs of the two branches of the same class. For instance, the parents and descendants form the first class, and are its two branches ; accordingly, a great-grandson, although he will not exclude the father, will take in preference to the grandfather or brother notwithstanding that these are nearer in kinship for they belong to different classes. Similarly, a grandfather cannot exclude a brother's grandson, for they belong to different branches of the same class. Thus the rule must be understood to be subject in its application to the classification of heirs, in which respect only there is a distinction between the two schools. It will be seen by and by that the Sunnis prefer the *nearer in degree to the more remote*, in the succession of *male agnates only*, whilst the Shiahs apply the rule of nearness or propinquity to all cases without distinction of class or sex. If a person die leaving behind him a brother's son and a brother's grandson, and his own daughter's son,—among the Sunnis, the brother's son being a *male agnate* and nearer to the deceased than the brother's grandson, takes the inheritance in preference to the others ; whilst among the Shiahs the daughter's son, being nearer in blood, would exclude the others.

It will be noticed, therefore, that the right of succession of the different relations who may survive a deceased person, varies according to circumstances. Some of them are absolutely excluded by the operation of the principles referred to, whilst others have their shares reduced by the fact of their co-existing with certain relations, who may or may not participate in the inheritance. But both among the Sunnis and the Shiahs there is one class of heirs who are never excluded from succession, however much their respective shares may vary. *This class of heirs comprises the father, the mother, the son, the daughter, the husband or wife.*

Principle of representation not recognised.

As a general rule, neither the Sunnis nor the Shiahs recognise the principle of representation. For example, if *A* had two sons one of whom died during his lifetime leaving several children, these children do not possess the right of representing their father on the decease of *A* but are "excluded" from the inheritance by their uncle.[1] Similarly, if there be two sons of one son or brother, and three of another (and no son or brother, as the case may be, living at the time), the five grandsons or brothers' sons will take the inheritance *per capita and not per stirpes*. There might exist a long established custom for the estate to descend to a single heir. In such a case the eldest son generally succeeds. But descent by lineal primogeniture is a recent innovation introduced in imitation of the feudal rules relating to estates in England.

---

1 Com. Moola Cassim bin Moola Ahmed *v.* Moolla Abdul Rahim and others (1905) L R 32 I A 177 ; Abdul Bari *v.* Nasir Ahmad A I R 1933 Oudh 142.

The right of representation, however, is recognised to a limited extent in the succession of the *cognates*. For example, half-sisters and brothers on the mother's side when they do succeed, take the mother's share. There are some other instances of the same kind.[1]

Rights of females.

Females, co-existing with males of the same degree (or of a lower degree, but entitled to succeed with them) take a smaller share than the males, but as regards dominion over property and the power of disposition and the *quantum* of interest derived by inheritance they stand on the same footing as the men.

Widow's interest.

So also a widow taking a share in her husband's estate acquires an absolute and indefeasible interest therein.

Renunciation of a vested right of inheritance.

According to the Mahommedan Law, the right to inherit may be renounced and "such renunciation need not be express, but may be implied from the ceasing or desisting from prosecuting a claim maintainable against another."[2]

Of an expectancy.

But can a person who would succeed to another if he survives the latter, renounce the inchoate right of inheritance or expectancy before it has become an absolute right? In the case of *Khanum Jan* v. *Jan Bibi*[3] two of the heirs of a deceased Mahommedan executed for a consideration a deed in favour of the other heirs, renouncing their right of inheritance to the ancestor's property, and for a period of nearly twelve years after her death they advanced no claim, but ultimately sued for their legal shares in the deceased's estate.

Khanum Jan v. Jan Bibi.

The Law Officers of the Patna Provincial Court on being questioned regarding the validity of the renunciation answered as follows :—

"Renunciation implies the yielding up of a right already vested, or the ceasing or desisting from prosecuting a claim maintainable against another. It is evident that, during the lifetime

1 In Pakistan the rule of representation has been introduced by section 4 of the Muslim Family Laws Ordinance, 1961.

2 Hurmoot-ool-Nissa Begum *v.* Allahdia Khan (1871) 17 W R P C 108, s. c. 2 Sutherland's P. C. Judgments 525.

3 (1827) 4 S D A Reps. 210; see also Samsuddin Goolam Husein *v.* Abdool Husein Kalimuddin (1906) I L 31 Bom. 165; Asa Beevi *v.* Karuppan 41 Mad. 365 : 46 I C 35; Suleman Sahib *v.* Kadir Ibrahim A I R 1953 Mad. 161.

of the mother the daughters have no right of inheritance and their claim on that account is not maintainable against any person during her lifetime. It follows, therefore, that this renunciation during the mother's lifetime of the daughters' shares is null and void, it being in point of fact giving up that which had no existence. Such act cannot consequently invalidate the right of inheritance supervenient on the mother's death or be any bar to their claim of the estate left by her. The omission to advance a claim for twelve years is no legal bar to the ultimate admission of such claim."

The opinion of the Muftis of the Provincial Court which was confirmed by the Law Officers of the Sudder Court, was followed by both Courts.

In the case of *Kunhi Mamod* v. *Kunhi Moidin*,[1] the Madras High Court has held that an agreement renouncing the prospective right for a consideration is valid and binding. Although the view taken by the learned Judges does not seem to be sustainable on the basis of the Mahommedan Law, yet the person who renounces his right on bringing a suit to recover his share should be called upon to refund the consideration received.

When it is sought to defeat the claim of a Mahommedan *pardanashin* female on the ground that she had renounced her right to a share in her deceased brother's estate it must be established that she had fully understood her rights and had validly relinquished her claim.[2]

A right of inheritance vests by operation of law and consequently, although a relinquishment of the right after it has vested may be binding on the person actually renouncing, it does not affect any one else. Thus an heir who refuses to take the share in a deceased person's interest to which he is entitled cannot deprive his own heirs of its benefit, and accordingly upon his death his right would devolve upon them, and they would be entitled to claim his share (subject, of course, to any bar resulting from the Statute of Limitation).

If the renunciation, however, is for a consideration, it may amount to a transfer of his interest and be binding on his heirs.

Vested estates in remainder not recognised.

The Mahommedan Law, pure and simple, does not recognise vested estates in remainder. In other words, whilst the property is in the hands of the owner, his heirs have no vested reversionary interest in it, such as would be assignable or pass to their heirs by right of inheritance.

1 (1896) I L 19 Mad. 176. *See also* Latafat Hussain *v*. Hidayat Hussain A I R 1936 All. 573: 161 I C 851; Qamar Din *v*. Mst. Aishabibi P L D 1956 Lah. 795 (F B).

2 Muhammad Kamil *v*. Mussumat Imtiaz Fatima (1908) L R 36 I A 210.

Abdul Wahid Khan v. Mst. Nuran Bibi.

This rule was enunciated by the Privy Council in the case of *Abdul Wahid Khan* v. *Mussumat Nuran Bibi.*[1] The facts of that case were somewhat peculiar, and though the

---

1 I L R 12 I A 91 : 11 Cal. 597 (P C). In this case, the property in dispute belonged to Mouzzum Khan who died on 22nd of January 1850, leaving a widow Mst. Gauhar Bibi, and also Abdus Subhan and Abdul Rahman who claimed to be his legitimate sons, with Gauhar Bibi who was in possession at the annexation of Oudh by the British (13th February 1856) the summary settlement was made, and after the general confiscation (15th March 1858) followed by restoration, and the summary settlement of that year, the settlement at the villages was again made with her. She continued in possession till her death on 18th October 1875.

In the course of proceedings at the regular settlement, litigation took place between the alleged sons on the one side, and Gauhar Bibi (widow) on the other resulting in compromise whereby it was agreed that the widow should, during her lifetime, continue to hold possession and remain proprietor, without power of alienation, and that after her death the two sons should possess each one-half of the property. Abdus Subhan died in 1868, and Abdul Rahman in 1874, Gauhar Bibi before her death, made a gift dated 30th April 1874 of the *talukas* to the daughter of Abdul Rahman named Murad Bibi who remained in possession till her death in January 1881, her husband Abdul Wahid Khan the appellant becoming her representative.

Nuran Bibi the principal plaintiff in the suit claimed as the sister of Abdus Subhan, and half sister of Abdul Rahman alleging that they were the sons of Mouzzum Khan. The plaint also alleged that by compromise above referred the brothers rights to the estate of Mouzzum Khan had been admitted and that it had been agreed that Gauhar Bibi should retain possession, during her lifetime, without power of alienation, and that after her death the sons should share the estate equally. The cause of action had arisen on the death of Gauhar Bibi, the termination of life possession, the interests of the two brothers having passed on their deaths to Nuran Bibi. The defence amongst other defences, besides disputing the legitimacy of Nuran Bibi, was that the compromise of 1866 created only rights contingent upon the brothers surviving Gauhar Bibi whereas they died before her so that no estate had passed to Nuran Bibi. The District Judge dismissed the suit while the Judicial Commissioner reversed the decision and decreed the suit. Their Lordships of the Privy Council on construction of the compromise deed came to the conclusion that on true construction of the compromise the title of the sons to succeed was contingent on their surviving the widow, and since they predeceased the widow, no interest passed to their heirs, on their death.

In Hasan Ali v. Nazo I L R 11 All. 456, the plaintiff brought a suit challeging the gift made by his uncle on the ground of undue influence, it was held, that the plaintiff had, during the donor's lifetime, no reversionary or vested interest in the estate, but a mere possibility of inheritance and consequently the donor, when he executed the deed, had full disposing power over his property, and the right which at his death accrued to the plaintiff came to the latter affected by the donor's acts and dispositions and that as a suit by the donor to set aside the deed would at the time of his death be barred under Art. 91 of the Limitation Act such a suit was barred against the plaintiff who claimed through him.

In Abdul Hussain *v.* Ghulam Hussain I L R 30 Bom. 304 it was held: "The right of son or daughter or other heir of a person to inherit his property is not an estate in remainder or in reversion in immovable property or an estate otherwise deferred in enjoyment. It is neither a vested nor a contingent right. It does not come within the definition of a vested interest in section 19 of the Transfer of Property Act or of a contingent interest in section 21 of that Act and section 107 of the Succession Act, 1865. So far from being vested or contingent right in present or in future it is in the language of clause (*a*) of section 6 of the Transfer of Property Act "the chance of an heir apparent succeeding to an estate or a "mere possibility" of succession which cannot be transferred".

arrangement upon which the decision proceeded was open to another construction, their Lordships thought that under it Gauhar Bibi had remained as full owner, and consequently her sons had no vested interest in the property.

Family arrangements or Tawris.

But as already observed, there is nothing in the Mahommedan Law to prevent an arrangement to the effect that *A* should have a life-interest in a particular property, or that an estate should be vested in him or her for life, and that upon his or her decease it should devolve upon *A's* heirs or any particular person or persons by way of a remainder. In fact, such family settlements are recommended under the head of *tawris* in order to prevent family disputes. An arrangement of this nature was recognised by the Judicial Committee in the case of *Khwajeh Solehman Quadir* (*sic*) v. *Nawab Sir Salimullah Bahadur*.[1]

---

1 (1922) L R 49 I A 153; In Amjad Khan *v.* Ashraf Khan A I R 1929 P C 149 (152) it was argued on behalf of the plaintiff, that under the Mahommedan Law which was applicable to the case, a transfer of life estate could not be made by means of a gift; in other words, it was argued that under the said law there could not be a transfer of any interest in property by way of gift *inter vivos* except an absolute interest. Their Lordships expressed no opinion on the point, because the appeal was disposed of on another ground.

In Nawazish Ali Khan *v.* Ali Raza Khan P L D 1948 P C 23 it was observed: "In general, Muslim law draws no distinction between real and personal property, and it does not recognise the splitting up of ownership of land into estates, distinguihed in point of quality like legal and equitable estates, or in point of duration like estates in fee simple, in tail, for life, or in remainder. What Muslim law does recognise and insist upon, is the distinction between the corpus of the property itself (*ayn*) and the usufruct in the property (*manafi*) Over the corpus of property the law recognises only absolote dominion, heritable, and unrestricted in point of time; and where a gift of the corpus seeks to impose a condition inconsistent with such absolute dominion, the condition is rejected as repugnant; but interests limited in point of time can be created in the usufruct of the property and the dominion over the corpus takes effect subject to any such limited interests. This distinction runs all through the Muslim law of gifts—gifts of the corpus (*hiba*), gifts of the usufruct (*ariyat*) and usufructuary bequests. No doubt where the use of a house is given to a man for his life he may, not inaptly, be termed a tenant for life, and the owner of the house, waiting to enjoy it until the termination of the limited interest, may be said, not inaccurately, to possess a vested remainder. But though the same terms may be used in English and Muslim law, to describe much the same things, the two systems of law are based on quite different conceptions of ownership. English law recognises ownership of the land limited in duration; Muslim law admits only ownership unlimited in duration, but recognises interests of limited duration to the use of property. There is no difference between the several Schools of Muslim law in their fundamental conception of property and ownership. But limited interest takes effect out of the usufruct under any of the Schools".

In Bai Saroobai *v.* Hussain Somji A I R 1936 Bom. 330 a Full Bench held that: 'Under Sunni Mahommedan Law a gift of a life interest is valid and it does not become automatically enlarged into a gift of the corpus of the property absolutely". Wadia, J. who wrote the main judgment observed: "A gift of the rents and profits, without more does not carry with it a gift of the entire property. Similarly a right to enjoy the usufruct of the property during the grantee's lifetime can also be conferred. *See also* Mst. Subhanbi *v.* Mst. Umraobi A I R 1936 Nag. 113; Achiruddin Ahmed *v.* Sakina Bewa A I R 1946 Cal. 288; Maitheen Bivi Umma *v.* Ithappiri Verkey A I R 1956 Tra.-Co. 268; Anjumanara Begum *v.* Nawab Asif Kadar (1933) 2 Cal. 109; Inayat Begum *v.* Maryam P L D 1953 Pesh. 1; Samir Sheikh *v.* Aijan Bewa P L D 1956 Dacca 143.

SECTION IV

FUNERAL CHARGES—DEVOLUTION OF THE RIGHT OF INHERITANCE.

Funeral charges.

FUNERAL expenses form the first charge on the estate of deceased person, and must be disbursed before payment of debts or legacies.

The funeral comprises the washing, shrouding and interring of the body together with the ceremonies connected therewith including the *chihlum* (funeral service performed on the fortieth day after the decease). All these are to be performed in a manner suitable to the deceased's position in life and means; and for the necessary expenses incurred therefor all his property is liable, except such as is held by somebody else in pledge, or is subject to any other special charge. Besides disbursements connected with the actual funeral all legitimate death-bed charges, such as fees of doctors attending the deceased, cost of medicine, etc., come in this category.

The debts of the deceased must be satisfied after the funeral charges.

After the funeral expenses are paid, the debts of the deceased must be satisfied.[1] For his debts, except such as are charged on some specific property, all his estate is liable, excluding those so charged. The *Fatawai-'Alamgiri* says: "Debts are of three kinds *viz.*, (*a*) those contracted in *health*; (*b*) those contracted at a time when the man was *in extremis* or labouring under an illness which ended fatally; and (*c*) those contracted partly in *health* and partly in *illness*.

"If they are all debts contracted in health, or all *in extremis* they are all alike, and none is entitled to any preference. If they are debts partly contracted in health and partly in illness, the former are preferred, if the latter can be established only by the acknowledgment of the deceased. But when the debts contracted in illness can be established by proof, or have been openly incurred for known causes, such as the purchase or destruction of property, or the proper dower of a wife, the latter debts are on the same footing as those contracted in health. Debts not actually due at the time of the debtor's death become payable immediately on the occurrence of that event, because the privilege of postponement is a personal right which dies with him. The death of a creditor has not the same effect, because the person to whom the right of delay belongs is still alive."

Debts cover the wages earned by and due to servants. The provisions of sections 101 to 105 of the Probate and Administration Act (V of 1881) which now govern the application of a

1 Nawab Mirza Mohammad Sadiq Ali Khan *v.* Nawab Fakhar Jehan Begum I L R 9 Luck. 701 : A I R 1934 Oudh 307 (payment of debts of the deceased take precedence over legacies)

deceased person's property, have amplified the prescriptions of the Mahommedan Law.

After payment of death-bed charges, funeral expenses and debts, any valid bequest is to be satisfied out of a third of what remains unless the heirs allow it beyond a third.

It is only after these legal duties have been discharged that the inheritance becomes divisible among the heirs.

Devolution of the right of inheritance.

But a partition before payment of debts does not invalidate the division of the property, the heirs remaining liable for the debts in proportion to the assets received by each.[1] For the estate of a deceased Mahommedan devolves upon his heirs immediately on his decease, and they acquire an absolute interest in their specific shares even before distribution or partition. The devolution of that interest is not dependent either on the division of the property among them or the payment of the debts left by the deceased.[2]

Right of the heir to deal with his share.

Unless it is found at the time of administration that the debts left by the deceased absorb the whole estate, and there is nothing in fact for the heirs to take, each heir has the right to deal with his share by sale or mortgage and pass a good title to the alienee notwithstanding any debts which might be due from the ancestor.[3]

Under the Mahommedan Law one heir is not entitled to represent his co-heirs in a suit by a creditor of the deceased, so as to make a decree binding against them, even though the heir who is sued is found to be in possession of the entire estate, unless such possession is with the consent of the other heirs and he is acting as their representative and manager.

Suit by creditors.

This principle has been adopted and followed by the High Court of Allahabad which has laid down that "a decree relative to the debts of a deceased Mahommedan passed in a contentious or non-contentious suit against only such of the heirs as are in

---

1 Jafri Begum *v.* Amir Muhammad Khan (1885) I L 7 All. 822, see pp. 838, 839.

2 Jafri Begum *v.* Amir Muhammad Khan, supra; Bussunteram Marwary *v.* Kamaluddin Ahmed (1885) I L 11 Cal. 421, 428.

The residue after satisfying debts and legacies is to be distributed among the heirs according to the law of the sect to which the deceased propositus belonged : Hayat-un-nissa *v.* Muhammad L R 17 I A 73 : I L R 12 All. 290.

3 Jafri Begum *v.* Amir Muhammad Khan, supra, followed in Muhammad Awais *v.* Harsahai (1885) I L 7 All. 716 ; Dallumal *v.* Hari Das (1901) I L 23 All. 263 ; Biland Sahai *v.* Begum Noor A I R 1943 Pesh. 62; Faizullah Khan *v.* Abdul Jabbar A I R 1943 Pesh. 65 and Ibrahim Abubakar *v.* Tekchand A I R 1953 S C 298.

possession of the whole or part of the estate, does not bind the other heirs who, by reason of absence or other cause, are out of possession, so as to convey to the auction-purchaser, in execution of such a decree, the rights and interest of those heirs who were not parties to the decree. But such heirs will not be entitled to recover from the auction-purchaser in execution of the decree, possession of their shares in the property sold, without such recovery of possession being rendered contingent upon payment by them of their proportionate share of the ancestor's debt for which the decree was passed and in satisfaction whereof the sale had taken place."[1]

Assamathennessa Bibee v. Roy Lutchmeeput Singh.

The same view was taken by the Calcutta High Court in the case of *Assamathennessa Bibee* v. *Roy Lutchmeeput Singh.*[2] In that case it appeared that one Buzloor Rohim died possessed of considerable property, both movable and immovable, and leaving a widow, Fatimatunnessa, a daughter, Shurfunnessa, and a sister, Sudderunnessa, his heiresses according to Mahommedan Law. Shortly after his death, Shurfunnessa obtained from the Court of the Judge of the 24-Pergunnahs a certificate under Act XXVII of 1860 to collect the debts, etc., of the deceased. A portion of the property of which Buzloor Rohim died possessed was an undivided moiety of certain premises in Calcutta being the property in suit, and the share of his sister, Sudderunnessa, in such property was, by Mahommedan Law, a one-sixth share of such undivided moiety. After the death of Buzloor Rahim, a suit was brought in the Court of the Judge of the 24-Pergunnahs by the Land Mortgage Bank of India against Shurfunnessa and her husband and two of her husband's brothers to realise certain mortgage securities executed by Buzloor Rohim to the Land Mortgage Bank of India, but to this suit neither Fatimatunnessa nor Sudderunnessa were made parties.

Sudderunnessa at that time was, and had been for some years, absent at Medina. In execution of the decree obtained by the Land Mortgage Bank the undivided moiety of the Calcutta property was attached and sold by the Sheriff of Calcutta on the 15th of June 1875, and was purchased by the defendant, who obtained possession thereof. The certificate of sale stated that what was sold was "the right, title, and interest of Buzloor Rohim, deceased, the ancestor, and of the defendants (naming them), the representatives, in a moiety of a piece of land situate in Jaun Bazar Street, etc."

On the 1st of December 1875, Sudderunnessa sold and assigned her share in (among other property) the undivided moiety of the premises in Calcutta to the plaintiff who brought a suit to recover the subject of his purchase, contending that the share of

---

1 Jafri Begum *v.* Amir Muhammad Khan, supra, followed in Muhammad Awais *v.* Harsahai (1885) I L 7 All. 716 ; Dallumal *v.* Hari Das (1901) I L 23 All. 263 and Abdul Majid Khan *v.* Krishnamachariar I L R 40 Mad. 243 (F B).

2 (1878) I L 4 Cal. 142.

Sudderunnessa did not pass and was unaffected by the sale of the 15th June, 1875. The defendant contended *inter alia*, that the property in suit was, by Mahommedan Law, subject to the payment of the debts of the deceased proprietor, and having been sold in payment of such debts, the deceased proprietor's heirs and representatives had no right, title, or interest in such property and the suit should therefore be dismissed.

The suit was decided by the first Court in favour of the plaintiff. On appeal, there being a difference of opinion among the Judges, the question was referred to a Full Bench. The Chief Justice in delivering the opinion of the majority, expressed himself thus :—

"The question, therefore, comes back to this : whether the decree, which was thus obtained, affected the share of Sudderunnessa, who was not a consenting party to it; and this question must in my opinion be determined by the Mahommedan Law, so far as that law upon the subject can be ascertained. It was strongly urged upon us by Mr. Jackson, on behalf of the appellant, that as the whole of the immovable property of Buzloor Rohim was in the possession of the defendants in the above suit, those defendants by Mahommedan Law represented the entire estate of Buzloor Rohim, and the decree against them bound the share of Sudderunnessa, as well as their own shares, and in support of that construction, he relied upon the following passages from the *Hedaya* :—"In Book XX, chapter 4 (relating to the duties of the Kazi), it is said : 'Any one of the heirs of a deceased person stands as litigant on behalf of all the others, with respect to anything due to or by the deceased, whether it be debt or substance, &c.' To this it is objected, 'If an heir be litigant on behalf of the others, it would follow that each creditor is entitled to have recourse to him for payment of his demand, whereas, according to law, each is only obliged to pay his own share.' Reply: The creditors are entitled to have recourse to one of several heirs only in a case *where all the effects are in the hands of that heir*. This is what is stated in the Iarna Kabeer, and the reason of it is, that although any one of the heirs may act as plaintiff in a case on behalf of the others, yet he cannot act as defendant on their behalf, unless the whole of the effects be in his possession.'

"Assuming that these passages do establish that, by the Mahommedan Law, if the whole of the immovable property of a deceased debtor be in the hands of one of his heirs, that heir may be sued by a creditor as representing the entire estate, and that a decree obtained against him would be binding as against the other heirs, it does not appear from the text of the *Hedaya* how far the rule thus laid down would be applicable in the case of a suit brought against two or more of several heirs who may be in possession of the property, nor whether the heir who is sued should be expressly charged as representing the whole estate of the deceased, nor whether the absent heirs should be mentioned in the proceedings.

"But it appears clear from another passage in the *Hedaya*, to which our attention has also been called, that an absentee heir would certainly not be bound by a decree obtained in such a suit, unless the proceedings are duly conducted, and the plaintiff's case proved in open Court; and that a decree by consent of the heir who is sued would not be binding on the other heirs. In Book XXXIX, chapter 1, on the subject of Partition, it is said: 'As where a man sues for a debt against an estate, and an heir or executor acknowledges his claim, in which case such acknowledgment as being to the detriment of the others, is not sufficient, but the claimant must produce evidence before the Kazi in his suit even against that heir or executor before he can establish his claim against the estate in general to the prejudice of the other heirs'.

"This appears to me a direct authority, that a decree by consent against one heir of a deceased debtor cannot legally bind the other heirs; and this rule is founded on the most manifest justice; because, although, for the sake of convenience, the share of an absentee heir may be bound by proceedings taken in open Court and in due course of law, as in such case the presence and sanction of the Judge, and the public nature of the proceedings, operate as a protection to the absentee, and as a guarantee for the *bona fides* and justice of the decree itself, it is obviously very different in the case of a decree made merely by consent, because there the absentee is entirely at the mercy of the consenting party, and there is no security whatever, either for the justice of the decree, or for the protection of the absent heir from any fraud or collusion, which may be practised against him."[1]

Varying decisions of the Indian Courts.

As usual, however, there is no uniformity in the decisions of the Courts even on this question. In the later cases the Calcutta High Court, proceeding on the analogy of the English Law, has regarded an action against one or more heirs in possession of the whole estate or that part of the estate which it was sought to charge, as an administration-suit, and a decree against the absent heirs in respect of the whole or part, as the case might be, to be valid unless such decree was obtained by fraud or collusion.

Muttyjan v. Ahmed Ally.

This was the view expressed in the case of *Muttyjan* v. *Ahmed Ally*,[2] where it appeared that after the death of a Mahommedan, several of his creditors had sued his widow and daughter, and obtained decree against the assets of the deceased, which assets had come into the possession of the mother and daughter. In execution of these decrees portions of the property left by him were sold; thereupon two married sisters of the deceased who lived with their husbands apart from the widow and daughter, sued as heirs of the deceased to recover their shares of the property sold. The Court held that the property of the deceased having been attached and sold in payment of his debts, the

1 See also Wahedun-nessa *v.* Shubrattun (1870) 6 B L R 54; Mazhar Ali *v.* Budh Singh (1884) I L 7 All. 297; Bachman *v.* Bachman (1884) I L 6 All. 583; Hamir Singh *v.* Zakia (1875) I L 1 All. 57.

2 (1882) I L 8 Cal. 370.

plaintiff's suit must be dismissed, for the learned Judges thought, when a creditor of a deceased Mahommedan sues the heir in possession, and obtains a decree against the assets of the deceased, such a suit is to be looked upon as an administration-suit; and those heirs of the deceased who have not been made parties cannot, in the absence of fraud, claim anything but what remains after the debts of the testator have been paid.[1]

This view, though alien to the Mahommedan Law, has been followed in a subsequent case by the same Court.[2]

The Bombay High Court has proceeded on a different analogy, *viz.*, that of the Mitakshara Law and has held to the same effect.[3] The Madras High Court seems inclined to the same view as the Bombay High Court.[4]

Principle.

The divergence referred to above arises only where there is no executor of the deceased or administrator appointed by the Court. For, when there is an executor or administrator legally representing the estate, the creditor must sue him and not the heirs.

After the estate has been divided among the heirs, they are liable for the debts of the deceased only to the extent of the share received by them respectively. A creditor, therefore, suing some

---

1 The practitioner may refer also to the following cases, though no principle can be gathered from them; Nuzeerun *v.* Ameeroodden (1878) 24 W R 3; Kishwar Khan *v.* Jewan Khan (1831) 1 Sel. Rep. 25; Khajah Hidayat Oollah *v.* Rai Jan Khanum (1844) 3 Moore's I A 295.

2 Amir Dulhin *v.* Baijnath Singh (1894) I L 21 Cal. 311; Abbas Naskar *v.* The Chairman District Board I L R 59 Cal. 2; A I R 1933 Cal. 80.

3 Khurshetbibi *v.* Keso Venayek (1887) I L 12 Bom. 101; Davalava *v.* Bhimaji Dhando (1895) I L 20 Bom. 338.

4 Pathummabi *v.* Vitil Ummachabi (1902) I L 26 Mad. 734.

The Madras High Court in a Full Bench decision Abdul Majid *v.* Krishnamachariar (1917) I L R 40 Mad 243 (F B) overruled its earlier decision in Pathmabi *v.* Vitil Ummachabi (1902) I L R 26 Mad. 734. The Bombay High Court has followed this decision in Mirkha *v.* Bhagirthebai I L R 43 Bom. 412 and later on Allisaheb *v.* Shesho Gobind Kul Karni A I R 1931 Bom. 545 and Virbhadrappa *v.* Shekabai A I R 1939 Bom. 188, the High Court of Lahore in Balak Ram *v.* Inayat Begum A I R 1935 Lah. 940, the Allahabad High Court in Manigir *v.* Amargoba A I R 1936 All 94, the Oudh Court in Mst. Sakina Begum *v* Mst. Shahr Bano A I R 1935 Oudh 62, the Nagpur Court in Suleman *v.* Abdul Shakoor A I R 1940 Nag. 99, Lakhmi Narain *v.* Saadat Ali A I R 1944 Nag. 99 and the Rangoon Court in Habib *v.* Swa Kyan A I R 1937 Rang 463. Even in Calcutta the view taken in earlier cases has been considerably toned down and in 59 Cal. 691 the decree was passed for a proportionate amount of the debt as against the persons who were defendants and not for the entire amount due from the deceased. This may now be taken as settled that a creditor cannot obtain a decree for the entire amount due by suing some of the heirs and if in execution of such a decree he sells the property of the deceased, the sale will not affect the interests of the heirs who were not parties to the suit. The same principle will apply to the execution proceedings.

of the heirs is entitled to a decree for a share of the debt proportionate to the shares received by them.[1]

The creditor's right to follow deceased's property.

The creditor of a deceased Mahommedan cannot follow his estate into the hands of a *bona fide* purchaser for value, to whom it has been alienated by the heir-at-law, whether the alienation has been by absolute sale or by mortgage.[2] But where the alienation is made during the pendency of a suit in which the creditor obtains a decree for the payment of his debt out of the assets of the estate which have come into the hands of the heir-at-law, the alienee will be held to take with notice, and will be affected by the doctrine of *lis pendens*.[3] The doctrine of *lis pendens* applies, of course, only to immovable property.

Where in execution of a money-decree against the heirs of a deceased Mahommedan for a debt incurred by him, a person *A* purchased certain property which had been allotted to the widow of the deceased in lieu of dower and of her share of the inheritance, and it appeared that previously to the purchase, the widow had mortgaged the same property to *B*, who, at the time of the mortgage, knew of the debt for which the decree was obtained; in a suit by *B* against *A* on the mortgage, it not being shown that there were no assets in the hands of the heirs-at-law to satisfy the debt due to *A's* vendor, it was held that *B* was entitled to recover.[4]

Under the provisions of the Indian Probate and Administration Act (V of 1881), the executor of a deceased Mahommedan cannot obtain a decree *until he has obtained probate*, although he may institute a suit to recover the assets due to the estate without proving the will.[5]

Succession Certificate Act.

Similarly, although Mahommedan heirs may prefer a claim to "debts" due to the ancestor and even bring a suit therefor without letters of administration there can be no

1 Pirthipal Singh *v.* Hussaini Jan (1882) I L 4 All. 361; Bussenteram *v.* Kamaluddin I L R 11 Cal. 421; Ramcharan Lal *v.* Mst. Hanifa Khatun I L R 54 All. 791 : A I R 1932 All. 591; Mauraj Mource *v.* Sh. Mohd. Hashim A I R 1941 Cal. 247. Where the estate of the deceased has not been distributed, and heirs are holding it jointly there should be decree against all heirs and decree-holder will be entitled to execute it against the property as a whole without interference with the extent of liability of decree *inter se*.

2 Syed Bazayet Hossein *v.* Dooli Chand; Mahomed Wajid *v.* Tayyuban (1878) I L 4 Cal. 402; L R 5 I A 211; Mussammat Wahidunnissa *v.* Mussammat Shubrattun (1870) 6 B L R 54; Campbell *v.* Delaney (1863) Marshall's Rep. 509.

3 Bazayet Hassain *v.* Dooli Chand. supra; Yasin Khan *v.* Muhammad Yar Khan (1897) I L 19 All. 504; Comp. s. 54 of the Transfer of Property Act (IV of 1882); and see Bholanath *v.* Maqbulunnissa (1903) I L 26 All. 28.

4 Narsingh Das *v.* Najmooddin Hossein (1881) I L 8 Cal. 20; 10 C L R 225.

5 Habiba *v.* Swa Kyan A I R 1937 Rang. 463. One heir of a deceased cannot be represented by another heir nor be bound by a decree against another heir. The heirs take as tenants in common, and each is an independent owner of his own share. Nor can the suit against one be regarded as an administration suit which can bind the interests of all the heirs.

decree in their favour unless they have obtained a certificate under the provisions of the Succession Certificate Act (VII of 1889).[1]

SECTION V

ANCIENT ARAB CUSTOMS—THE REFORMS OF MOHAMMED

Ancient Arab customs.

THE ancient Arab customs had, in the succession of a deceased person's property, one principal object in view, *viz.*, the maintenance of the goods in the family. With this view, the succession was confined exclusively to the male relations, and even among them to those who were capable of bearing arms. The daughters, the widows, the mothers, as well as the minors, were directly or indirectly excluded from succession; the daughters because their birth was regarded as a misfortune[2] and because they ceased upon their marriage to be members of the natural family; the widows, unless mother of children, because they possessed no recognised rights and were ordinarily treated as part of the husband's patrimony;[3] the minors, because they were unable to defend by their arms the tribal rights and privileges, and their goods therefore belonged to their tutors.[4]

Jewish rules.

Among the Jewish tribes who followed the Rabinical Law, the succession devolved in the first place on the sons, and the lineal male descendants, then on the daughters and their descendants, then on the father; fourthly, on the brothers and their descendants; fifthly, on the sisters and their descendants; and sixthly, on the grandfather, the uncles, the aunts, and so on.

Among the descendants, the sons had preference over the daughters, who occupied a secondary position even to their brothers' daughters. When a man died leaving the sons of a predeceased son and also the daughters of another predeceased son, the property was divided *per stirpes*, each group taking the share to which the person from whom they respectively received their title was entitled. The same rules applied to the succession of collaterals. The mother inherited nothing from her children. Illegitimate children when acknowledged had the same rights as the legitimate offspring. The succession of an illegitimate child

---

1 This Act has superseded Act XXVII of 1860. In Bombay, Reg. VIII of 1827 is in force and has the same object. Under this Regulation it has been held that a "certificate of heirship" cannot be granted to a minor: Bai Baiba *v.* Bai Daguba (1882) I L 6 Bom. 728. For the meaning of the words in section 4 of Act VII of 1889, see Kanchon Modi *v.* Baijnath Singh (1892) I L 19 Cal. 336.

Act VII of 1889 now stands superseded by Act XXXIX of 1925.

2 Koran, chap. lxxxi, v. 8.

3 *Ibid.*, chap. lxiii, v. 16.

4 *Ibid.*, chap. iv, vv, 2, 4, 5, 6, 7 and 11; chap. vi, v, 153; chap. xvii, v. 36.

devolved first upon the father, and, in his absence, passed to the State, or to the communal fund, as the case proved to be. Nor had the daughters any interest in the succession of their mother.

The uterine brothers and sisters had no right of succession.[1]

The Reforms of Mohammed.

The Arabian Legislator reformed the entire pre-Islamic customs. He gave, by express provision of the law, rights of inheritance to those who were excluded by the ancient institutions.[2] One of the great results of the new legislation was to raise women in the scale of civilisation, by elevating their moral and social position, and giving the widow, the mother, the daughters, and sisters heritable rights.

The provisions of the Mahommedan Law relating to succession are based on the following passages of the Koran:—

The Koranic rules.[2]

"God hath thus commanded you concerning your children. A male shall have as much as the share of two females; but if they be females only, and above two in number, they shall have two-third parts of what the deceased shall leave; and if there be but one, she shall have the half; and the parents of the deceased shall have each of them a sixth part of what he shall leave if he have a child; but if he have no child, and his parents be his heirs, then his mother shall have the third part; and if he have brethren, his mother shall have a sixth part, after the legacies which he shall bequeath, and his debts be paid.

"Ye know not whether your parents or your children be of greater use unto you. This is an ordinance from God, and God is knowing and wise. Moreover, ye may claim half of what your wives shall leave, if they have no issue; but if they have issue, then ye shall have the fourth part of what they shall leave, after the legacies which they shall bequeath and the debts be paid; they also shall have the fourth part of what ye shall leave, in case ye have no issue; but if ye have issue, then they shall have the eighth part of what ye shall leave, after the legacies which ye shall bequeath and your debts be paid; and if a man or woman's substance be inherited by a distant relation, and he or she have a brother or sister, each of them shall have a sixth part of the estate, but if there be more than this number, they shall all be equal sharers in the third part, after the payment of the legacies which shall be bequeathed and the debts, without prejudice to the heirs.

"They will consult thee for thy decision in certain cases; say unto them God giveth you these determinations concerning the more remote degrees of kindred. If a man die without issue, and

1 Comp. M. Sautayra.

2 See Koran, chap. iv, vv. 3, 12, 13, 14, 15, 57 and 175.

have a sister, she shall have the half of what he shall leave; and he shall be heir to her, in case she have no issue, but if there be two sisters, they shall have, between them, two-thirds part of what he shall leave; and if there be several, both brothers and sisters, a male shall have as much as the portion of two females."

Right of Inheritance.

"In these provisions", says Mr. Macnaghten, "we find ample attention paid to the interests of all those whom nature places in the first rank of our affections; and indeed it is difficult to conceive any system containing rules more strictly just and equitable."

The rules laid down in the Koran are to some extent amplified in the decisions of the Caliphs and Imams.[1]

Under the Musalman Law the right to inheritance is founded on three different rights—(i) *nasab* or *karabat*, kinship; (ii) *sabab*. special cause, *viz.*, a *valid* marriage, for the parties to a marriage which is either *void* or *invalid*[2] have no right of inheritance to each other;[3] and (iii) *wala*, which is of two kinds, *viz.*, *wala-ul-itak*, *i.e.*, the *wala* of emancipation, and the *wala-ul-mawalat*, or *clientage*.

CHAPTER II

HANAFI LAW OF SUCCESSION

SECTION I

CLASSIFICATION OF HEIRS

UNDER the Sunni Law of Succession the heirs connected to the deceased by the tie of blood are divided into three classes, *viz.*:—

(*a*) The *Zav-il-Furuz* (the "sharers,") persons whose shares are specified in the Koran, the traditions, or by the *Ijma'a-ul-Ummat*).

1 "The Muslim Law of inheritance", observes F. B. Tyabji "has always been admired for its completeness as well as the success with which it has achieved the ambitious scheme of providing not merely for the ...... of a single individual or homogenous group of individuals, on whom the estate of the deceased should devolve by universal succession, but for adjusting the competitive claims of all the nearest relations".

Sir William Jones, observed, "I am strongly disposed to believe that no possible question could occur on the Muslim Law of succession which might not be rapidly and quickly answered," while Mr. Rumsy was of the view, that "the Mohammedan Law of inheritance comprises beyond question the most refined and elaborate system of rules for the devolution of property that is known to the civilised world."

2 See following Chapter.

3 Durr-ul-Mukhtar, 852.

(*b*) The *'Asabah* (the "agnates").

(*c*) The *Zav-il-Arham* ("uterine relations).[1]

All relations by blood who are neither "sharers" nor *'Asabah* are included in this category.

No difference between Sunnis and Shiahs regarding "sharers".

With regard to the *Zav-il-Furuz* (the "Sharers"), there is no difference between the Shiahs and the Sunnis. But the former repudiate entirely an arbitrary classification of heirs into "agnates" and "uterine relations". Accordingly, they do not recognise the distinction of *'Asabah* and *Zav-il-Arham*; they group all the heirs together and treat them, as will be shown hereafter, according to their degree of propinquity to the deceased.

Thus under the Sunni Law, the uterine relations are placed in the last category; and it is only in the absence of sharers, and agnates that they receive any share in the inheritance.

Doctrine of "Return".

The "Sharers" take their specified portions, and the residue is then divided among the agnates. Should there be no agnates but only the "uterine relations" the residue would revert or *return* to the "Sharers" in proportion to their shares except in the case of the husband or wife. It is only when there are neither "Sharers" nor "agnates"[2] that the estate is divided among the "uterine relations".

The "sharers".

The "Sharers", or *Zav-il-Furuz*, are twelve in number. Their shares are liable to variation, according to circumstances, and some of them are subject also to entire exclusion owing to the operation of the two principles of elimination specified in Chapter I, Section III.[3] Four of these "Sharers" are males and eight females.

The four males are (*a*) the father; (*b*) the grandfather or *lineal male ascendant* (when not excluded); (*c*) the *uterine* brothers; and (*d*) the husband.

The females are; (*a*) the widow, (*b*) daughter, (*c*) son's daughter or the daughter of a *lineal male descendant* how-low-

---

1 Called by English writers "the Distant Kindred". The word literally means "uterine relations", and signifies, generally speaking, relations connected with the deceased through females. It is equivalent to the word bandhu in Hindu Law.

Until the reign of the Abbaside Caliph Mutazid u'Illah, "Uterine Relations" had no place in the succession; in default of "Sharers" and "Agnates" the estate of a deceased person escheated to the Bait-ul-Mal. Mutazid abolished this rule in 869 A C and gave to "Uterine Relations" their natural right in the inheritance of the propositus.

2 See Abdul Serang *v*. Putee Bibi (1902) I L 29 Cal. 738. See Gujjadhur Proshad *v*. Abdoollah (1870) 11 W R 220.

3 See ante.

soever, (*d*) mother, (*e*) true grandmother, (*f*) full sister, (*g*) consanguine sister, (*i.e.*,) half-sister on the father's side, and (*h*) uterine sisters, (*i.e.*), half-sisters on the mother's side.

The father.

1. *The father.*—The Sunni lawyers attribute to the father three characters—(*a*) the character of a simple "Sharer" when the deceased happens to leave a lineal male descendant; (*b*) the character of a simple residuary when he co-exists with a person who is only a "Sharer"—as a husband, a mother or a grandmother—when he takes the residue of the estate after the allotment of the share or shares; and (*c*) the character of both a "Sharer" and a residuary, as when he co-exists with a daughter or the daughter of a son or of any other *lineal* male descendant. In this case he takes first his share, and then becomes entitled to any residue after allotment of the daughter's or grand-daughter's share. For the sake of simplicity in the latter two cases, he may be said to take simply as a residuary.

The father's share.

The father's share, when the deceased leaves a son or son's son or any other lineal male descendant, like a son's son's son, is $\frac{1}{6}$.

The father's father, his share.

2. *The father's father* or any other lineal male ascendant (who is not excluded by the father or a nearer ascendant) takes the same share as the father, *viz.* $\frac{1}{6}$

[The Sunnis or rather the Hanafis divide the ascendants for purposes of succession into two classes, *viz.*, *true* and *false*.

A *true* grandfather is an ascendant in whose line of relationship to the deceased no female intervenes. For example, a father's father is a *true* grandfather; whereas a mother's father is a *false* grandfather.

True and false ancestors.

A *true* grandmother is a female ancestor in whose line of relationship with the deceased no *false* grandfather intervenes; thus a mother's mother or a father's mother or father's father's mother are *true* grandmothers, whereas mother's father's mother is a *false* grandmother. None of these distinctions exist in the Shiah Law.]

3. *The uterine brother* (when only one, and no child, or the child of a son[1] how-low-soever, father, or *true* grandfather), $\frac{1}{6}$.

When two or more, and no child or the child of a son how-low-soever, or father or *true* grandfather, $\frac{1}{3}$.

---

1 The word "son" here and in the following passages includes any lineal male descendant.

4. *The husband* (when the deceased leaves a child or the child of a son, how-low-soever), $\frac{1}{4}$.

Without them, $\frac{1}{2}$.

5. *The widow*, when the deceased has left no child or the child of a son, how-low-soever, $\frac{1}{4}$.

Co-existing with a child or child of a son how-low-soever, $\frac{1}{8}$.

In consequence of the limited and qualified recognition of polygamy, or more properly speaking, polygamy, by the generality of the schools, it sometimes happens that the deceased leaves him surviving more than one widow. In such circumstance the widows take the $\frac{1}{4}$ or $\frac{1}{8}$, as the case may be, between them.

A husband or widow co-existing with a *daughter's* child, (who is an *uterine relation*), takes his or her full share.

6. *The daughter* (when only one and no son, so as to render her a residuary), $\frac{1}{2}$.

Two or more (and no son), $\frac{2}{3}$.

7. *The daughter of a son* (or *daughter of a son's son*, how-low-soever)—

(*a*) when only one and no child or son's son or other lineal male descendant, $\frac{1}{2}$;

(*b*) when two or more and no child or son's son or other lineal male descendant, $\frac{2}{3}$.

The son's daughter.

(*c*) when co-existing with one daughter and no son or son's son or other lineal male descendant $(\frac{2}{3}-\frac{1}{2})=\frac{1}{6}$.

When there are two daughters, the son's daughters are excluded unless there happen to be with them a lineal male descendant of the *same or lower degree*.

The son's daughter or the daughters of any lineal male descendant are excluded by a son or by a lineal male descendant nearer in degree than themselves.

The mother.

8. *The mother* (when co-existing with a child of the *propositus*, or a child of his or her son, how-low-soever, or two or more brothers and sisters, whether consanguine or uterine, $\frac{1}{6}$.

When not, $\frac{1}{3}$.

But $\frac{1}{3}$ of *remainder* after deducting husband's or wife's share, when with *father*; $\frac{1}{3}$ of whole when with *grandfather*.

9. *The true grandmother*, how-high-soever (when not excluded by a nearer *true female* ancestor), $\frac{1}{6}$:

[Every one into whose line of relationship to the deceased a mother enters between two fathers is a *false* grandmother. The share of the *true* grandmother, on the father's or mother's side, is a sixth, whether there be one or more; all partaking in it equally who are in the same degree. When there are two grandmothers one of whom is related to the deceased on both sides, another only on one side. Abu Yusuf has said, and there is one report to the same effect from Abu Hanifa, that the sixth is to be divided between them equally, and the *Fatwa* is in accordance with this opinion.]

10. *The full sister* (when only one and no son, son's son howlow-soever, father, *true* grandfather, daughter, son's daughter or brother), $\frac{1}{2}$.

When two or more and no such excluder, $\frac{2}{3}$.

11. *The consanguine sister* (when only one and no excluder as above or full sister), $\frac{1}{2}$.

When one and co-existing with *one full sister*, $\frac{1}{6}$.

When two or more and no such excluder, $\frac{2}{3}$.

When there are two or more full sisters, the consanguine sister takes nothing unless there is a consanguine brother with her.

12. *The uterine sister* takes like the *uterine brother*.

These represent the "Sharers," persons whose shares are specified in the Koran, and with reference to whom, therefore, there is little or no difference between the Sunnis and the Shiahs.

Section II

'Asabah (Agnates) or "Residuaries"

Residuaries.

The residuaries or *'asabah* are divided into two groups, *viz.*, *'asabah* by *nasab* or kinship to the deceased, and *'asabah* by *sabab* or the special cause of *wala*.

The former group again is divided into three classes—

(1) residuaries in their own right;

(2) residuaries in another's right; and

(3) residuaries together with another.

The first class includes all agnatic male relations, that is, in whose line of relationship to the deceased no female enters; (for, if a female were to come in, the male is no longer a Residuary; he would belong to the category of either "Sharers" or "Uterine Relations" *e.g.*, a mother's son is not a Residuary but a "Sharer."[1]

[1] Durr-ul-Mukhtar 864.

These are the '*Asabah proprio jure* ('*Asabah-be-nafsihi*).

Residuaries in their own right.

(1) Residuaries in their own right are divided into four sub-classes:—

(*a*) The "offspring" of the deceased, meaning thereby the deceased's sons or lineal male descendants;

(*b*) his "root", *i.e.*, the ascendants; in other words, his father and *true* grandfather, how-high-soever;

(*c*) the "offspring" of his father, *viz.*, full brothers and consanguine brothers and their lineal male descendants;

(*d*) the "offspring" of the *true* grandfather *how-high-soever*; in other words, lineal male descendants however remote, of lineal male ascendants however removed.

Consequently, descendants in the male line of the paternal great-grandfather of an intestate are within the class of residuary heirs and entitled to take to the exclusion of the children of the intestate's sisters. Likewise descendants of a paternal grand-father's brother are residuaries and entitled to the inheritance in preference to grand-daughters in the female line.

It must be remarked that in the succession of the '*Asabah proper when the relations are of the same degree of affinity, preference is given to the strength of blood or consanguinity.* The *Durr-ul-Mukhtar* lays down as a legitimate conclusion from the Prophet's doctrine, "surely kinsmen by the same father and mother shall inherit before kinsmen by the same father only," that where relations are of an equal degree of affinity, regard is to be paid to the strength of blood. For example, when the deceased leaves a full-brother and a half-brother by the same father only, though the degree of affinity is the same, yet the tie of blood being stronger in the case of a full-brother than in that of the half-brother, preference is given to him. In the same way the son of a full-brother is preferred to the son of a half-brother on the father's side. So also when there is with the brother's son a paternal uncle, the uncle has no interest in the inheritance. Lineal male descendants exclude all agnates in the ascending as well as collateral lines.

The *Fatawai-Alamgiri* defines the '*asabah-be-nafsihi* to mean "every male into whose line of relation to the deceased no female enters." "Such residuaries are of four sorts—the offspring of the deceased, and his root, the offspring of his father, and the offspring of his grandfather. Hence the nearest of the residuaries is the son; then the son's son, how-low-soever; then the father; then the grandfather, or father's father, how-high-soever; then the full-brother; then the half-brother by the father; then the son of the full-brother; then the son of the half-brother by the father;

then the full-paternal uncle; then the half-paternal uncle on the father's side; then the son of the full-paternal uncle; then the son of the half-paternal uncle; then the full-paternal uncle of the father; then the half-paternal uncle of the father on the father's side; then the son of the father's full-paternal uncle; then the son of the father's half-paternal uncle on the father's side; then the paternal uncle of the grandfather; then his son how-low soever."

When there are several residuaries in the same degree, the property is divided between them "by bodies, not by families" (*i.e.*, *per capita* and not *per stirpes*). As, for instance, when there is a son of one brother and ten sons of another, or the son of one paternal uncle and ten sons of another, the property is to be divided into eleven parts, of which each takes one part.

Residuaries in another's right.

(2) The *Residuaries in another's right* are those females who become residuaries only when they co-exist with certain males, that is, when there happen to be males of the same degree, or who, though of a lower degree, would take as such.[1]

These are four in number, *viz.*:—

(*a*) Daughters (*with sons*).

(*b*) Son's daughters (*with a son's son or a male descendant still further removed in the direct line*).

This applies to the daughters of all lineal male descendants *however low*. For example, when there is a son's son's daughter co-existing with a son's daughter, the latter takes her half (like the daughter of the deceased), and the one-sixth goes to the son's son's daughter and so on. *If there are two son's daughters, the son's son's daughter will take nothing unless she has a lineal male descendant of the same or lower degree co-existing, such as a brother or a nephew.*

(*c*) The full sister (with her own *or full brother*).

(*d*) The sister by the same father, or, in other words, a consanguine sister (*with her brother*).

When the females are of the same degree as the males (or as in the case of son's daughters or the daughters of a son's son how-low-soever—when they co-exist with lineal male descendants though of a lower degree)—each female takes half the share of a male. For example, where there are two sons and three daughters or two brothers and three sisters, each daughter or sister, as the case may be, will take one-seventh. whilst each son or brother two-sevenths.

Residuary with another.

It must be remembered, however, that many males may become in certain contingencies, residuaries but it does not

1 Durr-ul-Mukhtar pp. 864, 865.

follow that in all cases their sisters would become residuaries *with* them. *It is only when the female is a sharer herself that, instead of taking a share, she takes as a residuary when co-existing with a male residuary.*

For example, if a man dies leaving behind him a widow, a paternal uncle, and an aunt, "be the latter by the same father and mother, or by the same father only", the aunt, not being a *sharer* according to law, is not entitled to any share in the inheritance of her deceased nephew, and her brother (the uncle) takes the entire estate after allotment of the widow's share.

When there is one sister of the whole blood, and consanguine brothers and sisters, the full-sister will take her half, and the residue will be divided among the half-brothers and sisters in the proportion of two to one.

When there are several full-sisters, they will take their two-thirds, and the remainder will be divided as above.

When the deceased leaves only a full-sister and a consanguine sister, they take a moiety and one-sixth respectively, and the residue is divided among them *pro rata*.

When there are two or more full-sisters and several consanguine sisters, but no (consanguine) half-brother, the full-sisters take the whole, the consanguine sisters take nothing.

Residuary with others.

(3) *The Residuaries with others are—*

(*a*) Full-sisters *with daughters or son's daughters.*

(*b*) Consanguine sisters, *with daughters or son's daughters.*

When there is one daughter or son's daughter with a full or consanguine sister, the daughter or son's daughter takes her moiety, and *the remainder goes to the sister.*

When there are several daughters or son's daughters, they take two-thirds, and the residue appertains to the sister.

When there are several daughters and full-sisters with son's daughters, the daughters and full-sisters exhaust the inheritance.

If there are two daughters, a son's daughter, and a lineal male descendant such as a son's son or a son's grandson, the two daughters take two-thirds between them; the son's son takes two-ninths, being two-thirds of the residue, and the son's daughter takes the remaining one-ninth.

When the deceased leaves a daughter and several daughters of a pre-deceased son, the daughter takes her half and the son's daughters one-sixth, and the residue is divided among the daughter and son's daughters *pro rata*; but if there are two or more daughters, they take two-thirds as their share and the remainder by return and "there is nothing for the son's daughters"; but if there is a male among them, he makes the females (whether they be his sisters or cousins) residuaries with him, so that if there were two daughters or more, they would have two-thirds between them, and the remainder would pass to the children of the son, in the proportion of two parts to the males and one part to the females. The male may be of a lower degree, still he would make them residuaries *with him*; so that the remainder would be between him and them in the same proportion, or two parts to each male, and one to each female.

Preference to propinquity.

When a person dies leaving behind him several relations who may be classed as residuaries of the different kinds mentioned, preference is given to propinquity to the deceased, so that the residuary with another when nearer to the deceased than the residuary in himself, would come first.[1]

Thus, when a man has died leaving a daughter, a full-sister, and the son of a half-brother by the father, one-half of the inheritance is given to the daughter and the other half to the sister, who is a residuary *with* the daughter and nearer to the deceased than the brother's son.[2] In the same way, a sister by the same father and mother (co-existing with a daughter) is preferred to a brother by the same father only, that is, the daughter will take her half share, and the remainder will be given to the full sister.

All residuaries other than these take the whole of the residue without the participation of the females of the same degree as themselves.

Where females, who, under the Mahommedan Law, are entitled to a share in the inheritance of the *propositus*, are excluded from succession by a valid custom, they should be treated as non-existent. For example, if a man were to die leaving a widow, a sister, daughters and nephews; and the daughters were excluded by custom, their exclusion would have the result of letting in the nephews to take as heirs in their default, in conjunction with the widow and sister, in lieu of the sister becoming the sole residuary.[3]

Residuaries of a disavowed child.

The residuaries of a *walad-uz-zina*, "a child of fornication", and of the son of an "imprecated" woman (a woman who has been repudiated by the husband by a proceeding for adultery and disavowal of parentage technically called *l'aan*)[4] are the kindred of their mother.

---

1 Durr-ul-Mukhtar 865.

2 Fatawai-'Alamgiri Vol. VI, p. 629.

3 Muhammad Kamil *v.* Mussummat Imtiaz Fatima (1908) L R 36 I A 210; I L 31 All. 557.

4 See post.

The "child of Imprecation".

So that if the son of an 'imprecated" woman should leave a daughter, a mother, and the "imprecator", the daughter would take a half, the mother a sixth, and the remainder would revert to them as if he had no father. If besides these there were also a husband or a widow, he or she would take his or her share, and the remainder would be distributed among the others, either as their share or by way of *return*. And if he should leave his mother, a half-brother by the mother and a son of the "imprecator", the mother would take a third, the half-brother by the mother a sixth, and the remainder would revert to them, there being nothing for the son of the "imprecator", as the deceased has no brother on the side of the father.

When the child of the son of an "imprecated" woman dies, the family of *his* father inherit to him, being his brothers; but the family of his grandfather, who are his paternal uncles, and their children, do not inherit to him. The same principle applies to the *walad-uz-zina*, "child of fornication", except that there is a difference between *walad-ul-mulainah* (disavowed child) and an illegitimate child in one respect, *viz*., that the *tawam*, or twin of the *walad-uz-zina*, inherits only as a half-brother by the mother, while the twin of an "imprecated" son inherits as a full brother.[1]

SECTION III

UTERINE RELATIONS OR "DISTANT KINDRED"

Uterine Relations.

WHEN there are no *consanguineous* "Sharers" or Residuaries, the "uterine relations" succeed to the inheritance of the deceased according to the class to which they belong and to their respective "rights".

Some writers have fallen into a mistake in supposing that the husband or wife also exclude the "uterine relations"[2] from sharing in the patrimony of the deceased ancestor. This is an erroneous idea. The *Zav-il-Arham* are always entitled to a share when co-existing with the husband or widow,.[3] In other words, a husband or widow, though a "Sharer", does not exclude "uterine relations" from inheriting.

Four classes.

The uterine relations, as in the case of the *Asabah proprio jure*, are divided into four classes, *viz.*:—

---

1. A man may deny one of twins and acknowledge the other, but in tha case the paternity of both is established (Hedaya, Vol. II, p. 325); so tha each is full brother or sister to the other.

2. See for *e.g.*, Shama Churn Sircar's Lectures, 1873.

3. Durr-ul-Mukhtar 873.

Class (1).

(1) The "offspring" of the deceased, *viz.*:—

(*a*) The children of daughters and their descendants how-low-soever.

(*b*) The children of son's daughters and their descendants how-low-soever.

Class (2).

(2) The "root" of the deceased or his ascendants, *viz.*:—

(*a*) Male ancestors however remote in whose line of relation to the deceased there occurs a female and who are therefore called, "false grandfathers;"

e.g., deceased's mother's father, father's mother's father, mother's mother's father, etc.

(*b*) Female ancestors technically called "false grandmothers";

e.g., mother's father's mother.

Class (3).

(3) The "offspring" of his parents, *viz.*:—

(*a*) The daughters of full brothers and of full brother's sons and their descendants.

(*b*) The daughters of consanguine brother (*i.e.*, by the same father only) and of consanguine brother's sons and their descendants.

(*c*) The *children* of half brothers by the same mother only and their descendants.

(*d*) The *children* of all sisters and their descendants.

Class (4).

(4) The offspring of grandparents and other ascendants however removed, *viz.*:—

(*a*) The daughters of full paternal uncles and of their sons;

(*b*) The daughters of half paternal uncles by the father (*i.e.*, father's consanguine brothers) and of their sons;

(*c*) Paternal aunts, full, consanguine or uterine and *their children*.

(*d*) Maternal uncles and aunts and *their children*;

(*e*) Paternal uncles by the mother, that is, the father's half brothers by the same mother only and *their children*; and their respective descendants however removed.

The enumeration not exhaustive.

The enumeration is by no means exhaustive. According to the most approved definition, all persons connected with the deceased through the persons mentioned are his "Uterine Relations" or Distant Kindred.

The general order of succession is according to their classification the first class succeeding first and so on.

Among the individuals of the various classes, succession is regulated by proximity to the deceased, the nearer in degree always excluding the more remote.

First class of uterine relations—Rules regarding their succession.

Accordingly, among the individuals of the first class of uterine relations or distant kindred, which comprises the children of daughters and the children of son's daughters:—

"(*a*) The *nearest in degree* to the deceased is the person preferably entitled to the succession. *Thus the daughter of a daughter will take in preference to the daughter of a son's daughter.*[1]

(*b*) If the claimants be equal *in degree*, that is, if all be related to the deceased in the second, third or fourth degree, as the case may be, in such circumstances, the child of a *sharer* or a *residuary* is preferred to the child of an *uterine relation*, *e.g.*, *the son's* daughter's daughter will take in preference to *the daughter's* daughter's son. It will be remembered that a son's daughter is a sharer, whilst the daughter's daughter is an *uterine relation*.

(*c*) *If the claimants be equal in degree and there be not among them the child of a sharer or a residuary*, or *if they all be related through a sharer or a residuary*, then the shares will be regulated by the number and sex of the persons existing at the time the inheritance opens, *provided the persons through whom the claimants are connected with the deceased are of the same sex*, or as it is technically said, "provided the sex of the roots agree".[2]

For example, if a man were to die leaving a daughter's son and a daughter's daughter, it will be noticed that the two claimants are not only equal in degree to the *propositus*, but that there is no difference in the sex of the persons through whom they are connected with the deceased. Accordingly, the daughter's son takes ⅔rds whilst the daughter's daughter gets ⅓rd. Similarly, if there were two sons of a daughter and two daughters of another daughter, the two grandsons would take ⅔rds between them, and the two grand-daughters ⅓rd between them.[3]

Imam Mohammed's rule followed by the Indian Hanafis.

(*d*) But if "the sex of the roots" differ, or, *in other words, if the persons through whom the claimants happen to be connected with the deceased differ in their sex*, then, according to Imam Mohammed, whose opinion on this point is followed by the Indian Hanafis, the shares are not regulated by the number and

1. Fatawai-'Alamgiri, Vol. VI, p. 637.
2. Durr-ul-Mukhtar 870.
3. *Ibid.*

sex of the claimants, but "by the roots", in other words, they take *per stirpes*.[1]

Abu Yusuf's rules.

According to the rule of Abu Yusuf which, being simpler and more intelligible, is followed throughout Western Asia, in every case where, the claimants are of an equal degree and *there is not among them the child of a sharer or a residuary,* the property is divided with reference to the sex and number of the claimants.[2]

A few examples may be of assistance to the student in understanding these divergent views:—

Suppose a man were to leave him surviving a daughter's son's daughter, and a daughter's daughters's son, thus—

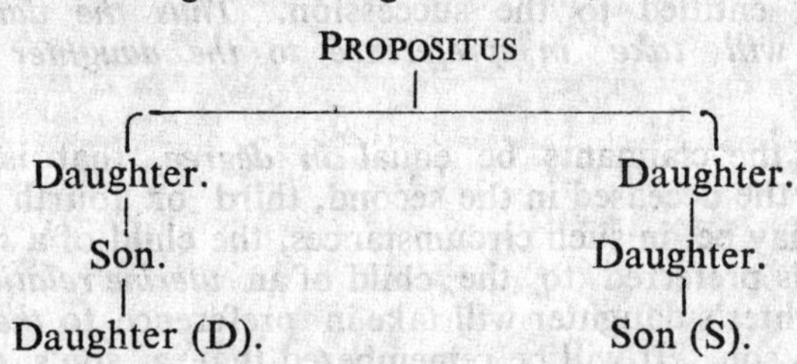

In that case according to Abu Yusuf, the distribution would be made according to the number and sex of the claimants, and the son (S) would get ⅔rds and the daughter (D) ⅓rd. According to Mohammed, the distribution would be made according to the sex of the "roots", *viz.*, of the intermediate ancestors. Thus the daughter's son being entitled to double the share of the daughter's daughter would pass his ⅔rds to his daughter (D), and the daughter's daughter would pass her ⅓rd to her son (S).

Examples.

Take another case. A man dies leaving one son of a daughter's daughter, and two daughters of a daughter's son, thus—

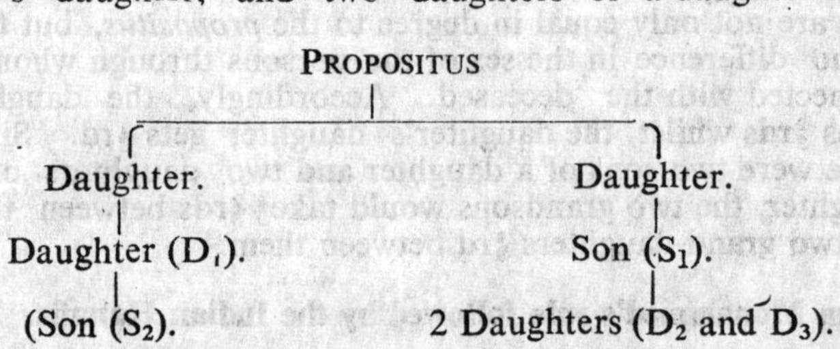

According to Mohammed S_1 takes ⅔rds and passes it on to his two daughters (D_2 and D_3), whilst D_1 takes ⅓rd and passes it on to her son (S_2).

According to Abu Yusuf, the property is divided into four shares of which S_2 takes 2, or half of the whole, and D_2 and D the remaining half equally between them.

1. Sirajia, 90, 131, Fatawai-'Alamgiri, Vol. III, 638.
2. *Ibid.*

(*e*) When the claimants are more than two in number and although equal in degree derive their descent from separate ancestors, differing in sex,, the distribution, according to Mohammed, will be made with regard to the sex of the ancestors in the first line of descent (from the deceased), when the difference in sex occurs. After which the males will be grouped in one class and the females in another class, and the shares of the males will be passed down in the aggregate to their descendants to be divided according to the usual rule, and the shares of the females similarly to their descendants. After the intermediate ancestors have been thus grouped, the aggregate shares of the two classes must be kept distinct through all the lines of descent. If there is one individual of one sex, and several of the other in the line where the difference first occurs, the share of that individual must be kept distinct for his or her descendant; and this process of differentiation must be carried through all the lines of descent.

For example, if a man died leaving the following relations:—

PROPOSITUS

Daughter.	Daughter.	Daughter.	Daughter.
Daughter.	Daughter.	Son.	Son.
Son.	Son.	Daughter.	Daughter.

According to Mohammed, the distribution would take place in the second line where the difference in sex first appears: the two sons are allotted $\frac{4}{6}$ths and the two daughters $\frac{2}{6}$ ths. The $\frac{4}{6}$ths of the sons are passed down to their daughters in equal shares and the $\frac{2}{6}$ths of the two daughters to their sons in equal shares.

Examples.

If instead of the two sons leaving daughters they had left a son and a daughter respectively, the son would have taken $\frac{2}{3}$rds of $\frac{4}{6}$ths $=\frac{8}{18}$ths, whilst the daughter would have taken $\frac{1}{3}$rd of $\frac{4}{6}$ths $=\frac{4}{18}$ths.

According to Abu Yusuf, the two male claimants would take $\frac{1}{3}$rd each and the two female claimants $\frac{1}{6}$th each.

Or take another instance: a man dies leaving five descendants, three of whom are females and two males, *viz.*, *two* daughters of a daughter's son's daughter, *one* daughter of a daughter's daughter's son, and *two* sons of a daughter's daughter's daughter, as in the following table:—

Daughter.	Daughter.	Daughter.
Daughter (D_1).	Daughter (D_2).	Son (S_1).
Daughter (D_2).	Son (S_2).	Daughter.
2 Sons.	Daughter.	2 Daughters.

According to Abu Yusuf, the property of the deceased will be divided into seven shares, out of which two shares will be given to each of the males and one share to each of the females.

The rule of Imam Mohammed.

According to Mohammed, the property will be divided into 28 shares, out of which eight shares will be given to each of the daughters of the daughter's son's daughter, six shares to the daughter of the daughter's daughter's son, and 3 shares to each of the sons of the daughter's daughter's daughter. The reason of this division is thus stated :

Here the sexes differ first in the second line. As S_1 (the son in the second line on the right hand side) has two descendants among the claimants,—by the strength of his sex, he will be treated as two males equivalent to four females); D_1 (the daughter on the left hand side) having two descendants among the claimants will on account of her sex, be treated as two females; and D_2 (the daughter in the middle) having one descendant among the claimants will be treated as one female; the property will therefore be divided into seven shares, of which four shares or $\frac{4}{14}$ will be allotted to S_1, who being by himself will be isolated and *his* share will descend to his descendants (his two grand-daughters) in aqual moieties, *i.e.*, $\frac{2}{14}$ each. The shares of D_1 and D_2 formed into a group will be dealt with in the aggregate and will descend to their immediate descendants (S_2 and D_3) in equal moieties, because S_2 is a male and is equal to two females and D_3 represents two females (her descendants).

Examples.

These must now remain apart or isolated, and thus the two sons of D get $\frac{8}{14}$ equally between themselves, and the daughter of S_2 gets $\frac{3}{14}$ for herself. In other words, the descendants of S_1 get 16 shares and the descendants of D_1 and D_2 six shares respectively.

Or take another example of a somewhat more complicated character.

A person dies leaving twelve relations, three males and nine females all standing in the same rank or degree of affinity, in the sixth generation from the common ancestor; thus:—

S	S	S	D	D	D	D	D	D	D	D	D
D	D	D	D	D	D	D	D	D	D	D	D
S	D_a	D_b	S	S	S	D	D	D	D	D	D
D	D	D	S_b	D_d	D_e	S	S	S	D	D	D
D	S_a	D_c	D	D	D	S	D	D	S	D	D
D_1	D_2	D_3	D_4	D_5	S_6	D_7	D_8	S_9	D_{10}	S_{11}	D_{12}

Abu Yusuf would divide the property into fifteen shares, giving one share each to the females and two shares each to the males.

But Mohammed would divide the property into 60 shares, giving to claimant No. 1, 12 shares; No. 2, 8 shares; No. 3, 4 shares; No. 4, 9 shares; No. 5, 3 shares; No. 6, 6 shares; No. 7, 2 shares; No. 8, 4 shares; No. 9, 3 shares; No. 10, 2 shares; No. 11, 1 share; No. 12, 6 shares.

And this division he would make on the following basis:—

In the first column there are three males and nine females; divide the property into 15 shares, which would give exactly 2 shares to each male and one share to each female.

In the second column, which implies the second generation, the members happen to be all of the same sex. Mohammed passes them over.

Examples.

When he arrives at the third column or the third generation, he finds under the three males of the first column, one male and two females, *viz.*, D_a and D_b. He takes the 6 shares of these three males and divides them among the one male and two females in the third column, in the proportion of two shares for the male and one share each for the females, so that the male gets 3 out of 6, and the two females get 1½ each.

Under the nine females of the first column, who each took one share we find in the third column three males and six females. Mohammed, in order to give each male a share double that of each female, would have to make the 9 into 12, but as 12 leaves a remainder when divided among 9, he takes the 4, the resultant of 12, by the common divisor 3, and multiplies the original shares by 4, so as to give 60. Accordingly, he would divide 60 now among the original heirs (of the first generation), by which the three sons would get 8 each, that is, 24 among the three, and the daughters 4 each.

The 24 shares of the three males of the first generation are brought down to the three persons just beneath them in the third generation and divided in the proportion of 2 to a male, and one to a female by which the male in the first perpendicular column and the third horizontal column gets 12 for himself and the two females, *viz.*, D_a and D_b, 6 each; the share of S, *viz.*, 12, there being no difference or break in the sex of his heirs, is received by his female descendant (D_1) in the sixth generation.

The 12 shares of D_a and D_b in the third column is divided in the same way in the generation in which the difference of sex occurs, that is, the fifth generation, by which S_a in the fifth horizontal column gets 8 and passes the same on to his descendant in the sixth generation, and the same is the case with D_c in the fifth horizontal and the third perpendicular column.

So that D_1 gets 12.
„ D_2 „ 8.
„ D_3 „ 4.

The 36 shares obtained by the nine females of the first

generation are divided in the third generation, when the break in the uniformity of the sex takes place, in the usual manner, by which three sons obtain among themselves 18 shares and the six daughters 18 shares. In the fourth generation, under the three males or sons, we find one male and two females, and the 18 shares are divided among them accordingly, giving 9 shares to S_b in the fourth column who passes it on without break to D . The 9 shares of the two females in the fourth generation, *viz.*, D_d and D_e, in the fifth and sixth perpendicular columns, come down as a whole to the two persons in the sixth column and underneath them, and then are divided according to the usual mode, by which D_5 gets 3 shares and S_6 gets 6, and so on.

Consideration paid to blood.

In addition to sex, consideration is also paid in the succession of uterine relations to the *sides* from which they are related to the deceased. In this also the two lawyers differ. According to Mohammed, the strength of blood of the persons from whom the surviving heirs derive their title, or what is called the sides in the "roots" is taken into consideration; whilst, according to Abu Yusuf, the strength of blood in the heirs themselves, or what is called the sides in the persons, is considered,[1] *e.g.*:—

Daughter.	Daughter.	Daughter.
Daughter.	Son.	Daughter.
2 Daughters.		Son.

Abu Yusuf in this case would divide the property into three equal shares (regarding each daughter by both sides as equal to the son who is connected by one side only). But Mohammed would divide the property into 28 shares, out of which 22 would be given to the two daughters and 6 to the son, in the following manner:—Two daughters carried to the son in the second line make four daughters, two daughters carried to the daughter on the left-hand side in the second line make two daughters, and one son carried to the daughter on the right-hand side stands as one daughter, making in all 7 shares, of which 4 shares should be given to the son in the middle in the second line; the remaining 3 shares (there being two daughters only in the second line) would be given equally to both, that is, $\frac{3}{14}$ each.

In this way 28 shares are required to give integral shares, that is, $\frac{4}{7}$ of 28, *i.e.*, 16 to the son which comes down to the daughters, and $\frac{3}{14}$ of 28, *i.e.*, 6 again, to the daughter on the left-hand side in the second line, which also comes to the two daughters; and $\frac{3}{14}$ of 28, *i.e.*, 6 to the daughter on the right-hand side in the second line, which comes to her son.

To state shortly according to Mohammed the estate will be divided into 28 parts, out of which the females take 22 shares (16 in right of their father and 6 in right of their mother), whilst the male descendant takes only 6 shares in right of his mother.

1 Imam Mohammed is followed in India.

To take another case; suppose a man (A) had two daughters, both of whom died during his lifetime, one leaving a son (*a*), and the other a daughter (*b*). These two intermarried, and had one male issue (S_1). Subsequently, on the decease of her first husband (*a*), the daughter (*b*) marries H, of which union there is one female issue (D_1). Now, A dies, leaving behind him only S_1 and D_1. How is the property to be divided?

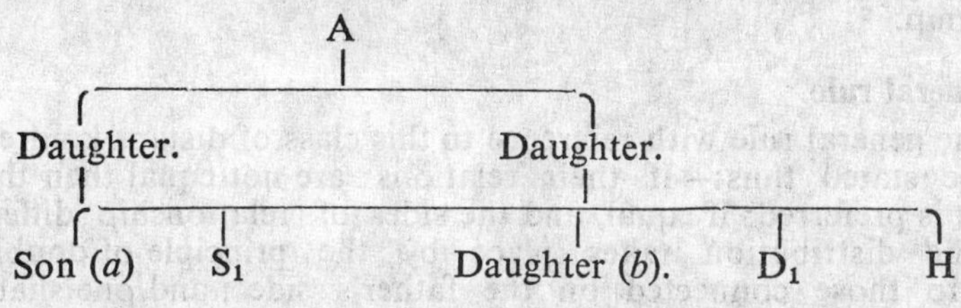

In this case Abu Yusuf would take the son, being doubly connected, as four daughters, and divide the property *per capita*, giving to the son 4 shares, and to the daughter 1 share. But Mohammed would divide it into 6 shares, and give 5 shares to the son and 1 to the daughter, in the following way:—The son in the second line takes $\frac{1}{3}$ and passes on to his son, the daughter in the second line takes $\frac{2}{3}$, a moiety of which also passes to her son, who thus gets ^{5}, and the remainder, $\frac{1}{6}$, goes to the daughter D_1.

Uterine Relations of the second class.

In the succession of uterine relations of the second class which comprises the excluded grandfathers and grandmothers, the same rules are to be observed, *viz.*:—

(*a*) Proximity to the deceased.

(*b*) The condition and sex of the person through whom the claimants are connected to the deceased, *viz.*, whether or not he or she is a sharer or a residuary, provided the *sides are equal, with this addition that,*

(*c*) *if the claimants are related through different sides two-thirds would go to the paternal and one-third to the maternal side without regard to the sex of the claimants.*

If the claimants be equal in degree of affinity and distance, and there be none among them who is related through a sharer or residuary, or all of them be related through heirs, then, if the sex of those through whom they are related agree, and their relation be also on the same side (either through the father or the mother of the deceased), then the property would be distributed equally among them.

If, on the other hand (notwithstanding equality in degree), the sexes of those through whom they are related differ, then the property is distributed according to the first rank that differs in sex, as happens in the first class: that is, the division will commence in the rank or line when the difference first appears, on the principle that a male has double the portion of a female; and then the males will be grouped in one class and the females in another, and their shares passed on in the usual manner.

If, however, the relation differs, that is, the claimants be connected respectively through the mother and the father (notwithstanding equality in degree), the property is divided on the principle of double shares to the claimants connected through the father, and one share to those related by the mother: that is, two-thirds would be given to those connected on the father's side as a group, and one-third to those connected on the mother's side as a group.

The general rule.

The general rule with reference to this class of distant kindred may be stated thus:—If their relations are not equal then the nearest is preferred; if equal, and the sides of relationship differ, then the distribution takes place by the principle of double shares to those connected on the father's side ; and one share to those connected on the mother's side if they agree in side, that is, in strength of blood and distance, and the "roots" agree throughout in sex, then the distribution takes place according to the number of claimants; but if the "roots" differ in sex, then the property should be divided according to the difference of sex in the highest rank, as in the first class.

For example, father's mother's father takes $\frac{2}{3}$, whilst mother's mother's father takes $\frac{2}{3}$.

Distant kindred of the third class.

The succession of the distant kindred of the third class, which includes sister's children, brother's daughters, and the sons of brothers by the same mother only, is also regulated by the rule that the nearest succeeds in preference to the more remote; *but when all are equal in degree, the child or children of a residuary is preferred to one who is not*: for example, if a man leaves a son of a sister's daughter and daughter of a brother's son,—both equidistant from him—the whole estate goes to the daughter of the brother's son, because she is the child of a residuary, namely, the son of a brother.[1]

With regard to the succession of this class it must be noted that—

(*a*) When the claimants are equal in degree the descendants of full brothers exclude those of half blood by the father (consanguine brothers), but not those of uterine brothers and sisters.

(*b*) But the descendants of full sisters do not exclude the descendants of consanguine brothers and sisters.

(*c*) The descendants of uterine brothers and sisters take the share of their ancestors (*viz.*, $\frac{1}{3}$).

Distant kindred of the fourth class.

Among the individuals of the fourth class, if the sides are equal preference is given to propinquity, but if the sides of consanguinity differ, then no regard is shown to the strength of relationship.

---

1 Sirajia, p. 45.

Those who are related both by the father and mother are preferred to those who are related by the father only; and they who are related by the father, are preferred to those who are related by the mother only, whether they be males or females; and, if there be males and females and their relation be equal, then the male has the allotment of two females.

For example, "if there be a paternal uncle and aunt, both by one mother, or a maternal uncle and aunt, both by the same father and mother, or by the same father or by the same mother only, and if the sides of their consanguinity be different, then no regard is shown to the strength of relation; as, if there be a paternal aunt by the same father and mother, and a maternal aunt by the same mother, or a maternal aunt by the same father and mother, and a paternal aunt by the same mother only, then two-thirds go to the kindred of the father, for that is the father's share, and one-third to the kindred of the mother, for that is the mother's share; then what is allotted to each set is divided among them, as if the place of their relationship were the same." Thus a full paternal aunt excludes father's uterine brother and half sisters, but not mother's half brothers and the half sisters; and a mother's brother or sister does not exclude father's uterine brother and half sister. Those on the father's side take two-thirds, while those related on the mother's side divide one-third among themselves.

SECTION IV

THE DOCTRINE OF WALA

BESIDES the heirs specified above the Musulman Law recognises the right of succession based on the relationship technically called *wala*.

"*Wala*", says the *Hedaya*, "literally means friendship and assistance, but in the language of the law it signifies that assistance, which is a cause of inheritance." It means, in fact, the peculiar and artificial relationship, which, in a state of society like that of the Arabs, came into existence when the master freed his slave, or when one person made himself the *client* of another, in both of which cases it was the duty of the parties to help each other; the master, in one case and the patron, in the other, continuing liable for the *Diat* (blood-money, *wehr-geld*) of the freedman or client.

As regards the right of inheritance founded on *wala* there is great divergence between the schools.

Wala-ul-'itk.

The Hanafis recognise two kinds of *wala*, *viz.*, *wala-ul-'itk*, "the right of inheritance acquired by emancipation", and the *wala-ul-mawalat*, "the right of inheritance by clientage". "Clientage" implies a responsibility on the part of the patron for the delicts of the *mawla* or "client".

The Shiahs recognise three kinds of *wala*, two of which are analogous to those recognised by the Sunnis; but whilst the Shiahs postpone the right of succession of the emancipator until after the blood-relations are all exhausted, the Sunnis give the preference to the emancipator over the uterine relations of the deceased. For example, if a man were to enfranchise his slave, and that slave were to die subsequently leaving certain heirs belonging to the class of uterine relations, the emancipator would exclude such relations under the Sunni Law. "By the *wala* of manumission", says the *Hedaya*, "' *asubat* is established; in other words, when a person emancipates his slave he is '*Asabah* to such slave, and is entitled to inherit of him in preference to his maternal uncles or aunts or other uterine kindred."[1]

Emancipator.

The emancipator is accordingly styled in Sunni Law "a residuary for special cause". In the absence of the manumittor, his male, but not the female, residuary heirs succeed to the deceased freedman. Females succeed, however, when they themselves have manumitted the slave. If the deceased freedman leave no sharer or residuary by blood, his entire estate goes to the '*Asabah* by *wala* (the emancipator or his *male* residuary heirs), to the absolute exclusion of the deceased's uterine relations. If he leave a sharer, then the specified share is allotted to such sharer and the residue goes to the residuary by *wala*; but if he leave a residuary *by blood*, then the latter takes nothing.

Whilst the Shiah Law restricts the rights of inheritance by *wala* exclusively to those cases where the emancipation has been granted voluntarily or as an act of charity, the Hanafi branch of the Sunni Law recognises no such restriction. For example, according to the *Sharifia*, "the manumittor inherits from the manumitted in general, whether he manumitted for the sake of God or for the sake of Satan, or upon the condition of continuing under the manumittor's control, or upon the condition of not taking his *wala*, or upon the condition of his giving or not giving some property, or as a *mukatib* or for other causes." So that whether the emancipation be for evil purposes or as an act of charity, whether it be sold to the emancipated or granted to him freely, the emancipator is always entitled to succeed to the inheritance of the emancipated, in case he dies without leaving residuaries by blood. Even if the right of *wala* was expressly abandoned at the time when emancipation was granted, it would not interfere with the emancipator's right of succession.

The Malikis and the Shiahs.

The Malikis agree with the Shiahs in holding that in case of manumission for an evil purpose, or when the manumittor has renounced his claim by *wala*, he has no title to succeed to the inheritance of the deceased freedman.

The emancipated slave is under no circumstance entitled to the inheritance of the emancipator.

But in the succession of the manumittor and his male residuaries to the emancipated slave, a variation is made by the

1 Hedaya Bk. xxiii.

Sunnis in the recognised order of succession. For example, in ordinary cases, when a man dies leaving behind him a son and a father, the father takes his specified share, *viz.*, one-sixth and the son takes the residue; but if a freedman were to die leaving behind no '*Asabah* by blood, but only his manumittor's son and father, the son of the emancipator would take the whole inheritance to the *exclusion of the father.*[1] So, also, in the case of the manumittor's son co-existing with a grandfather. The general principle is that in the succession of "residuaries for special cause, the nearest takes the whole in preference to the one more remote (as an agnate).

Under the Sunni Law, therefore, if a freedman leave a wife, a daughter's son, and his manumittor's son, the wife takes her specified share, and the residue goes to the emancipator's son as a "residuary for special cause" to the total exclusion of the freedman's grandson.

Wala-ul-mawalat.

The right of persons by virtue of the *wala-ul-mawalat* (or clientage), however, is postponed until all other heirs are exhausted. The patron, accordingly, does not exclude the uterine relations as happens in the case of the emancipator co-existing with the *Zav-il-Arham.* The Shafe'is regard this form of *wala* as implying a fraud on the *Baitulmal* or public treasury (for the benefit of all the Musalmans) and consequently consider it illegal and invalid.

The subject of *wala*, however, has now only an antiquarian interest, for section 3 of Act V of 1843 has removed all bar to the succession of the natural heirs of an emancipated slave to his or her inheritance. And in the case of *Sayad Mir Ujmuddin Khan* v. *Zia-ul-Nissa Begam*[2] the Privy Council declared in effect that the right of inheritance created by the relationship of *wala* to the exclusion of the emancipated slave's natural heirs was done away with by that Act. The result of that Statute is that the distant kindred (cognates) of a person, who was a slave at one time but was emancipated afterwards, take their natural place in the order of succession.

When the deceased leaves no relation by blood, but leaves him or her surviving a husband or a widow, as the case may be, *such husband or widow takes the entire inheritance.*[3]

In the absence of the heirs mentioned above, the succession devolves upon the person who has made himself responsible for the delicts of the deceased. As the peculiar relationship of clientage is unknown in India, this provision of the Sunni Law does not need discussion.

---

1 Hedaya Bk. XXIII.

2 (1879) L R 6 I A p. 137; I L 3 Bom. 422; 5 C L R 11.

3 Mahommed Arshed Chowdhry *v.* Sajida Banu (1878) I L 3 Cal. 712; Bafatun *v.* Bilaiti Khanum (1914) I L 31 Cal. 683.

Heir by acknowledgment.

Next comes the heir by acknowldgement. *An heir by acknowledgment is one in respect of whom the deceased (both the acknowledgor and acknowledged being persons of unknown descent) has admitted a tie of blood other than that of paternity.* For example, if two persons of unknown parentage call themselves brothers, and one of them dies without leaving any *known* heirs, the other person would be entitled to the deceased's inheritance.

Then comes the universal legatee or the person in whose favour the deceased has made a general devise.[1]

And lastly the Public Treasury (*for the benefit of all the Musalmans*).[2]

SECTION V

THE DOCTRINE OF RETURN OR *Radd.*

UNDER the Sunni Law, when there are "Sharers", and no Residuaries, the *residue* of the property, after the allotment of shares, is divided among the "Sharers" under the principle of *Return*, in proportion to their shares.

Return—Husband or widow entitled to—

The early lawyers were of opinion that neither a husband nor a wife was entitled to take by *return*, but later jurists have held that when the deceased leaves no other heir belonging either to the categories of sharers or residuaries (by blood) or uterine relations (distant kindred), the husband or widow takes by *return*. And this rule has been recognised and enforced by the British Indian and Algerian Courts.[3]

Among the persons to whom there may be a *return* are the following: (*a*) mother; (*b*) grandmother; (*c*) daughter; (*d*) son's daughter; (*e*) full sister; (*f*) half sister by the father; (*g*) half-brother; or (*h*) sister by the mother. *And a return may take place to one, two, or three classes at the same time. But no more than three can take by return at one and the same time.*[4]

Examples.

The residue after allotment of sharers is apportioned among the parties indicated, in the proportion of their shares, *e.g.*—

When there is a grandmother with a sister by the same mother of the deceased, the shares are $\frac{1}{6}$ each; therefore the residue is divided among them equally.

When there is a daughter with mother, the shares are $\frac{1}{2}$ and $\frac{1}{6}$; therefore the residue is divided among them in proportion to their shares, which will be $\frac{3}{12}$ and $\frac{1}{12}$.

---

1 This is due to the provision that a man cannot devise away the whole of his property from his heirs.

2 Under the Mahommedan Law the property of a person dying without leaving any heir goes to the State to be applied for the benefit of the general body of Moslems. See also Rumsey's Mah. Law of Inheritance, p. 179.

3 See Mahommed Arshed Chowdhry *v.* Sajida Banu, supra; Bafatun *v.* Bilaiti Khanum, supra.

4 Durr-ul-Mukhtar, pp. 868, 869.

When there are two widows, a mother, and three daughters, the widows take between them $\frac{1}{8}$.

Mother, $\frac{1}{6}$ of $\frac{7}{8} = \frac{7}{48}$.

3 daughters, $\frac{4}{6}$ of $\frac{7}{8} = \frac{28}{48}$.

L. C. D. $=$ 144.

$\therefore$ each widow $=$ 9, 2 widows $=$ . . . 18

Mother $=$ 21

Each daughter $=$ 35, 3 daughters $=$. 105

144

Or—Mother: daughter $= \frac{1}{6} : \frac{1}{2} = 1 : 3$.

$$\text{Mother} - \left(\frac{1}{6} + \frac{1}{12} = \frac{2+1}{12}\right) = \frac{1}{4}.$$

$$\text{Daughter} - \left(\frac{1}{2} + \frac{3}{12} = \frac{6+3}{12}\right) = \frac{3}{4}.$$

Or—Widow, mother and daughter.

Widow $= \frac{1}{8}$.

Mother: daughter $= \frac{1}{6} : \frac{1}{2} = 1 : 3$.

Mother $= \frac{1}{4}$ of $\frac{7}{8} = \frac{7}{32}$.

Daughter $= \frac{3}{4}$ of $\frac{7}{8} = \frac{21}{32}$.

Widow, 4; mother, 7; daughter, 21.

2 widows, 1 mother and 3 daughters.

2 widows $= \frac{1}{8}$, one widow $= \frac{1}{16}$.

Mother: 3 daughters $= \frac{1}{6} : \frac{2}{3} = 1 : 4$.

When there happen to be a mother, a daughter and son's daughter, the shares are respectively $\frac{1}{6}$, $\frac{1}{2}$ and $\frac{1}{6} = \frac{5}{6}$; the residue is then divided among them in proportion to their shares, that is, $\frac{1}{30}$ to the mother, $\frac{1}{30}$ to the son's daughter, and the daughter $\frac{3}{30}$.

Or—Mother and son's daughter together take $\frac{2}{6}$.

Daughter $= \frac{3}{6}$.

$\therefore$ Mother and son's daughter:

daughter $= \frac{2}{6} : \frac{3}{6} = 2 : 3$.

$\therefore$ Daughter takes $\frac{3}{5}$.

Mother and son's daughter, $\frac{2}{5}$.

And so when there is only a daughter with a son's daughter.

Or, put in the way adopted by the Arabian jurists, in which instead of adding afterwards a share of the residue to the original share, the shares are originally divided among the parties as they would be taken, by way of *return*.

For example—

4 widows, $\frac{1}{8}$, each $\frac{1}{32}$.

9 daughters and 6 *true* grandmothers have $\frac{7}{8}$ between them. To be divided in the ratio of $\frac{2}{3}$: $\frac{1}{6}$ =4: 1.

$\therefore$ 9 daughters $=\frac{4}{5}\times\frac{7}{8}=\frac{7}{10}$ each $\frac{7}{90}$.

$\therefore$ 6 grandmothers $=\frac{1}{5}\times\frac{7}{8}=\frac{7}{40}$, each $\frac{7}{240}$.

L. C. D. =1,440.

Each widow 45, each daughter 112, each grandmother 42.

Section VI

Double Inheritance or Vested Interests

Double inheritance or vested interests.

When a deceased leaves a certain number of heirs, and one of them, before distribution takes place, happens to die leaving heirs, in such cases these heirs take under both the deceased, if they are heirs of both; or under one of them if they are only heirs to one. For example, a man dies leaving a son, a daughter, and a half-brother by the father. In this case the son excludes the half-brother; but before distribution the son dies leaving only the sister and his half paternal uncle as his heirs. In this case the son's $\frac{2}{3}$ is divided equally between his sister and his uncle, the former getting half of $\frac{2}{3}$, *viz.*, $\frac{1}{3}$, and the latter the remaining $\frac{1}{3}$. This is called taking a "double inheritance".

Take another example of a more complicated character from the *Sirajia*:—

(1) A woman dies leaving

(*a*) A husband	$=\frac{1}{4}$.
(*b*) Daughter and mother	$=\frac{1}{2}:\frac{1}{6}=3:1$.
Daughter	$=\frac{3}{4}$ of $\frac{3}{4}=\frac{9}{16}$.
Mother	$=\frac{1}{4}$ of $\frac{3}{4}=\frac{3}{16}$.

(2) Afterwards the man dies leaving

(*a*) Daughter	$=\frac{9}{16}+\frac{1}{2}$ of $\frac{1}{4}=\frac{11}{16}$.
(*b*) Widow	$=\frac{1}{8}$ of $\frac{1}{4}=\frac{1}{32}$.
(*c*) Mother	$=\frac{1}{6}$ of $\frac{1}{4}=\frac{1}{24}$.
(*d*) Father	$=\frac{1}{4}-(\frac{1}{8}+\frac{1}{32}+\frac{1}{24})$
	$=\frac{24-19}{96}=\frac{5}{96}$

(3) Afterwards the daughter dies leaving

(*a*) Paternal grandfather	$=\frac{5}{96}+\frac{1}{6}$ of $\frac{11}{16}=\frac{16}{96}$.
(*b*) Paternal grandmother	$=\frac{1}{24}+\frac{1}{6}$ of $\frac{11}{16}=\frac{15}{96}$.
(*c*) Maternal grandmother	$=\frac{3}{16}+\frac{1}{6}$ of $\frac{11}{16}=\frac{29}{96}$.
(*d*) 2 sons (each)	$=\frac{2}{5}$ of $\frac{11}{32}=\frac{11}{80}$.
(*e*) 1 daughter	$=\frac{1}{5}$ of $\frac{11}{32}=\frac{11}{160}$.

Reducing these fractions to the L. C. D.—

```
  | 16, 32, 96, 80, 160
4 | 96, 160
4 | 24, 40
2 |  6, 10
     3,  5
```

$4 \times 4 \times 2 \times 3 \times 5 = 480.$

∴ Mother of the original deceased, that is maternal grand-mother of the last deceased $= \frac{29}{96}$ of $480 = 145.$

Father's widow	$= \frac{1}{32}$ of $480 = 15.$
Father's mother	$= \frac{15}{96}$ of $480 = 75.$
Father's father	$= \frac{16}{96} \times 480 = 80.$
Sons	$\frac{11}{80}$ each $= 132.$
Daughter	$\frac{11}{160} = 33.$
	Total 480.

SECTION VII

THE DOCTRINE OF INCREASE OR *Aul*

IT sometimes happens in practice that when there are several sharers co-existing, their fractional shares when added up amount to a great deal more than the integral quantity. In order to meet the difficulty thus arising, the Sunni lawyers make a proportionate abatement in all the shares by increasing the common divisor.

Increase.

This is called *Aul* "increase". *Aul* is thus a technical expression used by Sunni lawyers to signify *a proportionate increase in the common divisor for the purpose of yielding the requisite number of shares*. For example, if a woman leave behind her a husband, two daughters and a mother, their respective shares would be one-fourth, two-thirds, and one-sixth.

The common divisor in this case is twelve, which represents the shares into which the estate will have to be divided, three being the husband's share, eight the daughter's, and two the mother's.

Sunni Rule.

But three, two, and eight make thirteen. The Sunnis, accordingly, in order to give the exact number of shares to each heir, divide the property into thirteen shares.

The Shiah doctrine.

Among the Shiahs this arbitrary division of the property is not recognised. On the contrary, when they find that the property falls short in distribution of all the appointed shares, the deficiency falls upon the heir or heirs, whose share or right is liable to fluctuation or variation. For example, in the above case the mother and husband would get among the Shiahs, their full sharer, without any abatement, and the remainder, *viz.*, seven-twelfths, would be given to the daughters in equal proportion.

SECTION VIII

POSTHUMOUS CHILDREN, ETC.

A widow's period of probation or 'iddat.

WHEN a person dies leaving a widow, she is prohibited from marrying before the expiration of four months and ten days. This is called the '*iddat* or probation of widowhood, and is prescribed for discovering whether she is *enciente* or not. If she is, her probation will not terminate until she is delivered. If a child is born within the ordinary period of gestation[1] it would succeed to its father.

Posthumous children.

Where a child is born after the decease of any *other* relation to whose inheritance it would have been entitled had it been in existence at the time of such relation's death, it will succeed only if born *within* six months from such death, unless the other heirs acknowledge that the child's mother was pregnant when the deceased person died.

A child in the womb may belong to the category of (*i*) those who totally, or (*ii*) those who partially, exclude the other heirs; or (*iii*) those who participate with them. If he be a total excluder of all the heirs, as (for instance a son), the other heirs, being brothers or sisters or paternal uncles, the whole of the estate must be reserved to abide the event of his birth. When only some of the heirs are excluded, as when there is a grandmother and a brother, the grandmother's sixth is to be paid to her, and the remainder of the estate reserved. If the child be only a partial excluder, as when there is a husband or a wife besides him, the smaller of the shares to which the party may be entitled is to be paid to him or her, and the remainder is to be retained.

And when the heirs are persons who are not subject to partial exclusion, as a grandfather, or grandmother, their full shares are to be paid to them, and the remainder is to be retained.

If the child is only a participator with the other heirs, and neither a total nor a partial excluder, as when the deceased has left sons and daughters and a pregnant widow, the share of one son is to be reserved.

If the child is born dead he does not inherit, and there is no other legal effect or consequence. The signs of life are breathing making a sound, sneezing, crying, laughing, and motion, as of the eyes or hands.

If half of the child is protruded, and it then dies, it is entitled to inherit, but not if less than half be protruded. When the head

---

1 See post.

is presented, and the breast is protruded while the child is still living, it inherits; but if the feet are presented, regard is to be had to the navel.

When a child is born dead it does not inherit as already mentioned, but this is to be understood of a regular delivery; and "if violence has been done to the mother, as for instance, if she has been struck on the belly and has cast her progeny, such progeny is to be regarded as one of the heirs. For the law imposes a liability on the striker, and liability is incurred only for an offence against the living, not against the dead. When, therefore, we presume the child to have been alive, he is entitled to his share in the inheritance, and the share can be inherited from him, in the same way, as the exchange for his life, is inherited from him, and that is the fine."

Persons dying together in a common calamity.

Persons dying in a sudden calamity are supposed to have died together, so that they do not inherit to each other, but the property of each goes to his or her respective heirs, unless it is known in what order they died, when those who died last will inherit to those who died before them.

Agreement before marriage relinquishing rights of inheritance void.

An agreement entered into before marriage that the parties shall have no right of inheritance to each other, or that the husband shall not take a share in the inheritance of the wife in case she predeceased him, or *vice versa*, is void; and the right will accrue under the law.[1] But the husband or wife may renounce the right *after* it has accrued.

SECTION IX

MISCELLANEOUS EXAMPLES

When the father exists by himself, he takes the entire inheritance.

When the mother exists by herself, she takes the whole inheritance: one-third as her appointed share, and the remainder by right of *return*.

When the father and the mother exist together, the mother takes one-third, and the father takes the remainder.

When the deceased leaves behind him a father, a mother, and brothers (or one brother and two sisters, or four sisters), the mother takes one-sixth and the father takes the remainder, to the total exclusion of the brothers or brothers and sisters.

If the father and mother exist with the deceased's children, the father and mother take one-sixth each.

When there is only one son, he takes the entire inheritance.

1 Fatwai-Kazi Khan.

If there are several sons, they divide the inheritance equally among themselves.

When there is only one daughter, and no residuary, she takes the inheritance: half as her appointed share, and the remainder by right of *return*.

If there are two or more, they take the entire inheritance equally, two-thirds as their appointed share, and one-third by right of *return*.

When the two ascendants, or either of them, are co-existing with the descendants, then each of the ascendants, receive one-sixth and the remainder is distributed among the descendants equally, if they be all males; but if there be a female or females among them, then each male has the portion of two females.

When a husband or wife of the deceased co-exists with the parents and the children, then the husband or the wife takes his or her reduced share,[1] and the parents theirs, while the remainder goes to the children.

When there are two ascendants and a daughter, the ascendants receive their one-sixth respectively, and the daughter her moiety, and the residue is given to the father.

When the two parents co-exist with one daughter and a consanguine brother, the parents take their respective shares, *viz.*, one-sixth, the daughter her moiety, and the remainder is given to the father.

When the two ascendants co-exist with a daughter and the husband, there must be a proportionate abatement in the shares. For example, the share of a husband is one-fourth, that of the parents, one-sixth each, and of the daughter, one-half, total 13; and accordingly, instead of getting three-twelfths, the husband gets three-thirteenths, the daughter six-thirteenths, and the parents two-thirteenths each. In case of the deceased being a male leaving a widow behind co-existing with the daughter and the parents the father would take the entire residue.

If the deceased leave surviving her, her husband and the two ascendants (parents), the husband takes his half, the mother one-third of the remainder and the father the residue.

The lineal male descendants exclude from succession everyone connected with the deceased through them, and also everyone connected through the deceased's parents, but not the parents themselves. For example, they, (the male children) exclude the deceased's brothers, and their children, his grandparents and their ancestors, his paternal and maternal uncles and aunts and their children.

Under the Sunni Law, if the deceased leave behind him a daughter and a predeceased son's son, then the daughter takes her moiety, and the residue goes to the grandson.

---

1. *Viz.*, $\frac{1}{4}$ or $\frac{1}{8}$.

But if, instead of a son's son, there were only son's daughters, then these would take one-sixth equally among themselves. If, however, there were two or more daughters, the son's daughters would take nothing. But if there happened to be with the son's daughters a son's son also, then the daughters would take their two-thirds and the remaining one-third would be divided among the grandchildren in the proportion of two for each male and one for each female. A son, however, would exclude *in toto* the sons and daughters of a predeceased sons.

Under the Sunni Law, a daughter's daughter, as an *uterine relation,* has no place in the inheritance until all heirs with a residuary title are exhausted. For example, a father would exclude entirely, under the Sunni Law, a daughter's daughter.

If there be only one full brother, he takes the entire inheritance; when there are several, they divide the inheritance equally among themselves.

If there be sisters with the brothers, the brothers take two shares each, and the sisters one each.

If there are two or more uterine brothers or sisters co-existing with full brothers and sisters, the former receive one-third, which is divided equally among them without distinction of sex, whilst the full brothers and sisters take the remainder in accordance with the general principle.

When there are no full brothers and sisters, then consanguine brothers and sisters take their places.

The paternal or maternal grandfather, if alone, without any co-heir, takes the entire inheritance; so does the grandmother.

When there are ancestors of the paternal as well as of the maternal line, the former, without distinction of sex, take the entire inheritance.

The paternal grandfather and grandmother share in the succession according to the general principle of two shares for each male and one share for each female.

When the deceased leaves surviving only a maternal grandfather and maternal grandmother, the latter takes the entire inheritance.

When there are uterine brothers or sisters co-existing either with a maternal grandfather or maternal grandmother, they receive one-third among them, the remainder going to the grandfather or grandmother. If there is only one uterine brother, he receives one-sixth.

When there is a half brother by the same mother only and the son of a full brother, the half brother gets one-sixth, and the remainder goes to the son of the full brother.

When the deceased leaves nephews and nieces, consisting of the children of brothers and sisters, the children of sisters being uterine relations do not succeed until the agnates are exhausted,

When there are paternal uncles and aunts, the entire inheritance goes to the paternal uncles, to the execution of the paternal aunts.

When there are uncles and aunts, some of whom are the brothers of the full blood of the deceased's father and others of the half blood partly on the father's and partly on the mother's side, the uncles who have the same father, and mother as the father of the deceased, or who have the same father, that is, the full brothers and consanguine brothers of the deceased's father, exclude all other relations from the succession.

A divorcee.

If a woman be divorced by a husband during an illness from which he does not recover, and which eventually causes his death, her right to a share in his inheritance continues until the expiration of her *'iddat*, or period of probation, so that if the husband died within that time she would succeed, but if he recovered during that interval and died either of the same disease or any other complaint, she would not succeed.

Minors contracted in marriage by their guardians.

Minors contracted in marriage to each other by their fathers or paternal grandfathers have a mutual right of inheritance. But if the contract were entered into by a guardian other than the father or paternal grandfather, then the marriage remains in suspense until assented to or ratified by the parties on attaining majority,[1] and if one of them were to die in the interval before the ratification of the contract, the survivor would have a right of inheritance.

Neither the step-mother nor the step-daughter has any right in the inheritance of a deceased person.

When a person has died leaving him surviving a paternal half-uncle, a mother and a grandmother (father's mother), one-third will go to the mother, and two-thirds, to the paternal half-uncle, the grandmother being excluded. If there were several paternal half-uncles, they would take the two-thirds among them.

A has a son *B*, who dies in the life-time of *A*, leaving a son *D*. Afterwards *A* dies leaving him surviving *C*, his daughter, and *D*. Previous to partition *C* dies leaving two daughters, *E* and *F*. Under such circumstances *C* having become entitled to one-half as daughter, that share would go to her daughters *E* and *F* as well as to the nephew *D*; that is, two-thirds of the half will go to *E* and *F* in equal moieties, and the remaining third to *D*, who will also get the remaining half of the original estate, *e.g.*—

On the death of *A*,

$C=\frac{1}{2}$.

$D=\frac{1}{2}$.

On *C*'s death, *E* and $F=\frac{2}{3}$ of $\frac{1}{2}=\frac{1}{3}$

$D=\frac{1}{2}+\frac{1}{3}\times\frac{1}{2}=\frac{1}{2}+\frac{1}{6}=\frac{2}{3}$.

A man dies leaving a mother, paternal half-grand-uncles and

1 See post.

the daughters of a paternal grand-uncle. In this case, the mother takes her legal share, and the residue is given to the paternal half-grand-uncles, the daughters of the paternal grand-uncle not taking anything as they are *Zav-il-Arham.*

A person dies leaving two sisters and a daughter of a pre-deceased son. In this case, the grand-daughter would take a moiety, and the sisters the remaining moiety.

A woman dies leaving her surviving a husband, a daughter and a paternal uncle. In this case, the husband takes his $\frac{1}{4}$, the daughter $\frac{1}{2}$, and the paternal uncle the residue.

A man dies leaving him surviving a grandson and grand-daughter by a predeceased daughter. At the time of his death, the grandson is in a foreign country, and for a considerable time is *mafkud-ul-khabar*,[1] and no news is received of him. In such a case the property will be divided into three shares, of which the grandson will obtain two shares, and the grand-daughter one. Neither the husband of the daughter nor that of the daughter's daughter are entitled to any share. "An absentee, concerning whose place of abode, death or existence, no tidings can be learnt, is, as regards his own property, alive, and as regards that of others, defunct." The ruling power should appoint some one to take charge of his affairs, and his portion should be reserved for the usual period now recognised. None of his relations would be entitled to participate in his property.

Supposing the grand-daughter were to die, leaving a son, a daughter and a husband, her property will be made into four parts, and distributed among her heirs in the following manner:—

One share will go to her husband, two to her son, and one to her daughter; and if the original proprietor's son-in-law died possessing property distinct from that of such proprietor, it would devolve on his son.

A man dies leaving two daughters, a son's son and a daughter of a son. In such a case after the discharge of the legal liabilities attaching to the estate of the deceased, the partition will be effected thus:

Daughters	$=\frac{2}{3}$
Son's son and son's daughter (as residuaries)	$=\frac{1}{3}$
Son's son	$=\frac{2}{3}\times\frac{1}{3}=\frac{2}{9}$
Son's daughter	$=\frac{1}{3}\times\frac{1}{3}=\frac{1}{9}$

When the deceased leaves a mother, three sisters, a brother, and a widow, the division will be thus:—

widow	$=\frac{1}{4}$
mother	$=\frac{1}{6}$
brother and sisters (as residuaries)	$=\frac{14}{24}$
brother	$=\frac{2}{5}\times\frac{14}{24}=\frac{14}{60}$.
each sister	$=\frac{1}{5}\times\frac{14}{24}=\frac{7}{60}$.

1 See post.

When the deceased leave four daughters, a brother, two sisters and a widow, the division will be thus:—

widow	$=\frac{1}{8}$
daughters	$=\frac{2}{3}$
brother and sisters	$=\frac{5}{24}$
brother	$=\frac{2}{4}\times\frac{5}{24}=\frac{10}{96}$
each sister	$=\frac{1}{4}\frac{5}{2}+{}_{4}=\frac{5}{96}$

When the deceased leaves a widow, an uterine sister and four nephews (brother's sons), the division will be thus:—

widow	$=\frac{1}{4}$
sister	$=\frac{1}{2}$
nephews (as residuaries)	$=\frac{1}{4}$

A person dies leaving father, mother and daughter:

$$\left.\begin{array}{ll}\text{Father} & =\frac{1}{6}\\ \text{Mother} & =\frac{1}{6}\\ \text{Daughter} & =\frac{1}{2}\end{array}\right\}=\frac{5}{6}.$$

The residue goes to the father.

If there were two daughters, father $=\frac{1}{6}$, mother $=\frac{1}{6}$, and the two daughters $=\frac{2}{3}=\frac{4}{6}$.

(No residue).

Father, mother, daughter and son:

Father	$=\frac{1}{6}$.
Mother	$=\frac{1}{6}$.
Son	$=\frac{2}{3}\times\frac{2}{3}=\frac{4}{9}$.
Daughter	$=\frac{1}{3}\times\frac{2}{3}=\frac{2}{9}$.

If there are two daughters:

Father	$=\frac{1}{6}$.
Mother	$=\frac{1}{6}$.
Son	$=\frac{3}{9}$.
Two daughters	$=\frac{3}{9}$.

Father, mother and husband:

Husband	$=\frac{1}{2}$.
Mother	$=\frac{1}{3}\times\frac{1}{2}=\frac{1}{6}$.
Father	$=\frac{1}{3}$.

(As residuary).

Mother, father and one sister:

Mother	$=\frac{1}{3}$.
Father	$=\frac{2}{3}$.

(As residuary).

Sister excluded by father.

Mother, father and two sisters:

Mother owing to there being two sisters $=\frac{1}{6}$.

Father (as residuary) $\frac{5}{6}$.

Sisters excluded by father.

Father, mother, daughter and two son's **daughters (grand-**daughters):

Father $=\frac{1}{6}$.

Mother $=\frac{1}{6}$.

Daughter $=\frac{1}{2}$.

Two grand-daughters $=\frac{1}{6}$.

If there were two daughters, they would take two-thirds excluding the son's daughters.

Father's mother, mother's mother and paternal grand-father:

Father's mother and mother's mother $=\frac{1}{6}$.

Paternal grand-father $=\frac{5}{6}$.

Two daughters, son's daughter and son's son's son:

Two daughters $=\frac{2}{3}$.

Son's son's son $=\frac{2}{3}\times\frac{1}{3}=\frac{2}{9}$.

Son's daughter $=\frac{1}{3}\times\frac{1}{3}=\frac{1}{9}$.

Widow, mother, two sons and three daughters:

$$\left.\begin{array}{ll}\text{Widow} & =\frac{1}{8}\\ \text{Mother} & =\frac{1}{6}\end{array}\right\}\frac{14}{48}=\frac{98}{336}.$$

Two sons $=\frac{4}{7}\times\frac{34}{48}=\frac{136}{336}$.

Three daughters $=\frac{4}{7}\times\frac{34}{48}=\frac{136}{336}$.

Husband, mother, three full-sisters, four consanguine brothers and sisters and two uterine brothers and sisters:

$$\left.\begin{array}{ll}\text{Husband} & =\frac{3}{6}\\ \text{Mother} & =\frac{1}{6}\\ \text{Three full-sisters} & =\frac{4}{6}\\ \text{Two uterine brothers and sisters} & =\frac{2}{6}\end{array}\right\}=\frac{10}{6}.$$

The consanguine brothers and sisters have no shares, and the doctrine of *increase* comes into force.

∴ Husband $=\frac{3}{10}$.

Mother $=\frac{1}{10}$.

Three full-sisters $=\frac{4}{10}$.

Two uterine sisters and brothers $=\frac{2}{10}$.

These being legal shares divided equally and are preferred to consanguine ones.

Husband, father, mother and two daughters:

$$\left.\begin{array}{ll}\text{Husband} & =\frac{1}{4}\\ \text{Father} & =\frac{1}{6}\\ \text{Mother} & =\frac{1}{6}\\ \text{Two daughters} & =\frac{2}{3}\end{array}\right\}\frac{15}{12}.$$

The common divisor must therefore be increased to 15 and the shares reduced proportionately.

Husband $\frac{3}{15}$ father $\frac{2}{15}$ mother $\frac{2}{15}$ and the two daughters $\frac{8}{15}$

Father, mother, widow and two daughters:

Widow	$=\frac{1}{8}$
Father	$=\frac{1}{6}$
Mother	$=\frac{1}{6}$
Two daughters	$=\frac{2}{3}$

(total $\frac{27}{24}$.)

The common divisor must therefore be increased to 27 and the shares reduced proportionately.

Widow	$=\frac{3}{27}$.
Father	$=\frac{4}{27}$.
Mother	$=\frac{4}{27}$.
Two daughters	$=\frac{16}{27}$.

Widow, mother and daughter:

Widow	$=\frac{1}{8}$
Mother	$=\frac{1}{6}$
Daughter	$=\frac{1}{2}$

(total $\frac{19}{24}$.)

Mother and daughter $=\frac{1}{6}:\frac{1}{2}=1:3$.

Divide proportionately between mother and daughter$=\frac{8}{96}:\frac{18}{96}$

Widow	$=\frac{12}{96}$.
Mother	$=\frac{1}{6}+\frac{5}{96}=\frac{21}{96}$.
Daughter	$=\frac{1}{2}+\frac{15}{96}=\frac{63}{96}$.

Consanguine sister or sisters with one full sister and no excluder $(\frac{2}{3}-\frac{1}{2})=\frac{1}{6}$.

One full sister and several consanguine sisters:—Full sister, $\frac{1}{2}$; consanguine sisters, $\frac{1}{6}$, or as $\frac{3}{6}:\frac{1}{6}$, ∴ full sister$=\frac{3}{4}$, consanguine sisters divide $\frac{1}{4}$ equally.

Two daughters, two son's daughters, three consanguine sisters:—Two daughters $=\frac{2}{3}$; three consanguine sisters being residuaries with daughters, get $\frac{1}{3}$; son's daughters, not being sharers or residuaries with daughters, are excluded.

Two son's daughters, one full sister and several consanguine sisters; the full sister excludes consanguine sisters owing to propinquity to the deceased and takes the residue; two son's daughters$=\frac{2}{3}$; full sister $=\frac{1}{3}$.

Husband, two daughters, a sister and the son of father's paternal uncle.

Husband	$=\frac{1}{4}$.
Daughters	$=\frac{2}{3}$.
Sister	$=\frac{1}{12}$.

The son of the father's paternal uncle is excluded by the sister.

A woman dies leaving a daughter, a mother, a father, and a husband. In this case the denominator will be increased to 13:—

Husband	$=\frac{1}{4}=\frac{3}{13}$.
Mother	$=\frac{1}{6}=\frac{2}{13}$.
Daughter	$=\frac{1}{2}=\frac{6}{13}$.
Father	$=\frac{1}{6}=\frac{2}{13}$.

A person dies leaving an uterine sister and a half-sister by the same father. The division will be thus:—

Uterine sister	$=\frac{1}{6}$.
Consanguine sister	$=\frac{1}{2}$.

Remainder to be *returned* to them *pro rata*.

Hence the shares will be $\frac{1}{4}$ and $\frac{3}{4}$ respectively.

A man dies leaving a widow, a mother, a son, and a brother. The division will be as follows:—

Widow	$=\frac{1}{8}$.
Mother	$=\frac{1}{6}$.
Son	$=\frac{34}{48}$. Total $=\frac{48}{48}$.

The brother is excluded.

If the son dies, his inheritance will be thus:—

His mother (widow of the original deceased).

$$=\frac{1}{3}\times\frac{34}{48}=\frac{17}{72}.$$

The uncle, residue $=\frac{34}{48}-\frac{17}{72}=\frac{34}{72}$.

Hence the widow of the original proprietor gets—

$$=\frac{1}{8}\times\frac{17}{72}=\frac{26}{72}.$$

Mother	$=\frac{12}{72}$.
Brother	$=\frac{34}{72}$.

A woman dies leaving a husband, a daughter, a brother and three sisters. The division in this case will be as follows:—

Husband	$=\frac{1}{4}$.
Daughter	$=\frac{1}{2}$.
Brother	$=\frac{2}{16}$.
Each sister	$=\frac{1}{16}$.

A man dies leaving a wife, a mother, three sisters of the full blood, one sister of the half-blood, and two brothers of the half-blood. The division in this case will be as follows:—

Widow	$=\frac{1}{4}$.
Mother	$=\frac{1}{6}$.
Three sisters	$=\frac{2}{3}$; but $\frac{3+2+8}{12}=\frac{13}{12}$.

$\therefore$ Increase divisor to 13, which gives 3 shares to widow, 2 shares to mother, and the residue to the sisters; but as 8 cannot be divided equally among the three sisters increase divisor to 39; thus,

Widow $=\frac{9}{39}$.
Mother $=\frac{6}{39}$.
Each sister $=\frac{8}{39}$.

A person dies leaving a mother, an uterine sister and a consanguine sister. In such a case—

The mother takes $=\frac{1}{6}$.
The uterine sister $=\frac{1}{6}$.
The consanguine sister $=\frac{1}{2}$.

The remainder is *returned* to them in the same proportion.

In other words, the share would be as follows:—

The mother $=\frac{1}{5}$.
The uterine sister $=\frac{1}{5}$.
The consanguine sister $=\frac{3}{5}$.

CHAPTER III

CAUSES OF EXCLUSION FROM INHERITANCE

SECTION I

Partial Exclusion

Partial exclusion.

Exclusion is said to be of two kinds—*partial* and *total*. The former, though called *exclusion,* is in reality a reduction of the share receivable by one heir from the fact of co-existence with another heir.

As already stated, six persons can never be excluded from inheritance, *viz*., the father, the son, the husband, the mother, the daughter, and the widow.

Among residuaries the nearer always excludes the more remote. *But a nearer residuary does not always exclude a more remote sharer*, *e.g*., a mother's mother is not excluded by a father; nor does a nearer sharer exclude a more remote residuary nor even a more remote sharer, unless the right of succession is founded on the same relationship, as in the case of a mother and a grandmother, or a daughter and a son's daughter.

Full brothers and sisters are excluded by a son, son's son and a father, and by a grandfather also with some difference of opinion.

Half-brothers and sisters on the father's side are excluded by the same persons and also by full brothers and sisters ; and half-brothers and sisters on the mother's side are excluded by a child, the child of a son, a father and a grandfather. All grandmothers, whether maternal or paternal, are excluded by a mother ; and paternal grandmothers are excluded by a father, as a grandfather is excluded by him, and they are also excluded by a grandfather when anterior to him; but a paternal grandmother is not excluded by a grandfather, because she is not anterior to him.

Grandmothers on the side of the mother are not excluded by a father ; so that if one should leave a father, father's mother, and a mother's mother, the father's mother is excluded by the father, but there are different opinions as to the mother's mother, some saying that she has a sixth; whilst others hold that she has only the half of a sixth.

The nearer excludes the more remote, whether himself an heir or excluded. Thus, if one should leave a father, a father's mother, and the mother of a mother's mother, it is said that the father has the whole, because he excludes his mother, and she excludes the mother of the mother's mother, because she is nearer to the deceased. There is a difference of opinion about her right of succession along with her son, *viz.*, the paternal uncle to the deceased; but, according to the generality of our 'sheikhs', she does not inherit with her son, *viz.*, the paternal uncle.

It should be remembered that only one grandmother on the side of a mother can be considered an heir, for *true* grandmothers are only those in whose line of relationship a father does not come between two mothers; so that this single heir is the mother's mother how-high-soever, and the nearer excludes the more remote, so that only one grandmother can inherit. But among paternal grandmothers many may be heirs.

The circumstances which tend to exclude a person from inheritance either wholly or partially rest on the fact of his or her co-existing with some other preferentially entitled. The death of the latter would remove the cause of exclusion

SECTION II

Total Exclusion

Total disqualification.

Under the Musulman Law several causes debar a person from succeeding to the estate of the *propositus* notwithstanding that he may stand to the deceased in the relation of an inheriting kinsman.

(1) The first is difference of faith technically called *kufr*[1] (infidelity). *Kufr* means the *denial* of the unity of God (*wahdaniet*) and of Mohammed's Messengership (*risalat*), the

1 A believer in God or Theist who, although he does not call himself a Musulman, yet accepts Mohammed as one of the veritable "Messengers of God" can hardly be designated kafir. Many Moslem divines regarded Ram Mohan Roy as a Moslem—certainly not a kafir. Islam depends on the acceptance of the two doctrines mentioned in the text. The recognition of sectarian dogmas is a matter of detail. And hence whilst the ultra-Sunni regards a Shiah as a Moslem, he does not consider him a Momin (one having Iman or Faith), and *vice versa*. Iman, which originally meant a belief in the cardinal principles, is now applied to the acceptance of sectarian dogmas.

two cardinal principles on which Islam is founded. Every person who acknowledges the Divine Unity and the Messengership of the Arabian Prophet is regarded as within the pale of Islam ; nothing more is required. Those, however, who deny these cardinal principles are considered beyond the benefit of its rules. Accordingly, when a person dies leaving an heir who by birth or apostacy is a "denier", *i. e.*, repudiates God's Unity and Mohammed's Ministry, such heir would be excluded from succession in preference to another who does accept those doctrines. Consequently, those who profess a different faith from Islam have no title to the inheritance of a deceased Musulman . So that if a Musulman die leaving behind him an heir who does not profess the Islamic faith, he is debarred from inheriting, even though he be nearest to the deceased. For example, if a man die leaving behind him a son who is a non-Moslem, and a grandson who is a Moslem, the son would be evicted from the succession, and the grandson would take the inheritance to the absolute exclusion of his father.[1]

The Indian Act XXI of 1850 has made a variation in the Mahommedan Law of Inheritance. The principle by which non-Moslems were excluded from the inheritance applied equally to those who were born in a different faith, and those who abjured Islam.

Rules relating to "apostates" abolished—Act XXI of 1850.

For example, an apostate from Islam and an original non-Moslem came equally within the purview of this rule, so that if a deceased Moslem left behind him three heirs, one of whom was a non-Moslem, the other an apostate, and the third a Moslem, the first two, under the Mahommedan Law, would be absolutely excluded from succession, and the inheritance would go entirely to the Moslem heir, though he may be remotest of all of them in the degree of proximity to the deceased.

The change effected by Act XXI of 1850 is most important. This Act consists of only one section, but its operation has had the effect of diverting entirely in many cases the course of succession from the channel into which it would have otherwise run. It enacts that " so much of any law or usage now in force within the territories subject to the Government of the East India Company, as inflicts on any person forfeiture of rights or property, or may be held in any way to impair or affect any right of inheritance, by reason of his or her renouncing or having been excluded from the communion of any religion, or being deprived of caste, shall cease to be enforced as law in the Courts established by Royal Charter within the said territories."

The effect of this enactment has been to do away with the provision of the Mahommedan Law by which "apostates" were

1 These provisions do not own their origin to religious exclusiveness, but to the political necessities of the early Commonwealth, when an "unbeliever" was an inveterate enemy, and an "apostate", a traitor. They have their counterpart in Christian communities. In Russia, even now a convert from the orthodox church is debarred from the rights of inheritance.

excluded from the inheritance of deceased Moslems. But if the person renouncing the Musulman religion were to pre-decease the *propositus* leaving heirs belonging to his or her new creed, would they be entitled to succeed under this Act to their Moslem relation? The question is not free from difficulty. *Prima facie*, the prohibition against the succession of original non-Moslems would seem to remain intact. So that if an apostate were to die leaving children brought up in his or her own creed, they would have no right of succession to the inheritance of their Moslem relation, though had their apostate parent been alive, he or she would have been entitled under the Act to succeed.

The Allahabad High Court has, however, taken a different view. A member of a Hindu family, who had renounced Hinduism and had adopted the Mahommedan faith, died leaving a son born in the Musulman religion. On a claim by the latter to a share of the inheritance of his Hindu grandfather, the High Court held that the relief granted by the Act to the person renouncing his former faith extended to his issue.[1]

If the apostate were to die after the inheritance has opened and the right of succession has vested in him, then the succession of his own children, though non-Moslems, would not be prevented by the evicting provision of the Mahommedan Law.

Under the Sunni Law, a Moslem does not inherit from a non-Moslem, nor does a non-Moslem inherit from a Moslem.[2]

But in the case of succession to the inheritance of male apostate, Abu Hanifa made a distinction based on the time when the property was acquired.

For example, if the property was acquired before apostacy, it went to the Moslem heirs; but if it was gained subsequent to the apostacy, then it escheated to the *Bait-ul-Mal*, or if part was acquired before apostacy and part after apostacy, the part which was acquired before went to the Moslem heirs, and the part acquired afterwards to the *Bait-ul-Mal*. The view of Abu

---

1 Bhagwant Sing *v*. Kallu (1888) I L 11 All. 100.

[*N.B.*—This ruling has been overruled by the Privy Council in Metar Sen Singh *v*. Maqbul Hasan Khan 57 I A 313 wherein their Lordships relying upon Vaithilinga Odayar *v*. Ayyathorai Odayar I L R 40 Mad. 1118 accepted the narrower view, the view which in their Lordships' opinion is the correct view, namely, that the section in terms only applies to protect the actual person who either renounces his religion or has been excluded from the communion of any religion or has been deprived of caste. It is intended to protect such a person from losing any right of property or of succeeding as heir. In other words when once a person has changed his religion and changed his personal law, that law will govern the right of succession of his children. It may of course work hard to some extent upon expectant heirs, especially if the expectant heirs are the children and perhaps the unconverted children of the ancestor or who in fact does change the religion, but after all it inflicts no more hardship in their case than in any other case where the ancestor has changed the law of succession, as for instance, by acquiring a different domicile. Their Lordships did not find it necessary to consider any question of hardship that may arise. Sundramal *v*. Ameenal A I R 1927 Mad. 72, and Chidrambaran Chettiyar *v*. Ma Nyein and others A I R 1927 Rang. 179 also followed the same view.]

2 Fatawai 'Alamgiri, Vol. VI, p. 631.

Hanifa is followed in most Mahommedan countries where the *Bait-ul-Mal* exists for the benefit of the general body of Musulmans. But Abu Yusuf and Mohammed differ from Abu Hanifa on this point, and agree with the Shiahs in holding that the entire estate of an apostate descends to his Moslem heirs.[1] In the case of a female apostate, however, her entire property, whether acquired before or after apostacy, goes to her Musulman heirs.[2]

Difference of country.

Difference of country involving difference of allegiance is also a bar to succession under the Sunni Law ; but this is confined to non-Moslems only. *Moslems, among themselves, though owing different allegiance, succeed to each other*. The Musulman sovereigns, however, by special treaty regulations, have granted to the subjects of non-Mahommedan powers the privilege of acquiring property by inheritance in Mahommedan countries.

Homicide.

(2) The second cause which absolutely excludes a person from succession is homicide, in other words, a person causing the death of another cannot inherit to the latter. Under the Sunni Law the exclusion takes effect whether the person is killed intentionally or by accident.[3]

An act, however, committed by an infant or an insane person which causes death, does not exclude such infant or such insane person from succeeding to the estate of the deceased. Or, if a person were to kill another in justifiable war, or when inflicting punishment under the direction of the law, such person would not be excluded from the inheritance of the person killed.

Being the indirect cause of a person's death without any intention is not a sufficient ground for excluding from his inheritance ; as, for instance, when a person has dug a well into which another falls, or placed a stone on the road against which he stumbles and is killed in consequence.

In other words, any act committed by one person which causes the death of another leads to the forfeiture by the former of his right of inheritance to the latter, if the act is such as would render him punishable under the law. For example "when a father", says the '*Alamgiri*, " circumcises his child, and the child dies in consequence of the operation, the father is not deprived of his right in the child's inheritance".

"But if he should admonish him by stripes, and the child should die in consequence, he is responsible for the *diat* or fine, and loses his right to inherit, according to Abu Hanifa, though he is not responsible, according to the other two.[4] This is the

---

1 Compare Phear, J., in the matter of the application of Zynab Bibi O. C., September 1876, unreported.

2 Sirajia, p. 58; Fatawai 'Alamgiri, Vol. VI, p. 633.

3 Gul Khan *v*. Mst. Karam Nishan A I R 1940 Lah. 172.

4 *viz*., Imam Abu Yusuf and Imam Mohammed.

adopted doctrine. And if a teacher be the person who punished the child with the father's permission, he does not incur any liability according to all their opinions."

Homicide.

Under the Shiah Law, the homicide must be *intentional* and unjustifiable to be a bar to succession.[1]

Slavery.—(3) The status of slavery is also treated as a bar to succession under the Shiah as well as the Sunni Law.

If a person should die leaving one heir free and another a slave, the whole inheritance would go to the one who is free, though the other may be nearer to the deceased.

If the slave has a child who is free, it would inherit in preference to its parent.

As the status of slavery does not exist in India, this rule of Mahommedan Law has only an antiquarian interest.

(4) Under the Sunni Law an illegitimate child ("child of fornication")[2] cannot inherit to his father or relations on the father's side, although in the absence of legitimate issue he is entitled to inherit from his mother and relations on the mother's side.[3]

Under the Shiah Law a child of fornication is "*nullus filius*" and cannot inherit to either of its parents.[4]

The Mahommedan Law does not recognise any physical defect as forming an impediment to succession, and consequently a person who happens to be insane is not excluded from inheritance.[5]

Similarly, want of chastity in a daughter, before or after the death of her father, or whether before or after her marriage, is no bar to succession.[6] Nor does a widow lose her right to a share in her husband's estate by reason of unchastity in her husband's lifetime. This rule, however, is based on the assumption that the status of marriage subsists to the end.

---

1 Under the Musulman Law a person who is the *indirect* cause of another's death is not liable to any penalty, even what is called "expiative".

2 See post, p. 115.

3 Bafatun *v.* Bilaiti Khanum (1903) I L 30 Cal. 683. In this case a Mahommedan female died leaving a husband and an illegitimate son of a sister. The husband became entitled to half of the deceased's property, whilst the other half was taken by the sister's son as a distant kindred of the third class.

4 Sahebzadee Begum *v.* Himmut Bahadoor (1869) 12 W R 512, on review (1870) 14 W R 125; Keolapati *v.* Amar Krishna A I R 1939 P C 249.

5 Mir Mahar Ali *v.* Amani (1869) 2 B L R, A C 306, s c 11 W R 262.

6 Noronarain Roy *v.* Neemaee Chand Neogy (1866) 6 W R 303.

CHAPTER IV

THE MAFKUD OR MISSING PERSON

The mafkud or the missing person.

"THE *mafkud* is a person regarding whom it is not known whether he is dead or alive. In the *Muhit* it is stated that if a Moslem be captured by an enemy, and it be not known whether he is dead or alive though it be known that he is a captive in the *Dar-ul-Harb*, he should be designated a *mafkud*. But in the *Multeka* and other authorities it is clearly laid down, that in order to be designated a *mafkud* the place where he is abiding should also be unknown." The author of the *Radd-ul-Muhtar* observes that a knowledge of the place of abode involves a knowledge of the missing person being alive, for if it be not known whether he is living, it follows that the other fact would also be unknown.

The mafkud's agent.

When a person, who is missing, has left his property in the hands of an agent, neither the officer-in-charge of the *Bait-ul-Mal* (even when he has no heir), nor the Kazi can take the property away from that person. The latter can only do so if he is satisfied that the agent is destroying, or is likely to destroy or to embezzle the property. This also is the rule laid down by Mufti Abu S'aud in his Ordinances (*M'aruzat*).

When the missing person has expressly authorised his agent to recover his debts by suit, according to Abu Hanifa he can do so, but not otherwise.

If the *mafkud* or missing person has left no agent, the Kazi may appoint some one to take care of the property. But there is a difference of opinion regarding the Kazi's power to authorise the agent to recover by suit the missing man's debts. In the *Khulasa*, however, it is stated that if he be a *Mujtahid* Kazi[1] the authorisation is lawful.

The Kazi is not authorised to sell any property of the missing person excepting such as is likely to be lost or damaged or to deteriorate in any way. In the latter case he is to keep the proceeds in deposit. But he can out of such proceeds pay for the maintenance of the missing man's family.

If a person purchases some property, but before delivery of possession becomes a *mafkud*, in such a case if the property be movable the Kazi can sell it and pay, with the proceeds its price to the original vendor. But not if the property be *'akar*.

When a thing has been pledged by one person to another and, after such pledge, the pledgor has become a *mafkud*, the pledgee cannot sell it for the discharge of his debt, without an order of the Kazi.

1 Kazi learned in the law.

Maintenance of the missing person's family.

When the Kazi has appointed an *Amin* or trustee for the goods and property of a missing person, such trustee will pay out of the available property of the *mafkud* the maintenance of his family, his family meaning his wife and his children, and his parents if they are in want.[1]

Malik's doctrine.

According to Imam Malik the wife of a missing person is entitled to observe the *'iddat* of death on the expiration of four years from the date of his disappearance. In other words, his death would be presumed on the lapse of four years, and after observing the usual probation of four months and ten days prescribed as the period of *'iddat* in case of the husband's death, she would be entitled to re-marry. Imam Shaf'ei held the same opinion originally. As regards the partition of the missing man's property they agree with the Hanafis that it can only be done under a decree of the Judge, otherwise distribution is permissible only after 90 years.

Imam Ahmed (ibn Hanbal) says that when there is a strong presumption of death, the property should be divided among the heirs, just as the widow should be allowed to observe the *'iddat* of death after four years. For example, if a man is missing from the ranks of two fighting bodies or from a ship which is wrecked, the presumption is that he is killed or drowned. In such cases, the property should be divided after four years from the date of the accident, and his wife should observe her *'iddat*. But when no such presumption arises, *e. g.*, when a man has gone travelling on trade and has not been heard of, Imam Ahmed says, recourse must be had to the *Hakim* [Judge] to pronounce his judgment.

Recognised rules according to Malik.

In the *Bazazia* it is stated that "in our times", the *Fatwa* is according to the rule of Imam Malik. And the author of the *Radd-ul-Muhtar*, following Mufti Abu S'aud, adds "where there is no Maliki Kazi, the Hanafi Kazi is authorised to pronounce the *Fatwa* according to the exigencies of the times in conformity with the rule of Imam Malik."

Imam Malik's rule is based upon a decision of the Caliph 'Omar in accordance with the opinion of the Caliph 'Ali.

If a person die leaving two daughters, and the children of a son who is missing at the time of his death, in such a case if the property be in the hands of the daughters, they will be regarded as holding their brother's share in trust for him. If he should appear, a half will be given to him. If he be found to be dead, his half would be divided among his children in the proportion of two shares to a male and one share to a female.

If a person die leaving a legacy in favour of another who is missing, the legacy will be kept in abeyance until it is ascertained whether he is dead or alive, as in the case of a partition of inheritance.

1 See post.

Recognised rule.

"There is great difference of opinion as to the period during which the share of a missing person should be held for him; some have said 90 years; others 70, whilst 'moderns' generally have fixed 60 years." But the recognised rule as laid down in the *Fath-ul-Kadir,* is that the Judge may give any direction having regard to the circumstances of any particular case, as to the probability of the missing person's death, and the period for which the partition should be delayed.

Among the Hanafis, a missing person is "considered alive" before the adjudication of the Kazi "so far as regards his own property, but dead as regards the property of others." On the expiration of this period, "he is to be accounted dead with respect to his own property, and with respect to the property of others, as if he had died on the day of his being missing."

The decision of the Kazi must be obtained with regard to the death of a missing person. Should he appear alive after the declaration of death, he would not be entitled to take a share in any inheritance *which has opened since the declaration.*

If the wife of the missing man re-marries after waiting for four years and after observing the usual *'iddat* and he appears, "the wife would be for him", whilst any children born to her by her second husband would belong to the latter.

When a declaration of death is made regarding a missing person, the right to succeed to him will accrue from that date and not from the time when he has disappeared.

Should he re-appear, and the property be still in the hands of those among whom it was divided when his death was declared, it will be given back to him.

But if it has passed away from their hands, he would have no right to recover it.

When a person dies leaving certain heirs, one of whom is missing, the division would be made after excluding the share of the missing person. For example, if a man dies leaving two daughters, a son who is missing and the son of a predeceased son, the daughters will get one-fourth each, and a moiety will be kept in trust for the missing person. If he is not found and the Kazi pronounces him to be dead, another one-sixth will be given to the daughters and the remainder to the grandson.

Shiah and Shaf'ei doctrine.

Among the Shiahs the lapse of ten years gives rise to the presumption of death, whilst among the Shaf'eis the recognised period is seven years, which is the same as in the Indian Evidence Act.

Indian Evidence Act, s. 107.

Section 107 of the Indian Evidence Act runs as follows:—

"When the question is whether a man is alive or dead, and it is shown that he was alive within thirty years, the burden of proving that he is dead is on the person who affirms it."

Section 108.

Section 108 then provides "that when the question is whether a man is alive or dead, and it is proved that he has not been heard of for seven years by those who would naturally have heard of him if he had been alive, the burden of proving that he is alive is shifted to the person who affirms it."

The intention of the Legislature.

A Full Bench of the Allahabad High Court has held that the old Hanafi doctrine is a rule of evidence and not a part of the Mahommedan Law which the Courts are bound to administer.[1] It is submitted, however, that it could hardly have been the intention of the Legislature to vary the substantive rules of the Mahommedan Law. For example, if a Hanafi wife whose husband has been missing for four years, were to observe at the expiration of that period the *'iddat* of widowhood and afterwards to re-marry, it would be impossible, in my opinion, to hold that such marriage was invalid owing to the provisions of s. 108 of the Indian Evidence Act.

A "captive"[2] is subject to the same rules as other Moslems in respect of inheritance unless he renounces his religion; and if he renounces it, he is subject to the rules relative to "apostates", If it is not known whether he has renounced his religion, or whether he is dead or alive, he is subject to the same rules as a missing person.

CHAPTER V

MALIKI AND SHAF'EI RULES OF SUCCESSION

THE Malikis and Shaf'eis are in general accord with the Hanafis on the broad principles upon which the Sunni system of classification is based. For example, they also divide the heirs into the three classes, *viz.*, sharers, residuaries, and uterine relations, recognised by the Hanafis.

With reference to the *sharers* there is no difference. As regards the *'Asabah*, there are some points of divergence between the Hanafis on the one side and the Shaf'eis and Malikis on the other. Originally these allowed the right of succession to the *'Asabah-be nafsehi* (residuaries) *proprio jure* in the collateral branch up to the 6th degree only; see table on the following page.

Right of cognates recognised.

But later lawyers have recognised the right of the *'Asabah* of a lower degree. In default of the *'Asabah*, whether *'Asabah-be-nafsehi, be ghairahi*, in their own right, in another's right, or with another, or for *special cause*, as the manumittor or his residuary, the property of the deceased goes to the uterine relations.

1 Mazhar Ali *v.* Budh Sing (1884) I L 7 All. 297; Imdad Ali *v.* Ghulam Jilani 42 O R 1892 and Mairaj Fatima *v.* Abdul Wahid I L R 43 All. 673.

2 A Moslem held captive in a non-Moslem country.

TABLE of *'Asabah proprio jure* according to the MALIKI and SHAF'EI SCHOOLS.

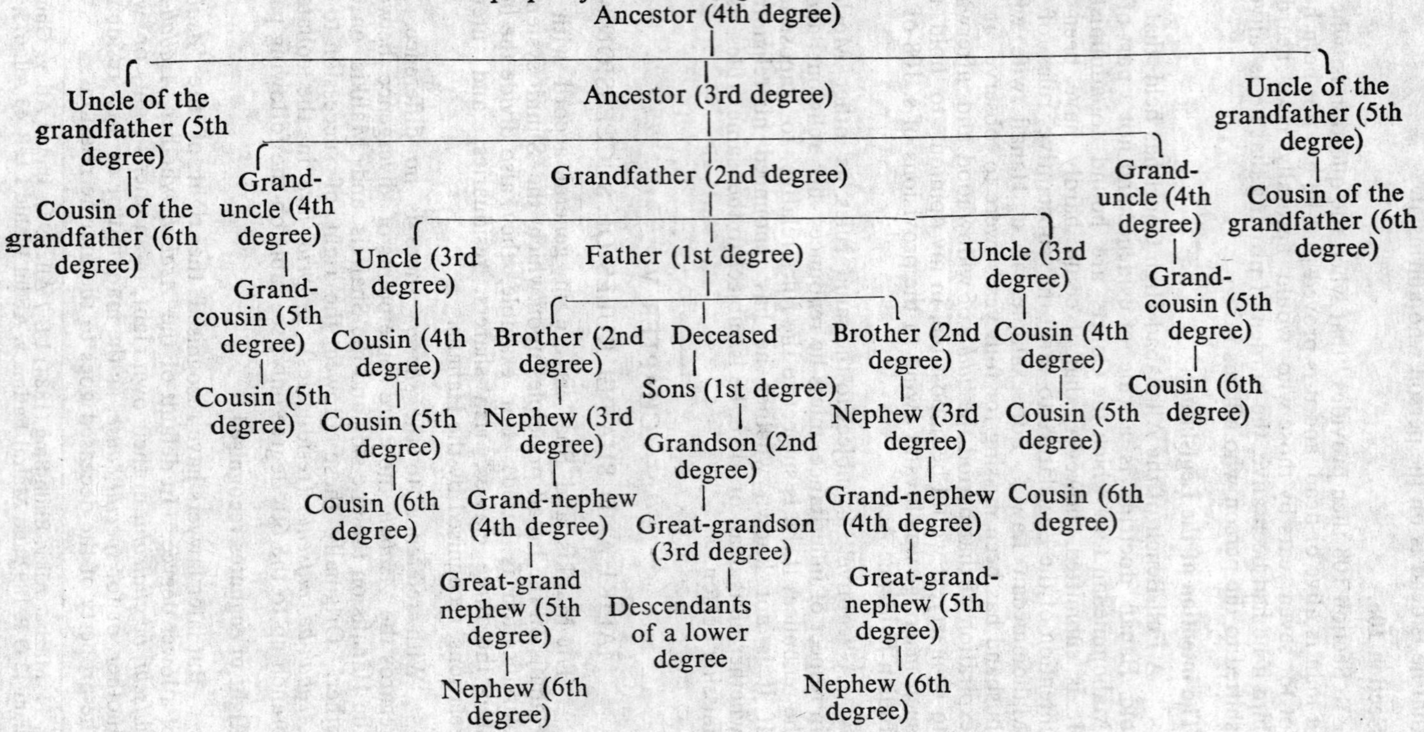

The right of succession is founded on four causes:—(1) kinship; (2) marriage; (3) clientage (*wala*) ; and (4) Islam, because in default of other heirs the general body of Moslems represented by the *Bait-ul-Mal*, become entitled to the estate of a deceased person.

Originally there were ten males legally entitled to succession: (1) son; (2) the son's son, how-low-soever; (3) the father; (4) male ascendants of a higher degree; (5) the brother; (6) the sons of the brother (excepting the son of an uterine brother); (7) the half-brother on the father's side; (8) his son; (9) the husband; (10) the emancipator. The female heirs were seven: (1) the daughter; (2) the son's daughter, how-low-soever; (3) the mother; (4) the grandmother and the other female ascendants called *true*; (5) the sister; (6) widow; (7) the emancipatress.

The succession of cognates.

"According to the primitive Shaf'ei doctrine", says the *Minhaj-ut-Talibin*, "the succession of uterine relations was not recognised, and even the *Zav-il-Furuz* could not take more than the share appointed for them in the Koran, the rest going to the *Bait-ul-Mal*. But it has been held by modern jurists that in the absence of all other natural relations the residue of the estate after allotment of the shares laid down in the Koran, should be divided among the sharers in proportion to their appointed shares. And the cognates are entitled to succeed to the exclusion of the *Bait-ul-Mal*."

As regards the "Sharers" and the classification of the *Zav-il-Furuz*, there is no difference between the Shaf'eis, Malikis and Hanafis.

When the "Sharers" exhaust the inheritance, the '*Asabah* take nothing. It is only when any residue is left after allotment of the shares, that the '*Asabah* take the residue.

The father takes the share allotted to him in the Koran when he co-exists with the son or son's son how-low-soever. In default of a son or son's son how-low-soever he takes as a residuary when he exists with a daughter or son's daughter: first he takes his $\frac{1}{6}$; and next the residue, after deducting the share of the daughter or son's daughter.

The mother can never claim more than $\frac{1}{3}$ or $\frac{1}{6}$; whilst her portion is only $\frac{1}{3}$ of what *remains* after allotment of the husband or widow's share, if she happens to co-exist with the father and husband or widow of the deceased.

The paternal grandfather's right is governed by the same rules as the father's subject to the following exceptions:—

(1) The brothers and sisters are always excluded by the father unless they become entitled with him as residuaries.

(2) The father excludes his own mother, whereas the grandfather does not exclude the paternal grandmother.

(3) The father reduces the share of the mother when with

a husband or widow to one-third of the residue after allotment of the husband or widow's share, but the grandfather does not do so.

When there is only one son he takes the entire inheritance; when several they take it equally among themselves.

A daughter with a son takes half the share of her brother, but when by herself, a moiety; when there are two or more daughters, and no son, they take two-thirds among them equally.

The children of sons, in the absence of other heirs, are governed by the rules applicable to the children of the deceased.

When there is a son co-existing with the children of a pre-deceased son the latter are excluded.

If the deceased has left only brothers and sisters they share the inheritance in the proportion of two to one in the case of sons and daughters.

The consanguine brothers and sisters are subject to the same rules as full brothers and sisters. There is one exception to this case, *viz.*, when a woman dies leaving as her heirs her husband, her mother, two uterine brothers or sisters, and a full brother. In this case the full brothers would share with the two uterine brothers or sisters in the third allotted to them in the Koran; but, if instead of a full brother, there had been a consanguine brother, he would have inherited nothing. This is called a case of *musharraka*.

When there are full brothers or sisters co-existing with consanguine brothers or sisters, the latter would be excluded unless the full sister or consanguine sister becomes an heir by the agnatic title in consequence of being with a brother.

An uterine brother or sister takes one-sixth; when there are several they take one-third among them equally without any distinction of sex.

The full sisters or consanguine sisters become "residuaries by right of another" when they co-exist with the daughters of the deceased or his son's daughters. They can claim a portion as if they were brothers, excepting that the consanguine sister is excluded by the full sister when there is a daughter of the deceased co-existing with them.

The sons of full brothers and consanguine brothers follow in general the rule relating to the succession of their fathers. They differ from them in the following particulars:—

(1) They do not reduce the mother's share to a sixth.

(2) They are excluded by the paternal grandfather.

(3) They do not render their sisters residuaries.

(4) They are excluded from succession in the case called *musharraka*, already referred to.

The full brother or consanguine brother of the father is subject to the same rule as the full brother or consanguine brother of the deceased.

In default of residuaries by blood, the emancipator (if the deceased was a freedman) becomes entitled in preference to the uterine relations of the deceased. There is no distinction on the ground of the sex of the emancipator. In the absence of the emancipator, his or her residuaries in their own right (*'Asabah proprio jure*) become entitled.

Non-Moslem.

There is no succession between a Musulman and a person who denies the unity of God and the Messengership of the Prophet. The apostate does not inherit from anyone nor does anybody from him. The slave cannot inherit, but according to a later doctrine of Shaf'ei, the slave who was partially enfranchised can have heir of his own, though he cannot inherit himself.

Homicide.

A person killing another has no right of succession to the latter's inheritance, though some make an exception to this rule in the case of a slayer who is not liable to a penalty.

When two persons entitled to succeed to one another in case of one predeceasing the other, die in a common calamity, such as drowning, etc., or when the time of their respective deaths cannot be ascertained, in other words, it cannot be known which of them died first, there is no succession between them, and their inheritance devolves on their respective heirs.

The mafkud.

The goods of a prisoner of war or of a person who is missing, and of whom no news can be obtained, should be kept in the custody of a trustee until his death has been established, or until a period sufficient to give rise to the presumption of his death has elapsed. In such a case the Judge must hold an enquiry and then pronounce a declaration about the death of the missing individual, after which he will proceed to divide the succession among those who have the right of inheritance at the time of declaration. If a missing person is an heir to another, his portion would be kept in trust whilst the other heirs would receive their legal shares.

If at the time when the succession opens, a woman is pregnant with a child who would be entitled to a share in the inheritance, the share of the infant would be reserved until his birth.

Aul recognised.

The doctrine of *aul* or increase in the denominator when the fractions amount to more than the integer is recognised as among the Hanafis. And the rules relating to partition are the same.

CHAPTER VI

SHIAH LAW OF SUCCESSION

SECTION I

Classification of heirs

WE have thus far seen the mode of classification and the principles of distribution in force among the Sunnis, and it must have become apparent that the rules of inheritance among them are highly complicated. Among the Shiahs, on the contrary, the law of inheritance is of the greatest simplicity and does not involve any discussion regarding the relative rights of *agnates* and *cognates* —the '*Asabah* and the *Zav-il-Arham.* The great distinction, in fact, between the Shiah and the Sunni Law of Inheritance consists in the question of agnacy. The Shiahs repudiate *in toto* the doctrine of *t'asib* (تعصيب); consequently the paternal relations of the male sex, or what are called '*Asabah* proper in Sunni Jurisprudence, have no especial privilege, nor are they preferred to the relations connected with the deceased through females.

For example, the Shiahs consider it as contrary to justice to exclude the daughter's children in favour of the remote descendants of a brother, on the fictitious ground of being connected with the deceased through male relations.

Shiah Law.

According to the Shiahs, there are two causes which give rise to the right of inheritance: (1) *Nasab* (consanguinity), and (2) *Sabab* (special cause). Consanguinity implies simply the tie of blood. All relations, therefore, connected with the deceased by the tie of blood, are entitled to share in his inheritance unless excluded by the operation of the rules which I shall presently define.

Nasab.

The relations, who are entitled to succession by virtue of consanguinity (*nasab*), are divided into three classes or groups, and each class again is divided into two sections. The members belonging to the first class of heirs exclude from succession those belonging to the second, whilst these, in their turn, exclude the members belonging to the third class. But the heirs of the two sections of each class succeed together. For example:—

(1) The first class of heirs entitled by *nasab* to inherit from the deceased consists (*a*) of the ascendants of the first degree, *viz.*, the parents, and (*b*) of the children and their offspring, including all lineal descendants of the deceased.

(2) The second class consists (*a*) of the ascendants of all degrees and (*b*) brothers and sisters and their descendants.

(3) The third class consists of the callaterals (*a*) on the father's and (*b*) on the mother's sides, being descendants, however low in the collateral lines of the ascendants, however high, such as uncles, aunts, grand-uncles, grand-aunts, etc., however high, and their descendants, however low.

Whilst there is a single member of the first class existing, those who belong to the second and the third class are absolutely excluded from the succession. In the same way, if there be any relation of the second class, co-existing with relations of the third class the latter take nothing.

But the members of the two sections of each class succeed together. For example, parents take a share in the inheritance of the deceased with the children of the deceased; grandparents with the brothers and sisters; and maternal uncles and aunts with the paternal uncles and aunts. A child or child's child entirely excludes the brothers and sisters and their descendants. And so brothers and sisters and their descendants exclude the uncles and aunts, but they inherit together with the ascendants of higher degree.

When a Sunni Musulman dies leaving behind him a daughter's daughter with a brother's son, the brother's son as an *'Asabah*, takes the entire inheritance in exclusion of the deceased's own grand-child. Among the Shiahs, the grand-daughter of the deceased, as a lineal descendant, takes the whole property to the exclusion of the brother's son.

When a Sunni Musulman dies leaving behind him a daughter and a brother, the daughter takes her specified share, *viz.*, a moiety, and the rest goes to the brother, as a residuary or *'Asabah*. Under the Shiah Law, she takes the whole—half as her specified share, and the other half by the doctrine of *return*.

Order of succession: Sabab.

The right of succession for special cause (*sabab*) or "affinity," is divided under two heads:—

(1) The right of inheritance by virtue of matrimony (*zawjiyet*); and

(2) The right of inheritance by virtue of *wala* or special relationship.

(1) The right of inheritance by virtue of *zowjiyet* appertains to the individual heir under all circumstances. The husband or the wife, accordingly, is never excluded from succession. If the deceased leave behind him a child and a widow, the latter takes her specific share, and the residue goes to the child. In the same way, a widow co-existing with the parents or grandparents or brothers and sisters of the deceased, is entitled to her specific share before the property is divided among the heirs, who succeed by virtue of *nasab*.

(2) The right of inheritance by *wala* (*al-miras bi'l wala*) has assumed a peculiar aspect among the Shiahs, owing to the political subjection in which they were kept in early times. The right is divided under three heads, *viz.* :—

(*a*) *Wala-ul-'itq*—"The right of inheritance possessed by the emancipator".

(*b*) *Wala-z-zamin-il jarirah*—"The right of inheritance for obligation of delicts committed by the deceased", (*c*) *Wala-'l-Imam*—"The right of inheritance possessed by the *Imam* by virtue of the *wala* of *Imamate* or spiritual headship".

'Itk. Difference between the Shiah and the Hanafi Law.

The first form of *wala* (*wala-ul-itq*) has its exact counterpart in the Hanafi Law, but the right which springs from it is regarded in different ways by the two schools. For example, under the Hanafi Law, if a slave were to buy his liberty, it would not affect the right of inheritance possessed by the emancipator; and if the slave were to die after enfranchisement, leaving no '*Asabah* proper of his own, the emancipator would take the whole inheritance to the exclusion of the emancipated slave's "uterine relations". Under the Shiah Law, the emancipator succeeds to the inheritance of the freedman only under certain well-defined conditions, *viz*. (*a*) when the enfranchisement is purely spontaneous and voluntary on his part. When the slave's enfranchisement is obtained by payment of a ransom, or when he is manumitted in performance of a vow, or as a propitiative offering to the Almighty, or when the emancipation is the result of law, then the emancipator has no right of succession. (*b*) The emancipator is entitled to succeed only when the freedman has left no blood-relations behind him; and (*c*) when, after enfranchisement, the master continues responsible for the delicts of the emancipated. If the emancipator's responsibility cease by operation of the law or by virtue of a special contract, at the time of manumission, he would have no right of inheritance to the estate of the emancipated slave, nor would he have any right if the deceased left any heirs connected to him by *nasab*.

Wala'z-zamin-il-jarirah.

The *wala'z-zamin-il-jarirah* is in some respects analogous to the *wala-ul-mawalat* of the Hanafis, for the Shaf'eis recognise no similar right. The history of the origin of the *wala-'z-zamin-il-jarirah* or, at least, the form it has taken among the Shiahs, throws considerable light on the state of manners and the conditions of society among the Musulmans in early times.

In certain stages of society it has been usual for a stranger on arriving in a foreign city to furnish guarantees for good behaviour. This custom appears to have existed during the Middle Ages in most of the Free Towns of Europe and there can be little doubt that its counterpart in the East gave rise to the doctrine of "the right of inheritance based on suretyship". The custom acquired a distinctive character under the Abbaside sovereigns, who invariably exacted security for good behaviour from all strangers who arrived in the city of Baghdad from Khorasan. Those who became sureties were responsible to the State for any offence committed by their clients, and were in return entitled to succeed to the inheritance of the latter when they died leaving no heir.[1] But this right was neither reciprocal nor transmissible.

1 During the reign of al-Mamun, the Imam 'Ali ibn-Musa ar-Riza used to stand zamin (surety) for all his people. He is therefore styled the Imam Zamin. The custom of tying a piece of gold on the arms of all persons leaving home or making long journeys and commending them to the Imam Zamin, dates from this epoch.

Wala-ul-Imam.

In the absence of the emancipator as well as the *Zamin* ("the surety"), the Imam, as the Spiritual Head of the Shiahs, becomes entitled to the inheritance, there being no escheat to the public treasury (*Bait-ul-Mal*) under the Shiah Law. The right of the Imam however, is not in the nature of an escheat to the sovereign. The property goes to him as the Spiritual Head of the Shiah Commonwealth, to be distributed among the poor and indigent of the locality where the intestate lived, or where he was born. In the absence (*ghibat*) of the Imam, as is practically the case at the present moment, the twelfth Imam having mysteriously disappeared near Surraman-Raa[1] the property goes to his representative (the *Mujtahid*), the chief expounder of the law, to be distributed by him equitably and properly among the poor and indigent of the place where the intestate lived or for such charitable and religious purposes as may seem consonant to his last wishes.

Right of the Imam. Statute of Limitation.

The right of the Imam is, accordingly, not *qua* sovereign, but *qua* spiritual leader, and would be subject to the ordinary bar of the Statute of Limitation. In India, the inheritance of a Shiah Mahommedan dying without leaving any possible heir of the various classes indicated above, goes to the *Mujtahid* of the locality nearest to the place where the intestate lived, as the representative of the Imam; but supposing the right was neither claimed nor advanced for the space of twelve years from the date of the intestate's death, it would be barred by the ordinary limitation applicable to the claims of private individuals.

On this point, a *Fatwa* contained in the *Jam'a-ush-Shittat* pronounced by a recent leading *Mujtahid* of Iran (Persia) is worth insertion.

Q. "What should be done with the property of a person dying without leaving any heir behind him (*mal-i-min-la-waris-lahu*) during the absence (*ghibat*) of the Imam; whether it is to be distributed among the poor of the locality where the deceased was born or where he died, or where the property is situated; whether it is to be given generally to the poor, or applied to specific purposes; or whether it is to be preserved until the appearance of the Imam; and in case it is required to be given to the poor, might it be given to one single individual whilst others are available, or must it be distributed among many; is the property to be given to the poor intact, or might it be sold and its proceeds distributed ?"

A. "The property of an intestate leaving no heir behind him does not go to the *Bait-ul-Mal*."

"It is the property of the Imam, whether he is present or absent (*ghaib*). If the deceased leave any heir behind him, even *zamin-i-jarirah* the Imam does not succeed. If the Imam be

1 See Short History of the Saracens.

absent, the property should be distributed among the poor of the deceased's village or native city (*balad-i-myet*). If it be considered advisable by the *Mujtahid* to sell it, it is valid to do so, especially when the property in itself is of no use to the poor; when the poor are many, it is wrong to give it to one only, though there is nothing in law to make it invalid. The distribution in those cases ought to take place under the direction of the *Hakim* (Judge) who is the delegate of the Imam, and such is the opinion of the *Kifayah*."

From the use of the word *Hakim* towards the end of the answer, it is clear that the *Mujtahid* acts in the capacity of a Judge in the administration of the estate of the deceased intestate. In Shiah countries not subject to foreign control, the *Mujtahid* who is the chief expounder of the law, is also frequently vested with the powers of the Kazi. When this is the case, no difficulty occurs in the application of the principle of the Shiah Law. But in India, where the Shiahs are subject to a non-Muslem power, the question may arise under whose direction the distribution contemplated by the Shiah Law should take place. These questions, it seems to me, are answered by the dictum quoted from the *Jama-ush-Shittat*. The Civil Court, representing the *Hakim* mentioned in the *Fatwa*, would assume the charge of the property, and make it over to the *Mujtahid* (if there be any), to be distributed among the poor and indigent of the deceased's village or native city, under the Court's own control and supervision, so as to leave no room for doubt as to its proper application. If there be no *Mujtahid*, some Shiah officer should be appointed for the purpose of effecting the distribution. It must also be remembered that the law does not *necessarily* contemplate the application of the proceeds in the shape of alms. If the object of the law, which has in view the benefit of the poor and the indigent, "who are always in need of help", can be attained by establishing an institution by which *regular* assistance can be rendered to them, it would be valid.

SECTION II

CONSANGUINEOUS RELATIONS

Consanguineous relations.

Under the Shiah Law, heirs to whichever class they may belong among the consanguineous relations, are divided into three categories in respect of the *right* which entitles them to participate in the inheritance of the deceased, *viz.* :—

(1) Those whose heritable right is acquired by virtue of the shares assigned to them in the Koran (*al-farz*),[1] and who are therefore designated *zu-farz*;

---

1 For example, among those entitled by virtue of nasab (consanguinity), the mother is one who takes her appointed share and also the residue when there are no other heirs; similarly the husband or widow takes his or her share, as the case may be, fixed in the Koran, and the residue in the absence of other heirs.

(2) Those who inherit sometimes as *zu-farz* and sometimes by virtue of their relationship (*karabat*) to the deceased;[1] and

(3) Those who take only by virtue of their relationship, and are, therefore, called the *zu-karabat*, and are entitled to the *saham-bi'l-karabat*.

The zu-farz.

The heirs who are entitled to appointed shares (the *zu-farz*) are :—

(*a*) A daughter or daughters, when without (the deceased's) father, and her or their own brother or brothers.

(*b*) Full sister or sisters, or a consanguine sister or sisters existing without a grandfather and brother, or brothers of the same degree as themselves.

(*c*) The father, with a child or children of the deceased.

(*d*) The mother.

(*e*) The husband, or

(*f*) The widow.

(*g*) The person or persons related by the same mother only.

When there is only one heir, whether a *zu-farz* or a *zu-karabat* or one entitled by virtue of the special relationship of *sabab*, such heir takes the entire inheritance.

When the heir is a *zu-farz*, he or she takes first the appointed share, and the remainder is *returned* to such heir.

When the heir is a *zu-karabat*, the entire inheritance goes to him by virtue of the relationship by blood ; and also when the relationship is one created by *sabab*.

For example, an only daughter takes her appointed share, *viz.*, one-half, and the remainder goes to her by *return*.

An only son takes the entire inheritance by right of *karabat*, there being no specific share assigned to him by the law.

When the deceased leaves behind him or her no relation excepting a husband or a widow, who is entitled to succeed by virtue of the *sabab-i-zowjiyet* (matrimony), he or she takes the entire inheritance, first his or her specific share, and the remainder by *return* (*radd*).

Shares of males and females—General rule.

When there are male and female heirs of the same degree in the order of relationship, belonging to the same class, and connected equally by the tie of blood, the male takes double the share of a female. For example, a son takes double the share of a

---

1 For example, the father, the daughter or daughters, a full sister or sisters and the uterine brothers and sisters.

daughter ; a grandson double the share of a grand-daughter, and so on.

Persons connected through father and mother respectively.

In the case, however, of heirs related on the mother's side, an exception is made to the above rule. For example, uterine brothers and sisters divide the share allotted to them, *viz.*, one-third, equally without distinction of sex.

When there are two or more heirs who inherit, not as *sharers*, but by *karabat* or *sabab*, they take the estate in proportion to their respective rights. For example, when there are two sons, they divide the estate equally; when there are only a son and a daughter, the son takes two-thirds and the daughter one-third.

When there are several heirs, some connected with the deceased through the father and others through the mother, then each party takes the portion of the person through whom they are related. For example, when there are paternal as well as maternal uncles and aunts, then those connected on the father's side take two-thirds, and one-third goes to those who are connected on the mother's side.

When the individuals so related to the deceased are themselves of different descriptions, then the share allotted to the group is divided according to their sex or respective individual rights. For example, if the deceased leave behind him several paternal uncles and aunts, they take two-thirds among them as a body, but the two-thirds is divided among them in the proportion of two to one, so as to give the males double the share of the females.

The children of consanguineous heirs if not in any way excluded, take the place of their deceased or disqualified parents, and receive proportionately the shares of their parents. For example, if a man die, leaving the children of a son and the children of a daughter, the first take two-thirds of the estate and divide it proportionately amongst them, according to their respective rights, whilst the children of the daughter take one-third (to which their mother was entitled) and divide it in the same way.

When there are two or more heirs, one or more of whom are entitled as *zu-farz* and the others as *zu-karabat*, the *zu-farz* take their respective shares before the residue is divided among the latter.

Full and half blood relations.

When there are several relations some of the full and some of the half blood, those connected on the mother's side *only* take one-third which is divided among them equally *without distinction of sex* (if only one, he or she takes one-sixth), and the residue is divided among the relations of the full blood in the usual proportions, *relations on the father's side being entirely excluded.*

For example, if the deceased leave some full brothers and sisters and some half brothers and sisters, both on the father's and the mother's side, *the uterine brothers and sisters take one-third of the inheritance among them and divide it equally without distinction of sex.* If there be only one such uterine brother or sister, he or she takes one-sixth. The residue is then divided among the full brothers and sisters in the proportion of two to one, the brothers of the half blood on the father's side being entirely excluded.

It is only in default of the relations of the full blood, that those connected on the father's side participate in the inheritance. For example, if a person die leaving a brother of the half blood on the father's side, and a sister by the same father and mother, the latter would exclude the brother *in toto*. This rule applies to all cases.

Husband or widow never excluded from succession.

The husband or widow is never excluded from succession.

In ancient times the widow did not take by *return*, but modern lawyers hold, and it has been decided that she, like the husband, takes by return in the absence of all consanguineous heirs.

When there are relations who are connected with the deceased on the father's side only, and others who are connected on the mother's side only, and both sets of relations are equal in degree and class, the two sets take their respective shares and divide the residue among themselves *pro rata*.

For example, if the deceased leave behind him a sister of the half blood on the father's side and a sister of the half blood on the mother's side, both of them take their respective shares, *viz.*, one-half and one-sixth ; and the remainder, *viz.*, one-third, is divided among them in the ratio of three to one.

The shares.

As far as the shares are concerned, they are six in number, *viz.*, a moiety, a fourth, an eighth, a third, two-thirds, and one-sixth.

(1) A moiety is taken by—

(*a*) The husband, when there are no children;

(*b*) Two or more full sisters, when there is no full brother;

(*c*) The daughter, when only one.

(2) The fourth is taken by—

(*a*) The husband *with* children ,

(*b*) The widow, when there are no children.

(3) The eighth is taken by the widow[1] with children or children's children, how-low-soever.

(4) The third is taken by—

(*a*) The uterine brothers and sisters, when two or more in number;

1 Or widows.

(*b*) The mother, when the deceased has left no children, or where there are *two or more* brothers or one brother and two sisters.

If there are children, or two or more brothers or one brother and several sisters, the mother's share is reduced to one-sixth, though in the latter case the brothers and sisters take nothing.

(5) Two-thirds are taken by—

(*a*) Two or more daughters, when there are no son or sons ;

(*b*) Two or more full sisters, when there is no full brother, or when there are no brothers of the half blood on the father's side only.

(6) A sixth is taken by—

(*a*) The father and the mother, when the deceased has left lineal descendants ,

(*b*) The mother, when there exist with her two or more brothers of the full blood, or one brother and several sisters of the full blood (or by the same father only the father himself being in existence) ;

(*c*) The single child by the same mother only, whether such child be male or female ; *viz*., a uterine sister or brother.

Section III

(*Miras-ul-ansab*)

The classes of heirs.

1. The heirs entitled by virtue of *nasab* are, as already mentioned, divided into three classes (*tabka*).

2. The relations of the first class consist of the immediate descendants of the deceased and their lineal descendants.

3. When the father exists by himself, he takes the entire inheritance.

(Same under the Sunni Law.)

4. When the mother exists by herself she takes the whole inheritance; one-third as her appointed share, and the remainder by right of *return*.

(Same under the Sunni Law.)

5. When the father and the mother exist together, the mother takes one-third, and the father takes the remainder.

(Same under the Sunni Law.)

6. When the deceased leaves behind him a father, a mother, and two brothers, or one brother and two sisters, or four sisters,

the mother takes one-sixth, and the father takes the remainder, to the total exclusion of the brothers or sisters.

(Same under the Sunni Law.)

7. If the father and mother co-exist with children, the father and mother take one-sixth each.

(Same under the Sunni Law.)

8. When there is only one son, he takes the entire inheritance. If there are several sons, they divide the inheritance equally among themselves.

(Same under the Sunni Law.)

Primogeniture partially recognised.

The Shiah Law recognises partly the principle of primogeniture holding that the eldest son is entitled to the sabre, the Koran, the signet, the robes of honour and other vestments of his deceased father.

9. When there is only one daughter, she takes the inheritance, half as her appointed share and the remainder by right of *return*. If there are two or more, they take the entire inheritance equally, two-thirds as their appointed share and one-third by right of *return*.

(Under the Sunni Law, they take the *entire* inheritance only when there are no other relations.)

10. When the two ascendants, or either of them, are co-existing with the descendants, then each of the ascendants receives one-sixth, and the remainder is distributed among the descendants equally if they be all males ; but if there be a female or females among them, then each male has the portion of two females.

(Same under the Sunni Law.)

11. When a husband or widow of the deceased co-exists with the parents and the children, then the husband or the widow takes his or her *reduced* share,[1] and the parents theirs, while the remainder goes to the children.

(Same under the Sunni Law.)

12. When there are the two ascendants and a daughter, the ascendants receive their one-sixth respectively and the daughter her moiety, and the residue is divided among them *pro rata*, that is, the parents take two-thirtieths and the daughter three-thirtieths in addition to their shares.

(Under the Sunni Law the father takes the entire residue.)

13. When the two parents co-exist with one daughter and with brothers consanguine or of the full blood of the deceased, the parents take their respective shares, *viz.*, one-sixth, the daughter her moiety, and the remainder is divided *pro rata*

---

1 *Viz.*, $\frac{1}{4}$ or $\frac{1}{8}$.

between the father and the daughter, *viz.*, in the proportion of one to three.

(Under the Sunni Law the father takes the entire residue.)

14. When the two ascendants co-exist with a daughter and the husband, the latter and the ascendants take their respective *reduced* shares, and the residue goes to the daughter. For example the husband takes one-fourth, the parents one-sixth each, and the remaining five-twelfths goes to the daughter.

But when the deceased happens to be a male and leaves a widow behind co-existing with the daughter and the parents, they all take their respective shares, *viz.*, one-eighth, one-half, and two-sixths, and the remainder is divided among the parents and the daughter *pro rata*.

(Under the Sunni Law, in the first case there would be a proportionate abatement in the shares of all the heirs, and the deficiency would not fall entirely upon the daughter. In the latter case, the father would take the entire residue.)

15. If, in the preceding case, there were brothers [1] co-existing with the relations mentioned above, then the residue would be divided only among the father and daughters.

16. When there are two or more daughters and one parent, then the latter gets his or her one-sixth, and the daughters get their two-thirds as their appointed shares, and the remainder reverts to them *pro rata* in the proportion of four to one.

17. If the deceased leave surviving her husband and the two ascendants (parents), the husband takes his half, the mother one-third of the *original* estate, and the father the remainder.

(Under the Sunni Law, the mother takes one-third of the remainder after the allotment of the husband's share. [2])

Likewise, if the deceased leave a widow behind.

Representation takes place in the descending line, or, in other words, on failure of the direct descendants (the deceased's children), the children of the children take the places of their respective parents in the distribution of the inheritance, with the immediate ascendants or parents of the deceased.

18. *The lineal descendants exclude from succession everyone connected with the deceased through them, and also everyone connected through the deceased's parents, but not the parents themselves.* For example the children how-low-soever, exclude the deceased's brothers and their children, his grandparents and their ancestors, his paternal and maternal uncles and aunts and their children.

(Under the Sunni Law, the lineal *male* descendants alone represent their parents in the succession.)

---

1 Or one brother and two sisters, or four sisters.

2 See ante.

19. Descendants nearer in degree exclude the more remote. For example, when the deceased has left a daughter and a predeceased son's son or daughter, the deceased's daughter takes the entire inheritance to the exclusion of his grandchild, on the principle of the nearer excluding the more remote.

(As already pointed out, the Sunni Law is very complicated on this point, and differs materially from the Shiah rule. Under the Sunni Law, if the deceased leave behind him a daughter and a predeceased son's son, then the daughter takes her moiety, and the residue goes to the grandson. But if, instead of a son's son, there were only son's daughters, then these would take one-sixth equally among themselves. If, however, there were *two or more* daughters, the son's daughters would take nothing. But if there happened to be with the son's daughters a son's son also, then the daughters would take their two-thirds, and the remaining one-third would be divided among the grandchildren in the proportion of two for each male and one for each female. A son, however, would exclude *in toto* the sons and daughters of a predeceased son.)[1]

20. Each descendant inherits the portion of the person whose place he or she takes in the succession. For example, if the deceased were to leave behind him the child, male or female, of a daughter, that child would inherit the portion of its mother whether alone or co-existing with the parents of the deceased ; and the remainder, after the allotment of the share or shares, would revert to the child in the same manner as it would have reverted to his or her mother if she had been in existence. A son's child, male or female, inherits that which is inheritable by its father—the whole, if it be alone, or the residue if it exists with the deceased's parents, husband, or wife.

(Under the Sunni Law, a daughter's daughter, as an *uterine relation*, has no place in the inheritance until all heirs with a residuary title are exhausted. For example, a father would exclude entirely, under the Sunni Law, a daughter's daughter. But under the Shiah Law, the father would take his one-sixth, and the daughter's daughter one-half (her mother's share), and the residue would be divided among them in the proportion of three to one.)

21. *When the children of a son co-exist with the children of a daughter, the son's children take two-thirds of the inheritance* (*in their father's right*), *and the daughter's children one-third* (*in their mother's right*.)

(Under the Sunni Law, the children of a daughter are *uterine relations*, and are postponed until the sharers and residuaries are exhausted.)

22. When there is also a husband or wife co-existing with the grandchildren, then the husband or wife receives his or her *reduced* share, *viz*., one-fourth or one-eighth, and the remainder is divided among the grandchildren, the son's children taking two-thirds of the residue, and the daughter's children one-third.

1 See ante.

The daughter's children divide their share of the inheritance in the proportion of two for each male and one for each female.

23. The grandfather or the grandmother takes no share in the inheritance whilst there is a child how-low-soever or an ascendant of the first degree existing at the time.

SECTION IV

THE SUCCESSION OF HEIRS OF THE SECOND CLASS

Consanguineous heirs of the second class.

1. The second class of consanguineous heirs comprises the ascendants of higher degrees than parents, *viz.*, (*a*) grand-parents and their ancestors, and (*b*) brothers and sisters and their lineal descendants.

2. If there be only one full brother, he takes the entire inheritance ; when there are several, they divide the inheritance equally among themselves.

(Same under the Sunni Law.)

3. If there be sisters with the brothers, the brothers take two shares each and the sisters one each.

(Same under the Sunni Law.)

4. In default of full brothers and sisters, the succession passes to the consanguine brothers and sisters, and the mode of distribution is the same as in the case of full brothers and sisters.

5. When there are full brothers and sisters co-existing with consanguine brothers or sisters, the latter take nothing.

6. When there is a uterine brother or a uterine sister alone surviving the deceased, he or she receives first the *saham-ul-farz*, *viz.*, one sixth, and the remainder by *return*.

7. If there are two or more uterine brothers or sisters co existing with full brothers and sisters, the former receive one-third, which is divided equally among them *without distinction of sex*, whilst the full brothers and sisters take the remainder in accordance with the general principle.

(Same under the Sunni Law.)

8. When there are uterine brothers and sisters co-existing with one full sister, the former take one-third, and the latter (the full sister) one-half, and the remainder is *returned* to her.

9. When there is only one uterine brother or sister and one full sister, the former takes one-sixth, and the latter the residue partly as her share and partly by *return*.

10. When there are uterine brothers or sisters and two or more full sisters, the former take one-third equally among them, and the latter two-thirds.

11. When there are no full brothers and sisters, then consanguine brothers and sisters take their places.

(Same under the Sunni Law.)

12. The paternal or maternal grandfather, if alone without any co-heir, takes the entire inheritance; so does the grandmother.

(Same under the Sunni Law.)

13. When there are ancestors of the paternal as well as of the maternal line, the former receive two-thirds, to be divided among them in the proportion of two shares to each male and one share to each female; whilst the latter, *i.e.*, the maternal ancestors, take one-third, to be divided equally among them without distinction of sex.

(Under the Sunni Law, the paternal ancestors[1] take the entire inheritance.)

14. The *paternal* grandfather and grandmother share in the succession according to the general principle of two shares for each male and one share for each female.

(Same under the Sunni Law.)

15. The *maternal* grandfather and grandmother share equally (without distinction of sex.)

(Under the Sunni Law, the maternal grandmother takes the entire inheritance.)

16. When there are uterine brothers or sisters co-existing either with a maternal grandfather or grandmother, or with both, then one-third of the estate is divided *equally* among them all.

(Under the Sunni Law, when there is only one uterine brother, he receives one-sixth ; when two or more, one-third; the remainder goes to the maternal grandmother.)

17. When there are paternal and maternal ancestors in conjunction with full brothers and sisters, or the children of such brothers and sisters, or with brothers and sisters of the half blood on the father's side, or their children, then the maternal ancestors take one-third, and the paternal ancestors take the remaining two-thirds with the brothers and sisters or their children (being treated in the distribution as brothers and sisters themselves), in the proportion of two shares for each male and one share for each female.

For example, if the deceased left behind him the mother's mother and the mother's father, also the father's mother and the father's father, besides a brother and sister, in this case one-third would be taken *equally* by the deceased's mother's mother and the mother's father, whilst the remaining two-thirds would be divided among the brother and sister of the deceased and his paternal grandparents, in the proportion of two shares for each male and one for each female, that is, four-eighteenths would be the share of the brother and the grandfather respectively, two-eighteenths of the sister and the grandmother respectively.

---

1 True grandfathers.

18. The ancestors, however remote, inherit with brothers and sisters and their children. But when there are several ancestors, the one nearest to the deceased excludes the more distant.

19. The husband or wife co-existing with brothers and sisters or their children, or with grandparents, always receives his or her *full* share.

20. When there is a full sister and a sister of the half blood on the mother's side, the latter takes one-sixth, and the residue goes to the full sister, partly as her appointed share and partly by *return*.

When there is a half-brother on the father's side (in other words, a consanguine brother) co-existing with a full sister, the latter will exclude the brother from any share in the inheritance. It would not be so, however, if he was a half-brother on the mother's side. In that case he would take his legal share, and the remainder would go to the full sister. The uterine relations have no right in the residue after allotment of shares when they co-exist with relations of the full blood.

When there is a half-sister on the mother's side, and a half-sister on the father's side, the former takes one-sixth and the latter one-half, and the remainder is divided among them in the proportion of one to three.

21. When there is a half-brother by the same mother only and the son of a full brother, the whole of the inheritance goes to the former.

(Under the Sunni Law, the half-brother gets one-sixth, and the remainder goes to the son of the full brother.)

22. The children of brothers and sisters represent their predeceased parents, and each one of them inherits the portion of the person through whom he or she is connected with the deceased, in other words, the part which is assigned to its parent.

(The children of sisters are uterine relations under the Sunni Law, and do not succeed until the agnates are exhausted.)

23. When there is only one child of a brother or a sister, it takes the share of its parent.

24. When there are several children of the brother or the sister, the share allotted to their predeceased parent is divided equally among them, if they be all of the same sex; when they are not all of the same sex, then the males receive double the share of the females.

25. In case there are several children of the uterine brothers or sisters, the share which they take in right of their parents is divided equally among them.

26. The surviving children of a full sister, who is predeceased, receive the moiety of the inheritance in right of their mother "besides what may revert by *return*".

27. The children of a brother take the remainder like their father, after allotment of the fixed shares. The children of two or more predeceased sisters take two-thirds, unless there is a husband or widow, when they take what remains after allotment of the husband's or widow's share.

28. In default of children of full brothers or sisters, the children of half-brothers and sisters on the father's side take their place.

29. The child of an uterine brother or sister takes one-sixth ; while if there be several children, they receive one- third.

30. When there are several children of uterine brothers and sisters as well as of full brothers and sisters and of half-brothers and sisters on the father's side, the latter are excluded entirely, one-third going to the first, and two-thirds to the children of full brothers.

31. If, in the above case, there were a husband or a wife co-existing with the relations mentioned, the husband or the wife would take his or her full share ; the children of uterine brothers and sisters would take one-third of the *original* estate (or if only one child, one-sixth) ; and the remainder would go to the children of full brothers and sisters ; in their default, to the children of consanguine brothers and sisters.

32. The lawyers are not agreed whether, when there are children of uterine brothers and those of a consanguine sister the residue, after allotment of their respective shares, should be divided among them *pro rata*, or should go to the latter entirely.

SECTION V

THE SUCCESSION OF RELATIONS OF THE THIRD CLASS

Consanguineous relations of the third class.

1. This class comprises the paternal and maternal uncles and aunts of the deceased, and their descendants, the nearest in descent always excluding the more remote.

2. The paternal uncle, when alone, takes the entire inheritance. When there are several uncles, they divide the inheritance equally among them. The same rule applies to paternal aunt or aunts.

3. When there are paternal uncles and aunts, they take the inheritance in the usual proportion of two to one.

(Under the Sunni Law, the entire inheritance goes to the paternal uncles to the exclusion of the paternal aunts.)

4. When there are uncles and aunts, some of whom are the deceased father's half-brothers and sisters on the mother's side and some are of the full blood, then the paternal uncles and aunts on the mother's side take one-third among them equally, or if only one, such uncle or aunt takes only one-sixth, whilst those

who are full brothers and sisters of the deceased's father take the remainder, in the proportion of two shares for each male and one share for each female. The consanguine brothers and sisters of the father are excluded by the full brothers and sisters.

(Under the Sunni Law, the uncles who have the same father and mother as the father of the deceased, or who have the same father, that is, the full brothers and consanguine brothers of the deceased's father, exclude all other relations from the succession.)

5. The children of uncles and aunts, paternal or maternal, do not take a share in the inheritance when they co-exist with uncles and aunts, on either side, for in this line also the nearest always exclude the more remote, except in one case, *viz.*, when there is a son of a full paternal uncle with a *consanguine* paternal uncle, the cousin excludes the uncle. This is the only example where the cousin has preference over the uncle; if instead of a consanguine paternal uncle, there were a maternal uncle or a paternal uncle of the half blood on the mother's side, the cousin would be excluded.

6. The maternal uncle takes the entire inheritance when by himself. So also, when there are two or more such uncles or aunts. When the maternal uncles and aunts of the same degree exist together, they share the inheritance equally without distinction of sex.

7. When there are uterine maternal uncles and aunts existing with maternal uncles and aunts of the full blood, the first receive one-third, which is divided among them equally without distinction of sex ; and the maternal uncles and aunts of the full blood receive the remaining two-thirds, to be divided in the proportion of two for each male and one for each female. The consanguine uncles and aunts are excluded by the full uncles and aunts.

8. When there is an uncle or aunt of the maternal line and an uncle or aunt of the paternal line, the first takes one-third and the latter two-thirds. So also when there are several of them.

9. When there are paternal and maternal uncles and aunts of the father co-existing with the paternal and maternal uncles and aunts of the mother, those related through the mother alone, *i.e.*, the uterine relations, receive a third, which is divided equally among them; whilst those related through the father alone, *i.e.*, the consanguine relations, receive two-thirds, one-third of which is divided *equally* among the father's maternal uncles and aunts, and the remaining one-third among his paternal uncles and aunts *unequally*, in the proportion of two shares for each male and one share for each female.

10. In default of the deceased's uncles and aunts of the paternal as well as maternal lines and *their descendants*, the succession passes to the paternal and maternal uncles and aunts of his father and mother and their children; such is the case with each generation, the nearer being preferred to the more remote.

11. Every person, related to the deceased on both sides, *viz.*, the father's and mother's, in any degree of consanguinity, excludes from inheritance a person in the same degree on the father's side only, whether a male or a female, but not a relation on the mother's side only.

Double title to inheritance.

12. With reference to those who have a double title in the inheritance of the deceased, the Shiah Law gives to such heir a share in virtue of each title, unless one title operates to the exclusion of the other, when the heir receives his or her share in virtue of the superior title.

For example, a woman dies leaving behind her a husband who is also her cousin (being the son of her paternal uncle): he will receive a share in the inheritance, in virtue of matrimony, as well as in virtue of the relationship of blood. But if the deceased left behind her a half-brother on the mother's side, who is the son of her paternal uncle, he succeeds as a uterine brother, for in law, an uterine brother excludes the cousin.

The example of an "impeding cause" is furnished by a paternal uncle's son who is also a half-brother as he succeeds by virtue only of his fraternal right.

SECTION VI

RULES RELATING TO THE SUCCESSION OF HUSBANDS AND WIVES

(*Ahkam-ul-Azwaj*)

Husband and wife.

1. As stated before, a husband or widow is never excluded from the succession. The husband receives his fixed share under all circumstances, and so does the widow, and it is only after the allotment of *their* shares, that the partition of the estate can take place among the other heirs.

2. When the marriage is of a *permanent* character, the husband and the wife succeed to each other mutually without any condition to that effect in the contract. But as a section of the Shiahs recognises the validity of *temporary* contracts of marriage, it is necessary to mention that persons so married have no reciprocal right of inheritance, unless there is a condition to that effect expressly entered into at the time of marriage.[1]

3. When the husband has irrevocably divorced his wife,[2] the marital relation between the two is absolutely at an end, and the right of inheritance based on matrimony is extinguished. It is otherwise in the case of a *revocable* or *reversible* divorce when the right subsists so long as the woman is in her '*iddat* or "period of probation". So that if either husband or wife should die during this period, the survivor would be entitled to his or her share in the deceased's inheritance.

4. Where a man suffering from an illness, whether dangerous or otherwise, marries a woman, and dies of that illness,

---

1 But see post.

2 See post.

without "intervenient" recovery or without consummating the marriage, the woman has no right to inherit to the deceased, as in such a case the marriage is inoperative or void.[1]

5. Where non-consummation is due to her death before the man, even if he was ill, or to her own illness at the time of the marriage if the man was in health, the right of succession would be established.

6. If a woman be irreversibly divorced by a husband during an illness from which he does not recover and which eventually causes his death, her right to a share in his inheritance continues for the space of one year, unless she marries another man in the meantime. If the husband died after the lapse of a year or if he recovered during that interval and died either of the same disease or of any other complaint, or if she remarried within the year, she would not succeed. The husband, however, would have no right to inherit from his wife even if she died *within* the year.[2]

(Under the Sunni Law, the right of inheritance continues only until the expiration of the woman's period of probation.)

7. The husband and the wife have a mutual right of inheritance so long as the marriage subsists in fact or constructively in law.

Marriage of minors.

8. Minors contracted in marriage to each other by their fathers or paternal grandfathers have a mutual right of inheritance. But if the contract were entered into by guardians other than the fathers or paternal grand-fathers, then the marriage remains in suspense until assented to or ratified by the parties on attaining majority;[3] and if one of them should die in the interval before the ratification of the contract, *the survivor would have no right of inheritance.*

(The Hanafis differ on the latter point.)

9. If one of the minors alone attained his or her majority and ratified the contract, and the other died before attaining his or her majority, the former would have no right of inheritance. But if the ratifier died, then the part which would fall to the share of the survivor would be reserved for him or her until the attainment of majority, in order to enable the survivor (husband or wife) to exercise the right of option.

10. When there are no children, the husband takes one-half of the deceased wife's inheritance.

11. When there are children, the husband takes a fourth.

(Same under the Sunni Law.)

---

1 Marriage contracted by a person who is ill is dependent upon consummation.

2 A death-bed divorce is pronounced to be improper and reprehensible although valid in law.

3 See post.

12. When there are several widows, they take the fourth or eighth equally among themselves.

13. The husband takes a share in all kinds of property left by his deceased wife, and so does the widow when she has a child "born of her womb", or child's child. But when she has no child, or when a child was born to her, but died before the decease of her husband, then she is entitled to a fourth share in the personal estate only, including *household* effects, trees, buildings, etc.[1] She takes no interest in the landed property. When there are several widows, they take the fourth of the personal estate *equally*. But when the widow has children, she takes an eighth of both personal and real property. If the children, however, be not of her womb, she is *not* entitled to an eight of the immovable estate.[2]

(Under the Sunni Law, the widow, in default of children, takes a fourth of the entire inheritance, both real and personal.)

14. If a woman die leaving her surviving her husband as her sole heir, he takes the entire inheritance, half as his specified share and the remainder by *return*. According to the ancient doctors, the widow, when sole heiress, did not take by *return*; according to them she took her one-fourth, and the residue went to the Imam.[3]

As stated already, according to the modern jurists the widow is entitled to take *by return. This is the rule now in force.*

In early times the Sunnis likewise allowed the residue to go to the husband, but not to the widow. For example, if a woman died leaving her husband as her sole heir, he took the entire inheritance; but if a man died leaving behind his widow as his sole heiress, she took her one-fourth, and the rest escheated to the *Bait-ul-Mal*. The modern jurists,[4] however, are of opinion that as the *Bait-ul-Mal*, which in early times existed for the benefit of the indigent Moslems, and for the promotion of the welfare of the Islamic Commonwealth, is now entirely shorn of that character, being simply the Government exchequer, the doctrine of escheat does not apply to either the case of a husband or a widow. They, accordingly, hold that where an intestate dies leaving no other heirs, excepting a wife or a husband, the entire inheritance goes to him or her. This view has been rightly adopted and upheld by the Indian Law Courts.[5]

---

1 Jam'a-ush-Shittat. See Toonanjan *v.* Mehndee Begum (1861) 3 Agra 13; Asloo *v.* Umdatoonnissa (1873) 20 W R 297; Umardaraz Ali Khan *v.* Wilayat Ali Khan (1896) I L 19 All. 169; Mir Ali Hussain *v.* Sajuda Begum (1897) I L 21 Mad. 27; Aga Mahomed Jaffer Bindanim *v.* Koolsom Beebee (1897) I L 25 Cal. 9; Muzaffar Ali Khan *v.* Parbati (1907) I L 29 All. 640.

2 Abu'l Kasim Ali ibn Abi Ahmed al-Hussaini surnamed, ibn-ul-Huda, commonly known as Shaikh Syed Murtaza, holds a different opinion.

3 As there is no machinery now to take charge of the Imam's share, the ancient doctrine enunciated in the Sharaya-ul-Islam is completely exploded.

4 See the Radd-ul-Muhtar, *in loco.*

5 See the case of Musst. Subhani 1 S D A Reports and the more recent decisions of the Calcutta High Court in the case of Mohammed Arshad Chowdhry *v.* Sajida Banoo (1878) I L 3 Cal. 702 and Bafatun *v.* Bilaiti Khanum (1903) I L 30 Cal. 683.

15. As has already been pointed out, the Shiah Law does not recognise the doctrine of escheat to the *Bait-ul-Mal.* In the *Sharaya-ul-Islam,* it is laid down that, "when the Imam is absent or *ghaib,* the property should be distributed among the poor and the indigent, and should not be given up to any but a *pious* Sultan"[1] for similar distribution.

When the deceased leaves no heir, not even a *zamin-ul-jarirah* (a surety), the whole of the property goes to the Imam, whether he be present or absent, for the relief of the poor and indigent of the deceased's city or village. 'Ali the fourth Caliph (the first Imam of the Shiahs), used to distribute the property among the poor and indigent of the deceased's native town and among the weak and infirm neighbours of the deceased.[2] The Imam being at the present moment absent or *ghaib,* the property would be taken charge of by the *Mujtahid* or the *Hakim* to be distributed among the indigent and helpless neighbours of the deceased belonging to the Shiah sect. Preference should always however, be given to the poor descendants of the Prophet.

As under the Sunni Law, funeral expenses must be first paid out of the assets of a deceased and then his debts. When a person has died involved in debt to the full amount of his property, it is not to be transferred to his heir, but will remain subject to the same conditions as if it still belonged to him. If the debts should not absorb the whole of his estate, so much of it as is required for the payment of his debts remains subject to the same conditions, while the surplus is to be transferred to his heirs.

The principles applicable to this subject under the Hanafi Law apply *mutatis mutandis* to Shiah estates.[3]

Section VII

Causes of Absolute Exclusion from Inheritance

(*Mawanah-ul-Irs*)

Kufr.

Like the Sunnis, the Shias recognise three causes of exclusion from inheritance, *viz.,* (*a*) denial of the Unity of God and the Messengership of the Prophet (*viz., kufr*); (*b*) intentional homicide or murder (*katl*) by the inheritor of the person whose inheritance is in question, (*c*) status of slavery (*rikkiyet*), and (*d*) illegitimacy.

Non-Moslems have no right of inheritance to Moslems.

1. Those who deny the unity of God and the Messengership of the Prophet have no title to the inheritance of a deceased Musulman. So that, if a Shiah Musulman were to die leaving an heir who is a "denier", he is debarred from inheriting, even though he be nearest to the deceased. For example, if a man were to die leaving behind him a son who is a non-Moslem, and

1 Jam'a-ush-Shittat.

2 Irshad-ul-Allamah; Sharaya-ul-Islam.

3 See ante.

a grandson who is a Moslem the son would be excluded from the succession, and the grandson would take the inheritance to the absolute exclusion of his father.

(Same under the Sunni Law.)

If a Moslem were to die leaving heirs who are non-Moslems, the estate of the deceased would go to the Imam.

Abjuration of Islam causes a forfeiture of the right of inheritance. I have already described the change effected in the Musulman Law by Act XXI of 1850, and those remarks apply, *mutatis mutandis*, to the Shiah Law.[1]

Apostacy.

If apostacy occurs after the inheritance has opened and the right of succession has vested in the "apostate", in that case he is not excluded from his share in the inheritance

A Moslem heir is preferred to non-Moslem heirs in the succession to a deceased non-Moslem. So that if a non-Moslem were to die leaving a Moslem and a non-Moslem heir, the Moslem heir though remote in the degree, should succeed in preference to the non-Moslem heir. Were the non-Moslem, however, to leave only non-Moslem heirs, the inheritance would go to them in preference to the Imam. If, however, any one of them should adopt the Islamic faith, the entire inheritance would descend to him to the exclusion of the non-Moslem heirs.

(Under the Sunni Law, a Moslem does not inherit from a non-Moslem, nor does a non-Moslem inherit from a Moslem.)[2]

As under the Sunni Law, when either of the parents is a Moslem, the law presumes the child to be a Moslem (until it is able to make a choice), and the right to its succession is regulated by the laws of Islam. So also should one of the parents of a child, both being non-Moslems, at the time of its birth, accept the Faith of Islam during its infancy, the presumption would be the same, *viz.*, that the child is a Moslem.

Moslems inherit from each other though they may belong to different sects.

(Same under the Sunni Law.)

Apostates; succession to their estate.

As regards the succession to the estate of a *murtadd* or "apostate", the same rule applies, that is, though an "apostate" may not succeed to the inheritance of a Moslem relative, Moslem heirs may succeed to his inheritance.

Among the Shaf'eis, the inheritance of an "apostate" escheats to the *Bait-ul-Mal*, whether he leaves any heir or not.

(Among the Hanafis, in the case of a male "apostate", a distinction is made in this respect having regard to the time when

---

1 See ante.

2 Fatawai 'Alamgiri, Vol. VI, p. 631.

the property was acquired.[1] For example, if the property was acquired before apostacy, it goes to the Moslem heirs; but if it was gained subsequent to the apostacy, then it escheats to the *Bait-ul-Mal.* In the same way, if a portion was acquired before apostacy that portion goes to the Moslem heirs, and the portion acquired afterwards would go to the *Bait-ul-Mal.* This is the view of Abu Hanifa, and the principle laid down by him is followed in most Mahommedan countries. But Abu Yusuf and Mohammed differ from him on this point, and agree with the Shiahs in holding that the entire estate of an "apostate" descends to his Moslem heirs.[2]

(Under the Hanafi Law in the case of a female apostate, her entire property, whether acquired before or after apostacy, goes to her Musulman heirs.[3])

As already stated, apostacy from Islam after devolution of property does not, according to both Hanafis and Shiahs, defeat the right of succession.[4]

(Difference of country involving difference of allegiance is also a bar to succession under the Sunni Law; but this is confined to non-Moslems only. Moslems, among themselves, though owing different allegiance, succeed to each other. The Musulman sovereigns, however, by special treaty regulations, have granted to the subjects of non-Mahommedan States the privilege of taking property by inheritance in Mahommedan countries.)

The Shiahs do not regard difference of nationality to be a bar to succession in any case.

Homicide.

(2) Under the Shiah Law the homicide must be intentional and unjustifiable to be a bar to succession. Unintentional homicide, resulting from inadvertence or accident, does not exclude the person who has committed the act from succession to the person killed. But the absence of intention must be clearly proved.

(Among the Hanafis, homicide, intentional or unintentional, invariably excludes from inheritance. An act, however, committed by an infant or an insane person which causes death, does not exclude such infant or such insane person from succeeding to the estate of the deceased. Or, if a person were to kill another in justifiable war, or when inflicting punishment under the direction of law, such person is not excluded from the inheritance of the killed. According to the Shaf'eis, the person who causes the death of another, under any circumstances whatsoever, is excluded *in toto* from the succession.

---

1 See ante.

2 Compare, Phear, J., in the matter of the application of Zaynab Bibi, High Court, Calcutta, O. S. September 1876, unreported.

3 Sirajia, p. 58; Fatawai 'Alamgiri, Vol. VI, p. 633.

4 See Wajeh-oon-Nissa Khanum *v.* Mirza Husen Ali, 30th Dec. 1806, 1 Sel. R 268.

If a person should slay his father, and the parricide has a child, this child may inherit from the grandfather, for the crime of a father is no bar to the succession of his children; but if the heir of the murderer be a *Kafir*, they are both excluded together, and the inheritance goes to the Imam, unless the "denier" should embrace the Faith, when he would be entitled to the inheritance.

Status of slavery.

(3) The status of slavery is a bar to succession under the Shiah as well as under the Sunni Law. Under the Shiah Law, if a person leave no other heir but a bondsman, his property is to be sold, and the proceeds applied to the emancipation of the slave. The Sunnis do not recognise this principle, but hold that the inheritance escheats to the *Bait-ul-Mal*.

If a person should die leaving one heir free and another a slave, the whole inheritance would go to the one who is free, though he be more remote, to the exclusion of the bondsman though he be nearer to the deceased.

If the bondsman has a child who is free, it would inherit in preference to its parent.

When the deceased has left an heir who happens to be a bondsman, the bondsman is to be purchased out of the estate and then emancipated, whereupon he would become entitled to the residue; and his proprietor may be compelled to dispose of him. Should the property left by the deceased be inadequate for the purchase, some doctors have said that the bondsman must be ransomed to the extent of the property, and left to work out the remainder of his price by emancipatory labour.

If there are two or more heirs, one of whom is a slave at the ancestor's death, but is emancipated before partition, he is entitled to participate in the succession if equal in degree to the others, or to take the whole alone if he is nearer to the deceased.

Illegitimacy.

(4) *Illegitimacy* is a bar to succession under the Shiah Law. But a distinction is drawn between a child of fornication (*walad-uz-zina*) and a child whose parentage has been formally disavowed by the father,[1] *viz.*, "a child of imprecation", *walad-ul-Malainah*.[2] An illegitimate child is regarded as *nullus filius*, as owning no *nasab* to either of its parents, and therefore incapable of inheriting from either. Nor, supposing the child died leaving him surviving his parents or relations connected through them, would they be entitled to his inheritance.[3]

But the *legitimate* offspring and the husband or wife, as the case may be, of an illegitimate person are entitled to inherit from such illegitimate person and from each other *reciprocally*. But where the *walad-uz-zina* leaves no *legitimate* issue or anyone connected by the tie of matrimony, the inheritance goes to the Imam. The law is otherwise as regards a "child of imprecation".

---

1 See the Chapter on Legitimacy.

2 See post.

3 Jam'a-ush-Shittat; Irshad-ul-Allamah; Shara'ya.

Such child owns a *nasab* to its mother and the maternal relations and consequently inherits from them and they, on their side, have the right of inheriting from such child. The disavowing father and those related through him do not inherit from such child, even though subsequently the father may acknowledge the parentage. But if the child is *acknowledged* after a formal disavowal, that is, the renunciation is withdrawn by the father, he would be entitled to succeed to his father's inheritance though not to the paternal relations.[1]

(Under the Sunni Law, a "child of fornication" is placed on the same footing as a "child of imprecation". The *walad-uz-zina* inherits, like the *walad-ul-malainah*, from his or her mother and the mother's relations, and they likewise inherit from him or her.[2])

It must be mentioned, however, that some Shiah doctors are in accord with the Sunnis in holding that a *walad-uz-zina* has a right of succeeding to his mother and the maternal relations. The other doctrine has, however, been adopted and enforced by the Indian Law Courts.[3]

SECTION VIII

RELATIVE EXCLUSION (الحجب) *al-hajab*

RELATIVE exclusion is of two kinds, *partial* or *absolute*, (الحجب عن البعض) or (الحجب عن الاصل)

Absolute Exclusion.

Absolute exclusion: As a general principle the nearer relative always excludes the more remote from succession.

(Same under the Sunni Law in the succession of agnates.)

The direct descendant of the second degree is excluded entirely by the descendant of the first degree, without distinction of sex. For example, the daughter excludes the grandson.

When there are lineal descendants of several degrees, the nearer in the order of descent excludes the more remote.

Direct descendants exclude all other relations excepting the deceased's father and mother, and husband or wife.

Brothers and sisters exclude the nephews and nieces from succession.

The nearer excludes the more remote.

In the collateral line, also, the nearer excludes the more remote. Thus, the collaterals of the second class, *viz.*, brothers and sisters, and their direct descendants exclude collaterals of the third class, *viz.*, paternal and maternal uncles and aunts and their descendants.

---

1 Shara'ya; Jam'a-ush-Shittat.

2 Fatawai 'Alamgiri, Vol. VI, p. 629.

3 See Sahibzadee Begum *v.* Himmat Bahadoor (1869) 12 Sutherland's Weekly Reporter, p. 512.

Full blood relations exclude the consanguine relations, provided they are equal in degree.[1]

(The principles of exclusion under the Sunni Law are analogous to those recognised by the Shiahs.

E. G.—Whoever is related to the deceased through another does not inherit whilst that other is living,[2] except the mother's children, who inherit with her (notwithstanding that they are related through her to the deceased), because she has no title to the whole of the inheritance. Among residuaries, persons nearest in the degree of propinquity entirely exclude the more remote. Sisters are excluded by sons and daughters; grandmothers are excluded by a mother.) .

A sister excludes the children of her deceased sister.

A daughter excludes the children of a deceased daughter.

Sons and daughters of a whole brother exclude half-brothers and sisters.

Full brothers and sisters are excluded by a son, son's son, and a father and grandfather.

Half-brothers and sisters on the father's side are excluded not only by the persons above-mentioned, but also by full brothers and sisters.

Half-brothers and sisters on the mother's side are excluded by a child, the child of a son, the father, and a grandfather.

---

1 "A child excludes all persons who are related to the deceased through his parents, or one of them,—as brothers and sisters and their children, grandfathers and their parents, paternal and maternal uncles and aunts and their children, and none can participate with children in the inheritance, except the immediate parents of the deceased and a husband or wife. Upon failure of parents and children of the deceased, brothers and grandfathers succeed, a brother excluding the child of a brother, and when there are several generations together, in different degrees of descent, the nearer is always preferred to the more remote.

"Brothers and sisters and their children, however remote, exclude all those who are related through the grandfathers—as paternal and maternal uncles and their children—but do not exclude the parents of these grandfathers, for a grandfather, how-high-soever, is always a grandfather, though when there are several generations together, in different degrees of ascent, the lowest in descent, or nearest to the deceased, is always preferred to the more remote.

"Uncles, paternal or maternal, and their children, how-low-soever, exclude the paternal and maternal uncles of the father; and in like manner, the children of the father's paternal or maternal uncles exclude the paternal and maternal uncles of the grandfather. Further, a person who is related to the deceased by the father only is excluded by one who is related to him by both father and mother, provided they are equal in class and degree.

"Lastly, a relation by blood, however remote, excludes an emancipator; and, in like manner, an emancipator, or his representative in the inheritance of the freedman, is preferred to the surety for offences, and the surety for offences is preferred to the Imam."

2 *E.g.*, the son's son does not inherit whilst the son is living.

All grandmothers, whether maternal or paternal, are excluded by the mother.[1]

Ascendants of the first degree exclude ascendants of the second degree and all collaterals.

A blood relation, however remote, entirely excludes a manumittor.

(Under the Sunni Law, a manumittor has precedence over the uterine relations.)

Partial exclusion.

Partial exclusion, or reduction of shares, takes place in three cases:—(*a*) When the children of the deceased reduce the share of the widow or the husband respectively from one-fourth to one-eighth or from one-half to one-fourth;[2] (*b*) when they reduce the share of the deceased's mother from one-third to one-sixth; (*c*) when brothers and sisters reduce the share of the mother from one-third to one-sixth, though they themselves take nothing.

The reduction of the mother's share[3] effected by the presence of brothers and sisters is subject to four conditions:—(*a*) That there should be two or more brothers or a brother and two sisters, or four or more sisters; (*b*) that they should be neither slaves nor non-Moslems, nor have been convicted of murder; if they are slaves or non-Moslems, or have been convicted of murder they would not reduce the mother's share; (*c*) that the father should be existing also; (*d*) that they (the brothers and sisters) should be either of full blood or consanguine.

If a person were to die leaving both parents, and the mother be pregnant at the time, and be subsequently delivered of twin male children, these children would not reduce her share from a third to a sixth.

Presumption of death when a person is missing.

When a person is missing from his home or country, and it is not known whether he is dead or alive, his property cannot be divided among his heirs until his death is fully established, or until such a period shall have elapsed as would remove all probability of his being still alive. His property may then be divided under the decree of the Judge among his heirs in existence at the time of the decree. Under the Shiah Law, the expiration of ten years gives rise to the presumption of death.

SECTION IX

GENERAL RULES OF SUCCESSION

WHILST the effect of disqualification incident on infidelity and the commission of the crime of homicide is confined to the

1 The principal examples of exclusion under the Sunni Law are given in the Fatawai 'Alamgiri, Vol. VI, p. 630.

2 A child, how-low-soever and whether male or female, excludes the parents of the deceased from more than two-sixths of the estate, except in the case where, with one daughter, or two or more daughters, there is only one parent; and reduces the share of the husband or wife.

3 The mother's share is a sixth with full or consanguine brothers and sisters, when they are two or more brothers, or one brother and two sisters not labouring under any bar against succession.

person who is the subject thereof,—so that as regards all other persons its effect is the same as if he were actually dead,—the action of the two principles of exclusion which arise from the existence of particular inheritors preferentially entitled, operates to the exclusion of a wider circle; so that a person excluded by another, may exclude others either entirely, or reduce their shares, which means that a person who is himself incapable of deriving any benefit from his relationship to the deceased is nevertheless the means of partially excluding others.

General rules.

The general rules regulating the succession of heirs may be stated shortly in the following words:—(*a*) The heir most nearly related to the deceased takes in preference to one more remotely connected; (*b*) one related by a double relationship is preferred to one connected by one tie (on the father's side); (*c*) whoever is related to the deceased through any person shall not inherit while that person lives; (*d*) when the relationship is equal, a male gets double the share of a female.

These general rules are recognised with very little variation by the Sunnis. The difference arises from the secondary position they give to the uterine relations.

Doctrine of "increase" not recognised by the Shiahs.

The doctrine of *Aul* or "increase" in force among the Sunnis is considered invalid by the Shiahs. *Increase* is a technical expression used by Sunni lawyers to signify a proportionate increase in the common divisor for the purpose of yielding the requisite number of shares. For example, if a woman leave behind her a husband, two daughters and a mother, their respective shares would be one-fourth, two-thirds, and one-sixth. The common divisor in this case is twelve, which represents the shares into which the estate will have to be divided, three being the husband's share, eight the daughter's, and two the mother's. But three, two, and eight make thirteen. The Sunnis accordingly, in order to give the exact number of shares to each heir, divide the property into thirteen shares.

Among the Shiahs this arbitrary division of the property is not recognised. On the contrary, when they find that the property falls short in distribution of all the appointed shares, the deficiency falls upon the heir or heirs whose share or right is liable to fluctuation or variation.[1] For example, in the above case, among the Shiahs, the mother and husband would get their full shares, without any abatement, and the remainder, *viz.*, seven-twelfths would be given to the daughters in equal proportions.

A child *en ventre sa mere* is entitled to inherit if born alive but if still-born, it has no title to any portion; whereas if born alive, though death should ensue immediately after its birth, its share belongs to its own heirs. If miscarriage is produced by violence, regard is to be had to any movement of the child to see whether it was born dead or alive.

The following synoptical table will illustrate the Shiah Law of Succession :—

1 The Mafatih and the Rouzat-ul-Ahkam, both agree in holding that the deficiency falls on the daughter or daughters or on the persons (as a sister or sisters) related by both parents or by the same father alone, and not on those related on the mother's side.

SYNOPTICAL TABLE OF SHIAH INHERITANCE

- *Nasab* (consanguinity).
  - 1st Class
    - Immediate ascendants, *viz.*, father and mother.
    - Lineal descendants.
  - 2nd Class
    - Ascendants of the 2nd and higher degree, *viz.*, grandparents and ancestors further removed.
    - Brothers and sisters and their descendants.
  - 3rd Class
    - Paternal uncles and aunts, and their children.
    - Maternal uncles and aunts, and their children.
- *Sabab* (special cause).
  - *Zoujiyat* (matrimony)
    - Husband or wife
  - *Wala.*
    - (Emancipation) *Wala-ul'Itk.*
    - (Clientage or suretyship) *Wala-uz-zamin-il-Jarirah.*
    - *Wala-ul-Imamate* (spiritual headship).

CHAPTER VII

THE KHOJAHS AND CUTCHI MEMONS

Borahs.

The Isma'ili sect is divided into two sub-sects both of whom are represented in India.[1] The Borahs of Western India are the representatives of the Western Isma'ilias, "*Isma'ilia-i-Maghrib*", who recognise the succession of the Fatimide Imams and Caliphs of Egypt, and whose religious head has his abode in Yemen with a deputy residing in the Bombay Presidency. Generally speaking they are subject to the Musulman Law.

But as already mentioned,[2] the Bombay High Court has held that the Sunni Borahs of the Dhanduka Taluka in Gujarat and the Molasalam Girasias in the Broach District, both of whom were originally Hindus and were converted to Islam by *Isma'ili* missionaries are, in matters of inheritance and succession, governed by the law of the religion they abandoned centuries ago.

The other division called the Eastern branch owes its origin to Hasan Sabah[3] of Alamut and is represented among the Khojahs of Bombay and the Hunzas of Gilgit, both of whom recognise a descendant of Hasan as their religious head.

The Khojahs.

The history of the Khojah community was involved in some mystery until the year 1866 when owing to certain disputes regarding the relative rights of the head of their church and of the members of the congregation, the matter was brought for settlement before a British Court of Justice. Mr. Justice Arnold in a luminous judgment[4] after referring to various incidents in the history of Islam, thus describes their origin :—

"The next question is, *Who and what are the Khojahs, and what have been their relations with the hereditary Imams of the Isma'ilis, the ancestors of Aga Khan ?*

"From the evidence adduced in this case, the more probable conclusion, I think, is that the Khojahs were originally Hindus of the trading class, inhabiting the villages and towns of Upper Sind. Their language is Sindi or Cutchi—a cognate dialect, and such ancient religious works as they possess are written in the Sindi language and character. Sind, an early Mahommedan conquest, has long had a large Mahommedan population, but a considerable portion both of the retail and wholesale business of the country has always remained in the hands of the Hindus. The position and circumstances of these remote and isolated Hindu traders were manifestly such as to favour their conversion to some form or other of Mahommedanism.

---

1 The spirit of Islam, Ed. 1923, p. 342.

2 See ante, Chap. I, Section II.

3 The founder of the order of "Assassins."

4 The Advocate-General ex relatione, Daya Muhammad *v.* Muhammad Husen Huseni (otherwise called Aga Khan) (1806) 12 Bom. H C R, p. 323.

"That they were so converted by Pir Sadr Din about 400 years ago, is admitted by both the contending parties in the Khojah community. It is also agreed that the tomb of this Pir (or saint) is at Ootch, a town of about 1,800 houses in the Native State of Bahawalpore, on the left bank of the Punjnud—the channel through which the collective waters of the five rivers of the Punjab flow into the Indus—and about 40 miles above its point of junction with the latter river. Here the agreement ends; according to the traditions of the great body of the Khojah community, Pir Sadr Din came from Khorasan and was an Isma'ili Dai, or missionary, sent by Shah Islam, one of the ancestors of Aga Khan, and the form of Mahommedanism which he taught his converts was the Shiah Imami Isma'ili faith.

"The term 'Khojah' means both 'the honourable or worshipfull person' and 'the disciple'. Its full meaning, as applied to the community converted by Pir Sadr Din, may, perhaps, fairly be taken to amount to this, 'the honourable or worshipfull converts'."

Memons.

The Memons, too, were originally Hindus, and admittedly were converted to Islam about three or four hundred years ago. But because these two communities were originally Hindus, they have been held by the British Courts of Justice immutably bound by Hindu customs; in other words though Mahommedans, they are still as regards succession, treated as Hindus. It is necessary, therefore, to refer to the cases bearing on the question.

The first case among the Khojahs in which the point was raised whether they should be governed by Hindu customs or by the laws of their religion arose in Bombay in 1842[1]. Sir Erskine Perry, then Chief Justice of the Supreme Court of Bombay, delivered a learned judgment in which he discussed at great length the force of customs. As the report of that case is not easily available, I set out here a portion of his judgment.

"The Khojahs", said that learned Judge, "are a small caste in Western India, who appear to have originally come from Sind or Cutch, and who, by their own traditions, which are probably correct, were converted from Hinduism about four hundred years ago by a Pir named Sadr Din. Their language is Cutchi; their religion Mahommedan; their dress, appearance, and manners, for the most part, Hindu. These latter facts, however, do not warrant the conclusion being drawn, if such conclusion is necessary for decision of the case (and I think it is not) that the Khojahs were originally Hindu, for such is the influence of Hindu manners and opinions on all castes and colours who came into connection with them, that gradually all assume an unmistakable Hindu tint. Parsis, Moguls, Afghans, Israelites, and Christians, who have been long settled in India,[2] are seen to have exchanged much of their ancient patrimony of ideas for Hindu tones of thought; and, in observing this phenomenon, I have been often led to compare it with one somewhat similar in the

1 Hirbai v. Sonabai (1845) Perry's Oriental Cases, 110.

2 Now Indo-Pakistan.

black soil in the Deccan, which geologists tell us possesses the property of converting all foreign substances brought into contact with it into its own material.

"However this may be, the Khojahs are now settled principally amongst Hindu communities, such as Cutch, Kathiawar, and Bombay, which latter place, probably is their head-quarters. They constitute, at this place, apparently about two thousand souls, and their occupations, for the most part, are confined to the more subordinate departments of trade. Indeed, the caste never seems to have emerged from the obscurity which attends their present history, and the almost total ignorance of letters, of the principles of their religion, and of their own *status*, which they now evince, is probably the same as has always existed among them since they first embraced the precepts of Mohammed.

"Although they call themselves Musulmans, they evidently know but little of their Prophet and of the Koran; and their chief reverence at the present time is reserved for Aga Khan, a Persian nobleman, well-known in contemporaneous Indian history, and whom they believe to be a *descendant of the Pir*, who converted them to Islam. But even to the blood of their saint they adhere by a frail tenure; for it was proved, that when the grandmother of Aga Khan made her appearance in Bombay some years ago, and claimed tithes from the faithful, they repudiated their allegiance, commenced litigation in this Court, and professed to the Kazi of Bombay their intention to incorporate themselves with the general body of Musulmans in the Island. To use the words of one of themselves, they call themselves Shiahs to a Shiah and Sunnis to a Sunni, and they probably neither know nor care anything as to the distinctive doctrines of either of these great divisions of the Musulman world. They have, moreover, no translation of the Koran into their vernacular language, or into Gujarati, their language of business, which is remarkable when we recollect the long succession of pious Musulman kings who reigned in Gujarat, and in the countries in which the Khojahs have been located. Nor have they any scholars or men of learning, among them, as not a Khojah could be quoted who was acquainted with Arabic or Persian, the two great languages of Mahommedan literature and theology; .and the only religious work of which we heard as being current amongst them was one called the *Das Avatar*, in the Sindi character and Cutchi language, of which Narayan, the interpreter, has procured me some translated passages, and which, as professing to give a history of the tenth incarnation in the person of their saint, Sadr Din, appears to be a strong combination of Hindu articles of faith with the tenets of Islam.

"No other fact of any material bearing on the case was proved; but the defendants brought forward evidence to show that Hirbai, the complainant in one case, and her cousin, Gungbae, the complainant in the other, had received jewels from the executrixes of Sajan Mir Ali, which, it was contended, amounted to a recognition and confirmation of the will of the latter, according to the rules of Mahommedan Law. But as I was clearly of opinion on looking at the sex, the tender age, and the helpless condition of these young women, that the simple fact of receiving jewels tendered to them by their elders in the family amounted to no compromise of their just and legal rights, the fact may be passed over without further notice.

"When this case was standing over for judgment, a suit was instituted in relation to the Memon Cutchi caste, in which it was intimated that exactly the same question arose.

"In this case, also, a suit was instituted by Memon Cutchi females, praying for a distribution of the paternal property in accordance with the text in the Koran, and a plea of exactly the same import as in the Khojah case, of a peculiar custom existing among the Memon Cutchis, was filed, upon which *viva voce* evidence was taken before me, by consent, in the last term.

"Amongst the Memon Cutchis, it was also clearly proved that the custom of excluding females from the inheritance prevailed amongst them exactly as it does amongst Hindus. The Memons were originally, and still are, settled in Cutch, from which they have spread themselves into many of the adjoining countries in Western India, and, by their own account, even into Malabar and Bengal. By their traditions they were originally Loannas, a Hindu commercial caste in Cutch; but they are not able, and no records are forthcoming, to indicate the period of their conversion, although there is every reason to believe it must have been some hundreds of years ago. They may be characterized as being more orthodox Mahommedans than the Khojahs, and in being in every way the superiors, so far as wealth, numbers, and learning are concerned. They make the pilgrimage to Mecca, which is unknown amongst the Khojahs; and a branch of the caste, the Hala Memons, who are settled in Kathiawar, are said to observe every portion of the Mahommaden Law, including the injunctions as to the division of an inheritance.

"These facts having been established, the first question which arises is, whether this peculiar custom of succession which has prevailed from time that may be called immemorial amongst these castes, can be sanctioned in a British Court of Justice? And secondly, it has been made matter of grave argument, whether any customs conflicting with the express text of the Koran can be valid amongst a Mahommedan sect. The importance of these questions, both to the castes themselves, from the large pecuniary as well as social interests involved, and as regards other castes and Courts in the interior, from the universality of the principles involved in the argument, has caused me to apply myself to the inquiry with more than usual anxiety and as it is unlikely, from the magnitude of the stakes at issue, that the parties against whom I have formed a conclusion will be satisfied with my decision. I am studious to set out the grounds of it fully, so as to enable a superior Court to judge of its validity."

Then after describing the origin of customs and their force in law and discussing other cognate subjects, the learned Judge proceeded thus :—

"This brings us to the second question in the case; for it has been contended, and indeed the main stress of the argument has rested on this point, that however valid this custom might be in other respects, it can never have validity with respect to the Mahommedans, as it is in conflict with the Divine Law as revealed to them by the Koran; that in this respect it is equivalent to a custom in England which conflicts with a subsequent Act of Parliament : and the passage from *Thibaut* also shews that the Roman Law allowed of no custom if the *lex scripta* had laid down a rule on the subject.

"This view of the question, as bringing the binding effect of Divine Law into discussion, opens up a very interesting field of enquiry, and one on which it becomes difficult to express oneself clearly, if any regard to conciseness is to be maintained. But in a juridical point of view I apprehend there is no difficulty in stating what the sound conclusions are.

"A jurist *qua* jurist has only to deal with human laws : he recognises the existence of Divine Laws, and their validity in *foro conscientioe* with those to whom they are addressed, or who believe in the revelation containing them; but he does not recognise them as enforceable in Courts of Justice any further than the secular power has ordained. Under a Government such as that of England which has established the principle of universal toleration as to religious belief, it is no doubt the duty of a secular Judge to pay the utmost respect to the religious opinions of every suitor who comes before the Court; and his judicial impartiality should be preserved within such inflexible limits, that on every controversy which is capable of arising within the bosom of society, the opinion should be universally diffused that a calm and just decision between the litigant parties would as surely issue from the judgment-seat as if it were occupied by a Judge of their own creed and colour. But the question on every such occasion for the Judge would be, what the law was which had been delivered to him for administration by his Sovereign." And he concluded by holding that in the two cases before him the parties were subject to the customs which prevailed in their families as part of the communities to which they belonged.

Hirbai v. Sonabai.

The case of *Abraham* v. *Abraham*[1] and that of *Jwala Bakhsh* v. *Dharam Sing*,[2] had not been decided then, or possibly the view of the learned Judge might, to some extent, have been modified. It is strange, however, that the conclusion arrived at in *Hirbai* v. *Sonabai* should still be regarded as absolutely binding. But the later decisions, with a natural tendency to *Hinduise* foreign elements, have gone far beyond Sir Erskine Perry's conclusions. It has been held that the Khojahs and Memons, though professedly Mahommedans, should be presumed to be subject to Hindu customs, *unless they prove some other custom;* whereas Perry, C. J., had, in the particular case before him, found in favour of the custom *dehors* the Mahommedan Law.

---

1 9 M I A 199.
2 10 M I A 511.

Hirbai v. Gorbai.

In the case of *Hirbai* v. *Gorbai*[1] it was held that in the absence of satisfactory proof of a custom, differing from the Hindu Law, the Courts of the Presidency will apply to the Khojahs, the Hindu Law of Inheritance and Succession, and that if a custom opposed to Hindu Law be alleged to exist amongst the Khojahs, the burden of proof rests upon the person setting up that custom. But it was added that the Khojahs, having been originally Hindus and converted from the Hindu religion by a *da'i* or missionary of the Imam of the Isma'ilis, to the Mahommedan religion of the Shiah division and Imami Isma'ili sub-division, and being partly regulated by Mahommedan Law, partly by Hindu Law, and partly by custom, occupy a position so peculiar, that the Courts do not apply to them, when seeking to prove a custom of inheritance or succession differing from the Hindu Law, the stringent rule that the custom must be proved to be ancient, invariable and submitted to as legally binding but will act upon satisfactory evidence that it has been the general custom and accepted as such by the great majority of the Khojah community.

In that case it appeared that a Khojah had died intestate and without leaving any issue. He was survived by his mother (a widow), his wife, and a married sister. It was held that, according to the custom of the Khojahs, his mother was entitled to the management of his estate, and therefore to letters of administration in preference to his wife or his sister.

Rahimatbai v. Hirbai.

In *Rahimatbai* v. *Hirbai* the Court went still further and held that in order to prove a custom of inheritance among the Khojah Mahommedans at variance with the rules of Hindu Law, evidence merely of the opinion of the leading members of the caste, is not enough. Instances must be proved in which the alleged custom has been observed and followed.

Ashabai v. Tyeb Haji Rahimtulla. Abdul Cadur Haji Mahomed v. Turner.

In another case,[3] although there was no evidence to show that the Hindu Law or custom was applicable to the particular people or the community among whom the question arose, it was "considered the settled rule in Bombay that in the absence of sufficient evidence of usages to the contrary, the Hindu Law is applicable in matters relating to property, inheritance, and succession among Khojah Mahommedans". Similarly, it was held in the cases of *Ashabai* v. *Tyeb Haji Rahimtulla*[4] and *Abdul Cadur Haji Mahomed* v. *Turner*.[5] In the first-mentioned case, Sargent, C. J., said as follows:—

"The first question of importance which presents itself for

1 (1875) 12 Bom. H C R p. 294.

2 (1877) I L 3 Bom. p. 34.

3 Shivji Hasam *v.* Datu Mavji Khoja (1878) 12 Bom. H C R, p. 281.

4 (1882) I L 9 Bom. 115.

5 (1882) I L 9 Bom. 158.

decision in this case is as to the Law of Inheritance applicable to Cutchi Memons, to which caste the parties interested belong. The ecclesiastical records of this Court show that Khojahs and Cutchi Memons have ever since the decree in the case of the "Khojahs and Memons" before Sir E. Perry in 1847 (*Hirbai* v. *Sonabai*) been regarded in the Supreme Court and subsequently in this Court as Hindus who had been converted to Mahommedanism, whilst retaining their Hindu Law of inheritance; and, so far as Khojahs are concerned, the decision of the Court of Appeal in the case of *Hirbai* v. *Gorbai* must be taken as conclusively deciding that the *onus* of proving a custom of inheritance not in conformity with Hindu Law lies upon those who set it up. The above records are even richer in instances of the application of Hindu Law of Inheritance to the estates of Memons than those of Khojahs, and establish a non-contentious practice extending over many years.

"I think, therefore, that in the absence of any special ground of distinction, and none was suggested, no sufficient reason exists for placing Memons on any different footing from Khojahs as regards the application of the Hindu Law of Inheritance in the absence of proof of any special custom, although undoubtedly it leaves the law, as pointed out by the Chief Justice in the above case (*Hirbai* v. *Gorbai*), in an incomplete state, which can only be satisfactorily dealt with by express legislation." And the division of certain personal effects was made on the authority of the *Mayukha* and treated as *Stridhan*.

In the second case, Mr. Justice Scott expressed himself thus:—

"The parties belong to the caste known as the Cutchi Memons who, like the Khojahs, are Hindus by origin, converted to Mahommedanism some centuries ago. It is a well-known principle of law in India, that, when a Hindu is converted to Christianity or Mahommedanism, the conversion does not, of necessity, involve any change of the rights or relations of the convert in matters with which Christianity or Mahommedanism has no concern such as his rights and interests in, and his powers over, property -*Abraham* v. *Abraham*. As regards the Khojahs, it has been decided by this Court that in questions of inheritance they are governed by Hindu Law in the absence of any proved special custom to the contrary—*Rahmatbai* v. *Hirbai*. But the point is not so clearly settled as regards Cutchi Memons. Sir E. Perry in *Hirbai* v. *Sonabai* treated the two castes on the same footing, and decided that, by their customary law, females were not entitled to a share of their father's property at his death, as they would have been according to Mahommedan Law, but only to maintenance and marriage expenses. This ruling has been followed and strengthened in the case of Khojahs, until now they are completely governed by Hindu Law in matters of inheritance. But in the case of Memons, this Court has decided *In re Haji Ismail Haji Abdula* that the Cutchi Memons are not Hindus within the meaning of section 2 of the Hindu Wills Act (XXI of 1870), and the late Chief Justice then added: 'We know of no difference between Cutchi Memons and any other Mahommedans, except that in one point, connected with succession, it was proved to

Sir E. Perry's satisfaction that they observed a Hindu usage which is not in accordance with Mahommedan Law.' This dictum was not, however, necessary to the decision of the point before the Court; and it has not been followed in subsequent cases. In *Ashabai* v. *Haji Tyeb* the question was raised, and the present Chief Justice distinctly ruled that 'Memons as much as Khojahs, although converts to Mahommedanism, still retain the Hindu Law of Inheritance'."

But Mr. Justice Scott proceeded to point out that in the question before him the Hindu Law was not different from the Mahommedan Law as enunciated "in a Code prepared by a Council of Pundits(!) from the University Mosque of el-Azhar at Cairo."[1]

And now these Khojahs and Memons are so tied down by judicial decisions to Hinduism that, unless they move the Legislature[2] to relieve them from subjection to Hindu rules of inheritance, they must continue to be treated as Hindus rather than Moslems.

In the case of *Mahomed Sidick* v. *Ahmed Abdul Haji Abdul Satoo*,[3] it was also held that Cutchi Memons are governed by the Hindu Law of Inheritance in the absence of proof of special custom.

Cassumbhoy Ahmedbhoy v. Ahmedbhoy Habibbhoy.

The applicability of the Hindu Law in its most archaic form, *viz.*, the *Mitakshara*, was carried to the extremist limit in the case of *Cassumbhoy Ahmedbhoy* v. *Ahmedbhoy Hubibbhoy and another*,[4] in which Jardine, J., held that amongst Khojah Mahommedans a son was entitled to obtain a partition of the ancestral estate in his father's lifetime without his father's consent and that by the law and custom of Khojah Mahommedans there is a distinction between ancestral and self-acquired property in reference to the power of the owner to devise or make a gift thereof similar to that which obtained under the ordinary Hindu Law.

The learned Judge also held that the presumptions of the Hindu Law apply to Khojah Mahommedans, and the burden of proving propositions opposed to that law lies on him who alleges them. And, therefore, in a suit for partition brought by a son against his father, who alleged that the customs and usages of the Khojah community in matters of partition were not identical with the Hindu Law, and did not confer on a son any right to demand in his father's lifetime a partition of the property in the father's hands, whether ancestral or self-acquired, the burden of proving the issues framed upon those allegations lay upon the defendants.

1 I never knew of the existence of Pundits at el-Azhar—Amir Ali.

2 By virtue of the Muslim Personal Law (Shariat) Application Act of 1937, the customary law of succession of Khojahs and Cutchi Memons (except as to agricultural land) stands abolished and they are now subject to the Mahommedan Law.

3 (1885) I L 13 Bom. p. 280.

4 (1885) I L 13 Bom. p. 534

On appeal.

But these wide presumptions were fortunately cut down by the Appellate Court,[1] which held that the rule that Hindu Law as administered in the Bombay Presidency, in the absence of proof of custom to the contrary is the law applicable to Khojah Mahommedans, was not to be understood in its widest sense, *but as confined to simple questions of inheritance and succession.* And the learned Judges declared that the right of a son to partition in the lifetime of his father, more especially where movable property is concerned, is one upon which the greatest doubt and difference of opinion has always prevailed, and consequently there was no presumption in favour of its inclusion in the Hindu Law, which, in the absence of proof of custom to the contrary, is applicable to Khojah Mahommedans, the *onus* lying on the party alleging such a right, in the case of Khojah Mahommedans, to prove it. They also held on the evidence, that it was not established that amongst Khojahs in Bombay there was any recognised right of a son to demand partition in the lifetime of his father, although it was proved to be customary in Kathiawar and Cutch for a father to give a son who wished for it his share of the family property, both ancestral and self-acquired.

And they laid down broadly that where wealth amassed in trade by an individual is said to be ancestral in the hands of that individual, it is not enough to show that he inherited some property; it must be shown that the property inherited contributed in a material degree to the wealth so amassed; a view somewhat different from that expressed by other Courts.

The Madras High Court refused, however, to give effect to the plea of a Hindu custom in a case which arose among the Ravathans of South Malabar, converts like the Memons from Hinduism to Islam. One Sheitha died leaving a widow and several daughters and sons. In a suit by the widow and the daughters, for their shares of his estate under the Mahommedan Law, it was contended by the other members of the family, that, according to a special custom obtaining among the Ravathans of that part of the country adopted from Hindu Law, females were excluded from inheritance by sons and son's sons. In two instances it was proved that women of this class had obtained shares under Mahommedan Law by suits without this plea having been put forward. The District Munsif described these cases as interruptions and found on the evidence that the custom was proved, and this decree was confirmed by the Subordinate Judge. On special appeal, the High Court held that no valid custom was established by the evidence. A custom to be valid must be consciously accepted as having the force of law.[2]

---

1 Mirabivi *v.* Vellayanna (1885) I L 8 Mad. 464.

2 *Ibid.*

[*N.B.*—The above discussion is now merely of historical interest, in view of section 2 of the Muslim Personal Law (Shariat) Application Act of 1937, applicable to both India and Pakistan. A Muslim, whatever his sect or caste, is governed by the Muslim Law of Inheritance. Section 2 of the West Pakistan Muslim Personal Law (Shariat) Application Act, 1964 also is to the same effect and abolishes custom in West Pakistan in matters of succession to agricultural land as well.]

CHAPTER VIII
THE BAIT-UL-MAL

THE term *Bait-ul-Mal*, according to the author of the *Multeka*, is an abbreviation of *Bait-ul-Mal-il-Muslemin*, literally treasury of the Musulmans, or property of the Moslem community and public treasury.

The *Bait-ul-Mal* consists of four departments or divisions *viz.*:—

(1) The chamber of alms, *bait-us-sadakat*.

(2) The chamber of booty, *bait-ul-ghanimet*.

(3) The chamber of the *kharaj*, or the tax levied upon the *Rayahs*.

(4) The chamber of uninherited property.

The revenues of the chamber of alms accrue from:—

(*a*) Landed estates found without a master after a conquest, those taken from the enemy, and those of which the former proprietors remain as tenants.

(*b*) Mines, treasure-troves, etc., etc.

The property of the chamber of the *ghanimet* is composed of:—

(*a*) The fifth part deducted from the spoils of war (Koran, chap. viii, v. 42).

(*b*) The tithes paid by Moslems as masters of the domains granted to the conquerors at the time of the conquest, or left at that period to the old proprietors after their conversion to Islam.

(*c*) The taxes paid by right of *ushr* and *zakat*.

The chamber of the *kharaj* comprises the taxes levied by the State, such as the capitation tax levied on landed property, annual tributes, the indemnities of peace, etc.

The fourth chamber contains the goods left by persons dying without an heir, or by one who has disappeared from the country.

This property corresponds to some extent to that which in European countries accrues to the State by right of escheat, waif, etc. It is necessary, however, to bear in mind that it is generally a sort of deposit in the *Bait-ul-Mal* as unclaimed property, and it can never be reckoned as the legitimate possession of the treasury though in fact, it frequently remains permanently in its trust.

The revenues are employed in the following manner:—

(1) Those of the department of alms, for the exclusive benefit of poor and indigent Moslems, or orphans, widows, and travellers in distress.

For the enfranchisement of slaves, or for other acts of piety. Finally, for the payment of salaries due to the collectors of tithes and other officers.

(2) Those of the department of *ghanimet* according to the disposition of the sovereign, who has the sole right to distribute the same ; but here the Imam is subject to rules which are impossible for him to violate, the first of which is that the booty must be employed in making public improvements and erecting new public buildings.

(3) Those of the department of *kharaj* for the benefit of the Musulman community at large, and in defraying the expenses of the public service, in paying the salaries of Kazis, Muftis, and the pensions of soldiers.

The revenues are also employed in the purchase of arms, horses, and other necessaries of war, as well as in the construction of mosques, bridges, roads, the cleaning of rivers, etc.

(4) Those of the department of unclaimed property, in the relief of those who are sick and poverty-stricken, the burial of the poor, the support of foundlings, in affording succour to the indigent and the helpless ; for the construction of bridges, roads, caravanserais when these have not been provided for by private endowments.

It is clear, therefore, that the British Government in India is not entitled under the Mahommedan Law to the property of the Musulmans dying heirless and intestate in that country. The claims advanced on its behalf are consequently not warranted according either to the Shiah, or to Sunni doctrines. The only ground on which the claim could be based would be that the property would remain in trust in the hands of the officers of Government for the benefit of the poor. But the Musulman Law insist that such property should be applied exclusively to the benefit of the Moslem poor; whereas the claim advanced on behalf of the Government does not entertain this object.

PART II

THE LAW RELATING TO STATUS

CHAPTER I

THE CONFLICT OF LAW

I HAVE thus far treated of the Musulman Law of Inheritance, with special reference to the differences existing between the Shiah and the Sunni schools on that branch of the subject.

The Musulman Law a personal law.

I now proceed to discuss the personal law of the Musulmans properly so called,—the law in fact which regulates the *status* of individuals subject to the Islamic system.

With the exception of certain principles, the operation of which is necessarily confined to the territorial limits of Islam, the Musulman Law generally is a *personal* law, that is, its incidents remain attached to the individual Moslem whatever the domicile, so long as he continues even outwardly faithful to the Islamic faith. "A Musulman", says the *Kifaya*, "is absolutely subject to the laws of Islam, whatever the domicile."[1] This is not the case with born Musulmans alone. As soon as a person belonging to a different persuasion changes his faith for the religion of Mohammed and adheres to the Islamic system, all the civil obligations and duties which the Musulman Law imposes, and the rights and privileges which it gives, become attached to the new proselyte.[2] According to the Mahommedan Law, therefore, a mere change of domicile when unaccompanied by a change of system, effects no alteration in the status or *legal capacity* of Moslems.

Claim to exclusive jurisdiction not peculiar to Islam.

It will be observed that this claim to exclusive jurisdiction is not peculiar to Islam. At least, analogous principles are to be found in several European systems of law. According to the Mahommedan jurists, adherence to Islam implies allegiance to the Islamic Commonwealth, and consequently such allegiance is the test of the civil rights and liabilities of Moslems. Under the Italian and the French Law it is the same—allegiance instead of domicile furnishing the test of civil rights. The difficulties, therefore, which would arise from a conflict between the English and the Musulman Law would not occur in Italy or in France. A Moslem Turk or a Moslem Persian domiciled in Italy, so long as he retained his religion, would be presumed to retain his allegiance to the sovereign of his native country, and his status and the succession to his property would be governed by the laws of his nation. But if he naturalised

1 Kifaya, Vol. II, p. 763.

2 Farooq Leivers *v.* Adelaide Bridget Mary P L D 1958 Lah. 431.

3 See Syed Ali Nawaz Gardezi *v.* Lt. Colonel Muhammad Yusuf P L D 1963 S C 51.

himself in either of these countries, without changing his faith, how would his rights and duties be regulated? Would the abandonment of his allegiance to the sovereign of his native country imply the renunciation of an adhesion to the Islamic system? The Musulman Law gives a categorical negative to the above question, and would insist upon his continuing subject to the jurisdiction of the laws of Islam. The case, however, will be regarded differently by the Italian or French Law, and the Moslem who settled in France or Italy and naturalised himself there would thenceforward be subject to the laws of that country.

The Dar-ul-Islam.

Owing to the state of belligerency which existed originally between the Islamic Commonwealth and the hostile nations of the East and the West, the early Moslem jurists, like the Christian jurists of later times,[1] divided the civilised world into two great parts the *Dar-ul-harb* and the *Dar-ul-Islam,*—the territories of war and the territories of peace. These two divisions, one of which represented the land of infidelity and darkness, the other that of light and faith, were supposed to be always inimically inclined towards each other. But the Mahommedan Law allowed ampler guarantees of personal safety to non-Moslems who entered the territorial limits of Islam for purposes of trade or commerce, than were recognised in Christendom. A non-Moslem entering a Moslem country was regarded as a guest, even if the *aman* or guarantee which he received on the frontier was granted to him by an ordinary villager. He was allowed to remain unmolested in the country for a year. At the end of this period, however, he was bound to leave, or to take up definitively the status of a *zimmi* or tributary, when he became liable to the payment of the usual *kharaj* or taxes, and also became entitled to the privileges which the Musulman Law gave to its own non-Moslem subjects.

In process of time, however, new relations sprang up between Moslem nations and various non-Moslem countries; a state of amity limited either to fixed periods or in permanence was established in such cases, under which by mutual agreement, Moslems and non-Moslems acquired reciprocal rights in the friendly States. These non-Moslem countries received the designation of *Dar-ul-Aman* or "the country of guarantee." The privileges which the Musulman sovereigns, in the plenitude of their pride or power, granted to the subjects of friendly non-Moslem sovereigns were far more valuable than those which the Moslems received in return; the immunities heedlessly bestowed at a time when Moslem power was at its zenith, have, under the name of Capitulations become the cause of infinite trouble in modern times to Moslem States.[2]

Animus revertendi.

A Musulman going to a foreign country was always presumed to have an *animus revertendi.* He could, under no circumstance,

---

1 Grotius and Puffendorf expressly excluded the Musulmans from all community of interest with the Christian nations of Europe; and even later international jurists countenance the views that international law is limited to Christendom—Woolsey, Int. Law, § 5.

2 The Angora Republic has set itself free from the Capitulations.

abandon the domicile of Islam; and if he did so, or acquired a foreign domicile in the *Dar-ul-harb*, he was presumed to have apostatised, and the law considered him civilly dead. This rigorous stricture on the comity of nations was the natural result of the hostilities in which the Moslems became involved with the neighbouring countries after the death of the Prophet. Since, however, the Moslem sovereigns have entered into treaty-stipulations with the Christian Powers of Europe, and Christendom itself, renouncing its former bigotry, has admitted, to some extent at least, the Musulman nations to the common enjoyment of the *jus gentium*, the rigor of the Mahommedan Law has been considerably relaxed. A Musulman, therefore, may now acquire a foreign domicile without ceasing to be a Moslem.

The new conditions of modern political necessities, when millions of Mahommedans are subject to non-Moslem Governments and are protected as *Mustamins*[1] in the enjoyment of their civil rights and privileges, would also materially affect the ancient view of the Musulman Law. Under these new circumstances, a Moslem residing in one particular dependency where the laws of Islam are strictly in force, may remove to another part of the same empire where the Islamic Law would be only partially recognised, and yet acquire there a permanent domicile, without contravening the spirit of the Mahommedan legislation. For example, a Mahommedan born within the territorial limits of British India may acquire a domicile in Great Britain or Ireland without ceasing to be a follower of the Faith, as a change of domicile in this case would not imply or necessarily involve a change of allegiance.

It would seem that the early Musulman jurists had in view cases of this nature when they declared that whilst Moslems could not absolutely forego their original domicile, they could remove from one province to another of the same empire subject to the same sovereign.[2]

Status depends on domicile.

According to the English Law status depends *prima facie* on domicile, subject, of course, to various exceptions and limitations, too numerous to detail. "The law of domicile", says Dicey, "affects, though it does not wholly govern, the rights" which relate to status, marriage, divorce, and movables. The status, therefore, of a Musulman temporarily residing in England would be governed by the provisions of the Mahommedan Law, unless they are in conflict with the English Law or "natural justice". His capacity for the acquisition and exercise of legal rights, and for the performance of legal acts, would depend necessarily on the law of his domicile. British India is, to all intents and purposes, in the eye of the Mahommedan Law, a portion of the *Bilad-ul-Islam*. And 21 Geo. III, c. 71, and

1 The non-Moslem subjects of a Mahommedan Government are called Zimmis. They are liable to the Jazia or capitation tax, unlike the Mustamins, who are either the inhabitants of the dar-ul-aman or mere temporary sojourners in the Bilad-ul-Islam, having entered the Musulman territories under specific guarantee.

2 Tatar-Khaniye; Tableaux Gen. de l'Empire Ottoman, Vol. III, *in loco*.

subsequent statutes of the Indian Legislature having expressly declared that in India the law relating to the Mahommedans shall, in all matters relating to them, be strictly and impartially administered, it may be assumed that, so far as the Indian Musulmans are concerned, the law of their domicile would mean the Musulman Law.[1]

As long as a Musulman retain his original domicile, so long his status and his personal capacity to do certain legal acts remain subject to the Islamic Law. The moment, however, he abandons the domicile of origin, or as soon as he acquires or adopts a new domicile, he ceases to be governed by the law of his nation. For example, an Indian Musulman when he once takes up his abode permanently in England, or shows distinctly by some conduct on his part that his stay in this country is not in the nature of a sojourn, but that he has what is called an *animus manendi*, is subject thenceforward, in all matters relating to succession and personal status, to the English Law. He ceases to be under the jurisdiction of the Musulman Civil Law. The moral and religious portions of the law remain binding upon his conscience, but his subjection to the jurisdiction of the English Law has the effect of withdrawing him from the *regime* of the secular law of his own nation. How far this is in accord with the spirit of the Mahommedan Law will be apparent from what has been stated before. Under the Italian, and probably under the French Law, he would remain subject to the Islamic system, in spite of a change of domicile, so long as he retained his allegiance.[2]

So, also, a Musulman whilst maintaining a constant association with the country of his origin, or being frequently in the habit of going to and fro, may, by establishing a permanent business or trade in England, evince an intention of adopting a domicile different from the domicile of origin and submitting himself to the jurisdiction of the new domicile.

Lex loci rei situs.

As the *lex loci rei situs* governs all questions which relate to immovable property, the succession to the real estate of a Moslem, whether temporarily residing in England or permanently domiciled, would be governed by the law of the place where the property is situated. So also in the case of *wakfs* and *hibas* (endowments and gifts) of real property. Here, again, arises a conflict between the English and the Musulman Law. Under the Musulman Law, as under the Code Civil,[3] a person cannot devise away his entire property to the prejudice of his natural heirs. Under the English Law he can. Consequently, if the property is situated in England, a Moslem, whether temporarily residing in England, or permanently domiciled, can leave his entire real estate by a testamentary disposition, regardless of the claims of his heirs under the Mahommedan Law. If the disposition relates to movable property, it would be governed by the Mahommedan Law, if the testator was not domiciled in England. Would a *wakf*, however,

1 The same is the position in Bharat. Pakistan, however, is being founded on Islamic Ideology is even otherwise a Dar-ul-Islam.

2 The rules of the "Code Napoleon" have been somewhat encroached on by later practice in France, but the new Indian Code is explicit.

3 Art. 913.

of what are called "chattels real" in English Law be governed by the Musulman Law or by the *lex situs*? Probably the latter. In the same way, succession to immovable property situated in England would be regulated according to the English Law, whether the deceased owner was domiciled in England or not. For example, if a Mahommedan died leaving certain real estate in this country,[1] and two sons, the elder of whom was a non-Moslem, such elder son would take the entire inheritance to the exclusion of the younger brother, despite the disqualification attached by the Mahommedan Law based on difference of faith.

Descent of real property.

Under the English Law, real property must go to the "heir." and a man must, in order to be an heir, not only be the eldest, living, legitimate son of his father, but must be born in *lawful* wedlock, "within the state of lawful matrimony" recognised by the Law of England.[2] It will be seen, therefore, that in the succession to real estate situated in England, the descent will be regulated strictly according to the provisions of the English Law, without the least regard to the rules which govern the question of inheritance under the Musulman Law. For example, suppose a Moslem, belonging to the section which recognises the lawfulness of polygamous unions and residing but not domiciled in England, dies leaving two children, the issue of two separate contemporaneous marriages, *viz.*, a daughter born of the first wife, and a son born of the second wife. He leaves also certain immovable property situated in England. The son, no doubt, fulfils the first condition required by the English Law, for the purpose of succeeding to the real estate of his father; that is, he is indisputably "the eldest, living, legitimate son of his father". His status of legitimacy is not affected nor altered by the English Law. It depends on the law of his father's domicile, and as under the Musulman Law the union of his parents was valid and legal, he is under the English Law, also, the legitimate son of his father. But as the English Law does not recognise the legality of contemporaneous unions, he would not be considered as "born in *lawful* wedlock", and therefore not entitled to succeed as "heir" to real property situated in England. Nor would he be entitled to transmit the right to land situated in England to his son or to collateral relations.[3] And yet being legitimate and the *nasab* being established according to the law of the father's domicile, *viz.*, the Musulman Law, he would not be regarded as a "stranger in blood" to his father.[4]

---

1 This was written in England.

2 Birtwhistle *v*. Vardill, (1840) 7 Cl. and Fin. 895.

3 See Re Don's Estate 4 Drew 194; 27 L J (Ch.) 98.

4 See Skottowe *v*. Young L R 11 Eq. p. 474; Re Hurel Angeline *v*. Dick (1932) Ch. 722.

[*N. B.* Descent to an heir at law has been abolished in respect of the estates of persons dying after (1925 15 and 16 Geo. s c 23) subject to an exception in case of persons of unsound mind, alive and of full age on 1st January 1926, and without prejudice to the devolution of any entailed interest. On the death of a person intestate after 1925, his real estate is held upon trust for sale and is distributed in the same manner as personalty modified in relation to deaths after 1952, by the Intestates Estate Act, 1952. Accordingly on an intestasy the right of a person legitimated by extraneous law for share will, it appears, be determined by the law applicable to the personalty.]

It will be seen, therefore, that there is little or no doubt as regards the position of a Moslem domiciled in England; nor is there any question regarding the law which is applicable to the succession or disposition of real estate in England. The position, however, of a Musulman temporarily resident in England requires consideration, as his status and personal capacity are entirely governed by his personal law or the law of his domicile.

Marriage between Moslems and non-Moslem females.

The Mahommedan Law recognises the lawfulness of unions between Moslems and non-Moslem females belonging to Scriptural creeds. As regards intermarriage with females practising idolatry, there is a prohibition[1] which is explained by the degrading heathenism that prevailed among the Arabs before the promulgation of Islam. The disastrous influence exercised by their peculiar idolatry over the people of the Peninsula led Mohammed to interdict unions between the Moslems and the pagan females with the sole object of keeping idolatry out of the Islamic body politic. In making this prohibition he was actuated by the same motives which led the more ancient Semitic legislator to prohibit all unions between the Israelites and the Phoenicians. An union between a Moslem female and a non-Moslem, on the other hand, was forbidden for political reasons, as a non-Moslem in those days was an alien and generally an enemy, and consequently the marriage of a Moslemah with a non-Moslem meant the adoption by her of a hostile domicile and complete expatriation from her domicile of origin—a result strongly disapproved of and reprehended by archaic communities.

But it is a mistake to suppose that under the Musulman Law, a Moslem may *only* marry a woman belonging to the revealed faiths by which are meant Islam, Christianity and Judaism.[2] Marriages are allowed between Moslems and the *Ahl-ul-Hawa* (freethinkers), the Sabaeans, Zoroastrians, as well as the Jews and Christians. A Moslem may, therefore, lawfully intermarry with a woman belonging to the Brahmo sect. Nor does there seem to be any reason why a marriage with a Hindu woman whose idolatry is merely nominal and who really believes in God should be unlawful. The Mogul Emperors of India frequently inter-married with Rajput (Hindu) ladies and the issue of such unions were regarded as legitimate and often succeeded to the imperial throne.[3] What the Mahommedan Law requires is that any such union should not lead to the introduction of idolatry in a Mahommedan household.

Lex loci contractus.

A marriage between a Moslem and a non-Moslemah celebrated in a foreign country is valid under the Mahommedan Law, if it is performed in accordance with the requirements of the *lex loci contractus* or the rites of the communion to which the wife belongs.

1 See Holy Quran II: 228.

2 See Holy Quran V: 5 (Matrimonial relations with Ahl-i-Kitab expressly allowed).

3 See Religion of Islam, page 614, which is of the view that Budhists, Parsis, Hindus etc. are the Ahl-i-Kitab with whom matrimonial connection is permissable.

This principle of the Mahommedan Law coincides with the English Law. According to the English Law the *capacity* to contract a marriage is judged by the respective *lex domicilii* of the parties, but the form of the contract, generally speaking, is governed by the place where the contract is entered into.

Locus reget actum.

"Just considerations", says Phillimore, "of the immense importance attaching to the validity of that contract which is the foundation of the State and the nursery of the Commonwealth, have induced all civilised nations to recognise universally the principle "*locus reget actum.*" In other words, whilst the capacity of persons contracting a *de facto* marriage depends on the law of their respective domicile, the law of the place of celebration is binding as to the outward form.

Brooks v. Brooks.

In the case of *Brooks* v. *Brooks*[1] Lord Campbell laid down the law on the subject of a marriage celebrated in a foreign country in the following terms:—

"There can be no doubt of the general rule, that 'a foreign marriage, valid according to the law of a country where it is celebrated is good everywhere'. But while the forms of entering into the contract of marriage are to be regulated by the *lex loci contractus*, the law of the country in which it is celebrated, the essentials of the contract depend upon the *lex domicilii*, the law of the country in which the parties are domiciled at the time of the marriage, and in which the matrimonial residence is contemplated. Although the forms of celebrating the foreign marriage may be different from those required by the law of the country of domicile, the marriage may be good everywhere. But if the contract of marriage is such, in essentials, as to be contrary to the law of the country of domicile, and it is declared void by that law, it is to be regarded as void in the country of domicile, though not contrary to the law of the country in which it was celebrated."

And he added in another part of his judgment that "it is quite obvious that no civilised State can allow its domiciled subjects or citizens, by making a temporary visit to a foreign country to enter into a contract to be performed in the place of domicile, if the contract is forbidden by the law of the place of domicile as contrary to religion or morality, or to any of its fundamental institutions".

Herbert v. Herbert.

In the case of *Herbert* v. *Herbert*,[2] Sir William Scott

1 (1861) 9 H L C 193 see p. 207; (Marriage with the deceased wife's sister in Denmark).

Re. De. Wilton (1900) 2 Ch. 481 (Marriage with niece in Germany).

Re. Paine (1940) Ch. 46 (Marriage with deceased sisters's husband in Germany).

Chetti *v.* Chetti (1909) P. 67. An English woman domiciled in England married a Hindu, temporarily resident in England, and on her petition for judicial separation the husband was not allowed to deny the validity of the marriage on the ground of religious capacity, he being a Hindu domiciled in India at the time of the petition. See also Macdogall *v.* Chitnuvis (1937) S C 390 ; Re Paine (1940) 1 Ch. 46 ; Kenward *v.* Kenward (1951) P. 1242 ; (1950) All E R 297.

2 2 Hagg. Consist p. 271.

pronounced emphatically in favour of the principle that "every marriage is to be universally recognised, which is valid according to the law of the country in which it was had, whatever that law might be."[1]

Following the principle laid down in *Brooks* v. *Brooks*, the Calcutta High Court has held that the Courts in India will not disallow a Roman Catholic of Indian domicile who has obtained the necessary dispensations from marrying his deceased wife's sister who by the law of her own church, may be incapable of contracting the marriage, as the husband's capacity rendered the marriage valid in law.[2]

Similarly, under the Mahommedan Law, the legal capacity to enter into the marital state is governed by the Islamic rules, but the form of the ceremony is regulated by local customs and rites. For example, the Mahommedan Law recognises the validity of a marriage between a male and a female who are *sui juris* and with reference to whose union there is no legal impediment, regardless of the particular form or mode in which such marriage is celebrated. A Mahommedan may marry a Hebrew or a Christian female, and such marriage may validly be celebrated either according to the rites or communion to which the wife belongs, or as a civil act before the officer of the State regularly authorised to perform the ceremony or register its *factum*. So long as the marriage is performed in accordance with the law of the place where it is solemnised, and there is no incapacity in the parties to intermarry, the law holds the union lawful.[3]

Under 6 & 7 Will. IV, c. 85, and 19 & 20 Vic., c. 119, when the parties do not belong to the Church of England they may be married by one of their ministers duly authorised therefor. Under the same Statutes when the parties do not wish to have the aid of any religious rite, or when either of them happens to be a non-Christian, they may intermarry by a civil contract registered in the presence of a duly authorised officer.

All such marriages are valid under the English Law, and would be valid under the Mahommedan Law, both civil and religious.

According to the English Law the domicile of the husband is the domicile of marriage. But the mere fact of a woman marrying a foreigner does not lead necessarily to the abandonment of her own domicile and the adoption of that of her hubsand. It depends entirely on the intention of the parties ; in other words, if there are circumstances tending to show that the woman before her marriage never intended to abandon her

1 See also Kent *v.* Burges (1840) 11 Sim. 361; s c 5 Jur. 166 and Lacon *v.* Higgins (1822) 3 Stark 178; Lavtour *v.* Teesdale (1816) 8 Taunt. 830. In re Knoz (1899) 23 L R Ir. 542. Marshall *v.* Marshall and St. Clair (1908) Times 10th March; Re Green Noyes *v.* Pitkin (1909) 25 T L R 222; Salveson (or Von Lorang) *v.* Austrian Property Administrator (1927) A C 641 (H L); Kenward *v.* Kenward (1950) 2 All E R 297. As regards a marriage in England between foreigners see Simonim (f. c.) Mallac *v.* Mallac (1860) 2 Sw. & Tr. 67; s c 29 L J Mat. 97.

2 H A Lucas *v.* Theodoras Lucas (1904) I L 32 Cal. 187; see also In re Bozzelli's Settlement; Husey-Hunt *v.* Bozzelli (1902) 1 Ch. 751; Suldhana *v.* Suldhana I L R 54 Bom. 288.

3 Halsbury Laws of England, III edition, Vol. VII, para. 165; Syed Ali Nawaz Gardezi *v.* Lt.-Col. Muhammad Yusuf P L D 1963 S C 51.

domicile of origin, or the man led her to believe that she should retain her own domicile and remain always subject to her own laws, or that he himself would settle in her country, the mere retenion by the husband of his domicile or his return thereto with or without her, would not affect her *status* or any rights created under or in connection with the contract of marriage.

Colliss v. Hector.

This principle was enunciated with great force in the case of *Colliss* v. *Hector*.[1] In that case a Turkish subject named Rassam intermarried in England with a lady who was born in India of English parents and had come over to England with the intention of permanently settling here. When Rassam made proposals of marriage to Mrs. Rassam, she objected to entertain them on the ground that she did not wish to spend her life at Mosul. To get over the objection, Rassam promised to reside permanently in England, and stated that he would simply go over to Mosul to realise his property there, and would then come back and settle in England for the remainder of his life. Upon the faith of that promise Mrs. Rassam became his wife. The marriage took place in a church in London, according to the rites of the Church of England.

Previous to the marriage an indenture of settlement was prepared and executed by both husband and wife, by which the former settled certain properties possessed by him on certain trusts in favour of his wife and of her children by a former marriage and of that marriage. Some time after the marriage Mr. and Mrs. Rassam went to Mosul, where they lived together for three years, and had one issue, a daughter. Mrs. Rassam returned to England and Rassam died shortly after when Mrs. Rassam was informed that before his death he had divorced her, in accordance with the Turkish Laws which rendered void the previous settlement. Mrs. Rassam had no notice of the proceeding taken by Rassam to obtain the divorce. Upon a bill by the children of Mrs. Rassam against the trustees of the settlement the Court (Hall, V. C.) held as follows :—

"As to the merits of the case, after the most careful investigation of the facts and circumstances on the part of the trustees, and their evident anxiety to leave nothing uncommunicated to the Court which could in any way tend to establish rights founded upon the invalidity of the settlement, I have not any doubt which would justify me in not dealing with the case upon the footing that the settlement is a perfectly valid one, and must have effect given to it. The answer of the trustees states, that, according to Turkish Law, something has taken place in Turkey which has done away with the settlement ; but I hold that this was, and remains, and must be construed as an English settlement. It has been said that when the parties married they anticipated going to reside in Turkey, but the evidence establishes that they must have contemplated living in England. What Rassam, in his own mind, contemplated I will not say ; but I am satisfied that he represented to Mrs. Rassam that he meant to leave Turkey and come to reside and be domiciled in England. The evidence of Mrs. Rassam, and of independent witnesses who had conversations with Rassam, proves that he made representations to

1 L R 19 Eq. 334.

Mrs. Rassam that he would reside in this country; and that she accepted his offer of marriage upon the faith of his doing so. There is nothing in the evidence or in the letters which she wrote to induce me to think that Mrs. Rassam's evidence is not trustworthy. The settlement, therefore, being an English contract, must be expounded according to English Law, and the rights of the parties claiming under it must be recognised and dealt with according to the same law. Assuming that, by the proceedings which took place in Turkey, the marriage was, by the Law of Turkey rendered null and void, and the contract and settlement became of no effect in Turkey, I must hold that the Turkish Court could not make void an English settlement in the absence of parties taking benefits under it, and, therefore, that the proceedings which took place in the absence of the plaintiffs and Mrs. Rassam are not, in this Court, worthy of any attention. But I am by no means satisfied that the proceedings in Turkey were either proper, or that they were before a Court having jurisdiction in the matter. The opinions which have been obtained in reference to Turkish Law are not worthy of consideration, for they are not based upon the English contract, but set forth hypothetical case. The trustees do not state that they took the opinion of English counsel upon the validity of the settlement, having regard to what took place in Turkey, and I hold that I ought not to deal with the case in any way upon the view that the validity of the settlement and the interests of the parties to the contract have been brought into question, but that, on the contrary, I must deal with the settlement as being a complete and perfect one, and as giving rights to parties who now claim under it."

The principle that the domicile of the husband is the domicile of marriage obtains only in a qualified shape in the Mahommedan Law, and extends to the right of the husband (unless there is any stipulation to the contrary) to insist upon the wife residing with him wherever he resides, or going with him wherever he goes. Beyond that the law does not go. If a Turkish subject were to intermarry with a Moslem female domiciled in Persia or British India, her domicile would not be changed by the marriage, nor would any contract entered into between them be governed by Turkish Law. In the same way, if a Moslem domiciled in one country were to marry a *kitabia viz*., a woman belonging to Judaism or Christianity whose domicile was in another country, she would not, by the mere fact of her marriage, lose her nationality or become subject to the Laws of Islam to which her husband may be subject. Nor would she become subject to his personal laws, apart from any territorial law, even if they were natives of the same country. *In both cases her inheritance would devolve according to her law and his according to his law.* For example, being a non-Moslem she would not inherit from him, and if he be a *Sunni* he would not inherit from her. If he be a *Shiah* he may inherit from her, if her law permitted such a devolution.

Polygamy.

There is great difference of opinion among the followers of Islam regarding the extent to which polygamy or, more properly speaking, polygyny is tolerated or allowed in the Islamic system. An influential and growing section holds that the conditions under which it was permitted are so difficult of compliance that they amount to a virtual prohibition and that the circumstances which rendered it permissible in primitive times having either passed away or not existing in modern times, the practice of polygamy is in contravention of the law.[1]

In Turkey, the Hanafi church may be regarded as the State Church; in Persia, Shiahism is the State religion. But in both countries, other creeds and faiths are treated with far greater toleration than in most European States. In British India there exists a variety of creeds and sects, each of which receives due recognition ; and their followers are subject to their own laws. Among the Hindus, a man is governed by the law of the *Mitakshara* or the *Dayabhaga* according to the *mantras* he pronounces, the rites he practises. Among the Mahommedans, he is a Shaf'ei, Hanafi, Usuli, Akhbari, or Mu'tazili, according to his own religious convictions ; and he is subject exclusively to the law of the school or sect to which he belongs. The differences in ritual and doctrine, though often small, divide one sect or school completely from the other. Between the Mu'tazili and the Usuli (Shiah)—in some respects analogous schools—and the older sects there is a wide gulf ; and at no point is the divergence greater than on the subject of marital relationship. The Mu'tazili is a strict monogamist ; according to him the law forbids a second union during the subsistence of a prior contract. In other words, a Mu'tazili marriage fulfils in every respect the requirement of an essentially monogamous marriage as "a voluntary union for life of one man and one woman to the exclusion of all others".

Brinkley v. Attorney-General.

In the case of *Brinkley* v. *The Attorney-General*[2] Sir James Hannen pointed out that what was meant by the phrase "Christian marriage, 'marriage in Christendom' and other equivalent phrases was simply a marriage of the exclusive kind mentioned." In the case referred to, an Englishman of the name of Brinkley temporarily residing in Japan, had married a Japanese woman *according to the laws in force in that country.* Upon a petition under the Legitimacy Declaration Act of 1858 (21 & 22 Vic., c. 93) presented by Brinkley for a declaration of the validity of his marriage celebrated in Japan, the President held as follows:—

"This case is clear from the difficulties which arose in the Mormon case and in the South African case,[3] because in both those instances it was an attempt to establish as a valid marriage one which admitted of the possibility of a marriage with another person than the first spouse. The principle which has been laid down by those cases is that a marriage which is not that of one

1 See Appendix.

2 (1890) 15 P D 76.

3 Bethell *v.* Hillyard post.

man and one woman, to the exclusion of all others, though it may pass by the name of a marriage, is not the status which the English Law contemplates when dealing with the subject of marriage. But in this case it has been proved in the most satisfactory manner by the deposition of a Japanese Professor of Law, that by the Law of Japan marriage does involve this, and that one man unites himself to one woman to the exclusion of all others. Therefore, though throughout the judgments that have been given on this subject, the phrase 'Christian marriage', 'marriage in Christendom', or some equivalent phrase, has been used, that has only been for convenience to express the idea. But the idea which was to be expressed was this—that the only marriage recognised in Christian countries and in Christendom is the marriage of the exclusive kind I have mentioned, and here it was proved that in Japan marriage is of that character. We all know that Japan has long taken its place among civilized nations, whose forms and laws and ceremonies are not to be treated as on the same footing with those of the Baralong tribe of South Africa. I have, therefore, come clearly to the conclusion that these cases do not apply, and that, as has been candidly admitted by Mr. James, a valid marriage can take place in Japan between an Englishman and a Japanese woman *according to the Law of Japan*, which would be a valid marriage in this country and everywhere else."

This case establishes the principle that a marriage, though celebrated in a foreign country according to foreign rites, will be recognised in England as a "Christian marriage", if the union is essentially of a monogamous character.

[But the English Law does not recognise any *form* of marriage which admits of a polygamous relationship. For example, if a person domiciled in England were to marry a woman belonging to a community or people who admit and practise polygamy, *by their form of marriage*, and there is no evidence to show that the husband intended to take her as his sole wife, the English Law will not recognise the relationship so as to confer on the wife the right of succession to her husband's property in England.]

Bethell v. Hildyard.

In the case of *Bethell* v. *Hildyard*,[1] the main question was whether a marriage contracted by an Englishman who had not abandoned his English domicile, with a South African woman of the Baralong tribe *according to their rites*, was valid under English Law, so as to give to the issue of the union a right to real property in England. The facts of the case are material for the due apprehension of the judgment, and I therefore set them out in detail.

One Christopher Bethell who was born in England had gone to the Cape of Good Hope in 1878. In 1884 he went through a form of marriage with a girl of a South African tribe according to their rites. Shortly after his marriage he was killed in a

[1] 38 Ch. D 220.

skirmish. At the time of his death the girl whom he had married was bearing him a child born a few days afterwards. Under the will of his father, Christopher Bethell was entitled to a life-interest in certain real estate situated in England, with remainder to his children. In their default the property was to go to his eldest brother William Bethell.

Some time after the death of Christopher Bethell, William Bethell took out an originating summons in this matter, in which the trustees (the defendants) of the testator's will were respondents, asking for a declaration that he was entitled to the property on the ground that Christopher Bethell had died without leaving any issue, and on the 12th of June, 1885, an inquiry was directed whether Cheristopher Bethell was ever married, and if so, when, and to whom, and whether he left any, and what children him surviving, and when they were respectively born. The Chief Clerk in answer to that enquiry made a certificate that Christopher Bethell in October, 1883, being then a resident at Mafeking in Bechuanaland, went through the form of marriage *according to the custom of the Baralong tribe with Teepoo*, a Baralong girl, and had issue by her, a female child, who was born ten days after his death ; that the Baralongs had not any religion nor any religious customs, and that polygamy was allowed in that tribe ; that at the time of the marriage the domicile of Christopher Bethell was English, and that, save as aforesaid, he never was married. Upon that certificate the matter came on to be heard for further consideration. It was then considered desirable that the infant child mentioned in the certificate should be represented ; and in order that that might be done, the official solicitor was appointed her guardian, and notice of the Order of 12th of June, 1885 was served upon him in accordance with the Rules of the Supreme Court, 1883, Order XVI, Rule 44, and Order IX, Rule 4. The infant had appeared by her guardian, who had taken out a summons asking that the certificate might be varied by finding that Christopher Bethell was married to Teepoo, and left one child him surviving, a girl, born on the 9th of August, 1884. The evidence which had been taken by commission in Bechuanaland, was to the effect that Christopher Bethell *refused to be married in a church*, though, as stated, there was a Wesleyan church at Mafeking, and a minister ; and also an English church and a clergyman at Kimberley, a large English town not very far off ; that he did not intend to remain in Bechuanaland, but to return to England ; *that in none of his communications to his relations or friends had he intimated or led them to infer that he was married*, and that he called Teepoo "that girl of mine". It was also in evidence that in the Baralong tribe "each male is allowed one great wife and several concubines, who have almost the same status in the home as the great or principal wife." And Montsioa, the chief of the tribe, said :— "There are those who have two, three or four wives, but the first is the principal wife." The marriage-ceremony was thus described :—"When the consent of the parents has been obtained, the bridegroom slaughters a sheep, a buck, an ox, or cow. The head of the animal is taken to the bride's parents, as also is the hide, which is cleaned and softened. They are then considered married, and after the birth of the first child the number of the cattle previously agreed upon is handed over to the wife's parents." Christopher Bethell in October, 1883, went through that ceremony with Teepoo, a niece of Montsioa, who in his depositions, gave this account of what took place :—

"Behtell came to me and said he wanted a woman to take and marry according to the Baralong custom. I said to him, 'You know we Baralongs have a different custom from other tribes. The custom is that during courtship and after marriage, the man when he kills an ox, sends the head to the girl's mother, so if you do this the mother will know your intentions are honourable.' Bethell said:—'Well I want to marry a Baralong, and I will do so according to Baralong custom'; also 'I am a Baralong', I said, 'Will you not marry her in church?' He said, 'No : I am a Baralong ; did you marry your wife in church, did you not also marry in the custom I am about to do'? I said, 'Very well, if that is the case you can take one', and of a truth he did take one. He slaughtered an ox, and sent the head to Makwas, the mother of Teepoo. I then went to Makwas, and said, 'Give your daughter to Bethell ; you see he really means it. See, he has sent you the head.' She did, and he married exactly in accordance with our customs. There is no other ceremony except taking the girl. The paying of the cattle is no part of the ceremony of marriage, and may be done years after the consummation of the marriage. Bethell took the girl to his house. Bethell gave a span of oxen and trekgoad and plough to Teepoo's father, saying, 'Plough Makwas' garden with this.' It is one of our customs for the son-in-law to plough the mother-in-law's garden, or have it ploughed. I know that Bethell really married Teepoo, and that she was his wife and not his paramour."

On the 3rd December 1883, Christopher Bethell wrote and signed the following document making some provision for Teepoo and any child she might have by him :—

"I hereby desire that in the event of my decease here in Mafeking, and in the absence of any other will, Mr. E. Rowland shall take over all my arms, ammunition, cannon wagon, oxen, horses, and any other property that may be in my possession, and shall sell them to the best advantage. I desire that he will realize all the property as quickly as possible, and shall apply the proceeds to the payment of Taylor and Leark's (Klerksdup) account, the balance he shall have and hold as a bequest and present from me. And he shall inform my relatives in England of my decease and of manner in which my property is disposed of. Always providing that before disposing of any of the proceeds of the sale of my property he shall purchase or put aside (30) thirty heifers, (10) ten three years old (10) ten two years old, (10) ten one year old, and shall use them for the benefit of Teepoo in the following manner—he shall keep the heifers for the space of one year from my decease, and in case she (Teepoo) has no child by me he shall hand the said (30) thirty heifers over to her for her own property and use. If she has a child after my decease, he shall keep the heifers and their produce until the said child be arrived at the age of (21) twenty-one years, selling any full-grown oxen and old cows, and investing the proceeds in land or English Government securities. The milk of the cattle and the use of the young oxen to be applied to the use of Teepoo and the child. At the end of eight years the child is to be removed from its mother and placed at a school for the time of ten years, either in the colony or in England, and if a boy shall be taught a profession, or enter Her Majesty's service as soldier. In order to repay the work of Mr. Rowland in the case of a child being born I desire that he shall take (20) twenty per cent. of all sales of oxen and cows as before mentioned. In case Teepoo re-marries or has any more children, or conducts herself in an improper way, she shall be debarred from any participation in heifers and shall give up the guardianship of the child at once to E. Rowland and shall receive ten yearly heifers only as a dowry. But in case she have no child by me at the expiration of the year, she will be at liberty to do so as she likes, and will receive the (30) thirty heifers as before mentioned. And Ragnassie, her father, shall receive eight young heifers as dowry and thereby relinquishes by Bechuana law all command over Teepoo and the child."

Mr. Justice Stirling's judgment is as follows :—

"The question thus raised is whether a marriage valid according to English Law took place between Christopher Bethell and Teepoo, and it has been very fully and ably argued by counsel on behalf both of the infant and of William Bethell. The facts which gave rise to it, so far as the same appear by the evidence are shortly these : Christopher Bethell, who left England in 1878, was, shortly after his arrival in South Africa, appointed British Resident with Montsioa, the chief of the Baralongs, a barbarous or semi-barbarous tribe who inhabit a portion of Bechuanaland beyond the limits of the British dominion. That appointment was afterwards cancelled, but he continued to reside among the Baralongs and became a store-keeper at Mafeking within their territory. Upon the breaking out of the disturbances in Bechuanaland he joined the Bechuana mounted police, a corps in the employment of the British Government, and he met with his death in an encounter between that force and the Boers. At the time of his death a commission appointing him to a command in the corps had been made out, and was on its way to him, but he did not actually receive it.

" As was found by the Chief Clerk, polygamy prevails among the Baralongs. According to one witness ' Each male is allowed one great wife and several concubines, who have almost the same status in the home as the great or principal wife'. And the chief of the tribe said : ' There are those who have two, three or four wives, but the first is the principal wife'.

" Christopher Bethell in October 1883, went through that ceremony with Teepoo, a niece of Montsioa, who gave an account of what took place."

Then after referring to the will of Christopher Bethell the learned Judge proceeded :—

" Christopher Bethell kept up communication with various

members of his family down to shortly before his death. He from time to time expressed his intention to return to England; and that portion of the Chief Clerk's certificate which finds that his domicile was English has not been excepted to. He never mentioned the marriage to any of his relatives; and there is no evidence that he ever introduced Teepoo, or spoke of her to any European, as his wife. One of the witnesses stated that he always called her 'that girl of mine'. Although it was not formally in evidence, it was stated at the Bar, and the statement was accepted by counsel on behalf of the infant, that the contents of the testator's will[1] were communicated to Christopher Bethell shortly after his father's death in 1879; and that the income of the property, amounting to about £600 a year, was regularly remitted to him down to the time of his death.

"I have now to inquire what is the law applicable to the case. In *Warrender* v. *Warrender*, Lord Brougham, said: 'A marriage, good by the laws of one country, is held good in all others where the question of its validity may arise. For the question always must be: Did the parties intend to contract marriage? And if they did that which in the place they were in is deemed a marriage, they cannot reasonably, or sensibly, or safely, be considered otherwise than as intending a marriage contract.' This is the general rule of law and is relied on by the counsel for the infant. His Lordship, however, afterwards qualifies his statement of the rule as follows: 'The rule extends, I apprehend, no further than to the ascertaining of the validity of the contract, and the meaning of the parties, that is, the existence of the contract and its construction. If indeed there go two things under one and the same in different countries—if that which is called marriage is of a different nature in each there may be some room for holding that we are to consider the thing to which the parties have bound themselves, according to its legal acceptance in the country where the obligation was contracted. But marriage is one and the same thing substantially all the Christian world over. Our whole law of marriage assumes this; and it is important to observe, that we regard it as a wholly different thing, a different *status* from Turkish or other marriages among infidel nations, because we clearly never should recognise the plurality of wives, and consequent validity of second marriages, standing the first, which second marriages the laws of those countries authorize and validate . . . . Indeed if we are to regard the nature of the contract in this respect as defined by the *lex loci*, it is difficult to see why we may not import from Turkey into England a marriage of such a nature as that it is capable of being followed by and subsisting with another, polygamy being there of the essence of the contract'. That statement of the law was acted upon by Lord Penzance in the case of *Hyde* v. *Hyde and Woodmansee*, in dealing with the case of a Mormon marriage celebrated at Salt Lake City. He there says:[2] 'The Matrimonial Law of this country is adapted to the Christian marriage, and it is wholly inapplicable to polygamy' and, 'I

1 Meaning Christopher Bethell's father's will.

2 1 L R P & D 130 (1866).

conceive that marriage as understood in Christendom, may for this purpose be defined as the voluntary union for life of one man and one woman, to the exclusion of all others.'

" I conceive that, having regard to these authorities, I am bound to hold that a union formed between a man and a woman in a foreign country, although it may there bear the name of a marriage, and the parties to it may there be designated husband and wife, is not a valid marriage according to the law of England, *unless it be formed on the same basis as marriages throughout Christendom* and be in its essence ' the voluntary union for life of one man and one woman to the exclusion of all others.' Now, it is plain that Christopher Bethell intended that Teepoo should have a status different from and higher than that of a mere concubine. Indeed the attempt to form such a connection with any woman of the tribe, and still more with one nearly related to its chief, would probably have been attended with unpleasant, not to say dangerous consequence. The evidence clearly proves *Christopher Bethell* intended that the relationship between himself and *Teepoo* should at least be that of husband and wife in the sense in which those terms are used among the *Baralongs*. That relationship, however, is essentially different from that which bears the same name in Christendom, for the *Baralong* husband is at liberty to take more than one wife ; and it must therefore be determined whether the union between Christopher Bethell and Teepoo was a marriage in the Christian or merely in the Baralong sense. In my opinion, the latter alternative is the conclusion to be arrived at upon the evidence before me. *To begin with, the cohabitation between Christopher Bethell and Teepoo lasted for only a few months. During that time both resided in the Baralong country. Christopher Bethell, although he kept up communication with his relatives at home, never mentioned his marriage to them. He never introduced Teepoo or spoke of her to any European as his wife. In short, there is an entire absence of that reputation of marriage (in the Christian sense) which has in many cases afforded weighty evidence of the actual existence of such a union.*[1] Next it is to be observed that Christopher Bethell positively and emphatically refused to marry Teepoo in church, and that not on the ground that there was any difficulty in finding a place of religious worship where the marriage ceremony might have been performed, but upon the allegation, which he repeated more than once, that he was a Baralong, and wished to be married according to Baralong customs. He thus desired to be regarded as being, for the purpose of the relationship he was about to form, a member of the tribe. I think that the proper inference is that he meant to enter into no higher or other union than that which between members of the tribe was regarded as a marriage. This conclusion appears to me to be strongly confirmed by the document of the 3rd December of 1883. It can scarcely be supposed that if Christopher Bethell regarded his union with Teepoo as a marriage, in the sense in which it is understood among Englishmen, and the child, referred to in that document, as legitimate, he would have made such provisions as are therein contained for the maintenance, education, and advancement in life of the child. He was in receipt of an

1 "The italics are mine to show that the gist of the judgment lies here"—Amir Ali.

income of £600 a year from an estate in Yorkshire ; and he knew of the provisions of his father's will, under which a legitimate child of his would succeed to the property ; yet he directed that his child by Teepoo should be maintained and educated up to the age of twenty-one on the proceeds of thirty heifers to be purchased out of the proceeds of a sale of his property at Mafeking, to be effected by his friend Mr. Rowland, who was a resident among the Baralongs. It is true that he speaks of the ' re-marriage ' of Teepoo and makes provision for the ' dowry ' to be received by her, and by her father ; but in my opinion he used those terms in the sense in which they were understood among the Baralongs, and his instructions were directed simply to ensure the fulfilment of obligation which he conceived to be cast upon him by their laws or customs. Finally, *Teepoo* herself has given us testimony in this case. No doubt the evidence was completed before her child was made a party to the cause, but I should willingly have listened to any application on the infant's behalf for leave to adduce further evidence. No such application has been made ; and there is nothing to show that Teepoo regarded herself as entering into any other union than such as prevails among the tribe to which she belongs, or that she would have been, or would have considered herself to be, aggrieved if Christopher Bethell had availed himself of the Baralong custom and introduced a second or third wife into his household. I am, therefore, of opinion that the union between Christopher Bethell and Teepoo was a marriage in the Baralong sense only, and was not a valid marriage according to the law of England. In the view which I have taken it is unnecessary for me to express an opinion on many of the numerous points relating to the law of marriage which were discussed before me, but I ought, perhaps, to refer to two cases which were cited in support of the contention on behalf of the infant, *viz.*, *Johnson* v. *Johnson's Administrator* and *Connolly* v. *Woolrich.* Those decisions are not of course, binding upon me, but they are entitled to most respectful consideration, and, in the absence of direct English authority might have exercised a weighty influence upon my decision. The former of those cases was decided in 1860, before *Hyde* v. *Hyde and Woodmansee*, and in the latter judgment was given on the 9th of July 1867, but *Hyde* v. *Hyde and Woodmansee*, which was decided on the 20th of March, 1866, was not referred to. I am not sure that the learned Judges who decided those cases took the same view of the law as is expressed by Lord Penzance, by which I consider myself to be bound ; but in both cases the facts were very different from those in the present case ; and circumstances were proved which might, in my judgment, well lead to the conclusion, consistently with the doctrine laid down in *Hyde* v. *Hyde and Woodmansee*, that the marriages there under consideration were valid according to the Law of England."

It will be seen that in the case under reference Bethell refused to marry the girl according to his own rites ; that he never designated her as his wife ; never introduced her as such to any of his English friends ; and never communicated that fact of his marriage to his relations or friends in England. There was neither such performance as would give to the union the status of a valid marriage under the English Law, nor recognition on the part of the man that the woman was his wife in the sense in which it is understood in European countries. The conclusion was therefore irresistible that he had only taken the woman as a wife in the Baralong sense.

Hyde v. Hyde and Woodmansee.

In *Hyde* v. *Hyde and Woodmansee*, the marriage was between two Mormons in the Mormon country according to Mormon rites.

After the marriage the husband went to the Sandwich Isles, and there abandoned Mormonism. He was thereupon excommunicated by his former sect, and his wife was declared free to marry again which she did according to Mormon rites. Upon a petition by the husband for a dissolution of marriage on the ground of adultery, Lord Penzance held as follows :—

" The petitioner in this case claims a dissolution of his marriage on the ground of the adultery of his wife. The alleged marriage was contracted at Utah, in the territories of the United Sates of America, and the petitioner and the respondent both professed the faith of the Mormons at the time. The petitioner has since quitted Utah, and abandoned the faith, but the respondent has not. After the petitioner had left Utah, the respondent was divorced from him, apparently in accordance with the law obtaining among the Mormons, and has since taken another husband. This is the adultery complained of. Before the petitioner could obtain the relief he seeks, some matters would have to be made clear and others explained. The marriage, as it is called, would have to be established as binding by the *lex loci*, the divorce would have to be determined void, and the petitioner's conduct in wilfully separating himself from his wife would have to be accounted for. But I expressed at the hearing a strong doubt whether the union of a man and woman as practised and adopted among the Mormons was really a marriage in the sense understood in this, the Matrimonial Court of England, and whether persons so united could be considered ' husband ' and ' wife ' in the sense in which these words must be interpreted in the Divorce Act. Further reflection has confirmed this doubt, and has satisfied me that this Court cannot properly exercise any jurisdiction over such unions.

" Marriage has been well said to be something more than a contract, either religious or civil—to be an institution. It creates mutual rights and obligations, as all contracts do, but beyond that it confers a status. The position or status of ' husband ' and ' wife ' is a recognised one throughout Christendom ; the laws of all Christian nations throw about that status a variety of legal incidents during the lives of the parties, and induce definite rights upon their offspring. What, then, is the nature of this institution as understood in Christendom? Its incidents vary in different countries, but what are its essential elements and invariable features? If it be of common acceptance and existence, it must need (however varied in different countries in its minor incidents) have some pervading identity and universal basis. I conceived that marriage, as understood in Christendom, may for this purpose be defined as the voluntary union for life of one man and one woman to the exclusion of all others."

Then after referring to some inconveniences, more ingenious than real, which might follow in England from the recognition of polygamous unions contracted in foreign countries, the learned Judge proceeded as follows :—

" In conformity with these views the Court must reject the prayer of this petition, but I may take the occasion of here observing that this decision is confined to that object. This Court does not profess to decide upon the rights of succession or legitimacy which it might be proper to accord to the issue of the polygamous unions, nor upon the rights or obligations in relation to third persons which people living under the sanction of such unions may have created for themselves. All that is intended to be here decided is that as between each other they are not entitled to the remedies, the adjudication, or the relief of the Matrimonial Law of England."

The Supreme Court of the United States.

The view of the Supreme Court of the United States is more in conformity with the requirements of the *jus gentium* and the dictates of natural justice than the enunciations of the English Law Courts. The United States Supreme Court has held that when a man belonging to a polygamous community but unmarried at the time, contracts according to the rites of his people and in his own country, a marriage with a woman belonging to the same community who also is unmarried at that time, the marriage is, and ought to be, held valid by the *jus gentium*.[1]

But when a marriage is contracted by an Englishman or any other person subject to monogamous rules with a woman belonging to a polygamous community according to the English form or any other form recognised among monogamous communities, such marriage would, upon the principle laid down in *Brinkley* v. *The Attorney-General*, be recognised as a marriage in the English sense. Similarly, if a man belonging to a polygamous community were to marry an English woman or any other woman belonging to a monogamous community, according to the English form or any other monogamous form, it would be recognised as a marriage in the English sense.

[Suppose a person belonging to a polygamous community but subject to the laws of England marries according to rites recognised by the English Law, a Christian woman domiciled in England or any other woman belonging to a monogamous body of people such as the M'utazalite sect of Musulmans, can he enter into a bigamous relationship with any other woman ? I submit not, and I think the fact of his belonging to a polygamous community would make little difference in his liability to a prosecution for bigamy under the English Law. If I am right in this view, it would probably make no difference whether the man is domiciled in England or in a dependency of England where polygamy is recognised. For it seems to me that by

1 See Bishop, Husband and Wife, *in loco*.

entering into a marriage-relationship with a woman belonging to a monogamous community according to monogamous rites, he takes upon himself all the obligations springing from a monogamous relationship.][1]

Accordingly, it would seem advisable for a woman belonging to a monogamous community entering into a marriage with a man belonging to a polygamous community in India[2] where polygamy is not unlawful, to marry according to rites exclusively in force among monogamous communities, or before the Registrar, and, at the same time to obtain from the man a declaration to the effect that the union is absolutely monogamous, and that he would never have, at any time, and under any pretext, the right of contracting another lawful union during the subsistence of the first. No such declaration would probably be needed in the case of a marriage celebrated in England according to any form authorised by English Law.

Among Musulmans, even of the polygamous sect, it is usual nowadays to insert in the contract of marriage a clause to the effect that should the husband marry another wife, the first marriage would become *ipso facto* void, and the wife would become entitled to recover her dower as upon divorce.

In Persia, Turkey, and other Mahommedan countries generally, the State Regulations insist upon the registration of marriage as well as of divorces in the books of the Kazis. In Bengal there is an optional law for the registration of marriages and divorces. The Koran lays down certain rules for effectuating a dissolution of the marriage-contract, but does not provide for the enforcement of those rules. Accordingly, among many Islamist communities whilst a marriage may be contracted without the assistance of the expounder of the law, its dissolution cannot be effected without the sanction of the Judge or *Hakim-ush-shar'a*. There seems no reason why the Indian Legislature should not frame rules, in the interests of public morality, to require all sections of Musulmans to obtain the *imprimatur* of a Mahommedan Judge to the effectuation of a divorce.[3]

Marriage of a Moslem with a non-Moslem female.

When a man, although not a Christian, marries in England a Christian woman according to Christian rites, all the rights and obligations springing from the marriage relationship will be governed by the English Law.[4] But a purely Jewish marriage, contracted according to Jewish rites, will be governed by the laws of the Jews.[5]

1 *See* Risk *v.* Risk (1950) 2 All E R 973. In this case, Bernard, J. refused to make a declaration of nullity in case of an English woman domiciled in England who went through a marriage ceremony in Egypt according to Muslim Law.

2 Now Indo-Pakistan.

3 See Muslim Family Laws Ordinance, 1961.

4 Jones, falsely called Rabinson *v.* Rabinson, 2 Phillimore's Rep. 285.

5 Lindo *v.* Belisario 1 Hegg. 216; Goldsmid *v.* Bromer, 1 Hegg. 324. In both these cases though the parties were Jews and the marriage was performed according to Jewish rites, the English Consistory Court entertained the suits.

In *Goldsmid* v. *Bromer*, which was a suit of jactitation of marriage, instituted on behalf of Miss Goldsmid against Bromer, both parties being of the Jewish religion, on suggestion that the asserted marriage was not valid, by reason of non-conformity of the ceremony to the Jewish Law, Sir William Scott commenced his judgment with the following remarks:—

"The parties are both Jews, and both appeal to the jewish Law, by which this question must be decided, for on the mere fact there is no question. The Jews, though British subjects, have the enjoyment of their own law in religious ceremonies; and the Marriage Act acknowledges this privilege, by excepting them out of its provisions: to deny them the benefit of their own law, upon such subjects would be to deny to a distinct body of people the full benefit of the toleration to which they have long been held to be entitled."

In re Ullee, the Nawab Nazim of Bengal's infants.

Would the same principle apply to Mahommedans residing in England? Considering that the Mahommedan Marriage Law does not require any religious ceremony, the question has little or no practical importance. Marriage among Islamists is essentially a civil contract, and may be solemnised before a civil officer duly authorised therefor, and in the presence of witnesses. Among the Sunnis, proposal on one side and assent on the other recorded in the presence of witnesses is sufficient; among the Shiahs, the presence of witnesses even is not necessary. It is purely a *per verba de praesenti* contract. Suppose, however, a marriage is contracted between two Musulmans residing in England belonging to the polygamous section, or between such a Musulman residing here and an English woman, according to the forms and rites generally practised among his sect, what would be the consequences of such an union? *In re Ullee, the Nawab Nazim of Bengal's infants*,[1] it appeared that the father of the infants was the late Syed Munsoor Ullee, Nawab Nazim of Bengal. The Nawab, in 1870, came to England for the purpose of prosecuting certain claims against the British Government. On the 15th May 1870, whilst in London, Nawab Munsoor Ullee who, it appeared in the course of the proceedings, belonged to that section of the Mahommedans which recognises polygamy, and who had at the time several wives living in India, went through the ceremony of marriage with an Englishwoman, according to the forms and rites in vogue among his community. In 1875 the Nawab Nazim and the lady made a declaration before the then Lord Mayor of London in avowal of the said marriage and aknowledging the children thereof as being the Nawab Nazim's children, and the Nawab Nazim acknowledged them among his heirs according to the Mahommedan Law. In or about the year 1880 the Nawab Nazim went through a similar ceremony of marriage with another Englishwoman, and the first lady thereupon declined to live with him. The children remained in the Nawab Nazim's house, and in November 1880 were sent by him to India without the consent of their mother.

It appeared that S. Ullee, and N. Ullee, the two boys, had been afterwards sent to England and were residing with one

1 53 L T Rep. N S 711.

Mr. Mowbray Walker at Forest Hill. The two girls had remained in India in the harem of the Nawab Bahadoor of Moorshidabad, the eldest son of the Nawab Nazim, and their half-brother. The Nawab died in 1884.

Upon an application by the first English wife for the custody of her children, her contention being that they were illegitimate, Mr. Justice Chitty delivered the following judgment:—

"This case presents several peculiarities, including the admission of the applicant as to the invalidity of her marriage; such admission, however, is made with the view of establishing the illegitimacy of her children. The marriage was undoubtedly invalid according to the English Law. The Nawab was already married, and had already at least one wife in his own country, when the ceremony of marriage according to Mahommedan rites was performed with the applicant in this country. The marriage was a Mahommedan and by consequence a polygamous marriage,[1] and not intended to be monogamous. Even if the ceremony were according to the Mahommedan Law a marriage binding on the husband, yet still, according to the English Law, it was not a marriage binding on any spouse of English domicile, the reason, being that it was not intended to be a marriage. That was so decided in the case of *Hyde* v. *Hyde*,[2] where Lord Penzance held that the English Courts could not take judicial cognisance of a Mormon marriage. The ceremony there was celebrated by Brigham Young at Salt Lake City, and, as stated in the report, recognised as a valid marriage in the United States because both parties were single at the time of the marriage. Lord Penzance declined to adjudicate upon or give relief in respect of such a marriage, on the ground that marriage as understood in Christendom was the voluntary union for life of one man and one woman to the exclusion of all other connubial unions. Lord Penzance, however, observed (p. 138) that while thus treating the so-called marriage he was not professing to decide upon any rights of succession or legitimacy which it might be proper to accord to the issue of polygamous unions. He, therefore, left the question of the status according to English Law of such issue open and untouched. The same question I also am able to set aside as immaterial for the present decision, with the observation that, had I had to determine it I should have required fuller arguments upon it than I have had addressed to me on the present occasion. Upon the facts of the case it is apparent that the infants were treated as the children of the Nawab—as to the two eldest (being girls born before 1875) by the joint statutory declaration of the parents made before the Lord Mayor in 1875, and as to all four by the award of the British Government in 1880 and the will of the Nawab in 1884. That the Mahommedan Law allows recognition to establish legitimacy is clear from the authorities referred to by Mr. Macnaghten in his argument. To what extent the English Law would in that respect yield to the Mahommedan Law is, as already stated, an open question. The legitimisation

1 The learned Judge has fallen here into an error, resulting from want of acquaintance of the Musulman law. He was not aware that large numbers of Mahommedans are, by their view of the law, as monogamous as Christians.

2 L Rep., 1 P & D 130.

of children by subsequent marriage, as allowed by the Law of Scotland and many European communities, is for purposes of International Law recognised in this country, and has been recently extended in the Appeal Court so as to entitle a child born before wedlock of parents domiciled in Holland to share as next-of-kin under the Statute of Distribution in the personal estate of a sister born of the same parents after wedlock. I am by no means satisfied that, according to the principles of International Law as now understood, I ought to hold the infants now in question to be for the purpose of the application illegitimate, but it is immaterial to give any decision on that point. I will, however, in favour of the mother's contention, assume that the children are illegitimate, and thereby reduce the issue to the question as to the position which, according to English Law, a mother occupies in respect of children who are not legitimate." The learned Judge after mentioning that under the English Law the mother is not their guardian, and after discussing at great length the law relating to the right of the mother to the custody of her illegitimate children, held that in the case under reference she was not entitled to the right she claimed.

It will be seen that in this case the marriage was not in accordance with the form recognised in England; it was performed according to rites generally observed by the polygamous section of Mahommedans. The Nawab himself had several wives before he contracted this union, and entered into a similar relationship shortly after. As in the case of *Bethell* v. *Hildyard* already referred to, there could be no question under the circumstances that the marriage was not one which the English Law could recognise as a lawful marriage so far as the status of the wife was concerned.[1]

But there can also be no doubt that though such a marriage may not, for certain purposes, be recognised as a valid marriage under the English Law, the issue would be regarded as legitimate.

A Moslem marriage is a civil act.

Suppose a marriage is contracted by a Musulman in a foreign country according to foreign rites, would it be necessary, in case of the return of the husband to his native land, to go through any other ceremony to validate the previous marriage? The French Courts have answered this question in the negative, and their decisions are in conformity with the principles of the Mahommedan Law. *A Moslem marriage is a purely civil act. Its validity depends on the legal capacity of the parties to enter into a binding contract. Proposal and acceptance are the sole essential ingredients which constitute a valid Mahommedan marriage.*[2] If the man is "adult" and "discreet" that is, if he is over fifteen years of age, and is capable of understanding the nature and legal consequences of his acts—in fine, if he is not a *sarir* (minor) or a *safih* (*non compos mentis*); if the woman also is adult and

---

1 "To fail to recognize a marriage which was valid by a man's lex domicili (which is generally accepted as governing his status) seems the height of absurdity. Moreover, it is clear that Peuzance (in Hyde *v.* Hyde (1866) L R 1 P & D 130) had himself intended no such result"—Bromley on Family Law, p. 5.

2. *See* the Chapter on Marriage.

discreet, and they both contract themselves in marriage, it is valid in law, either with or without evidence. So that an union contracted in a foreign country, before a civil officer expressly authorised to register marriages, is sufficient to constitute a valid marriage, and no fresh ceremony is needed on the return of the husband to his native country.[1]

The child of a Moslem father follows his status.

According to the Mahommedan Law, when one of the parents is a Moslem, the child born of a mixed union shall be presumed to be a Moslem.[2] Under the English Law, a legitimate child is presumed to belong to the communion of the father and follows his domicile. As the Islamic system recognises the lawfullness of unions contracted between Moslems and non-Moslem females, no conflict is possible between the English and the Musulman Law respecting the religious belief of a child born of a mixed union. For, if a Musulman were to marry a Christian woman in England according to Christian rites such marriage would be validly contracted both under the English as well as the Mahommedan Law, and the child of such union would belong to the creed of the father. If, before entering into a contract of marriage, the parties should enter into a specific agreement with regard to the rearing of the children, such agreement would be valid under the Mahommedan Law, even though it may be stipulated that some of the children should be brought up as non-Moslems. But such children will be "excluded" from the inheritance of their Moslem father, by the operation of the disqualifying provisions of the Musulman Law, unless the father were domiciled in England, or the estate were real and situated in England. But the father may, though domiciled in the *Bilad-ul-Islam,* by a testamentary disposition, leave to such children and the wife not more than one-third of his entire property.

Effect of a change of domicile.

If a Moslem belonging to the polygamous section, who acquires a foreign domicile in a country where polygamy is prohibited, has at the time two wives co-existing, the mere fact of a change of domicile will not annul or render void the second union, but neither the husband nor such wife will have any enforceable rights against each other. But though she may not be entitled to sue him for maintenance or restitution of conjugal rights, there is no rule of law to show that she would be precluded from sharing in his inheritance upon his decease. The right of succession possessed by her came into existence on her marriage—a marriage validly contracted and never set aside; and she would therefore, be entitled to take a share in her husband's estate (*miras*), despite the fact that the law of the present domicile did not recognise her original status.

If a Musulman temporarily residing in England does an act, which, though valid under the English Law, is invalid under the Islamic Law, what would be its effect upon his return to his

1 See the precedents in Sautayra; all the schools are in accord on this point. See the Jam'a-ush-Shittat.

2 *See* Hedaya, p. 64; Baillie, Vol. II, p. 265. But such a presumption may be rebutted by general conduct and surrounding circumstances as held in Bhaiya Sher Bahadur *v.* Bhaiya Ganga Bakhsh Singh I L R 36 All. 101.

native land? For example, suppose a Moslem were to marry an idolatrous woman in England—such a marriage would be valid under the English Law, but invalid under the Mahommedan Code. What would be the effect of such an union on the return of the husband to the territorial limits of Islam? As the prohibition against Moslems intermarrying with idolatrous females was founded on special reasons which were the outcome of the times, probably the union would be recognised as lawful.[1]

Can a Moslem belonging to the polygamous section of Mahommedans contract a second marriage contemporaneously with another previously contracted, under any form recognised by English Law whilst temporarily residing in England? I submit not, and I should think that in doing so, he becomes liable to a criminal indictment for bigamy.

Nor can a Moslem belonging to the polygamous section once domiciled in England exercise the power on a temporary return to the *Bilad-ul-Islam*. This has been expressly h ld by the French Courts in Algeria, and it is not unlikely that the same view would be taken by the English Courts.[2]

The majority of the schools give to the parties to a marriage-contract, subject to certain special conditions, the power of dissolving the matrimonial tie by their own consent or free will. According to them, no proceeding in a Court of Justice is necessary for the dissolution of the contract.[3] Would a Musulman belonging to those schools residing in England but domiciled in an Islamic country, have the power of dissolving the status of marriage, without the intervention of the English Divorce Court? The general course of English decisions points by analogy to the conclusion that he *cannot* do so for any purposes of English Law; that is, the English Law will neither recognise nor give effect to such dissolution of the marriage-tie.

Wilson v. Wilson.

As a general rule, jurisdiction in matters of divorce depends on the domicile of the husband at the time of the institution of the proceedings. In *Wilson* v. *Wilson*,[4] Lord Penzance said: "It is the strong inclination of my own opinion that the only fair and satisfactory rule to adopt on this matter of jurisdiction is to insist upon the parties in all cases referring their matrimonial differences to the Courts of the country in which they are domiciled. Different communities have different views and laws respecting matrimonial obligations, and a different estimate of the causes which should justify divorce. It is both just and reasonable, therefore, that the differences of married people should be adjusted in accordance with the laws of the community to which they belong, and dealt with by the tribunals which alone can administer those laws."

Niboyet v. Niboyet.

The same view of the law was enunciated by Lord

1 Comp. Dicey on Domicile.
2 *See* Baindail *v.* Baindail (1946) 1 All E R 342 C A; Sirinivasan *v.* Sirinivasan (1945) 2 All E R 21.
3 See the Chapter on Divorce, post.
4 (1872) L R 2 P & D 435.

Justice Brett in *Niboyet* v. *Niboyet*,[1] who stated that "the domicile of the wife, so long as she is a wife, is the domicile which the husband selects for himself", and that "the only Court which, on principle, ought to entertain the question of altering the relation in any respect between parties admitted to be married or the status of either of such parties arising from their being married, on account of some act which by law is treated as a matrimonial offence, is a Court of the country in which they are domiciled at the time of the institution of the suit."

Hyde v. Hyde.

In the case of a marriage, essentially monogamous in its nature and fulfilling the exact conditions laid down by the learned Judge in the case of *Hyde* v. *Hyde*,[2] that is "a voluntary union for life of one man and one woman to the exclusion of all others", there seems to be no principle of law which would lead the English Divorce Court to decline entertaining a suit for the dissolution of the matrimonial status upon grounds recognised by that Court. An analytical consideration of the judgment in *Hyde* v. *Hyde* would point to the conclusion that Lord Penzance in refusing to grant the relief prayed for in that case, did not expressly or even by implication decide that the English Divorce Court would not entertain a suit for the dissolution of a *monogamous* marriage *contracted* in England by a person *domiciled* in England belonging to a persuasion other than the Christian.

Goldsmid v. Bromer.

On the contrary, all the cases, especially that of *Goldsmid* v. *Bromer*, show that it would grant relief in such cases.

When a Moslem, belonging to the section which recognises the power of divorce in the parties, is only temporarily residing in England, how would the power be regulated? Supposing the Moslem husband wanted to dissolve the marriage-tie on the ground of incompatibility of temper on the part of the wife, or supposing a wife wanted a divorce for ill-usage, would the parties be entitled to dissolve the status by mutual consent, or would they be required to have a formal decree to that effect? If the marriage was contracted in England, the English Courts would recognise no divorce granted under the jurisdiction of a purely Musulman Court, unless such divorce was for a ground "recognised as such in this country, and the process of the foreign country was not resorted to for the collusive purpose of calling in the aid of its tribunals."[3] But if the marriage was contracted abroad, and

1 (1878) 4 P D 1, 13. The correctness of the ruling of the majority of the Court in Naboyet *v.* Naboyet and Sottomayor *v.* De Barras, has been doubted by some of the leading English Jurists.

2 (1866) L R 1 P & D 130 per Lord Penzance.

3 Shaw *v.* Attorney-General (1870) L R 2 P & D 156. But See Halsbury's Laws of England, 3rd Edition, para. 200, where it is stated that a declaration of divorce made under Muhammadan Law made by a person domiciled in India or Egypt, has not the effect in England of dissolving a marriage contracted in England according to English law, with a woman *domiciled in that country*. The authorties cited in support of this proposition are Rex *v.* Hammersmith Ex parte Anwaruddin (1917) 1 K B 634 C A and Maher *v.* Maher (1951) P 342. In Russ *v.* Russ (1962) 2 W L R 708, it has been held that as a general rule English law looks to the law of the domicile to determine the status of the parties. It is added, however, that the Courts have discretion, and may in a proper case refuse to recognize a status conferred or imposed upon a person by the law of his domicile and will reach their decision with due regard to common sense and in some sense to reasonable policy.

the parties were resident in England, even then the English Court will refuse to recognise a divorce not obtained through a validly constituted Court of Justice.[1] So that a Mahommedan residing in England, though belonging to the section, which gives to the parties the power of dissolving the contract, cannot effect a dissolution of the status of marriage of his own free will, though it may be valid in his own country.[2]

A Musulman marriage.

Under the Sunni Law witnesses are necessary to the contracting of a valid marriage, though the absence of witnesses does not invalidate the marriage. If a Musulman of the Sunni sect were to marry a Moslemah, the witnesses under the Mahommedan Law ought to belong to the same faith; but when the parties to the marriage-contract differ in faith, then it is not necessary that the witnesses should be the professors of Islam.

Under the Mahommedan Law, as under the Scotch Law, a marriage *per verba de praesenti* is sufficient to constitute a valid contract. But if the marriage is celebrated in England, it must be performed in the mode or according to the rites or ceremonies requisite by the English Law to enter into a valid contract. The validity of the ceremony must, in fact, be regulated by the laws of England on the subject. The consent of parents or guardians, necessary under certain conditions to the validity of a Mahommedan marriage, is treated by the English Law as part of the ceremony or form of the marriage.[3] For example, whilst a Hanafi or a Shiah male or female, if *sui juris*—that is, if over fifteen years of age and possessed of discretion—can contract himself or herself without the consent of the guardian, a Shaf'ei girl, though "adult and discreet", can, under no circumstance, enter into a contract of marriage without such consent. If however, she contracted herself in marriage in England, against the wishes or without the consent of her guardian, it would be valid.

Registration of a marriage.

In Algeria it has been held that the Kazi is not bound to register a marriage between a Moslem and a non-Moslemah, but such marriage can be registered before the civil officer, who in fact, is compelled by law to give effect to the wishes of the parties and make a record thereof in the registry office. Under the Mahommedan Marriage Registration Act, which is in force in several parts of the Province of Bengal, it is optional with Musulmans to register their marriage; but as the Kazis under the Act are especially appointed for the purpose of registering the marriage of the Mahommedans, they would be bound to do so if an application were made to them for the purpose. Supposing therefore, that a Moslem either permanently domiciled in Bengal,

1 See Shaw *v.* Gould (1868) L R 3 H L 55. See Appendix.

2 "In spite of earlier dicta to the contrary, it is now clear that English Courts will recognize non-judicial divorces obtained unilaterally by one party to the marriage in accordance with a religious law (e.g., jewish ghet) provided the parties are domiciled in a country the territorial laws of which permit such a method"—Dicey's Conflict of Laws, 7th Edition, page 307.

See also Ali Nawaz Gardezi *v.* Lt.-Col. Mohammed Yusuf P L D 1963 S C 51.

3 Sottomayor *v.* De Barros (1877) 3 P D 1—7.

or only temporarily resident there, married a non-Moslem woman, and applied under the Marriage Registration Act to have the contract registered the Kazi will have no option; though if there had been no such law in force, or if the office of Kazi had existed under the same conditions as under a purely Mahommedan *regime*, a refusal on his part would have been justifiable.

A curious point bearing on this part of the question came up for discussion before the Court of Algiers on the 14th of October 1874. A Musulman resident of Algeria married a Spanish lady named Marie Moll, who had embraced the faith of Mohammed. The marriage was contracted in the presence of the Kazi of Tlemcen. A child was born of this union, who was registered as the legitimate offspring of the husband Yusuf and the wife Marie Moll. Subsequently, on the death of her husband, Marie Moll, in her own right and that of her child, attempted to take possession of the deceased's estate, but was opposed by his brothers, who contested that the marriage contracted before the Kazi was invalid, inasmuch as though the lady had adopted the Musulman faith, she continued to be a Spanish subject, and that, therefore, the ceremony ought to have taken place before the Spanish Consul or the French authorities. The Court, consisting of three French Judges and two Musulman assessors, unanimously upheld the validity of the marriage, and declared that Marie Moll and her child were entitled under the Mahommedan Law to the patrimony of Yusuf the deceased.[1]

A Musulman, therefore, marrying a non-Moslemah in those parts of India where the Mahommedan Marriage Registration Act is in force, can do so either before the Kazi appointed under the Act, or privately before two witnesses belonging to his or her faith. If the woman is a foreigner the contract may be entered into either before the Consul of the State to which she is subject, or a Registrar or an ordinary Justice of the Peace, or the Kazi. If the marriage takes place in England or any other European country, the formalities of the *lex loci contractus* with reference to a civil marriage must be complied with. [Of course, no law would prevent a Mahommedan resident in England from marrying a Moslemah or a non-Moslemah according to the terms of the Musulman Law *per verba de praesenti*, but no Court of Law would take cognisance of it unless the requirements of the English Law for the purpose of contracting a *valid civil marriage* were gone through.]

In India a marriage between a Moslem and a Christian female in order to be valid must be solemnised according to the provisions of the Christian Marriages Act (XV of 1872).[2]

A Musulman domiciled in England cannot marry his deceased wife's sister;[3] but if he were only temporarily residing in England, it is open to question whether he would be debarred from doing so. The American authorities certainly maintain that such a marriage would be valid.[4] But, according to the English

1 2 Sautayra, p. 126.

2 See Tasaduq Hussain *v.* Tasaduq Hussain P L D 1953 Lah. 112.

3 Since this was written a marriage with a deceased wife's sister has been legalised in England.

4 See Wharton, sec. 141.

jurists, it would appear that any marriage *contracted* in England within the degrees of consanguinity prohibited by the English Law would not be regarded as valid for any purpose by the English Courts.[1]

The *patria potestas*, under the Mahommedan Law, cannot be exercised by parents resident in England over their children, unless such powers are in conformity with the provisions of the English Law.

Morris v. Davies. Piers v. Piers.

Under the English Law, as under the Mahommedan Law, when the parties cohabit together as husband and wife there is a presumption in favour of marriage. The principle was laid down in the case of *Morris* v. *Davies*,[2] followed afterwards and re-enunciated in *Piers* v. *Piers*.[3] In the latter case the Lord Chancellor used the following important words:—

"I have not found that the rule of law is anywhere laid down more to my satisfaction than it is by Lord Lyndhurst in the case of *Morris* v. *Davies* as determined in this House. It is not precisely the same presumption as exists in the present case; but the principle is strictly applicable to the presumption which we are considering. He says, 'The presumption of law is not lightly to be repelled. It is not to be broken in upon or shaken by a mere balance of probability. The evidence for the purpose of repelling it must be strong, distinct, satisfactory and conclusive'. No doubt, every case must vary as to how far the evidence may be considered as 'satisfactory and conclusive; but he lays down this rule that the presumption must prevail unless it is most satisfactorily repelled by the evidence in the cause appearing conclusive to those who have to decide upon that question."

"Then we have the subsequent conduct of the parties, proving beyond all questions that they supposed that a valid marriage had been celebrated. The children are treated as legitimate children; the wife is treated as the lawful wife; and the conduct of the parties, from beginning to end, shows that they believed a valid marriage to have been solemnized. This is not at all shaken by the fact of a subsequent marriage having taken place in Ireland. We know that that does frequently happen without the slightest imputation on the validity of the first marriage."

Sastry Velaider Aronegary v. Sembecutty Vaigalie.

And in *Sastry Velaider Aronegary* v. *Sembecutty Vaigalie*,[4] Sir Barnes Peacock thus summarised the principle, "that the presumption of marriage from cohabitation with habit and repute can only be rebutted by the clearest and most satisfactory

---

1 Dicey, however, seems to doubt the absolute correctness of this doctrine.

2 5 Clark & Fin. 163.

3 2 H L Cases 331 ; Spwack *v.* Spwack (1930) 142 L T 492; Russel *v.* A. G. 1949 P. 391.

4 6 Appeal Cases, p. 372 ; In re Taplin 1937 All E R 105.

evidence." "In *De Thoren* v. *Attorney-General*" to use the words of Sir Barnes Peacock in *Sastry Velaider*, "Lord Caires, then Lord Chancellor, stated that the presumption of marriage is much stronger than the presumption raised with regard to other facts; and he referred to the *Breadalbane case*[1] in which it was held that the presumption was one which not only might, but ought to be drawn from cohabitation with habit and repute, although the cohabitation commenced with a ceremony which was not only invalid by reason of the real husband, of the woman being alive at the time, but was known by both parties to be invalid".

"Their Lordships having come to the conclusion that Pattenier and the second plaintiff lived together as man and wife, and that Pattenier held her out as his wife, the presumption of their marriage is not lightly to be rebutted."

This principle is in accordance with the rule of the Mahommedan Law.

The King v. The Inhabitants of Brampton.

In the case of *The King* v. *The Inhabitants of Brampton*[2] it appeared that two British subjects in a foreign country, being desirous of intermarrying, went to a chapel for that purpose, where a service in the language of the country was read by a person habited like a priest, and interpreted into English by the officiating clerk; which service the parties understood to be the marriage service of the Church of England, and they received a certificate of the marriage, which was afterwards lost. Lord Ellenborough held the presumption to be strongly in favour of the marriage, and Mr. Justice Grose put his decision very tersely in the following words:—

"The question is whether this was a good marriage? And in determining that, I have no objection to consider whether it be a good marriage either according to the Law of England, or according to the law of the country where it took place. Upon the former ground, I rather think that it was good by the Law of England for the reasons which have been stated by my Lord. But considered as a marriage by the law of the country where it was celebrated, I think there can be no doubt. The parties meant to be married; they went openly to a chapel in the country where they were; they found there a person appearing as a priest of the country, and they were married by him; the service was performed in French, but it was translated to the parties, and they understood it to be the marriage ceremony. From these facts the presumption would be that it was a marriage according to the law of that country, by a priest of that country cognizant of its laws in that respect and who, it must be presumed would celebrate according to the law of his own country. There is, therefore, a fair and reasonable presumption that these parties were regularly and legally married according to the Law of Saint Domingo. I should think the marriage might be sustained according to the

1 Law Rep. Sc. & Div. 2 H L s c 269. But in a prosecution for bigamy the presumption of the prisoner's innocence outweighs the presumption of marriage to be drawn from cohabitation, and the marriage must be strictly proved by the prosecution. See Archbold's Criminal Pleading, 33rd Edition, page 1377.

2 10 East. 282.

Law of England, but I have no doubt that it is sustainable by the law of the country where it was celebrated."

The issue of polygamous unions, legitimate.

The English Law does not recognise the validity of polygamous unions, but the status of the issue of such unions, if such unions are valid by the law of the parents' domicile, remains wholly unaffected. For example if a Musulman, domiciled in Algeria, where the Shaf'ei branch of the Sunni law is in force, married two wives, the children of the second marriage, according to the principle laid down in *Re Goodman's Trusts*[1] would be treated as legitimate, for the purpose of taking under the Statute of Distributions, albeit the English Law does not recognise a second union contemporaneously with the first as lawful or valid. But if a Moslem belonging to the polygamous section and domiciled in England were to contract a second marriage in Algeria the children of such marriage would apparently be excluded from the operation of the statute.

Re Goodman's Trusts.

In *Re Goodman's Trusts*, the dispute related to the personal estate of one Rachel Goodman who died domiciled in England. At the date of her death her sole relatives were the children of her two deceased brothers, Issac and Leyon Goodman. Leyon Goodman whilst in England had cohabited with one Charlotte Smith, by whom he had several children. He removed afterwards to Holland and domiciled himself there where another child (afterwards Mrs. Pieret) was born to them. Subsequent to the birth of this child, Leyon Goodman married Charlotte Smith, and under the Dutch Law the children born before marriage were legitimated.

The question then arose whether Mrs. Pieret could take as next-of-kin any share in the personal estate of the deceased under the English Statute of Distribution.

The Master of the Rolls decided against her. On appeal this decision was reversed. The judgment of Lord Justice Cotton is extremely important. His Lordship, after stating the facts, proceeded as follows:—

"It is urged in support of the decision of Jessel, M. R., that the Law of England recognises as legitimate those children only who are born in wedlock. This is correct as regards the children of persons who, at the time of the children's birth, are domiciled in England. But the question as to legitimacy is one of status, and in my opinion, by the law of England, questions of status depend on the law of the domicile. For this proposition there is authority. It is stated by Story, J., in his book on the *Conflict of Laws*, s. 93, that foreign jurists also generally, although not universally, maintain that the question of legitimacy, or illegitimacy, is to be decided exclusively by the law of the domicile of origin. And in paragraph 93(*e*), he states that 'the same general

---

1 44 L T Reports 527: (1881) 17 Ch. D 266 C A; Re Bischoff Shein Cassel *v.* Grant (1948) Ch. 79: (1947) 2 All E R 830.

doctrine is avowedly adopted by the Courts of England', and he refers to the opinion expressed by Lord Stowell in *Dalrymple* v. *Dulrymple*[1] that by the Law of England the status or condition of a claimant is tried by reference to the law of the country where that status originated. Moreover, in the case of *Birtwhistle* v. *Vardill*[2] when it first came before the House of Lords in the year 1830, Alexander, C. B., when giving the unanimous opinion of the Judges who were consulted, refers with approval to the opinion so expressed by Lord Stowell, as applicable to the case before the House. In *Fenton* v. *Livingstone* Lord Wensleydale in a passage which I do not repeat without qualification, expresses himself thus: 'The laws of the State affecting the personal status of its subjects travel with them wherever they go, and attach to them in whatever country they are resident.' Kindersley, V. C., in his judgment in *Re Don's Estate*, to which I shall afterwards refer, lays down the same rule. If, as in my opinion is the case, the question whether a person is legitimate depends on the law of the place where his parents were domiciled at his birth, that is, by his domicile of origin, I cannot understand on what principle, if he be by that law legitimate, he is not legitimate everywhere, and I am of opinion that, if a child is legitimate by the law of the country where at the time of its birth its parents were domiciled, the Law of England, except in the case of succession to real estates in England, recognises and acts on the status thus declared by the law of the domicile. In fact, the respondent wishes to use the proposition that, in an English Act of Parliament, those only are next-of-kin or children of a deceased brother whom the Law of England recognises as legitimate as if it were whom the Law of England would recognise as legitimate if, at the time of their birth, their domicile, that is, the domicile of their parents, had been English. *But, in my opinion, in deciding questions of legitimacy, that is, of status, the Law of England looks to the law of the actual not of an hypothetical domicile.* I am of opinion that, on principle as by the Law of Holland, where the parents of Hannah Pieret, were in fact domiciled at the time of her birth, she is legitimate, the Law of England, for the purpose of succession to personal estate, ought to hold her to be legitimate. This, on principle, is very obvious, but the cases may have established a different rule, and it is necessary to consider the authorities which were relied upon in argument in support of the decision of Jessel, M. R." His Lordship then proceeded to consider the authorities. "The case which was much discussed was that of *Birtwhistle* v. *Vardill*, which in the year 1830, and again in 1840, came before the House of Lords. All that was actually decided in that case was, that the eldest son, born in Scotland before marriage of the parents domiciled there, though by Scotch law legitimate by reason of subsequent marriage of his parents, was not capable of taking land in England as heir of his father. The unanimous opinion of the Judges, as expressed on two occasions, was that he could not; but Alexander, C. B., states the question to be considered, as being, whether, by the Law of England, a man is heir of English land merely because he is the eldest legitimate son

1 2 Hagg, Consist, 54.

2 2 Cl. & F 571.

3 33 L T Rep., O S . 35; 2 Macq. 548.

of his father, and, though he gives his opinion that he is not, he, particularly in the passage to which I have already referred, treats the general question of his status, that is, of his legitimacy, as one to be determined by the law of the place where the parents were domiciled at the time of his birth. He was then delivering the unanimous opinion of the Judges who had been consulted. When the case was before the House of Lords in the year 1840 (7 Cl. & F., 925), Tindal, C. J., delivered the unanimous opinion of the Judges then consulted, and he stated the ground of their opinion to be that they held it 'to be a rule or maxim of the Law of England, with respect to the descent of land in England from father to son, that the son must be born after actual marriage between his father and mother'. Tindal, C. J., does not, it is true, so distinctly as was done by Alexander, C. B., state the proposition that legitimacy must depend on the law of the country of the parents' domicile, at the time of birth, but he treats the Statute of Merton as referring only to the question of the right to inherit land in England, and in 7 Cl. & F., p. 932, there occurs this passage: 'The contest above adverted to was a contest between the ancient law and custom of England on the one hand, and the canon law on the other, which should prevail as to the hereditary succession to land in England, canon and civil law being acknowledged and prevailing in England in all other respects with the single exception of its application to the descent of land.' The decision in that case, therefore, was not at variance with the rule which, in my opinion, is, on principle, the correct one, and the opinion expressed by the Judges strongly supports my view. But it was urged that the opinion expressed by the Judges as to the legitimacy of the son born before marriage was intended to apply only to his right to share in the personal estate of the father domiciled in Scotland, as the eldest son was admittedly legitimate by the Law of Scotland, by which the succession to the father's personal estate must be governed. This construction would reduce to a nullity the opinion there expressed by the Judges, and, in my opinion, they did intend to express their opinion that the claimant, being legitimate by the Law of Scotland where his parents were domiciled at his birth and at the date of their marriage, must be considered as legitimate in England, except for the purpose of succession to real estate, and that this depended on a special rule of the feudal law as adopted in England. This, in my opinion, was the view taken by Lord Cranworth in *Shaw* v. *Gould*, which, however, has been quoted in a different sense. Kindersley, V. C., took the same view in *Re Don's Estate*.[1] He says: 'It appears to me that on the authorities applicable to this question the principle is this, that the legitimacy or illegitimacy of any individual is to be determined by the law of that country which is the country of his origin. If he is legitimate in his own country, then all other civilised countries, at least all Christian countries, recognise him as legitimate everywhere. He then refers to the case of *Birtwhistle* v. *Vardill*, and treats it as an exception to the general rule above stated by him founded on the rules of inheritance attached to land in this country. But although the decision in *Birtwhistle* v. *Vardill* is not against the

---

1 4 Drew. 194; 30 L T Rep. O S 190.

appellant, and the opinion expressed in that and the other cases to which I have referred are in his favour, the case of *Boyes* v. *Bedale*[1] and the opinions expressed by Wood, V. C., in that case are undoubtedly in favour of the decision of Jessel, M. R., in the Court below. In *Boyes* v. *Bedale* the question was on the construction of a bequest in the will of a domiciled Englishman to the children of a person named, and Wood, V. C., held that a child exactly in the same position as Hannah Pieret was not entitled under this bequest. He said that the will being that of a domiciled Englishman, must be construed according to English Law, which, in my opinion, is correct so far as to require that this word 'children' shall be construed 'legitimate children'. But the Vice-Chancellor held that English Law recognised as legitimate only those children born in wedlock. This, though correct as regards the children of persons domiciled in England at the time of their birth is, in my opinion, erroneous as to children born of parents who at the time of their birth were domiciled in a country by the law of which the children were legitimate. At the end of his judgment in *Boyes* v. *Bedale* the Vice-Chancellor expressed his opinion that any claim under the Statute of Distributions would be dealt with in the same way. *Re Wright's Trusts*[2] also a decision of Lord Hatherly when Vice-Chancellor, is not inconsistent with the opinion already expressed by me, and explains how the children of Leyon Goodman who were born while he was domiciled in England make no claim. They, like the children excluded by the Vice-Chancellor in *Re Wright's Trusts*, were born while their parents were domiciled in a country by the law of which no subsequent marriage of persons domiciled there could legitimate children born before their marriage. The exclusion of these children is, therefore, in accordance with the rule as to status already expressed by me. The judgment in *Re Wilson's Trusts*[3] affirmed by the House of Lords under the name of *Shaw* v. *Gould*[4] is not an authority on the questions involved in the case, for there, by the Law of England, the mother of the children had not been effectually divorced from her first husband, and her marriage with the father of the children was void, and the children were illegitimate. *Boyes* v. *Bedale*, though mentioned with approval by Kindersley, V. C., in *Re Wilson's Trusts*, is really the only decision which supports the judgment of Jessel, M. R., and *Skottowe* v. *Young*[5] is certainly a decision in favour of the appellants. In that case Stuart, V. C., held that the children of a testator domiciled abroad, who were in exactly the same position as regards legitimacy as Hannah Pieret, were under the Legacy Duty Act, liable to pay duty at the rate of 1 per cent. only, that is, as children of the testator within the meaning of that Act. Moreover, though in *Goodman* v. *Goodman*[6] the point raised on this appeal is not

1 10 L T Rep. N S 131; 1 Hem. & Mil. 798.
2 27 L T Rep. O S 213; 2 Kay & J 595.
3 13 L T Rep. N S 576; L R 1 Eq. 247.
4 18 L T Rep. N S 833; L R 3 E & I App. 55.
5 24 L T Rep. N S 221; L R 11 Eq. 474.
6 6 L T Rep. N S 641; 3 Giff. 463.

mentioned in the judgment, Stuart, V. C., who decided that case, and the counsel who argued it, appear to have assumed that, if Hannah Pieret was born after her father acquired a domicile in Holland, she was to be considered as a legitimate child according to the Law of England, and entitled as such under the will of the testator in that case. There is, therefore, a conflict of decisions, and, as in my opinion the decision in *Boyes* v. *Bedale* is contrary to principle and erroneous, I think that we ought not to follow that case, and that Hannah Pieret is to be treated as a legitimate child of Leyon Goodman, and as such entitled to share in the personal estate as to which Rachel Goodman died intestate, as one of her next-of-kin."[1]

CHAPTER II

THE STATUS OF LEGITIMACY

Section I

Sunni Doctrines

Under the Mahommedan Law, as in all civilised systems of law, "the child follows the bed", that is, the *paternity of a child born in lawful wedlock is presumed to be in the husband of the mother without any acknowledgment or affirmation of parentage on his part and such child follows the status of the father.*

Presumption of legitimacy.

According to the Sunni schools, the presumption of legitimacy is so strong, that in cases where a child is born six months from the date of marriage[2] and within two years[3] after dissolution of the marital contract, either by the death of the husband or by divorce, a simple denial of paternity on the part of the husband would not take away the status of legitimacy from the child.

Of course, presumption based on the "bed" is subject to the right of disavowal on the part of the husband for want of access.

The Musulman Law on the subject of legitimacy is analogous to the English Law.[4] According to the English Law, a child born anywhere in lawful wedlock is legitimate. The presumption in favour of legitimacy arising from that circumstance, however, is not a *presumptio juris et de jure*, but, may be rebutted by evidence which must be clear and conclusive and not resting

---

1 I have quoted from these cases at some length as the reports are not easily available in India, and because I consider it necessary that Indian lawyers should have some knowledge of the decisions of the English Courts on the subject (Amir Ali).

See also on the subject of mixed marriages Ogden *v.* Ogden (1907) P. 107; also in 96 L T 505.

2 See post, p. 169.

3 According to the modern rule, ten months; see post, p. 169 postnotes.

4 Fatawai 'Alamgiri, Vol. I, p. 727; Kanz-ud-Dakaik,

merely on probabilities.[1] It is not necessary, however, to prove that generative access was physically impossible; it is enough to show circumstances in the conduct of the parties and otherwise which render the moral presumption against such access irresistible.[2]

Probably the same rules would apply to a question of legitimacy arising under the Mahommedan Law.

The *Fatawai 'Alamgiri'* says:

"Paternity does not admit of positive proof, because the connection of a child with its father is secret. But it may be established by the word of the father himself, or by a subsisting *firash*" that is, a legally constituted relationship between him and the mother of the child.

It then goes on to add :—

"There are three degrees in the establishment of paternity,—the first is a valid marriage; the second an invalid marriage that comes within the meaning of one that is valid; and the third, bondage.

'The effect of the first degree is to establish paternity without a claim, and to prevent its rejection by a mere denial, though it may be rejected by *l'aan* or imprecation, in the case of valid marriage, but not where the marriage is invalid, but if the case does not admit of *l'aan*, the paternity of the child cannot be rejected."

Shortest period of gestation.

The shortest period of gestation, according to all the schools, is six months. This period is fixed in the Koran, and consequently there is little room for divergence among the jurists. The *Radd-ul-Muhtar* says the shortest period of gestation is six months according to all the four Imams without difference.[3] But they differ considerably as to the longest period of pregnancy.

The old Hanafi lawyers, upon the authority of a tradition reported by 'Ayesha, hold two years as the longest term of gestation.[4] On the other hand, Malik, Shafe'i and Ahmed ibn Hanbal extend the term to four years. Several others have considered the longest period to be five, and sometimes seven years.[5] The Imams, Shafe'i and Malik based their opinions on the legendary birth of Buer-asp, surnamed Zuhak Tazi, who

---

1 Bosvile *v.* Attorney-General, 56 L J P 97; s c 12 P D 177. See Russell *v.* Russell.

2 Gurney *v.* Gurney; 1 Hem. & M 413; s c 32 L J Ch. 456.

3 Koran, chap. xlvi, v. 14; Radd-ul-Muhtar, Vol. I, p. 1027.

4 Durr-ul-Mukhtar, p. 282; Fatawai Kazi Khan, Vol. I, p. 422.

5 *Ibid.*, p. 828; Fatawai Kazi Khan, Vol. I, p. 422.

is said to have been born in the fourth year of his conception, like Ibn Rab'ia and Ibn 'Ajlan.[1]

The Shiahs, upon the basis of a decision pronounced by 'Ali during his Caliphate, recognise ten lunar months as the ordinary period of gestation.[2]

Hanafi doctrine relating to ascription of paternity.

According to the Sunni schools, therefore, where a child is born to a woman within the period indicated, *viz.*, six months or more from the date of marriage, and within ten months after dissolution of the marital contract either by the death of the husband or divorce, such child is *affiliated*, without an express acknowledgment on the part of the father. Nor will a simple denial of paternity by the husband take away the status of legitimacy from the child.

"And if a man should", says the *Fatawai 'Alamgiri* " marry a woman, and she be delivered of a child *within* six months from the day of marriage, the paternity of the child from him is not established, because conception must have taken place before the marriage; but if she is delivered at six months or more, its paternity is established, because of the subsisting *firash* or bed

1 The author of the Sharifia ridicules these legendary stories, whilst the Radd-ul-Muhtar says that certain diseases show the same symptoms as pregnancy, and that, therefore, Malik was misled into thinking that gestation may extend to four years; but even the author of the Radd adopts two years as the ordinary period.

Mr. Baillie thinks that the ancient Sunni doctors, in laying down such long periods, had in view those abnormal conditions which "sometimes perplex the most skilful of the medical faculty in Europe". D'Ohsson and Sautayra, on the contrary, are of opinion that the old jurisconsults of the Sunni schools "were actuated by sentiments of humanity, and not by any indifference to the laws of nature, their chief desire being to prevent an abuse of the provisions of the law regarding divorce and the disavowal of children".

Notwithstanding that the Shafe'i and Maliki doctrines are in force in Algeria, the Algerian Kazis have adopted the same view as D'Ohsson, and in their decisions seem invariably to have held that ten months was the maximum term recognised by law. The Court of Algiers, by several decrees, dated the 16th of April 1861, the 13th of November 1861, and the 1st of September 1868 respectively, has supported and confirmed the Kazis' decisions. Although the early Hanafi jurists have laid down two years as the maximum period for gestation, the view of the Algerian Kazis is in accord with the modern rule recognised universally by Mahommedan Judges and Doctors of Law.

See Tableaux Gen. de l' Empire Ottoman, Vol. III, pp. 102, 103. Under the Roman Law, the longest period of gestation was ten months. Under the Code Napoleon (Art. 312), the shortest term of pregnancy is one hundred and eighty days, and the longest three hundred days.

2 Jam'a-ush-Shittat; Mafatih; Irshad-ul-'Allamah.

The Shar'aya has the following on this point:—"All children born under a contract of permanent marriage appertain to the husband, upon condition of coition and the lapse of not less than six months nor more than the longest period of gestation from the time of its occurrence till the birth of the child. That period is nine months, according to the most common opinion; but some of our doctors have extended it to ten months, and this is considered to be correct. Others, again, have gone so far as to extend the period to a year; but their opinion is now abandoned". As stated in the text, the ordinary period is ten lunar months, but in exceptional cases, according to several eminent jurists, the period may extend somewhat longer.

and the completion of the term of pregnancy, whether he acknowledged the child or remained silent; and if he should deny its birth, that may be established by the testimony of one woman bearing witness to the fact."

Presumption of legitimacy.

"If a man committed fornication with a woman and she became pregnant and he then married her, after which she gave birth to a child. If the child was born at six months or more from the date of marriage, its *nasab* would be established in the father"; *i.e.*, it would be regarded as the legitimate offspring of the woman's husband; but if it was born within less than six months no ascription would take place "unless the man acknowledged it to be his issue, but did not say 'it was his by fornication.' "

Acknowledgment.

In other words, it is the right of the man to legitimate a child born *within* the time by acknowledging *expressly* or *impliedly* that the *conception* took place in wedlock.

Shiah doctrine.

As will be seen later, the Shiahs hold that in order that *ascription* should take place (independently of acknowledgment), the birth of the child must be at six months from the date of the *consummation of the marriage*. But they agree with the Sunnis in holding that when the child is born under circumstances which give rise to the natural presumption that it is his offspring, nothing short of a proceeding in which the husband and wife are put on their oaths, can take the status of legitimacy from it.[1]

[The Musulman Law in allowing the parties to pledge their oaths on the question of paternity seems to proceed on more reasonable grounds than the English Law, under which neither husband nor wife can be examined for the purpose of proving non-access during marriage, nor can they be examined as to any collateral fact for the purpose of proving non-access[2] although previous statements by the mother regarding the illegitimacy of the child have been held to be admissible.][3]

Similarly, the *Radd-ul-Muhtar* says, " *when there is subsisting relationship*, according to the Disciples the evidence of the midwife alone is sufficient for the establishment of *nasab*. Some have held that the evidence of a man is sufficient, but this must be if he was present at the birth".[4]

Birth after dissolution of the marriage-relationship.

When a woman is divorced *after consummation* of the marriage and she is subsequently delivered of a child, its

1 See post, p. 172.

2 Rex *v.* Stourton, 5 A & E 180; In re Sinclay 17 Beav. 523; Patchett *v.* Holgate; 15 Jur. 308; Atchley *v.* Sprigg 3 N R 360.

3 The Aylesford Peerage (1885) 11 App. Cases H L 1. See Russell *v.* Russell L R Appeal Cases (1924) 687.

4 See Razia Begum *v.* Sahebzadi Anwar Begum A I R 1958 And. Pre. 195 where it has been held that acknowledgment or long co-habitation as husband and wife raises a mere presumption. Where it is definitely proved that there was no marriage at all when children were begotten, the issue cannot be legitimated by acknowledgment.

descent would be established up to ten months. In other words, if the child is born within ten months from the date of the divorce, it would be affiliated to the husband.

Further cases of ascription by presumption.

A fortiori, if the birth were to take place within six months from such dissolutions, the paternity of the child would be ascribed to the husband of the mother, without any affirmation on his part.

Nor would any statement by the woman, on the expiry of the prescribed period of probation that she was not pregnant, affect the question.

The Sunni Law contains other instances of ascription of the paternity of a child to "the husband of the mother" based on presumption or on the acknowledgment of the putative father. For example, it is stated that "if a child be born *at* two years after divorce, affiliation would take place if the husband claimed the child as his own, although Kohastani and Tahawi are of opinion that when the birth takes place *after* two years then only a claim is necessary for affiliation. But the author of the *Tanwir-ul-Absar* in accordance with the text-writers, has adopted the other opinion".[1]

And, according to the *Fath-ul-Kabir*, "affiliation would take place if the husband *should claim* a child born two years after divorce, even though the wife should deny its being his."

All the old rules regarding affiliation must be taken subject to the provision already stated that the maximum period of gestation now recognised is ten months, unless there is any exceptional circumstance retarding the bitth of the child.

So also if a child be born *after* six months from date of divorce but *within* six months from a declaration that she had completed her probation, the child would be affiliated, but not if the birth took place *after* six months from such declaration.

When there has been no assertion of pregnancy on her part [at the time of the dissolution of the marriage], nor subsequent declaration that she had completed her probation, the child would be affiliated if born within nine months from the date of divorce.

A child born to an adult woman, who is observing the '*iddat* incumbent on a widow, would, be affiliated to her deceased husband, whether he consummated the marriage or not, for *firash* is established by the contract and not by *copula*. This rule, however, must be taken subject to the condition that the other heirs of the deceased have a right to impugn the legitimacy of the child.

But if the widow, be a young girl (*as-saghira*) whose puberty is doubtful, and who made no assertion of being pregnant, and a child be born to her in less than ten months and ten days from the date of her husband's death, the child would be affiliated to

1 Radd-ul-Muhtar, Vol. II, p. 1027.

him, because in this case there is the presumption that she was pregnant before the expiration of her *'iddat* of widowhood (which is four months and ten days), and six months is the shortest time of gestation. But if the child be born at ten months and ten days or more, its conception will not be ascribed to him.

If an adult woman or adolescent girl were to admit after four months and ten days from the death of her husband, in other words, on the expiry of the *'iddat* she has to observe in consequence of the death of her husband, that she was not *enciente*, and a child should be born to her thereafter, such child would not be affiliated to the deceased husband unless the birth occurs at less than six months from such declaration, when ascription would take place.

These statements also must be taken subject to the rule that in the absence of any exceptional circumstance the maximum period of gestation now in force is ten months.

Disavowal of paternity.

But a husband can disavow or disclaim a child born in wedlock, within the period recognised by law, on the ground of impossibility of cohabitation whether the impossibility arose from disease, physical incapacity or want of access.[1]

According to the *Fatawai 'Alamgiri,* a disavowal on the ground of the absence of cohabitation requires the performance of the formalities which surround the proceeding by *l'aan* or imprecation. M. Sautayra, however, is of opinion that a disavowal of paternity should be enforced by a simple judicial action, instituted by the husband or his representatives, against the wife or those who represent the interests of the child, and that such an action instituted for the purpose of establishing illegitimacy is subject to the ordinary rules of procedure, and does not require the formalities of the *l'aan* or "imprecation"

This view, however, seems to be founded on a misconception of the true nature of a proceeding by *l'aan.*

According to the older schools the husband has the power *suo motu* of dissolving the marriage, without any option on the part of the wife. But he cannot so easily discard a child born by the wife in wedlock. If he denies the child to be born of his loins, the disclaimer can be effectuated only by a formal proceeding before the Judge (*Kazi* or *Hakim-ush-Shara*) in which he and the wife would be arrayed against each other as *challenger* and *challenged.* On one side the charge of adultery, which the denial of paternity implies, on the other the refutation is to be made on oath. And to show that the allegation involving such grave consequences is not made lightly, the parties have to invoke imprecation (*l'aan*) against each other for perjury.[2]

---

1 Fatawai 'Alamgiri, Vol. II, p. 722; Sharay'a-ul-Islam, p. 300; Jam'a-ush-Shittat; Radd-ul-Muhtar, Vol. II, p. 1028; see post.

2 Radd-ul-Muhtar, Vol. II, p. 963; Fath-ul-Kadir, Vol. II, p. 317; Fatawai 'Alamgiri, Vol. I, p. 703.

Lex fori British Indian Procedure.

Such a proceeding operates as a definitive or irreversible divorce. Under the Hanafi Law the husband can re-marry a woman separated by *l'aan*. The Shiah Law, in order to accentuate the solemnity of the proceeding, prohibits a re-marriage.

The *lex fori* in British India neither contemplates nor will probably countenance such a proceeding. Where, therefore, the husband denies the legitimacy of a child born by his wife in wedlock the procedure will be the same as in declaratory suits.

A mere declaration of illegitimacy of the child under the *lex fori* may not effectuate a divorce between husband and wife, but if it is coupled with a decree for dissolution of the marital tie, it would be valid.

A proceeding by *l'aan* is resorted to only where the husband makes the charge. Where a child is born after his death, and some other person impugns its legitimacy, he must proceed in the usual way, and, as under the English Law, the *onus* of proof would be on him.[1]

The Indian Law Reports furnish no instance of a suit by a husband questioning the legitimacy of a child born of the wife in wedlock. The cases in which the status of legitimacy has been discussed have arisen chiefly on the suit of a child, after the decease of the alleged father, to establish its right of inheritance to the paternal estate.

But even in these cases the main question has proceeded on the basis of the wife's position, whether she was legally married or not.[2] The principles formulated in the decisions of the Judicial Committee of the Privy Council contain important and explicit declarations regarding the unwillingness of the Musulman Law to bastardise children, *when the surrounding circumstances lead to an irrebuttable inference that the child was the offspring of the father or that he acknowleged and recognised it as such during his lifetime.*[3]

Upon a careful analysis of the cases which bear upon the legitimacy of a child, it will be found that the matter in dispute invariably turns either upon the validity of the marriage of the parents, or on the proof of the fact that the child was *born in wedlock*.[4]

---

1 Plowes *v.* Bossey 2 Dr. & Sm. 145.

2 Comp. Dicey, The Law of Domicile.

3 Khajah Hedayut Oollah *v.* Rai Jan Khanum (1844) 3 Moo I A p. 295; Khajurunnissa *v.* Roshan Jehan (1876) L R 3 I A 291; s c I L 2 Cal. 184. In the latter case their Lordships dealing with the question of the child's legitimacy, as well as the position of the mother said as follows:—"Where a son has been uniformly treated by his father and all the members of the family as legitimate, a presumption arises that the son's mother was the father's wife"; see also Jeswunt Singhjee Ubby Singhjee *v.* Jet Singhjee Ubby Singhjee (1845) 3 Moo. I A p. 245 and Muhammad Ismail Khan *v.* Fidayatunnissa (1881) I L 3 All. p. 723.

4 See Habib-ur-Rahman *v.* Altaf Ali (1921) 48 I A 114 : A I R 1922 P C 159. There is no legitimation in Mohammadan Law. In order to be legitimate a son must be the offspring of a man and his duly wedded wife. If direct proof of marriage is not available indirect proof may suffice. Acknowledgment must be not only of sonship but must be made in such a way that the acknowledgment to accept the other not only as his son but as his legitimate son,

Under the Jewish Law, the right of disavowal possessed by the husband is absolute.[1]

The Code Civil of France also permits a disavowal on the ground of the physical impossibility of cohabitation.[2] The Musulman Law, it will be seen, is analogous to the Roman and the French Law in recognising certain specific grounds as justifying the disavowal of a child born in lawful wedlock; *those grounds being physical impossibility and want of access.*

Right of disavowal a terminable right.

But the Musulman Law goes further and holds that the right of disavowal is a *terminable* right. It ceases on the occurrence of certain contingencies which the law always keeps in view.

If the father has taken part in the customary ceremonies[3] which in a Musulman family attend a birth; or has, by his conduct, led people to believe that he considered the child his *legitimate* offspring; and has accepted their formal congratulations, then his right to deny its legitimacy falls to the ground.[4] *unless he can prove, that at the time he was unaware of his wife's infidelity.*

Maliki doctrines.

If the husband is on the spot, and is aware of his wife's confinement, the Malikis allow him two days and the Hanafis a week, for the purpose of disavowal.[5]

Hanafi doctrines.

Among the Hanafis, the lapse of a week implies the performance of all the ceremonies attending the birth, and therefore, should no denial take place within that period, the presumption, of course, is that the husband has no ground to question the legitimacy of the child.

The Fatawai 'Alamgiri.

" The right of rejection", says the *Fatawai 'Alamgiri* "continues only until the husband has expressly acknowledged the paternity of the child, or has made some manifestation of acquiescing in it, by the acceptance of congratulations, or the

---

1 Code Rabbinique (Ebn.-Haezer) Vol. II, p. 63.

2 Arts. 312—318.

3 Such as the 'akika & c. See Herklot's Qanoon-i-Islam.

4 Fatawai 'Alamgiri, Vol. I, p. 703; Sharaya p. 346.

"When a man has denied the child of his wife after its birth, or at the time when he is accepting congratulations, or when the necessaries" (connected) "with the birth are being purchased, his denial is valid, and the l'aan should be administered to him; but if he should not deny it until after this, though the l'aan would still be administered to him, the nasab (of the child) would be established in him. But if he were absent from his wife, and not aware of the child's birth until informed of it, he would have, according to Abu Hanifa, as much time for denial as is occupied with congratulation; or, according to the two Disciples, the whole period of the *nifas* after receiving the intelligence";—Fatawai 'Alamgiri.

5 Tab. Gen. de l' Empire Ottoman, Vol. III, p. 103.

purchase of things necessary in connection with its birth; or a long time has elapsed with knowledge of the event; or until something has happened that cannot be undone, as for instance, the commission of an offence by the child, and the imposition of a fine in consequence on the father."

"In fixing the length of time which precludes the father from denying the child, *regard is to be had to custom; and if a time has elapsed after which it is not usual for a father to deny his child, the denial would not avail, according to Abu Hanifa, by one report, though by another he left it to the discretion of the Judge;* while Abu Yusuf and Mohammed fixed it at forty days, after which the denial would not be valid."[1]

"If the delivery be of twins", says the *Hedaya*, and one is born a day within the six months and the other a day beyond them, the paternity of neither is established.[2] If a dispute should arise between the husband and wife, he saying 'I married thee since four months', and she saying, 'since six months', the word of the wife would be preferred, and the paternity of the child would be established, because appearances testify in her favour, the birth being apparently in consequence of the marriage."

Absence of the husband.

If the husband be absent, the law gives him as much time as would be usually occupied with congratulations, from the receipt of the information concerning his wife's confinement.

Shiah doctrine. Period of disavowal.

Among the Shiahs, the term allowed to the husband for the purpose of disavowing a child is forty days (the whole period of the *nifas*), whether the husband is on the spot or is absent from his wife. In the latter case, the period commences from the moment he receives the information of the child's brith.[3]

Legitimation per subsequent matrimonium.

According to the Law of England, of the Northern States of America and of all countries where the English Common Law is in force, ante-nuptial children or children born "out of wedlock" cannot be legitimated by the subsequent marriage of the parents. According to the Scotch Law, and that of most countries which have adopted, or have been influenced by the Roman Law, as the Law of France, such children are legitimated by the subsequent marriage of the parents. These systems of law, in short, recognise and allow what is technically called *legitimatio per subsequens matrimonium.*

Under the English Law, a child born in lawful wedlock is legitimate, though conception may have taken place before the actual marriage.

Not recognised in Mahommedan Law.

The Muhammedan Law, like the English Common Law, does not recognise the legitimation of ante-nuptial children

1 See also the Fath-ul-Kadir, Vol. II, p. 317.

2 This must be read with the qualification in the Radd-ul-Muhtar.

3 Jam'a-ush-Shittat.

by the subsequent marriage of the parent; but it goes further than the English Law in refusing to attach the *status* of legitimacy to any child not *conceived*, though born in wedlock. It insists that the intercourse between the parents, of which the child is the fruit should, in order to render him *legitimate*, take place under lawful contract.[1]

Sunni Law.

If the birth takes place six months from the marriage, the Sunni Law presumes that the conception was in wedlock. Whilst the Shiah Law requires that, in order to be legitimate, the child should be born six months from the *consummation*.

"If a man", says the *Fatawai 'Alamgiri*, "should commit *zina*[2] with a woman and she should become pregnant, and he should then marry her, and she be delivered of a child *within* six months of the marriage, its paternity from him would not be established, unless he should claim it, and should not say, 'It is of fornication', but if he should say, 'It is mine by fornication', parentage would not be established."[3] So also the *Hedaya*, "If a man marry a woman, and she bring forth a child *within* less than six months from the date of marriage, the parentage of the child is not established in the husband, as pregnancy in that case appears to have existed previous to the marriage and consequently cannot be derived from him".[4]

Muhammad Allahdad Khan v. Muhammad Ismail Khan.

In the case of *Muhammad Allahdad Khan* v. *Muhammad Ismail Khan*,[5] the Allahabad High Court appears to have had this principle in view, but there is so much confusion in the decision that the observations of the learned Judges require to be received with considerable qualification.

Shiah doctrines.

The (Shiah) *Shara'ya-ul-Islam* and the *Jam'a-ush-Shittat* declare that "If a man should have carnal connection with a woman, get her with child, and then marry her, there would be no *nasab* between him and the child".[6]

---

1 See Habib-ur-Rahman *v.* Altaf Ali L R 48 I A 114: A I R 1928 P C 159.

See Abdul Rehman Kutty *v.* Aisha Beevi A I R 1960 Kerala 101. In this case a married woman was driven out by the husband within a few days after the marriage, on the ground at her concealed pregnancy, and a child was born to her within about four months after her being driven out. It was held that no presumption under section 42, Evidence Act could be raised, as there was no valid marriage.

2 Fornication.

3 Fatawai 'Alamgiri, Vol. I, p. 727; Fatwai Kazi Khan, Vol. I, p. 421.

4 Hedaya, Vol. I, p. 382.

5 (1888) I L 10 All. 289. Petheram, C. J., seems to have thought that according to the Mahommedan Law, the effect of an acknowledgment by a Mahommedan that a particular person, born of the acknowledgor's wife before marriage is his son in fact, though the acknowledgor may never have treated him as a legitimate son or intended to give him the status of a son capable of inheriting as legitimate, unless conditions exist which make it impossible that such person can have been the acknowledgor's son in fact, which is, I submit, an incorrect notion.

See also Sadiq Hussain Khan *v.* Hashim Ali Khan (1916) 43 I A 212.

6 Shara'ya p. 300.

Two points deserve attention in the dicta given above. Not only is there a great divergence between the Sunni and the Shiah Law, but a certain amount of difference is observable between the views entertained by the *Fatawai 'Alamgiri* and the *Hedaya*, respectively, though, on careful consideration, it would seem that the difference is more apparent than real. The Shiah Law excludes all possibility of a child being affiliated to the father if the conception has taken place *before* marriage. The *Fatawai 'Alamgiri* holds that when the conception takes place before marriage, and the child is born *within* six months of that time, it is not legitimate; by implication, therefore, it leads to the conclusion that in the converse case, that is, when it is conceived before marriage, but is born *after* six months, it would be legitimate. It thus gives the benefit of the doubt to the child. The *Hedaya* apparently proceeds on a different basis, but in the result it coincides with the ruling of the *Fatawai 'Alamgiri*. It seems to hold that, as the shortest period of gestation is six months, if a child be born *within* that time, it cannot be supposed to be the child of the husband, and its parentage must be ascribed to another person, *unless the husband claims it as his own*.

As a general rule, therefore, it may be said that the Shiah Law is stricter than the Sunni Law, for whilst the latter recognises, as legitimate, children born at six months from marriage, even though conception may have taken place before marriage, the Shiah Law attaches the status of legitimacy only to such children as are *actually conceived* in wedlock.[1]

Section 112 of the Indian Evidence Act embodies the English rule of law, and cannot be held to vary or supersede by implication the rules of Mahommedan Law.[2]

Ashrufooddowla Ahmed Hossein Khan v. Hyder Hossein Khan.

In *Ashrufooddowla Ahmed Hossein Khan* v. *Hyder Hossein Khan*,[3] the Judicial Committee of the Privy Council expressly laid down the principle that under the Mahommedan Law "the presumption of legitimacy from marriage follows the bed and is not ante-dated by relation." This principle only proves what has already been stated, namely, that the Musulman Law does not recognise the doctrine of *legitimatio per subsequens matrimonium*.

Under the Code Napoleon, when a contract of marriage is entered into in good faith, the children of such marriage are legitimate in the eye of the law, though the union may be declared null and void subsequently.[4]

How the presumption of legitimacy arises.

The presumption of legitimacy is so strong in the Mahommedan system that according to the *Fatawai 'Alamgiri* "only the offspring of a connection where the man has no right or *semblance* of right in the woman, either by marriage or by the relationship of master and bonds-woman, is a *walad-uz-zina* or a child of

---

1 Jam'a-ush-Shittat; Mufatih; Irshad-ul-'Allaamah; Shara'ya.

2 In Sibt Muhammad *v.* Muhammad I L R 48 All. 625: A I R 1926 All. 589 and Mst. Rahim Bibi *v.* Chiragh Din A I R 1930 Lah. 97 it was held that section 112 of the Evidence Act supersedes Mahommedan Law and that it applies to Mahommedans.

3 (1866) 11 Moo. I A 94, 113.

4 Arts. 201 and 202.

fornication." As regards the child born of slaves, the Mahommedan system is far more humane than any other. In the Southern States of North America, until the abolition of slavery, the child of a slave-woman begotten by her master was always a slave and could be, and was, in fact, sold as a part of his property.

Abu Hanifa.

According to Abu Hanifa, legitimacy is established by a valid marriage or an invalid contract of marriage whether the connection be radically illegal or not.

Abu Yusuf and Mohammed differ from him, and their opinion, which is given in this work, is recognised as law by the Hanafis. According to them *nasab* is established (*a*) by a *valid* marriage, (*b*) by an *invalid* marriage, and (*c*) by the *status* of bondage. A marriage without witnesses, a marriage with an idolatress or fire-worshipper or with the wife's sister, and such like are regarded as *invalid* marriages.[1]

Principle. Difference between an invalid marriage and a marriage void ab initio.

There is great difference between a marriage which is void *ab initio* (*batil*) and one which is *invalid* (*fasid*). If a man were to contract a marriage with a woman related to him within the prohibited degrees, the marriage would be void *ab initio*. Under the Hanafi Law, the children of such an union would not have the status of legitimacy, unless the man was wholly unaware of the relationship or he was the subject of *ghurur* or *deception*. For example, if a man were to marry a woman related to him within the prohibited degrees, on the representation that she was not so related, and the marriage was consummated, the issue of such an union would be legitimate.

An invalid marriage.

But it is different in the case of an invalid marriage. An invalid marriage is one where the parties do not labour under an inherent incapacity or absolute bar, or where the disability is such as can be removed at any time. *The issue of such unions are legitimate.*

"An invalid marriage", says the *Fatawai 'Alamgiri*, "is like a valid marriage in some of its effects, one of which is the establishment of parentage".

In these cases the six months will run from *copula* and not from marriage.

Invalid marriages : Issue Legitimate.

The subject of invalid marriages, unions that are merely invalid (*fasid*) but not void (*batil*) *ab initio* under the Sunni Law, will be dealt with later in detail, but it may be stated here that *the issues of invalid marriages are without question legitimate according to all the sects.*

---

1 See Bibi Amu *v.* Asiat P L D 1958 Kar. 420. The continuous cohabitation of alleged parents and acknowldgement of the child by the father is presumptive evidence of marriage between the parents and of legitimacy of the offspring. Legitimacy of children may be proved or inferred from circumstances without any direct proof either of the marriage or any formal act of legitimation.

For example, if a man were to marry a non-scriptural woman[1] the marriage would be only invalid, for she might at any time adopt Islam or any other revealed faith, and thus remove the cause of invalidity. The children of such marriage, therefore, are legitimate.[2]

A man belonging to the older sect might marry first one sister, and thereafter, whilst the first marriage is subsisting, might marry another sister. The marriage with the second sister would only be *invalid*, for the first might either die or be divorced, when an union with the second would be lawful. *The issue, therefore, of the union with the second sister would be legitimate and would be entitled to succeed to the inheritance of their father along with the children born of the first mother.*

Azizunnissa Khatoon v. Karimunnissa Khatoon.

In *Azizunnissa Khatoon* v. *Karimunnissa Khatoon*[3] the learned Judges have under a misconception of the Mahommedan Law, held that where a man marries two sisters, the children of the second union are illegitimate. This enunciation, which is in conflict with the recognised law, is evidently due to mixing up two questions, *viz., the title of the second wife to inheritance* and *the status of the children born of her. There is no question that she is not entitled to inherit*; *but there is equally no question that the children are legitimate.*

Principle.

A marriage contracted in the *bona fide* belief on the part of the husband that the woman was a widow or the divorcee of another man (when, as a matter of fact, the former husband of the woman was not dead, or had not divorced her, as the case may be) gives rise to the same consequences as an *invalid marriage*. The man is not subject to *hadd* or the punishment for fornication, and the issue of the union are held to be his legitimate offspring. *A fortiori* when both parties enter into the contract *bona fide* believing that the first husband is either dead or has divorced the woman the children are affiliated to the second husband.

Principle.

Though *the issue of an invalid marriage are legitimate and have a right to the inheritance of the father, the mother has no such right.*

---

1 A woman not belonging to the revealed faiths, in other words, an idolatress; Fatawai 'Alamgiri, Vol. I, p. 722; Radd-ul-Muhtar, Vol. I, p. 577.

2 In view of this recognised principle, it seems to me that in the case of Abdool Razak *v.* Aga Mahomed Jaffer Bindanim (1893) I L 21 Cal. 66; s c L R 21 I A 56, the real question for determination was missed both in the Recorder's Court as well as before the Judicial Committee. For if there was a *de facto* marriage, the prior conversion of the woman. so far as the legitimacy of the child was concerned, was immaterial, As regards conversion to Mahomedanism, also, there seems to have been some misapprehension; for, all that is required under the Mahommedan Law is profession and not conviction.

3 (1895) I L 23 Cal. 130; the elaborate arguments at the bar seem to have given rise to some of the confusion in the minds of the learned Judges.

In Taliamand *v.* Mahamad Din I L R 12 Lah. 52; A I R 1930 Lah. 907 it was held that marriage with a wife's sister during the subsistence of the previous marriage was only invalid (fasid) and not void *ab initio* (batil) and that the issue of such marriage was legitimate and inherited the fathers property.

Again an invalid marriage has no legal effect before consummation so that if the parties are separated by the Judge before consummation, the woman has no right to dower; *but after consummation she is entitled to her proper dower or the specified dower, whichever is less.*

There is no divorce in such a marriage, but after consummation the husband may relinquish his marital right, provided it is done in express terms.

According to some authorities, if a Moslemah were to marry a non-Moslem, both being unaware of the unlawfulness of the union, the marriage would be only invalid, for the unlawfulness is founded on the accident of the man being an "unbeliever", which may cease at any time. The issue of such marriage would, according to this view, be legitimate.[1]

The Hanafi Law gives further details regarding the affiliation of children born of *invalid* relationships.

Shubhat-ul-akd: Semblable contract.

It divides *semblance* (*shubh*) into three categories.—(1) *Semblance in the fact;* (2) *Semblance in the subject* and (3) *Semblance in the contract.*

Principle: Shubh-(semblance.)

An example of *semblance in the fact* is given when a man cohabits with his divorced wife, who has been absolutely separated, before the expiration of her terms of probation. The issue of such connection would be affiliated to the father.

If the *iddat* had expired, there would be no *semblance* even of this kind; and all are agreed that the parties would be liable to the *hadd* (the punishment for adultery) "even though the husband had recalled his wife after the triple repudiation".

An example of the second kind of semblance is given by a man cohabiting with a woman whom he had completely repudiated by any of the *kinayet*, or ambiguous expressions.[2]

In such case there is no infliction of the *hadd*, even though the man should not claim that he thought the intercourse to be lawful, and the paternity of the offspring is established if claimed by him.

Abu Hanifa's doctrine.

The third kind of *shubh*, or *semblance* is that to which I have already referred, *viz.*, that which is established by a contract of marriage. According to Abu Hanifa, it is established whether the contract be lawful or unlawful, and "whether all are agreed as to the illegality, or there is a difference of opinion on the subject, and whether the party be conscious of the illegality or not."

1 But see post.

2 In this case there was a difference of opinion among the Companions, the Caliph 'Omar holding the repudiation to be reversible—Hedaya, Vol. II, p. 22.

Principle : Abu Yusuf and Mohammed.

According to the Disciples there is no *semblance when the marriage is one which is universally recognised as unlawful.* For example, if a man were to contract a marriage with a female related to him within the prohibited degrees,[1] or the wife or the *muataddah* of another man (*i. e.*, a woman whose marriage was dissolved either by death or divorce, but who had not completed her period of probation) *with the knowledge* that she was prohibited to him or was the *muataddah* of another man; and if a child is born, that child, according to Abu Yusuf and Mohammed, will not be affiliated to him.

It would be otherwise, however, if at the time of marriage the man believed or was led to believe that the woman was lawful to him.

Principle.

But where there is no inherent bar to a valid union, the mere existence at the time of the marriage of some accidental circumstance will not render the union void, and the issue of the union will consequently be legitimate.[2] I have already given examples of this principle, and it is unnecessary to dwell upon it further.

Ghurur or deception.

The instances of "deception" given in the law-books spring from the social conditions of the people and the seclusion of women. Among most Eastern races, it is not customary to see the future wife before the marriage. Hence one rule about *ghurur* is thus stated "If a strange woman be introduced into the bed of the bridegroom who is assured by her female attendant that she is the bride, and cohabitation ensue, the man would not be liable to punishment for adultery, and the issue, if any, will be affiliated to the father and the woman should have to go through the probation".

But a casual relationship by a married man with a strange woman would not relieve him from punishment, even though he may assert he understood she was his wife.[3]

Principle.

When a trustworthy person has informed a woman that her absent husband is dead, or that he has repudiated her three times or a letter of *talak* (or repudiation) has come to her from him by the hands of a trustworthy person and she has a strong conviction of its truth, she need be under no apprehension in keeping *'iddat* and, upon expiration thereof, marrying another man.

---

1 Maharim, pl. of Mahram.

2 See post.

3 It is important to bear in mind that when there is no punishment, the children are legitimate. Ghurur, in fact, covers cases in which the parties have acted *bona fide*.

In like manner, if a woman should say to a man, "My husband has repudiated me, and my *'iddat* is past", he need be under no apprehension in marrying her; and if she should be delivered of a child at more than six months from the marriage, the paternity is established in him.[1]

Principle.

But if a man married a woman knowing that she was the wife of another (which marriage was still subsisting to his knowledge), and she should bear a child to the second husband, *the child would not be affiliated to him,* though she may have told him that she was unmarried or divorced. But if *A* were to marry *B* knowing that she was married to *C*, on *C's* assurance that he had divorced her, the issue of such an union would be legitimate, even though it may turn out that the assurance was untrue.

As already stated, when a divorce takes place after cohabitation any child born according to the modern rule, within ten months of the divorce, is affiliated to the father. "If the birth should take place at more than ten months, and the divorce were revocable, the child's descent would still be established, and the repudiation would be held to have been revoked. And even though the repudiation had been irrevocable, still the descent of the child from the husband would be established if it were claimed by him."[2]

Similarly, in the case of a posthumous child born of the womb of the deceased's wife, it is affiliated to the husband if the birth take place at any time within ten months from the death. And the law is so jealous in preserving legitimacy that even where the man has died before actual cohabitation but after marriage, and a child is born within that period, the child would be regarded as legitimate.

This state, however, is subject to the right of the other heirs, to question the legitimacy of the child on evidence.

In other words the presumption in both cases may be rebutted. But the evidence in the first case, *viz.*, where consummation has taken place, must be strong to displace the presumption of law.

It must be remembered that whether cohabitation has taken place or not (after marriage), the wife has to observe the *'iddat* after the death of the husband to see whether she is or is not *enceinte*. "If the woman were to make a declaration at any time when the *'iddat* may reasonably be supposed to have expired, that the *'iddat* had been completed, whether it were for death or for divorce, and she were subsequently delivered of a child, the paternity of the child would *not* be established unless it was born in less than six months from the date of the declaration, for there might possibly be a mistake on the part of the woman in supposing she was not *enceinte* and yet it may not be right to give her the longer term."

---

1 Durr-ul-Mukhtar, p. 274.

2 See Ismail Ahmed Peepadi *v.* Momin Bibi A I R 1941 P C 11.

If a widow or divorcee were to contract a second marriage before the expiration of her *'iddat*, and were to have a child ten months from the date of her divorce, or from the death of the first husband, and at less than six months from her marriage with the second, the child would belong to the first because the second marriage is invalid.[1]

But if the delivery is at more than two years [ten months] from the divorce or death, and at six months or more from the second marriage, that marriage is lawful, and the child belongs to the second husband. If, again, the birth is at more than ten months from the first event, and at less than six months from the second, the child is not affiliated either to the first husband or to the second.

Nevertheless the second marriage is lawful, according to Abu Hanifa and Mohammed. Because the birth of the child being at more than ten months from the dissolution of the first marriage, it is evident the woman was not pregnant and therefore not in her *'iddat* at the time of the second, unless it was known at the time of the marriage that the woman was in her *'iddat* when contracting. If that were known at the time, the second marriage would be invalid, and the child would be affiliated to the first husband, "if that were possible, by its being born at less than two years [ten months] from the death or repudiation, and at six months or more from the date of the second marriage, because the second marriage being invalid, preference is given to the valid one, if possible".

Where, again, it is impossible to ascribe the paternity to the first husband, while it is possible to ascribe it to the second, by reason of the date of the first being more than ten months from that of the death or divorce and at six months or more from the second marriage, the descent of the child from the second husband is established; because, though the second marriage is invalid,[2] there is an objection to the descent being ascribed to the valid marriage, and "it is preferable to ascribe the pregnancy to an invalid marriage than to *zina*".

It must be noted that most of these dicta involve questions of evidence.

SECTION II

SHIAH DOCTRINES

Shiah Law—legitimacy how established.

UNDER the Shia Law, marriage without cohabitation does not affiliate the child of the woman to her husband as under the Sunni Law. Even where consummation has taken place, but the woman gives birth at less than six months from its occurrence to a perfect and living child, there would be no affiliation. If both the parties concur in declaring that its birth has happened

1 Durr-ul-Mukhtar p. 279; the delivery, in the circumstances, being evidence that she was pregnant, and therefore in her 'iddat at the time she contracted the marriage. See Abdul Rahman Kutty *v.* Aisha Bibi A I R 1960 Kerala 101.

2 It is assumed that the woman was known to be in 'iddat at the time of her marriage, which might be if she believed herself to be pregnant.

at more than ten months or, in exceptional cases, eleven months, from consummation, or this fact can be established by the husband's absence from his wife for a period longer than the longest period of gestation, the child to which the woman gives birth would not be affiliated to her husband. It is a matter of evidence whether affiliation under such circumstances would take place even if the husband were to claim the child as his own. But where the marriage has been consummated, and a child is born to the woman at six months, or more, *after such consummation*, it becomes affiliated of right to the husband; even though the woman may have committed adultery with somebody else, and such child cannot be disavowed by the husband, "otherwise than by *l'aan* or imprecation"[1]; and if the parties differ as to the fact of consummation or the birth of the child, preference is given to the words of the husband when confirmed by his oath.

Principle.

When consummation has taken place, and the woman has been delivered at six months or thereafter, it is unlawful for the husband to deny the parentage, on suspicion of the mother's misconduct or even though he "should know her with certainty to have committed adultery; and if he would deny her offspring to be his child, its parentage as from him cannot be rescinded in any other way than by going through the process of *l'aan*". In other words, according to the *lex fori* of British India there must be a judicial declaration in a formal proceeding.

If a man should divorce his wife, who thereupon observes an '*iddat* or period of probation, and gives birth to a child within the longest period of pregnancy from the date of the divorce, such child belongs to him, if its mother has not cohabited with another person under a valid or an invalid contract of marriage.

It is incumbent on a husband to acknowledge the child of his wife when he admits that he has had conjugal intercourse with her, and if he should deny the child, his denial is of no avail to the rescinding of its parentage[2] *unless he goes through the process of l'aan*, in other words, without a judicial proceeding where both parties are put on their oaths. And the same rule holds good, though the parties should differ as to the period between the birth of the child and the date of their intercourse.

When a man has divorced his wife, who, after observing the '*iddat* has married again, and the woman gives birth to a child at less than six months from the divorce, the child belongs to the first husband, whereas, if it is born at six months or more, it belongs to the second husband.

As regards the issue of *invalid* unions, the *Shara'ya* says: "*If a man were to cohabit with a strange woman erroneously, supposing her to be his wife, and she should give birth to a child, its parentage would be established in him.*"

If a man believing a woman to be unmarried, or a widow, or divorced from her former husband, should enter into a contract of marriage with her, and it should afterwards appear that the former husband was not dead, or had not divorced her, the

---

1 See ante.

2 *Ibid.*

woman must be restored to her first husband, after observing an *'iddat* on account of her connection with the second; but her child, if she is pregnant, belongs exclusively to the second, subject to the conditions already mentioned, "whether she acted, in the matter of the supposed death or divorce, on the decree of a Judge or the information of a single person, or the testimony of witnesses".

Nasab.

The Shiah Law on the subject of *nasab* is explicit. *Nasab*, according to the jurists of this school, is established by a *valid* marriage or by an *invalid* contract of marriage. If a man should enter in good faith into a contract of marriage which turns out to be invalid, or if a man cohabits with a woman, erroneously, but *bona fide*, believing her to be his wife, the offspring of such marriage or such intercourse would be legitimate in the eye of the law.[1]

Similarly, would *nasab* be established though the union was *ab initio* null and void. For example, if a man married a woman who was forbidden to him, or with whom marriage was unlawful, either *radically*, that is, from the relationship of blood existing between the parties, or by some incidental circumstance, such as fosterage, matrimonial affinity or any other cause, the issue of such an union would be legitimate, *if the marriage was contracted in error, or the parties were not aware of the hurmat* (illegality).[2]

If a man married, *by a pure mistake*, a woman within the prohibited degrees of consanguinity, such marriage would be *radically* illegal but the issue of the union would *not* be illegitimate.

Difference between the Hanafi and Shiah doctrine.

As already mentioned, Abu Hanifa not only agrees with the Shiah doctors, but even goes beyond them in some respects, whilst Abu Yusuf and Mohammed, whose views have been adopted by the great jurist Abu'l Lais, and are in force among the Indian[3] Hanafis, hold a contrary opinion. According to them, the children of a *radically* illegal union, *e.g.*, an union within the prohibited degrees would be illegitimate, *unless* the marriage was contracted in good faith and in absolute ignorance of the prohibition or illegality.

When a woman, whose former husband is alive, enters into a second contract of marriage under the *bona fide* belief that the husband is dead, and man whom she marries acts under the same belief, a child born of such marriage is legitimate according to the Shiahs.

Principle.

But if the parties were to marry with the knowledge of the fact that the woman's first husband was alive, the intercourse being *ab initio* adulterous, the child would have no *nasab* with his father, according to both the Hanafis and the Shiahs.

1 Irshad-ul-'Allamah; Shara'ya-ul-Islam, p. 301.

2 Jam'a-ush-Shittat; Shara'ya-ul-Islam, p. 457.

3 Now Indo-Pakistan.

The Jam'a-ush-Shittat.

This position appears clearly in a case stated in the *Jam'a-ush-Shittat* where the following question was put to the *Mujtahid.*

Q.—"A woman of the name of Hind became pregnant three years from the time her husband became a *mafkud-ul-khabar* (missing), and gave birth to a child who was named 'Umar; and people say that the child was begotten by one Bakr. Shortly after Hind intermarried with Bakr in spite of her husband being still missing. Some years later Hind died. Can 'Umar claim from Bakr the dower due to his mother"?

A.—"According to the case stated, 'Umar is not the child of the missing husband; and when it is known that he was begotten by fornication it cannot be affiliated to the adulterer, or claim the inheritance of its mother. As regards the marriage of Hind with Bakr, if both knew of its illegality, and that the husband was missing, the woman was unlawful [to Bakr] and the marriage unlawful; and such marriage cannot be the subject of dower, because for fornication there is no dower; and, therefore, even if 'Umar should be ascribed to the mother, he would not be entitled to claim.

"If Hind and Bakr, or either of them were not aware of the illegality of their union, then she would be entitled to her *mahr-ul-misl*, and her legal heirs can claim the same. But 'Umar cannot claim. If 'Umar, however, was begotten under *shubh* (deception or semblance of right) he would be affiliated to the mother and can claim her dower."[1]

Principle.

Under the Shiah Law, "a child of fornication" (*walad-uz-zina*) owns no *descent* to either of its parents. It is regarded as *nullus filius*; "so neither the man who has unlawfully begotten, nor the woman who has unlawfully borne, the child, nor any of their relations can inherit from such child; nor has the child any title to inherit from them."[2]

Musst. Sahebzadi Begum v. Mirza Himmat Bahadur.

The principles of the Shiah Law of legitimacy were discussed at some length in the case of *Musst. Sahebzadi Begum* v. *Mirza Himmat Bahadur*, which came before the High Court of Calcutta.[3] It appeared in that case that a Hindu Rajah, called Modenarain Singh, had contracted an alliance with a Shiah woman of the name of Burati Begum. There were several children born of this union, all of whom were brought up in the Mahommedan faith and the Shiah communion. Upon the decease of one of the sons, leaving behind him his wife Sahebzadi Begum, and a brother and sister, the question was raised whether the latter were entitled to any interest in the estate of the deceased. It was decided that as, under the Shiah Law, there was no *nasab* between them and the *propositus* they had no heritable right in his property.

---

1 Jam'a-ush-Shittat.

2 See ante ; Fatawai 'Alamgiri, Vol. II, p. 210.

3 Supra. See also Bailie, Vol. II, p. 305.

Principle. Walad-ul-mala'inah.

Whilst the offspring of illicit intercourse—a *walad-uz-zina*—owns no relationship or *nasab* under the Shiah Law to either of its parents, the rule is otherwise with reference to the "child of imprecation" *walad-ul-mala'inah*, the child whose affiliation has been "cut off" by the proceeding of *l'aan*, or who has been bastardised by a judicial proceeding. "The child of imprecation is cut off from the man, not from the woman, so that the mother and those related through her retain their right of inheritance reciprocally."[1] But if the father were to make a retractation of the *l'aan*, the *nasab* or the status of legitimacy will be re-established so far as to restore to the child the right of inheritance to its father, but not *vice versa*[2] that is, the father cannot, by a retractation, recover his right of inheritance to any property that may be left by the child.

Sunni doctrines.

Under the Sunni Law there is no difference in the status of a *walad-uz-zina* and a *walad-ul-mala'inah*—a "child of fornication" and a "child of imprecation". Both have a *nasab* with their mother and with persons related to them through her, and consequently they can inherit from her and all relations connected through her, just as the latter can inherit from them.[3] For example, if, in the case of *Musst. Sahebzadi Begum* v. *Mirza Himmat Bahadur*, the parties had been Sunnis instead of Shiahs, the brother and sister would undoubtedly have taken a share in the inheritance of their deceased brother.

SECTION III

PRESUMPTION OF LEGITIMACY

THIS is a very important branch of the Mahommedan Law, and in many instances the principles have been misunderstood in the Indian Courts.

Status of legitimacy—presumption.

When the parties are married, and the marriage is a matter of notoriety and capable of distinct proof, any dispute as to the status of the children resolves itself into a mere question whether the children were *conceived and born* in lawful wedlock. But there may be cases in which the marriage is not capable of being easily proved. It may have been contracted in a distant country, or under circumstances which preclude the possibility of securing documentary or oral testimony as to the *factum* of the marriage. *In these cases the Mahommedan Law presumes a legal marriage from continued cohabitation and the acknowledged position of the parties as husband and wife, provided there is no insurmountable obstacle to such a presumption and provided the relationship existing between the parties was not "a mere casual*

---

1 Irshad-ul-'Allamah; Jam'a-ush-Shittat; Shara'ya, p. 349.

2 *Ibid.*

3 Kanz-ud-Dakaik; Fatawai 'Alamgiri, Vol. VI, p. 629; Sice, Lois Musulman.

concubinage", but was permanent in its character, justifying the inference that they were lawfully married.[1]

Principle.

For example, if a woman, married to a man from whom she is not divorced, contracts a union with a second person, and lives with him continuously, such continuous cohabitation in the face of the legal bar to their lawful union, will not give rise to the presumption of a legal marriage;[2] or, if the woman were related to the man within the prohibited degrees, their living together as husband and wife, will not lead to the presumption of a lawful marriage.

Principle.

If, however, there was no such bar to their being lawfully married, and the connection was not in the nature of a casual concubinage, the law will presume from continuous cohabitation that they were lawfully married and would attach the status of legitimacy to the offspring of the connection.[3]

Should the presumption be based on continuous relationship, the issue of the connection can be legitimated only by the father's acknowledgment, *express or implied.* It is not necessary that he should acknowledge the child *expressly*. If it can be inferred from his conduct towards and his treatment of the child that he acknowledged it to be his legitimate issue, the law will attach the status of legitimacy to the child.[4]

---

1 Buker Hoossain Khan *v.* Shurfoon Nissa Begum (1860) 8 Moo. I A 136. See also Khajah Hidayut Oollah *v.* Rai Jan Khanum (1844) 3 Moo. I A 295; and *Musst.* Husnoo *v.* *Musst.* Wahedunnissa, Agra Sudder Dew. Ad. Decisions for 1864, 380. See also Habib-ur-Rahman Chowdhury *v.* Altaf Ali Chowdhury (1921) L R 48 I A 114; Ma Khatoon *v.* Ma Mya A I R 1936 Rang. 448 ; Zamin Ali *v.* Aziz-un-Nissa A I R 1933 Lah. 329 : I L R 55 All. 139.

2 See Muhammad Shafiqullah Khan *v.* Nuhullah Khan I L R 48 All. 58. It is only where direct proof of marriage is not available that indirect proof of marriage by way of acknowledgment of legitimacy in favour of a child is allowed to take the place of direct proof of marriage. When direct proof is available to establish that marriage was impossible or a marriage would be invalid (the woman being already married and her husband who was alive not having divorced her) no question of presumption of marriage on account of an alleged acknowledgment can arise.

Rashid Ahmad *v.* Anisa Khatun A I R 1932 P C 25: L R 59 I A 21. In this case a Hanafi Muhammadan had repudiated his wife by three pronouncements (irrevokable talak). The parties afterwards lived together and five children were born to them whom the father acknowledged as legitimate. After his death the children claimed their share of his estate as heirs. A remarriage between the parties was not proved but the Court was asked to presume it from the acknowledgment of legitimacy. It was held that an acknowledgment of legitimacy, no doubt, raises a presumption of marriage but that is only when there is no legal bar to the marriage. There is such a bar in this case created by the divorce which can only be removed by proving that the mother of the children had, after the divorce, married another man and the latter had died or divorced her after actual consummation of the marriage. If these facts are not proved, remarriage cannot be presumed and the children cannot be held to be legitimate.

3 See Bibi Amu *v.* Asiat P L D 1958 Kar. 420.

4 See Mohabbat Ali Khan *v.* Mohammed Ibrahim Khan 56 I A 201. An acknowledgment which involves the assertion that the father was married to an acknowledgee's mother immediately raises a presumption in favour of marriage and legitimacy.

Presumption of legitimacy from continued cohabitation.

This position was laid down with considerable distinctness by the Judicial Committee in the case of *Ashrufood Dowlah Ahmed Hossein Khan* v. *Hyder Hossein Khan*.[1] In this case their Lordships said as follows:—

"The presumption of legitimacy from marriage follows the bed and whilst the marriage lasts, the child of the woman is taken to be the husband's child; but this presumption follows the bed, and is not ante-dated by relation. An ante-nuptial child is illegitimate. A child born out of wedlock is illegitimate; if acknowledged, he acquires the status of legitimacy. When, therefore, a child really illegitimate by birth becomes legitimated, it is by force of an acknowledgment express or implied, directly proved or presumed. These presumptions are inferences of fact. They are built on the foundation of the law, and do not widen the grounds, of legitimacy by confounding concubinage and marriage. The child of marriage is legitimate as soon as born. The child of a concubine may become legitimate by treatment as legitimate. Such treatment would furnish evidence of acknowledgment. A Court would not be justified, though dealing with this subject of legitimacy, in making any presumptions of fact which a rational view of the principles of evidence would exclude. *The presumption in favour of marriage and legitimacy must rest on sufficient grounds, and cannot be permitted to override overbalancing proofs, whether direct or presumptive.*"[2]

Principle.

As already stated, the acknowledgment need not be express; it may be inferred from *treatment*, but the treatment of the child by the father must be such as to give rise to the inference that the child was treated as a *legitimate* child.

The legal effects of an acknowledgment.

When the child born of the *ventre* of a woman between whom and the father there has existed continuous relationship, has been acknowledged by the latter as his *legitimate* offspring, such acknowledgment will have the effect of giving to the mother the status of a married wife, entitling her to succeed to the inheritance of her child's father.[3]

In other words, the acknowledgment by a man of the paternity of a child as his legitimate offspring has the effect of giving not

1 (1866) 11 Moo. I A 94; see also Buker Hoossain *v.* Shuroon Nissah Begum (1860) 8 Moo. I A 136; *Musst.* Husnoo *v. Musst.* Wahedunnissa Agra Sudder Dew. Ad. Decisions for 1864, 380 supra.

2 See Ihsan Hasan Khan *v.* Panna Lal A I R 1928 Pat. 19. If there is no definite evidence of valid marriage between the parties, acknowledgement by father is sufficient to make the issues legitimate.

Muhammad Sadiq *v.* Mohammed Hasan A I R 1943 Lah. 225. The effect of a valid acknowledgement would be that the marriage of the mother of the acknowledgee with the acknowledger would be held proved unless it is disproved. Until the claimant establishes his acknowledgment the onus is on him to prove a valid marriage. Once he establishes an acknowledgment, the onus is on those who deny the marriage to negative it in fact.

3 **Radd-ul-Muhtar, Vol. II, p. 1035.**

only to the child but also to the mother the right of inheritance to the father, the law presuming from the acknowledgment of the *legitimacy* of the offspring a lawful union between the parents.[1]

For example, *A* and *B* live together as husband and wife and have issue, there is no evidence that they were married; at the same time there is no "insurmountable bar" to their contracting a lawful marriage; *A* acknowledges the children, either in express terms or by conduct, that they are his *legitimate* offspring, such acknowledgment has the effect of giving a right of inheritance to the children as well as to *B*. It is not necessary that the man should expressly state that the children are his legitimate offspring. It is sufficient if he treats them *as such*.[2] Some of the lawyers have derived the presumption so far as to lay down the rule that if a man were to say 'this is my child' and do not say that 'it is mine by fornication,' the law will presume it to be legitimate. But, this rule must be received with caution.[3]

---

1 See Mohabbat Ali Khan *v.* Mohammed Ibrahim Khan 56 I A 201 ; Habibur Rahman Chowdhry *v.* Altaf Ali 48 I A 114. The law presumes in favour of marriage and against concubinage, when a man and a woman have cohabited continuously for a number of years.

A claimant son who has in his favour a good acknowledgment of legitimacy is in this position, the marriage will be held proved and his legitimacy established, unless the marriage is disproved. Until the claimant establishes his acknowledgment, the onus is on him to prove a marriage. Once he establishes an acknowledgment the onus is on those who deny a marriage.

Abdur Razzaq *v.* Agha Mohammed Jaffer 21 I A 56 : 21 Cal. 666 P C The Mohammedan doctrine of acknowledgment does not apply to every case of admission of paternity. An intention to confer the status of legitimacy must be found or presumed. The reason for this doctrine is to be found in the possibility under Muslim Law of proving the existence of a valid marriage in cases where no ceremony has been performed but evidence is adduced from which it appears that the parties intended to be united in the marriage bond. See Ashraf-ud-daulah *v.* Hyder Hussain Khan 11 Moo. I A 94 and Habib-ur-Rahman *v.* Altaf Ali 48 I A 114: A I R 1922 P C 149.

2 See Imambandi *v.* Mustaddi (1918) L R 45 I A 73.

Habib-ur-Rahman *v.* Altaf Ali 48 I A 114. The acknowledgment must be not merely of sonship but of legitimate son.

3 See Sadiq Hussain Khan *v.* Hashim Ali Khan 43 I A 212. No statement made by one man that another (proved to be illegitimate) is his son can make that other legitimate, but where no proof of that kind has been given, such a statement or acknowledgment is substantive evidence that the person so acknowledged is the legitimate son of the person who makes the statement provided his legitimacy is possible.

But as observed in Ahsanullah *v.* Najabat Ali A I R 1929 Cal. 682, a declaration by a person that another person is his legitimated son born of his loins and in the womb of his married wife in an acknowledgment not merely of sonship but of legitimate sonship. And if direct evidence of marriage is adduced and the Court disbelieves it, the effect of presumption arising from the acknowledgment is not lost and the failure does not absolve the opposite-party from disproving the impossibility of marriage and thereby rebutting the presumption).

In Feroz Din *v.* Nawab Khan A I R 1928 Lah. 432, it was held that acknowledgment by the father gives rise to a presumption of fact that there was a marriage between the parents and thus it may be rebutted by positive proof that there was no marriage between the parents.

[Continued on next page]

Mahatala v. Prince Ahmad Haleemuz Zuman—Acknowledgment of a child.

The point was decided in the case of *Mahatala* v. *Prince Ahmad Haleemuzzuman.*[1] In this case two ladies named respectively Mahatala and Imtazunnissa claimed to be the widows of Prince Gholam Mohammed. As there was no proof of Mahatala's marriage the Court held against her. As regards Imtazunnissa the Chief Justice (Sir Richard Garth) said as follows:—

"And we should probably have had some difficulty in the case of Imtazunnissa but for the legal presumption which we consider arises in her case and which does not arise in the case of Mahatala. There is no direct proof of Imtazunnissa's marriage; there is no evidence of her being treated with any special favour or distinction, except as the mother of Prince Haleem; and there is no doubt that towards the close of his life, and especially in the *wakfnama*, Imtazunnissa was considered as in the same category as Mahatala. But the fact that she was the mother of Prince Haleem and that Prince Haleem was from the first acknowledged and treated by Prince Gholam as his lawful son, makes all the difference we think to the right of Imtazunnissa.

"We have been referred in the course of the argument to a long current of authorities upon the subject of the presumption both of marriage and legitimacy, which arises under the Mahommedan Law, either from express acknowledgment or from a course of treatment, which amounts to such acknowledgment. This doctrine of presumption is in the present case of great importance. It appears to us to constitute the most essential distinction between the respective claims of these two ladies, whose rights and status we have to determine.

"In many respects the evidence of actual marriage in the case of Imtazunnissa may not appear more cogent than in the case of Mahatala. They may both have received from Prince Gholam (at any rate towards the close of his life), the same amount of attention and kindness; the provision which he may have made for them may have been equal; and they may have been treated both by the Prince himself, and after his death by

---

In Jiand Khan *v.* The Province of Sind A I R 1948 Sind 130 the same principle was propounded.

But as observed by their Lordships in Fatima Benti Hafedah *v.* The Administrator General, Zanzibar A I R 1949 P C 254, the mere admission of paternity in no way establishes anything but a casual union and more is required to show the existence of the marriage bond if the existence of that bond is to be derived from association alone without any preceding ceremony. The father may accept his parent-hood without intending to make the child legitimate. Once, however, marriage is established acknowledgment of paternity is enough. Similarly in their Lordships' opinion once it is proved that relationship of master and slave concubine has been proved a connection is established which leads to the inference that the child is legitimate if its paternity is acknowledged.

1 (1881) 10 Cal. L R 293; Comp. Campbell *v.* Campbell L R 1 H L (Sc.) 182. Of course if the mother is a non-Moslemah the bar which is created by difference of faith precludes her from taking a share in the inheritance of the husband, but the offspring of the connection are, without any question, legitimate.

the family, with an equal share of respect and consideration. But having regard to the law of presumption, the great advantage which the one lady possesses over the other consists in this,—that she has a son, who has been clearly and indubitably acknowledged from first to last by Prince Gholam as his legitimate offspring.

"And, as a matter of legal presumption, full effect could not possibly be given to this acknowledgment of the legitimacy of Prince Haleem, unless his mother were also presumed to have been his father's lawful wife."

After referring to several cases, the learned Chief Justice proceeded as follows:—

"In this latter case[1] it is said: 'When a man has openly, and for a long course of time, lived with a woman as a man lives with his wife, and has habitually and openly treated the children as his children before the world, or when he has publicly and advisedly said, of a boy begotten by himself, 'this is my son', then the presumption takes its fullest effect. In that case, we think that the law not only raises a presumption of marriage, but in practice prohibits any counter-proof short of establishing a legal impossibility. In such a case, we may not really believe that there was an actual celebration of marriage; we may have little doubt that there was nothing of the kind, but still marriage is legally possible, and it must be presumed, not as much by presumption of fact, as by presumption of law'.

"This appears to meet the case of Imtazunnissa. She undoubtedly cohabited for years with Prince Gholam as his wife; and she had a child by him who has been openly acknowledged and treated by the Prince as his lawful son. We may not find in her case any evidence of the actual fact of marriage more cogent than in the case of Mahatala, and yet we would be justified

---

1 *Musst.* Nawabunnissa *v.* *Musst.* Fuzloonissa (1863), Marshall's Rep. 428. See also Rook Begum *v.* Walagawhur Shah (1865) 3 W R 187 approved by the Privy Council in 45 I A 73.

Mohammad Sadiq *v.* Mohammad Hasan A I R 1943 Lah. 225. The Mohammedan Law of acknowledgment of parentage with its legitimating effect has no reference whatsoever to cases in which illegitimacy of the child is proved and established either by reason of impossibility of lawful union between the parents of the child or by reason of their marriage being disproved. The doctrine relates to cases where either the fact of the marriage itself or the exact time of its occurrence with reference to the legitimacy of the acknowledged child is not proved. In other words it applies only to cases of uncertainty as to legitimacy and in such cases acknowledgment has its effect, but that effect always proceeds upon the assumption of a lawful union between the parents of the acknowledged child. In the case of a good acknowledgment of legitimacy, the marriage between the parents of the child will be held proved and his legitimacy established unless the marriage is disproved. Until the child establishes his acknowledgment the onus is on him to prove a marriage between his parents. Once he establishes his acknowledgment the onus is on those who deny a marriage to negative it in fact.

See also Tyebhoy Essofalle Thingna *v.* Collector of Allahabad A I R 1944 Bom. 91; Rafiqa Begum *v.* Aisha Begum A I R 1945 All. 363 and Roshanbai *v.* Suleman A I R 1944 Bom. 213.

under the circumstances in presuming almost conclusively her marriage with the Prince."

The case of *Ghazanfar Ali Khan* v. *Kaniz Fatima*[1] furnishes an illustration of the converse doctrine. In that case the mother of the child—whose legitimacy was in question—was proved to have been a prostitute before she was brought to the house of the child's father; there was no sufficient evidence of marriage or of acknowledgment of her as a wife or of the child as the father's legitimate offspring. The Judicial Committee on the facts declined to raise a presumption of marriage from long cohabitation.

CHAPTER III
THE DOCTRINE OF ACKNOWLEDGMENT

SECTION I
ACKNOWLEDGMENT OF PATERNITY

Adoption not recognised.

ADOPTION in the sense in which it is understood by the Hindus and as it was practised among the Romans, is not recognised by the Mahommedan Law. Among the Romans, as among the Hindus of the present day, it was intimately connected with religious ideas "having relations to the repose of the souls of the departed and the preservation of the household divinities." It existed also among the pre-Islamic Arabs and, no doubt, had a similar origin.[2]

The Prophet appears to have recognised the custom at the time he adopted Zaid, the son of Haris. Later, when he had weaned the idolatrous tribes from the revolting practices to which they were addicted, and had given them higher ideas of domestic relationship, he explained in fuller terms that adoption similar to what was practised in the "Days of Ignorance" created no such tie between the *adopted* and the *adopting* as resulted from blood relationship.[3]

The Musulman Law, accordingly, does not recognise the validity of any mode of *filiation where the parentage of the person*

---

1 (1910) L R 37 I A 105; Dhan Bibi *v.* Lalon Bibi I L R 27 Cal. 801.

See Gangadhar *v.* Rachappa A I R 1929 Bom. 246. The ordinary case which the English authorities had in mind was that of a man and woman living together as man and wife in the ordinary way, and regarded as such by their friends and neighbours. When the status of the man is lower than that of the woman, and the intercourse between them was necessarily illicit for a large number of years, a presumption of legitimate marriage cannot be raised.

Ismail Ahmad Peepadi *v.* Momin Bibi A I R 1941 P C 11. Where the husband marries a poor wife of lower social standing and keeps his marriage with her to some extent secret and never takes her to live at his father's house the child's claim as the only child of the marriage does not necessarily fail because the father is not shown to have treated him as one would ordinarily expect an only child to have been treated by his father. By far the most important question in such circumstances is whether the father maintained and supported the child.

2 Caussin de Percival Histoire des Arabes Vol. I. p. 364.

3 Koran, Chap. xxxiii; Tabari (Zotenberg's Translation), Vol. III, p. 58.

adopted is known to belong to a person other than the adopting father, and an *adopted child* (or *mutabanna*) has no rights in the estate of his or her *adoptive parents*.[1]

Ikrar or acknowledgment.

The only form of filiation which is recognised by the Mahommedan Law is the one which is created by *ikrar* or "acknowledgment". Under the Sunni Law, the father alone has the right to establish the relation of sonship to the total exclusion of the mother or any other relative.

The Calcutta High Court has laid down that the doctrine of acknowledgment is an integral portion of the Mahommedan family law and the conditions under which it will take effect must be determined with reference to Mahommedan Jurisprudence, rather than the Evidence Act.[2]

Acknowledgment may be either express or implied.

Such acknowledgment may be either express or *implied*; it may be made in express terms, or may be implied from the father's conduct towards, and his *continued* treatment of, the child as his own *legitimate* child.[3]

Conditions of valid acknowledgment.

But in order to render the acknowledgment valid and effectual in law, three conditions must be fulfilled, *viz.* :—

(1) The acknowledgor and the acknowledged must be of such ages respectively as would admit of the possibility of their standing in the relation of parent and child to each other. For example, a man cannot establish the relationship of father and son between himself and another, unles he is at least twelve and a half years older than the son he intends to filiate or acknowledge.

(2) The person acknowledged must be of *unknown descent* (*majhul-un-nasab*).[4] If the parentage is *known* to belong to somebody else no *ascription* can take place to the acknowledgor.

---

1 See Muhammad Allahdad Khan *v.* Muhammad Ismail Khan (1888) I L 10 All. 289, 340; Muhammad Umar Khan *v.* Muhammad Niazuddin Khan (1911) I L 39 Cal. 418. See also Bai Machhbai *v.* Bai Hirbai (1911) I L 35 Bom. 264, which was the case of an adoption by a convert to Hinduism.

2 Fazilatunnissa *v.* Kamarunnissa (1904) 9 Cal. W N 352.

3 Fatawai 'Alamgiri Vol. I, p. 703; Sharh-i-Vikaya Vol. II, p. 438, Hedaya Bk. xxv, chap. iii; Sharaya'ul-Islam p. 376; Khaja Hidayat Oollah *v.* Rai Jan Khanum, supra; Ashrufood-Dowla Ahmed Hossain Khan *v.* Hyder Hossein Khan, supra; Nawab Muhammad Azmat Ali Khan *v.* Lalli Begum (1881) I L 8 Cal. 922; s c L R 9 I A 8; Syed Sadakat Hossein *v.* Syed Mohammed Yusuf (1883) I L 10 Cal. 663; s c L R 11 I A 31; Abdool Razack *v.* Aga Mohammed Jaffer Bindaneem (1893) I L 21 Cal. 666; s c L R 21 I A 56; Masit-un-nissa *v.* Pathani (1904) I L 26 All. 295; Mohammed Sadiq *v.* Mohammad Hasan A I R 1943 Lah. 225.

4 *i.e.*, of unknown paternity, at the place of his birth or at the place where he is residing.—Durr-ul-Mukhtar, p. 604.

The Bombay High Court has laid down that a person can acknowledge a son where there is no proof of the latter's legitimacy or illegitimate birth and his paternity is unknown in the sense that no specific person is known to be his father. It is not permissible to acknowledge a child known to be the offspring of an unlawful connection.[1] This enunciation, however, requires a certain qualification and must be viewed in the light of the facts of the particular case.

Principle.

For if there was no bar to a lawful connection between the parents and they had lived together for a long time as husband and wife acknowledging each other as such, the mere absence of direct proof of marriage would not invalidate an acknowledgment of sonship. *The acknowledgment, however, must be of legitimate sonship.*[2]

(3) The acknowledged must believe himself *to be the acknowlegor's child*, or, at all events, assent to the fact.[3]

The *Hedaya,* with reference to this, latter condition, says: "It is also a condition that the boy verify the acknowledgment, because he is considered to be his own master, as he is supposed to be able to give an account of himself. *It would be otherwise if the child could not explain his condition.*"[4]

An infant who is too young to understand what the relationship implies, or to give an account of himself, is not required to agree to the acknowledgment, nor is his assent a condition precedent to the validity of an acknowledgment, as it is in the case of an adult.

Assent on the part of an infant not necessary.

The *Jouharat-un-Nayyireh* says: "The assent is required only from a young person who is possessed of discretion and is able to give an account of himself.........it is not necessary in the case of an infant".

The *Jam'a-ush-Shittat* says: "No regard is paid to the assent of a young child"; and the *Shara'ya-ul-Isam* adds: "If an infant is acknowledged and afterwards, on attaining his majority, he denies the paternity, such denial is of no effect."

Capacity to acknowledge subject to limitations.

An acknowledgment can take place only when the person acknowledging possesses the legal capacity of entering into a

---

1 Mardan Saheb *v.* Rajak Saheb (1909) I L 34 Bom. 111; Feroz Din *v.* Nawab Khan A I R 1928 Lah. 432.

2 Abdur Razaq *v.* Agha Mahommed Jaffar 21 I A 56; Fatima Benti Hafedah *v.* A. G. Zanzibar A I R 1949 P C 254.

3 There is no difference between the Shiahs and the Sunnis on these points, Shara'ya-ul-Islam, p. 376.

4 Hedaya, Bk. xxv, chap. iii, Vol. III, pp. 168, 169. The rule applies to both male and female children. See Omda Bebee *v.* Syed Shah Jonab Ali (1866) 5 W R 132; Fazeelun Bibee *v.* Omdah Bebee 10 W R 469; Waheedun *v.* Wassee Hossein 5 W R 402.

valid contract. The person must be adult, sane, and free. An acknowledgment made by an infant (under the Mahommedan Law, one who has not attained the age of puberty), or by a person who is in *duress*, or who is *non compos mentis*, is absolutely invalid. An insane person, however, may be *acknowledged* without regard to his or her assent, in the same way as an infant.[1]

Regard must always be paid to the fact that when an acknowledgment is in favour of a child or an insane person who cannot assent to the relationship so created, the interest of such child or such person should not in any way be affected.

Acknowledgment must be legally established.

"All that has been said is subject to this qualification, that the acknowledgor is not suing for property. When property is sued for on the ground of the relationship, as, for instance, when a woman sues a man on the ground of his having married her for such a dower and then repudiated her before consummation and thereupon claims half her dower; or a woman sues a man for maintenance, declaring herself to be his wife, the Judge (it is generally agreed) is to put her oath". In other words, the mere "acknowledgment" which is involved in the claim is not sufficient to establish the relationship.

For example, if a person were to die leaving property and some one else were to put forward a claim to a share in his inheritance on the ground of being the father of the deceased, the allegation would have no effect until the relationship was judicially established.

An acknowledgment of parentage may be considered therefore, as analogous, in certain of its legal effects under the Mahommedan Law, to the doctrine of *legitimatio per subsequents matrimonium*. But there is this marked difference between the two doctrines, that whereas *acknowledgment* presumes a *prior marriage*, the legitimation of ante-nuptial children by a subsequent marriage proceeds upon a different hypothesis. So far, however, as the status of legitimacy is concerned both doctrines lead to the same result—of legitimating the issue of an invalid connection or of a marriage of which there is no proof that it was validly contracted.

Muhammad Allahdad Khan v. Muhammad Ismail Khan.

In the case of *Muhammad Allahdad Khan* v. *Muhammad Ismail Khan*[2] Edge, C. J., and Straight, J., laid down somewhat broadly that the rules of the Mahommedan Law relating to acknowledgment by a Mahommedan of another as his son are rules of the substantive Law of Inheritance. Such an acknowledgment, unless certain impediments exist, confers upon the person acknowledged the status of a legitimate son capable of inheriting. Where there is no proof of a legitimate birth or of illegitimate birth, and the paternity of a child is unknown, in the sense that no specific person is shown to be the father, then the acknowledgment of him by another who claims him as a son affords a conclusive presumption that he is the legitimate child of

1 Shara'ya p. 376.

2 (1888) I L 10 All. 289.

the acknowledgor and places him in that category. Such a status once conferred cannot be destroyed by any subsequent act of the acknowledgor or of any one claiming through him.[1]

The enunciation of Mahmood, J., were more exact. The learned Judge held, that although, according to the Mahommedan Law, *ikrar* or acknowledgment in general stands upon much the same footing as an admission as defined in the Evidence Act, acknowledgments of parentage and other matters of personal status stand upon a higher footing than matters of evidence, and form a part of the substantive Mahommedan Law. So far as inheritance through males is concerned, the existence of consanguinity and legitimate descent is an indispensable condition precedent to the right of succession, and such legitimate descent depends upon the existence of a valid marriage between the parents. Where legitimacy cannot be established by direct proof of such a marriage, acknowledgment is recognised by the Mahommedan Law as a means whereby the marriage of the parents or legitimate descent may be established as a matter of substantive law. Such acknowledgment always proceeds upon the hypothesis of lawful union between the parents and the legitimate descent of the acknowledged person from the acknowledgor, and there is nothing in the Mahommedan Law similar to adoption as recognised by the Roman and Hindu systems, admitting of an affiliation which has no reference to consanguinity or legitimate descent. A child whose illegitimacy is proved beyond doubt, by reason of the marriage of its parents being either disproved or found to be unlawful, cannot be legitimised by an acknowledgment. Acknowledgment has only the effect of legitimation where either the fact of the marriage or its exact time, with reference to the legitimacy of the child's birth, is a matter of uncertainty.

Rule of legitimation by acknowledgment.

Thus the rule relating to the legitimation of children by *acknowledgment* is based on the *assumption of legitimacy* and its establishment by the avoidance of the hypothesis of unlawful relationship between the parents.[2] To use the language of the Judicial Committee in the case of *Ashrufood Dowla Ahmed Hossein* v. *Hyder Hossein* "acknowledgment of paternity under the Mahommedan Law is a recognition, not simply of sonship, but of legitimacy as a son". *Accordingly, a child proved to be the offspring of fornication or of a casual and adulterous connection cannot be legitimated by the father.*[3]

Principle.

But if a man were to cohabit with a woman (not by way of a casual relationship), and to have issue by her and were to acknowledge such children as his *legitimate* offspring, such

1 See Mohammed Azmat *v.* Lalli Begum 9 I A 8; I L R 8 Cal. 422; Sadaqat Hussain *v.* Mohammed Yusuf 11 I A 31: 10 Cal. 663.

2 The Calcutta High Court, misapprehended the Mahommedan Law in the matter of the Petition of Najibunnissa Bibi (1869) 4 B L R A C 55.

3 See Habibur Rahman *v.* Altaf Ali L R 48 I A 114: A I R 1922 P C 159; Feroz Din *v.* Nawab A I R 1928 Lah. 432; A I R 1929 Lah. 55.

acknowledgment would supply any defect in the evidence of marriage.[1]

The acknowledgment of legitimacy proceeds upon the basis of a prior lawful relationship between the parents. If the marriage, however, is alleged and disproved, the effect of an *implied* acknowledgment as deducible from mere treatment is minimised, for, as already stated, *an acknowledgment to be effective must directly or indirectly point to the children as the legitimate issue of the acknowledgor.*[2]

In some of the cases decided, the principle has been stretched further than what is warranted by the Mahommedan Law, and has given rise to confusion in the Indian Courts. The enunciations, however, in the cases of *Hyder Hussain* and *Habib-ur-Rahman Chowdhury* clearly define the principles and the limits of the Mahommedan Law of acknowledgment.[3]

SECTION II

ACKNOWLEDGMENT OF OTHER RELATIONSHIP

THE disavowal of a son after an established acknowledgment is "untenable"[3] in the sense that the affirmation of legitimacy by the father once made *so as to satisfy the requirements of the law* cannot be revoked by him or questioned by his heirs.

As already stated, the mode of filiation known as adoption is not recognised under the Mahommedan Law; an adopted child (or *mutabanna*) has no rights in the estate of his or her adoptive parents.

Acknowledgment of a child by a married woman. Sunni doctrine.

According to the Sunni doctrine the acknowledgment of a child by a *married* woman is *not valid*, inasmuch as it affects another person, *viz.*, the husband, unless it is confirmed by the husband's own declaration. For example, if Hind, the wife of Zaid, were to say that Amr, a person of unknown parentage, was her son, her statement would have no legal effect, for, were it otherwise, liability might be attached to the husband, prejudicially perhaps, through his wife's statement. If, however, he were to confirm her acknowledgment it would be valid, and the son Amr would acquire the status of legitimacy.

This rule is intended to guard against the imposition of fictitious children as the offspring of a particular person; and with this object it is also laid down that maternity can be estab-

---

1 Imambandi *v.* Mustaddi L R 45 I A 73; Habibur Rahman *v.* Altaf Ali Chowdary L R 48 I A 114; Sadiq Hussain Khan *v.* Hasham Ali L R 43 I A 212; Ahsanullah Khan *v.* Nejabat Ali A I R 1929 Cal. 682.

2 Comp. Dhan Bibi *v.* Lalon Bibi (1900) I L 27 Cal. 801; Fazilat-unnissa *v.* Kamarunnissa, supra; Masilunnissa *v.* Pathani, supra and Oomda Beebee *v.* Syud Shah Jonab Ali (1866) 5 W R 132; Khushal Singh *v.* Jaimal 190 P L R 1908; Habibur Rahman Chowdery *v.* Altaf Ali 46 Cal. 259

3 Comp. Ashrufood-Dowlah Ahmed Hossain Khan *v.* Hyder Hossein Khan, supra; see post p. 226; Habib-ur-Rahman Chowdhury *v.* Altaf Ali Chowdhury (1921) L R 48 I A 114.

lished by the testimony of the midwife, when it is necessary to ascertain that the child with reference to whom a claim is advanced, "is the identical child which the said woman brought forth."[1]

It will be seen, therefore, that a woman, who is married or who is observing the '*iddat* or probation during which she cannot contract a second marriage, is precluded from acknowledging a child, unless her acknowledgment is confirmed by her husband, or the child is proved to be her own.

"A woman's acknowledgment", says the '*Inaya*, "with respect to child, is not valid, inasmuch as the parentage affects another, namely, the husband, unless her statement is confirmed by him (as the right appertains to him), or the birth be proved by the testimony of a competent woman, namely, the midwife"; or, it may be added, any other evidence that may be procurable to connect the child with the mother.

If she is married, and her husband confirms her in what she had said about the child being hers, its descent is established from both, and there is no necessity for any proof; but if he deny what she has said, she is not to be believed without proof, because she is burdening another with the descent. The testimony of the midwife, however, is sufficient for this purpose, because all that is required is to identify the child as hers, the ascription to the husband being an inference from the existing *firash* or bed.

If she is undergoing her '*iddat*, full proof is required, according to Abu Hanifa, unless the pregnancy was manifest or the husband had previously acknowledged it, though, in this case also, the two Disciples were of opinion that the testimony of one woman would be sufficient. If she be neither married nor a *m'uataddah*[2] the descent of the child would be established by her word, because it is obligatory on none but herself, *according to the approved opinion*, though some jurists maintain that, whether married or not, her assertion is not to be received without proof.[3]

Mother's declaration as to a posthumous child.

But supposing the husband be dead, the mother's declaration as to the legitimacy of a posthumous child born during the '*iddat*, or longest period of gestation recognised by law, is of effect only if unsupposed by other heirs to the deceased. In case of opposition it must of course be established by legal evidence.

---

1 Hedaya Bk. xxiv, chap. v.

2 M'uataddah is a woman who is observing the '*iddat* or period of probation (after either the death of the husband or divorce) to see whether she is with child.

3 'Inaya, Vol. III, 215. Maternity admits of positive proof; because the separation of a child from its mother can be seen ('Inaya, Vol. III, p. 588). The testimony of one woman is sufficient to establish that fact. Descent from her is therefore, established by birth (Jouharat-un-Nayyireh, Bk. on Ikrar). All that is required is identification of the child and the Prophet himself accepted the testimony of the midwife to the birth of a child (Hedaya, Vol. III, p. 549).

If the actual birth of the child be not in dispute, if there be no question as to its legitimacy, if the mother's statement that the child born to her Is her deceased husband's be assented to expressly or impliedly by those heirs, who would otherwise exclude it from succession, "the child should be held to be descended from the husband" . . . . . . "though no person bears evidence to the birth."[1]

Such child would succeed, of course, to its deceased father. But a question may arise whether the parentage so established would affect the rights of heirs other than those who acknowledged him to be the child of the deceased. Would their acknowledgment, in fact, establish conclusively the legitimacy of the child and impart to its status the character of a right *in rem*? The opinion on this point seems to be, that if there be no doubt as to the credibility of the acknowledging heirs, if their acknowledgment cannot be impeached in any way, then "the parentage which is established affects others as well as themselves,[2] and is conclusive against all the world."[3] This does not refer to the legitimacy of a child established in a contentious proceeding in a Court of Justice. In such a case the judicial declaration *ipso facto* imparts to it a conclusive character and constitutes the status a right *in rem* which cannot be questioned in any other proceeding.

Acknowledgment of nasab or paternity under the Shiah Law.

As we have already seen under the Shiah Law, the first cause which gives rise to a right of inheritance is *nasab*. A man may establish to himself the *nasab* of a child whose paternity is not known, provided there is sufficient disparity of age for the one to be the father of the other.

But a man cannot affiliate to himself the child of a woman between whom and himself there has been such a distance as to preclude his having access to her for a period equal to the age of the child. If there is any dispute as to the paternity of the child the person acknowledging must establish the acknowledgment on proof.

Principle.

After a conclusive acknowledgment of paternity and legitimate sonship neither the child on attaining puberty can render it void by repudiating the acknowledgment nor can the acknowledgor render it void by a subsequent disavowal.

1 Radd-ul-Muhtar *in loco*.

2 Hedaya (Eng. Transl.) p. 381.

3 Abu Hanifa says that if a woman, separated from her husband, be delivered of a child during the period of probation, "the parentage is not established in a husband, unless the birth be proved by the evidence of two male witnesses, or one male and two female witnesses". The author of the Hedaya, however, explains this by saying that this rule applies to a case "where there is no apparent pregnancy". As a matter of fact, however, it would appear to be now settled that the evidence of the midwife is sufficient in law to establish the actual birth. Comp. Abu Hanifa's views with the Shiah doctrines. I take it that when it is stated that the midwife's evidence is sufficient to establish birth it implies that her statement is accepted as true to connect the child with the mother.

Assent on the part of an infant not necessary.

No assent on the part of an infant is necessary to give him a right of inheritance to the acknowledgor, but if the person acknowledged be adult, in that case assent would be requisite. So that if the adult should deny the *nasab* it would not be established.

The *nasab* of any relation other than a child cannot be established by acknowledgment, without the assent or concurrence of the person in whose favour it is made.

Acknowledgment of other relationships.

Principle.—In order that an acknowledgment of any relationship other than that of paternity may give rise to a mutual right of succession the parties must be of unknown descent and have no known heirs, for such an acknowledgment cannot affect the right of others. If the acknowledgor has any known heir, his acknowledgment of *nasab* to another cannot be accepted.

Shiah Law.

When one person acknowledges another as the issue of his deceased father, and the two acknowledge a third, the *nasab* of the third is established, provided the two first are persons whose evidence can be accepted, but if the third should deny the second, the *nasab* of the second would not be established, and the third would take half the estate, the first a third, and the second a sixth, being the complement of a share of the first. Similarly, if the two first being of known paternity were to acknowledge a third, his *nasab* would be established, provided the two are persons whose evidence can be accepted. But in this case the denial by the third of the *nasab* of either of the other two will have no effect, and the estate of the deceased must be divided among them all in thirds.

If a person were to die leaving him surviving his wife and a brother, and the widow were to acknowledge a child to be his, her share would be reduced to an eighth, and the child would take the other eighth, unless the brother should assent to her acknowledgment, when the whole of the remainder would go to the child. When the presumptive heir acknowledges another to be nearer to the deceased than himself, he must surrender to such person the whole of whatever may be in his hands that belonged to the deceased.

When a person of unknown paternity dies without leaving any *known* heir and another person were to affirm that he was the father of the deceased, the *nasab* would be established and the inheritance of the deceased would belong to the acknowledgor.

In this case it is not necessary that the deceased should be an infant so long as there is sufficient disparity of age between the two.

But if the person acknowledged is equal in degree to himself, he has only to surrender out of his own share a due proportion for the share of the person so acknowledged.

In the case of a deceased person, the absence of assent does not affect the validity of the acknowledgment even though he were adult, for being dead, he comes within the rule applicable to the case of a child. So also, if a person should acknowledge an insane person to be his son, the absence of his assent is of no consequence as no regard can be had to the words uttered by a person in such circumstances.

It will be observed that the Shiah Law coincides with the Sunni doctrines regarding the conditions necessary to constitute a valid acknowledgment of a child. It requires also that, in the first place, the child acknowledged must be of unknown descent or parentage.

If it should be generally known that the *acknowledgor* and the *acknowledged* were not related to each other by the tie which they allege, or if it should be known that the parties belong to different families, or that the child has a *known* father or mother other than the *acknowledgor*, the acknowledgment is not valid.

In the second place, there should be such a difference of years between the parties as to render it possible that they could stand towards each other in the acknowledged relationship. No particular limit of age is specified in the Shiah Law, the law of nature furnishing the guiding principle in such cases. Nor is the acknowledgment of a child by a man valid when he could not possibly have had access to its mother during the age of such child.[1]

In the third place, there should be no dispute as to the parentage of the child, that is, no other person should claim the child to be his own; in which case, the acknowledgment is not valid without proof.[2]

Acknowledgment of a child by a married woman: Shiah rule.

An acknowledgment, therefore, of a child by a married woman is valid in law, provided her husband confirms her statement and the requisite conditions, as stated above, are complied with.

But where the husband is dead, and the widow is delivered of a child, the question seems to be involved in great doubt. If there be no dispute as to the birth of the child, the parentage would, of course, be ascribed to the husband; but when the child's legitimacy is questioned, difficulties arise which cannot be easily solved by a literal interpretation of the Shiah doctrines. Recourse must then be had to equity and to a liberal construction of the rule of law as explained and adopted by the more modern jurists of the Shiah school in Persia.[3]

---

1 Shara'ya, p. 376; Irshad-ul-'Allamah.

2 Jam'a-ush-Shittat.

3 Compare most of the dictai n the Jam'a-ush-Shittat.

Shiah doctrines.

For example, the Shiah Law declares that descent or *nasab* cannot be established except by the testimony of two *just* men;[1] "nor can it be established by the testimony of two profligates, even though they be the heirs",[2] except in so far as the "profligates" themselves are concerned. The *raison d'etre* of this restriction is obvious. It is laid down with the object of preventing the perpetration of fraud by the collusion of unscrupulous heirs. This is shown in the following rule: "If two brothers being *just*[3] persons, should testify to another being a son of their deceased brother, his *nasab* or descent, and his right to the inheritance of the deceased, would be established; but such right would create no reciprocity." The son so acknowledged would inherit *from the deceased*, but he would not inherit from the deceased's brothers, nor would they from him. Even if two "profligate"[4] brothers were to acknowledge a certain child to be their deceased brother's offspring, such child would succeed to his inheritance in preference to them.

It will be seen, therefore, that where the legitimacy of a posthumous child is questioned, the Shiah Law requires more ample guarantees than the Hanafi Law against fraud and collusion. So long as this is kept in view, and the conception and birth of the child are satisfactorily proved, the technicalities of the Shiah Law may safely be disregarded.

Acknowledgment by the heirs of a deceased.

Under the Shiah Law, however, a woman whose husband is dead, may acknowledge a child as the lawful issue of her marriage with her deceased husband. *But if the fact that the child is her husband's child rests only on her acknowledgment it will only affect her share in the inheritance of the deceased.* If a deceased person were to leave a widow and brothers, and the widow were to acknowledge a child to be the child of her deceased husband, her share in the estate of the husband would be reduced from one-fourth to one-eighth; and the *acknowledged* child would take the other eighth, even when the descent is disputed by the deceased's brothers. *When the descent is established in a Court of Justice or assented to by the brothers, the child would take the entire residue.*

Acknowledgment of relationship other than filial.

An unmarried woman, or a woman who has no husband, can create the relationship of mother and child between herself and another person by a simple *Ikrar* or acknowledgment, provided the other conditions are fulfilled.

Sunni doctrines.

As already stated, acknowledgment also establishes certain

---

1 'Adil, *i.e.*, a man leading an honest life, never accused nor convicted of any serious civil or moral offence.

2 Shara'ya, p. 377.

3 Men whose evidence is impeachable.

4 Hedaya, Bk. xxv, chap. iii.

other relationships beside parentage; and in these cases there is no distinction between an acknowledgment made by a man and that made by a woman. For example, a person may acknowledge another as his or her father or mother, or husband or wife; and such acknowledgment, if *assented* to or confirmed by the acknowledged, whether during the lifetime of the acknowledgor or after his or her disease, would constitute a valid relationship, *in so far as the parties themselves are concerned.*[1]

"The acknowledgment of a man", says the *Fatawai 'Alamgiri*, "is valid with regard to five persons—his father, mother, child, wife and *mawla*[2]; because in all these cases he acknowledges an obligation [of maintenance], but it is not valid except for these. The acknowledgment of a woman is valid with regard to four persons—her father, mother, husband and *mawla*. But it is not valid with regard to a child, unless assented to by her husband, for it is burdening him with paternity".

In the case of these acknowledgments, *express* assent on the part of the acknowledged is necessary to constitute a valid relationship; when no such assent is proved, the acknowledgment falls to the ground and creates no right on either side.

In these cases, also, the parties must be of unknown descent in order to stand to each other in the alleged relationship without disregard to obvious facts.

Shiah principle. Acknowledgment of a wife.

"The descent of any other than a child cannot be established", says the *Shara'ya*, "without the assent or concurrence of the person acknowledged";[3] and the right of inheritance created by such an acknowledgment is restricted to the acknowledging parties themselves and does not extend to their heirs. It is otherwise in the case of parent and child. "If one person acknowledges himself the father of another, who, if able to do so, verifies and avows the filial tie, these are not only by law the heirs of each other, but this right extends to all the heirs or descendants of both." But if "a person declare another to be his brother, who, on his part, avows the relationship, *and they are not known to be the contrary, the right of inheritance is established between them as to each other, but does not extend to the brothers of either nor to any other relation*".[4]

If the acknowledgor has any *known* heir his acknowledgment of *nasab* in favour of another does not exclude the former from his natural rights of inheritance, or vest any right in the acknowledged. The *Shara'ya* lays down as a general rule that, in such a case "his acknowledgment of *nasab* is not to be accepted".

---

1 Hedaya Bk. xxv, chap. iii.

2 A client, as in the Roman system.

3 Shara'ya, p. 376.

4 See Himmat Bahadoor *v.* Sahebzadee Begum (1873) 13 B L R 182; s c L R 1 I A 23. Same under the Hanafi Law, Hedaya Vol. III, p. 169; collateral acknowledgment is also allowed under the Maliki Law, 1 Sautayra p. 339.

The acknowledgment by a man of a woman as his wife is valid when confirmed by her, provided she is not already married to some one else nor is in her *'iddat,* and the acknowledgor is not under a legal incapacity to marry her.

Difference between the acknowledgment of a child and any other relation.

Acknowledgment is valid with respect to all these persons whether it is made "in health or in sickness",—in other words, whether it is made *inter vivos* or *in extremis* because it is of a matter binding on the acknowledgor himself, and the burden of the descent is not cast on any other.[1]

Principle.—The acknowledgment of a man with respect to persons other than those before-mentioned, such as a brother, or a paternal or maternal uncle, or the like, affects only the acknowledgor and acknowledged. But in the case of a child it is obligatory not only on the acknowledgor and the person acknowledged, but on other persons also.

Acknowledgment of a child—its effects on other relations.

For instance, if one were to acknowledge a son, the person acknowledged would inherit together with all the other heirs of the acknowledgor, though they should all deny his descent, and he would inherit also from the father of the acknowledgor, that is, the grandfather of the person acknowledged, though the grandfather should deny his descent. As regards any other relationship the acknowledgment only binds the person concerned. And, accordingly in the *Fatawai Kazi Khan* the matter is explained thus:—

"And when it has been said that the acknowledgment of a man is not valid with respect to those above-mentioned, it is only meant that it is not obligatory on any other except the acknowledgoı and the acknowledged; but with regard to such rights as affect them only, the acknowledgment is valid."

Where no other heir.

For instance, if a person were to acknowledge another as his brother, having other heirs beside, who deny the alleged relationship, and the acknowledgor should die, the person so acknowledged would not inherit with the other heirs, nor would he inherit from the acknowledgor's father if he should deny the descent, but [if decrepit] he would be entitled to maintenance as against the acknowledgor himself during his life.

If the acknowledgor left no heir, the person acknowledged would be entitled to his succession, because the acknowledgment comprehends two things,—descent and a right to the acknowledgor's property after his death, and though the first cannot be entertained as it affects another party, the second is not open to the same objections, because it is only against himself, and a man has the power of disposing of the whole of his property when he has no creditor nor heir.[2]

---

1 'Inaya, Vol. I, p. 616; Jouharat-un-Nayyireh, Bk. on Ikrar

2 'Inaya, Vol. III, p. 616.

If a person whose father is dead should acknowledge another as his brother, though the descent would not be established by reason of his statement, yet the person acknowledged would be entitled to share *with* him in the father's inheritance.

Woman's acknowledgment of a husband.

If a woman were to acknowledge, either in health or in illness, that she married a particular individual for so much dower, and were then to deny the marriage, and the husband were to assent to it during her life, the marriage would be established; but if he should not assent till after her death, it would not be established, according to Abu Hanifa, nor would the man be entitled to any share in the inheritance; though according to Abu Yusuf and Muhammad, it would be established. And this is still further explained by what follows.

"In a case of parentage, confirmation by the person acknowledged is valid after the death of the acknowledgor, because the relationship continues after death. So also, assent or confirmation by a wife is valid after the death of the acknowledging husband, because the effect of the marriage continues after death till the expiration of the '*iddat*. In like manner, assent or confirmation by a husband is valid after the death of his wife, according to Abu Yusuf and Muhammad, because of his right of inheritance, which is one of the effects of marriage; but, according to Abu Hanifa, it is not valid, because the marriage itself is cut off by the death, and the assent cannot be founded on the right of inheritance, which was not in existence at the time of acknowledgment, to which the assent must necessarily be referred."[1] The *Fatwa* is with Abu Hanifa, that is, decrees are passed according to his opinion.

The effect of contradictory statements as to legitimacy.

Descent, according to Abu Hanifa, is one of those things which cannot be dissolved after it has once been established; and, consequently, when once a child has been acknowledged, its status cannot be reversed by a subsequent rejection, but will continue as a bar to any other claim. Similarly, if a person were to testify that a particular child of a particular man, and should afterwards, on his testimony being rejected, claim the child as his own, such claim will not be accepted. Or, if one were to say with respect to a child in his custody: He is the son of my absent slave so-and-so", and should afterwards say, "He is my own son", there would be no *nasab* between the boy and the man—not even, according to Abu Hanifa, though the slave should deny the boy to be his son.

If a man were to acknowledge that he married a particular woman for a certain dower, and after making such admission were to deny the marriage, supposing such acknowledgment is assented to by the woman either during his life or after his death, such acknowledgment would be lawful and she would be entitled to her share in the inheritance, and also to the dower, with this

1 Hedaya and Kifaya, Vol. III, p. 582; Jouharat-un-Nayyireh, Bk. on Ikrar.

difference, that if the acknowledgment were made by the man *in extremis* and the dower admitted by him exceeded her proper dower, the acknowledgment would be of no avail as to the excess.

Shiah Law.

Under the Shiah Law, if a child of unknown paternity (*nasab*) were to die without leaving any heir except the Imam, and some person were to make a *declaration* to the effect that the deceased was his child, the inheritance of such child would go to the declarant, instead of the Imam.

Foundlings (*lakit*) are recommended to the especial care of all Musulmans. The person who takes charge of some children occupies the position of a father towards them, and is entitled to inherit from them.[1]

CHAPTER IV

THE *WILAYET-UL-IJBAR*, THE PATRIA POTESTAS

THE RIGHT OF GUARDIANSHIP FOR MARRIAGE

Most of the provisions relating to the *patria potestas* are not peculiar to the Muhammedan Law.[2] The distinguishing feature of Islamic Jurisprudence, as compared with modern systems of law, consists in the power of the father to *impose* the status of marriage on his minor children. It is known as the right of *jabr* and is recognised with various modifications by all the schools.

The right of jabr among the ancient Arabs.

The right of *jabr* is founded on the original *patria potestas* which existed among the Arab tribes from the earliest times. Among them the father had the right of compelling his sons to marry until such time as they were capable of bearing arms, and the daughters until their *emancipation*, by marriage or otherwise, from his control.[3]

Among the Jews.

Among the Jews, the father could give his daughter in marriage without her consent as long as she was a minor, that is, had not attained the age of twelve.[4]

---

1 For fuller information on the subject, see D'Ohsson's Tableaux General de l'Empire Ottoman, Vol. III. The law relating to foundlings is set out at great length in the Radd-ul-Muhtar; see post.

2 The *patria potestas* of the Civil Law as regards the marriage of the children was abrogated by the Cannon Law which is the law by which marriages excepting so far as they are affected by the Marriage Act, are governed in England; see Sherwood *v*. Ray, 1 Moor P C 353.

3 Perron, Femmes Arabes, pp. 191-226.

4 Code Rabbinique, Ebn. Haezer, Vol. I, p. 123.

Under the Mahommedan Law.

Under the Mahommedan Law, according to all the schools,[1] the power of the father to give his children in marriage without their consent can be exercised in the case of sons until they have attained their *bulughyet* or puberty, when they are emancipated, so far as their personal rights are concerned, from the *patrias potestas*, and are at liberty to contract themselves in marriage. As regards female children, there is considerable divergence among the several schools.

Persons not *sui juris* labour under the same legal disabilities as in other systems of law. They cannot enter into any contract or legal transactions without the consent of their natural guardians.[2]

The want of capacity, which results from minority, is founded on the principles of right reasoning and the desire to protect people not competent to exercise sound discretion in the affairs of everyday life from the consequences of their own acts.

An infant, accordingly, is incompetent to enter into a contract of marriage without the consent of his or her guardian. A marriage contracted by a minor, who is possessed of understanding (*rushd*), is not, however, absolutely invalid, but its validity, like that of any other act committed or contract entered into by an infant, is dependent on its ratification by the guardian, or by the person who stands in *loco parentis*.[3]

Right of Jabr ends with puberty.

The power, which the Musalman Law vests in the father, of imposing the status of marriage on his minor children is, in principle, absolute and unlimited. But the power is surrounded with so many conditions and formalities, that the mischief, which otherwise might arise from it, rarely occurs in practice. The right of *jabr* in its harsher form, terminates practically with puberty.

The provisions of the Indian Majority Act (IX of 1875) have left untouched the rules of Mahommedan Law relating to marriage, dower and divorce. The majority of the person, therefore, on which the status of marriage is sought to be imposed, and consequently the competency of the person who wants to give him or her in marriage will be judged on the basis of the Mahommedan Law.

Puberty is presumed on the completion of the fifteenth year, according to most of the schools,[4] unless there is evidence to the contrary. As a general rule, however, a person who completes the fifteenth year is considered, without distinction of

1 See Muslim Family Laws Ordinance (VIII of 1961).

2 Fatawai 'Alamgiri, Vol. I, p. 377; Kanz-ud-Dakaik; Jam'a-ush-Shittat.

3 Hedaya, Vol. III, pp. 482-483; Jam'a-ush-Shittat.

4 The presumption may be rebutted. The Muslim Family Laws Ordinance, 1961 has fixed marriageable age at 16 years.

sex, to be adult and *sui juris*, possessed of the capacity to enter into legal transactions.

After the age of fifteen every contract of marriage entered into on behalf of a youth or a girl is dependent upon his or her *express* consent; and, among the Hanafis and Shiahs, the children of both sexes on attaining majority are free to contract marriages without the consent of their guardians.[1]

There is no divergence between the several schools as regards the capacity of a son to contract himself in marriage after he has completed his fifteenth year, though there exists considerable difference of opinion as regards the capacity of female children.[2]

Hanafi and Shiah doctrines.

The Hanafis and the Shiahs hold that the right of *jabr* in the case of males, as in that of females, continues until they have arrived at the age of puberty.[3]

Right of an adult girl to enter into marriage.

"It is not lawful for a guardian", says the *Hedaya*, "to force an adult virgin into marriage. None, not even a father nor the sovereign, can lawfully contract a woman in marriage who is adult and of sound mind without her permission, whether she be a virgin or not."[4]

Similarly, the Shiah Law declares that neither a father nor a grandfather has authority over an adult and discreet virgin, who is herself competent to enter into a marriage contract. This rule applies also to a woman who is not a virgin.[5]

Maliki and Shaf'ei rules.

The followers of Malik and Shaf'ei, on the other hand, are of opinion that the exceptional right of *jabr*, in the case of females, continues in force until they are married, and, consequently emancipated from paternal control.[6]

But as the followers of the different schools can easily change from one to the other by a simple change of ritual or doctrine, the hardship which might possibly arise from the rigid application of the Shaf'eite and Malikite doctrines are obviated.[7]

These schools also hold that the right of *jabr* does not cease when a girl is a *safiha* (devoid of intelligence), or when she has

---

1 Radd-ul-Muhtar; Jama'a-ush-Shittat; Muharrar (Shaf'ei).

2 Al-Wafi; Ikhtilaf-ul-Aimmah (India office copies).

3 Hedaya, Vol. I, p. 96; Fatawai 'Alamgiri, Vol. I, p. 399; Kanz-ud-Dakaik; Shara'ya, p. 263; Jam'a-ush-Shittat.

4 See also the Fatawai 'Alamgiri, Vol. I, p. 406.

5 Shara'ya, p. 263.

6 Kitab-ul-Anwar la'amal-ul-abrar, Book on Nikah (Marriage).

7 See post

been married whilst yet a minor, and has been divorced before arriving at maturity.[1]

Limitations on the right of jabr.

Though the right of *jabr* is theoretically an absolute right, in practice, there are numerous conditions attached to its exercise. The father, without any difference among the jurists, is prohibited from marrying his child to those who are diseased, to slaves, idiots and other ineligible persons. But Abu Hanifa and his two Disciples differ on the questions, how far a marriage contracted by a father on behalf of a girl for less than her proper dower is valid in law. Abu Hanifa appears to think that inadequacy of consideration is no ground for holding the marriage to be invalid. Abu Yusuf and Mohammed, however, are of opinion, that when the dower is out of proportion to her proper or customary dower the contract is not valid. And there seems to be a general consensus of opinion among all the jurists that where the father has acted "wickedly or carelessly", the marriage is invalid.[2]

Improper marriage contracted for a minor.

If a man should agree on behalf of his minor son to pay a dower in excess of the infant's means, or of the wife's proper dower or marry him to a woman of low position, the marriage would similarly be invalid.

The discretion of the Judge.

In fact, the law is particularly attentive to the interests of the child. It takes care that the right of *jabr* should never be exercised to the prejudice of the infant; any act of the father which is likely to injure the interests of the minor is considered illegal, and entitles the Kazi or Judge to interfere in order to prevent the completion of such act, or, if complete, to annul it.[3]

Nor can the father indefinitely abuse his authority by systematically refusing his consent to the marriage of his children. Such cases are necessarily rare, the Islamic system being opposed to monasticism and celibacy; still, as cupidity may prompt a father to refuse successive suitors for his daughter's hand, the Judge is authorised to interpose, provided on inquiry he finds *sufficient* and *reasonable* cause for so doing. In India[4], this function would probably be assumed by the Civil Court upon the application of the guardian next in order to the father. For example, a case may occur in which a mother is quite willing that her daughter should marry an eligible suitor, but the father without any good reason and simply from caprice, withholds his consent. Under these circumstances the Civil Court would, under the Mahommedan Law, be authorised to restrain him from any

1 Fatawai Kazi Khan, section on Guardians.

2 Fatawai 'Alamgiri, Vol. I, p. 412; Kitab-ul-Anwar; Jam'a-ush-Shittat.

3 Comp. Sautayra.

4 Now Indo-Pakistan.

interference with the marriage, and the order of the Court would be tantamount to the consent of the father.

What would be *sufficient* and *reasonable* cause to justify or warrant the interference of the Judge would depend, of course, on the special circumstances of each individual case.[1]

Emancipation from the right of jabr.

Among the Hanafis and the Shiahs, the children are emancipated from the right of *jabr* on attaining puberty; an abuse of the paternal authority among the followers of these two sects is impossible where the children are adult and discreet. Should a father persist in refusing his consent to the marriage of his adult daughter, she can validly enter herself into a contract of marriage even against his will and without his consent. "If the guardians of an adult and discreet virgin should refuse to marry her to an equal, when desired by her to do so, there is no doubt that she may enter into the contract of marriage against their will."[2] The *Jam'a-ush-Shittat* says, in answer to the question.[3] "Is the consent or permission (*izn*) of the father *necessary* to the marriage (*'akd*) of a virgin who is adult and discreet (*baligha* and *rashida*)?" that such permission is not necessary, her own consent being enough, to make the contract valid in law.

An unequal marriage.

If the marriage contracted by her is unequal, that is, should she contract herself in marriage to a person far inferior in rank or position, the father would have a right to object, but such objection must be urged before the Kazi.

Among the Shaf'eites and the Malikites, with whom a girl is not absolutely emancipated from the *patria potestas* until she is married, the abuse of the paternal authority is probably more frequent. The hardships occasionally entailed by the Shaf'ei and Maliki doctrines are obviated by the facility accorded to the followers of the several Sunni schools to attach themselves either to one school or the other, as inclination or conviction may suggest. For example, an unmarried girl of eighteen, who, according to the Malikis would remain subject to the father's authority until she was married, may at any time emancipate herself by declaring herself to belong to the Hanafi school.[4]

This point was discussed at some length in the case of *Muhammad Ibrahim bin Muhammad Sayad Parkar* v. *Gulam Ahmed bin Muhammad Sayad Roghe and others*.[5] In this case a girl, named Khadija, whose family were of the Shaf'ei sect, had, on arriving at puberty, made a declaration before the Kazi of Bombay that she had renounced the Shaf'ei doctrines

---

1 De Menerville, Jurisprudence de la Cour d' Alger, p. 451.

2 Shara ya, p. 263.

3 Jam'a-ush-Shittat. See Sibt Ahmad v. Amina Khatun A I R 1929 All. 18.

4 This discussion is now merely of historical interest. See Appendix.

5 (1864) Bombay, H C R O C J 236.

and had adopted the tenets of the Hanafis. Shortly after this she was married to the plaintiff, apparently with her own consent and in accordance with the Hanafirites. Her father, however, had never consented to her marriage with the plaintiff. In a suit brought by the plaintiff against the father for the unlawful detention of his wife, the principal legal question raised and discussed turned on the point whether the marriage contracted with the plaintiff was void in consequence of the girl's father not having consented to it. The Court, consisting of Sausse, C. J., and Couch, J., in an exhaustive and well-considered judgment, held (*i*) that, according to the Mahommedan Law, a Musulman female belonging to any one of the four Sunni schools, "can, after attaining puberty, elect to belong to whichever of the other three sects she pleases, and the legality of her subsequent acts will be governed by the tenets of the Imam whose follower she may have become" ; (*ii*) that, according to the doctrine of the Hanafis, "a Musulman female, after arriving at the age of puberty, without having been married by her father or guardian . . . . . can select a husband without reference to the wishes of the father or guardian, though according to the doctrines of Shaf'ei, a virgin whether before or after puberty, cannot give herself in marriage without the consent of her father" ; (*iii*) that consequently the marriage contracted by Khadija, by her own consent, was valid and binding. The same principle would have applied had she become a Shiah.[1]

Incompetency of the father.

When the father of a family is incompetent, by reason of mental incapacity, to exercise the right of *jabr*, the guardian next in order to him exercises that right.[2] Similarly, when the father is absent or at such a distance as precludes him from acting, the guardian next in order can lawfully contract a child in marriage.[3]

The *Jam'a-ush-Shittat* gives examples of cases where marriage contracted by the mothers of infant children, during the absence of the fathers in distant townships, have been held to be valid.

Hanafi doctrines.

The nature of the absence or the distance, which would justify the exercise of the right of *jabr* by the guardian next in order to the father, is of particular importance, and has attracted the special attention of the Musulman jurists.

1 "There is not any ceremonial required", added the learned Judges in the course of their judgment, "to indicate the change of sect; the only outward difference between a follower of Shaf'ei and a follower of Abu Hanifa consists in the former, at the conclusion of prayer in a mosque. saying Amin in a loud tone, whilst the latter pronounce it softly, and also that in praying, a Shaf'ei extends his arms whilst a Hanafi keeps them down".

2 Kallo Shaikh *v*. Gureeboollah Shaikh (1868) 10 W R 12.

3 Fatawai 'Alamgiri, Vol. I, p. 401; Fatawai Kazi Khan. Vol. I, p. 406. According to the Shaf'eis, in the absence of the "preferential guardian", the right passes to the "Sultan and the Kazi",—Kazi Khan, Vol. I, p. 406.

The meaning of Ghibat-ul-munkata'.

The *Hedaya* says, "if the father or the first natural guardian of an infant should be removed to such a distance as is termed *ghibat-ul-munkata'*, it is in that case lawful for the guardian next in degree to contract the infant in marriage". And then it explains". By the absence termed *ghibat-ul-munkata'*, is to be understood the guardian being removed to a city out of the track of the caravans or not visited by the caravans more than once in every year. *Some, however, have defined it to signify a distance amounting to three days' journey.*"[1]

According to the *Radd-ul-Muhtar*, *ghibat-ul-munkata'* implies such a distance, or such an absence, as precludes the possibility of obtaining the father's sanction to any contract entered into by the next guardian on behalf of the infant, without serious inconvenience.[2] The *Fatawai 'Alamgiri*[3] and the *Fatawai Kazi Khan* seem to point in the same direction. The general conclusion arrived at from the authorities quoted is that each case must be decided on its own individual basis.

Where a father was undergoing a long term of imprisonment, it has been held that the mother and grandmother were entitled to give the daughter in marriage.[4]

Apostacy of the father—General rule.

Nor is the consent of the father necessary to the marriage of his infant daughter, when he has abandoned the Mohammedan Faith, as the renunciation of Islam leads to the forfeiture of all parental right of *jabr*. The point was decided *in the matter of Mahin Bibi.*[5] In that case a Mahommedan female had married a Jew convert to Islam. A female child was born of the union, who was brought up in the Shiah doctrines professed by the mother, although the father soon after her birth had returned to his former faith. Subsequently, the mother contracted the girl in marriage to a Shiah Musulman. Upon an application of the father to obtain possession of the person of the child, on the ground that the marriage contracted by the mother was invalid, inasmuch as he had not assented thereto, Macpherson, J., decided that, under the Mahommedan Law, an apostate is not entitled to exercise the right of assenting to the marriage of his children, who have been contracted by the guardian next in order to him ; and that, therefore, the marriage of the applicant's daughter was valid without his assent.

---

1 Hedaya.

2 See the Chapter on Marriage.

3 Fatawai 'Alamgiri, Vol. I, p. 401; Fatawai Kazi Khan, Vol. I, p. 406.

4 Kaloo Shaikh *v.* Gureeboollah Shaikh, supra.

5 (1874) 13 B L R O C 160. See also Gul Muhammad v. Mst. Wazir (1901) 36 P R 191 : Hedaya, p. 392.

A similar case is given in the *Jam'a-ush-Shittat*. The question there put to the *Mujtahid* was, whether the marriage contracted by the mother on her daughter's behalf was valid without the consent of the father, who had become a convert to Christianity. The answer was in the affirmative.

Grandfather—Shiah doctrine.

In the absence of the father, the Shaf'eis and the Shiahs allow to the grandfather[1] the right of *jabr*, *i.e.*, the power of imposing the status of marriage.

Maliki dotrine.

The Malikis consider the right essentially personal, and belonging exclusively to the father in his quality of father. In the absence of the father, the right, according to this school, passes to his executor or to the Kazi.

Hanafi doctrine.

The Hanafis allow the right of *jabr* to all natural guardians.

Improper marriage may be interdicted by the Judge.

They give the right in the first instance to the nearest paternal relations. In the absence of paternal relations, maternal relations within the prohibited degrees can exercise the power. For example, when the father's brother is present, he is the preferential *wali* (guardian), and neither the mother nor the mother's relations have any right, *though if the proposed union be improper, the mother or the maternal relations can move the Judge for an injunction to restrain the wali from entering into the contract*. And they can do so, even if the father is entering into the contract.

"The guardians in marriage", says the *Sharh-i-Vikaya*, "are the '*Asabah* or agnates according to the same order as in inheritance and exclusion. By '*Asabah* is meant '*Asabah* in their own right, that is, males related without the intervention of females; then the mother, then the distant kindred in order of proximity; then the successors by contract (*mowla-al-mawalat*) and then the Judge." "The guardianship (*wilayet*) in marriage belongs", says the *Fatawai 'Alamgiri*, "in the first place to the '*Asabah* in the order of inheritance, the more remote being excluded by the nearer."[2]

Hanafi doctrine.

According to the Hanafis, in the absence of the '*asabat-un-nasabiye* (residuaries by blood), the right of *jabr* becomes

1 Al-Muharrar; Kitab-ul-Anwar; Mafatih; Sharay'a; Ikhtilaf-ul-Aimma; Fatawai Kazi Khan, Vol. I, pp. 405, 407.

2 See post, Chapter on Marriage.

vested in the *sababiye*; in other words, the emancipator or emancipatress, "for in this case male and female are alike."[1]

Shiah and Shaf'ei doctrines.

The Shiahs, as stated before, accord the power to the father and the grandfather, but deny it to every other relation ; in this they agree with the Shaf'eis. According to the *Shara'ya* "an executor has no authority in marriage, even if it were expressly given by the testator ; nor has the Judge any power over a person who is not adult."[2]

In the case of one who is devoid of intelligence, both the testamentary guardian and the Judge have a qualified authority.

If the marriage be for the benefit of the *non compos mentis*, or for the protection of his interest it would be valid. If otherwise, it would be invalid.

Hanafi doctrine.

Among the Hanafis, in the absence of the agnates, the power is passed on to the uterine relations.[3] According to Abu Hanifa as currently reported; failing the *'Asabah* every near uterine relative who may inherit from a minor, whether a boy or a girl, has the power of giving him or her in marriage. Mohammed does not agree in this view ; and the opinion of Abu Yusuf is not certain. Among the uterine relations the nearest, says Abu Hanifa, is the mother, then follows an enumeration not necessary to refer.[4]

---

1 The Radd-ul-Muhtar gives the rule in the following terms:—the nearest guardian to an insane woman is her son; then her son's son, h. l. s.; next, her father; then her grandfather, that is her father's father, how-highsoever. When an insane woman has a father and a son, or a grandfather and a son, the guardianship belongs to the son, according to Abu Hanifa and Abu Yusuf, but to the father according to Mohammed. It is better, however, that the father should direct the son to give her in marriage, so that it may be lawful without any difference of opinion. After the above persons, comes the full brother, then the half-brother on the father's side; then the full brother's son ; then the consanguine half-brother's son ; how-lowsoever; then the full uncle; then the half-uncle on the father's side; then the son of the full uncle, then the son of the half-uncle on the father's side and their descendants; then the father's full paternal uncle; then his paternal half-uncle on the father's side then the sons of both in the same order; then the grandfather's full paternal uncle; then his paternal half-uncle on the father's side, and then the sons of both, in the same order; then any 'Asabah still further removed.

The order of these agnatic guardians may be stated shortly thus; (*a*) the lineal male descendants; (*b*) the lineal male ascendants, and (*c*) the male relatives in the order of succession; those related by both parents having precedence over those related by the father only. "All these guardians have the power of jabr," says the Fatawai 'Alamgiri. "over a female or male during minority", Vol. II, p. 583.

2 "An adult who has discretion" Shara'ya, p. 263.

3 The mother comes in after the 'Asabat-un-nasabiye and the 'Asabat 'us-sababiye.

4 These rules like those relating to the powers of an infinite number of agnatic relations are merely the outcome of a desire to carry logical considerations to the utmost limit and have no practical application.

The powers of the Judge.

The judge has the power of contracting a person in marriage, who requires a guardian, when it is within his *commission* and authority ; but when it is not within his commission, he is not the guardian. If a Judge should contract a minor in marriage when he has no authority from the Sultan for that purpose, and should afterwards, upon receiving such authority, give his sanction to the marriage, it would be lawful on a liberal construction of the law, "and this is correct".

"When the Judge marries a young girl to himself, it is a marriage without a guardian ; for, in his personal concerns, he is a mere subject, and the guardianship devolves on the person above him, that is the *wali* or governor, who also is but a subject in his own matters. Nay, the Khalifa (Caliph) himself is no more than a subject in things that regard himself."

It is lawful for the son of a paternal uncle to marry his uncle's daughter. Supposing the Kazi were to marry a young girl to his own son, the transaction would not be lawful, and is contrary to the case of all other guardians.

The authority of the executor.

An executor has no authority to enter into a contract of marriage for or on behalf of an infant in marriage, whether he be appointed by the father or not, unless he happens to be the natural guardian, in which case he would have the power by virtue of his relationship and *not of his executorship*.[1]

Guardianship of foundlings.

And if a boy and girl be both under the care or custody of a person who has brought them up, as, for instance, in the case of foundlings or orphans, he will have no authority to marry them to each other.

"A slave cannot be the guardian of any one ; nor can a *mokatib*[2] be guardian to his own child. A minor or an insane person has no power of guardianship, and a non-Moslem cannot be guardian to a Moslem, whether male or female ; nor a Moslem to an infidel, whether male or female." All this, it must be remembered, is for purposes of imposing the status of marriage, and not for guardianship in the sense in which the term is ordinarily used in the English language ; the reason is obvious, for difference of faith may well furnish grounds for apprehension that the power will not be properly exercised.

The guardianship of an insane person.

"When a guardian becomes permanently insane, his guardianship ceases. But if he be one with lucid intervals, his guardianship does not cease, and his acts during a lucid interval have legal operation. Abu Hanifa is reported to have said, that if the

1 Fatawai 'Alamgiri, Vol. I, p. 399.

2 *i.e.*, a slave who has been partially enfranchised.

madness continues for a month without a lucid interval, it is to be regarded as permanent, and the *Fatwa* is thereon."

According to the *Fatawai 'Alamgiri*, the guardianship of the father continues over the person and property of a son who, though arrived at majority, is either a confirmed madman, or has lucid intervals. But when a youth has attained his majority in a state of sanity, and subsequently thereto became either a confirmed lunatic or mad with lucid intervals, in such a case, according to Abu Yusuf the guardianship does not revert to the father but passes on to the Judge ; so that if the father should intermeddle with his property, or contract him in marriage, the act would not be legal.[1] And though there seems to be some difference of opinion among the lawyers, this view seems most conformable to right reasoning.

Two guardians equal in degree.

According to the Hanafis, when a minor, whether male or female, has two guardians equal in degree as, for instance, two brothers or two paternal uncles, and either of them contracts the minors in marriage, the transaction is lawful "And", adds the *Fatawai 'Alamgiri*, "it makes no difference whether the other of them allows or cancels the marriage. If they both contract her to different persons at the same time, or it is not known which contract was first, both contracts are void."

Contract by remote guardians.

Principle.—When a minor, whether male or female, is contracted in marriage by a more distant guardian, while a nearer is present and competent to exercise the right, the contract is dependent on the sanction of the nearer ; but if the nearer be incompetent by reason of minority or insanity, the contract would be lawful. Similarly, if the nearer guardian be away at such a distance as precludes him from acting, the marriage contracted by the more remote would be lawful.

Ghibat-ul-munkata'.

The Imam Sarakhsi and Mohammed ibn-ul-Fazl have held that the distance is to be calculated by the possibility of losing a present suitable match while inquiry is made for the opinion of the absent guardian. The *fatwa* is to that effect, *i.e.*, decisions are passed according to that principle. So if a nearer guardian be living in the same city, but concealed, "he is not to be waited for, and the absence is to be accounted as a precluding one."

Validity of contracts made by the remoter guardian.

If a more remote guardian should contract a minor in marriage while a nearer guardian is present, the marriage would be dependent on the latter's sanction, and if he should then absent himself, in consequence of which the guardianship devolves upon the former, the marriage first contracted by the remoter guardian

---

1 Fatawai 'Alamgiri, Vol. I, p. 400.

would not be valid until sanctioned by him after such devolution of the guardianship.

The guardianship of the nearer ceases during his absence and is transferred to the more remote, so that if the nearer guardian were to contract the minor during his absence, the contract would be unlawful, while if the more remote were to enter into the contract, it would be lawful. The authority of the more remote guardian is annulled by the return of the nearer, but not so the contract which he may have actually made, for that was entered into while the authority was complete. All the jurists, however, are agreed that when the nearer guardian prevents a woman from marrying, or when a father or grandfather is profligate, the Judge may contract the woman to a *Kufu* (an equal).

The guardian of a minor boy and girl may marry them to each other against their will.

Would a mother, who happens to be a testamentary guardian or an executrix to her deceased husband, have under the Hanafi law the power of contracting her minor children in marriage? [1] The Algerian Courts have construed the law in her favour.

Under the Shiah Law the mother has no power.

Under the Shiah Law the mother has no power of contracting her children in marriage, not even as executrix of the father.

Generally speaking, whilst a *wali-al-akrab*[2] is present, and is qualified to exercise the right of *jabr*, or to give his consent to a marriage contracted for his infant child, the mother has no power to marry such child against the wishes of the "preferable guardian." All the schools, however, seem to agree in holding that when the right is exercised by the *wali* prejudicially to the interests of the child, the mother has "a right to interfere." "When the father marries his poor daughter to a man equally poor," says Sidi Khalil, "the mother has the right of intervention."

There are passages of like import in the (Shiah) *Jam'a-ush-Shittat* and the (Hanafi) *Radd-ul-Muhtar* and the *Fatawai Kazi Khan*. A comparison of the views enunciated by the jurists of the various schools leaves no doubt that the mother's right of interference will be regulated according to the exigencies of each particular case.

Right of the minor to rescind contract on attaining majority.

Where a minor is contracted in marriage by any person other than the father or grandfather, *such minor on attaining puberty has an absolute right to ratify or rescind the contract.*[3]

But the minor has an option even in the case of a marriage contracted by a father or grandfather *if the latter was a prodigal*

1 See the Jurisprudence de la Cour d' Alger, 1864.

2 *i.e.*, the nearest guardian.

3 Now a minor given in marriage even by the father or grandfather has option of puberty. See Dissolution of Muslim Marriages Act (VIII of 1939).

or *addicted to evil ways or the marriage was manifestly to the minor's disadvantage.*[1]

Shiah doctrines.

The Shiah Law on the subject of the *patria potestas* has been already sufficiently indicated. A few more examples taken from the *Shara'ya* and the *Kitab-ul-Intisar* may not be without value. "No person", it is stated emphatically, "has any authority to contract another in marriage except a father, a paternal grandfather or other lineal male ascendant, an executor or a Judge." (I am leaving out the "master", as slavery, even in the mild form recognised in the primitive Mahommedan Law, does not exist in India.[2]) The authority of a father and a paternal grandfather to contract the daughter or grand-daughter in marriage independently of her own wishes subsists so long as she is a minor[3]; and she has no option of cancelling the contract on attaining majority.[4] And this rule is applicable to a male child.

Option of puberty.

A contract entered into on his behalf by the father or grandfather would be binding on the minor, and he would have no option to cancel it on attaining puberty and discretion. But neither the father nor the grandfather has any power over an adult virgin who is descreet, for she is perfectly competent to contract a *permanent* marriage, and if her guardians should refuse to marry her to an equal, when desired by her to do so, she has the power of contracting herself, even against the will of both, and they have no power whatever over a woman who is not a virgin, and has attained puberty and discretion, nor over an adult male. But when a person, though adult, happen to be *non compos mentis*, the father or grandfather may contract him or her in marriage, and "he has no option after restoration to reason".

Powers of the Judge.

The Judge is vested with authority only with respect to a person who has attained puberty without discretion, or one who has become insane, *when marriage is for his benefit.*

An executor has no authority in marriage, according to the most approved tradition, even if it were expressly given to him by the testator. But an executor may contract a person, who, though arrived at puberty, is deficient in understanding, when there is any necessity for contracting him in marriage.

The following provision throws considerable light on the manners of the people when these rules were promulgated. It is with reference to a person against whom the *fiat* of the Judge has issued declaring him to be a *mahjur*. A person who has been inhibited for prodigality cannot lawfully marry, unless it is needed for reasons of health ; and if he should do so, the marriage would be valid. "But if he be desperately bent on marriage, the Judge may lawfully grant him permission to marry, either specifying a particular woman, or leaving the permission

---

1 Aziz Bano v. Mohammed I L R 47 All. 823: A I R 1925 All. 720.

2 Now Indo-Pakistan.

3 Aziz Bano v. Mohammed, *supra*. (Shia girl given in marriage to a sunni husband by her father can exercise option of puberty before consummation).

4 But see Dissolution of Muslim Marriages Act (VIII of 1939).

general, and if he should be impatient, and contract himself before obtaining the permission, being in the condition before mentioned, the marriage would be valid : but if the dower be more than what is proper for a person of the same condition as the woman, it would be void as to the excess."

NOTES

The Indian[1] readers of this treatise will perhaps find it of some interest to know that, under the French Law, a man cannot marry until he has attained the age of eighteen, nor a woman until she is fifteen. The consent of both parents is required, by a son under twenty-five years of age, and a daughter under twenty-one. If the parents disagree as to the consent, the father's sanction is held sufficient. If the parents are dead, then the consent of the grandfather and grandmother is requisite to contract a valid marriage. In their absence, the consent of the family council *conseil de famille*[2] must be obtained. Even when a man has attained his twenty-fifth year, and the woman her twenty-first, both are still bound to ask, by a formal notification, the consent of their parents, and until the man has attained his thirtieth year and the woman her twenty-fifth, this formal act must be repeated thrice at the interval of one month ; and one month after the third application, it is lawful for the parties to marry with or without consent. After the age of thirty a man or woman may legally marry without the consent of his or her natural guardians, a month after formal notice has been served upon them by two notaries or by one notary and two witnesses.

Under the English Law, a person, whether male or female, cannot marry without the consent of the parents until the age of twenty, though amongst the operatives and colliers in Lancashire and amongst the agricultural labourers in England, they do contract such marriages in thousands.

CHAPTER V

THE CUSTODY OF CHILDREN (*AL-HIZANAT*)

"The *hazina*", says the *Tanwir-ul-Absar*, "is the woman to whom belongs the rearing up of a child." And Khair-ud-din Ramli (the author of the *Khairiyeh*) says that the conditions of *hizanat* are that the *hazina* should be free, adult, trustworthy and capable of bringing up the child, and not married to a stranger.[3]

1 Now Indo-Pakistan.

2 In Code Napoleon, Art. 183.

3 Radd-ul-Muhtar, Vol. II, p. 1042; the Radd-ul-Muhtar is an extremely valuable and authoritative work on Mahommedan Law (see Vol. I, the Introd.). It purports to be a commentary on the Durr-ul-Mukhtar, which again is a gloss on the Tanwir-ul-Absar. The texts quoted in the Radd-ul-Muhtar are chiefly from the latter, whose author is referred to as the Author, whilst the author of the Durr-ul-Mukhtar is referred to as the Commentator (Sharih). The Radd represents to a large extent the developed Hanafi principles. At the same time it must not be supposed that the doctrines it expounds are accepted in their entirety.

[The word *hizanat* is given as *Hazanat* in the *Misbah*, the *Bahr-ur-Reik* and the *Nahr-ul-Faik*.]

The mother.

"The mother is of all persons", says the *Fatawai 'Alamgiri*, "the best entitled to the custody of her infant children during the connubial relationship as well as after its dissolution."[1]

So also the *Radd-ul-Muhtar*:—"The right of the *mother* to the custody of her child is established whether she be a *Moslemah* or *Kitabia* or a *Majoosia* and even though she be separated from her husband. But it does not belong to one who is an apostate."

It will thus be seen that this right belongs to her *qua* mother, and nothing can take it away from her except her own misconduct.

The paternal power, over the infant children discussed in the previous chapter is based on the assumption that it is for their benefit. Similarly when the tenderness of their age, or the weakness of their sex, renders a mother's care necessary, the Mahommedan Law supports the mother's natural right to the custody of her children and allows it to take precedence of the paternal right for a certain specified time.

When the children are no longer dependent on the mother's care, the father has a right to educate and take charge of them, and is entitled to the guardianship of their person in preference to the mother.

Hanafi doctrines.

Among the Hanafis the mother is entitled to the custody of her daughter until she arrives at puberty:[3] among the Malikis, Shaf'eis and Hanbalis the custody continues until she is married.[4] According to the judgments of the Court of Algiers it appears that, in several notable instances, the Hanafi Kazis have followed the Maliki doctrines, and decided that the mother is entitled to the custody of her daughters until their marriage.

1 Fatawai 'Alamgiri, Vol. I, p. 728.

2 An example of a Majoosia mother is given thus:—"If both parents were Magians and the father adopted Islam, and the mother remained in the old faith, still the mother would be entitled to the custody for her maternal love."

3 Fatawai 'Alamgiri, Vol. I, p. 730; Fatawai Kazi Khan, Vol. I, p. 478.

4 Sautayra, p. 348; Sidi Khalil; Radd-ul-Muhtar, Vol. II, p. 1054. The Radd-ul-Muhtar says, that according to Fakih Abu Lais, a mother and a grandmother (maternal as well as paternal) are entitled to the custody of a girl until puberty; but an aunt only up to nine or eleven, for she cannot exact the same amount of respect in teaching manners. According to Zailye, "owing to the evil manners of the times", this rule should apply also to a grandmother. But as regards the mother this has reference to a woman who has been divorced from her husband:" comp. Fatawai Kazi Khan, Section on Hizanat.

Maliki rule.

An analysis of the dicta contained in the authorities recognised among the eastern Hanafis leads to the conclusion that the difference between the doctrines of the Malikis and the Hanafis respecting the term during which the mother's custody lasts is not so great nor so marked as would at first appear. The *Fatawai 'Alamgiri* which gives the opinions of several jurists, points to the conclusion that the right of *hizanat* terminates when the girl is *marriageable*. The Malikis hold that it should continue until she is *actually married*. As, in eastern countries, girls are generally contracted in marriage as soon as they are marriageable, and occasionally before they have arrived at maturity, it is apparent that there is practically no difference between the two schools. It may be remarked, however, that the Maliki doctrines are more conformable to right reasoning and furnish a definite standard for the guidance of those who have to administer the law. Probably the Anglo-Indian[1] Courts, in deciding questions bearing on this point, would follow the precedents of the Algerian Court, which have adopted the Maliki rule as the guiding principle in all such cases.

As regards an adult girl who has been once married, the father or grandfather alone can insist upon her remaining with them if there is any fear of danger to her character or person. If the girl has no person with whom she may stay, the Judge, as the custodian of the interests of the public, may appoint some honest and proper Moslem female with whom she may live.[2]

Custody of a male child: Maliki rule.

There is greater divergence among the different Sunni schools with reference to the mother's custody of her male children. The Malikis hold that the right of *hizanat*, in respect of a male child, continues until such time as he arrives at puberty. "This is the formal text of Sidi Khalil", says Sautayra, "constantly applied in jurisprudence".

Shaf'ei doctrines.

The Shaf'eis and Hanbalis allow the boy, at the age of seven, the choice of living with either of its parents. Should he prefer to continue with his mother, he is allowed to do so until he attains the age of puberty, when he has no option and his guardianship devolves on the father. In practice, however, the father's right to the custody of the boy's person terminates with his puberty, for he is then *personally* emancipated from the *patria potestas*.[3]

Hanafi rule: The Judge's powers.

According to the Hanafi doctrines even when a boy has attained puberty, the father may insist on his remaining in the

1 Now Indo-Pakistan.

2 See Note at end of Chapter.

3 Sautayra, Vol. I, p. 348; Raddul-Muhtar, Vol. II, p. 1055.

paternal care if he be thoughtless or likely to go wrong. If the father is covetous of the property or earnings of the son, the Kazi should appoint a trustee.

Principle.

Among the Hanafis the accepted doctrine is that the mother's *hizanat* of a male child ends with the completion of his seventh year. "The mother and the grandmother," says the *Fatawai 'Alamgiri*, "are entitled to the custody of a boy until he is independent (of their care) that is, until he is seven years old."[1] But, adds the *Fatawai 'Alamgiri*, "Kuduri has declared that the custody lasts until the boy is able to eat and drink and perform the necessary ablutions by himself; Abu Bakr-ar-Razi puts the limit at nine years; the *Fatwa* (however) is according to the first doctrine.[2]"

So also the *Radd-ul-Muhtar* "the period when the male infant becomes independent of female care is seven years, and on this is the *Fatwa*".

The mother, therefore, is entitled in preference to the father to the custody of her infant male child under seven years of age.[3] *A fortiori* she has a better title to the guardianship of his person than the paternal uncle.[4]

Shiah doctrines.

Among the Shiahs, the mother is entitled to the custody of her children without distinction of sex until they are weaned.[5] During this period, which is limited to two years, the children cannot under any circumstance be removed from their mother's care without her consent.[4]

Custody of a female child.

After the child has been weaned, its custody, if a male, devolves on the father, and if a female on the mother. The mother's custody of a female child continues to her seventh year. After she attains that age, the father is entitled to her custody in preference to the mother ; but the father may allow the mother to retain the custody of the children of both sexes beyond the period specified by the law.[6]

Principle.

It will be seen that, though the period of *hizanat* varies among the different schools, the general principle, which governs

---

1 Fatawai 'Alamgiri, p. 730; Fatawai Kazi Khan, Vol. I, p. 478. In the matter of Tayheb Ally (1864) 2 Hyde, 163.

2 D'Ohsson says. "The mother's right lasts in the case of male children up to the age of seven, eight or nine years: in the case of female children until their majority or their marriage." Tab. Gen. de l'Empire Ottoman, Vol. III, p. 104.

3 Lardli Begum *v*. Mahomed Amir Khan (1887) I L 14 Cal. 615.

4 As to the right of the grandmother against the paternal uncle, see Bhoocha *v*. Elahi Bux (1885) I L 11 Cal. 574.

5 Jam'a-ush-Shittat; Jam'a-i-Abbasi; Shara'ya-ul-Islam. *See* Salim-un-nissa *v*. Saadat (1914) I L R 36 All 466. If the mother dies during the weaning period, the father is entitled to the custody of the child.

6 Jam'a-ush-Shittat.

its duration, is founded essentially on the interests of the child. "At the age of nine,"[1] says D'Ohsson, "a boy passes from the care of his female relations into the hands of his father, in order to receive from the father, a masculine education analogous to the paternal status, condition, and fortune."[2]

When both the parents are of the same school it is easy to determine the period of the *hizanat*; but if they belong to different schools, the principle upon which the question of custody should be determined is not entirely free from difficulty.

Right of hizanat has in view the exclusive benefit of the child.

It may be stated, as a general rule, that as the right of *hizanat* has in view the exclusive benefit of the infant, each particular case would be governed by the doctrine in force among the sect to which the child is supposed to belong; or, *if that cannot be ascertained, by a consideration of what would be best for the child as a Moslem child.* This rule has been adopted by the Court of Algiers, and no difficulty has been found in its application to individuals cases.

Judgment of the Court of Algiers.

The terms of the judgment delivered by the Court of Algiers on the 15th of April 1872, leave no room for doubt on the question. In the case referred to, it appeared that one Lakhal bin Mohammed, married a girl of the name of Ayesha bint Mustapha. A boy was born of this union who bore the name of Mohammed, after which a separation took place between Lakhal and Ayesha. When the boy reached the seventh year of his age, Lakhal applied to the Hanafi Kazi to obtain possession of the child's person. The Kazi of Algiers gave a decree in favour of Lakhal, but on appeal to the Court of Algiers, this judgment was reversed, and the child was allowed, in accordance with the Maliki doctrines, to remain with the mother.

Subject to the limitation already pointed out as regards the duration of the *hizanat*, the custody of infant children devolves, in the first place, upon their female relations; and it is only when there are no female relations that the right goes to the male relatives.

Maliki doctrines.

The Malikis differ to some extent from the Hanafis respecting the order in which the right of custody is possessed by the various relations. For example, they hold that, failing the mother of the child, the right passes (*i*) to the maternal grandmother; (*ii*) to the great grandmother; (*iii*) to the maternal aunt and grand-aunt; (*iv*) to the full sister; (*v*) to the uterine sister; (*vi*) to the consanguine sister; and (*vii*) to the paternal aunt. "When there are no relations of these degrees, or none qualified or willing to

1 The Hanafis of Turkey seem to extend the duration of the hizanat up to nine years.

2 *See also* Muhammad Bashir *v.* Ghulam Fatima P L D 1953 Lah. 73; Anwar Ilahi *v.* Mst Rashida Akhtar P L D 1955 Lah. 412.

exercise the right of *hizanat*, it passes to the father, and failing him to his executor, his son, his nephew, his uncle, and his cousin."

Hanafi doctrines.

According to the Hanafis, the order runs thus:—(*i*) the mother; (*ii*) the mother's mother-how-remote soever; (*iii*) then the father's mother how-high-soever;[1] (*iv*) then the grandfather's mother how-high-soever; (*v*) full sister; (*vi*) uterine sister; (*vii*) full sister's daughter; (*viii*) uterine sister's daughter; (*ix*) consanguine sister; (*x*) full maternal aunt;[2] (*xi*) uterine maternal aunt; (*xii*) consanguine maternal aunt; (*xiii*) consanguine sister's daughter; (*xiv*) brother's daughter; (*xv*) full paternal aunt; (*xvi*) uterine paternal aunt; (*xvii*) consanguine paternal aunt; (*xviii*) mother's maternal aunt of the full blood; (*xix*) mother's uterine maternal aunt; (*xx*) then the consanguine; (*xxi*) father's maternal aunt of the full blood; (*xxii*) uterine; (*xxiii*) consanguine; (*xxiv*) mother's paternal aunt of the full blood; (*xxv*) uterine; (*xxvi*) consanguine;[3] father's father's sisters. The general principle upon which the right is founded, is common to both the schools, *viz.*, that "the custody of an infant belongs by right to the mother's relations, and those connected through her (that is, *uterine* relations) are preferred to those connected with the child on the father's side only (that is, the consanguine relations)."[4]

According to the Hanafis, if there be no female relations, *or if none of them be legally qualified to exercise the right*, it passes (*a*) to the father; (*b*) failing him, to the paternal grandfather; (*c*) to the lineal male ascendant of the third degree, or still higher; (*d*) to the full brother; (*e*) to the consanguine brother; (*f*) to the full brother's son; (*g*) to the consanguine brother's son; (*h*) full paternal uncle; (*i*) to the half-paternal uncle on the father's side, and (*j*) to the son of the paternal uncle in the same order.[5] *Among these relations, also, the nearer always excludes the more remote.*

No male has a right to the custody of a female child unless within the prohibited degrees.

No male has a right to the custody of a female child unless he is a mahram, that is, stands to her within the prohibited degrees of relationship and cannot under any circumstance marry her.[5] Though a boy may be entrusted to the care of the paternal uncle's son, a girl cannot be placed under his guardianship, he not being a *mahram* to her.[6] The sons of aunts and uncles have no right to

1 Nur Begum *v.* Mst. Begum A I R 1934 Lah. 274. If the minor's mother has lost her right by remarriage, the mother's mother has a right preferential to the father's mother.

2 Tamina Khatoon *v.* Gohar Jan I L R 1941 Cal. 419; A I R 1942 Cal. 281. A maternal aunt has a preferential right to the custody of a minor over the father's step-mother.

In re Isso I L R 1942 Kar. 215: A I R 1942 Sind 113. Rights of female relations of the mother cannot be taken away by father's will.

3 Durr-ul-Mukhtar; Fatawai 'Alamgiri, Vol. I, pp. 728, 729.

4 Radd-ul-Muhtar, Vol. II, p. 1050.

5 *See* Muhammad Bashir *v.* Ghulam Fatima P L D 1953 Lah. 73, *also* Nur Begum *v.* Mst. Begum A I R 1934 Lah. 274; Kundan *v.* Aisha Begum A I R 1939 All. 15; Muhammad *v.* Mujeeb-un-nissa A I R 1952 Mad. 280.

6 Radd-ul-Muhtar, Vol. II, p. 1051.

the custody of a female child not being within the prohibited degrees. Nor is an *'Asabah* who is profligate entitled to the custody of a female child.[1]

Rights of the 'Asabah.

When there are no *'Asabah* qualified to take charge of the child, then the male *uterine* relations are given the charge *e.g.*, the uterine brother; uterine brother's son; father's uterine brother; mother's full brother.

If there are several male uterine relations entitled to the custody of the child, then the one who most tenderly looks after the child's interests is entitled to preference, then the one most virtuous, and then the one senior in age.

But this principle is not restricted to the male *uterine* relations, for it is explicitly enunciated that when there are several relations of the same line or degree, all equally qualified and willing to take charge of the child, the custody should be entrusted to the one who shows the greatest tenderness to it.[2]

The *Radd-ul-Muhtar* states the principle thus, "when there are several persons equally entitled to the *hizanat*, as full brothers or full paternal uncles, then the most virtuous among them should be given the charge, and if all are equally virtuous, then the senior among them in age has preference."[3]

The Judge.

In the absence of the natural guardians, or when none of them are qualified or willing to take charge of a minor, the custody of the child devolves on the Judge, who should place the infant in the care of a trustworthy person of the same sex as the infant.[4]

A non-Moslem mother.

As stated already, the right of *hizanat* appertains equally to Moslem and non-Moslem mothers. When, therefore, a Moslem marries a non-Moslemah, and there are issue of that marriage, the mother is entitled to exercise the *hizanat* over her children, like a Moslem mother. Al-Karkhi explains that the right of *hizanat* belongs to a mother in her capacity and character of mother; and consequently she does not forfeit that right by the fact of belonging to any faith other than the Moslem faith. A non-Moslemah mother's right to the custody of her infant children is restricted to a woman belonging to another faith at the time of her marriage.

Principle.

Where a Moslemah renounces Islam she forfeits at once the right of hizanat.

---

1 Fatawai 'Alamgiri, Vol. I, p. 730. The sons of uncles and aunts have no title to hizanat.

2 Durr-ul-Mukhtar.

3 Fatawai 'Alamgiri, Vol. I, p. 730; Radd-ul-Muhtar. About male relations, see Fuseehun v. Kajo (1883) I L 10 Cal. 15.

4 Radd-ul-Muhtar. Vol. II, p. 1051.

The Shiahs.

The Shiahs are in agreement with the Sunnis with regard to the general principles governing the right of *hizanat*. But among them, in the absence of the mother the right passes to the father, and failing him to the grandparents and other ascendants. When there are no ascendants, the right passes to the collaterals within the prohibited degrees, the nearer excluding the more remote.

Although the right to the guardianship of the minor passes in the order mentioned above, in the case of a contest between two persons one *preferentially* entitled as against the other, the Judge has to consider not only the respective qualifications of the claimants, but also the interests and well-being of the minor as a Musulman child.[1] The provision in the Guardians and Wards Act (VIII of 1890) which directs the Court in appointing a guardian to keep in view the "welfare of the minor" is in harmony with the Mahommedan Law.[2]

Qualifications necessary for the Hazina.

The qualifications necessary for the exercise of the right of *hizanat* are the following:—(*i*) that the *hazina*[3] should be of sound mind; (*ii*) that she should be of an age which would qualify her to bestow on the child the care which it may need; (*iii*) that she should be of good moral conduct; and (*iv*) that she should live in a place where the infant may not undergo any risk morally or physically.

Hizanat how lost.

The right of *hizanat* or custody, according to all the schools, is lost—

(1) by the subsequent marriage of the *hazina*, with a person *not related to the infant within the prohibited degrees*;

(2) by her misconduct;[4]

(3) by her changing her domicile so as to prevent the father or tutor from exercising the necessary supervision over the child; and

(4) by her abjuration of Islam.

(5) by her neglect of or cruelty to the child.

1. The right of a woman to the custody of an infant child is made void by her marriage with a "stranger", the presumption

1 Comp. Durr-ul-Mukhtar and Idu *v*. Amiran, supra ; see also in the matter of Ameerunnissa (1869) 11 W R 297; Abasi *v*. Dunne (1878) I L 1 All. 598.

2 *See* Mohammed Bashir *v*. Ghulam Fatima P L D 1953 Lah. 73 and Amar Ilahi *v*. Rashida Akhtar P L D 1955 Lah. 412.

3 *i.e.*, the female of hazin or person entitled to the hizanat or custody.

4 *See* Abasi *v*. Dunne (1878) 1 All. 598 and Khushi Mohammed *v*. Mohammed-un-nissa P L D 1961 Lah. 768.

of law being that a woman entering a new family will not have the same love or affection for the child as before.[1]

The author of the *Radd-ul-Muhtar* says, "the right of *hizanat* is lost by the mother (or any other woman) marrying a *ghair-mahram* of the infant, that is, one *not* related to the infant within the prohibited degrees, for a stranger would not be agreeable to her bringing up the child with affection and care."

But if she were to marry a *mahram* or a relation of the infant within the prohibited degrees, the right of *hizanat* would not fall to the ground. For example, if a mother were to marry the child's paternal uncle, such marriage being valid under the Mahommedan Law, she would not forfeit her right to the custody of her infant children. *But the mahram must be one by consanguinity.*

Although ordinarily the woman entitled to the custody of a child forfeits her right on contracting a marriage with a stranger, special considerations regarding the interests of the child may require that its custody should be retained by her. For example, if a woman separated from her first husband, were to marry a second time in order to secure for her infant child better and more comfortable living, she would not forfeit her right of *hizanat*.[2]

The Courts would preserve to the mother the custody of the child if it be in its interest that it should remain with her.

So also where the *hazina* contracts a second marriage, and the father does not, within a reasonable space of time from the date of such marriage, or from the date of his knowledge thereof, claim the person of the infant, he should be supposed to have abandoned his right over it, and it should remain thenceforward definitely under her care.

When the right of a mother or any other female relation lapses by marriage, it revives when the marriage is dissolved.[3]

Misconduct on the part of the Hazina.

2. The right of *hizanat* is lost by the misconduct of the *hazina*. For example if she be found leading an immoral life or frequenting the society of women of ill-fame, or if she be convicted of theft, she forfeits her right to the custody of the infant.

---

1 See Beedhun Bibi *v*. Fuzaloolah (1873) 20 W R 411; Fuseehun *v*. Kajo (1883) I L 10 Cal. 15.

2 The Decrees of the Court of Algiers, although no authority for the British Courts in India, (now the Courts of Pakistan), furnish useful illustrations of the general principle. See the Decrees, dated 8th of October 1862, 29th of June 1865, and 9th of December 1867 quoted in Sautayra, Droit Musalman.

See also Anwar Ilahi *v*. Rashida Akhtar P L D 1955 Lah. 412.

3 Fatawai 'Alamgiri, Vol. I, p. 728; Radd-ul-Muhtar *in loco*; Fatawai Kazi Khan, Vol. I, p. 478. There is no difference between the Shias and Sunnis on these points.

Fuseeheen *v*. Kajo (1884) 10 Cal. 15; Bhoocha *v*. Ilahi Bakhsh (1885) 11 Cal. 574 and Ansar Ahmed *v*. Samidan A I R 1928 Oudh 220: 106 I C 822.

4 *See* Khushi Muhammad *v*. Muhammad-un-nissa P L D 1961 Lah. 768.

The *Fatawai 'Alamgiri* says, as already stated, that of all persons the mother is the best entitled to the custody of her infant children, "unless she be an apostate, an immoral woman, or one unworthy of being trusted."[1] It goes on to add that a woman who habitually leaves her home and neglects her children, and allows them to starve, is unworthy of trust, *i.e.*, of having the custody of infants confided to her. The *Nahr-ul-Faik* says, "a woman has no right to the custody of a child, if she be a thief, an adulteress, a public singer, or a professional mourner". The odium attached to the two latter classes of women originated in the fact that in Eastern countries, immorality is generally associated with the profession or calling they follow.

Principle.

The *dicta* in the *Fatawai 'Alamgiri* supply the general principle governing these cases, by declaring that the misconduct which would disqualify a mother, or any other female relation from exercising or claiming the *hizanat* of a child, is "such wickedness as would prove injurious to the child"[2].

An adulteress, who is in the habit of leaving her house and neglecting her child, is disentitled from claiming the right of *hizanat*.[3]

The author of the *Bahr-ur-Raik* has stated that when the mother is a *Kitabia* and next to her is a *Moslemah* who is ill-conducted, the latter would, nevertheless, have preference. The author of the *Tanwir-ul-Absar* has not approved of this opinion, and has declared that no such distinction should be made, for the *Kitabia* only follows her faith. Some jurists have stated that the distinction between a *Moslemah* and a *Kitabia* is beside the point, for what must be considered in each case is what is good for the child, and its proper bringing up. Mufti Abu Sa'ud has laid down that all cases of misconduct do not necessarily destroy the right of *hizanat*; what must be considered is the detriment to the child, the question being, is the woman's misconduct likely to injure the child? So also it is stated in the *Hashiat-ul-Madani*.[4] The injury to be considered may be either physical or moral.

If the mother is *ghair-mamunah* or untrustworthy she is not entitled to the custody of her child. According to the *Mujtaba* a woman who goes out of the house at all time and leaves the child in a *neglected* condition, whether the going be with or without necessity is a *ghair-mamunah*, for example, as when she is a peasant woman and goes out to cultivate her field, or is a midwife, or washer of corpses. If she has to go out to work for her living she must make some provision for the care of the child during her absence.

Improper conduct on the part of a woman disentitles her to claim the right of custody. Similarly, if she were to misconduct

1 Fatawai 'Alamgiri, Vol. I, p. 728.

2 See the judgment of the Kazi of Constantine, 16th November 1860; Jurisprudence de la Cour d'Alger, De Menerville.

3 Radd-ul-Muhtar, Vol. II, p. 1042. *See also* Khushi Muhammad *v.* Muhammad-un-nissa P L D 1961 Lah. 768.

4 Radd-ul-Muhtar; see note II.

herself *after* the right had vested in her and the child had been confided to her care, she would forfeit the *hizanat*, and the person next in order would take charge of the infant.

In the *Kinia*, it stated that a woman, even though immoral may have the custody of a child, *so long as no evil effect may be apprehended to the infant*, and so long as her nurturing may be necessary for its benefit.[1] This, however, refers clearly to the custody of an infant of very tender years, like a child at the breast who cannot be taken away from its mother without serious risk of life.[2]

Abasi v. Dunne.

In the case of *Abasi* v. *Dunne*[3] it was held by the Allahabad High Court that a public prostitute was disqualified from having the custody of her infant sister. This was no doubt in accordance with the Muhammedan Law; but no attention seems to have been paid in the decision of that case to the allegation of the plaintiff, that her sister was being brought up in the tenets of Christianity by the people to whom her custody had been entrusted by the Magistrate.

Principle.

Except in the case of a non-Moslemah mother[4] the Muhammadan Law does not permit the custody of a Moslem child to be confided to any other than a Moslem or Moslemah. The order of the Magistrate, therefore, in the case of *Abasi* v. *Dunne* in pursuance of which the child was placed in a Christian orphanage and brought up as a Christian was absolutely illegal.

Principle.

Although the fact that the original faith of the mother is not Islam does not disentitle her from the right of *hizanat*, she cannot interfere with the religion of the child as Moslem child. Any tampering with it will amount to "misconduct" and will involve a forfeiture of the right.

Apostacy.

3. As already stated, abjuration of Islam is also a bar to the exercise of the right of *hizanat*. Consequently, a woman, who abjures the Islamic faith, whether before or after the right vests in her, is disentitled from exercising or claiming the right of *hizanat* in respect of a Moslem child.

Act XXI of 1850.

The provisions of Act XXI of 1850 make no alteration in the principles of the Muhammadan Law bearing on this subject: The

1 Radd-ul-Muhtar, Vol. II, p. 1042.

2 *See* Mst. Bibi *v*. Mst. Bibi A I R 1934 Lah. 287 (2). Where the mother of Muslim minors aged 11, 9 and 8 was not of good character and married a Hindu, the interests of the minors required that she be deprived of the custody of children being not so young that they could not be separated from her.

Mst. Aisha *v*. Barkat Ali A I R 1934 Lah. 221 (1). A Muslim woman who was not of good character and had married a Hindu was deprived of the custody of her daughter aged 5 but allowed to retain custody of daughter aged 2 years who could not be separated from her.

3 (1878) I L 1 All. 598.

4 Radd-ul-Muhtar *in loco*.

effect of that Act is confined to questions of inheritance. Consequently a convert to Christianity, though she may not lose her right of inheritance, would still forfeit her right of guardianship in respect of her infant relations.[1] For example, if a man were to die leaving two daughters, one of whom is an infant, the elder would, in the absence of other female relatives, be entitled to the custody of her sister. If, however, it appeared that she had apostatised from Islam previous to the disease of her father, she would be disqualified from claiming the *hizanat* of her sister, though her right of inheritance would be preserved to her by Act XXI of 1850.

Under the Hindu Law, unchastity in a woman is a bar to succession, but if property has once vested in her it would not be forfeited by her subsequent unchastity.

Under the Musulman Law, unchastity does not disqualify a woman from succession, though in the interests of the child it disqualifies her from exercising the right of *hizanat*.

Removal of the child by the hazina.

4. The right of *hizanat* is also liable to forfeiture in case the *hazina* removes the child, without the consent of its father or guardian, to such a distance from his usual place of residence as would prevent him from exercising the necessary supervision or control over her.[2]

But this rule is subject to qualification. When the change of residence is caused by unavoidable exigencies, or when it has been made for the benefit of the child, the right of *hizanat* is not lost. For example, a woman, who earns her livelihood by going into service, may be obliged to follow her employers from one place to another and take her child with her. The frequent change of residence resulting from the necessities of employment will not lead to the forfeiture of her right of custody. If a woman were to attempt to remove with her child from the usual place of residence, and the husband were to apply to the Judge to obtain the person of the infant upon the ground of its removal, he would be bound to inquire into the facts of the case, and, on being satisfied that the removal is only temporary or undertaken in the interests of the child, to allow it to remain in the mother's custody.[3]

While the marriage subsists "the conjugal domicile is the place of *hizanat*;" thus the home where the parents usually reside and live together as husband and wife is the place where the child should be brought up. Accordingly, the father cannot leave the city where they are residing and take the child with him out of the custody of the mother without her consent.[4]

---

1 Mulla's view expressed on the point at pages 234 and 294 of 15th Edition is wholly erroneous and misleading.

2 Fatawai 'Alamgiri, Vol. I, p. 731; Jam'a-ush-Shittat.

3 Jurisprudence de la Cour d'Alger, de Menerville.

4 Fatawai 'Alamgiri, Vol. I, p. 731; Kitab-ul-Anwar.

When a separation has taken place between the parents, the mother is entitled to return with her infant child to her native city (if the marriage took place there), however distant it may be from the residence of the father. "But", adds the *Fatawai 'Alamgiri*, "she cannot do so if the marriage did not take place there, unless it is so near the place of separation that if the husband should leave his own residence in the morning to visit the child he can return home before night;" nor can she "remove to any other city on any other condition".

Principle.

The following passage from the *Hedaya* explains the principle more fully:—"To the propriety of the woman carrying her child from one place to another, two points are essentially necessary, *first,* that she be a *native* of the place to which she goes, and, *secondly*, that her marriage took place there".[1]

Maliki doctrines.

"This, however, means only where the places are considerably distant; but if they be so near that the father may go to see his child and return the same night, there is no objection to the wife going to the place with the child and there remaining; and this whatever be the size and degree of the places, whether cities or villages." According to the Maliki jurists a distance of six *birids*[2] implies such distance as would prevent the father from exercising control or supervision over the mother.

Principle.

These dicta which were more or less the outcome of local conditions have not the force of rules, and each case has to be decided upon its own merits.

If the father were to remove from his usual place of residence or from the place where the *hazina* is residing and exercising the rights of *hizanat*, he would have, under certain circumstances, the power of withdrawing the child from the *hazina's* custody. This power, also, is strictly subordinated to the interests of the child. If the infant be independent of the mother's care, if it be doubtful whether she would, when freed from the supervision of the father, bestow the same care and tenderness on the child as before, then the Judge may, in his discretion, grant the father's application to remove the child.

The principle which should guide the decision of the Judge in these cases is laid down in explicit terms in a decree of the

1 Hedaya (English Translation), Vol. I, p. 391. The passage which follows is worthy of note:—"Nor is there any objection to her removing from the village to the city or chief town of a district, as this is in no respect injurious to the father, and is advantageous to the child . . . . . . but the reverse (that is, her removal from a city to a village) would be injurious to the child, as he would thereby be liable to acquire the low manners and mean sentiments of villagers: wherefore a woman is not at liberty to carry her child from a city to a village," unless it is her native place and the marriage was celebrated there.

2 A birid is equal to four farsangs, each farsang being equal to three miles of 1,700 metres each.

Court of Algiers dated the 11th of February 1862. "Considerant," it says, "qu'il s'agit de savoir si le pere, voulant parti pour la Macque et s'y etablir definitivement, peut, ainsi qu'il le pretend et que l'a decide le jugement attaque, emmener sa fille avec lui, malgre les protestations de sa mere; considerant qu'il est de principe en droit musulman comme en droit francais, que lorsqu'il s'agit de statuer sur le sort d'un enfant appartenant a des parents divorces, on doit rechercher principalement quel est le principal interet de l'enfant, et decider en consequence a qui, du pere ou de la mere, il doit etre remis; considerant a cet egard, qu'independament des hasards que le voyage projete entraine pour la jeune fille, sa translation et son establissment a la Mecque presentent des dangers encore plus reels; qu'en effet le pere et la nouvelle epouse sont l'unet l'autre d'un age avance; que dans un temps prochain ils pouraient venir a manquer a la jeune fille et la laisser isolee, sans appui dans un pays lointain, *tandis qu'a Alger elle resterait sous lee yeux de sa mere*, qui lui a toujours prodigue les soins les plus tendres, et dont la conduite est irreprochable; qu'elle y trouverait encore la protection les secours et les conseils des freres et des autres parents de sa mere, qui tous lui portent le plus vif interet; . . . . ordonne que la fille restera sous la grade de sa mere."[1]

Lardli Begum v. Mohammed Amir Khan.

This decision shows plainly the governing principle in all questions of *hizanat*. The right is founded primarily for the benefit of the child and is to be exercised by those relations who are most likely to bestow care and kindness on it. The case of *Lardli Begum* v. *Muhammad Amir Khan*[2] does not seem to have looked at the question of *hizanat* from this point of view.

According to the *Sirajia*, the father can take his infant child away with him *only* when the *hazina* has lost her right and there is no one else upon whom it devolves in succession to her. But the moment the right reverts to the *hazina*, the child must be brought back and made over to her. For example, if the mother had separated from the father of the child, and lost the *hizanat* owing to her having married another person, and this husband dies, the right reverts to her.[3] But in the *Sharnibilalieh* it is stated

1 Sautayra, p. 355.

2 Supra, p. 223.

Mohammed Bashir *v.* Ghulam Fatima P L D 1953 Lah. 73. All rules of Mohammedan Law relating to guardianship and custody of the minor are merely the application of the principle of benefit of the minor to diverse circumstances. Welfare of the minor remains the dominant consideration and the rules only try to give effect to what is minor's welfare from Muslim point of view.

Amar Ilahi *v.* Rashida Akhtar P L D 1955 Lah. 412 (416). It would be wholly wrong to suppose that the Muslim Law of guardianship creates rights in respect of minors for the benefit of their guardians. On the contrary, that branch of law was evolved for the benefit and welfare of the minor; and certain relations were given preferential right to the custody of the minor because normally those persons are more interested in the welfare of the minor and are, therefore, better suited to act as guardians.

3 *See* Fusseehen *v.* Kajo (1884) I L R 10 Cal. 15; Bhooch *v.* Elahi Bux (1885) I L R 11 Cal. 574; Ansar Ahmad *v.* Samidan A I R 1928 Oudh 220; Amar Ilahi *v.* Rashida Akhtar P L D 1955 Lah. 412.

that the father has no such right of removal; and in the *Hawi* it is laid down that he cannot remove the child to such a distance that the mother cannot see it every day if she chose. "This must be borne in mind.[1] In other words, this is the principle which must govern all such cases.

Hizanat a personal right. Act VIII of 1890.

The right of *hizanat* is a personal right, which the parties entitled can enforce by a judicial proceeding. Act VIII of 1890 (the Guardians and Wards Act, which has repealed Act IX of 1861 and Act XL of 1858, lays down the procedure for the appointment of guardians for the person and property of minors, being persons who have not attained their majority under the provisions of Act IX of 1875 (the Indian Majority Act). The provisions of section 17 of Act VIII of 1890 are worthy of note. It says:—

(*a*) "In appointing or declaring the guardians of a minor, the Court shall, subject to the provisions of this section, be guided by what, consistently with the law to which the minor is subject, appears in the circumstances to be for the welfare of the minor.

(*b*) "In considering what will be for the welfare of the minor, the Court shall have regard to the age, sex, and religion of the minor, the character and capacity of the proposed guardian and his nearness of kin, to the minor, the wishes, if any, of a deceased parent, and any existing or previous relations of the proposed guardian with the minor or his property.

(*c*) "If the minor is old enough to form an intelligent preferene, the Court may consider that preference."

As observed before, these provisions are in conformity with the Muhammedan Law.

Under this Act, therefore, the discretionary powers, vested in the Kazis under the Musulman Law, are vested in the High Courts and the principal Civil Courts of original jurisdiction in a district, and such Courts are bound to administer strictly, in all questions affecting the custody of Moslem children, the provisions of the Musulman Law regarding *hizanat*.

Mother's right of custody of her minor married daughter.

The mother is entitled to the custody of a minor married daughter in preference to the daughter's husband until the girl attains the age of puberty.[2] In the case of *Khatija Bibi*,[3] a husband applied that his wife, stated in the return to a writ of *habeas corpus* to be "an infant under the age of sixteen years, to wit of the age of eleven years or thereabout", might be delivered over into his custody. The Court, on the ground that she had not attained the age of puberty and that her dower had not been paid, refused

1 Radd-ul-Muhtar, Vol. II, p. 1058.

2 Comp. Radd-ul-Muhtar, Vol. II, p. 1056.

3 In the matter of Khatija Bibi (1870) 5 B L R 557. See In the matter of Mahin Bibi (1874) 13 Bom. L R 160; Nur Kadir *v.* Zuleikha Bibi (1885) I L 11 Cal. 649.

to order her to be taken from the custody of the mother, although the mother had taken her away secretly, in the absence of her father and husband from Bandari, where they were all living together, to Calcutta. The Calcutta High Court has held that when a person acting at the instance of and under the instigation of the mother takes away a minor wife from what is in law the custody of the husband, it is not taking from lawful guardianship under the Indian Penal Code and does not amount to kidnapping.[1]

If a mother were not to agree to nurture or take care of an infant without remuneration or compensation, and the father be not in a position to pay any, and some other woman, relation or stranger, be willing to bring up the child free of charge, the custody will be given to the latter. So in the *Hashiat-ul-Manadi.*[2]

Similarly, where an infant has no female relation other than one who is not willing to bring it up without being paid for the same, but has a paternal uncle's son who is willing to bring it up without payment, the infant may be confided to his care. No compulsion should be exercised on any woman to whom the right of nurture belongs to take charge of the child, if she herself be unwilling, for her unwillingness may arise from inability, unless the child will not take any other breast or the father has no means to employ a nurse.[3]

In the *Zahiria* it is stated that if the child has no other female relation excepting one to undertake its charge, she may be compelled to do so.

Principle.

The mother can on no account give up her right of *hizanat* for even if she were to obtain a *khula* in lieu of abandoning her right to her child's custody, the *khula* will be valid, and she will retain her right of *hizanat*.[4]

If the woman has no house, the father will have to provide her with one with such attendants as the child may require according to his means. According to the Shaf'eis, if the child is possessed of means, the habitation and attendants must be provided from its property. But if it has no property, all its expenses will appertain to the person who is liable for its maintenance. Khair-ud-din Ramli (the author of the *Karieyeh*) has stated that this rule obtains also amongst "us", *viz.*, the Hanafis.

Miscellaneous principles.

When a non-Moslemah, even though she be a Magian or Zoroastrian, is entitled to the *hizanat*, she stands on the same footing as a Moslemah, until the child is able to understand religious matters.

---

1 Korban *v.* King-Emperor (1905) I L 32 Cal. 444. *See also* Sultan Khan Mangal Khan *v.* Gullu A I R 1959 Madhya Pradesh 99.

2 Radd-ul-Muhtar, Vol, II, p. 1045. Comp. Fatawai 'Alamgiri, Vol. I, p. 73.

3 Fatawai Kazi Khan.

4 Radd-ul-Muhtar, Vol. II, p. 1050.

Principle, when the mother is a non-Moslemah.

In the *Nahr-ul-Faik* it is stated that it is proper to fix the age for the comprehension of religion at seven years or at such period when it is apprehended the child might become attached to infidelity or *Kufr*, owing to companionship with one who is an unbeliever in Islam.[1]

Principle.

As the right of the *hazina* becomes void by her marrying a "stranger", that is a person not related to the child within the prohibited degrees, so does it become liable to be forfeited on her taking up her abode with some one who has no affection for the child or whose interests are opposed to those of the child. For example, as is stated in the *Kinia*, if a woman, after the death of her husband leaving an infant child, were to marry a "stranger", and the mother's mother were to keep the child in the same house with the "stranger", the executor of the father would be entitled to insist that the *hazina* (the mother's mother) should live with the child at some other place. According to the *Nahr-ul-Faik*, the *hazina* is entitled to keep the child with her in the house of her own husband. For example, if an aunt is entitled to the custody of an infant, no objection can be raised to *her* husband on the ground of his being a person not related to the child within the prohibited degrees.[2]

A paternal uncle's son is in the position of a "stranger", so that if the mother of a child were to marry the son of its paternal uncle, her right of *hizanat* would become void. So also with foster-relations, *e.g.*, if the woman were to marry a foster-uncle or foster-father of the child, the position would be the same, and the right of *hizanat* would fall to the ground.

When the second husband dies, or becomes absolutely separated from the woman, the right revives.

Illegitimate children.

The custody of illegitimate children appertains exclusively to the mother and her relations.[3] If a child be a foundling, its custody belongs to the person who found it, or to the State.[4]

Though a mother is entitled to take her child to her native city, no other female hazina has a similar right.[5]

A foundling—Religious duty.

A foundling is called a *lakit*, something taken up from the ground, and the person picking it up is called the *multakit*. "A *lakit*", says the *Radd-ul-Muhtar*, "is an infant who has been thrown away or abandoned by its parents, or one of them, either from want, or to conceal the shame of adultery. Any one who finds

1 Radd-ul-Muhtar, Vol. II, p. 1052.

2 *Ibid.*

3 *See* Gohar Begum *v.* Suggi A I R 1960 S C 93.

4 Tab. Gen. de l' Empire Ottoman, Vol. III, p. 101.

5 Comp. Fatawai 'Alamgiri, Vol. I, p. 731; Baillie's Dig., p. 440, (2nd Ed.).

a *lakit* and does not pick it up, *i.e.*, allows it to die, commits a great sin; and he who picks it up will get his reward [from God]. To pick it up is a religious duty (*Farz-ul-kifaya*), and if the *multakit* is certain that its being neglected will cause the child's death, and there is nobody else there, its picking up is an obligatory religious duty (*Farz-ul-ain*). . . . . . . Kindness to children is the best of human actions, and to save one life is to give life to mankind, for God has said, 'he who has saved a life has saved the human kind'. The *lakit* will be free, enjoying all the privileges of being a Musulman . . . . The food, raiment, lodging, medicine, all that the foundling needs appertain to the *Bait-ul-Mal*. . . . . And when the boy has grown up, and has been contracted in marriage by the Sultan, the dower he may have to pay will be paid out of the *Bait-ul-Mal*".

"If the *lakit* has any property, its expenses will be paid out of the same, or if any relation of his is discovered anywhere, such expenses will be paid by such relation. . . . . And fine incurred by the *lakit*, in case it has no property and no known relation, will be paid from the *Bait-ul-Mal*. . . . . ."

"It is not lawful for anybody else to take child away from the *multakit*. Whether the sovereign can do so is a subject of discussion. In the *Fath-ul-Kadir* it is stated it is not lawful, and the author (of the *Tanwir-ul-Absar*) has, following the author of the *Bahr-ur-Raik*, maintained the same view. In the *Nahr-ul-Faik* it is stated that the Sultan may remove the child from the custody of the *multakit*, if he considers the latter to be not fit for having its custody. . . . . . ."

"If anyone were to take away forcibly a *lakit* from the *multakit*, and he were to sue for the child, the *lakit* will be restored to him, but it will not be restored to him if he made over the child voluntarily to the person whom he now sues."

The foundling—his custody.

"When two persons claim the person of a *lakit*, it will be given to him who has preference over the other: *e.g.*, if a Moslem and a Christian are the rival claimants, the child will be given to the Moslem.[1] But if they are both equal, then it is left to the decision of the Kazi to consider whose custody will be most beneficial to the child; and this is according to *Bahr-ur-Raik*. If one of them claim to be the father of the child, in that case, if the child be alive, *nasab* would be established. If it be dead, he will have to establish it by proof.[2] This is according to the *Khanieh*.[3]

"In the *Munia* it is stated that if more than two persons claim the *nasab* of a child, then, according to Abu Hanifa, it may be adjudged to them all if they are not more than five." In other words, all of them would have to contribute to its support.

1 This is according to Kazi Khan.

2 Because when the child is alive any property found with him will be applied to its needs. But in case it is dead, it is possible that the person alleging himself its father may do so from greed. Hence, the necessity of proof.

3 Fatawai Kazi Khan.

"If a married woman were to claim a *lakit* as her child, her claim would be valid, if her husband affirms her statement or the midwife proves the birth, or one man and two women establish the same. But if the woman has no husband, in that case she may establish her claim by the evidence of two males. . . . ."

"When two women are rival claimants to a *lakit*, the one who establishes her claim by evidence, will get the child. If they both produce evidence, the child will be adjudged as the child of both. On this the Disciples differ; they think the child will not be adjudged as the child of either. All this is from the *Khanieh*. If two persons claim to be the *multakit* of a foundling child, and one is able to describe some special marks on the person or clothing of the child, then the Kazi may give the child to him, unless there are reasons in the evidence of the other to counterbalance the weight of these matters. . . . But if their claims are equal, the Kazi may give (the support of) the child to both. . ."

"If a child is found to be in the quarters of the Moslems, or at the door of their mosque, or any place chiefly frequented by them, it will belong exclusively to Islam. . . . .

"Any property found with the *lakit* will belong exclusively to the child, and the *multakit* or any person to whom its custody is entrusted will spend it over the foundling under the directions of the Kazi."

"The *multakit*, *i.e.*, the person who has found the child, is entitled to apprentice the foundling to learn some craft or to put him to school and to take charge of anything given to the child by others by way of gift or alms. But he cannot have him circumcised. . . . . ."

"The *multakit* can take the foundling with him from one place to another, but he ought not to remove him from the city into the country, as that may be prejudicial to the child. . . . . . The guardianship of a *lakit* belongs primarily to the sovereign."[1]

NOTE

According to the *Muhit* the guardian is entitled to protect a young girl who has attained puberty—but is yet a virgin although there should be no apprehension of her doing wrong. But when she has advanced in age and has formed her judgment and is chaste he has no right to retain her, and she is entitled to reside where she pleases without any hinderance. In the case of a girl who is no more a virgin [*i.e.*, has been once married and is either a widow or divorced] the guardian is entitled to protect her if she cannot be trusted to take the care of herself. But if she can be trusted to take care of herself he has no right to keep her and she should be allowed to reside wherever she likes. *Fatawai Alamgiri*, Vol. I, p. 730.

---

1 Radd-ul-Muhtar, Vol. III, pp. 484—490; comp. the Hed., Bk. X.

CHAPTER VI
THE STATUS OF MARRIAGE

SECTION I
GENERAL OBSERVATIONS

"Marriage", says the *'Ashbah,*" is an institution ordained for the protection of society, and in order that human beings may guard themselves from foulness and unchastity. . . . ."

"No sacrament but marriage has maintained its sanctity since the earliest time [*lit*. the days of Adam]. It is an act of *ibadat* or piety for it preserves mankind free from pollution. . . . . ."

"It is instituted by divine command among members of the human species. . . . . . ."

"Marriage when treated as a contract is a permanent relationship based on mutual consent on the part of a man and a woman between whom there is no bar to a lawful union. . . . . ."

"It does not give the man any right over the person of the wife except for mutual relationship according to the law of nature and not contrary to it.[1] This is clearly laid down in the *Baday'a*. . . . . . ."

"It is allowed between two people of different sexes to whose mutual cohabitation there is no natural or legal bar or prohibition. For example, a man cannot marry a hermaphrodite nor any woman within the degrees prohibited by divine law. . . . . . ."

"And being ordained among members of the human species a man cannot marry a being of another kind."

The object of marriage.

"Marriage is obligatory on a person whose passions cannot otherwise be restrained from the commission of wrongs or from hankering after what has been prohibited, and who can provide the dower and maintenance of a wife. But it is not sinful for one, who is continent and, has no means, to abstain from it. . . . . ."

Asceticism, however, is disapproved of as it leads to many evils.

"If two people of different sexes intermarry with the object of guarding themselves from foulness and unchastity and procreating children and rearing them up tenderly, the act is pious. If it is only for self-indulgence, the act is not pious. . . . . . ."

"It is unlawful to oppress or coerce a woman into marriage or to obtain her consent by force or coercion, or to compel her to marriage."[2]

---

1 The Musulman Law is far more stringent than either the Civil or the Canonical (Christian) Law in protecting women from injuries.

2 The above is a paraphrase from the Durr-ul-Mukhtar and the Radd-ul-Muhtar.

"Marriage is a contract which has for its object the procreation of children." And the *Kifaya* lays down that it is one of the original necessities of man (*al-hawaij-ul-aslia*) instituted for the good ordering of life. It is, therefore, lawful on the part of an old man (*sheikh-ul-kabir*) or who has no hope of offspring, and even in the last or death illness."[1]

"The intercourse of a man with a woman who is not his wife", says the *Hedaya*,[2] "is unlawful, and prohibited absolutely. When there is neither the reality nor the *semblance* of this relation between the parties, their intercourse is termed *zina* or fornication, and subjects them both to the *hadd*,[3] or a specific punishment for vindicating the rights of Almighty God."[4]

Principle.

"A knowledge of the illegality, however," says the *Fatawai Alamgiri*, "is a condition essential to the infliction of the *hadd*. So that if the person was not aware of it, the punishment cannot be inflicted. And when there is a semblance of right, in some cases even where it amounts to a doubt (fiction) punishment is avoided."

Shubh or semblance of right.

The *Fatawai 'Alamgiri* goes on to add:—"Semblance is of several kinds: First, *shubh fi'l f'il*, or *semblance* (*doubt*) *in the fact*, also termed *shubh ishtibah* or semblance of assumption; which is, when a person supposes that something is a proof of right which is not so *in reality*." [An instance of this is furnished in the case of a man who imagines that the slave of his wife is lawful to him, because he may make use of her services.] "The benefit of this kind of semblance or doubt is allowed only when the person who entertains the doubt claims that he thought the intercourse to be lawful. If he does so, he would be exempted from the *hadd*; but otherwise it must be inflicted, because the intercourse is in reality *zina* (fornication)."

Semblance of right avoids the punishment of adultery.

"Second, *shubh fi'l mahal* or *semblance in the subject*, also termed *shubh hukmia* (legal semblance), because there is some actual proof of lawful right in the woman, though connection with her may, for some reason, be prohibited. Regard is, therefore, to be had to this semblance with reference to all persons, and its establishment is not dependent on the conception of the offender

1 Kifaya, Vol. III, p. 577, Chapter on Acknowledgment by the sick.

2 Hedaya, Vol. II, p. 586.

3 Fatawai 'Alamgiri, Vol. II, p. 202.

4 The hadd of zina in early times, used to be the old Rabbinical punishment stoning to death, if the offending party was "muhsin", and if not, scourging, with a hundred stripes for one who was free, and fifty for a slave. A muhsin "with a (ص) is a person who is free, sane, adult, a Moslem, and married by a valid contract that had actually been consummated, to a woman in whom the same qualities are combined." But under a ruling of the Caliph 'Ali, the stoning to death was commuted to flogging.

and his claim of legality *for the connection is not positively zina.*" [An example of this is to be found in a marriage with the wife's sister, whilst the first marriage is still subsisting.][1]

"Third, *shubh fi'l 'akd* or *semblance in the contract*; and, according to Abu Hanifa, wherever a contract of marriage has taken place, whether it be lawful or unlawful, and whether the illegality be one on which all are agreed, or with respect to which there is some difference of opinion, and whether the party be aware of the illegality or not, he is not liable to the *hadd*; but, according to the two Disciples when the marriage is one that is generally admitted to be unlawful there is no *shubh* or semblance of right, and the party is liable to the *hadd, if he was aware that there is none,* though otherwise he would be exempted." It follows, therefore, that, in the opinion of Abu Hanifa, connection under any contract of marriage is not *zina*; and that in the opinion of the Disciples, whenever an union is by consensus unlawful, connection under it is *zina, if the contract was entered into with a knowledge of its illegality.*[2]

Walad-uz-zina.

The offspring of a connection where the man has no right nor semblance of right in the woman, by marriage or bondage, is termed *walad-uz-zina*, or child of *zina*, and is necessarily illegitimate.[3]

"According to a tradition of the Prophet reported in the *Jam'a-ut-Tirmizi*,[4] the Faithful are directed to contract marriages in mosques and to give publicity to the same. . . . . . ."

"And it is most commendable to contract a marriage on a Friday."

"It is not sinful to have music at a wedding."[5]

Principle.

Regarded as a social institution, marriage, under the Muhammedan Law, is essentially a civil contract. Its validity depends on proposal on one side and acceptance on the other. The law does not insist upon any particular form in which the contractual performance should be affected or that the union should be evidenced by any writing, nor is the presence of witnesses essential for its legality. For, though among the Sunnis the presence of witnesses is considered necessary to the validity of a marriage, their absence only renders it *invalid* which is cured by consummation. In fact, a marriage-contract, as a civil institution, rests on the same footing as other contracts. The parties retain their personal rights against each other as well as against strangers; and, according to the majority of the schools, have power to dissolve the marriage-tie, should circumstances render this desirable.[6]

1 See post.

2 Fatawai 'Alamgiri, Vol. II, p. 208.

3 Fatawai 'Alamgiri, Vol. II, p. 209.

4 Radd-ul-Muhtar, Vol. II, p. 429.

5 *Ibid.*, p. 420.

6 See post.

Marriage as a civil institution.

"Marriage, like other contracts", to use the words of Mr. Baillie, "is constituted by *ijab wa kabul* or declaration and acceptance", but it confers no rights on either party over the property of the other. The legal capacity of the wife is not sunk in that of the husband; she retains the same powers of using and disposing of her property, of her entering into all contracts regarding it, of suing and being sued without his consent, as if she were still unmarried. She can even sue her husband without the intervention of a trustee or next friend, and is in no respect under his legal guardianship.

Principle. The contract of marriage.

"In the language of the law", as in the common parlance, the formal conclusion of the contract is called '*akd* conveying the same meaning as the terms *obligation* in the Roman Law. In fact, '*akd* is the completion of the contract which commences with the proposal or demand in marriage and ends with the consent.

The *Radd-ul-Muhtar* says that '*akd* signifies both proposal and assent, and that the word means the contract of marriage as well as cohabitation.[1]

Capacity of the parties to marry each other.

The validity of a marriage under the Mahommedan Law depends primarily on the capacity of the parties to marry each other. The performance of the marriage according to the form prescribed in the place where the marriage is celebrated, or which would impress on the woman by the customary law of the Musulmans the status of a wife in a matter of secondary consideration.

Principle.

It is a recognised principle of law that the capacity of each of the parties to a marriage is to be judged of by their respective *lex domicilii*. If they are each, whether belonging to the same country or to the different countries, capable, according to their *lex domicilii*, of marriage with the other, they have the capacity required by the rule under consideration. In short, as in other contracts so in that of marriage personal capacity must depend on the law of domicile.[2]

Prohibitive Capacity of a Moslem domiciled in England.

The *capacity* of a Musulman domiciled in England will be regulated by the English Law, but the capacity of one who is domiciled in Islamic countries or in countries where the Musulman Law is in force, by the provisions of the Musulman Law. It is, therefore, important to consider what the requisite conditions are to vest in an individual the capacity to enter into a valid contract of marriage.

1 Radd-ul-Muhtar, Vol. II, pp. 425, 429.

2 Dicey on Domicile.

The capacity to contract marriage.

As a general rule, it may be remarked, that under the Islamic Law the capacity to contract a valid marriage rests on the same basis and depends on the same conditions as the capacity to enter into any other contract.

(1) In the first place the parties must be able to understand the nature of their act. For, if either of them is *non compos mentis* or is incapable of understanding the nature of the contract, it is void.

(2) In the second place they must be adult (in cases where the marriage is not contracted for them by their guardians), and

(3) In the third place, they must be acting of their free will and not under compulsion.[1]

"Among the conditions which are requisite for the validity of a contract of marriage," says the *Fatawai 'Alamgiri*[2] "are understanding, puberty and freedom in the contracting parties, with this difference that whilst the first requisite is essentially necessary for the validity of the marriage, as a marriage cannot be contracted by a *majnun* (*non compos mentis*), or a boy without understanding; the other two conditions are required only to give operation to the contract, as the marriage contracted by a (minor) boy (possessed) of understanding is dependent for its operation on the consent of his guardian".

Age of discretion.

Puberty and discretion constitute, accordingly, the essential conditions of the capacity to enter into a valid contract of marriage. A person who is an infant in the eye of the law is disqualified from entering into any other legal transaction (*tasurufat-ush-shari'yeh*), and is consequently incompetent to contract a marriage. Like the English Common Law, however, the Mahommedan Law makes a distinction between a contract made by a minor possessed of discretion or understanding (a *sarir*), and one made by a child who does not possess understanding (a *saghir*). A marriage contracted by a minor who has not arrived at the age of discretion, or who does not possess understanding or who cannot comprehend the consequences of the act, is a mere nullity. The same conditions are necessary in the case of a girl as in the case of a boy; she, also, in order to contract a valid marriage, must be major and sane.

The Mahommedan Law fixes no particular age when discretion should be presumed. Under the English Law, however, the age of seven marks the difference between want of understanding in children and capacity to comprehend the legal effects of particular acts. The Indian Penal Code[3] also has fixed the age of seven as the period when the liability for offences should commence. It may be assumed, perhaps not without reason, that the same

---

1 What is coercion must depend on circumstances; comp. Wortham's Case, 2 H L Cases 73.

2 Fatawai 'Alamgiri, Vol. I, p. 377; Fatawai Kazi Khan, Vol. I, p. 380.

3 Now Pakistan Penal Code.

principle would govern cases under the Muhammadan Law; that is, when a contract of marriage is entered into by a child under the age of seven, it will be regarded as a nullity.[1]

It is otherwise, however, in the case of a marriage contracted by a *sarir*. "It is valid", says the *Fatawai 'Alamgiri*, "though dependent for its operation on the consent of the guardian."[2]

A contract entered into by a person who is insane or whose mind is so diseased that he cannot comprehend his act, is null and void, unless it is made during a lucid interval.

The English Courts have laid down that in deciding whether a person has sufficient mental capacity to contract a marriage, the question for the Court is whether the mind of the contracting party was diseased or not at the time of the contract; and if the evidence establishes that the mind was, at the time of entering into the contract, diseased, the Court will not enter into the consideration of the extent of the derangement.[3]

The same principle would govern cases arising under the Musulman Law.

A bondsman cannot enter into a contract of marriage without the consent of his master. The Musulman lawyers, therefore, add freedom (*huriyat*) as one of the conditions to the capacity for marriage.

Age of majority.

Majority is presumed among the Hanafis and the Shiahs on the completion of the fifteenth year, in the case of both males and females, unless there is any evidence to show that puberty was attained earlier.

Shamsunnissa v. Ashrafunnissa and others.

In the case of *Shamsunnissa* v. *Ashrafunnissa and others*[4] it was held by the Sudder Court of Calcutta that the declaration of a girl that she was adult, when there was nothing in her appearance to lead to the contrary conclusion, would be accepted to establish majority.

There must be no legal disability.

Besides puberty and discretion, the *capacity to marry* require that there should be no legal disability or bar to the union of the parties[5] *viz.*:—

---

1 Comp. Bishop on Marriage and Divorce (3rd Ed.), s. 194.

2 Fatawai 'Alamgiri, Vol. I, p. 377. A sarir is a youth who has not attained majority but is possessed of understanding. The Fatawai 'Alamgiri calls such a minor sabi-ul-'aakil.

3 Hancock (f. c. Peaty) *v*. Peaty 36 L J Matr. 57; S C L R 1 P 33; 16 L J 182.

4 See Morleys' Digest, Vol. I, p. 303.

5 Fatawai 'Alamgiri, Vol. I, p. 378: Irshad-ul-'Allamah; Jam'a-ush-Shittat.

(*a*) that they should not be within the prohibited degrees or so related to or connected with, each other as to make their union unlawful;

(*b*) that the woman must not be the wife or *mu'ataddah*[1] of another man.

SECTION II

THE LEGAL DISABILITY TO MARRIAGE (*Asbab-ut-Tahrim*)[2]

Capacity: legal disabilities.

THE prohibitions against certain kinds of marriage are more numerous in the Musulman Law than in the Code Civile, but they present, in the main, the same features as the French and English Law with respect to the prohibited degrees.

These prohibitions may be divided under four heads, *viz.*, (*A*) *absolute*, (*B*) *relative*, (*C*) *prohibitive* and (*D*) *directory*.

Absolute prohibition.

(*A*). The absolute prohibitions arise in the first place from legitimate and illegitimate relationship of blood (*consanguinity*)[3]; secondly, from alliance or affinity (المصاهرت *al-musa-heret*)[4]; thirdly, from fosterage (الرضا *arraza*).

According to Caussin de Perceval the ancient Arabs permitted the union of step-mothers and mothers-in-law on one side, and step-sons and sons-in-law on the other.[5] The Koran expressly forbade this custom. "Marry not women" says the Koran, "whom your fathers have had to wife (except what is already past), for this is an uncleanness, an abomination, and an evil way."[6] Then come the more definite prohibitions: "Ye are forbidden to marry your mothers, your daughters, your sisters[7] and your aunts, both on the father's and on the mother's side; your brother's daughters and your sisters' daughters; your mothers who have given you suck and your foster-sisters; your wives' mothers; your step-daughters born of your wives with whom ye have cohabited".

"Ye are also prohibited to take to wife two sisters (except what is already past), and to marry women who are already married."

---

1 A woman who is observing the 'Iddat or probation for a deceased husband or on account of divorce.

2 Fatawai 'Alamgiri, Vol. II, p. 385; Fatawai Kazi Khan, Vol. I, p. 380; Shara'ya, p. 263; Mafatih.

3 The cause of prohibition (tahrim-un-nasab) arising from consanguinity; Shara'ya, p. 266; Fatawai 'Alamgiri, Vol. I, p. 385 (al-Mahramat-bin-nasab).

4 *Ibid.*, p. 386.

5 Hist. des Arabes, Vol. I, p. 351.

6 Koran, Chapter iv, v. 2.

7 Among the ancient Egyptians and Persians such marriages were allowed.

Prohibitions founded on consanguinity.

(I) The prohibitions founded on consanguinity (the *tahrim-un-nasab*) are the same among the Sunnis as among the Shiahs. No marriage can be contracted, (*a*) with the ascendants, (*b*) with the descendants, (*c*) with relations of the second rank, such as brothers and sisters or their descendants, (*d*) with paternal and maternal uncles and aunts. Nor can a man marry his father's or any other ascendant's or his son's or any other descendant's widow. Similarly, it is prohibited to contract any union with one's illegitimate child or his or her descendants, for illegitimate relationship creates the same *prohibitions* as legitimate relationship.

According to the *Bahr-ur-Raik*, marriage is forbidden on the ground of consanguinity with the following women:—

(*a*) mother and all female ascendants;

(*b*) daughter and all female descendant, how-low-soever;

(*c*) sister and her female descendants, how-low-soever;

(*d*) brother's daughters, how-low-soever;

(*e*) father's sister (but not her daughter or any other descendant);

(*f*) mother's sister (but not her daughter or any other descendant).

Similarly marriage is lawful with an uncle's daughter. "These rules are applicable to both men and women. For example, as a man is forbidden to marry his sisters' or brothers' daughters, so is it forbidden for a woman to marry her brother's or sister's son, and so on"

Hanafi prohibitions for affinity.

(II) According to the Hanafis the second ground of *absolute* prohibition is founded on *affinity*, and this is created not only by a valid or invalid contract of marriage, but also by adulterous intercourse. "Even a woman who has been 'touched with desire' by a man becomes forbidden to his ascendants and descendants, and her female descendants and ascendants become forbidden to him."[1] And when a *valid* marriage has been contracted with a woman, her mother and other female ancestors and her daughter become forbidden to the man even though there may not have been consummation.

Affinity, therefore, prohibits to the man the following women:—

(*a*) Mother-in-law, how-high-soever.

(*b*) Wives' daughters, how-low-soever.

(*c*) Son's wife, how-low-soever, that is, son's son's wife. &c., or any woman with whom a son or grandson, &c., has cohabited or "whom he has touched with desire."

---

1 "Touching with desire" means any act of familiarity between a man and a woman. The age of nine, on the part of girl, is presumed to be the earliest age when this may occur. All these provisions are intended for the protection of women.

(*d*) So also step-mothers, or any woman with whom the father or any other ancestor has committed fornication.

The rule is applicable to both men and women. As a man cannot marry his son's wife, so a woman cannot marry her daughter's husband.

Accordingly, sisters, full, consanguine or uterine, by valid or invalid marriage or adulterous connection, are forbidden.

So the daughters of such sister, as well as the aunts by *nikah* or adulterous connection. This applies to both men and women.

Shaf'ei doctrine.

According to the Shaf'eis, however, an adulterous connection does not give rise to the *prohibition* of affinity. In this, they differ from both the Hanafis and the Shiahs.

Shiah rule.

According to the Shiahs, any act of impudicity between two adolescent youths creates a "perpetual prohibition" against either of them intermarrying with the female relations of the other.[1]

Fosterage.

(III) Among the Shiahs, marriage is forbidden for fosterage in the same order as in the case of *nasab*.

The Sunnis, however, permit marriage in spite of fosterage in the following cases:—

(*i*) The marriage of the father of the child, with the mother of his child's foster-mother;

(*ii*) with her daughter;

(*iii*) the marriage of the foster-mother with the brother of the child whom she has fostered;

(*iv*) the marriage with the foster-mother of an uncle or aunt.

Durr-ul-Mukhtar: exceptions.

According to the *Durr-ul-Mukhtar* there are twenty-one exceptions to this rule. For example, the foster-mother of a child and her mother are lawful to the child's grandfather. Similarly, a man may marry his brother's or sister's foster-mother; his son's foster-sister; paternal or maternal uncle's foster-mother; son's paternal aunt by fosterage, etc. The husband of the foster-mother may marry the natural mother or sister of his wife's foster-child.[2]

---

1 This is apart from the severe punishment for which the offence itself is liable.

2 Durr-ul-Mukhtar (Hoogly Ed.), p. 220.

Shiah rule.

The relationship by fosterage arises among the Shiahs when child has been actually nourished at the breast of the foster-mother.[1]

There is no difference among the Sunnis and the Shiahs regarding the prohibitions arising from affinity.

As already stated, the prohibitions springing from *consanguinity*, *fosterage* and *affinity* are applicable to both man and woman. What is forbidden to the man is forbidden to the woman.[2]

So far the absolute prohibitions.

Principle.

A marriage contracted within the prohibited degrees is null and void.[3]

Relative prohibitions—Hanafi Law. An invalid marriage.

(*B*) The *relative* prohibitions spring from causes which render the marriage only invalid, for the cause which creates the bar may be removed at any time thus rendering the union lawful *ab initio* without the necessity of a fresh contract. This in fact is the test of an *invalid* marriage. For example:—

Principle.

(*a*) Among the schools which recognise polygamy it is forbidden to marry *contemporaneously*, or one after the other during the subsistence of the first contract, two women so related to each other, that, supposing either of them to be a male, a marriage between them would be illegal (under the rules relating to absolute prohibition).

Thus a man may not marry two sisters or a woman and her niece by the same contract or one after another whilst the previous marriage is subsisting. But if such a marriage is contracted *in fact*, it is *invalid* (*fasid*) but not void (*batil*), for the prior marriage may become dissolved at any time by the death or divorce of one of them and thus validate the second union. Accordingly, although the Judge may separate the parties on the ground of the invalidity of the marriage, if it is consummated the issue would be affiliated to the father, in other words they would be his legitimate children.

In such cases whilst the children inherit from the father, their mother does not.[4]

---

1 Among the Shiahs, it is required that the child should have been suckled at least fifteen times, or at least a day and night; among the Hanafis it is enough if it had been suckled only once; among the Shaf'eis, it is necessary that it should have been suckled four times.

2 Manah-ul-Ghaffar.

3 See Chapter VII on Void and Invalid Marriages.

4 See post.

(*b*) Nor, according to these schools, can a man marry a fifth wife when he has completed the number tolerated in the Koran, *viz*., four. This is called illegality springing from *completion of number*. But, again, this is only invalid, for the man may, (as these schools allow), divorce one of the previous four wives, or any one of them may die, when the fifth connection would become valid.

(*c*) A woman may not marry her own slave. But she may emancipate him, and then marry him if she chooses. If a marriage, however, is contracted whilst the slave is unemancipated, the connection is *only invalid*.

(*d*) Similarly a man may not enter into a contract of marriage, according to the *Bahr-ur-Raik*, with his slave-girl whilst he has a lawful wife. But he may enfranchise her and then marry her if he chooses.

Law regarding intermarriages between Moslems and non-Moslems. Sunni doctrines.

(*e*) The fifth *relative* prohibition springs from *shirk* or polytheism. The observant student of the law of the two principal sects which divide the world of Islam cannot fail to notice the distinctive peculiarity existing between them in respect of their attitude to outside people. The nations, who adopted the Shiah doctrines, do not seem to have come into contact to any marked extent with the Chiristian races of the West, whilst their relations with the Mago-Zoroastrians of the East were both intimate and lasting. The Sunnis, on the other hand, seem always to have been more or less influenced by the Western nations. In consequence of the different positions which the followers of the two sects occupied towards non-Moslems, a wide divergence exists between the Shiah and Sunni schools of law regarding intermarriages between Moslems and non-Moslems.

It has already been pointed out that the Koran, for political reasons, forbade all unions between Musulmans and idolators. It said in explicit terms, "Marry not a woman of the polytheists (*mushrikin*) until she embraces Islam." But it also declared that "such woman as are *muhsinas* (of chaste reputation) belonging to the Scriptural sects, or believing in a revealed or moral religion, are lawful to Moslems."

Principle.

From these and similar directions two somewhat divergent conclusions have been drawn by the lawyers of the two schools.

The Sunnis recognise as legal and valid a marriage contracted between a Moslem on one side and a Hebrew or a Christian woman on the other.[1]

---

1 Hedaya, Vol. I, p. 85; Fatawai 'Alamgiri, Vol. I, p. 398. Jews and Christians are, by consensus. Scripturalists as both received a Dispensation. Abu Hanifa permits a Musulman to marry a Sabean woman, but Abu Yusuf and Mohammed and the other Sunni Imams hold such unions illegal.

Akhbari Shiahs.

They hold, however, that a marriage between a Musulman and a Magian or a Hindoo woman is invalid. The Usulis, the M'utazilas and a large section of the Akhbaris agree with the Sunni doctors. They recognise the validity of a permanent contract of marriage between a Moslem and a female belonging to "the Scriptural sects" or believing in God. Some of the Akhbari Shiahs, however, do not recognise as legal a *permanent* contract of marriage between a Moslem and a woman following any other creed.[1]

They allow, however, temporary contracts (*muta'a*) extending over a certain specified period with a Christian, Jew, or a Magian female.[2]

Principle.

This does not mean, however, that if a permanent marriage (*nikah*) be contructed *in fact* it would be unlawful.

Both schools prohibit a Moslem male from marrying an idolatrous female, or one who worships, the stars or any kind of fetish whatsoever.

Principle.

These prohibitions are relative in their nature and in their effect. *They do not imply the absolute nullity of the marriage. For example, when a Mahommedan marries a Hindoo woman, the marriage is only invalid and does not affect the legitimacy of the offspring,*[3] *as the polytheistic woman may at any time adopt Islam which would at once remove the bar, and validate the marriage.*

Marriage with a Hindoo woman; children legitimate.

In some of the cases it has been supposed that when a Moslem marries a non-Scriptural woman, in order that the marriage may be valid she must first adopt Islam. This was apparently the governing idea in *Abdur Razak* v. *Agha Mohammed Jaffer Bindamin.*[4] The notion, however, is erroneous. If there is an actual marriage, subsequent adoption of the Islamic Faith would make the union valid and no fresh ceremony would be needed.

I have already described the reasons which led to the prohibition of intermarriages between Moslems and idolatrous females (which is the real signification of *Mushrikin*); and also between non-Moslems and Moslemahs.[5]

Prohibitive incapacity.

(*C*) *Prohibitive incapacity* springs from the fact that the woman is already the wife of another man. In other words, a

1 See Syed Ali Nawaz Gardezi v. Lt.-Col. Muhammad Yusuf P L D 1963 S C 51.

2 Mafatih; Shara'ya, p. 274. According to the Shiahs, Zoroastrianism is one of the revealed religions.

3 See post.

4 Supra.

5 Ante.

married woman cannot marry again so long as the first marriage is subsisting.

The same rule, however, does not apply to a man, for except among the M'utazilas who do not recognise the unconditional lawfulness of polygamy, a man may have four wives at one and the same time, but not more, provided he can deal equitably with all. Nor can a man marry the widow or divorce of another man during her *'iddat*.

Another example of *prohibitive incapacity* is furnished by the rule that a Moslemah cannot enter into a lawful contract of marriage with a non-Moslem. Here, again, two Hanafi authorities[1] lay down that the union is only *invalid*. But all the Shiah schools forbid the marriage of a Moslemah with a non-Moslem.[2]

Examples of directory prohibitions.

(*D*) According to all the sects, it is unlawful to contract a marriage with a woman who is *enceinte, if it be known that the pregnancy is from her husband or "master"*, whether he be a *Moslem*, *Zimmi* (non-Moslem subject) or *harbi* (an alien enemy), and whether it is by a valid or an invalid marriage, or a mere semblance of marriage or "ownership by the right hand."[3] "It is reported from Abu Hanifa that a marriage with a refugee woman coming from the enemy's country is valid, though she may be pregnant by her husband, but Zailye has held its prohibition to be correct, and this is reliable and in the *Fath-ul-Kadir* it is laid down that the prohibition is the accepted doctrine."[4]

Lawful with one pregnant by fornication—Hanafi doctrine.

According to the Hanafis, it is lawful for a man to contract a marriage with a woman who is pregnant by *fornication* with somebody else, though connubial intercourse is forbidden until she is delivered.[5] This is the opinion of Abu Hanifa and Mohammed. Abu Yusuf differs from them and holds such an union to be invalid, but "the *Fatwa* is with Abu Hanifa and Mohammed".

The Shaf'eis, Malikis and Hanbalis hold the same doctrine as Abu Yusuf.

Principle.

Where a woman is pregnant by fornication with the same man who marries her, the marriage is lawful, and connubial

---

1 The Muit and the Muntaka; but see post.

2 Comp. Bakhshi Kishen Prasad *v.* Thakur Das (1897) I L 19 All. 375.

3 Radd-ul-Muhtar Vol. II, p. 474. "Ownership by the right hand" means right by capture in lawful warfare, the only form of bondage recognised by the law. But it has been extended by the legists to all bonds-women.

4 *Ibid.*, Comp. Hedaya, Bk. II, Ch. I, Grady's Ed., p. 32.

5 Radd-ul-Muhtar, Vol. II, p. 478.

intercourse is not forbidden between them. On this there is *consensus*. The Shaf'eis and Shiahs agree with the Hanafis on this point, and Abu Yusuf holds the same opinion as Abu Hanifa and Mohammed.

"And the *nasab* of the child born of the womb of the woman would be established in the man if it is born at six months or more from the date of marriage".[1] "But if born within six months its *nasab* would not be established, and it will not inherit to the husband or its mother, *unless* he says that it is his child and does not add that it is his by fornication. In that case, *nasab* will be established. This is according to the *Khanieh* (*Fatawai Kazi Khan*)...... If he says it is by *zina*, *nasab* will not be established. But if he does not mention *zina* distinctly, *nasab* will be established, for in this there is the possibility of the pregnancy having taken place from a previous marriage [between him and the woman] or from an invalid contract; and as the conduct of a Moslem should always be attributed to proper motives, so possibly there might have been a prior contract."[2]

Shiah rule—Marriage with a pregnant woman.

Among the Shiahs, there seems to be some difference of opinion regarding the validity of a marriage contracted by a man with a woman who is pregnant by adulterous intercourse with *another*. One writer (the Fazil-ul-Kashani), seems to think there ought to be no marriage, until the woman is delivered. The weight of authority, however, is in favour of the lawfulness of the union. The *Jawahir-ul-Kalam* says, "If a (married) woman became pregnant by fornication, after which her husband divorced her, in such a case her '*iddat* would be according to the ordinary probation as if she had not committed fornication and was not pregnant thereby. For what has been stated as to the '*iddat* of a pregnant woman lasting until her delivery does not apply to pregnancy by fornication. In this case the ordinary probation should be calculated. And I have found no difference on this point. If such a woman were to marry another person after the (ordinary) '*iddat* it would be lawful; and I have found no difference thereon, for the delivery is not the period of probation for a woman pregnant by fornication. Similarly, if a woman who has no husband, is pregnant by *zina*, there is no difference (*i.e.*, all are agreed) as to the validity of her marriage (during such pregnancy) with a person [other than the adulterer]".

Principle.

Similarly, it is stated in the *Hadaik*, that "if a woman is pregnant by *zina*, there is no '*iddat* for her, and she can lawfully intermarry with another before delivery".

In the *Mafatih* also it is laid down that, "the accepted doctrine is there is no '*iddat* for an adulteress whether she be pregnant or not by fornication ..... and if she be pregnant it is lawful for her to marry before delivery".

---

1 Radd-ul-Muhtar, Vol. II, p. 478.

2 *Ibid*.

At the same time, in order to keep the *nasab* pure it is recommended that a man should not marry a woman who is pregnant by fornication with another until she is delivered.[1]

Re-marriage with a woman separated by l'aan forbidden by the Shiah doctrines—Allowed under the Hanafi Law.

Under the Shiah Law, a woman against whom a proceeding by *l'aan* has taken place on the ground of her adultery and who is thereby divorced from her husband, cannot under any circumstance re-marry him. The Shaf'eis and Malikis agree in this opinion with the Shiahs. The Hanafis, however, allow a re-marriage with a woman divorced by *l'aan*.

Some Shiahs think that the niece of a wife may be validly married with the consent of the wife. But this union is considered invalid by the majority of this sect as well as by the Sunnis.

Marriage during Ihram.

Among the Shaf'eis, Malikis and Hanbalis, marriages are prohibited during the state of *ihram* (pilgrimage to Mecca), so that when a marriage is contracted by two persons either of whom is a follower of the doctrines of the above-mentioned schools whilst on the pilgrimage, it is invalid.

The Hanafis regard such marriages to be legal. The *Fatawai 'Alamgiri* says distinctly that "it is lawful for a *Muhrim* and *Muhrimah* to intermarry while in the state of *ihram*".

With the Shiahs though a marriage in a state of *ihram* is not lawful, the woman is not prohibited to the man always, unless he was aware of the illegality of the union.

SECTION III

THE FORM OF MARRIAGE

The form of marriage.

THERE are several other conditions laid down in the treatises on Musulman law for the contractual performance of marriage, all of which when properly considered resolve themselves to a mere question of form.

For example, it is required (*a*) that the parties to the contract "should hear each other's words," that is, the contract should be understood by both; (*b*) that, if *sui juris*, they should actually consent to the contract; and (*c*) that the husband and wife should be distinctly specified, so that there should be no doubt as to their identity.[2]

Regarding these formal conditions the Sunnis and the Shiahs are agreed, but whilst the former insist that the declaration and acceptance "should take place at one and the same meeting", and that "the acceptance should not be discrepant from the

1 Mafatih.

2 Fatawai 'Alamgiri, pp. 377, 378 and 381; Shara'ya p. 263.

declaration" the latter hold that "it is not a condition that the acceptance should *verbally* agree with the declaration".[1]

Sunni Law—Presence of witnesses—

It is also necessary under the Sunni Law, that there should be witnesses present to attest the conclusion of the contract. Two witnesses at least should be present to testify that the contract was properly entered into, and was in accordance with the conditions laid down above.

When the wife is a non-Moslemah the witnesses may be of the same faith as herself or any other faith.

A marriage contracted without witnesses, however, is not illegal.

Shiah Law does not require witnesses.

Under the Shiah Law, "the presence of witnesses is not necessary in any matter regarding marriage; and if a marriage were contracted by the spouses themselves or their guardians in private, it would be valid; even if there were an *injunction* to secrecy, that would not invalidate it".[2]

Difference between the Sunnis and Shiahs.

In fact, the great point of difference between the Sunnis and the Shiahs on the subject of marriage is, that whilst the former require the presence of witnesses at the contractual performance, they do not require any testimony for the dissolution of the contract by the husband; on the other hand the Shiahs do not require any evidence of marriage so long as the parties agree that it was performed regularly, *but they insist upon the presence of witnesses for the dissolution of the contract.*

General Principle.

The law appoints no specific ceremony for the contractual performance of a marriage; and no religious rites are necessary for contracting a valid marriage.[3]

But according to recognised custom, marriages among all the sects are solemnised by a person conversant with the requirements of the law, who is designated for the occasion, the *Kazi*. Two other persons, formally appointed for the purpose, act on behalf of the contracting parties, with a certain number of witnesses, and the terms are usually embodied in a deed of marriage called *Kabin-nameh* or *Mahar-nameh*. These formalities are also observed in the marriages of Mahommedans with women belonging to other Faiths.[4]

---

1 Jam'a-ush-Shittat; Mafatih; Shara'ya, p. 262.

2 Shara'ya, p. 262.

3 *See* Maung Kyi *v.* Ma Shawe Baw A I R 1929 Rang. 341: I L R 7 Rang. 777; Jogu Bibi *v.* Mesel Shaikh I L R 63 Cal. 415: 164 I C 957 and Mohammed Zaman *v.* Naima Sultana P L D 1952 Pesh. 47.

4 *See* Mst. Ghulam Kubra Bibi *v.* Mohammed Shafi A I R 1940 Pesh. 2 and Mst. Bibi Ahmed-un-nissa *v.* Ali Akbar Khan A I R 1942 Pesh. 19.

Christian Marriage Act (XV of 1872).

Under the Christian Marriage Act (XV of 1872), however, when one of the parties is a Christian the marriage in order to be valid under that Act, has to be solemnised in accordance with the provisions of Ss. 4 and 5 of that Act.

Nikah in the Arabic language means marriage, but in Bengal a first marriage is commonly called *shadi*[1] and the first wife a *shadi* wife. A second marriage is usually called *nikah*. The word thus used is supposed to imply an inferior kind of marriage which is altogether erroneous.

In India[2] as well as in other Mahommedan countries, many local forms have become associated with the performance of the matrimonial contract.

Performance of ceremonies not essential to a valid marriage.

The validity or invalidity of a marriage, however, does not depend in any way on the performance or non-performance of the forms and ceremonies that have been engrafted on Moslem manners and customs by contact with outside races.[3]

Legally a marriage contracted between two persons, possessing the capacity to enter into the contract is valid and binding, if entered into by mutual consent, in the presence of two witnesses. As already stated, the Shiah Law dispenses even with the latter provision.

"When a man," says the *Shara'ya*, "has declared himself to be the husband of a woman, and she has assented to the truth of the declaration, or when a woman has declared herself to be the wife of a man, and he has acquiesced therein, they are judged to be ostensibly married."[4]

As stated already as a general principle, a Mahommedan marriage requires no particular or formal rites to constitute it valid in law; and a marriage is legal and binding if celebrated *per verba de proesenti*.

In consequence, however, of the ceremonies practised in India,[2] it is usual to find two *distinct local* forms existing side by side. The first is the *'urfi* (customary) form; the second the *shar'ai* (or strictly legal form). The *'urfi* marriage is celebrated among the Shiahs and the Sunnis with elaborate ceremonies, similar to those practised in Turkey, and described with so much particularity by D'Ohson. The *shar'ai* marriages require no

1 Shadi is a Persian word and means rejoicing. As the first marriages are usually celebrated with much pomp and ceremony, it has received the designation of shadi.

2 Now Indo-Pakistan.

3 For the ceremonies usually performed at Mahommedan marriages, see Van Lennep's Bible Lands; Lane's Manners and Customs of the Egyptian People; Mrs. Mir Hassan Ali's Observations on the Musulmans of India and Herklot's Qanoon-i-Islam.

See also cases of Mst. Ghulam Kubra and Mst. Bibi Ahmad-un-nissa *mentioned in* foot-note 4, p. 254 ante.

4 Compare the cases cited in the Jama'a-ush-Shittat.

ceremonies (the *rusumat*). In the *shar'ai* form of marriage, the simple directions of the law are only complied with.

'Urfi and Shar'ai marriage.

As the terms *'urfi* and *shar'ai* occur frequently in cases where the legitimacy of a child is in dispute or the fact of its mother's marriage is questioned, it is necessary to bear in mind the difference between these two forms of marriage. At the same time, it must not be forgotten that so far as the legal consequences of a marriage are concerned, it is equally valid whether it is celebrated in the *'urfi* or in the *shar'ai* form. Of course, in the case of an *'urfi* marriage, the publicity with which the rites are performed ensures the probability of satisfactory evidence forthcoming, should a dispute arise at any time regarding the *factum* of the contract.

A Shar'ai marriage.

In a *shar'ai* form, on the contrary, the legal forms only are complied with, and consequently there is little publicity; and therefore, when it becomes necessary in such cases to produce reliable testimony of the marriage, the task is by no means so easy as in the *'urfi* form, unless the marriage has been registered.[1]

First marriages, even among the poorer classes, are frequently solemnised in the *'urfi* form. It must be added, however, that the *'urfi* form is rapidly falling into disuse, owing to the extravagance and waste connected with it.

In India[2] there is little difference between the rites that are practised at the marriage ceremonies of the Shiahs and the Sunnis. All marriages commence with betrothal (*mangni*) which extends over years, months or weeks, as the case may be. They may take place between minors as well as between grown-up people.

Marriage how celebrated.

Marriages are celebrated, generally speaking, in the house of the bride's father or guardian in the presence of the agents (*wakils*), if any, of the parties, and the guests, some of whom become witnesses to the deed of marriage. In this document are embodied all the conditions to which the husband binds himself, together with the amount of the ante-nuptial settlement, the nature of its payment, questions regarding the custody of the children, and other cognate matters. It is attested by the *walis* (guardians), by the *wakils* (agents), if any, of the bride and the bridegroom, and by the witnesses.

---

1 Under the Mahommedan Marriage Registration Act (Bengal Act I of 1876) which is in force in some parts of Bengal, it is optional with the parties or their guardians to register the marriage. At the time the Bill was about to be passed into law, the author pressed on the authorities the advisability of making the registration compulsory, but other counsels prevailed. It has since been acknowledged that great difficulties arise in the administration of justice from the permissive character of the Act. In Algiers, and in most Mahommedan countries, registration is compulsory. In Pakistan Registration of Marriages has been made compulsory under section 5 of the Family Law Ordinance.

2. Now Indo-Pakistan.

Kabin-nameh or deed of marriage.

In certain parts of India,[1] notably in Lower Bengal, the absence of a deed formally embodying the terms of the marriage-contract is an unusual circumstance in respectable families, especially in the case of a first marriage or when both the parties belong to the same rank or occupy the same position in life. The document is called a *Kabin-nameh.*

But *Kabin-namehs* are not so common in Behar, in the North-West Provinces and other parts of the country. Among the Shiahs of Lucknow and several other places, the *Mujtahid's* register is practically the sole record of the amount of dower and conditions of marriage.

As stated before, in practice, there is little or no difference between the ceremonials (*rusumat*) observed by the Shiahs and the Sunnis on these occasions. Theoretically, however, there is a difference which ought not to be lost sight of in dealing with the question of *form*. Whilst the Sunnis simply *recommend* the use of the *Khutba* before the contract is finally executed, and of the *Surat-ul-Fatiha* (the opening chapter of the Koran) at the conclusion of the marriage, the Shiahs consider the use of these to be, to some extent, obligatory.

The sigheh.

Among them, the ceremony commences as well as concludes with a prayer, and after the *sigheh*[2] has been pronounced, the person who officiates as minister or priest, reads the *Khutba* and the *Surat-ul-Fatiha* to sanctify and bless the union.

Marriage how contracted—Hanafi Law.

"Marriage is contracted", says the *Hedaya*, "by means of declaration and consent, both expressed in the preterite."[3] According to the *Hawi-ul-kudsi*, it is not necessary that the proposal should always precede assent, or that the proposal should come from one side particularly. So long as there is intelligent assent to the proposal for a permanent contract, it is valid. In making the proposal as well as in expressing assent, the past tense is used, says the *Radd-ul-Muhtar*, in order that the contract may not be referred to a future time. But it adds significantly, *marriage does not depend on the use of any express terms so long as the purpose is distinctly understood*; *and may, therefore, be contracted in the present tense.*

Shiah Law.

Under the Shiah Law, however, it is not necessary that both parties should use the past tense. So long as the acceptance

1 Now Indo-Pakistan.

2 The sigheh is common to both Sunnis and Shiahs. It is the oral declaration of the engagement, and is pronounced in words almost sacramental in their character on the completion, or conclusion of the ceremony, to mark it as irrevocable.

3 Hedaya Vol, I (Eng. Transl.), p. 72. "There are only two tenses in the Arabic verb, the preterite and the aorist. The latter being employed to express present and future time, is ambiguous, and the preterite is commonly used in contracts, for though its proper function is to relate to the past, it is employed in law in a creative sense to meet the necessity of the case."

is a natural consequence of the proposal or declaration and sufficiently expresses the intention of the consenting parties, it is valid in law.[1]

Declaration, in the language of the law, signifies the proposal made by one of the contracting parties, and *consent*, the acceptance of the declaration by the other.

Proposal and acceptance may be made and given either by the principals or their proxies or guardians.

The words by which marriage may be contracted—Sunni doctrines.

Among the Sunnis, marriage may be contracted by the use of the words *nikah* or *tazwij* (marriage), which are express in their meaning; or of the terms *hiba* (gift), *tamlik* (appropriation), or *ba'i* (sale), which convey the sense of the intended matrimonial contract implicatively.

The *Kifaya* is very explicit on this point. "The words by which marriage is contracted are of two kinds, *sarih* or plain, and *kinayet*, or implicative. The *sarih* or plain, are *nikah* and *tazwij*. All the others are *kinayet*, or implicative, and they comprehend every word that is employed to effect an immediate ownership in a specific thing. Thus, marriage, is contracted by *hiba* or gift, *tamlik* or transfer, and *sadakah*, or alms. So also by the word *ba'i* or sale; as if a woman should say, 'I have sold myself to thee,' or a father should say, "I have sold my daughter to thee for so much" and in like manner it is contracted by the word *shirra* or purchase; as if a man should say to a woman, 'Thou art mine,' or 'hast become mine,' and she should answer 'yes.' So also if he should say, 'Be my wife for a hundred,' or 'I have given you a hundred that you may be my wife,' and she should accept, it is a marriage. If a woman irrevocably repudiated should say, 'I have restored myself to thee,' and the husband should answer, 'I have accepted,' in the presence of witnesses, that is marriage. So also if a man, after he has repudiated his wife three times, or irrevocably, should say, 'I have recalled thee on so much,' and the woman is content, and the transaction takes place in the presence of witnesses, it is a valid marriage; and it would be so even though no mention were made of any property, provided that both parties are agreed that the husband intended marriage. But if the same words were addressed to a stranger, and the woman should consent, there would be no contract."

Shiah doctrines.

The Shiahs, on the contrary, hold that a valid marriage can only be contracted by the use of the words *nikah* or *tazwij* (both of which imply exclusively matrimony). They declare all marriages contracted by the use of any other expression as *invalid*.[2]

But when a marriage has been contracted by the expressions recognised as illegal under the Shiah Law, and has been consum-

1 Shara'ya.

2 Shara'ya, p. 262; Mafatih.

mated, the law attaches to it all the incidents and liabilities of marriage validly contracted.[1]

Both Sunnis and Shiahs agree in holding that a marriage cannot be contracted by the use of the expressions *ijara* (lease) or *'ariyet* (loan).

Any expression conveying intention sufficient.

Any expression, in fact, which conveys the idea of the two persons agreeing to cohabit piously and chastely with the object of procreating children and rearing them up is sufficient for a valid contract of marriage. And, therefore, implicative expressions are allowed as sufficient.

Arabic terms not necessary.

Foreign words, also, are sufficient if they convey the meaning of marriage, and it is not necessary that the words used should be Arabic.

Similarly, if an illiterate person were to mispronounce a word, or if a member of a non-Arabic community were to pronounce incorrectly the Arabic words in ordinary use among Arabic-speaking people, the validity of the contract will not be affected thereby so long as the intention is to contract a marriage.[2]

"And the Shaikh-ul-Islam Abu S'aud, Mufti of Turkey, has given *Fatwa* to the effect that where among communities or people, wrong words are in vogue or the Arabic words are mispronounced and they are used with the object of contracting marriage, such marriage is lawful."[3]

"The common use of wrong words among ignorant people may be regarded as a new language. *And the words, therefore, are to be taken as valid, for the chief point to be regarded is the intention. For prayers, even, are not vitiated when a foreigner or an ignorant person mispronounces his words.*"[4]

Where an [Arabic-knowing] individual *knowingly* mispronounces his words, the author of the *Tanwir-ul-Absar* holds such marriage not to be valid.

Marriage contracted by expressions not authorised.

According to both the Hanafis and the Shiahs, a marriage cannot be contracted by the use of the expression *ijara* (lease), or *'ariyet*, or such like words as give rise to temporary obligations. The *Durr-ul-Mukhtar* says a marriage contracted by such expressions is not valid, because there is no permanency in them, but they refer only to the enjoyment of the usufruct, whereas in *nikah*, permanency is an absolute condition.[5]

1 Jama'-ush-Shittat.

2 Radd-ul-Muhtar, Vol. I, p. 442.

3 *Ibid.*

4 *Ibid* p. 443.

5 Radd-ul-Muhtar Vol. I, p. 443.

Principle.

But if a marriage be, as a matter of fact, contracted by any such expressions, and the parties cohabit after such marriage, the man will not be liable for the *hadd* or punishment for adultery, and the woman will get her dower but less than that specified, unless the specified dower is less than the *mahr-ul-misl* (dower customary in her family), in which case she would get the specified dower.[1]

When the term marriage (*nikah*) is used, it is not necessary that the parties should have a knowledge of the legal effects of the contract. Nor, when the word "marry" or "marriage" is used, is it necessary to go further and enquire into the intention.[2] But where an union is effected by implicative expressions, the parties must intend *marriage*. In the *Durrar-ul-Ahkam*, however, it is laid down that if the implicative expressions are known to the parties to mean marriage, no further knowledge or intention is required.

The *declaration* and *acceptance*, or, in other words, proposal and consent, may be expressed in any language known to the parties.[3]

Sunni Law.

Under the Sunni Law it is required that the declaration should precede the acceptance, in order to demonstrate conclusively the intention of the parties.[4]

Shiah Law.

Under the Shiah Law, however, it is not necessary that the declaration should precede the acceptance.[5]

Marriage may be contracted by signs in the case of the dumb.

As marriage is contracted by speech, so also it may be contracted in the case of the dumb by signs, when the signs convey their meaning intelligibly.[6]

When a marriage is contracted through an agent or by correspondence, under the Sunni Law, the receipt of the message or of the letter must be attested by two witnesses, and so also the *consent*.

According to all the schools the bridegroom is entitled to see his wife before the marriage,[7] but Eastern customs very rarely allow the exercise of this right, and the husband, generally

1 Radd-ul-Muhtar Vol. I, p. 443.

2 *Ibid.*

3 Mafatih; Fatawai 'Alamgiri Vol. I, p. 382.

4 See Fatawai 'Alamgiri Vol. I, p. 382; Fatawai Kazi Khan Vol. I, p. 379; Fusul 'Imadiya.

5 Jam'a-ush-Shittat; Shara'ya p. 362.

6 Jama'a-ush-Shittat; Shara'ya p. 262. With regard to the validity of a contract of marriage between deaf and dumb persons under the English Law, see Harrod *v.* Harrod, *infra.*

7 Durr-ul-Mukhtar, p. 196; Perron, Femmes Arabes, pp. 525—530.

speaking, sees his wife for the first time when leading her into the nuptial chamber. In order to obviate the drawbacks which naturally spring from the restrictions imposed by Oriental manners on social intercourse between the two sexes, custom has devised the institution of *mushattas*, who serve as intermediaries and help in bringing together the families of the future bride and bridegroom. The *mushattas* arrange the visits of the members of the two families to each other, settle the outlines of the marriage settlement and the *paraphernal* accessories, discover the fortune and means of the parties, and act generally as agents on behalf of the people interested in the arrangement.

SECTION IV

CONSENT

Consent of an adult person necessary to the validity of marriage.

No contract can be said to be complete unless the contracting parties understand its nature and mutually consent to it. A contract of marriage also implies mutual consent; and when the parties see one another, and of their own accord agree to bind themselves, both having the capacity to do so there is no doubt as to the validity of the marriage.[1] Owing, however, to the privacy in which Eastern women generally live, and the difficulties under which they labour in the exercise of their own choice in matrimonial matters, the Mahommedan Law, with somewhat wearying particularity, lays down the principles by which they may not only protect themselves from the cupidity of their natural guardians, but may, also, have a certain scope in the selection of their husbands.

For example, when a marriage is contracted on behalf of an *adult* person of either sex, it is an essential condition to its validity that such person should consent thereto; or, in other words, marriage contracted without his or her authority or consent is null, by whomsoever it may have been entered into.[2]

Among the Hanafis and the Shiahs, the capacity of a woman, who is adult and sane, to contract herself in marriage is absolute.

Shiah Law. Hanafi Law.

The Shiah Law is most explicit on this point. It expressly declares, that in the marriage "of a discreet female (*rashida*, who is adult), no guardian is required." The *Hedaya* holds

---

1 "The contract of marriage is, in its essence, a consent on the part of a man and woman to cohabit with each other and each other only. The religious element does not require anything more of the parties"; Harrod *v.* Harrod 1 Kay & J 4; s c 18 Jur. 853: 2 W R 612.

2 Fatawai 'Alamgiri, Vol. I, p. 405; Fatawai Kazi Khan, Vol. I, p. 481; Shara'ya, pp. 262, 263; see the case of Asgur Ali *v.* Munaffat Ali (1874) 22 W R 403, in which the marriage of an adult girl contracted by the father was held to be invalid because she had not consented to it.

Begum *v.* Faiz Bakhsh 60 I C 734 (Lah.). A marriage without the bride's consent and in her absence is invalid.

the same opinion: "A woman", it says, "who is adult and of *sound mind*, may be married by virtue of her own consent, although the contract may not have been made or acceded to by her guardians, and this, whether she be a virgin or *saibbah*."[1]

Shaf'ei and Maliki Law.

Among the Shaf'eis and the Malikis, although the consent of the *adult virgin* is as essential as among the Hanafis and the Shiahs to the validity of a contract of marriage entered into on her behalf, she cannot contract herself in marriage without the intervention of a *wali*.

Wali or guardian.

Among the Shaf'eis,[2] a woman cannot personally *consent* to the marriage. The presence of the *wali* or guardian is essentially necessary to give validity to the contract. The *wali's* intervention is required by the Shaf'eis and the Malikis to supplement the presumed incapacity of the woman to understand the nature of the contract, to settle the terms and other matters of similar import, and to guard the girl from being victimised by an unscrupulous adventurer, or from marrying a person morally or socially unfitted for her.

SECTION V

GUARDIANSHIP FOR PURPOSES OF MARRIAGE

Rules relating thereto

It is owing to the importance and multifariousness of the duties with which a *wali* is charged, that the Sunni Law is particular in ascertaining the order in which the right of *wilayet* is possessed by the different individuals who may be entitled to it.

Hanafi doctrines.

The schools are not in accord with reference to the order. A *wali* or guardian must be major, sane and free. He must not be a minor or lunatic, with or without lucid intervals. Nor can a *wasi* or executor, under the Hanafi Law, act as a *wali* unless he comes within the category of *walis* pointed out by the law.[3]

If a father who is not "just", or who is addicted to evil ways were to marry his infant daughter to her *manifest* disadvantage,

---

1 Hedaya, Bk. 1 (Eng. Trans.), p. 95; a Saibbah is a woman who has been once married and lived with her husband—thus ceasing to be a virgin.

See Jainan *v.* Rulia 145 P L R 1914: 25 I C 43. Where the father, the mother or brother consents to the marriage, and she remains silent, it is tantamount to her consent.

2 Hasan Kutty *v.* Jainaba 52 Mad. 39 : A I R 1928 Mad. 1285. Under the Shaf'ei and Maliki law the consent of adult virgin is not sufficient for the completion of the marriage contract. It must be given through the guardian.

3 Radd-ul-Muhtar, Vol. II, p. 486.

or to a *ghair kufu, to one unequal to her* (by birth or position), such marriage will not be operative or valid, and the Judge will have the power to set it aside at the instance of another *wali* (guardian) although remote.[1]

A *wali*, who is a *fasik-ul-mutahattik*, that is, *addicted to evil ways and extravangance*, is not entitled to the *wilayet-ul-ijbar* (the guardianship in marriage). *Wilayet-ul-ijbar* means the right of a guardian to impose on his ward the status of marriage.

A sui juris-woman.

A woman, who is sane, free and adult, can marry herself to an equal, with or without the consent of any person who might be her *wali*. This is the *mazhab* (doctrine) of Abu Hanifa, Abu Yusuf and Mohammed, the general principle being that any one who has the capacity to deal with his or her property, can also deal with his or her person.[2]

Shaf'ei and Maliki doctrines.

"Shaf'ei and Malik hold a contrary opinion", says the *Radd-ul-Muhtar*, "but there is no authentic *hadis* in support of their views."[3] At the same time, it is recommended, as more consistent with decorum, that an adult virgin should entrust the negotiations of her marriage to a *wali* in whom she trusts.

The *'asabah-be-nafsihi* have the *wilayet*, provided the individual claiming the right is free, possesses the capacity and is a Moslem.[4]

Hanafi Law.

The Hanafis entrust the office first to the *'asabah-be-nafsihi* (the *'asabah proprio jure*) in the order of succession, *viz.*, the son, then the son's son, then the father, then the father's father, then the full brother, then the consanguine brother, then the full brother's son, then the consanguine brother's son, then the full paternal uncle, then the consanguine paternal uncle, and then their sons, and so on.

When there are no *'asabah-be-nafsihi*, the *wilayet* devolves on the mother, then on the grandmother (father's mother), then on the daughter, son's daughter, daughter's daughter, and so on; then on the maternal grandfather (*jadd-ul-fasid*), then on the sister, then on the half-sister, then on the uterine relations, then on the *mowla-ul-mawalat*. For example, suppose a man of the name of Khalid, is converted to Islam by one Zaid, a *majhul-un-nasab*,[5] who has no known relations; and Khalid dies leaving an infant daughter, Zaid would be her *wali*. "In the absence of

1 Radd-ul-Muhtar, Vol. II, p. 486.

2 *Ibid.*

3 *Ibid.*

4 Ante, p. 242.

5 A person of unknown paternity.

all these, the *wilayet* is to the Sultan and then to the Kazi, who is vested with the jurisdiction by his *sanad* or commission."[1]

Marriage by a minor girl where there is no wali or Kazi.

When a minor girl, who has no relation that can stand in the situation of a *wali*, contracts herself in marriage, and there is no Kazi from whom sanction may be obtained, the marriage is not void, but *will take effect on her attaining majority and ratifying the contract*.[2]

This relates to a case where the marriage is with one who is *suitable* or is the *girl's equal* (*kufu*) and on a proper dower. But when the dower is small, and the man is not her equal, the marriage is ineffective.[3]

Also, when a minor girl has been married without the intervention of a *wali* or the sanction of a Kazi in the country of the enemy (the *Dar-ul-Harb*), or on the sea, or when travelling in the desert and such like places, the marriage is null. But if the marriage is contracted in a village or a city, it remains subject to her option.[4]

Marriage contracted by two walis standing in the same degree of equality.

If two *walis* standing in the same degree like two brothers or two paternal uncles, were to marry a minor girl to two different individuals, the first marriage in order of time will take effect; but if they are contemporaneous, or if it cannot be ascertained which is prior in time, both will be void.[5] Or, the girl may, on attaining puberty, declare that one is the first, which will then be operative.

Marriage to different persons by different walis.

And if the *wali* were to contract her in marriage before obtaining her permission, and on learning of it she were to remain silent, it would amount to ratification. If there be two or more *walis*, and they were all to contract her in marriage with two different people, and she was to remain silent after hearing of both of them, that is, say neither "yea" or "nay", both marriages will remain dependent on her express ratification. And if she were to assent to both, both will be void. If the marriages were contracted after obtaining permission, the one prior in time would take effect.[6]

---

1 Radd-ul-Muhtar, Vol. II, p. 512.

In the Radd-ul-Muhtar it is stated that according to Abu Hanifa and Abu Yusuf, the son takes precedence over the father, "but in the Hindieh (Fatawai 'Alamgiri), it is laid down that it is proper that the father should have precedence." Mohammad differs from the Imam Abu Yusuf; See the Radd-ul-Muhtar, Vol. II, p. 510; and Fatawai Kazi Khan, Section on Guardians; comp. Baillie's Dig., p. 45.

2 Radd-ul-Muhtar, Vol. II, p. 515.

3 *Ibid.*, p. 551.

4 *Ibid.*

5 *Ibid.*

6 *Ibid.* p. 490.

The executor cannot contract a minor in marriage.

The executor (*wasi*) of the father has no right, in his character of executor, to impose the status of marriage on the infant children of the testator, even though the father may have given him the power in his will. In the *Khanieh*,[1] however, it is stated that Hisham has reported in his work called the *Nawadir*, an opinion of Abu Hanifa to the effect, that if the father had made a *wasait* (testamentary direction) in his will, then the executor would have the power. And Zailye had adopted this view, but *this report* [from Abu Hanifa] *is weak*. And in the *Fath-ul-Kadir* this matter is explained ; it is there laid down that, if the father had in his lifetime fixed upon a bridegroom and distinctly mentioned him in his will, the executor may marry the testator's daughter after his death to the bridegroom so chosen. But this view, again, is combated in the *Bahr-ur-Raik*, which lays down that the executor can marry the girl to the boy in the lifetime of the testator as his *wakil* or agent, and not after his death as his executor. The author of the *Radd-ul-Muhtar* then winds up by saying that, if the executor be a *wali de jure*, he can contract the minors in marriage, otherwise not. If there are no natural *walis*, he must do it with the sanction of the Kazi.[2]

The Kazi.

But the Kazi cannot marry a minor girl to his own son or any other relative whose evidence would not, under the Musulman Law, be admissible against himself. Nor can he marry her himself. And so is the case with the Sultan himself.[3]

Ibn Nujaim has declared judicially that, when the Kazi has given his sanction to the marriage of a minor, there can be no further dispute, and no outsider can again question it. And similar *Fatwas* are to be found in the *Anf'a-ul-Wasail*.

Principle.

It is laid down in the *Khanieh* (*Fatawai Kazi Khan*), that if a youth who has not attained puberty were to disappear after his marriage with an adult girl and she were to marry during his absence somebody else, such second marriage would be lawful even though the boy may choose to ratify the contract entered into by him or on his behalf during his minority, provided the second marriage is contracted before he has signified his ratification.[4]

Principle.

In the *Fath-ul-Kadir*, it is laid down that when the father of an *adult* girl has married her to *A* with her permission, and

---

1 The Fatawai Kazi Khan is so called in the Radd-ul-Muhtar.

2 Radd-ul-Muhtar, Vol. II, p. 514.

3 *Ibid.*

4 *Ibid.*, p. 515. See also Badal Aurat *v.* The Queen-Empress I L 19 Cal. 79, post; see Fatawai Kazi Khan, Section on Conditions of Marriage.

the girl contracts herself in marriage with *B*, in such a case whichever marriage is *declared by* her to be prior in time will be lawful . . . . . but if the woman says she does not know which one is prior in time and which subsequent, both marriages will be annulled.[1]

Principle.

It is lawful for a remote *wali* to contract a girl in marriage when the nearer is absent. When the father is absent, and the paternal uncle and paternal grandfather are present, the *wilayet* belongs to the grandfather.[2]

When the *nearer wali* (*wali-ul-akrab*) is present, but labouring under a disability, *e.g.*, is a minor or a lunatic, the marriage by the more remote will be lawful.

If the more remote marries a girl or a boy when the nearer is present, the marriage is dependent upon the latter's ratification, which ratification must be distinct. Mere silence is not sufficient.[3]

Ghibat-ul-munkata'.

As regards the distance, which would justify a remote *wali*, marrying a minor in the absence of the nearer *wali*, the author of the *Tanwir-ul-Absar*, following the *Kanz-ud-Dakaik*, has held it to be three days' and nights' journey, and this is called a *ghibat-ul-munkata'*.[4]

In the *Multeka* it is stated, that when a suitable match is arranged for a boy or a girl with a bride or bridegroom of equal position, and the nearer *wali* of either is at such a distance that his approval cannot be obtained without the risk of the match falling through owing to delay, such a distance would be a *ghibat-ul-munkata'*. Ibn-Kamal has given *Fatwas* in accordance with this doctrine. And in the *Bahr-ur-Raik* it is stated from the *Mabsut* that this principle is correct. In the *Nihaya* it is laid down that all the jurists have adopted this view, and in the *Fath-ul-Kadir* it is mentioned that there is no difference on this point.[5]

According to the *Multeka* a marriage contracted by the remoter guardian is valid when the nearer though living in the city where the parties are residing happens to be concealed, and his whereabouts cannot be ascertained, nor can his sanction be obtained, and the *kufu*[6] will not wait for his appearance.

---

1 Radd-ul-Muhtar, Vol. II, p. 515.

2 See ante, Chap. IV.

3 Radd-ul-Muhtar, Vol. II, p. 516.

4 *Ibid.*

5 *Ibid.*, See ante, Chap. IV.

6 The equal in match to the bride or bridegroom.

If the absent *wali-ul-akrab*[1] marries the minor to some person at the place where he himself happens to be, the marriage will not be valid according to the *Nahr-ul-Faik*, the *Muhit* and the *Mabsut*.

If a *wali* refuses to give his ward in marriage, it is an act of oppression; then the sovereign or his representative, the Kazi, (Judge) would marry the minor.[2] But not when the *wali* is absent on *Hajj*.

If the *wali-ul-akrab* altogether prohibits the marriage, then the Kazi would authorise the next guardian to contract a marriage for the minor.

And if a marriage has been contracted by a remoter guardian in the absence of the nearer, it will not be annulled when the latter returns, but will remain valid.

Principle : An acknowledgment of marriage between minors made by walis.

An acknowledgment of marriage between minors made by their *wali* or *walis* is not effective and will be set aside if, on attaining majority, the minors or either of them should deny the same. But if the *wali* should make the acknowledgment during their minority, *and they should not say anything on coming to know of it after attaining majority, the acknowledgment would be valid.*

Shaf'ei doctrines—order of guardians.

The Shafi'es adopt the following order; the father, the father's father, the son (by a previous marriage), the full brother, the consanguineous brother, the nephew, the uncle, the cousin, the tutor, and lastly, the Kazi, thus entirely excluding the female relations from the *wilayet* (the guardianship).[3]

Maliki doctrines.

The Malikis agree with the Shaf'eis in confinding the office of *wali* only to men, but they adopt an order slightly different. They assign the first rank to the sons of the woman (by a former marriage), the second to the father, and then successively to the full brother, nephew, paternal grandfather, paternal uncle, cousin, manumittor, and lastly, to the Kazi.

Modern Maliki rules.

Among the Malikis and the Shaf'eis the presence of the *wali* at a marriage is always necessary, and this condition has given birth to two different systems.

The first of these considers the *wali* to derive his powers entirely from the law. It, consequently, insists not only on his

---

1 The nearest guardian.

2 Radd-ul-Muhtar, Vol. II, p. 517.

3 *Ibid.*, p. 518.

presence at the marriage, but on his actual participation in giving the consent. According to this view, not only is a marriage contracted through a more distant *wali* whilst one more nearly connected is present, invalid, but the latter cannot validate a marriage contracted at the time without his consent, by according his consent subsequently.

This harsh doctrine, however, does not appear to be enforced in any community following the Maliki or Shaf'ei tenets.

The second system is diametrically opposed to the first, and seems to have been enunciated by Shaikh Ziad as the doctrine taught by Malik.

An adult woman.

According to this system the right of the *wali*, though no doubt a creation of the law, is exercised only by virtue of the power or special authorisation granted by the woman; for the woman once emancipated from the *patria potestas* is mistress of her own actions. She is not only entitled to consult her own interests in matrimony, but can appoint whomsoever she chooses to represent her and protect her legitimate interest. If she thinks the nearer *wali* to be inimically inclined towards her, she may appoint one more remote to act for her in respect of her marriage. Under this view of the law the *wali* acts as an attorney on behalf of the woman, deriving all his powers from her and acting solely for her benefit.[1]

This doctrine has been adopted by Al-Karkhi, Ibn-ul-Kasim, and Ibn-i-Salamun and has been formally enunciated by the Algerian Kazis in several consecutive judgments.

When the *wali* preferentially entitled to act is absent, and his whereabouts are unknown; or when he is a prisoner or has been reduced to slavery; or is absent more than ten days' journey from the place where the woman is residing; or is insane, or an infant, then the *wilayet* passes to the person next in order to him.[2]

Hanafi rule.

The Hanafis hold that an adult woman is always entitled to give her consent without the intervention of a *wali*.[3] When a *wali* is employed and found acting on her behalf, he is presumed to derive his power solely from her, so that he cannot in any circumstance act in contravention of his authority or instructions.[4]

When the woman has authorised her *wali* to marry her to a particular individual, or has consented to a marriage proposed to her by a specific person, the *wali has no power to marry her to another*.

1 Muhammed Assem, Traite de Marriage, Traduction de B. Lasalle, chap. ii; Kitab-ul-Anwar; Hedaya, Vol. I, Bk. ii, chap. ii.

2 Radd-ul-Muhtar, Vol. II, p. 519.

3 Fatawai 'Alamgiri, Vol. I, p. 405.

4 Fatawai Kazi Khan, Vol. I, p. 380.

Shiah Law—Marriage of a sui juris woman.

Under the Shiah Law, a woman who is "adult and discreet" is herself competent to enter into a contract of marriage. She requires no representative or intermediary through whom to give her consent. "If her guardians"[1], says the *Shara'ya*, "refuse to marry her to an *equal* when desired by her to do so, there is no doubt that she is entitled to contract herself even against their wishes."[2]

The Shiahs agree with the Hanafis in giving to females the power of representing others in matrimonial contracts. "In a contract of marrige full regard is to be paid to the words of a female who is adult and sane, that is, possessed of sound understanding ; she is, accordingly, not only qualified to contract herself, but also to act as the agent of another in giving expression either to the declaration or to the consent."[3]

The *Mafatih* and the *Jam'a-ush-Shittat* also declare that "it is not requisite that the parties, through whom a contract is entered into, should both be males, since with us (the Shiahs) a contract made through (the agency or intermediation of) a female is valid".

Recapitulation.

To recapitulate :—Under the Maliki and Shaf'ei Law, the marriage of an adult girl is not valid unless her consent is obtained to it, but such consent must be given through a legally authorised *wali*, who would act as her representative. Under the Hanafi and Shiah Law, the woman can consent to her own marriage either with or without a *wali*. "When a girl is adult and discreet, no one has a right to be her guardian, but it is nevertheless becoming and proper for her to authorise her father or grandfather to settle the terms of the contract for her. If she have no father or grandfather, it would be well for her to appoint her brother to act on her behalf."[4]

SECTION VI

EXPRESS OR IMPLIED CONSENT

Consent how given.

The consent may be given either in express terms or by implication.

In the case of a girl who has been once married or is aware of the nature of the matrimonial contract,[5] *the consent is required*

---

1 *Viz.*, the father and the grandfather, who under the Shiah Law are the only wali-ul-jabir.

2 Shara'ya, p. 268.

3 *Ibid.*, p. 266.

4 Jam'a-ush-Shittat.

5 Saibbah, a girl who has lost her virginity.

to be express. When this is not the case, or, in other words, when the girl is a virgin, the jurists of all the schools hold that "smiling, laughing, or remaining silent, may be construed to imply consent".

"When the guardian", says the *Hedaya*, "being the person empowered to engage in the contract, requires the consent of an adult virgin to a marriage, if she smile or remain silent, this is compliance; because the Prophet has said, 'a virgin must be consulted in everything which regards herself ; and if she is silent, it signifies assent'; and also because her assent is rather to be supposed as she is ashamed to testify her wish, and laughter is a still more certain token of assent than silence ; contrary to weeping, which expresses abhorrence. . . . . . Some have said that if the laughter be in the nature of jest or derision, it is not compliance."[1]

According to the *Radd-ul-Muhtar*, if the laughter is in ridicule, then it will not amount to consent ; nor will crying aloud be taken as assent. But if the girl merely weeps slightly, it may be taken as if she was sorry to leave her relations.

Remaining silent, with a distinct knowledge of the fact, is tantamount to consent. But silence at first, owing to some accidental cause or illness, must not be taken as assent.[2] "When a father consults his daughter before marriage", says the *Fatawai 'Alamgiri*, "and says to her, 'I am going to contract you in marriage', and does not mention the dower or the name of the husband, and she remains silent, silence is not consent in such a case, *and she may afterwards repudiate the marriage.*"[3]

If the consent of an adult virgin is obtained by any person other than the father, brother, or uncle, such consent is required in *express* words.[4]

Consent of a woman suffering from a serious illness.

Similarly the consent is not valid if given when the woman is suffering from a serious illness likely to endanger life.[5]

Betrothal.

The institution of *mangni* or betrothal, though it exists in India, is not legally binding on either side. A marriage

1 Hedaya, Vol. I, p. 97; Fatawai 'Alamgiri, Vol. I, p. 408.

2 Radd-ul-Muhtar, Vol. II, p. 489.

3 Fatawai 'Alamgiri, Vol. I, p. 406.

4 Hedaya, Vol. I, p. 96 : Grady's Ed., p. 35.

5 This point was decided by the superior tribunal of Algiers on the 9th of November 1836. In that case it appeared that one Al-Taib married a woman of the name of Zuhra, who was at the time in an advanced stage of consumption. The woman, in fact, died four months after the marriage. Upon a suit by Al-Taib to establish his rights as husband in respect of the property left by Zuhra, the Majlis-ul-Kaza of Algiers made a decree in his favour. On appeal, however, the Kazi's order was reversed, and the marriage was pronounced invalid.

engagement which has not been completed by the actual *'akd,* and when the *sigheh* has not been pronounced, cannot be enforced.

An action for breach of promise cannot, therefore, lie under the Mahommedan Law. *It is only after the 'akd has been performed and the contract actually executed, that a suit can lie on behalf of either of the married parties for restitution of conjugal rights.*

Principle: Consent obtained by compulsion.

As under the English Law,[1] consent to the marriage obtained from the woman by fraud or compulsion has no effect, and the *nikah* is not valid; and if she has been induced or compelled to consent to a small dower, the Kazi must give her full customary dower or else separate the parties.

Silence on the part of an adult girl, after learning that a marriage has been contracted for her, amounts to ratification whilst the marriage is subsisting. If the husband were to die before the news has been communicated to the girl, her silence would not amount to consent, and she would not be entitled to inherit from the man, though she will have to observe the *'iddat*. This is a case in which the marrige was contracted without her previous permission or consent. But if her consent was taken before the marriage, she would be entitled to inherit.[2]

If an adult girl is married to a man by her wali, and on being informed of it, she says she would prefer anybody else, this is tantamount to repudiation.

Express assent when required.

If the paternal uncle's son were to contract a marriage for an adult girl, her silence is tantamount to refusal.[3] In other words, her express assent is necessary to validate a marriage contracted for her by her cousin (her paternal uncle's son) and of which she is informed after it has been contracted.

This applies to a case where it is done *without* her previous assent. But if the marriage is contracted with her express assent, it is valid by consensus.[4]

So long as the adult woman knows the specific individual to whom she has been married or is going to be married by the father, brother or uncle, her silence is tantamount to consent.

---

1 Scott, falsely called Sebright *v.* Sebright 56 L J P 11; S C 12 P D 21; Clarke (otherwise Stier, otherwise Ford) *v.* Clarke 65 L J P 13.

See also Abdul Latif Khan *v.* Niaz Ahmed I L R 31 All. 343 and Kulsumbi *v.* Abdul Kadir I L R 45 Bom. 151.

2 Radd-ul-Muhtar, Vol. II, p. 490; see Note 1 *Ibid.*

3 *Ibid.*, p. 457.

4 *Ibid.*, p. 496.

Principle.

When consent or permission is sought for by any other person her silence is not consent. Express assent is necessary in such a case both on the part of a virgin and of a girl who has lost her virginity.

Various other acts amount to assent, such as removing her furniture to her husband's house and so on. But mere acceptance of his presents is no evidence of assent.

A girl who has accidentally injured herself by jumping or riding or otherwise, is a virgin under the law. So also a woman who has been separated from her husband on the ground of his impotency, or has become divorced by his death before consummation.

Definition of a virgin.

A girl who has lost her virginity by fornication is also a virgin in law.[1] In short a virgin in fact and one in law (*hukmi*) stand on the same footing.

In the matter of denial of assent, the woman's statement is to be accepted as against that of her walis.[2]

The girl's statement as to puberty will be preferred to that of the guardian.

If a father of a girl were to marry her to a person on the supposition that she was a minor (under puberty), and the girl were to assert that she had attained puberty, and that consequently her *nikah* was not "valid" ; and the father and husband were to assert that she was under puberty, *her statement should be accepted if the girl be nine years of age or over.*[3]

Similar statement by a boy or youth.

Similarly, if a youth, whose property is sold by his father, were to say that he had attained puberty and that his father had no right to deal with his property, the boy's assertion would be accepted and the sale would be annulled.[4]

When assent need not be express.

But when two adult persons themselves enter into a contract of marriage, acceptance need not be express. If a man were to call a woman in the presence of witnesses, "my wife" and she

---

1 Provided her fornication has not formed the subject of a judicial proceeding.

2 Radd-ul-Muhtar, Vol. II, p. 496.

3 *Ibid.*, p. 497.

4 Tatar-Khanieh,

answered, "Yes, my husband", it will amount to a valid marriage.[1]

Principle : Assent implied by conduct sufficient.

The *Bazazia*, quoting the *Badaia*, states that assent implied by mere conduct is sufficient. For example, if a man were to propose marriage to a woman on a dower of 1,000 dirhems, and the woman says nothing, but merely accepts the dower, according to the *Bazazia* this would amount to a valid assent. But the author of the *Muhit* dissents from this view.

When assent should be given.

When the parties are present, the assent must follow immediately upon the proposal. If the woman or woman's proxy takes time to consider the proposal, the assent is not regarded as effective.

Marriage must not be dependent on a contingency.

"Among the conditions of proposal and consent are that the marriage should not be dependent on a contingency, nor suspensive on the happening of a future event, and the woman must not be unknown."

"If a man were to say, 'I shall marry thee three weeks hence', or 'on Zaid's coming', or if a woman were to say, 'I shall consent three weeks hence', or 'when Zaid arrives', there is no marriage. But if assented to, the proposal and assent will amount to a promise of marriage, and if consummated, will take effect as a valid marriage.

When a proposal is made in writing, the assent may be given on receipt of the writing or afterwards.

---

1 Compare the following remarks of Mr. Bishop on the subject of marriage: "Lord Stowell says, in terms the general correctness of which cannot be doubted that 'a marriage is not a mere carnal commerce; nor would it be so even in the law of nature. A mere carnal commerce, without the intention of cohabitation and bringing up of children, would not constitute marriage under any supposition. But when two persons agree to have that commerce for the procreation and bringing up of children, and for such lasting cohabitation,—that, in a state of nature, would be a marriage, and, in the absence of all civil and religious institutions, might safely be presumed to be, as it is popularly called, a marriage in the sight of God'. And perhaps we cannot object to a decision which holds—that a written instrument between a man and a woman by which they mutually promise to live together as husband and wife as long as they can agree, does not constitute marriage; at least the question should be, whether the parties did take each other as, in substance, husband and wife and did so live. But a mere understanding that they might divorce each other at pleasure, whether the understanding was written or verbal, should certainly not be construed to prevent the status of matrimony from attaching to them. Of course, an agreement of this sort between the parties would be void; but not unfrequently the Courts hold to be void some contract entered into at the time of marriage, while the sufficiency of the marriage itself is not denied."

"The consent essential to marriage must contemplate a present assumption of the status, in distinction from a mere future union. The agreement of future marriage is termed espousals de futuro, or a contract per verba de futuro, while the agreement which superinduces the status is termed espousals de proaesenti, or a contract per verba de proaesenti."

When a man makes a proposal in these terms : "I marry you on 1,000 dirhems", and the woman answers, "I accept the marriage, but not the dower", it is not a valid contract, for there is no reciprocity. But she may say, "I accept the marriage, but demand a dower of 2,000 dirhems" which, on acceptance by the man, would complete the marriage.

But if a man were to say, "I marry thee for 1,000 dirhems", and the woman were to say, "I consent for 500", no fresh acceptance on the husband's part is necessary. The husband has no right to reduce the dower, he can only increase it; but the woman may take less if she likes.

Proposal in writing.

The *Radd-ul-Muhtar* says the substance of the letter should be read to the witnesses, and so also the consent when given by letter. But when a proposal is made by letter, and the answer is merely 'I accept,' the *Bahr-ur-Raik* thinks it is not sufficient, for it is difficult to apprehend whether the acceptance refers to the proposal of marriage. But if the assent is worded thus, 'I accept thee for or as my husband', or 'I accept thy proposal of marriage', it would be sufficient.

In the *Fath-ul-Kadir*, it is stated that when a woman receives the letter, she should read it out to the witnesses or explain its purport to them; and that she should say, "I accept his proposal", or "I marry myself to him". All this will constitute a valid marriage.

But when a proposal is couched in these terms "marry me to thyself", in such a case it is not necessary for the woman to read the letter to the witnesses, for the man has made her his proxy. It is enough for her to say, "I marry myself to so-and-so".

It is also a condition that the contracting parties or their proxies should hear each other's words, or *see the proposal and acceptance in writing*. This of course does not apply to a case where one or the other is both deaf and blind. In such a case the proxy of the party who is labouring under the physical incapacity or the proxies of both, if they are both incapable, must hear the words or see the proposal and acceptance in writing.

SECTION VII

TESTIMONY

The presence of witnesses—divergence between the schools.

Under the Shiah and the Maliki doctrines the validity of a marriage does not depend on the presence of witnesses, whilst under the Hanafi Law it is a necessary condition.[1] The Hanafi rule insisting on the presence of witnesses at a marriage is based on a traditional saying of the Prophet, the authenticity of which, however, is not accepted by the Shiahs or the Malikis. Not only, under the Hanafi rule, must they be present at the time of the execution of the contract, but they must know of its actual terms. They must also be able to speak to the identity of the persons from whom the proposal and consent respectively emanate. If a woman was so concealed or veiled that neither of the witnesses could recognise her, or was able to tell whether she or any other female in the room gave the consent, their testimony would not be sufficient.

Hanafi doctrines.

The time when the presence of the witnesses is required, is when the contract is being actually entered into, *viz.*, when the proposal is made and the consent given. And it is insisted upon that both the witnesses should hear the words of both the contracting parties simultaneously. So that if one witness was to hear the words of one and not of the *other*, the contract would be invalid.[2] Similarly, it is laid down in the *Radd-ul-Muhtar* :—"The witnesses should be two free men or one free man and two free women, that they should be sane and adult and *hear the words of the contracting parties together.*" "This is the correct doctrine."[3]

"Nor can a marriage be validly contracted in the presence of two persons who are asleep or who are dumb. And this is the opinion of the generality of 'our' doctors. What Zailye has stated, that it is valid in the presence of two sleeping persons and not in the presence of two dumb people has been contradicted in the *Fath-ul-Kadir* and the *Bahr-ur-Raik*."

"It is further a condition of marriage", says the *Fatawai 'Alamgiri*, "that the witnesses should hear together the words of both the contracting parties. Hence, it cannot be contracted in the presence of two sleepers who have not heard the words of both the contracting parties, nor of two persons so deaf that they cannot hear; though it can be contracted on the testimony of a person who has lost his powers of speech or is dumb but can hear. If the witnesses should hear the speech of one of the parties, and not that of the other, or if one of the witnesses should hear the speech of one of the parties, and the other that of the other, the marriage is not valid. So also, if both the witnesses should hear both the parties, but hear them separately, as for instance, if the marrige should first take place in the presence of one of the witnesses, and should then be repeated in the presence of the other, who was absent on the first occasion, it would not be valid ; and if it should take place in the presence of two men, one of whom is deaf, and if the hearing witness

1 Radd-ul-Muhtar, Vol. II, p. 444; see post.

2 Fatawai 'Alamgiri, Vol. I, p. 378.

3 Radd-ul-Muhtar, Vol. II, p. 446.

should hear, but not the one who is deaf, and the former, or a third party should shout the words to the deaf person, the marriage would not be lawful until they both hear the contracting parties at once . . . . ."[1].

Marriage contracted in the presence of witnesses who are drunk.

"If two persons hear the words of the contracting parties, but do not understand their meaning, it has been said that the contract is valid, although *prima facie* it would be otherwise, and Imam Mohammed is reported to have held, that when a marriage is contracted in the presence of Turks or Hindis (Indians) [who do not understand Arabic], yet if they can explain what they heard, [in other words, if they could understand the nature of the ceremony,] the contract is lawful, but otherwise not so. In some of the *Fatawas* it is laid down, that comprehension is not a condition so long as the witnesses hear the words, so that if one should marry with *Ajmis* [non-Arabs], for witnesses, Zahir has stated that the contract would be lawful, if they understood the contract to mean marriage ; . . . . . *and this is correct* according to the *Jouharat-un-nayyireh.* Were a man to marry a woman in the presence of witnesses who are drunk, if they apprehended the matter of the marriage at the time, it would take effect even though they may not recollect [it] on becoming sober. In the *Fatawa* of Abu Lais it is stated that if a man were to address people saying, 'Bear witness that I have married the woman who is in this house', and the woman should answer, 'I have accepted', and the witnesses should hear her speech without seeing her person, and she alone were in the house, the marriage would be lawful ; but not so if there was another woman in the house with her at the same time. A person marries his daughter to a man in a house, and there are several persons in another house who hear the transaction, but are not called upon to bear witness to it, yet if there be an opening between the houses through which the persons can see the father, their testimony will be accepted, but otherwise not.[2]. . . . ."

"If a man and woman were to acknowledge a marriage in the presence of witnesses, saying [in the Persian language], 'we are wife and husband', no marriage would thereby be contracted between them, and this is approved.[3] And if he should say, in the presence of witnesses, 'This is my wife', and she should say, 'This is my husband', there never having been any marriage between them, there is a difference of opinion, but the correct view is that this would be no marriage[4] *unless judicially pronounced to be a marriage* or unless the parties were to say, 'Yes', in answer to the question of the witnesses, "Have you made this marriage?' when according to the approved doctrine,

1 Fatawai 'Alamgiri, Vol. I, p. 378. I have omitted the authorities cited such as Fath-ul-Kadir, Fatawai Kazi Khan, Khulasa, &c.

2 Fatawai 'Alamgiri, Vol. I, p. 379.

3 *Ibid.*, pp. 383-4.

4 Fatawai 'Alamgiri, Vol. I, pp. 383-4; see also the Sharh-i-Vikaya p. 106.

as stated in the *Sharh-ul-Jussas*, it would be tantamount to a marriage ; so in the *Mukhtar-ul-fatawa*."[1]

[*These statements refer to the contemporaneous acknowledgment of a marriage and not to the acknowledgment of a marriage previously contracted.*]

Other examples are given in the law books of expressions by which marriage may or may not be contracted. For example, if a man were to say to a woman, '*Salam uleki* (peace be to thee) O my wife', and she were to answer, 'and to thee *Salam*, O my husband', or if a woman were to say to a man, 'I have married myself to thee', intending to add 'for a hundred dinars', but before she can utter the latter words, he answers, 'I have accepted'; "in these cases", says the *Fatwai 'Alamgiri*, "according to Imam Ali as-Sughdi, there is no marriage. If a man were to send some people to another to solicit the hand of his daughter and they were to say [in Persian], 'Hast thou given the daughter to us', and he answers, 'I have given', whereupon they reply, 'we have accepted'; this is no contract of marriage for want of reference to the suitor."

Principle: Presence of witnesses necessary only for authentication.

It must not be supposed, however, that when Hanafi lawyers say that "a marriage without witness is not valid" or that "the presence of witnesses is necessary to the validity of a marriage", they mean to imply that a marriage without witnesses is void. The Hanafi rules relating to testimony in marriage have in view the *authentication of its factum*; the absence of witnesses, therefore, affects only its contractual completeness. For that reason it is declared that a marriage contracted without witnesses is *invalid*.[2] The condition of testimony, therefore, is not so essential that it cannot be dispensed with; and should a marriage be contracted at a place where compliance with it is impracticable, it would not be void on that ground. But where it is possible to obtain testimony, and the ceremony of marriage is gone through without the presence of witnesses to attest its performance, it is declared to be *invalid*. And the Kazi is authorised under such circumstances to decree *separation* on the application of either party, or, if they are minors, of their guardians. But once the marriage is consummated and the parties have cohabited, the contractual defect is removed; and the issue are declared to be legitimate.

Conditions necessary to the competency of witnesses.

"There are four conditions requisite to the competency of witnesses, *viz.*, freedom, sanity, majority, and Islam."[3] This is the general rule and is not confined to the case of marriage. The evidence of a bondsman is not admissible in a Court of Justice

1 Fatawai 'Alamgiri, Vol. I, p. 384.

2 Comp. the 'Inaya, Vol. II, pp. 74, 269, Cal. Ed.

See Shahzada Begum *v.* Abdul Hamid P L D 1950 Lah. 504,

3 Fatawai 'Alamgiri, Vol. I, p. 377,

nor of a person who has not attained puberty or is devoid of understanding.

Principle.

Islam also is a necessary condition, as a non-Moslem is declared to be incompetent to give evidence in a Moslem cause or against a Moslem.

Explanation.

This exclusiveness is not confined to Musulmans. Lord Coke declared that an "infidel" was not a competent witness on the ground that "all infidels were in law perpetual enemies, for between them, as with the devil whose subjects they are, there is perpetual hostility and can be no peace." Although the disqualification which the Musulman Law attaches to difference of faith is not now in force in India,[1] and the fact that the witnesses at a marriage were not Moslems may not, under the territorial law, affect its contractual completeness or render it invalid, it would be unnatural that when both parties are Moslems, all the witnesses should be non-Moslems. The condition requiring the witnesses to be Moslems, is not a part of the substantive law and the difference in their faith does not go beyond their competency to give evidence, nor does it affect the obligation itself. The rule aims only at securing *admissible* testimony.

Marriage with a non-Moslemah.

But when a Moslem contracts a marriage with a non-Moslemah, it may be contracted in the presence of two non-Moslems, belonging to her faith or any other faith, provided they do not labour under any legal disability.[2]

Sunni rule.

In marriage, under the Sunni Law, it is not necessary that the witnesses should bear an irreproachable character. The testimony, accordingly, of persons who have been accused of any crime or who have suffered punishment for delicts, such as slander, adultery, or fornication, is admissible. The deaf are not competent witnesses as they are incapable of hearing the words of either party. The Hanafis admit the testimony of the blind.[3]

If the woman is present before the witnesses, even though they may not see her face owing to her being veiled, yet if she is pointed out to them as the person assenting to the marriage, it is valid.

Evidence of identity.

But if she be in a room where there are other women at the same time, and the witnesses are unable to see or identify her, it is not valid for fear of mistake.

---

1 See s. 118 of the Indian Evidence Act (I of 1872).

2 Fatawai 'Alamgiri, Vol. I, p. 377; Fatawai Kazi Khan, Vol. I, p. 330; Radd-ul-Muhtar, Vol. II, p. 448.

3 Fatawai Kazi Khan, Vol. I, p. 380; Fatawai 'Alamgiri, Vol. I, p. 377; Radd-ul-Muhtar, Vol. II, p. 447.

It would not be right for the witnesses to testify to the marriage, under such circumstances, if the woman were to deny the marriage.

The case, however, is different when the woman is known to be by herself in the room and there is no fear of any mistake.

If the witnesses know the woman, it is enough for her proxy, or for any one who is acting for her in contracting the marriage to mention only her name. But when she is not known to the witnesses, even then, according to Khassaf and Kazi Khan, the mere mention of her name is sufficient. For example, if a man were to say, in the presence of witnesses, "I marry myself to the lady who has appointed me her agent for marrying her"—according to these jurists such a declaration would be sufficient.

Witnesses should know the names of the parties.

According to the author of the *Tanwir-ul-Absar* such a declaration is not sufficient, and when the woman is not known to the witnesses or is not before them, her name and her father's and grandfather's names must be mentioned in their presence for purposes of identification. "And this is correct and on this is the *Fatwa*." The *Bahr-ur-Raik* also states that the received doctrine is contrary to that of Khassaf. And Imam Ibn-ul-Fazl has laid down that when the bridegroom is not present, his name and his father's and grandfather's names should be mentioned ; and similarly in the case of the bride.

The author of the *Durr-ul-Mukhtar* adds that when the bride is known to the witnesses, and they know as a fact that she has consented to the marriage, it is enough to mention her name ; but, according to Imam Ibn-ul-Fazl, even when she is known to the witnesses, her name and the names of her father and grandfather should be mentioned.

They must understand that a marriage is meant.

If a man were to marry a woman taking God and his Prophet as his witnesses, some of the jurists have held that this will not be valid, and Abu'l Kasim Saffar has gone so far as to declare it to be *kufr* (blasphemy). Others have said that this is too rigid a view of the question, for the man may have intended to mean that God, who is the Knower of all things, knows that he means marriage, and invoking the name of the Prophet he may have meant that he was marrying in accordance with the laws of Islam. The *Tatar Khanieh*, quoting the *Multeka*, says that he will not be considered guilty of *kufr*.[1]

It is not necessary that all the witnesses present at a marriage ceremony should know the bride. It is sufficient when her name

1 Radd-ul-Muhtar, Vol. II, p. 452.

is mentioned that two of them should know her, in other words, both of them should know who the particular person is who is contracting the marriage, that she is so-and-so and the daughter of so-and-so. It is not necessary that they should see her face.

Both witnesses must understand what is said. But suppose a marriage is contracted in Arabic and the witnesses do not understand the Arabic language, in such a case there is a difference of opinion. "And it is most correct that the contract will be operative . . . . . What is required is that by the words used marriage is intended ; it is not necessary that they should understand the actual words."[1]

"When the proposal of marriage is made by letter, it is necessary that the witnesses should hear the contents of the letter. And this should be done in this way ; the woman on receiving the proposal should read out the letter to the witnesses or explain its meaning to them, *e.g.*, that so-and-so asks me in marriage and then say 'bear ye witness that I have married him'."[2]

Number of witnesses:

Among the Shaf'eis and the Hanafis the testimony of two men or of one man and two women is considered sufficient, but no marriage can be celebrated in the presence of females alone.[3] The Malikis insist that all the witnesses should be males.

All these rules as to testimony as to the factum of the marriage have the object of securing reliable evidence in case of dispute.

Although the law requires the presence of two witnesses only, and the early Caliphs always contracted marriages strictly in accordance with the requirements of the law, it is rare to find among Musulmans, especially in India;[4] nuptials celebrated so unostentatiously that more than two witnesses are not present.[5]

According to both the Shiahs and the Sunnis, a proposal of marriage may be made by proxy or by letter, but when it is made by letter, it is necessary, under the Sunni Law, that the woman should give her consent in the presence of two witnesses who have seen the letter delivered and are aware of its contents.[6]

In the same way when a proposal is made by proxy, the witnesses should hear the message delivered and the consent given. The proxy or the messenger need not be an adult person.[7]

---

1 Radd-ul-Muhtar, Vol. II, p. 447.

2 *Ibid.*, p. 446.

3 Hedaya; Fatawai Kazi Khan, Vol. I, p. 380; Fatawai 'Alamgiri, Vol. I, p. 373.

4 Now Indo-Pakistan.

5 The Shiahs, whilst holding that a marriage may be contracted in private without witnesses, enjoin the preservation of testimony to avoid disputes—Jam'a-ush-Shittat.

6 Fatawai 'Alamgiri, Vol. I, p. 380; Fatawai Kazi Khan, Vol. I, pp. 381, 382.

7 *Ibid.*

Agency in marriage.

Marriages may be contracted among the Sunnis and the Shiahs through the agency of proxies or *wakils*. As already stated for their appointment witnesses are not necessary, and their powers are governed by the same rules of law as apply to other contracts.

If two persons are appointed to act jointly, neither of them can act independently of the other. Should an agent exceed his authority, a contract entered into by him is not valid until ratified by the principal. It is illegal for an agent to contract the principal (if she be a female) to himself or to any of his own relations, unless empowered to the effect by the woman herself.

The same rule applies to a woman who acts as agent for a man. She cannot contract him in marriage to any of her own relations unless specifically authorised. If a marriage agent should act *mala fide* towards his principal, or prejudicially to the interests of such principal by marrying her to a slave, an eunuch, a lunatic or such like, the marriage is invalid.[1]

An unauthorised person (*fazuli* فضولی), may enter into a contract of marriage for another, *but it is not valid until ratified by the parties concerned.*

Shiah rule.

Under the Shiah Law, every person acting for an adult and discreet girl is a *fazuli*, unless specially authorised by her.[2]

SECTION VIII

CONDITIONS OF MARRIAGE

A promise of marriage not enforceable in law.

Though a promise of marriage has no legal effect under the Mahommedan Law, a stipulation after the marriage has taken place to the effect that it will not be consummated until the lapse of a specified period, is valid. Such a stipulation is invariably inserted in contracts of marriage, between minors. Conditions of this nature, however, are not needed under the Mahommedan Law, inasmuch as a Musulman husband is not entitled to the custody of his wife's person until she has attained puberty.[3]

A promise, however, of marriage made by a Musulman, even though temporarily residing in England, would give rise to the same legal consequences as though he were a native of the country.

---

1 Fatawai Kazi Khan, Vol. I, p. 382; Jam'a-ush-Shittat.

2 Jam'a-ush-Shittat.

3 In re Khatija Bibi (1870) 5 B L R O C J 530.

See Nur Kader *v.* Zulekha Bibi (1885) 11 Cal. 649; Korban *v.* Emperor (1904) 32 Cal. 444.

Illegal conditions.

The conditions in a marriage contract may be either legal or illegal. The illegal conditions are those which affect the validity of the marriage and render the contract voidable, unless consummation takes place.

When the marriage has been consummated, the condition alone is voided.

Principle : Temporary contracts illegal under the Sunni Law.

The condition which limits the duration of the marriage to a specified time is illegal under the Sunni Law.[1]

Such temporary marriages (*nikah-ul-muwakkat*) were admitted by the pre-Islamic institutions, and at the time the Islamic laws were promulgated were allowed equally among the Jews, the Sabeans and the pagan Arabs; and instances of such unions were not rare even in Christendom.[2] These unions were forbidden by the Prophet in the tenth year of the Hejira as contrary to the Islamic principles.

"And", says the *Tanwir-ul-Absar*, "a *nikah-ul-muta'a* (a temporary or usufructuary marriage) and a *nikah-ul-muwakkat* (a marriage for a fixed term) are both void".

The comment of the *Radd-ul-Muhtar* on this passage is as follows:—"In the *Fath-ul-Kadir* it is stated that the Shaikh-ul-Islam has thus pointed out the difference between these two marriages, *viz.*, that in the *nikah-ul-muwakkat*, the words *nikah* and *tajwiz* are mentioned, whereas in *mutta'a* the term (استمة) or (اتمتع) is used. . . . . and also that in the *nikah-ul-muwakkat* the term is fixed, whereas in *muta'a* the parties may live together so long as they wish to enjoy each other's company and no witnesses are required. And there is no doubt of this that though these (forms of marriage) were allowed at first, they were prohibited afterwards."[3]

Meaning of a Muta'a union—under the Hanafi Law a temporary contract takes effect as a permanent marriage.

Then follows a further definition of the word *muta'a*. "The accepted meaning of *muta'a* is a union between a man and a woman not with the objects which are the objects of marriage, *viz.*, the procreation of children and their rearing up, but a contract of mutual enjoyment which is to cease on the termination of the term fixed, or if there is no term specified, upon the man leaving the woman. . . . And in this definition, therefore, a temporary marriage is included in the term *muta'a* . . . . In the *Fath-ul-Kadir* the proofs for its being prohibited are stated. It was prohibited during the *Hajjat-ul-Wida'a* (the Last

---

1 Fatawai 'Alamgiri, Vol. I, p. 398.

2 Perron, Femmes Arabes, p. 171; Code Rabbinique, Vol. II, p. 232.

3 Radd-ul-Muhtar, Vol. II, p. 480.

Pilgrimage of the Prophet),[1] and the prohibition is for ever, and there is no difference on this point among the Imams and the learned of the various countries, though one section[2] admits the validity of *muta'a*. What has been stated in the *Hedaya* that Malik held it lawful is incorrect."[3]

Principle: Only condition invalid, not the marriage.

"Regarding the effect of a *nikah-ul-muwakkat* (a marriage for a fixed term), the doctrine of Imam Zuffar is to be preferred, *i.e.*, such a marriage will take effect as a permanent marriage, and the condition as to its being temporary will be invalidated for a *nikah-ul-mawakkat* is in effect a *muta'a* and this was abolished, but the meaning of abolition is that it existed before and was afterwards abrogated, and therefore the effect of the abrogation is that it avoids the condition as to the temporary character, but upholds the contract itself, as in the case of a *nikah-ush-shighar*.[4]

Nikah-ush-Shighar—its definition.

A *nikah-ush-shighar* is a marriage in which two women are married by one contract, the cohabitation of one being the dower of the other, in such a case, the marriage of both will be valid and each of them will get their customary dower, *mahr-ul-misl*. But the case is different with a mere contract for cohabitation, in other words, a union contracted with the word *muta'a*."[5]

Any condition which is dehors the contract of marriage is void in itself and does not invalidate the contract.

For example, if two persons were to marry each other on the condition that they should become separated after a month, the condition would be null and the marriage would take effect as a permanent contract, "but a man who has work to perform at night, like a watchman, may contract to live with his wife in the day".

Conditional marriage.

A conditional marriage is invalid. For example, if a man were to say, "I marry thee if my father will consent", and the bride were to say, "I consent", there would be no contract. So also a marriage to take effect at a future time. In both these cases *copula* will effectuate a marriage.

Principle.

As already stated, a marriage with an invalid condition is not invalid, the condition being void and the marriage operative,

---

1 Also called the Hajjat-ul-Balagh; see the Spirit of Islam (Ed. 1904), p. 106.

2 A section of the Shiahs.

3 Radd-ul-Muhtar, Vol. II, p. 480.

4 See post.

5 Radd-ul-Muhtar, Vol. II, p. 483.

e.g., if a man said, "I marry thee on condition that there shall be no dower or maintenance", and the woman were to consent, the marriage will be valid, and the wife will be entitled to both dower and maintenance.[1]

Judicial declaration of marriage—accepted doctrine.

"If a woman is not within the prohibited degrees, or another man's wife or another man's *mu'ataddah*,[2] and a Kazi were to declare her, upon the evidence of witnesses, to be the wife of so-and-so, she will be lawful to him, although in reality there may have been no marriage between the man and the woman. This is according to Abu Hanifa and on this is the *Fatwa*.

In other words, a judicial declaration of the status of marriage by a competent tribunal upon legal testimony would establish the relationship of husband and wife, even when the witnesses have deposed falsely, provided the woman is not prohibited to the man for any cause recognised by the law.

Temporary marriage—Akhbari doctrines.

The Akhbari section of the Shiahs and also some of the Usulis admit the validity of temporary marriages (*nikah-ul-muwakkat* and *muta'a*) or contracts for limited terms. According to them, a man and woman (possessing the capacity to marry) may enter into a contract of marriage for any period they like. The term (*muddat*) may vary from a day to a hundred years. Such marriages become dissolved either by efflux of the period fixed or may be put an end to by mutual agreement. They insist on the same conditions for the validity of a temporary as for a *permanent marriage* (*nikah-ad-daim*). There is, however, this difference, that whereas in the case of a permanent marriage, the non-mention of dower does not render the contract itself null and void, in a *muta'a* marriage it has that effect.[3] If the dower is mentioned, but not the term, the contract although intended to take effect as a *muta'a* operates as a permanent marriage.

Principle—Sunni Law.

As already pointed out, under the Hanafi Law, a marriage for a term of years is invalid, but if the parties live together as husband and wife *it takes effect as a permanent contract and gives rise to all the consequences of a valid marriage*.[4]

Hanafi Law. Nikah-ush-Shighar.

It was customary in pre-Islamic times for men to arrange to marry their daughters or other female relations reciprocally, "the person of one forming the dower of the other".

---

1 Radd-ul-Muhtar, Vol. II, p. 483. Comp. Fatawai Kazi Khan, Section on Dower.

2 *i.e.*, is observing the period of probation for another man.

3 Mafatih; see Chapter on Temporary Marriage, post.

4 Radd-ul-Muhtar, Vol. II, p. 481; see however, Imam Zuffar's opinion, ante.

This form of marriage was called a *nikah-ush-shighar*[1] and was prohibited by the Prophet according to a *hadis* (traditional saying) admitted to be authentic by all the sects. The Shiahs, the Shaf'eis and Malikis consider such marriages invalid, unless *consummation has taken place*, when the condition of dower is held void, and the *mahr-ul-misl* is presumed to be the dower of the woman.[2] The Hanafis regard this form of marriage as valid, *mahr-ul-misl* being presumed from the outset.[3]

Conditions opposed to public morality.

Void Conditions.—Conditions opposed to public morality are illegal and void without touching the validity of the marriage. For example, a condition made to the effect that the husband shall have no right to prevent his wife from frequenting immoral places is void.

If a woman should forgo her right to maintenance, or contract that she will not be entitled to any dower, the stipulation is of no effect in law, and is equally void.

An illegal condition annexed to a marriage void in itself.

An illegal condition annexed to a marriage does not cancel the marriage, but is in itself void. An agreement entered into between the husband and wife before marriage, that neither of them should inherit from the other is invalid, and upon the death of either, the survivor would become entitled to his or her legal share in the deceased's inheritance, even if there was no consummation.

Examples of legal conditions.

The legal conditions are the following, amongst others :—

(*a*) That the husband shall not contract a second marriage during the existence or continuance of the first.[4] In the case of *Poonoo Bibee* v. *Fyez Baksh* there was a condition to that effect, and it was upheld by the High Court of Calcutta.

Some of the Shiah doctors are of opinion that this condition is not legal. It would appear, however, that even in Persia, where their doctrines are chiefly in force, this condition is frequently imposed.

(*b*) That the husband shall not remove the wife from the conjugal domicile without her consent.

(*c*) That the husband shall not absent himself from the conjugal domicile beyond a certain specified time.

---

1 Shighar, suppression.

2 See Chapter on Dower.

3 Radd-ul-Muhtar, Vol. II, p. 481.

4 Comp. Radd-ul-Muhtar, Vol. II, p. 566, et seq., Malik Shah (the Seljukian) imposed this condition for the first time on Caliph Muktadi, to whom he gave his daughter in marriage; Von Hammer, Hist. de l'Empire Ottoman, Vol. III, p. 17 ; Tarikh-i-Wassaf; see the case of Poonoo Bibi *v.* Fyez Baksh (1876) 15 B L R App. 5.

(*d*) That the husband and the wife shall live in a specified place.

(*e*) That a certain portion of the dower shall be paid at once or within a stated period, and the remainder on the dissolution of the contract by death or divorce.

(*f*) That the husband shall pay the wife a fixed maintenance.

(*g*) That he shall maintain the children of the wife by a former husband.

(*h*) That he shall not prevent her from receiving the visits of her relations whenever she likes.

All these conditions being antenuptial agreements, made in consideration of marriage, are valid and enforceable in law.

In order to constitute a legal marriage, it is not absolutely necessary to reduce the terms into writing, or to embody the proposal and consent in a formal document. And in many parts of India, such as Behar, it is customary not to have any writing. Nevertheless, it has always been recommended that the conditions should be entered in a deed of marriage. The Caliphs, notably Harun-ar-Rashid,[1] insisted on all Moslems and Zimmis, subjects of the Caliphate, registering their marriages before the Kazis.

In Algeria, the deed of marriage is required by law to be registered and a copy kept in the Kazi's *mahkama*.[2]

The deed of marriage is called in India[3] the *Kabin-nameh* or *mahar-nameh* and when there is one, it is always placed in the keeping of the woman. The custom of handing the document to the wife or her guardians dates from pre-Islamic times, and is necessary for the protection of her interests in countries where no copies of marriage-contracts are kept in the public records.

SECTION IX

VALID RETIREMENT

(*Khilwat-us-Sahih*)

Presumption of consummation.

As in many cases invalid marriages are rendered valid by consummation, and as the dower does not become due in its entirety until the marriage has been actually or constructively consummated, the question of consummation forms often an important element in the discussion of the status of marriage.

---

1 De Sacy, Chrestomathie Arabe, p. 22.

2 The Mahommedan Marriage Registration Act is only optional; see ante. In Pakistan registration of marriage is compulsory.

3 Now Indo-Pakistan.

Hanafi and Maliki Law.

Under the Hanafi and the Maliki Law, a presumption of consummation is raised from the retirement of the husband and the wife into the nuptial chamber, under circumstances which lead to the natural inference of matrimonial intercourse. This is what is called *valid retirement* or *khilwat-us-sahih*. But when there is some legal, moral, or physical impediment to such intercourse no presumption is raised, and the retirement is not valid.[1] For example, when the parties are observing the obligatory fast of the Ramazan or either the husband or the wife is suffering from an illness which prevents connubial relationship, or a third ("discreet") person is present in the room though he may be blind, the retirement into the nuptial chamber does not give rise to the presumption of consummation.[2]

In Western Musalman countries, *khilwat-us-sahih* goes by the name of *bina*.[3]

The author of the *Radd-ul-Muhtar* following the *Bahr-ur-Raik* states that "there are four conditions necessary to make a retirement tantamount to actual *copula*, *viz*., (*i*) that the retirement must be real; (*ii*) that there must not be any physical ; (*iii*) moral ; (*iv*) or legal bar."

Real retirement means that there should be no third person at the place and that the place itself should not be a public one, like a public bath, public road, a mosque, etc. Moral and legal impediments include a woman being in her courses or in her *nifas* (after child-birth) or the parties being on a *hajj* or subject to the rules of *ihram*.

Physical impediment includes the malformation of the woman which prevents *copula*. It also includes infancy on the part of either or both, which prevents conjugal intercourse.

The place, also, must be fitting for retirement. It must not be exposed to public view or public access. An open or unclosed room will not give rise to the presumption.

If the husband does not know his wife, it amounts to . legal impediment.

---

1 Fatawai Kazi Khan, Vol. I, p. 383; Fatawai 'Alamgiri, Vol. I, p. 429; Radd-ul-Muhtar, Vol. II, p. 554 et seq.

2 In the Fath-ul-Kadir, it is suggested that the illness of the wife is to be considered, but the Radd-ul-Muhtar states that illness on either side likely to prevent cohabitation is to be taken into consideration. The author of the Radd-ul-Muhtar says that the presence in the room of a dog which bites would prevent the presumption from arising,—Radd-ul-Muhtar, Vol. II, p. 554.

3 This word, literally, means an edifice, and as the ancient Arabs used to erect a special tent to conduct their newly-married wives into, the retirement of the bride and the bridegroom into the nuptial chamber has come to be called by the name—De Sacy, Anthologie Arave.

Legal consequences resulting from a valid retirement.

When these impediments are not present, retirement is tantamount to actual *copula* for certain purposes even though the husband may be impotent.

Among the Hanafis and the Malikis, the *Khilwat-us-sahih* has the same character, and gives birth to the same legal consequences as the Hebrew ceremony of leading a bride to the nuptial bed.[1] It gives completion to the marriage and marks the time when the conjugal rights commence, and assures her entire dower to the wife. "Our masters", says the *Fatawai 'Alamgiri*,[2] "have placed the *khilwat-us-sahih* in the same category as actual consummation in respect of certain of its consequences, but not others. They have done so in the matter of confirmation of dower, the establishment of paternity, the observance of probation (*'iddat'*) the (wife's) right to maintenance and domicile (or lodgment), and the unlawfulness, of marriage with her sister or with four other women besides her, and the observance of the time for repudiation in respect of her. But they have not placed it on the same footing as actual consummation in making a person *muhsan*[3] or a daughter unlawful, or a divorced woman lawful to her first husband, or for the purpose of revoking repudiation or for inheritance. And retirement does not come into the place of consummation in impairing virginity ; so that, if a man should retire with a virgin and then repudiate her, she would subsequently marry as a virgin."

The following summary from the *Radd-ul-Muhtar* will further explain the subject.

"Valid retirement establishes the *nasab* of the child, entitles the woman to her dower, maintenance and lodgment, makes it incumbent on her to observe the *'iddat*, renders her sister unlawful to the man, creates the unlawfulness arising from the *completion of number*, and makes it incumbent on him to observe the time for *talak* in respect of her. But it does not create *ihsan* (احصان) as actual consummation, that is, if the man were to commit fornication with any other woman he would not be liable to the *hadd* (punishment for adultery), as he would be if he had consummated the marriage with the woman, nor does it render her daughter unlawful to him unless there was actual *copula* or he had "touched her with desire"; or, if the woman had been married to another man who had divorced her irrevocably, and she had afterwards contracted a second marriage, mere retirement with the second would not make her lawful to the first man who had divorced her. Nor does a *talak* given after a valid retirement entitle the husband to recall the wife as in the case of a consummated marriage. Nor should a man *talak* his wife after a valid retirement only, does she become entitled to a share in his inheritance in case of his death, before the expiration of her *'iddat*.

---

1 Code Rabbinique, Vol. I, p. 167.

2 Fatawai 'Alamgiri, Vol. I, p. 431.

3 Derived from ihsan; see ante, Sec. I of this Chap.

Nor, in the case of a virgin does retirement alone take her out of the legal position of a virgin."[1]

Shiah and Shaf'ei doctrines.

Under the Shiah as well as under the Shaf'ei Law, no absolute presumption arises from simple retirement, actual consummation alone giving rise to the rights and duties which spring from marriage.

At the same time, the parties place themselves in such a situation that cohabitation may take place, the mere denial by the husband of the *copula*, should the wife assert conjugal intercourse, will not be sufficient to contradict the wife without corroborative evidence.

SECTION X

PROOF OF MARRIAGE

MARRIAGE may be proved directly or presumptively. *Directly*, by means of the oral testimony of the witnesses present at the marriage, or by documentary evidence in the shape of a deed of marriage :

Presumptively, by statement of the parties or by evidence of conduct and reputation.

According to English Law, *general* reputation is admissible to establish the fact of the parties being married.[2] Section 50 of the Indian Evidence Act (I of 1872), however declares that "when the Court has to form an opinion as to the relationship of one person to another, the opinion expressed by conduct as to the existence of such relationship of any person, who as a member of the family or otherwise, has special means of knowledge on the subject, is a relevant fact".

It seems, therefore, to narrow the ground by limiting it to "opinion *expressed by conduct*".

Statement or conduct of the parties.

The Musulman Law does not go so far as the English Law, nor is it so limited as the Indian Act. For under the Musulman Law, marriage may be proved presumptively by the statements of the parties, or their general conduct towards each other. " When a person ", says the *Fatawai 'Alamgiri*, "has seen a man and woman dwelling in the same

---

1 Radd-ul-Muhtar, Vol. II, pp. 554-570. Comp. Plowts *v.* Bossey 2 Dr. & Sm. 145, "when a husband and wife have been in such a situation that access may have taken place, the presumption of law is in favour of the issue, but may be rebutted by strong evidence."

2 See Taylor, Ev., s. 578; Ameer Ali & Woodroffe, Indian Evidence Act, 3rd Ed. 506.

house (*bait*), and behaving familiarly towards each other as husband and wife, it is lawful for him to testify that the woman is the man's wife".[1]

According to Kazi Khan, if a man and woman were to say that a marriage had been celebrated between them at some previous time, though [in reality] there was no marriage between them, such a statement would not amount to a marriage "for that is a mere falsehood". "But if a man were to say 'this woman is my wife', and the woman were to say, 'this man is my husband', that would amount to a marriage", the acknowledgment of the two constituting a valid relationship.[2]

Or, "if a man were to say of a child 'this is my child', (meaning his legitimate child) and he were to die, and thereupon the mother of the child being a free woman, were to say 'he was my husband', she would be his wife, and would be entitled to inherit from him".[3]

A contemporaneous acknowledgment of a child, as a *legitimate* child, by a man and a woman has the same effect. For example, it is laid down that "if a man were to say to a free woman, 'this is my son by thee', or 'this is our son', implying that he was their *legitimate* child, and she were to reply, 'yes', it would amount to an acknowledgment of marriage".[4]

A man contracts his adult daughter in marriage, and it is never determined till the death of her husband whether she assented to or rejected the marriage; his heirs then allege that she was married without her authority, knew nothing of the transaction, and never consented to it, and that therefore, she has no right to any share in the inheritance; the woman insists, on the other hand, that the contract was entered into by her father with her authority; in these circumstances her word is to be preferred, and she is entitled to a share in the inheritance, being also obliged to observe the '*iddat*. But if she were to say : My father, indeed, contracted me in marriage without my authority, but on receiving the intelligence I declared my consent, she would not be entitled to her dower nor to any share in the inheritance.[5]

The legal effect of marriage.

Marriage legalises connubial relationship; it imposes on the husband the obligation of paying the antenuptial settlement

1 Comp. also the provisions of s. 108 of the Indian Evidence Act as to presumption; and Khajah Hidayatoollah *v.* Rai Jan Khanum (1844) 3 M I A 299; Nawabunnissa *v.* Fuzuloonissa (1863) Marshall 428; Wise *v.* Sanduloonissa Chowdranee (1867) 11 M I A 177; Mohatala Bibee *v.* Ahmed Haleemoozzoman.

2 Comp. Radd-ul-Muhtar, Vol. II, p. 435.

3 Fatawai 'Alamgiri, Vol. I, p. 727, see however post.

4 *Ibid.*; Baillie's Dig., p. 413, 2nd Ed.

5 Baillie's Dig., p. 60, 2nd Ed.

and of fulfilling all the antenuptial agreements made in consideration of marriage ; it establishes on both sides the prohibition of affinity and the rights of inheritance ; it obliges the husband to be just towards his wife, to treat her with respect and affection ; and exact from her in return obedience and faithfulness to him.[1]

CHAPTER VII

ILLEGAL AND INVALID MARRIAGES—OPTION OF PUBERTY—CAUSES FOR WHICH MARRIAGE MAY BE CANCELLED—EFFECT OF CHANGE OF RELIGION ON THE STATUS OF MARRIAGE

SECTION I

ILLEGAL AND INVALID MARRIAGES

Hanafi doctrines.

No part of the Musulman Law is perhaps more difficult to apprehend than the rules that relate to connections which, although not regarded as quite valid (*sahih*), give rise, on consummation, to some of the consequences resulting from a valid marriage. It is to these unions that French writers on the subject give the name of *semblable* contracts—an expression for which there is no synonym in the English language. The difficulty in apprehending the rules has increased owing to the desuetude of the practice which was observed by lawyers and judges in the early part of the nineteenth century, to deduce principles from a comparison, from a juridical standpoint, of the statements, often not easily reconcilable, of text-writers and commentators. And this criticism applies to the judicial application of other branches of the Musulman Law.

Azizunnissa Khatoon v. Karimunnissa Khatoon.

I am induced to make these remarks by the decision of the High Court of Calcutta in *Azizunnissa Khatoon* v. *Karimunnissa Khatoon*.[2] In this case it appears that one Golam Ally, a wealthy Mahommedan landholder of the Sunni sect, residing in the district of Fureedpore, had married two sisters, Azizunnissa and Izzatunnissa, one after the other by both of whom he had issue. In an administration suit brought after his death, the first Court held that the children born of Izzatunnessa were legitimate and entitled to share in his inheritance. Azizunnissa appealed to the High Court on the ground of the illegitimacy of her sister's children.

1 Like the English Law, the Sunni Law allows the husband a moderate power of correction over a refractory wife. The Shiah Law absolutely prohibits a husband to touch his wife in anger; Jam'a-i-Abbasi : Nail-ul-Maram.

2 Supra.

Examination of the case.

On the facts, therefore, the learned Judges had two questions to decide :—

(1) Whether the marriage contracted by Golam Ally with Izzatunnissa during the subsistence of his marriage with her sister was valid or not?

(2) Whether, if the marriage was not valid, the children were affiliated to the father and *nasab* was established under the Musulman Law?

Any one who has studied Musulman Law with approximate care will notice that these two questions are entirely distinct, for a marriage may be admittedly illegal or invalid and yet the children may unquestionably be *legitimate*. To illustrate my meaning I will give only one example. If a man were to marry the widow or divorcee of another whilst she was observing the *'iddat* or probation[1] for the latter, the marriage would not be valid; and yet if the parties cohabited and there were issue, *nasab* would be established.

The learned Judges, speaking with respect, apparently confused by the mass of texts quoted before them, mixed up the two questions and came to a conclusion in absolute conflict with a well-established and well-recognised rule of Mahommedan Law. They held that the marriage of a man with the sister of his wife who is legally married to him, is "void", and that the children of such marriage are illegitimate. And by way of a corollary they added that as the marriage was unlawful the issue of the second union could not be legitimated by the acknowledgment of the father.

I shall endeavour to show that the first and third propositions are based on a misconception, whilst the second is wholly wrong.

It is extraordinary that none of the authorities on which reliance is placed in the judgment enunciate the doctrine propounded by the learned Judges relative to the question of *nasab* or legitimacy. They declare either that the marriage is *fasid* or *batil* (*invalid* or *void*), but in no instance is it stated that the issue are *illegitimate*. On the contrary, one important authority, the *Fatawai 'Alamgiri*, among those cited at the bar, expressly lays down that where in such a marriage there has been *copula*, the issue are legitimate ("*nasab* would be established").

It, however, was brushed aside on purely inferential reasoning, which, analysed, amounts to this, that because some of the text-writers and commentators appeared to lay down that a marriage with a wife's sister was *batil* (ineffective or void), therefore the children must be illegitimate.[2]

---

1 See ante.

2 See Taj Bi *v.* Maula Khan (1917) 41 Bom. 845: 39 I C 603 ; Rahiman Bibi *v.* Mahboob Bibi I L R 1938 Mad. 278 : A I R 1938 Mad. 141 ; Mst. Kaniza *v.* Hasan I L R 1 Luck. 71 : A I R 1926 Oudh 231 ; Talimand *v.* Mohammad I L R 12 Lah. 52 : A I R 1930 Lah. 907, where it has been held that such a marriage is merely irregular and the issue is not illegitmate.

The rule in the Fatawai 'Alamgiri.

This view, however, as the learned Judges admit is entirely opposed to the rule laid down in the *Fatawai 'Alamgiri.* In going against this authority they forgot that it is a Digest of the Hanafi Law compiled under the authority of the Emperor Aurungzeb 'Alamgir by a selected body of jurists and judges, and embodies the rules and principles which were recognised and enforced in the Musulman Courts of justice under the Mogul rule ; whilst the other works, however learned and valuable or useful in elucidating the law, were after all the works of legists and jurisconsults who wrote or commentated as private individuals without the official imprimatur which gives the *Fatawai 'Alamgiri* its importance and value. But, as I shall presently show, even those authorities do not support the proposition enunciated by Petheram, C. J. and Beverly, J.

The Musulman Marriage Law.

In dealing with the principles of Musulman jurisprudence respecting this branch of the family law it would be well to bear in mind that the toleration accorded in the Islamic system to polygamy under certain limitations, and the recognition of relations with bondswomen, combined with the severity of the punishment to which adulterous connections are liable, have imparted an extraordinary complexity to the rules relating to the status of marriage and legitimacy.

The Koranic rules.

The Koranic rules regulating the relations of the sexes are extremely simple. In the first place it interdicts all relations which are not based on same *right*. In the second place, it prohibits unions with certain classes of women.

Supplementary rules and doctrines.

From these directions there has grown up a large mass of legal doctrines ; the enunciations of the early jurists have been amplified, commented upon and occasionally, although unavowedly, modified.

Definition of zina.

The first principle that required elucidation was that which related to adulterous relations, for *zina* or fornication carried with it a severe penalty. "The connection", says the *Hedaya,* "which gives rise to punishment is *zina,* and this, both in its primitive sense and also in its legal acceptation, signifies the relations of a man with a woman who does not belong to him either by right of marriage or of bondage, and [or] in whom he has no erroneous right or semblance of right based on error or doubt."[1]

1 Hed. Bk. VII, Chap. 2; Comp. Grady's Ed. of Hamilton, p. 182.

A child of fornication.

In other words, where a man cohabits with a woman in whom he has no right or semblance of right, it is *zina* ; and he makes himself liable to the specific punishment provided for the offence (*hadd*). The issue of such a connection *and such a connection alone, is a walad-uz-zina* ("child of fornication").

To explain more clearly the legal consequences resulting from lawful and unlawful relations the lawyers proceeded to define the conditions under which the right arises either (*a*) actually or (*b*) constructively. In order to create the status from which the first right may spring they required capacity—the man was to be *ahal* possessed of the necessary capacity ; the woman was to be *mahal,* a fitting subject.[1] Where these two requisites were present the right came into existence either upon marriage or from the status of bondage.[2]

Absolute or perpetual prohibition (hurmut).

Certain woman were under no circumstance "fitting subjects" of marriage to a man ; *they were absolutely prohibited to him and he could have no relations with them either as wife or bondswoman* ; whilst others were temporarily or relatively prohibited. For example, a man cannot marry an idolatress so long as she worships idols or the widow or divorcee of another man so long as her period of probation has not expired or his wife's sister so long as his marriage with the wife is in existence and her '*iddat* has not terminated and so forth. In these cases there is no *permanent* or *absolute* prohibition as in the other.

But the social conditions made it possible for a man to marry or become possessed of a woman as his bondswoman without knowing that she was absolutely forbidden to him. Not only might there be ignorance as to the relationship, but there may be doubts as to the legality of the relationship.

For example, a man was permitted to have relations with his own bondswoman but not with those of his wife or father; suppose he did so believing that he had a right he would not be guilty of fornication[3].

---

1 Hed. Bk. VII, Chap. 2; 2 Hamilton's Trans. 18.

2 1 Kifaya, Vol. II, Cal. Ed., pp. 1-2; 'Inaya, Vol. II, Cal. Ed., p. 7.

"Nikah (marriage)", says the Kifaya "cannot be effected except by its pillar emanating from an ahal (one who is competent to contract) and in reference to one who is the mahal (fitting subject) as in the case of all legal contracts. The pillar (nikah) consists of proposal and acceptance. The ahal (person competent to contract marriage) is one who is ahal (competent) for all contracts. The mahal is she who is a fit subject for the effect of it": Kifaya, Vol. II, Cal. Ed., pp. 1-2. Similarly it is stated in the 'Inaya, "the general ('aam) condition of nikah (marriage) is capacity (ahliat) as regards sanity and puberty, and fittingness in the subject (mahal)" 'Inaya, Vol. II, Cal. Ed., p. 7.

3 Fatima Binte Hafideh *v.* Administrator-General, Zanzibar A I R 1949 P C 254.

Doctrine of legal error or semblance, shubh.

It was for this purpose that the rules as to *shubh* (semblance, doubt or error) were framed. The learned Judges, it is submitted with respect, not only misunderstood the reason of the rules but failed to apply them correctly.

The *Hedaya* deals with the subject of "error" in the following terms :—

"*Error* in cohabitation is of two kinds, *viz.*:—

(1) *error* in respect to the act, which is termed *shubh-ishtibah* (error or misconception with regard to the legality of the act) ;

(2) *error* in respect of the subject, which is termed *shubh-hukmia* or *shubhat-ul-milk* (error with regard to the right in the woman). The first of these errors is established with respect to a man who mistakes an unlawful connection to be a lawful connection, because *ishtibah* (misconception) signifies a man having connection with a woman, under the supposition of the same being lawful to him...........The second kind of error is established *where the argument of the legality of the connection exists in itself, but yet practice cannot take upon it, because of some obstacle,*[1] *and* this does not depend upon the belief of the person who commits the unlawful act ; whence this kind of error is regarded in respect *to* all men, those who so conceive and those who do not ; and punishment drops in consequence of the existence of either of these kinds of doubt (error) on account of a well-known tradition of the Prophet."[2]

Then, after giving a few examples of relations with bondswomen in which doubt as to the lawfulness of the act might exist—examples which the learned Judges apparently understood to be exhaustive, it adds—" in all these situations the person who has relations does not incur punishment, provided he declare ' I conceived that this woman was lawful to me' ".

What then is *zina* (an adulterous connection) ? Let us see what the *Radd-ul-Muhtar* itself says on the subject.

As I have already pointed out the *Radd* is a commentary on the *Durr-ul-Mukhtar* which again is a commentary on an earlier work called the *Tanwir-ul-Absar*. The *Radd* cites both texts. In the chapter on *punishments* (*hudhud*)[3] occurs the following passage from the *Durr-ul-Mukhtar*—" the chapter relating to connections which make punishment incumbent[4]

1 The italics are mine.

2 Hed. Book VII, ch. 2 : Grady's Ed. (Hamilton's Transl.) p. 182.

3 Durr-ul-Mukhtar, Vol. II, Chapter on Connections with Punishment, etc. ; Radd., Vol. III, p. 231.

4 *Ibid.*

and which do not—on account of the existence of *shubh* (doubt or error) by reason of the traditional saying (*hadis*) of the Prophet, 'Remit punishment in cases of doubt (*shubh*) so far as possible'—

"Doubt is that which resembles a *shai* (object), but is in reality (فى نفس), not *shai* itself. It is of three kinds (انواع) :—(*a*) *hukmia* that which relates to the subject (محل) (*b*) *shubhatu-ishtibah* (doubt regarding the act), (*c*) *shubh-fi'l-'akd* (doubt regarding the contract) [*i.e.*, whether it is valid or not] . . . . thus when a man who has relations with a woman claims a doubt the punishment is not established in case of doubt in the *mahal* (subject), that is, regarding the right [ownership by marriage or bondage] and this is called *shubh-hukmia*, that is to say, a doubt in which it is a matter of doubt, whether according to the *Shar'a* (the Law) the *subject* is lawful . . . . . . " and there is no *hadd*. Also when there is a doubt as to the act [whether it is lawful] . . . ."[1] "And also except in the case of a woman who has been sent to a man to whom the woman represents that she is his wife, although she is not in reality ; in this case also *nasab* would be established according to the *Bahr* (*ur-Raik*)".

Shubhat-ul-'akd.

"And similarly there is no punishment in the case of *shubhat-ul-'akd* that is a doubt as to the lawfulness of the contract according to the Imam [Abu Hanifa]. As for instance when a man cohabits with a woman within the prohibited degrees whom he has married. And they [Abu Yusuf and Mohammed] have declared that if he was aware of the unlawfulness, he shall be subject to *hadd* and on this is the *Fatwa* according to the *Khulasa*." "But preferable according to all the commentaries is the doctrine of the Imam [Abu Hanifa], and, therefore, it is preferable to give *fatwa* according to it, so it has been stated by [Sheikh] Kasim in his *Tashih*".

The author of the *Radd-ul-Muhtar* takes up the passage "and there is no punishment also in the case of doubt with regard to the validity of the contract (*shubhat-ul-'akd*)", and discusses the question as follows :—"there is *shubhat-ul-'akd* where there is a contract in semblance and not in reality

---

1 Durrul-Mukhtar, Vol. II, Chapter on Connections with Punishment, etc.; Radd., Vol. III.

In the translation of the passage inserted in p. 169 of the report words have been interpolated which give it a totally different complexion from the original. The original runs as follows:—"If the man who had relations with the woman mentioned immediately before, *i.e.*, the M'uataddah wife, and the M'uataddah bondswoman but who has been emancipated claims the nasab (of the child born of the connection); in the first case nasab would be established, for it is shubhat-ul-mahal, but not in the second, as it is shubhat-ul-f'il and simply zina." In the translation words have been interpolated to lead to the conclusion that the first and second refer to the classes generally, which, it is submitted, is incorrect. The context shows clearly that the interpolations convey a wholly erroneous meaning of the passage.

. . . . . Therefore, a contract which is in reality a contract does not fall within the category of *shubhat-ul-'akd*; and for this reason it is laid down in the *Tatar-Khanieh* that when connection takes place by virtue of the right of marriage or bondage, and the unlawfulness is due to something else, there is no liability to *hadd* . . . . . And so also if a man has connection with his bondswoman, who is unlawful to him on account of fosterage or affinity (*masahirat*); *or in consequence of her sister being, for instance, in his marriage*; or on account of her being a Magian or apostate;[1] there is no *hadd* on him, even if he knows of the unlawfulness."

Then follows the substance of a passage from the *Fath-ul-Kadir* :—"Lawyers whose traditions and writings are reliable, as for instance Ibn-i-Manzar, have said that the man shall be subjected to *hadd* according to the two Disciples only in case of those who are *maharim*[2] [within the *prohibited degrees*] and not in the case of others than these; as for instance [if he marries] a Magian woman or a fifth wife or the *m'uataddah* of another."

Later on the author of the *Radd* identifies " the doubt regarding the contract" with the "doubt regarding the subject" (*shubhat-ul-'akd*)[3] and *shubhat-ul-mahal* and declares that in both cases "the punishment drops and *nasab* is established."[4]

The Jam'a-'r-Ramuz.

The *Jam'a-'r-Ramuz*[5] lays down the principle in these terms—" The punishment of *hadd* drops in respect of a man who cohabits with a woman under *shubh* (doubt or semblance of right). And doubt is of several kinds; one of them is the *shubhat-ul-'akd*, as if a man marries a woman without witnesses, or a slave girl without the permission of her master, or a slave girl upon a free woman, or a Magian woman or five women in one contract, or *joins two sisters*; or marries his *maharim* . . . . there is no punishment owing to the doubt (error) according to Abu Hanifa . . . . . . according to the two Disciples that is so, *except when he is aware of the unlawfulness* [*i.e.*, in the case of the marriage with a *mahram*]."[6]

Summary of the foregoing doctrines.

When a man marries a woman who is perpetually or absolutely prohibited to him, either he is aware of the illegality or

1 In both these cases marriage is forbidden.

2 Zat-ul-Moharim, *i.e.*, women who are perpetually prohibited, see ante.

3 "Shubh is what resembles a thing established and is not itself established."

4 Vol. III.

5 Quoted by the Radd-ul-Muhtar, under the name of the author, Kahastani.

6 Vol. IV.

he is not. With regard to the latter position there is *consensus*, *viz.*, that if he cohabits with her not knowing that she was unlawful (*haram*) to him, it is not *zina* and he is not liable to the punishment of fornication. But where the cohabitation has taken place with the knowledge on the part of the man of the illegality of the connexion, there is a difference of opinion between Abu Hanifa and his two disciples. Abu Hanifa holds that the connection is not *zina* and the man is not liable to the *hadd*; although he may receive some lighter punishment (*t'azir*) at the discretion of the Kazi. Abu Yusuf and Mohammed on the other hand, declared that the connection is nothing less than *zina* and the man ought to receive the specific punishment for *zina*. As already pointed out the *Fatwa*, according to the *Khulasa*, is given, *i.e.*, decrees made, according to their views.[1]

In the case of a marriage contracted with a *mahram* [a person within the prohibited degrees] *with a knowledge of its illegality on the part of the man only or on the part of both man and woman*, if there is consummation the woman is not entitled to any dower nor is she bound to observe the probation; but where it is otherwise, *viz.*, without knowledge of the illegality the observance of *'iddat* becomes obligatory on her and she becomes entitled to some dower.

Relative or temporary prohibition.

But where the prohibition is relative or temporary (*muwakkat*) *or the illegality springs from an accidental circumstance such as the absence of witnesses, the position is quite different.* Although the doctrine of *shubh* was sometimes brought to bear on these unions, as they were not inherently or radically unlawful the question of knowledge of their relative illegality did not enter into consideration—for under no circumstance, by consensus, the parties contracting such marriages were liable to *hadd*.[2]

"The author of the *Tanwir-ul-Absar* has used the word *maharim* generally [*i.e.*, without any qualification], and therefore, the word *maharim* includes those women who are prohibited on account of *nasab*, fosterage or affinity (*sahriat*), and he implies that if a man marries the wife (*mankuha*) of another, or the *m'uataddah* of another [a woman observing probation for another man either on account of death or divorce] . . . . . . or a Magian woman . . . . or two sisters by one contract and cohabits with them both or marries two sisters *one after another and cohabits with the second*; in these cases there is no *hadd* [punishment for unlawful cohabitation]. And this is by consensus, *bi'l-itifak*, [*i.e.*, Abu Hanifa and his disciples are agreed on the doctrine] according to the most approved report."

---

1 Ante ; see the Jam'a-'r-Ramuz, Vol. IV, p. 644, Chapter on Punishment.

2 Radd-ul-Muhtar, Vol. III, p. 236, "when the unlawfulness is in consequence of something else the connection does not involve liability to hadd."

"According to Abu Hanifa the reason [for not inflicting *hadd*] is manifest ; according to them [Abu Yusuf and Mohammed] it is based on *shubh* (doubt or error) which, according to them, is negatived only when the person prohibited is one regarding whose unlawfulness there is *consensus* and who is unlawful permanently (علي التائيد)."

[*From this it is perfectly clear that cohabitation after marriage with the sister of a wife is not zina.*][1]

Batil and fasid.

The early lawyers, in describing unions of either kind, often called them both *batil*, or used the term *batil* (null) and *fasid* (invalid) indiscriminately.[2]

In the *Hedaya* and *Fatawai Kazi Khan* the term *batil* is sometimes employed in respect of both classes of marriage. From one point of view both are *batil* as they are both nugatory and have no effect *until consummated*, and even then the result is of a limited character.

In later times a sharp distinction came to be recognized between marriages which were *radically illegal* and those which were illegal from some accidental or temporary circumstance. The reason of this is obvious ; in one case the marriage could not, under any circumstance, be contracted ; in the other there was no bar to the connection if the circumstance which made it unlawful for the time did not exist.

So early as the latter end of the 14th century one of the foremost commentators on the *Hedaya*[3] said as follows :—

Distinction between unions unlawful in themselves and those unlawful for something else.

"Know thou—that unlawful (*haram*) intercourse according to the first classification are of two kinds ; one of them is unlawful in itself (لعينه) ; and the other unlawful for something else (لغيره). As regards the first the reason of its unlawfulness consists in two things, one being the absence of right in its entirety (من كل وجه) as cohabiting with a strange woman, (الا تمبينه), or of the absence of

1 See Tajbi *v.* Maula Khan I L R 411 Bom. 845: 39 I C 603; Rahiman Bibi v. Mahboob Bibi I L R 1938 Mad. 278: A I R 1938 Mad. 141; Mst. Kaniza *v.* Hasan I L R 1 Luck. 71: A I R 1926 Oudh 231 and Taliamand *v.* Mohammad I L R 12 Lah. 52: A I R 1930 Lah. 907. Such marriage is only Fasid (irregular) and not Batil (void) and the issue of such marriage is legitimate and inherits from the father. The Calcutta view expressed in Azizunnissa *v.* Karimunnissa I L R 23 Cal. 130 is no longer good law.

2 Fath-ul-Kadir, pp. 33-34; and Jam'a-'r-Ramuz, Vol. II, p. 248. The old formula is thus given:—"it is permissible that unlawfulness be explained by fasid or batil."

3 'Inaya (Cal. Ed.), Vol. II, p. 496.

right in "a restricted manner", as cohabiting with a bondswoman whom he owns in partnership with another. The other is cohabiting with a woman who is prohibited to the man by perpetual unlawfulness, as for instance, cohabiting with a bondswoman who is his foster-sister."

" All connections other than those belong to the second class (*viz.*, being unlawful for something else), as for instance, cohabiting with one's bondswoman who is a Magian or with two bondswoman who are sisters to each other."[1]

"If a man were to accuse another [of committing *zina*], in the first class of connections in both its kinds he shall not be subjected to the punishment [of slander] because chastity of repute is not applicable to the person against whom the accusation [of *zina*] is made, for this is a condition of *ihsan* (احصان)[2] and also because the accuser in this instance speaks truly, for *zina* is a connection which is unlawful in itself (الزنا هو الوطئ الحرام لعينه). And in the second class [*viz.*, where a person accuses another of committing *zina* in cohabiting with a woman whose unlawfulness falls in the second category] the accuser shall be liable to punishment, for the unlawfulness in this class depends on a temporary cause which is capable of being removed (destroyed). *Dost thou not see that when a Magian woman accepts Islam or when one of the sisters [married or in bond] goes out of the milk (right or ownership) of the man, then it shall be competent to him to cohabit with the other ; therefore the cohabitation is not ina, and the accuser shall be subjected to the punishment of slander.*"

Paraphrased it amounts to this:—

Summary of the doctrines enunciated in the 'Inaya.

There are two kinds of unlawful intercourse between the sexes—one that is unlawful in itself or in other words, *absolutely* ; the other that is unlawful for something else, that is, *relatively*; the former is *zina*, the later is not *zina*. When the man has no right in the woman, or having such right, she is *perpetually* prohibited to him either on account of the relationship of blood or fosterage or that affinity which creates perpetual unlawfulness,[3] the intercourse is unlawful *in itself* ; when the prohibition is temporary or relative, the intercourse is unlawful for "something else", that is, some extraneous and accidental cause. Thus, with regard to women

---

1 The relative prohibition regarding cohabitation with a Magian or any non-scripturalist woman applies both to the status of bondage and of marriage. Similarly in the case of two sisters. The examples here given, therefore, apply, mutatis mutandis, to the woman over whom a man acquires a right by marriage.

2 See ante.

3 See ante. Affinity does not create perpetual prohibition in all cases.

who cannot be married by a man at the same time, or to use the language of Arabian lawyers, " who cannot be lawfully joined together", connection with them is not unlawful in itself but only for a temporary or incidental circumstance. For example, a man is not allowed to marry two women so related to each other that if one of them had been a man they could not intermarry, but he can at any time make the second woman lawful to himself by divorcing the first, or the first may die which would remove the bar to the second marriage.

Similarly, with regard to women prohibited on the ground of difference of religion. Though it is unlawful for a Musulman to unite himself to a Magian woman, the connection is not unlawful *in itself*, for the objection to it may be removed, as already observed, by her adopting the Moslem Faith; the cohabitation, therefore, is not *zina*. The same reason is applicable to his connection with an idolatress, for the objection is equally removable by a change of religion.

Invalid marriages—the Fatawai 'Alamgiri.

The *Fatawai 'Alamgiri*[1] which, so far as this question is concerned, represents the developed Hanafi Law, devotes a special chapter to "Invalid Marriages and the rules relating thereto."[2] "When an invalid marriage has taken place (اذا وقع النكاح فاسدا) the Kazi[3] must effect a separation between the husband and wife; and if there has been no *copula* she has no dower due to her nor has she to observe the *'iddat* (probation). If there has been *copula* she is entitled to whichever may be less—her customary dower[4] or the dower specified, when any has been named; and when no dower has been named (specified) she will get her customary dower whether it is great or small ;

'Iddat of separation obligatory in an invalid marriage.

and *'iddat* becomes obligatory on her . . . . which is to be calculated from the time of separation between them according to our three masters (*viz.*, Abu Hanifa, Abu Yusuf and Mohammed) so in the *Muhit* . . . . . .

But not of death.

"The *'iddat* of death[5] is not obligatory in an invalid marriage nor is maintenance (*nafka*)." In other words the woman is not bound to observe the *'iddat* prescribed for widows nor is she entitled to maintenance. "And if there is

---

1 Compiled in 1660 A C; see Vol. I, Introduction.

2 Vol. I, Chap. viii, p. 466.

3 The Kazi in the Islamic system is not only a Judge but a custodian of the morals of the people.

4 Mahr-ul-misl, see post.

5 The period of probation which a widow has to observe.

an agreement for maintenance in an invalid marriage it is not valid.

Establishment of the paternity of the children of an invalid marriage.

So [it is laid down] in the *Wajiz-l'il-kurdi.*" "And the *nasab*[1] of the child (*walad*) is established from the father in an *invalid* marriage, and the period of legitimate descent (*nasab*) is to be reckoned from the time of *dukhul* (*copula*) according to Mohammed (may his soul be blessed) and on this (*viz.*, his doctrine) is the *Fatwa,* as stated by Abu Lais. So in the *Tabiin.* "And an invalid marriage has no effect before consummation."

Example of an invalid marriage.

I have already given examples of an invalid marriage: it may, however, be useful for purposes of illustration to re-state some of them. A marriage with a divorcee or a widow of another man whilst she is observing her *'iddat,* "with a slave girl upon a free woman", with an idolatress or Magian ("*Majusi*"), or a woman "who has been forced" into the contract, or some of the instances mentioned in the law books. I have purposely left out the case of a man marrying two sisters by the same contract or separate contracts as that is the question which we are considering.

Marriage with a woman in her 'iddat—Shiah doctrines.

There is a wide divergence between the Shiah Law and the Hanafi doctrines on the subject of a marriage contracted during a woman's probation. Both schools forbid such unions. Under the Shiah law, however, if a man were to marry a woman whilst she was observing the *'iddat* of death or divorce for another husband, and were to cohabit with her, she would become unlawful to him in perpetuity—apparently by way of punishment for the attempt to confuse *nasab*[2]. But if there was no cohabitation, he can remarry her on the expiration of her *'iddat.*[3]

Under the Hanafi law there is no such penalty. Although the *m'uataddah*[4] of one man is as unlawful to another as his wife (*mankuha*) there is this important difference. A union with a married woman if contracted with the knowledge of that fact is an adulterous connection. A marriage during a woman's *'iddat* under the Hanafi law, is only *invalid.* Thus whilst the husband and wife are to be separated, if cohabitation takes place, the issue, if any, would be legitimate, and the parties can enter into a fresh contract of marriage.

Why is a marriage during the *'iddat* of a man only *invalid* under the Hanafi law? It is not because the woman's temporary

1 *i.e.*, Legitimate descent.

2 The children, if any, would not be punished for the mistake of their parents; they would be affiliated to the father.

3 Jam'a-ush-Shittat.

4 A woman observing the 'iddat.

unlawfulness is based on any inherent incapacity, but because *'iddat* is prescribed for the establishment of legitimate descent and "the prevention", as the *Hedaya* puts it, "of confusion of blood."

The true test of legitimacy.

Hence it is that where the connection is adulterous (*zina*) no *'iddat* is obligatory on the woman. The true test therefore, for judging whether the issue of a particular connection are legitimate or otherwise is to discover whether the mother *after separation*, has to observe the prescribed probation or not.[1]

Marriage with two sisters—Fatawai 'Alamgiri.

With regard to the marriage of two sisters, the *Fatawai 'Alamgiri* lays down the following rule: "When a man marries two sisters by one contract, separation must be effected between them and him (the man); if that is done before cohabitation, each of them will be entitled to the smaller amount of the two, *viz.*, customary and specified dowers. So in the *Muzmirat*."

"But if he marries them by two [separate] contracts the second marriage is *fasid*,[2] and it will be incumbent on him to separate from her and if the Kazi comes to know of it he must separate them. If then she [the second sister] is separated before consummation (*dukhul*), nothing will be established of the rules [of marriage].[3] But if she is separated after cohabitation dower becomes due to her, and the lower of the two, the specified amount and the customary dower will become obligatory [on the husband], and [the observance of] *'iddat* will be incumbent on her, and *nasab* [the paternity of her children] will be established [in the husband], and he should abstain from [cohabitation with] his wife [*i.e.*, the other sister] until the expiration of the *'iddat* of her sister [*i.e.*, the separated wife]; so in the *Muhit* of Sarakhsi."[4]

Azizunnissa Khatoon v. Karimunnissa Khatoon.

The learned Judges, after quoting this passage, proceed as follows:—

"The authority for this opinion,[5] which is cited in the *Fatawai 'Alamgiri*, but is not given by Baillie, is the *Muhit* of Sarakhsi, who died in A. D. 1096. We have not been referred to the original text, and we are informed that no copy of the *Muhit* is available in Calcutta. We are, therefore, unable to judge of the passage by its context or to see for ourselves how far it corresponds with the opinion expressed in the *Fatawai 'Alamgiri*. It appears, however, as pointed out by Moulvi Mohammad Yusoof, that some of the opinions

1 Not the 'iddat of death, see ante.

2 This is important.

3 In other words, the marriage will be ineffective.

4 Fatawai 'Alamgiri, Vol. I, p. 391.

5 It would have been more correct to say "rule".

expressed in the *Fatawai 'Alamgiri*, as well as in the *Muhit*, are directly challenged in the *Radd-ul-Muhtar*, and it is clear therefore that neither of these authorities is considered to be infallible or conclusive. Be that as it may, the passage in question is a solitary authority, and it is not shown that it has been accepted by any commentator other than the *Fatawai 'Alamgiri*[1] during the last 800 years, or that it has been acted on in practice.[2] Moreover it is distinctly opposed to the authorities which lay down that when a man marries two sisters by one contract, and one marriage is to precede the other, the marriage which is the later of the two is absolutely void. We do not think, therefore, that upon the authority of the *Fatawai 'Alamgiri* alone, and in the face of so many conflicting opinions in other commentators, we ought to hold that a marriage which is distinctly forbidden in the Koran[3] which rests on precisely the same basis as a marriage with a mother-in-law or a daughter-in-law[4] and which is so opposed to the customs of the people as to be rarely or never met with in practice,[5] is such a legal and valid marriage that the children are capable of inheriting."

Conclusion based on misapprehensions.

The above conclusion is founded on several misapprehensions. In the first place, the author of the *Radd-ul-Muhtar* never challenges directly or indirectly the "opinions", it would be more correct to call them the rules, enunciated in the *Fatawai 'Alamgiri*. And it is only with respect to the marriage of a non-Moslem with a Moslemah that he has professed to differ from the author of the *Muhit*, one of the greatest authorities on Hanafi Law.[6]

In the second place, it is an error to say that the marriage of a second sister "rests precisely on the same basis as a marriage with a mother-in-law or a daughter-in-law". The learned Judges naturally imported English ideas into the consideration of the question and looked at it through English spectacles for the English Law as it stands regards the wife's sister as being within the

1 It is difficult to understand what is meant by "any commentator other than the Fatawai 'Alamgiri". The Fatawai 'Alamgiri is not the name of an author, nor it is even a commentary. It is a Digest of rules collected from recognised authorities.

2 It does not appear that any proof was required of the practice spoken of here. I think I have abundantly shown that there is absolute agreement on the question which the learned Judges were considering.

3 The Koran forbids the marriage, but does not say what would be the status of the issue if such a marriage were contracted.

4 This statement is based on a misconception as I shall presently show.

5 There does not appear to have been any evidence to support this statement.

6 See Morley's Digest.

prohibited degrees, and as one with whom a marriage is illegal even after the wife's death.[1]

Misunderstanding of the Musulman Law.

They forgot that under the Musulman Law whilst a mother-in-law (by which I suppose was meant the wife's mother) and the daughter-in-law are *perpetually* and *absolutely forbidden*,[2] *the wife's sister is forbidden only so long as the first marriage is not terminated by death or divorce.* If the wife is divorced, the moment she has completed her *'iddat*, the man can lawfully marry the sister.

In the latter part of the passage quoted, there is a confusion of ideas which shows that Court failed to apprehend the distinction under the Musulman Law between the validity of a marriage and the establishment of *nasab* which creates the right of inheritance.

Conclusion unwarranted.

Under the Hanafi law, without any difference, the "child of fornication" alone, who is declared to own no *nasab* to the father,[3] is excluded from his inheritance.

Nowhere is it laid down that where a man marries two sisters (one after the other, the marriage with the second taking place during the subsistence of the union with the first), and cohabits with her, that the connection is *zina* or fornication, or that the man exposes himself to the punishment of *zina* provided under the Musulman Law, which is the only test for finding whether the connection is adulterous or not. There is absolutely no authority for such a contention, nor do the learned Judges proceed to lay down such a proposition which alone could justify the conclusion at which they arrived.

Examination of the authorities.

An examination of the authorities, however, will show that there are no "conflicting opinions" on the *nasab* or legitimacy of the issue of such an union. Just as there is agreement regarding the invalidity of the connection, so there is absolute *consensus* with regard to the legitimacy of the children born of the marriage.

"If a man", says the *Hedaya*, "engage with a woman in an invalid marriage and cohabit with her, she becomes entitled to her customary dower but not more than the

1 This was written before the law legalising a marriage with a deceased wife's sister was placed on the Statute-book in England.

According to the Marriage Act 1949 (English), First Schedule, the deceased wife's sister is listed at No. 1 of relations who are enumerated as statutory exceptions from prohibited degree of relationship.

2 Karim Bakhsh v. Mst. Mukabuar 16 P R 1917.

3 Under the Shiah Law, a walad-uz-zina, a child of fornication, owns no nasab to either parent, see ante.

specified amount."[1] "The descent of a child born of a woman enjoyed in an illegal marriage is established (in the reputed father). And Mohammed holds, and decrees are passed agreeably to this doctrine, that in the establishment of paternity under an *invalid* marriage the time is calculated from *copula* and not from the date of the marriage."[2]

The Fatawai Kazi Khan.

Kazi Khan[3], writing about the same time, says—"If a man marries a woman by an invalid marriage and cohabits with her and gets a child by her the *nasab* (parentage) will be established from him if the child is born six months thereafter (*i.e.*, after *copula*)".[4]

The Kanz-ud-Dakaik.

The *Kanz-ud-Dakaik*[5] lays down the rule in the following terms—"in a *nikah-ul-fasid* the customary dower becomes obligatory upon *copula*. But the customary dower should not exceed the *mussama* (specified dower); and *nasab* will be established and also "*iddat*". On this the comment[6] is "and *nasab* is established in a valid marriage because the child must be taken care of. The same reason applies to the case of an *invalid* marriage. And *nasab* is reckoned in an invalid marriage from *dukhul* (*copula*) according to Mohammed . . . . . and on this is the *fatwa*."

The Sharh-i-Vikaya.

The principle is laid down in similar terms in the *Sharh-i-Vikaya*.[7]

"In the case of an invalid marriage nothing will be obligatory unless there be cohabitation, even if there be valid retirement. (But) if he were to cohabit he will have to pay the customary dower if it does not exceed the dower fixed." "If the customary dower be equal to or less than the fixed dower, then the customary dower will have to be paid. But if the customary dower is greater than the fixed one, the excess will not be obligatory, *and the parentage will be established from the time of cohabitation according to Mohammed*[8] (may peace be on him) and on this is the *fatwa*."

The 'Inaya.

The *'Inaya*, which also is a commentary on the *Hedaya*, first gives the rule laid down in the latter work. "The Kazi will separate the husband and wife[9] in the case of a *nikah-ul-fasid*."

---

1 Book II, chap. III; Grad'y Ed. of Hamilton's Hed., p. 52.
2 *Ibid.*
3 See Vol. I, Introduction.
4 Fatawai Kazi Khan, p. 421.
5 The Lucknow Ed., p. 102.
6 *Ibid.*, p. 103.
7 Vol. II, p. 128.
8 The italics are mine.
9 It will be noticed that the expression used is (زوجين) "the husband and wife" thus indicating that the marriage is not void.

It then comments on it as follows:—

"A *fasid* marriage, like a marriage without witnesses (مثل النكاح بلا شهده), a marriage of a sister during the *'iddat* of another sister irrevocably divorced [*i.e.*, before the relationship with the other sister has definitely terminated],[1] a fifth marriage during the *'iddat* of the fourth[2] and such like (نحوها)."[3]

Then after stating the rule as to dower and *'iddat*, that they both become incumbent after *copula* and giving the reason therefor, the commentator proceeds to add:—

"The author [of the Hedaya] has said 'the *nasab* of her child [*viz.*, of the woman married by an invalid contract] will be established'; this is clear from what has preceded, and he [the author of the *Hedaya*] says, 'and the period of *nasab* will be reckoned from the time of *copula* (من وقت الدخول) according to Mohammad (may the peace of God be with him); and Abu Hanifa and Abu Yusuf (may the peace of God be with them) have said that it is from the date of marriage as in the case of a valid marriage, (كما في النكاح الصحيح) because the effect of the *fasid* (invalid) is drawn from the *sahih* (valid) and the *fatwa* is on the doctrine (*kawl*) of Mohammed (may the peace of God be with him)' ".[4]

The Radd-ul-Muhtar.

That the marriage of two sisters simultaneously or one after another is an *invalid* marriage is proved by the very authority on which the learned Judges seem to have relied in coming to the conclusion they did. After stating the rule from the *Tanwir-ul-Absar*—"and the *mahr-ul-misl* (customary dower) becomes obligatory in an invalid marriage (نكاح فاسد)", and the comment of the *Durr-ul-Mukhtar*, *viz.*, "and an invalid marriage is one [*viz.*, a marriage] in which is wanting any condition among the conditions for its validity *such as witnesses*", the *Radd-ul-Muhtar* proceeds as follows—"his[5] saying 'such as witnesses' and similar to it is *the marrying of two sisters together* [simultaneously] (معا) and marrying one sister during the *'iddat* of another sister, and marrying a *m'uataddah* [*i.e.*, a woman who is observing the *'iddat* of death, or divorce for another man] and [marrying] a fifth [wife] during the *'iddat* of the fourth, and marrying a bondswoman upon a free woman (*i.e.*, when he has a freewoman in matrimony]".

---

1 See ante.

2 Because a man cannot validly marry more than four wives; see ante.

3 'Inaya, Vol. II, p. 74.

4 *Ibid.*, p. 75.

5 "His" refers to the author of the Durr-ul-Mukhtar.

The Radd-ul-Muhtar is a commentary on the Durr-ul-Mukhtar which again is a commentary on the Tanwir-ul-Absar.

And again when dealing with the subject of *'iddat* and the circumstances which make it obligatory, the very first instance that is given is "marriage with the wife's sister".[1]

The Tahtawi.

The *Tahtawi* which, like the *Radd-ul-Muhtar*, is a commentary on the *Durr-ul-Mukhtar*, quotes first the passages in the latter work—"the *mahr-ul-misl* (customary dower) is incumbent in the case of a *nikah-ul-fasid* (*an invalid marriage*), *which is one in which any condition among the conditions necessary to constitute a valid marriage is wanting, such as witnesses.*" On this the commentator, a high authority in the Hanafi world, observes as follows:—The expression 'such as witnesses' includes a marriage with two sisters *together* or with one sister during the *'iddat* of another sister[2] [whom the man has married before], with a woman who is a *m'uataddah* [one observing the *'iddat* of death or divorce for anothor man], with a fifth during the *'iddat* of the fourth wife, with a bondswoman upon a free woman, of a *Kafir* [an infidel or non-Moslem] with a Moslemah. So no *hadd* will be inflicted on them [if they cohabit] and the *nasab* will be established and *'iddat* will be obligatory."[3]

From the above, two points are clear, *first*, that when a man marries two sisters, whether simultaneously or one after the other, the marriage is only *invalid* like a marriage "without witnesses"; in other words, it is only relatively contrary to law, but not radically, or absolutely prohibited; *second*, that there is no conflict of opinion among the jurists, as the learned Judges imagine.

Absolute consensus.

This may at first sight appear to be contradictory of the earlier statement that when a man marries two sisters by one contract, the marriage performed last is *batil* or void. But in reality it is not; what is really meant is that the second union, whether contracted at the same time as the first or afterwards, is nugatory or inoperative; but if consummated has the effect of a valid marriage in three particulars, *viz.*, (*a*) in the establishment of the *nasab* of the issue *in the father*, (*b*) in making *'iddat* incumbent on the woman, and (*c*) some dower obligatory on the man. Nevertheless the parties must be separated. *There is absolutely no difference on these points between the jurists, text-writers and commentators of the Hanafi school.*

1 " 'Iddat, according to its legal signification, means waiting which becomes obligatory on a woman . . . . . Therefore there is no 'iddat for zina. There are twenty cases in which 'iddat becomes obligatory, *viz.*, (1) in a marriage with the wife's sister . . . . . (6) with a fifth wife; (7) with a bondswoman upon a free woman; (8) with the sister of a woman with whom the man has cohabited under an invalid marriage or in a doubt of marriage; . . . . . (10) with a M'uataddah of another man; (11) with his own *irrevocably* divorced wife before she has been made lawful to him (*see post*) . . . . (20) with a Magian woman or one who has abandoned Islam."

2 In all these cases the tie is not completely severed until the probation is completed.

3 Tahtawi, Vol. II, p. 59.

Difference among the jurists as to the marriage of a non-Moslem with a Moslemah.

It is only with regard to the effect of a marriage between a non-Moslem man and a Moslem woman that there is a difference between the legists. "And in the *Muhit* it is stated", says the *Radd-ul-Muhtar* "that 'when a *zimmi*' [a non-Moslem subject] marries a Moslemah, separation shall be effected between them because the marriage that takes place is *fasid* (لانه وقع فاسدا)." There is no mention of *nasab* in this passage quoted from the *Muhit*, but the commentator draws the right inference and deals with it in this way, "From this it would be inferred that they shall not be liable to *hadd*, and that *nasab* and *'iddat* would be established from it [the union] if the parties have cohabited.[1] I say that the commentator [*i.e.*, the author of the *Durr-ul-Mukhtar*] will presently state towards the end of the section dealing with the establishment of *nasab* (parentage), on the authority of the *Majm'a-ul-Fatawa*, that 'if a *Kafir* [non-Moslem] marries a Moslemah and the woman bears a child to him, the *nasab* shall not be established from him, and *'iddat* shall not be obligatory on her, because the marriage is *batil* (void) and this [namely, what is laid down in the *Durr-ul-Mukhtar*] is clear (*sarih*), and therefore, it is to be preferred to an inference [the inference he has drawn from the *Muhit*].' This then thou should understand.[2]

There is not the slightest reference here to the case of a marriage with two sisters, simultaneouly or otherwise and it is difficult to understand how the learned Judges came to think that this passage had any bearing on the question they had to try.

Firash (bed) established in an invalid marriage.

Another passage in the *Radd-ul-Muhtar*, which was apparently not quoted before the Judges, places it beyond doubt that the author was confining his remarks solely to the marriage of a non-Moslem with a Moslemah. "In the *Majm'a-ul-Fatawa* it is stated that if a *kafir*[3] marries a Moslemah and she gives birth to a child, its *nasab* will not be established, nor will *'iddat* become incumbent on her, for the marriage is *batil*[4]—his[5] saying that the marriage is *batil* means this, that cohabitation in such a case is *zina*, and therefore *nasab* will not be established contrary to the case of a *fasid* [marriage], for in the case of a *fasid* (invalid) marriage the *copula* is subject to *shubh* (legal doubt or semblance); so *nasab* will be established; and therefore it is that an *invalid* marriage creates the *firash* (*i.e.*,

---

1 The result, in every instance, of a fasid marriage.

2 Radd-ul-Muhtar, Vol. II, p. 574.

3 An unbeliever in the cardinal doctrines of Islam, *viz.*, one who denies the Unity of God and the Messengership of the Prophet, see ante.

4 Here is one opinion opposed to another—the Muhit against the Majm'a-ul-Fatawa.

5 The "his" refers to the author of the Durr-ul-Mukhtar.

the bed),[1] whereas it is not so in the case of a *batil* [connection]."[2]

I have already pointed out that only when the connection is adulterous, when it amounts to *zina*, that the issue are illegitimate, or in the language of Arabian lawyers there is no *nasab*—that peculiar tie which binds the child to the father, the *walad* to the *walid*.

The Hanafi law may, therefore, be summarised thus:

Hanafi doctrines. Nikah-ul-batil.

Connections which are unlawful in themselves are null and void *ab initio* (*batil*) and create no civil rights and obligations between the parties. The wife has no right of dower against the husband (*unless the marriage is consummated*), and neither of them is entitled to inherit from the other, in case of the death of either, during the period when the contract is supposed to have existed. The illegality of such unions commences from the date when the contracts are entered into, and the marriage is considered as totally non-existing "in fact as well as in law".

Examples.

A marriage contracted within the degree prohibited by the Musulman Law falls under the head of marriages which are null and void *ab initio*; it carries no civil rights and produces no legal effect, unless it was contracted *unknowingly*. "If", says the *Radd-ul-Muhtar*, the man cohabits with the woman after his marriage, she will be entitled to her *mahr-ul-misl*, whatever that be, and this is correct. In the *Ziadat* it is stated that it should not exceed the specified dower, and this is the doctrine of the Disciples. So it is according to the *Tabiun*."

According to the Imams Abu Yusuf and Mohammed, if the marriage is contracted in good faith and in ignorance of the cause which renders the parties unlawful (*haram*) to each other and is followed by cohabitation the issue would be affiliated to the father and *nasab* would be established. But if it is entered into with a knowledge of its illegality the offspring, if any, would not acquire the *status* of legitimacy, though the woman would have to observe the '*iddat* or prescribed probation before she can marry again.

If, however, the man was led to believe that the woman was lawful to him, *nasab* would be established.[3]

All this, as shown already, is according to Imam Abu Yusuf and Imam Mohammad, for according to Abu Hanifa,

---

1 Firash is the marital relationship which validates connection.

2 Radd-ul-Muhtar, Vol. II, pp. 1041-2.

3 This is the rule of ghurur; see ante.

every marriage which is vitiated for some reason or other, either in consequence of an illegality, or an informality, or some supervenient incapacity, is only *invalid*, and the children are in every case legitimate.

Invalid marriages.

Marriages, which are not vitiated and rendered illegal by a radical defect of the character above described, stand on a different footing. In such cases also, if consummation has taken place *the children conceived and born during the existence of the contract are legitimate*. But whereas all marriages between two persons who are perpetually interdicted to one another by reason of consanguinity, affinity or fosterage, are illegal and void; the other unions are merely *invalid*, for the supervenient objection may be removed at any time. A Magian woman may be rendered lawful by conversion to Islam, Christianity or Judaism; a *m'uataddah* of another, by the expiration of her *'iddat*[1] an idolatrous woman by conversion to Islam. It is only in the first class of unions that the parties are liable to *hadd, if the marriage is contracted with knowledge of its illegality*, for it is *zina*.

In a *nikah-ul-fasid*, either of the parties may set aside the contract before consummation, but after consummation, according to most of the authorities, the separation must be effected in the presence of both.[2]

Mere abstention on the part of the husband to approach the wife is not a sufficient separation; he must expressly state to the woman that the marriage is set aside.[3]

If the parties do not agree to separate, the Kazi is authorised to decree separation.

According to the *Ghait-ul-Bayan*, a woman cannot contract a second marriage after she has been *invalidly* married until separation has actually taken place, or in case the marriage has been consummated until the probation has terminated.[4]

In an invalid marriage, *'iddat* does not become incumbent, as is the case in a valid marriage, by mere "retirement"[5] but only after actual consummation.[6]

Period of probation in an invalid marriage.

The period of probation runs from the time of separation; and the woman would be subject only to the *'iddat* of *talak*,

1 Ashbah-wan-Nazair, p. 58.

2 Radd-ul-Muhtar, Vol. II, p. 575.

3 *Ibid.*

4 Zailye seems to differ on this point.

5 See ante.

6 Radd-ul-Muhtar, Vol. II, p. 576.

viz., three months, and not to the *'iddat of death*, which is four months and ten days.[1]

In a *nikah-ul-fasid* the woman becomes entitled to her dower if the marriage is consummated. If the specified dower is less than her *mahr-ul-misl* she gets the same; if it is in excess, she will receive the customary dower only.

Issue of an invalid marriage legitimate.

As already stated, the issue of an invalid marriage are, in every instance, legitimate. The *nasab* is calculated from the date of *copula*, *dukhul*, and not from marriage. This is according to Mohammed "with whom is the *Fatwa*", that is judicial decisions are passed according to him. Whilst Abu Hanifa and Abu Yusuf have declared that, in the case of an invalid marriage, *nasab* would be calculated from the date of the marriage as in the case of a *valid* contract.

A child born at six months from consummation and within two years [ten months] from separation would be legitimate.[2]

Marriage of a Moslemah with a non-Moslem.

Like most other systems, the Musulman Law discountenances a marriage between a Moslem woman and a man professing another religion, whether he be a Scripturalist or otherwise. Under the Shiah law the issue of a marriage between a Moslemah and a non-Moslem are illegitimate, for the union is regarded as nugatory *ab initio*. In the Hanafi system, as we have seen, there is a great difference of opinion regarding the *status* of the children. According to the *Muhit* and apparently the *Bahr-ur-Raik* and the *Tahtawi*, the union is treated as an *invalid* marriage, for the man may at any time abandon his own religion and accept the Faith of Islam, and thus remove the bar to matrimony with a Moslem woman.

According to the *Majm'a-ul-Fatawa*, the *Durr-ul-Mukhtar* and the *Radd-ul-Muhtar* such a marriage is absolutely nugatory, and if there is cohabitation, it is tantamount to *zina*. Naturally, in the opinion of these jurists, the children would be illegitimate. This is an extreme doctrine, the enforcement of which in India,[3] would not only be attended with difficulty, but lead to consequences of anomalous character. For example, if a non-Moslem, whose personal law recognised a marriage with a woman of a different persuasion,[4] or who could contract such a marriage under the *lex loci* or Municipal Law,—were to marry a Musulman woman, she probably can get the marriage set aside on the ground that it was unlawful according to her personal law. But if she chose to abide by it, there is no machinery by which it can be cancelled. The

---

1 Radd-ul-Muhtar, Vol. II, p. 576.

2 *Ibid.*, p. 577.

3 Now Indo-Pakistan.

4 A Hindu of one caste cannot marry a woman of another caste, much less of a different creed.

issue of such a union, being regarded as illegitimate, would not be entitled to inherit to their Musulman relatives but would certainly inherit from their father, as they would be legitimate according to his personal law. Neither would they inherit from their mother, if she died in the Faith of Islam.

None of these consequences arise under the doctrine enunciated in the *Muhit*, which declares that the children would be treated as the children of an *invalid* marriage owning *nasab* to their father. Of course, if they too were non-Moslems, they would be excluded from the inheritance of their Moslem mother and their Moslem relations, not because they were illegitimate but because they were followers of another faith (*kibla*).

Shiah doctrines.

According to the Shiah law, if a man marries two sisters by one contract, the marriage is void as regards both; but if he marries them by separate contracts or one after the other, the first union would be effective (valid) whilst the second would be void.[1] If the husband has connection with the second wife under the "semblance of right" created by the marriage, the issue, if any, would be legitimate.[2]

According to the author of the *Mabsut* (*Shaikh-ul-'Allamah* Abu J'afar of Tus) "connection under *shubh* (semblance of right) stands in the position (منزله) of a *valid marriage*, [that is, gives rise to the same consequences as a valid marriage]." According to the *Shara'ya*, the prohibition of affinity would not be created by it, but the *nasab* of the children would be established in the father.[3]

Under the Shiah law, a man can marry his wife's niece or aunt, only with the wife's consent. If the contract is entered into without her permission, it is void, and the parties must separate. If there has been cohabitation under *shubh* (doubt) the issue, if any, would be affiliated to the father.

SECTION II

FURTHER PRINCIPLES RELATING TO INVALID MARRIAGES

Contracts entered into by mandatories.

If a man were to charge two mandatories (*wakils*) to marry him to a woman, and they acting independently of each other marry him to two sisters, the contract prior in

---

1 Shara'ya, p. 271.

2 *Ibid.*

3 *Ibid.*, 272.

date will be held valid, whilst the other will be voided without the formality of the Kazi's judgment, or a regular divorce from the supposed husband. When it is impossible to discover which of the two contracts was first entered into, both marriages would be nullified.[1]

When two sisters have been married to one man by one and the same contract, both marriages are void, and the women are not entitled to any dower, if separation has taken place before consummation; should the marriages, however, have been consummated, both the women would be entitled to their customary dowers, in spite of the dissolution of the contracts. If they were married by separate contracts, and it is not known who was married first each would be entitled to half the dower, if the separation took place before consummation,—but if after, then to their respective specified dowers if it is less than the customary dower; if it is in excess, they will get only the customary dower. When one marriage is consummated and not the other, the one which is consummated will be held valid though posterior in date.

Hanafi doctrines.

According to the Hanafi doctrines, when two women, one related to the man within the prohibited degrees, and the other not,—are married by the same contract and under one dower, the contract with the first is void, but with the second valid, and the entire specified dower belongs to her. According to the Disciples, if the marriage is consummated with both, the prohibited woman will be entitled to the customary dower.[2]

A girl married to two persons, first marriage valid.

When a girl is married to two men successively, to one by her father and to the other by another guardian, or when two men claim to be married to one woman, then the marriage first in date is alone considered legal and regular and the other is dissolved without divorce or decree. In case, however, it is impossible to discover which of the two contracts is prior in date, then both marriages are held null and void, and the woman is not entitled to claim any dower or right of inheritance on the death of the alleged husband or husbands.

Qualifications to the rule.

Should the second marriage, however, have been consummated, then on grounds of public morality, it will be considered valid.[3]

---

1 Fatawai 'Alamgiri, Vol. I, p. 392; Hedaya *in loco.*

2 Radd-ul-Muhtar, Vol. II, p. 480.

3 *Ibid.*, p. 485.

Marriage with a woman observing 'iddat—Hanafi doctrine.

Should a man contract a marriage with a woman during her *'iddat*, or period of probation, with knowledge of the fact that she was observing the *'iddat* being the widow or divorcee of another, such marriage would be invalid. After the expiration, however, of the probationary period, he can enter into a contract of marriage with her *de novo*. If the marriage is followed by cohabitation, the separated woman would be entitled to her dower, and any child born of the connection would be legitimate.

Maliki doctrine.

It is a doubtful point in law, whether, under the Maliki rule, a man contracting a marriage with a woman in ignorance of her *'iddat*[1] would be absolutely forbidden to cohabit with her. Several cases which have been decided in Algeria serve to show, that when a contract has been entered into in good faith, without the parties being aware of the unlawfulness of the act, it is regarded, by a liberal interpretation of the Maliki Law, as valid.

Shiah Law.

Under the Shiah Law, if a man commit adultery with a married woman knowing that she is married, he cannot marry her after the decease of her husband. Her person is "for ever unlawful to him".[2] Should he marry her in ignorance of the prohibition and there is issue of the union, such issue will be regarded as legitimate.[3]

Again, under the Shiah Law, if a man were to marry a woman observing the *'iddat* for another, the marriage is nugatory and the parties must be separated. If he cohabits with her under the contract, her person becomes absolutely prohibited to him "for ever" and he cannot enter into a fresh contract with her.

As under the Hanafi law, *the issue of the connection, however, would be legitimate.*

If the marriage is not followed by cohabitation, he can remarry her on the expiration of her *'iddat*.[4]

---

1 The extreme solicitude of the Musulman Law with respect to the legitimacy of children, and its aversion to bastardise the offspring of valid or invalid unions, has led to the formulation of the rule of 'iddat. Every woman separated from her husband, and every widow is required to abstain for a specific period from contracting a fresh union, until it is known with certainty whether she is enceinte or not. In the case of a widow this period is four months and ten days, whereas, in the case of a woman separated from her husband by divorce, it is only three months. This prohibition guards against confusion of parentage.

2 Mafatih.

3 Comp. the cases in the Jam'a-ush-Shittat.

4 *Ibid.*

Marriage with a pregnant woman.—General doctrines.

A marriage with a woman, who is bearing a child whose paternity or *nasab* is known, is placed in the same category as a marriage contracted during the period of *'iddat*. In other words, when it is known by whom she is *enceinte*, and the pregnancy is consequent upon a lawful contract, nobody else can marry her until after her delivery. The illegality of such a marriage is founded on an express direction contained in the Koran, and has frequently been enforced by the Kazis' Courts in Algeria.[1]

Marriage with a woman pregnant from fornication—Hanafi doctrine.

But where it is not known by whom a woman, who has no husband, is pregnant, in other words, when the pregnancy is consequent upon fornication, the rule is different. "Abu Hanifa and Mohammed have said", says the *Fatawai 'Alamgiri*, "it is lawful for a man to marry a woman pregnant by fornication, though he must refrain from matrimonial intercourse with her till her delivery. Abu Yusuf, however, was of opinion that the marriage is not valid, but the *Fatwa* is in accordance with the opinion of the two others." As it is not permitted to have connection with her, so also it is not permitted to "solicit" her. "When a man marries a woman", says the *'Alamgiri* quoting the *Majmoo'a*, "with whom he has already had illicit intercourse, and it appears that she is pregnant, the marriage is lawful, and he may cohabit with her, and she is entitled to maintenance according to all their opinions."[2]

Shiah doctrine.

The Shiahs are in accord with the Hanafis on this point. In the *Jawahir-ul-Kalam* it is stated that if the pregnancy is due to fornication, no *'iddat* is incumbent on her; and her marriage during pregnancy is valid. The same doctrine is laid down in the *Masalik-ul-Afham*, the *Irshad-ul-Azhan* and the *Mafatih*, which say there is a *consensus* of opinion on the point, although it is preferable (حوط) in order to prevent "confusion of *nasab*" to abstain from intercourse.

Hanafi doctrine.

"When a man is absent from his virgin wife for years and she marries and has children; or a woman is taken captive and married to an enemy and has children; or a woman claims to be divorced, keeps *'iddat* and afterwards re-marries and has children; or her husband's death is announced to her, and she keeps *'iddat*, marries another and has children, in such cases [the children] according to the Imam [Abu Hanifa] belong to the first [husband], whether he denies or claims

1 The Kazi, as the general conservator of law and morality in a Musulman community, has the power to annul or punish an illegal act, without a formal complaint being preferred before him. See the Fatawai 'Alamgiri and the Jam'a-ush-Shittat, Kitab-ul-Kaza; Sautayra, Vol. I, p. 142.

2 Baillie's Dig., p. 38, 2nd Ed.

them or whether the second denies or claims them or the children are born within six months or at the distance of more than two years, and the second [husband] may spend his *zakat* (obligatory alms) on such children and thus their testimony may be received on his behalf; so according to *al-Wajiz-lil-Kurdari.*" This opinion Abu Hanifa appears to have abandoned later on. "And it is stated by Abdul Karim Jurjani from Abu Hanifa that the offspring would belong to the second husband, that he (the Imam) came back to this opinion and on this is the *Fatwa*; so in the *Tajnis*."

"Similarly it is laid down in the *Fatawai Kazi Khan* and the *Sirajia*, and Sadr-ush-Shahid used to decide in accordance therewith."[1]

Although a passage is quoted from Zahir-ud-din to the effect that the *Fatwa* is with the first opinion of Abu Hanifa, the weight of authority is in favour of the doctrine stated in the *Tajnis*, the *Fatawai Kazi Khan* and the *Sirajia*.

Re-marriage with a divorcee according to the Hanafis.

When a man re-marries a woman from whom he has been irrevocably divorced,[2] *without or having been married to another man in the interim and separated from him*, such remarriage is illegal. Mere marriage would not be sufficient, there must be consummation. This rule was prescribed to arrest the scandal of indefinitely repeated divorces and remarriages which had become frequent in Arab society, and were opposed to the interests of public morality. The violation of this law, therefore, leads to the nullity of the marriage.[3]

Shiah doctrines.

According to the Shiahs, when a man divorces his wife irrevocably and then marries her again, *talaks* her and again re-marries her and again *talaks* her, he cannot re-marry her without submitting to the ordeal of her being married to another person and being divorced by him. This was prescribed as a punishment for the man's outrageous conduct towards the woman.

Should the separation, however, have taken place under circumstances giving rise to the inference that both parties, at the time of disagreement, had lost all self-control, some lawyers are of opinion an allowance should be made in their favour, and that they should be permitted to re-marry, without the wife having to undergo the disagreeable ordeal of a marriage ceremony with another man.

---

1 Fatawai 'Alamgiri, Vol. I, p. 467.

2 See Chapter on Divorce.

3 The scandalous condition of morality in the Arabian Peninsula, among the Jews, the Christians, and the Pagan Arabs, at the time of Mohammed's advent, is apparent from the prohibition pronounced by him against the re-marriage of a woman to a man who had divorced her three times.

According to the doctrines of the schools which recognise the lawfulness of polygamy, a man may enter into four contemporaneous contracts of marriage.[1] A contract of marriage with a fifth woman is invalid; if the marriage be consummated, though she would be separated from the man, *nasab* would be established and she would be bound to observe the *'iddat*. She would, at the same time, be entitled to her customary or specified dower whichever is less.[2]

SECTION III

INVALID MARRIAGES (*continued*)

THERE are certain other unions which are included under the head of *invalid* marriages and are governed by the rules relating to them.

Marriage by an infant.

For example, although a marriage contracted by an infant, who has not attained the age of discretion is null and void according to all the schools, a contract entered into by a minor possessed of discretion, is dependant for its operation on the ratification (*ijazat*, sanction) of the guardian.[3]

By an insane person.

Nor is a contract of marriage entered into by an insane person or one who, without being a confirmed lunatic, is labouring under mental hallucinations, valid under the Sunni Law.

Shiah Law.

Under the Shiah Law also the contract has no legal effect and is absolutely void.[4]

A marriage contracted during intoxication—Hanafi and Shiah doctrines.

A marriage contracted by a person whilst in a state of intoxication is invalid, according to the Shiah as well as the Sunni Law, unless confirmed after the recovery of consciousness The Shiah view is according to the *Mafatih*. The *Shara'ya*, however, makes a distinction between the case of a male and that of a female. A marriage contracted by a drunken man, according

---

1 See the Introduction. Even the Radd-ul-Muhtar states that if a man were to marry a woman, and in order to please her does not marry any other, his act is pious and he will be rewarded by God. Comp. the Shara'ya, p. 274.

2 A section of the Shiahs think that besides four wives permanently married; a man may contract several temporary marriages. The Sunnis repudiate this doctrine as immoral. The M'utaziles agree with the Sunnis.

3 Fatawai 'Alamgiri, Vol. I, p. 377; Shara'ya, p. 262.

4 Shara'ya, p. 262; Jam-'ush-Shittat; Kitab-min-la-Euhazzar-al-Fakih.

to the *Shara'ya*, is not valid, even though he may ratify it on regaining consciousness; whilst in the case of a female it is held to be otherwise. Consequently, a female who has been induced to consent to her marriage whilst in a state of intoxication, can, on becoming conscious, ratify the contract and it becomes valid. The opinion of the 'Allamah given in the *Mafatih* is the more correct and is supported by the cases cited in the *Jam'a-ush-Shittat*.

Marriage contracted in extremis—Shiah Law.

A marriage contracted by a person *in extremis* or by one suffering from a disease in which there is imminent danger of death, is invalid. If the disease, however, be such that the person recovers from it, and consummates the marriage, the invalidity is removed. "A marriage contracted by a sick person (مريض) is dependent on consummation", says the *Shara'ya*, "so that if he die of *that illness* without consummation, the contract is void and the woman has no right to dower or succession." The *Jam'a-ush-Shittat* says, "When a contract is entered into by a man suffering from an illness, and he dies of it *after* consummation, or if after recovering from that illness he dies of some other disease, then the marriage is valid, and the wife is entitled to her dower as well as to her right of succession." Again, when a woman in health marries a sick man and dies before consummation, the majority of the doctors hold that the husband is entitled to the right of succession in her estate, "though there is some difference of opinion." When a woman *in extremis* or suffering from a dangerous illness marries a man in health, who dies without consummating the marriage, the contract is held to be valid, and the wife has a right to her dower and to a share in the inheritance of her deceased husband. These principles are common to both Shiahs and Sunnis.

Consent obtained by fraud or force.

Where consent to a contract of marriage has been obtained by force or fraud, such a marriage is *invalid*,[1] unless ratified after the coercion has ceased, or the duress has been removed, or when the consenting party, being undeceived, has continued the assent.

The Shiah and Shaf'ei Laws are explicit on the point. Among the Hanafis the doctrine of the *Jam'a-'r-Ramuz* is the recognised law. The author of the *Radd-ul-Muhtar*, however, expressed a different opinion regarding the effect of a marriage contracted under duress or compulsion (*ikrah*).

The Judicial decrees (the *fatwa*) are passed according to the *Jam'a-'r-Ramuz*.

1 Jam'a-'r-Ramuz, p. 264.

The *Jam'a-'r-Ramuz*[1] of Kahastani dealing with the subject of dower in an *invalid* marriage states as follows:—"And in a *nikah-ul-fasid*, that is *batil*,[2] as for instance a marriage with a woman perpetually or temporarily prohibited to a man, or by compulsion *on her* (بالاكراه من جهتها) or without witnesses, or of a slave upon a free woman, or of a woman in her *'iddat* and others besides, nothing becomes obligatory [before *copula*] either on account of fixed or customary dower nor *'iddat* nor maintenance."

The words (من جهتها) have been construed by the great jurist Mufti Abu S'aud, frequently quoted by the author of the *Radd-ul-Muhtar*, to mean compulsion of the woman. "And Syed Abu S'aud has laid down that consent is conditioned on behalf of the woman and not on behalf of the man, and he has relied for proof on what has been set forth in Kahastani in the chapter on dower where it is stated that 'the marriage is invalid, where there is compulsion of the woman.' "

"But", says the author of the *Radd-ul-Muhtar*, "this requires consideration, because it is stated in the *Nikaya* that in a *fasid* marriage nothing [by way of dower] is obligatory when there has been no *copula*; otherwise the customary dower becomes obligatory. Then Kahastani commenting on this passage says 'in a *fasid* marriage . . . . such as a marriage with a woman prohibited perpetually or temporarily or a marriage where there has been *compulsion of the woman, &c.*' "[3]

Principle.

It is clear, therefore, that the author of the Jam'a-'r-Ramuz and the Mufti Abu S'aud distinctly regard free consent on the part of the woman as forming the very essence of the contract.

The author of the *Radd-ul-Muhtar* is rather casuistal on this point. In the first place he tries to show that (الاكراه من جهتها) refers to compulsion *by* the woman. Then he suggests that the expression is ambiguous, and that there is no reason why a marriage contracted under compulsion, should be invalid, when a divorce given under compulsion or by way of a joke is valid. Again, he suggests that the word *mukrah* (*person compelled*) is general and should not be used in a restricted sense (as applicable only to the woman). He concludes by referring to the *Kafi* of Hakim-ush-Shahid, which he says clearly holds that a marriage contracted under compulsion is

1 Jam'a-'r Ramuz, p. 264.

2 According to this commentator fasid and batil are interchangeable expressions in marriage.

3 Radd-ul-Muhtar, Vol. II, p. 444.

valid. The passage in the *Kafi* is as follows:—"And if the woman is compelled to marry a man for a dower of one hundred, whilst her customary dower is ten thousand, *and she has been given in marriage by her guardians who are the persons using the force*[1] then the marriage is valid; and the Kazi shall say to the husband 'you may, if you choose, complete her *mahr-i-misl* and she will remain your wife', if the husband is the *equal* (*kufu*) of the wife; but if the husband is not her *equal* the Kazi shall cause separation between them, and there shall be nothing [due] to the woman."[2] This clearly refers to a case where a woman's consent to the marriage has been extracted by pressure *on the part of her guardians*, and has no application to duress or coercion exercised by a stranger.

The passage in the *Kafi* explains the following statements in the *Fatawai 'Alamgiri*, which in their bare form are no less astounding than contrary to the generally equitable principles of the Musulman Law.

Compulsion—marriage by.

"When the Sultan compels a man to give his female ward[3] in marriage to one who is her equal for less than her proper dower, the woman herself assenting, and the constraint is then withdrawn, the guardian has the right of action (حق الخصومت) against the husband either to make up the dower to the customary amount (*mahr-ul-misl*) or for separation between them by the Kazi (though according to Abu Yusuf and Mohammed he has no right in such a matter)."[4] "And similarly, when the woman is compelled, and the compulsion is subsequently withdrawn, according to Abu Hanifa, she as well as the guardian have the right of action[5] [in the matter]. According to the other two (Abu Yusuf and Mohammed) the right of action appertains exclusively to the woman; so [it is stated] in the *Muhit* in the section relative to matters concerning guardians."[6]

The above passage deals with coercion or compulsion exercised by a stranger even though he be the sovereign. What follows refers to pressure or constraint brought to bear on a woman by her guardian.

"When a woman is constrained to marry herself to a man who is her *equal* on her customary dower,[7] and then the constraint is withdrawn, she has no option. But if she be constrained to marry herself to a man who is not her *equal* or the dower is less than the customary dower [in the case of an

1 The italics are mine.

2 Radd-ul-Muhtar, Vol. II, pp. 444-5.

3 مولية

4 As the woman who is evidently sui juris assents to the marriage.

5 حق لخصومت

6 Fatawai 'Alamgiri, Vol. I, p. 414; see also Baillie's Dig., p. 72,

7 Mahr-ul-misl, *i.e.*, the dower of her equals, see post.

equal], she has an option on the removal of the constraint; so in the *Muhit*. When a woman is constrained to enter into a marriage and does so, the contract is lawful, and no responsibility attaches to the person constraining.[1] If the husband be her equal and the specified dower more than or equal to the customary dower, and she demands that it may be raised to the customary amount, he shall be required to raise it or to separate. If he raises it [the dower] to the customary amount good and well (فبها). If separation occurs before consummation, he is not liable for anything; but if consummation has taken place and it was against her will, that would mean consent on his part to raise the dower to the customary amount; if it was with her consent, it would be an assent on her part to the specified dower, although it would still be open to her guardians, according to Abu Hanifa, to object to the dower, but according to the other two [Abu Yusuf and Mohammed] they would have no such right. All these relate to a case where the husband is her equal. But when he is not her equal, the guardians may separate the parties."[2]

It will be noticed that these passages deal exclusively with the question of dower and equality; and the effect of compulsion on the *status* of marriage is only incidentally referred to.

Probably the Indian[3] Courts, which are governed by principles of equity, justice and good conscience, will follow the rule laid down in the *Jam'a-'r-Ramuz* and affirmed by the Mufti Abu S'aud.

Shiah Law.

Under the Shia Law should a person, who has made a proposal or declaration, subsequently lose his consciousness and understanding (though only for a time), his proposal of marriage would, if accepted, be invalid.[4]

Limitations on the power of the father.

The right of the father under the Musulman Law to impose the *status* of marriage on his minor children has already been discussed. A marriage contracted by the father or the grand-father, who, in the absence of the father, stands in his place, is *prima facie* supposed to be in the interests of the child. A minor, therefore, contracted in marriage by a father or a grand-father according to the Hanafis, the Shaf'eis and the generality of the Shiahs (Malikis and M'utazilas differing), has ordinarily no right of option on arriving at puberty to ratify or cancel the contract of marriage.

---

1 This can hardly refer to coercion exercised by the person whom she is compelled to marry; for responsibility certainly attaches to him if the marriage is consummated.

2 Tatawai 'Alamgiri, Vol. I, p. 414; comp. Baillie's Dig., 2nd Ed., pp. 72-73.

3 Now Indo-Pakistan.

4 Shara'ya, pp. 262, 263; Jam'a-ush-Shittat; Irshad-ul 'Allamah.

Improper marriage contracted by father.

But there are important provisions qualifying the otherwise unlimited and irresponsible power of the father. It is held that a contract of marriage entered into by a father or any person standing *in loco patris*, must not be prejudicial to the interests of the minor. When a father, who is not just or is a *fasik-ul-Muta-hattik*, *i.e.*, extravagant in his habits or immoral in his life, enters into a contract of marriage for his child, it is invalid;[1] so also if it is manifestly to the disadvantage of the child. If the father were to contract his child to an eunuch,[2] to a slave, or a leper, or to one suffering from elephantiasis, or any other malady of such a nature as would prevent connubial relationship, the marriage would be invalid, and would be set aside at the motion of any friend of the infant or the guardian, next in degree to the father, of the child, or of the mother.[3] If the father were to marry the child to one very much beneath him or her in rank or quality or to one who cannot maintain the wife, such marriage would also be invalid.

Although Abu Hanifa is stated to have held that where it is not known that a father has acted carelessly or wickedly in marrying his infant child to one not an *equal* or for an unsuitable dower, the marriage is lawful, the enunciations of his Disciples are explicit; they declare such a marriage to be unlawful. "If a man were to marry his young child to one who is not an *equal* . . . . or to contract the child for *improper* dower as for instance, if the child be a daughter at less than her (*proper*) dower or if the child be a son at a dower in excess of the wife's (*proper*) dower, the marriage is lawful according to Abu Hanifa . . . . . . but unlawful according to the other two . . . . . . The difference between them has reference to a case *where it is not known* that the father acted carelessly or wickedly in the matter *but when this is known*, the marriage is void according to all their opinions; and in like manner there is consensus that if he were drunk (*sakran*) [at the time of contracting the marriage], it would not be valid (لا يصح); this according to the *Siraj-ul-wahaj*."[4]

It is clear therefore that there is no difference of opinion when it is "known" that the marriage was contracted carelessly or "wickedly," or is to the manifest disadvantage of the infant. The *Fatawai 'Alamgiri* then proceeds to add that when the excess or deficiency [in the dower is not *gross*, the marriage is lawful according to general agreement. The later enunciation refers to a case where deficiency in the dower forms the *sole* objection to the marriage.

1 Radd-ul-Muhtar, Vol. II, p. 484; Fatawai 'Alamgiri, Vol. I, p. 415; Shara'ya, pp. 263, 264; Jam'a-ush-Shittat; de Menerville, Jurisprudence de la Cour d'Alger.

2 Radd ul-Muhtar, Vol. II, p. 484.

3 *Ibid.*

4 Fatawai 'Alamgiri, Vol. I, p. 415; Baillie's Dig., 2nd Ed., p. 74.

The *Radd-ul-Muhtar* also is very distinct on this point. It lays down that by *consensus* a contract of marriage entered into for a minor child by a father or grandfather, whilst inebriated, is invalid and unlawful. Similarly, if the child is a girl and the father or grandfather were to marry her to a man who is either immoral, or wicked, or in want, or who cannot pay her maintenance or dower, or who carries on a low profession, such as that of a scavenger, or cobbler, or weaver, the contract would be unlawful.[1]

Necessity of obtaining an order from the Kazi.

There is no provision in the law that an order should be obtained from the Kazi declaring the invalidity of such a contract. In India, however, where there is no uniformity in judicial determination, it is advisable to apply for and obtain a declaration from the Civil Court.

As regards such a marriage contracted by any *wali* other than the father or grandfather, there is no question. The *Radd-ul-Muhtar*, following the *Fath-ul-Kadir* and the *Ghait-ul-Bayan*, says that a contract fraudulently or wickedly or even carelessly entered into by any person other than the father or grandfather is void. It would follow from this that it would not be necessary for the minor on attaining majority to annul or ratify it.[2] At the same time it is always advisable to obtain a judicial declaration regarding the inoperativeness of the contract.

SECTION IV

AL-KAFAT, OR EQUALITY IN MARRIAGE

Reason why equality is insisted upon.

THE Arabian Legislator appears to have viewed with disapprobation ill-assorted marriages. He is said to have declared that women should not be contracted in marriage except to their equals.[3] "Take ye care", said he, "that none contract women in marriage but their proper guardians, and that they be not so contracted except with their equals", "because", adds the *Hedaya*, cohabitation, society, and friendship cannot be completely enjoyed excepting by persons who are each other's equal (according to the customary estimation of equality), as a woman of high rank and family would abhor society and cohabitation with a mean man; it is requisite, therefore, that regard be had to equality with respect to the husband, that is, the husband should be the equal of the wife."

Hanafi doctrines relating to equality.

The Hanfis, accordingly, hold that *equality* between the two parties is a necessary condition in marriage, and that an

1 Radd-ul-Muhtar, Vol. II, p. 499; comp. Fatawai Kazi Khan, Sect. on Guardians.

2 Radd-ul-Muhtar, Vol. II, p. 501.

3 Hedaya, Vol. I, p. 110.

ill-assorted union is liable to be set aside by a decree of the Judge.

The Hanafi doctrines regarding equality are founded chiefly on Arab analogies. For example, it is declared that the husband should be the equal of the wife in lineage and rank, should not be a slave, should be a Moslem, should be possessed of sufficient means "to pay the wife's dower and provide for her maintenance", should be virtuous and pious,[1] should be the wife's equal in trade or business.[2] A profligate is not the equal of a good woman." . . . . "A person marries his young daughter to a man under the impression that he is virtuous. It afterwards appears that he is a habitual drunkard, and the girl on attaining puberty declares she is not content with the marriage. Under these circumstances, if the father was not aware of his being a drunkard, the marriage is liable to be cancelled."

Equality is not necessary in the case of a wife, for a husband can raise her to his own rank, however high.[3] But this refers to the case of an adult, for a man who is *sui juris* can marry any one he likes. But if a father or grandfather were to marry an infant to a low-born girl, such marriage would not be valid[4].

Equality is insisted upon at the outset, so that if the man was equal to the woman at the time of the marriage, and becomes lowered afterwards either morally or in material circumstances, the marriage cannot be invalidated.

Nor can a marriage be invalidated on the ground of discovery of inequality on the part of the man, if the *walis* of an adult girl have entered into a contract of a marriage with her express assent, unless at the time of the marriage the *walis* insisted upon equality and the man gave them the assurance about equality, or they required an assurance from him that he was well behaved, or not given to drinking, and he gave that assurance which is found to be untrue. In such cases both the girl and the *walis* will have the power to have the contract cancelled.[5]

A minor girl contracted in marriage by the father.

This is different from the case of a minor girl. If she is married by a father or grandfather to a person whom they believe either socially or morally to be her equal, and he turns out to be low-born or depraved or addicted to drinking, the right of having the contract cancelled is established in her as well as in her *walis*.[6]

---

1 Fatawai 'Alamgiri, Vol. I, p. 411.
2 Fatawai Kazi Khan, Vol. II, p. 399.
3 Radd-ul-Muhtar, Vol. II, p. 519.
4 *Ibid.*; comp. Fatawai Kazi Khan, Sect. on Guardians.
5 Radd-ul-Muhtar, Vol. II, p. 521.
6 *Ibid.*, p. 519.

Under the Hanafi Law there are six requisites to equality:—

(1) *Nasab*, family or descent.

(2) Islam.

(3) Profession.

(4) Freedom.

(5) Good character.

(6) Means.

(7) According to the *Fatwai Hamadia*, potency,—so that if a father married his minor daughter to a person known to be impotent, it will not be valid; though, according to the *Bahr-ur-Raik*, if the girl is adult, the marriage will be lawful (if the man is in other respects her equal), but the woman will have the power to obtain a nullity of the marriage on the ground of impotency.[1]

(1) The Koreish are each other's equal, but or superior to all other Arabs; so that a Koreishite woman is superior to all other Arabs.

Other Arabs are each other's equal, but they are superior to all non-Arabs. "Even a non-Arab King is not equal, to an Arab woman."[2]

Among Arabs, it is not necessary to look to the profession the man follows.[3]

Persons, who trace their descent to the Caliphs, though born and bred in foreign countries, are in the matter of descent, on the same footing as the domiciled Arabs.[4]

Equality in marriage.

An Alide is superior to all Arabs. So is a learned Ajami (non-Arab) the equal of an ignorant Arab or even an Alide. "The worth of learning is greater than the worth of family."[5]

Malik gives the preference to all the descendants of the Prophet over everyone else; but the Hanafis and Shaf'eis will not give any opinion as to who was superior to the other, *viz.*, 'Ayesha or Fatima't-az-Zahra (the daughter of the Prophet).

A Hanafi male is the equal of a Shaf'ei female, and a Hanafi may lawfully marry a Shafi. So if a Shaf'ei adult virgin were to marry a Hanafi, the marriage would be valid according to the Hanafi Law.[6]

A merchant is superior to a tradesman; a Kazi or *Fakih* (jurist) to a merchant.

If the boy has no means, but his parents or grandparents have, he must be accounted to have means.[7]

1 Radd-ul-Muhtar, Vol. II, p. 522.

2 *Ibid.*, p. 529.

3 *Ibid.*, p. 523.

4 *Ibid.*

5 *Ibid.*, p. 536; Fatawai Kazi Khan, Sect. on Equality

6 *Ibid.*, p. 530.

7 *Ibid.*, p. 531.

The Malikis and the Shiahs.

The Malikis and the Shiahs differ materially from the Hanafis in their estimate of the character of these conditions. According to them, Islam and an ability to support a wife are the two necessary conditions to constitute a well-assorted marriage.[1] A Moslem possessed of sufficient means to maintain a wife may, among the Malikis and the Shiahs, marry any Moslem woman, without question of lineage or rank; "for, are not", it is pertinently asked, "all Moslems equal?"[2]

If an adult woman contracts herself in marriage to one who is not her *equal* the *walis* have a right to object.[3]

Ability to support a wife.

The question of ability to support a wife has been a fruitful subject of discussion among the early lawyers. The *consensus* of opinion seems to be that if the husband possesses means to maintain his wife for one month, besides paying the prompt portion of the dower, it is sufficient "ability" in law.[4]

It is needless to add here that cases bearing on the point of equality required under the Hanafi Law rarely arise in India, inasmuch as the family of the bride and bridegroom take very great care to ascertain the *nasab* (descent) and *hasab* (character) of the parties, and yet contingencies may arise which may lead to serious discussions on the subject of equality.

"Except Islam and freedom", says the *Fatwai 'Alamgiri*, "equality in any other respect is not invariably observed in a country other than Arabia."

It has already been mentioned that the Shiahs and the Hanafis allow the greatest freedom to women, who are, if *sui juris*, free to contract themselves in marriage. But such freedom is restrained by the power of veto or objection possessed by the guardians in case of a alliance.[5] Among the Shiahs this right of veto is almost *nil*, owing to the fact that the conditions of equality,

1 Radd-ul-Muhtar, Vol. II, p. 519; Shara'ya, p. 278; Jam'a-ush- Shittat.

2 According to the Hanafi doctrines, an Arab of any tribe but the Koreish is not the equal of a Koreishite woman; a non-Arab is not the equal of an Arabian woman, a slave is not the equal of a free woman. So that all unions between such people are theoretically ill-assorted marriages. The marked distinction between the Shiah and Hanafi doctrines on the point is shown by the Shara'ya. "It is lawful", says the Shara'ya, "for a free woman to marry a slave, for an Arabian woman to marry a Persian, or for a woman of the tribe of Hashim to marry a non-Hashimite and *vice versa*", p. 278. So also the Mafatih.

3 *Ibid.* "It is abominable for a woman to marry a profligate, and the abomination is aggravated by his being a habitual drunkard."

4 See post, Chapter on Dower ; Fatawai 'Alamgiri, Vol. I, p. 411 ; according to Abu Yusuf if his daily earnings are sufficient to support the wife, it is enough.

5 Fatawai Kazi Khan, Vol. I, pp. 401, 468; and Fatawai 'Alamgiri, Vol. I, p. 412.

according to their doctrines, have reference only to the Islam of the husband and his ability to support the wife. If an adult woman of the Shiah school were to marry a non-Moslem, her relations would have the same right of objection as relations have under the Sunni Law.

Hanafi Law right of veto possessed by the wali.

Among the Hanafis, this right of objection has far greater importance. In the case of the rule laid down for the guidance of the guardians, when entering into a contract of marriage for their wards, the principle and the limits are easily definable; *e.g.*, guardians are directed to have regard to the ages of the parties; not to marry a young girl to a very old man and *vice versa*; not to allow a marriage to take place between a female of a noble family and a man for beneath her in rank or *status*,[1] should he not possess some qualification to justify the alliance; and not to marry minor girls on grossly inadequate dowers.

Unequal marriage contracted by an adult woman.

In the case of a mesalliance contracted by an adult woman, the question of *inequality* is one of some difficulty. An analysis of the various decisions collected together in the several digests, notably the *Fatwai 'Alamgiri* the *Fatwai Kazi Khan* and the *Radd-ul-Muhtar*, leads to the conclusion that in Musulman communities, outside the peninsula of Arabia, great disparity in rank, refinement, culture social position or means, would furnish reasonable and proper grounds for a guardian or *wali* to object to a marriage contracted by a female who is *sui juris*. For instance, if a woman were to contract a run-away marriage with a servant of her family, the marriage would be annulled by the Kazi on the application of the *wali*. Difference of faith would always justify an objection to a marriage. It is only the *asabah*, whether within the prohibited degrees or not, who can raise any objection to a marriage contracted by an adult girl on the ground of inequality.[2]

An *ill-assorted* marriage or a mesalliance contracted by a woman remains intact with all its consequences until annulled by the order of the Kazi.[3] A judge alone has the power of cancelling marriages on the ground of inequality. The judicial separation effected by the Kazi is not equivalent, however, to a *talak*, so that if the marriage has not been consummated, the woman is not entitled to any part of the dower. But if consummation has taken place or there has been "valid retirement" into the nuptial chamber, then the husband is liable for the whole dower and for maintenance during the '*iddat*.[4]

---

1 It must be added, however, that a man who is "rich in learning" is regarded as "the equal" of the noblest born woman.

2 Radd-ul-Muhtar, Vol. II, p. 486; comp. Fatawai 'Alamgiri, Vol. I, p. 412.

3 Fatawai Kazi Khan, Vol. I, pp. 401-468; Radd-ul-Muhtar, Vol. II, pp. 486, 531.

4 Fatawai 'Alamgiri, Vol. I, p. 412; Fatawai Kazi Khan, Vol. I, p. 401; Kanz-ud-Dakaik.

The delay of a guardian in instituting proceedings to set aside a marriage on the ground of a mesalliance does not lead to the forfeiture of his right.[1] "But after the woman has actually borne a child to her husband, the guradians have no right to have the marriage cancelled", "for", adds the *Radd-ul-Muhtar*, "it would damage the interests of the child; so in the *Durrar*."[2]

When the guardian has once, by word or deed, expressly or impliedly, acquiesced in the marriage, he loses absolutely his right of objection; or, when one guardian has consented, none other, except one higher in degree, can object.[3] The *Radd-ul-Muhtar* says, if some of the *walis* agree, it is tantamount to all agreeing, as the *aman* [guarantee of safety] given by one Moslem to a *harbi* [enemy] holds good against all Moslems.

The power of objecting belongs exclusively to the '*Asabah* of the woman and not to the uterine relations.[4]

There is no reason why the Civil Courts in British India[5] should not entertain a judicial proceeding or suit by a Moslem father to set aside, on the ground of inequality, a marriage contracted by an adult daughter.

If either of the married parties should die before the decree of the Judge is issued cancelling the marriage, the survivor would be entitled, as in an ordinary case, to a share in the inheritance of the deceased.

SECTION V

THE OPTION OF PUBERTY (*Khyar-ul-Bulugh*)[6]

Khyar-ul-Bulugh.

Under the Mahommedan Law there are two kinds of "option" in marriage, one is called the "option of puberty" (*Khyar-ul-Bulugh*) the other the "option of emancipation" (*Khyar-ul-Itk*). The first is the right vested in an infant in law to ratify or rescind on attaining majority (puberty) a contract of marriage entered into on his or her behalf during minority. The "option of emancipation" is the right vested in a bondswoman who has been given by her master in marriage during infancy to ratify or dissolve the contract on arriving at puberty after enfranchisement.

---

1 Fatawai Kazi Khan, Vol. I, p. 401.

2 Fatawai 'Alamgiri, Vol. I, p. 412; Radd-ul-Muhtar, Vol. II, p. 487.

3 The Fatawai 'Alamgiri, Vol. I, p. 412, says that if the wali take possession of the dower and provide the jahaz (in common parlance, jahez) it amounts to acquiescence.

4 Fatawai 'Alamgiri, Vol. I, p. 412.

5 Now Indo-Pakistan.

6 "There is no option of inspection or defect in marriage", says the Fatawai 'Alamgiri.

As the *status* of slavery is not recognised in British India,[1] and prevails only in a limited sense in countries governed by Musulman sovereigns, the rules relating to the "option of emancipation", possess only an antiquarian interest. The "option of puberty", on the other hand, is a subject of considerable importance and requires careful consideration.

Shiah doctrines.

As already pointed out, under the Shiah Law, no person other than a father or grandfather has any authority to contract an infant (a *saghir*) in marriage. When the contract is entered into by the father or, in his absence, by the nearest living paternal ancestor, the minor, whether male or female, has no "option" on attaining "puberty" unless the contract is to the *manifest* disadvantage of the minor, or has been "carelessly" or "wickedly" entered into,[2] *e.g.*, when the father of a girl has married her to a lunatic or an eunuch, or if a boy, has married him to a female who is unfit for connubial intercourse or has bound him to pay a dower which is utterly beyond his means, the contract is subject to the minor's *option* on attaining puberty. These examples are not exhaustive.

But a marriage contracted by any other relative, even a mother, is wholly inoperative unless expressly ratified by the infant on attaining puberty. In other words, all relations, other than the father or grandfather, are mere *fazulis*, unauthorised agents, and contracts of marriage entered into by them are treated as the acts of persons who have no legal authority to bind the infant.

Hanafi Doctrines—Difference in the powers of guardians.

According to the Hanafi Law, as we have seen, the power of giving an infant in marriage is vested in a number of relations besides the father and grandfather, but there is a great distinction between contracts of marriage entered into for minors by the latter, and those entered into by other *walis* or guardians.

When a marriage is contracted by the father or grandfather for his minor children or grandchildren with their *equals* (*kufu*) "even at a slight deficiency in the dower", the children have no option of setting aside the contract on attaining majority.

Principle.

In other words, if the marriage is in all respects suitable, the bride and birdegroom are equally matched in rank, position and age, and there is no deformity or evil habits on one side or the other, the dower is not unreasonably low und so on, in such a case the minors on attaining majority have no option; for it is presumed that all these cirumstances combining, the love which a father or grandfather bears to his children or grand-children must have actuated him in making his choice, which ought not to be set aside

1 Now Indo-Pakistan.

2 Comp. the Jam'a-ush-Shittat.

at the mere caprice of the young people after they attain the age of puberty.[1]

Option of Puberty.

But when the father or grandfather "carelessly" or "wickedly" contracts a minor boy or girl in marriage with a person who is not his or her *equal*, or if the father or grandfather is not honest or is a prodigal, or of bad behaviour, or it appears that the marriage is to the manifest disadvantage of the minor, the contract is not *valid*, and unless set aside before by the *wali* next to him in order, remains dependent on the ratification of the minor on attaining puberty. The *minor may either adopt it or rescind it as he or she chooses.*[2]

Ratification on attaining majority—Express.

In the case of a male, the option must be express. Similarly in the case of a woman who is a *Saibba* (not a virgin) the ratification must be explicit.[3] "When the option of puberty is established in favour of a *Saibba*", says the *Fatawai Kazi Khan* "it is not rendered void except in express words, or by cohabiting with the husband, or by asking for her dower or maintenance."

Implied ratification.

In the case of a virgin girl, the ratification may be either *express or implied.* For example, acquiescence in the marriage relationship or remaining silent a long time after attaining puberty would be regarded as ratification.

Marriage contracted for a minor by any guardian other than the father or grandfather.

But when a marriage is contracted for a minor by any person other than a father or a grandfather, "whether it is the mother or the Judge", it remains dependent on the "option of puberty", irrespective of the *bona fides* of the person contracting the marriage or any question of inequality.

Hanafi Law—Kazi's declaration when required.

According to the Hanafi Law, where a contract is dependent on the "option of puberty", it remains intact for certain purposes until a formal declaration has been made by the Kazi setting it

---

1 Comp. the Radd-ul-Muhtar, Vol. II, p. 501.

But see the Dissolution of Muslim Marriages Act, 1939, s. 2 (*vii*) which gives option of puberty where the minor girl below 15 is contracted in marriage even by the father or paternal grandfather—Ghulam Sakina *v.* Falek Sher P L D 1949 Lah. 75.

2 See Aziz Bano *v.* Mohammad I L R 47 All 823: A I R 1925 All. 720. A Shia girl given in marriage by her father to a Sunni husband has an option of repudiation on attaining puberty unless it has been ratified by consummation or otherwise. The reason given being that it would be contrary to all rules of equity and justice to force such a marriage on her, if on attaining puberty she considers the marriage to be repugnant to her religious sentiments.

Zubeda Begum *v.* Wazir Mohammad A I R 1940 Sind 145: 190 I C 94. Where the husband was convicted of theft and was under trial on a charge of enticing away a married woman, the wife was entitled to repudiate the marriage.

3 Comp. the Radd-ul-Muhtar, Vol. II, p. 501.

aside: that is, it will be regarded as subsisting for purposes of cohabitation and inheritance.

In other words, if they choose to cohabit together, they may do so without renewing the contract; and should one of them die before the decree of the judge, the survivor would be entitled to inherit from the deceased, "for death is tantamount to consummation", and if the husband dies, the woman would be entitled to her full dower.

The *Fatawai 'Alamgiri* following the *Hedaya*, states as follows:—

Option of Puberty.

"Where minors are contracted in marriage by a father or grandfather, they have no option on arriving at puberty; but when contracted by any other than a father or grandfather, they may, according to Abu Hanifa and Mohammed, on arriving at puberty, if they wish it, either abide by the marriage or cancel it. It is a condition, however, that there shall be the decree of a judge in the matter, contrary to the case of "the option of emancipation." And if a boy or girl should exercise the right of option, after arriving at puberty, but the judge has not made the order directing the separation between them until one of them dies, they have reciprocal rights of inheritance; and until the Kazi has effected the separation between them, the husband may lawfully cohabit with her. This is according to the *Mobsut*."[1]

Option of Emancipation.

It will be noticed that in the case of "the option of emancipation" no order of the judge is needed to give effect to the power which the law vests in the minor bondswoman, given in marriage by her master during her minority, to cancel the marriage on arriving at puberty *after she is enfranchised*. This right is restricted to bondswomen only and does not extend to bondsmen, "because", says the *Hedaya*, "it is intended as a security against an evident injury to herself (the wife) as the husband's power over her is extended and his authority, as well as her obligations, enlarged by her emancipation." "But", it goes on to add, "it is otherwise in the case of the option of puberty, because that option is reserved with a view to guard against injury to the other rights of the parties, which might occur in a variety of instances and which, if admitted (as if the marriage were absolute, they must be), would be calculated to introduce many evils into the married state, since the guardian might, for instance, in executing the contract, agree to an inadequate dower or to an unequal match; and as the dissolution of the marriage thus tends to affect other rights, a decree of the Kazi is 'essential' thereto."[2]

1 Fatawai 'Alamgiri, Vol. I, p. 402.

2 Hamilton's Hedaya (Grady's Ed.), p. 37. This is a free paraphrase of the Persian version of the Hedaya.

It must be noted here that the word "essential" does not occur in the original, which only speaks of the decree of the judge as a condition (Shart).

Examination of the dicta relating to the Judge's decree being requisite to the effectuation of the cancellation.

With regard to the 'condition' that in order to create an effective cancellation or separation, there should be a decree from the Kazi, the *Radd-ul-Muhtar* states as follows:—

"When two minors are contracted in marriage and the girl attains majority before the boy, if she desires to rescind the contract and to obtain the judge's decree *confirming* the cancellation the proceeding must be in the presence of the boy's father or his executor. If neither of them be forthcoming, the judge shall appoint a *wasi*[1] [to represent the minor]. He will make the *wasi* attend and will demand from him the arguments (proofs) on behalf of the minor against the wife's claim for separation, on the ground of her acquiescence in the marriage after attaining puberty or delay in demanding separation. If not [*i.e.*, if these defences are not available] the contesting party (*the guardian ad litem*) will put the wife on her oath, and if she take the oath, the Kazi shall separate them [in other words shall make a decree confirming the cancellation] in the presence of the *khasam* [the contesting party] without waiting for the boy to attain puberty."[2] The author then goes on to add "the executor of the father has precedence over the grandfather", and in support of his statement cites the following passage from the *Jam'a's Suffar*: "And if he [the boy] has no father or father's executor, then the grandfather or his ex ecutor shall contest the matter, and if there be no such person, in that case the Kazi shall appoint a contestor on his [the minor's] behalf."[3]

"As the *option* is, in its essence, a week right, its effectiveness depends on the decree of the judge like the revocation of a gift. And this indicates [implies][4] that if the husband be absent, separation shall not take place between them until he presents himself[5] [or is represented] because the decree must necessarily go against the absent party (*al-ghaib*)."

Principle.

"The condition [relative to the decree of the judge] is required for the purpose of confirming the cancellation, not for establishing the power (ikhtiar) [to cancel the marriage]."

---

1 The term wasi in this connection evidently means a guardian *ad litem*.

2 Radd-ul-Muhtar, Vol. II, p. 502.

3 *Ibid.*

4 Or "it is hinted herein".

5 That is "attends by a representative"—for being a minor he can only contest the action by a representative who in the last resort would be appointed by the judge. If the husband is adult and does not appear to defend, judgment must go by default.

"In short, when a minor boy and gril are married to each other by any person other than the father or grandfather, then they have an option to cancel the marriage on [attaining] puberty or on becoming cognisant of it [the marriage]. If they decide on cancellation, such cancellation shall not become confirmed (لا يثبت الفسخ) except by the decree of the Kazi. This is why the author [of the *Durr-ul-Mukhtar*] bases on this the observation, 'and they shall inherit from each other in this, that is in this marriage, before the confirmation of its cancellation."[1]

Examination of the doctrine.

Upon the above dicta arise two questions: (*a*) what is the reason for requiring the Kazi's decree in such cases? (*b*) what would be the effect if the woman were to re-marry without obtaining a judicial declaration?

There can be no question regarding the right itself; no decree is required to affirm it. It is also quite clear that the Kazi cannot make any declaration unless the party who claims the right has himself or herself exercised and asserted the right. Then, what does the condition imply? It means simply this—that in order to cause an effective cancellation or to impress on the act the judicial *imprimatur*, an order of the judge is necessary. Until that has been obtained, the *status* remains in an inchoate condition; the parties may lawfully cohabit which would amount to a recantation of the "option," or if either of them were to die, a right of inheritance would be established in the survivor.

Error in its conception.

But it does not follow from this that if a woman who has exercised the option were to contract another marriage, believing that she was entitled to do so, she would make herself liable to punishment under the criminal law. The validity of the rescission does not depend on the *imprimatur* of the Kazi, as the judicial declaration is needed to provide judicial evidence in order to prevent disputes, and judicial confirmation and authentication of the exercise of the right. *Ex hypothesi*, when a girl, who was given by her mother in marriage during infancy, on attaining puberty, rescinded the contract, and married another person, she could not be convicted of bigamy although the judge had not made his decree.[2]

Illegal convictions for bigamy.

The Indian Law Courts have often convicted of bigamy girls, who, in their infancy had been contracted in marriage by their guardians, but who, on attaining their majority, had married other men. In any case, these convictions would be wrong; for, supposing even consummation had taken place after the first marriage, the subsequent marriage being *shubhat-ul-'akd*, neither the women nor the men marrying them would, under the Mahommedan Law, be liable to any punishment; though the Kazi

1 Radd-ul-Muhtar, Vol. II, p. 502.

2 See Badul Aurat *v.* Queen-Empress (1891) I L 19 Cal. 19.

might give back the woman to the first husband. But, when there has been no consummation, and the girl, on attaining puberty and during the absence or imprisonment of the man to whom she was contracted in infancy, marries another person, the second marriage would be valid.[1]

When a minor girl marries a person who was her equal, she having no guardian, and there being no Kazi from whom sanction could be obtained, the marriage is lawful, but is dependent on her approval after arriving at puberty.[2]

When the option should be exercised—How it is lost.

Most of the text-books as well as digests of decisions lay down certain principles for the consideration of the question, when and how the right is lost. For example, it is said that mere silence, when the woman is a virgin, is sufficient to extinguish this option upon her part: so that if a woman, being a virgin, after attaining puberty, were to remain silent, her option would be lost. But if she were not a virgin at the time of marriage, or if then a virgin and her husband had directed her to be conducted to his house, and she had arrived at maturity while living with him, her option would not be cancelled by silence, nor even by her rising from the *majlis*,[3] but it would be cancelled by her assenting explicitly to the marriage or doing anything from which her assent might be clearly inferred, as, for instance, permitting cohabitation, or asking for maintenance or the like. She would, however, still retain her option, if she merely continued to eat his food or "serve him" as before. When a woman is aware of the contract at the time of arriving at puberty, but is ignorant that she has an option, and remains silent, her option is lost; but when she is not aware of the contract at the time of arriving at puberty, she has an option on receiving intelligence of it. "When a woman attains to puberty, and inquires the name of her husband, or the amount of the specified dower or salutes the witness, the option of puberty is extinguished."[4]

"When a woman perceives the arrival of her puberty she should exercise her option immediately on seeing the signs

---

1 See Mohammad Bakhsh *v.* Crown P L D 1950 Lah. 203; Vulanda *v.* Crown 33 P W R 1910; Ghulam Mohammad *v.* Emperor A I R 1933 Lah. 88; Mst. Haji *v.* Palio 33 Cr. L J 88; Mafizuddin Mandal *v.* Rahiman Bibi A I R 1934 Cal. 104; Shafiullah *v.* Emperor (1934) A L J 387. The Court's order is not essential for imparting validity to the exercise of option of puberty and that in any case declaration can be given by the Court itself in the course of criminal proceedings initiated under section 494, P. P. C. to the effect that the first marriage stands dissolved by the option of puberty having been exercised.

See also Pir Mohammad *v.* The State of Madhya Pradesh A I R 1960 M. P. 24.

2 Radd-ul-Muhtar, Vol. II, p. 515; Fatawai 'Alamgiri, Vol. I, p. 403.

3 The place or company in which she may happen to be at the time of her attaining maturity.—Hedaya, Vol. I, p. 105 note.

4 Fatawai 'Alamgiri, Vol. I, p. 403; Radd-ul-Muhtar, Vol. II, p. 508.

thereof;[1] when she observes it at night, she should say, 'I have cancelled the marriage' and take witnesses on arising in the morning, saying 'Surely I saw the sign now', for she would not be believed if she said, 'I saw it at night and cancelled'. This is reported in the *Majm'u-'un-Nawazil*, where the author says, 'in case it be false, although in some cases falsehood is permissible [in this matter] according to the *Khulasa*. Hisham has said, 'I inquired of Mohammed regarding a girl whose paternal uncle had contracted her in marriage, and who, on the appearance of her puberty, exclaimed, 'Praise be to God, I made my choice', and (he answered) she has her option; but if she had sent a servant on the appearance of her puberty, to get witnesses and the servant was unable to procure any, and by reason of her residing in a place cut off from people, she delayed for some days, for want of witnesses, he said the marriage would be binding on her, as that would not be a sufficient excuse.' Ibn Sama'at reports from Mohammed, that when a woman exercises her option and calls on witnesses to attest the fact, but delays for two months to bring the matter before the judge, she may still avail herself of it unless she has in the meantime cohabited with her husband."

The burden of proof.

"When there is difference between the parties with regard to the option of puberty, the woman saying, I elected to be free, and rejected the marriage when I arrived at puberty, while the husband says, 'nay, but you were silent, and your option has fallen to the ground', the husband's word is to be preferred."[2] In other words the burden of proof is cast on the wife. If cohabitation takes place and the woman asserts that it was by force, preference is to be given to her statement.

Principle.

It will be noticed, however, that these *dicta* refer to cases where the position of the parties is such that the husband may avail himself of his right of cohabitation, the main object of the enunciations being the avoidance of delay on the part of the woman in the exercise of the right. But when he is absent at a great distance, or has not been heard of for a considerable time or is undergoing imprisonment for a protracted period, the mere fact that the woman does not give expression to the rescission of the contract immediately on attaining puberty would not annul her right, so long as it is expressed in unequivocal terms or by conduct as soon thereafter as possible and before the return of the husband.

---

1 See Daulan *v.* Dossa P L D 1956 Lah. 712. The Dissolution of Muslim Marriages Act of 1939, has expressly fixed the age of puberty without any opportunity of rebuttal. Therefore a woman who was given in marriage by her guardian before the age of *fifteen* may repudiate her marriage within a period of three years after she attains the age of fifteen. Clause 7 of section 2 of the Act thus eliminates the fight over the proof of puberty.

2 Fatawai 'Alamgiri, Vol. I, p. 403; Baillie's Dig., p. 52, 2nd Ed.; comp. the Radd-ul-Muhtar, Vol. II, p. 508.

The option of puberty a substantive civil right.

Suppose a girl is married to a man in her infancy, and before she attains her puberty he is transported for a criminal offence for life, it can hardly be contended that she could not exercise the right of rescission, unless she expressed the fact immediately on attaining puberty. The option of puberty is a substantial right, and it seems to me it would not be consistent with equity to hold that delay, under, such circumstances, to notify the cancellation should lead to the forfeiture of the right.[1]

Time when the option should be exercised.

If the woman is unware of the marriage at the time of attaining puberty, the period for the exercise of the right is extended by *consensus* to the time when she becomes aware of the fact or is informed of it. But, according to Abu Hanifa and Abu Yusuf, a free woman loses her option of puberty even if she was unaware that she has such a right or that "it cannot be prolonged", "for the *Dar-ul-Islam* is the *Dar-ul-ilm* or 'country of knowledge,' and she, being free, is in a position to acquaint herself with the rules of the *Shar'a* (Law)."[2] In other words, in a Moslem country every follower of the Faith is presumed to know the law; and ignorance of its provisions is no excuse for abstention from the exercise of the right. According to Mohammed, however, the woman's right of option will be "prolonged" until she is acquainted that she has such a right, in other words, if she does not know that she has the right of rescinding the marriage, she will have the power to do so when she becomes aware of it.[3]

In a country like India, where the women are mostly ignorant and which is nominally Dar-ul-Islam, the rule of Imam Mohammad is certainly more reasonable and equitable.

Mulka Jehan Sahiba v. Muhammad Uskuree Khan.

The Judicial Committee of the Privy Council in the case of *Mulka Jehan Sahiba* v. *Mahommed Uskuree Khan*[4] laid down the principle which seems to be in absolute accord with the spirit of the Musulman Law. Their Lordships held that "where a minor girl has been contracted in marriage, the matter ought to be propounded to her on her attaining majority so that she may advisedly give or withhold her assent."

No period is prescribed within which the matter should be brought before the Kazi, although, as we have already seen, certain rules are laid down regarding the time when the right or option of cancellation should be exercised.[5]

1 See footnote 1 on p. 338.

2 Radd-ul-Muhtar, Vol. II, p. 509.

3 *Ibid.*, p. 508; "Variation from the truth" in claiming the right is permissible for extending the right; Durr-ul-Mukhtar.

4 (1873) L R I A Suppl. Vol. 192.

5 See Behram Khan *v.* Akhtar Begum P L D 1952 Lah. 548 and Allah Diwaya *v.* Kammon Mai P L D 1957 Lah. 651. The option of puberty is lost if marriage is consummated after puberty but not if it is consummated before puberty.

Principle—Shiah doctrine—Absolute abeyance.

The Shiahs differ materially from the Sunnis on this point They hold that a marriage, contracted on behalf of minors by any unauthorised person (*fazuli*), *i.e.*, any person other than a father or a grandfather, remains in absolute suspension or abeyance until assented to by the parties on arriving at puberty; that, in fact, no legal effect arises from it until such ratification, and if, in the interval previous to ratification, one of the parties should die, the contract would fall to the ground and there would be no right of inheritance in the survivor.[1]

It may be added that, under the Shiah Law, every person, other than a father or grandfather, contracting a minor for an infant, is a *fazuli*. Even a mother contracting a minor child is regarded as a *fazuli*. A contract of marriage entered into by *fazulis* is validated by the assent of the father or grandfather, if present and competent, or by the subsequent ratification of the minor or minors.[2]

In numerous instances, adult married women have been entrapped or decoyed into British colonies in South America and elsewhere, and once there, have never been able to return to India. With respect to these women, a question has arisen whether they could enter into lawful contracts of marriage in those countries. I think that if the women wrote to India (as was alleged they had done), and received no replies, in fact if they were unable to ascertain whether their husbands were alive or dead, they may, after observing the usual *'iddat*, validly re-marry in those countries.[3]

SECTION VI

CAUSES FOR WHICH A MARRIAGE MAY BE CANCELLED

Causes for cancellation of marriage.

When one of the parties to the marriage-contract is suffering from some disease, which prevents the consummation of the marriage, and this fact was not known to the other contracting party, the latter has the right of asking for a cancellation of the marriage.

Divergence between the schools.

There is great divergence between the Sunni and the Shiah doctrines regarding the power of cancellation given to the parties for the causes referred to, as well as regarding the procedure to be

1 Mafatih; Jam'a-ush-Shittat.

2 *Ibid.*

3 See Alauddin *v.* Farkhanda Akhtar P L D 1953 Lah. 131. In certain circumstances even a mere denial of marriage may amount to its repudiation. The only question is whether the woman is prepared to accept the man as her husband and if she unequivocally says she is not, the option of puberty is thereby exercised.

adopted for enforcing the cancellation. The question of procedure will be discussed in a future chapter;[1] here, attention will be simply directed to the causes for which a marriage may be cancelled among both Sunnis and Shiahs.

Impotency.

Both schools allow a wife to claim a cancellation on the ground of confirmed and incurable impotency, if she married him in ignorance of this circumstance.[2] The principle applies equally to those whose impotence arises from permanent infirmity and those whose incapacity is the result of mutilation, self-inflicted or otherwise. But in the first case, if the debility be only temporary and capable of being cured, it is not a sufficient cause for cancellation of the marriage.[3]

Sunni doctrines. Shiah rule.

According to the Sunnis, the wife is entitled to separation if the husband is unable to consummate the marriage with her, notwithstanding that the inability is *special* in her case.[4] According to the Shiahs, if the inability is only *special*, or, as it is called in English Law, *ad hoc*, the wife has no option.[5] Both schools deny the right of cancellation if incapacity supervened after consummation of the marriage, and also if the woman had entered into the contract with a knowledge of the fact that the man was impotent.[6]

General principles—Right to separation not defeated by delay.

It is not necessary for the wife to apply for separation immediately she becomes aware of his inability to consummate. Her right to claim a dissolution of the marriage is not forfeited, "however long the time may be till she is dissatisfied with his condition."[7]

Insanity of wife.

If the wife has any malformation which prevents connubial intercourse or if she happens to be insane at the time of marriage

1 See post.

2 It is the same under the Hebraic Law. Pothier uses almost similar words in describing the right of the wife to claim a divorce for impotence. "Il n'y a qu'une impuissance perpetuelle et incurable, telle que celle qui resulte de la privation de quelqu'une des parties necessaire a la generation qui forme un impechement de marriage"—Pothier, Cont. de Marriage. Same under the Canonical Law.

3 Comp. Pothier; "celle qui n'est que passagere, et dont on peut esperer la guerison ne rend pas la personne en qui elle se rencontre incapable de mariage." Incurable impotency existing at the time of marriage, under the English Law entitles a wife to a nullity of the marriage.

4 Fatawai 'Alamgiri, Vol. I, p. 707; see also Baillie's Dig., 2nd Ed., p. 347.

5 Shara'ya, p. 278.

6 Fatawai 'Alamgiri, Vol. I, p. 709; Fuzul-'Imadia; Fatawai Kazi Khan, Vol. I, p. 298; Shara'ya, p. 298; Jam'a-ush-Shittat.

7 Fatawai 'Alamgiri, Vol. I, p. 709.

See Ghulam Sakina *v.* Falak Sher P L D 1949 Lah. 75. Mere refusal of the wife to have herself examined by a lady doctor cannot be taken to be proof of consummation of marriage. Consummation must be proved by positive evidence.

or suffering from leprosy, the husband has no right to claim separation and thus avoid her claim to dower. He can, however, divorce her; but in that case he has to pay her a moiety of her dower, if the divorce is given before consummation or "valid retirement".

Husband a leper—wife's remedy. Hanafi doctrines.

According to Abu Hanifa and Abu Yusuf, if the husband be a lunatic or suffering from leprosy[1] of either kind, the wife has no right to seek separation. The injustice of this doctrine is obvious, for whilst a husband can easily get rid of a leper wife by divorcing her, Abu Hanifa and Abu Yusuf would give the wife, if the husband should be a leper, no such power.

Fatwa according to Imam Mohammed.

But Imam Mohammed enunciates a different rule. He has laid down, and on this is the *fatwa*, that "the wife is entitled to the option (خيار) in order that she may remove an evil from herself; contrary to the case of a husband, he having it in his power in similar circumstances, to relieve himself by divorce."[2]

It is clear that the jurists who compiled the *Fatawai 'Alamgiri* following the *Hawi-l'il-Kudsi* have adopted Mohammed's rule on the subject. They first quote a part of Mohammed's opinion, *viz*., "that if the madness be occasional, the case is to be adjourned for a year like that of an impotent person; and if at the expiration of the year, the madness is not cured, the woman has an option; and that if the madness be continued, the case is like that of a mutilated husband and *we* have adopted this (opinion)."[3]

Shiah doctrines. Lunacy of the husband.

Under the Shiah Law, in the case of lunacy, the right of a wife is more extended than that possessed by the husband. She is entitled to ask for a cancellation of the marriage on the ground of his mental derangement, whether permanent or occasional, whether it existed before marriage or supervened after marriage.[4]

In the case of the insanity of the wife, the derangement must be *cofirmed* and must have existed from before marriage in order to entitle the husband to have the marriage cancelled. Occassional

1 (جنون او برص او جذام)

2 Hedaya, chap. XI, Grady's Ed., p. 128.

3 Fatawai 'Alamgiri, Vol. I, p. 711. In any case, it is clear that the enunciations of Abu Hanifa and Abu Yusuf have not been acted upon in their entirety. And I submit that having regard to the rule of the Musulman Law which declares it to be the duty of the judge to follow the enunciation of any of these Imams that he considers most conformable to equity, the rule of Mohammed should furnish the governing principle in British Indian Courts.

4 Shara'ya-ul-Islam, p. 287.

See section 2(*vi*) of the Dissolution of Muslim Marriages Act, 1939. Insanity of 2 years' duration is a ground for dissolution of marriage.

aberrations or stupors, though of frequent occurrence, do not give to the husband that right.[1]

Wife's insanity.

Thus *continued* and *confirmed* insanity gives the husband, under the Shiah Law, the right to cancel the marriage.

He has the same right if the woman is afflicted with blindness or leprosy or is so malformed that cohabitation is impossible. In the case of lunacy, blindness and leprosy, his right of cancellation depends on the fact that he was unaware at the time of the marriage that the wife was deranged, blind or diseased. If he knowingly entered into the contract the right naturally falls to the ground. In the case of malformation the right comes into existence on his discovering the fact—"provided the defect cannot be removed or has resisted the usual remedies."[2]

Husband a leper—Shiah doctrines.

Whether the wife can cancel the marriage if she finds after marriage the husband to be a leper or afflicted with blindness is not clearly stated in the *Shara'ya*, but inferentially it would appear that she would have such a right—for in the case of a woman, it is declared that "she cannot be *rejected* for any other than the seven blemishes mentioned above". But in the case of a man, it is stated that the wife can cancel the marriage for the husband's insanity, eunuchism or impotence—but it is not stated that she may not obtain relief for any other cause.[3]

In all the cases referred to, the married parties have only an option. The husband or the wife may, on becoming aware of the nature of the disease with which the one or the other is afflicted, agree either to abide by the contract or to ask for a cancellation.

In the latter contingency the right must be exercised with as little delay, as possible. Unreasonable delay in availing one's self of the right would give rise to the presumption of acquiescence and waiver.

Fraud and misrepresentation—Shiah doctrines.

If one of the parties to a contract has been induced by the other to enter into it on fraudulent misrepresentations, he or she has the right to ask for a cancellation, or, under the Shiah Law, to cancel it of his or her own motion, on becoming aware of the fraud (*tadlis*). Even in the Shiah Law, however, it is recommended to obtain the *imprimatur* of the *Hakim-ush-shar'a* (the judge).

---

1 Jam'a-ush-Shittat; comp. Baillie's Imameea Law, p. 59.

2 Shara'ya, p. 288.

3 See section 2(vi) of the Dissolution of Muslim Marriages Act, 1939, Insanity, leprosy or a virulent venereal disease in the husband is a ground for dissolution of marriage.

Sunni doctrines.

Where legitimacy or equality is a special condition of the marriage contract and the man represents himself as legitimate, and it is proved afterwards that he is illegitimate, or represents himself as his wife's equal in birth when in fact he is much her inferior, the woman has a right to cancel the marriage.[1]

In all cases where marriage is cancelled by the exercise of the right of option vested in one or the other party, the separation has not the same effect as a divorce. Accordingly, when there has been no consummation, actual or constructive, the wife has no right to dower.

CHAPTER VIII

EFFECT OF CHANGE OF RELIGION ON THE STATUS OF MARRIAGE

Native Converts' Marriage Dissolution Act (XXI of 1866).

THE Native Converts' Marriage Dissolution Act (XXI of 1866) was specially designed to meet the case of converts to Christianity from Hinduism and other cognate systems which do not recognise the dissolution of a marriage once contracted. It exempts, however, from its purview Mahommedans, Christians and Jews. It defines a "native husband" to mean a married man domiciled in British India, who shall have completed the age of sixteen years and shall not be a Christian, Mahommedan or Jew: a "native wife" to mean a married woman domiciled in British India, who shall have completed the age of thirteen years and shall not be a Christian, a Mahommedan or a Jewess; and "native law" to mean any law or custom having the force of law, of any person domiciled in British India other than Christians, Mahommedans and Jews. And it lays down certain rules under which a "native husband" or "native wife" adopting *Christianity* may obtain release from the marriage-tie previously contracted. But the benefits of those rules are not extended to conversions to any other Faith.

Conversion to the Islamic Faith—The injustice of the provisions of the Act.

Christianity and Islam are the only two proselytising religions in India, and conversions to Islam are frequently as sincere as conversions to Christianity. But no "native husband" or "native wife" adopting Islam is entitled to come to the Court to obtain the relief provided in the Act. Their *status* is not allowed to be governed by the laws of the new Faith, but continues to be subject to the law or custom to which they were subject before.

According to the Musulman Law conversion to the Islamic Faith on the part of a man following any of the revealed or

---

1 Fatawai Kazi Khan, Sect. on Equality.

Scriptural (*Kitabia*) religions, such as Judaism and Christianity,[1] does not lead to a dissolution of his marriage with a woman belonging to his old creed. For example, if a Hebrew or a Christian husband were to adopt Islam and the wife were to continue to follow the religion of her people the marriage remains *lawful and binding*.[2]

Conversion to Islam of a non-Scripturalist.

When the parties are non-Scripturalist and one of them embraces the Musulman Faith in a country subject to the laws of Islam, the *Dar-ul-Islam*, Islam should be offered to the other, and if the latter adopts it, the marriage will remain intact, otherwise the judge should separte the couple. If the party to whom Islam is offered "remains silent and says nothing", the judge is to offer Islam for his or her acceptance three times in succession, and on his or her still remaining obdurate to decree separation. There is no difference between a discreet youth and one who is adult; so that a separation is to be made equally on the refusal of the former as of the latter, according to Abu Hanifa and Mohammed. But, if one of the parties be young and without sufficient discernment, it is necessary to wait till he attains discretion; and when he attains the age of discretion Islam is then to be offered to him; should he adopt it the marriage will remain intact, if not; a separation is to be made without waiting for his arriving at puberty. And if he be mad, Islam is to be presented to his parents; and if they or one of them should embrace it, the marriage will continue binding, if not, a separation is to be made between the married parties. If the husband should embrace the faith and the wife should refuse, the separation does not amount to *repudiation*, but if the wife should embrace the faith, and the husband were to decline, and a separation is made in consequence, the separation amounts to a *talak*, according to Abu Hanifa and Mohammed.[3] When a separation takes place between them by reason of his refusal, and it is after consummation, she is entitled to the whole dower; and if it is before consummation, and through his refusal, she is entitled to half the dower but if through her own refusal, she has no dower at all.[4]

In other words, if the conversion to Islam takes place in an Islamic country, the Kazi must be moved to summon the other party to adopt the Moslem Faith. In case of compliance the marriage remains intact and valid *ab initio*; and

1 Some Mahommedan lawyers make a distinction between Zoroastrianism, the religion of Zartusht or Zardahusht (Zoroaster) and Magianism (pyrolatry). The one is regarded as a revealed or scriptural religion, whilst the other is considered no better than idolatry. This view is now becoming general in the Islamic world.

2 See Farooq Leivers *v.* Adelaide Bridget Mary P L D 1958 Lah. 431.

3 Islam being an act of piety, is not a ground for separation, but the obdurate rejection of it.—Hedaya, Vol. I, p. 178. There is an exception, when the husband is a convert to Islam and the wife a Kitabia (Scripturalist), because the marriage is, as stated above, still lawful.

4 Because the cause of saparation proceeds from her.

there is no need for renewing the contract, though in practice it is sometimes done. Until the Judge has made his decree separating the parties the connection remains *invalid* and has all the consequences flowing from an invalid connection.

Conversion of a Scripturalist woman to Islam.

But when the adoption of Islam (in the case of non-Scripturalists) takes place in a country where the Laws of Islam *are not in force,* the dissolution of the marriage is suspended until the wife has completed three of "her terms", whether cohabitation had taken place or not.[1] And on the completion of the "terms" the marriage is definitely dissolved, and she can marry again. Where the parties are Scripturalists and the wife becomes a convert to Islam, the same procedure has to be followed, *viz.*, if the conversion takes place in a country subject to the laws of Islam, the Faith will be offered for acceptance to the husband, and on his refusal the Judge will make a decree for separation or cancellation of the marriage. But if the wife were to become a Moslemah, in a non-Islamic country, and the husband should also adopt the Faith before the completion of three of "her terms," the marriage would remain subsisting, otherwise they would become separated on such completion *without any decree or order of the Judge.*[2]

The Calcutta High Court has held[3] that India is not a non-Islamic country, and that consequently when a married non-Moslem woman adopts the Mahommedan Faith, and thereafter, contract a fresh marriage without applying to a Judge or a Magistrate to call upon the husband to adopt Islam, she is guilty of bigamy. As Act XXI of 1866 does not apply to conversions to Islam, if such an application were made to the civil or criminal court, it would certainly be rejected. The learned Judges in the case referred to do not say what would happen on the refusal of the Judge or Magistrate to listen to the prayer of the woman, or if the husband declined to accede to her demand. It is to be presumed, that the principle was enunciated for satisfying the Court's conscience and that on her making the application, the first marriage would be regarded as dissolved on the expiration of three *courses* or three months.

---

1 *Viz.* three courses of nature. As Islam cannot be formally presented for acceptance in a foreign country, the separation is effected by abstinence for three successive occurrences of the courses.

2 If the woman is past the age, the marriage would come to an end on the expiration of three months.

This authority has been dissented from in Ayesha Bibi *v.* Subodh Chakravarty A I R 1949 Cal. 486 where Ormond, J. on the basis of the proposal put forward by the All India Muslim League under the heading of a proposed establishment of Independent sovereign State in India to be known as Pakistan, held that the then British Government in India was not a Government of Islamic rule, and that India was not Darul Islam at least for the matters of law and procedure concerned in the matter of offering Islam by the converted spouse to the other.

3 In the matter of the Petition of Ram Kumari (1891) I L 18 Cal. 236.

Conversion of the wife to Islam.

When a non-Moslem female married to a husband who also is a non-Moslem, adopts Islam, and her union becomes dissolved under the provisions of the Mahommedan Law, as stated above, she is entitled to contract a valid marriage in accordance with the Musulman rites. The issue of such second marriage are legitimate. The decision, therefore, in *Sundari Letani* v. *Petambari Letani*[1] is in absolute conflict with the recognised rule of the Mahommedan Law.

When a non-Moslem husband and wife, married according to the rites of their professed faith, subsequently adopt Islam, their marriage remains intact; but in practice, it has been considered safer to contract a fresh marriage according to Mahommedan rites. After their adoption of the Musulman religion their rights and *status* are subject to the rules of the Musulman Law. This principle has received judicial recognition in the case of *Skinner* v. *Skinner*.[2]

In this case it appeared that two persons, a man and a woman, were married as professed Christians in a Church, and that subsequently they had adopted Islam and gone through the Mahommedan form of marriage. The husband died leaving a will excluding the wife from all participation in his estate. It was held by the Judicial Committee that the personal *status* of the deceased being at the time of his death that of a Mahommedan, and the plaintiff's personal *status* being that of his wife under the same law, she was entitled to a share in his estate notwithstanding his will which purported, but under the Mahommedan Law was inoperative, to exclude her.

"When both the parties are *mustmins* [Non-Moslems who have taken up their abode in an Islamic country under the guarantee of protection], absolute separation is effected between them by presenting Islam to the other, or by the expiration of three 'terms'. The 'terms' in these instances do not constitute an '*iddat*, and for that reason there is no difference between a wife with whom cohabitation has taken place and

---

1 (1904) 9 C W N 1903.

2 (1897), L R 25 I A 34; s. c. I L 25 Cal. 531; 2 C W N 219. Comp. Gobardhan Dass *v.* Jassodamoni Dassi (1891) I L 18 Cal. 252, in which it was held that the adoption of Christianity by a Hindu husband and wife did not *ipso facto* dissolve their previously contracted union. The same rule is in force in the Mahommedan Law.

See Noor Jehan *v.* Eugene Tischence A I R 1941 Cal. 582. The main distinction which has been drawn by the Muslim jurists is between a conversion which takes place in an Islamic country where both parties to the marriage may be brought before the Kazi, and a conversion which takes place in a country, which is not subject to the laws of Islam. In the former case it is laid down in the Hedaya that Islam is to be presented to the unconverted party by the Kazi and on refusal to embrace the faith, the Kazi must pronounce a decree of divorce. In the latter case the dissolution of marriage takes place automatically after the completion of the wife's three terms.

one with whom it has not, and whenever a separation takes place on this account before consummation, there is no *'iddat*; nor is there any though the separation should take place after consummation, if the woman be an alien non-Moslem; and even though she were a Moslemah, the result would still be the same, according to Abu Hanifa. If the woman, from extreme youth or advanced age, is not subject to the courses, the separation cannot be effected except by the expiration of three months, and if the woman be the convert to Islam, and her husband should come from the *Dar-ul-Harb* as a *Mustamin*, there can be no separation, except by the completion of three 'terms'. And in like manner if he should become a *zimmi*, after having come out a *Mustamin*, so that if his wife should afterwards follow him, Islam is to be presented to him; and if he adopt it, no separation is to be made between them. And so also if the husband be the convert, and the wife comes out as a *zimmia* there is no separation till she has had her 'terms' and should separation take place by the completion of three 'terms', this would amount to a separation by *talak*, according to Abu Hanifa and Mohammed."[1]

These rules refer to the adoption of Islam by one of the non-Moslem emigrant couple in Islamic countries.

Apostasy from Islam.

There is hardly any religious system which does not regard secession from the established religion of the State as tantamount to treason, or does not visit the culprit with punishment of the severest character. So late as the close of the eighteenth century of the Christian era, the Christian churches in Western Europe condemned "heretics" to the stake or the gallows; no distinction was made on the score of sex or age. Even when the growing conscience of the people led to the relaxation of the penalty of death, renunciation of the particular communion to which the seceder belonged was attended with forfeiture of civil rights and exposure to social ostracism and obloquy.

The peculiar and difficult circumstances under which the Church of Islam came into existence made "apostasy" a danger to the State; the abandonment of Islam was tantamount to the renunciation of allegiance to the Islamic Commonwealth; it was nothing short of treason. The law consequently prescribed the death-penalty for the offence but not at the stake, nor by drowning or hanging. The extreme penalty was, however, reserved only for the adult male *murtedd*, the traitor-apostate, and that only when he was a Moslem born. A woman, a youth, a man who had adopted Islam under compulsion, a young man whose parents were not Moslems and a number of other persons similarly circumstanced, were exempt from the death-penalty.[2]

---

1 Fatawai 'Alamgiri, Vol. I, p. 477; the authorities cited have been omitted.

2 Durr-ul-Mukhtar; Fatawai 'Alamgiri, Vol. II, p. 357.

When a woman abandoned Islam, she was to be imprisoned until she returned to the Faith.

These provisions have given birth to a body of rules regarding the matrimonial *status* of persons renouncing Islam.

Shiah doctrines.

Under the Shiah Law, if either of the married parties were to renounce Islam *before* connubial intercourse, the marriage is cancelled *on the instant* and the wife has no right to dower if she be the pervert; but if the husband were to apostatise, she would be entitled to half the dower.

If the renunciation of Islam takes place *after* the parties have cohabited, the cancellation is *suspended* until after the expiration of her *'iddat* whether the apostasy is on his or her part and no part of the dower abates, for the right to it is established by consummation (*dukhul*).[1]

When a Shiah Moslem abandons Islam after consummation of the marriage, it is unlawful for him to have connubial intercourse with his Moslemah wife, and the marriage remains in suspense until the expiration of her *'iddat*. If he has intercourse with her under *shubh* (the semblance of right) and continues in his denial of the Faith till the expiration of her *'iddat*, "the Shaikh,[2]" says the author of the *Shara'ya* "lays down that he (the husband) would be liable for two dowers, one the original dower for the contract, and the other for intercourse under the semblance of right." "With respect to

1 The author of the Shara'ya adds an extraordinary qualification to this rule. He says, "if the husband is born in the religion of *fitrat*, the marriage becomes dissolved instantly although cohabitation may have taken place, for his return (to the Faith) cannot be accepted."

Mr. Baillie construes *fitrat* by the word 'Islam', the use of which is carefully avoided by the author of the *Shara'ya*. He also renders (لا يقبل) by the words "is not allowed" which is not correct: see Baillie's Dig. of the Imameeah Law, p. 29.

To understand the meaning of the word *al-fitrat*, it is necessary to bear in mind the traditional saying of the Prophet—"every child [of man] is born (على الفطرة) religiously constituted [or born in the religion of nature]: it is his parents who make him a Jew, Christian or Magian':' (see the Siprit of Islam, p. 376). The evident meaning is that every human being is naturally a worshipper of God; training and education make him the professor of particular creeds. The author of the *Shara'ya* adopts the expression in the *hadis* and uses it in an exclusive sense. His qualification is not a rule of law, but rather a theoretical enunciation of ecclesiastical discipline. It may well be that the passage itself is an interpolation by some zealous Mujtahid, a suggestion which, from the context, appears to be more than plausible.

As may be imagined the harsh doctrine embodied in the qualification has not received support from other legists. A large body of jurists among them Ibn Idris make no distinction between a Moslem by birth and a Moslem by conversion.

2 The author of the Mabsut, Shaikh-ul 'Allamah Abu J'afar of Tus.

this, (however), there is a difficulty for she is still subject to the rules of a wife [until the expiration of her '*iddat*]."[1]

The issue of the connection if any, would be legitimate, and their *nasab* would be established in the father.[2]

Shaf'eite doctrines.

The Shaf'eis agree with the Shiahs that when either of the spouses renounces Islam after consummation, the marriage would become dissolved on the expiration of three courses of the woman. *It follows, therefore, that until then the marriage is in suspense.*

Hanafi doctrines.

Among the Hanafis, according to the old lawyers, whose views are enunciated in the *Hedaya*, the *Fatawai 'Alamgiri* and other works, apostasy from Islam of either husband or wife whether it takes place before or after consummation dissolves, *ipso facto*, the marriage-tie. And the Indian Courts have given effect to this doctrine without, it is submitted, sufficient consideration of the development that has taken place within the last three centuries in Hanafi legal conceptions regarding the effect of apostacy of one or other of the married parties on the marriage relationship. For example, in *Amin Beg* v. *Saman*[3] the High Court of Allahabad has held that under the Mahommedan law a wife's conversion from Islam to Christianity effects a complete dissolution of the marriage with her husband and the fact of such conversion was, therefore, a "bar" to a suit on his part for restitution of conjugal rights.[4]

Similarly, in a criminal case in which it was found that a Musulman husband had abandoned Islam, and his wife had after his apostasy contracted a second marriage, the Calcutta High Court held that a charge of bigamy brought by him on his return to Islam could not lie against her as her marriage with the complainant had become dissolved immediately on his renunciation of Islam.[5]

---

1 The author of the Shara'ya then adds the same qualification as before, "provided he (the husband) was born in the *fitrat*." The manner in which these words are introduced strengthens the belief that they have been interpolated.

2 See ante, Chapter on Legitimacy.

3 (1910) I L 33 All. 90. This case followed a previous decision of the N.-W. P. High Court, Zubardust Khan *v.* His Wife (1870) 2 N.-W. P. H. C., 376 and a Punjab case, Imamdin *v.* Aman Bibi (1906) Punjab Records 809.

See Ghaus *v.* Mst. Faiji A I R 1915 Lah. 14: and Sardar Mohammed *v.* Mst. Maryam Bibi A I R 1936 Lah. 666.

4 *See* section 4 of the Dissolution of Muslim Marriages Act, 1939 according to which the renunciation of Islam by a married Muslim woman or her conversion to a faith other than Islam shall not by itself dissolve her marriage.

5 Abdul Ghani *v.* Azizul Huq (1911) I L 39 Cal. 409.

As already observed, these decisions are founded on the enunciations of the older jurists. The modern lawyers, on the contrary, hold that when the husband renounces Islam and the wife continues in the Faith, the connection becomes unlawful, but if the man were to return to Islam *before* the expiration of the wife's *'iddat* [the probation she has to observe as if he were dead], there would be no need for a re-marriage between the parties. This seems clear from the doctrine enunciated in the *Radd-ul-Muhtar*[1] that if a Moslem were to abandon the Faith and to take refuge in a Non-Moslem country and were then to divorce his wife, the divorce would not be effective. But if he were to return to Islam whilst she was still in her *'iddat* and were then to give the divorce, it would be operative.

The passage quoted above shows conclusively that the marriage does not become dissolved instantly the man abandons Islam, for if it were otherwise a divorce pronounced by him after his return to the Faith could have no effect whatever as the status of marriage had already come to an end. In other words, the *status* of marriage remains in suspense until the wife has completed her probation.

As regards the effect of the wife's abjuration of Islam on the *status* of marriage there is the same divergence of opinion between the ancient and the modern jurists. The lawyers of Bokhara, who adhere to the doctrines of the ancients (*mutakkadamin*) hold that whatever the religion she adopts, she should be imprisoned until she returns to the Faith, when she should be constrained to re-marry her former husband on a very small dower. The object of the doctrine they propounded as they declared, was to prevent woman from trying to escape from the bonds of matrimony by the abandonment of Islam. The jurists of Balkh and Samarkand, on the other hand, have laid down that when a woman abjures Islam for a Scriptural or revealed religion like Judaism or Christianity, *her renunciation of the Faith does not dissolve the marriage*. Their arguments in support of their contention are as already stated, two-fold. In the first place they say that as a marriage between a Moslem and a Scripturalist woman (*Kitabia*) is lawful under the Musulman Law, the adoption of a revealed religion by a Moslem woman cannot affect the *status* of marriage. In the second place, they contend that when the circumstances of the age are such that a woman abandoning Islam can neither be imprisoned nor constrained to re-enter the fold of the Faith, to hold that abjuration of the Islamic Faith dissolves the marriage-tie would further the very object for

---

1 Radd-ul-Muhtar, Vol. II, p. 643, and Vol. III, p. 465. In the original the words are "if an apostate removes to the Dar-ul-Harb (an alien country where the laws of Islam are not in force), and there divorces his wife, it will not be effective, &c." His removal to an alien country makes no difference in the principle; for this removal is merely with the object of escaping the penalty of death.

which she apostatises, *viz.*, to "release herself of the burden of marriage."[1]

Although the Indian Courts have preferred to follow the extreme Bokhariot view, I submit the more reasonablee nunciations of the jurists of Balkh and Samarkand, furnish the guiding principle for tribunals who have by their constitution to act according to "justice, equity and good conscience."

The decisions of the British Indian Courts seem to overlook a fundamental difference between the case of a man and that of a woman abjuring Islam. In both cases the apostates are liable to punishment and forfeiture of civil rights, with this difference that whilst a man is subject to the penalty of death, a woman may only be imprisoned until she recants.

The ancient lawyers held that apostasy on the part of the husband "occasions" a *talak bain*, that in other words it amounts to an irrevocable divorce. But nowhere is it laid down that the effect of the apostacy on the marriage relationship absolves the wife from the rule relating to the observance of the prescribed *'iddat*. A woman is prohibited from remarrying during her *'iddat*. The question then arises what is the position of the parties during the term of the *'iddat* in the case of a *talak bain*? Suppose the parties resume cohabitation during the *'iddat*, will the Indian Courts be justified by their constitution to hold that such cohabitation was unlawful or that the issue of the connection born after such cohabitation were illegitimate? I consider any such conclusion would be most unwarrantable.

If after the expiration of the *'iddat*, whether it be in consequence of the husband's apostasy or of a *talak*, the woman re-marries, such marriage would be unquestionably valid. A re-marriage within the *'iddat* however, would not be valid, but the woman cannot be convicted of bigamy, not because the marriage was dissolved on the instant of the apostasy, but because the second marriage was contracted under *shubh*. This was evidently the line of argument adopted by Mr. Justice Holmwood in the Calcutta case referred to above, in conformity with the Musulman Law which declares that where less a marriage is contracted under such circumstances the parties are not liable to *hadd*.[2]

As regards the case of a woman, the position is different. She is not liable to the death-penalty; by apostatising she makes herself subject to incarceration until such time as she abandons the new faith and returns to Islam. One of the reasons, therefore,

---

1 The whole argument is set forth in the Radd-ul-Muhtar, Vol. II, p. 644, see also the Fath-ul-Kadir and Nahr-ul-Faik.

2 Abdul Ghani *v.* Azizul Huq, supra.

on which is based the doctrine of instant dissolution of the marriage-tie on apostasy, does not apply to her case.

Where the ancient doctors say that on the apostasy of a husband or wife there "occurs a *talak bain*", it means that the rights which spring from marriage cease ; this is a logical consequence of the deprivation of civil rights as part of the penalty for abjuration of Islam. But they do not lay down that, where the man apostatises, the wife is absolved from the obligation of observing the '*iddat* before she can re-marry, or that the husband has no right of condoning the wife's apostasy from Islam.

The Indian Courts in their adherence to the strict letter of the ancient doctrine have, it is submitted, missed the spirit of the enunciation; and have, accordingly, treated in the case of a wife as a privilege what was intended to be a punishment. By the interpretation put on the rule, a Musulman woman is thus enabled to obtain by a simple abjuration of Islam a dissolution of the marriage-tie which had become irksome. The enforcement of the Musulman Law in its entirety regarding apostates has become impossible under existing conditions in most countries inhabited by Moslems. A husband abandoning Islam cannot be punished by death; nor a woman abjuring the Faith can be liable to incarceration. Shortly stated, apostasy has ceased, especially in these countries, to be a State offence. It is absured and contrary to the principles of justice that one part of the rule should be enforced whilst the other should be ignored.

The legal position of the married parties one of whom abandons Islam must therefore be determined on principles of the Musulman Law other than those relating to apostasy. For example, it is the general rule that a non-Moslem cannot contract a valid marriage with a Moslemah; according to the majority of lawyers it is an illegal union. Consequently, when a Moslem husband abandons Islam, his connection with his wife becomes an illegal or at any rate an invalid connection. And the woman, accordingly, on the expiration of her '*iddat* can marry someone else.

But a Moslem can enter into a valid contract of marriage with a woman following any of the Scriptural faiths. All the legal cousequences (save as regards the right of inheritance, the reason for which is to be found in another principle) which flow from an union between two Islamists, arise out of such marriage. Suppose, then, a Musulman wife abandons Islam and embraces Judaism or Christianity, there is no inherent vice in the continuance of the contract as a valid contract. It is only as a State offence that the ecclesiastical law pronounces against her a forfeiture of civil rights. But when that law is unenforceable, the union remains as valid as it would be were the wife a Jew or a Christian at the time of marriage.[1]

When the Musulman husband and wife both abandon Islam and adopt another faith the marriage remains intact by consensus.

---

1 See section 4, Dissolution of Muslim Marriages Act, 1939.

CHAPTER IX

MARRIAGE UNDER THE SHIAH LAW

The Shiah Law has already been sufficiently indicated in the preceding pages, but it may be useful to give a few more principles.

Marriage how contracted.

According to the *Mafatih*.—"In contracting a marriage, it is allowable to use an expression in the imperative mood, or in the future tense, but not any other."

"If either of the contracting parties be unable to speak the Arabic language, then he or she should employ any language that must be best known to him or to her. And if either of them be unable to speak at all, or be dumb, in such a case it would be sufficient if he or she were to indicate the contract by a sign or hint".

This is amplified in the *Tahrir-ul-Ahkam*: "The contracting parties, if able (to speak), are required to use such expression as would indicate declaration and acceptance. But if both are, or one of them is, unable to speak, then a sign on the part of the person unable to speak, such as would indicate his or her assent, would be sufficient."

Acknowledgment of marriage.

When a man has declared himself to be the husband of a woman, and she has assented to the truth of the declaration, or when a woman has declared herself to be the wife of a man, and he has acquiesced therein, they are adjudged to be ostensibly married, as having mutual rights of inheritance. "But", says the *Shara'ya*, "if one of them alone made such declaration, judgment for the effects of the contract is to be given against him or her alone, and not against the other."[2] This refers to a case where a claim is put forward to the estate of a deceased person on the ground that the claimant is the widow or husband of the deceased. In such a case, though a liability would attach to the claimant, no right would accrue to him or her as against the other.

As under the Sunni Law, it is necessary that the bride, contracted in marriage, should be distinguished from others by some distinguishing characteristics either by name or by description.

1 Shara'ya, p. 262.

2 *Ibid.*, p. 263.

A marriage contracted by a *mariz* (a person suffering from a serious illness) does not give rise to any right unless there has been *copula*; so if he should die of that illness without consummating the marriage, it would have no effect, and the woman would not be entitled either to dower or to inheritance.

Prohibited degrees.

Seven classes of women are prohibited to a man for consanguinity, namely: (*i*) the mother, and all female ancestors; (*ii*) the daughter and daughter's daughter how-low-soever, and son's daughters to the lowest degree in descent, in other words, all female descendants; (*iii*) sisters, whether by the same father or by the same mother only, or by both parents; (*iv*) sisters' daughters, and their female descendants; (*v*) paternal aunts, whether they be the father's sisters of the whole or of the half-blood, as also the sisters of his grandfathers how-high-soever, (*vi*) maternal aunts by the same father or by the same mother alone, or by both parents; as also father's as well as mother's maternal aunts how-remote-soever in ascent ; (*vii*) female descendents of his brother of the whole or half-blood.[1]

All consanguineous relatives are prohibited, except the children of paternal and maternal uncles and aunts how-high-soever.

The like classes of men are prohibited to a woman; so that her father and all male ascendants, all male descendants, her brother and his male descendants, her sister's male descendants, her paternal uncle how-high-soever, and her maternal uncle how-remote-soever, are unlawful to her.

Affinity.

By reason of affinity a man is prohibited from marrying the mother and all female ancestors how-high-soever, and the daughters and female descendants, how-low-soever, of a wife. So also is a man prohibited from marrying his father's wife or the wife of any ancestor how-high-soever.[2]

The prohibitions of affinity spring both from a valid marriage as well as from fornication. For example, if a man has illicit intercourse with a woman, her daughter is forbidden to him, as if the woman was actually married to him. So also if a man marries a woman who happens to have a daughter by a prior marriage, the latter will be forbidden to him.

"If a man married a woman, but did not consummate the marriage, still her mother is for ever unlawful to him, and all her female descendants how-low-soever, are also prohibited to be married to him in conjunction with herself."

If there has been only a contract of marriage but no consummation, the woman, nevertheless, would be unlawful to the father

1 Shara'ya, p. 266.

2 Mafatih.

and the son of the man, but the woman's daughter is unlawful to him not in herself, but only in conjunction with her mother, so that if the man should separate himself from the woman [before consummation], he may lawfully marry her daughter.[1]

Zina.

Zina or fornication, though a prohibitory cause, has no retrospective effect. In other words, an illicit intercourse with any female relative of the wife, subsequent to the marriage, does not vitiate her marriage.

If a man were to marry a woman who was observing the probation (*'iddat*), whether for divorce or death, with a knowledge on his part of that fact and also of the unlawfulness of the union, under such circumstances the parties should be separated. If the marriage was followed by cohabitation, the woman would become unlawful to him "for ever". If the parties separated before cohabitation, according to the *Jam'a-ush-Shittat* he can enter into a fresh contract after the expiration of her *'iddat*. The same view is enunciated in the *Shara'ya-ul-Islam*.

But if he were to marry her in ignorance of her being in the state of *'iddat* or in ignorance of the fact that such a marriage was illegal, and cohabitation followed and a child was born of the union, within the period provided by law, such child would be affiliated to the man.[2]

The parties must, nevertheless, be separated, but the husband must pay the wife the dower specified in the contract. After separation, the woman must complete the *'iddat* for the first marriage and afterwards observe another for the second.[3]

If a man were to commit adultery with a married woman whose husband was alive, or who was in her *'iddat* for a *revocable* divorce, she would become perpetually unlawful to him, according to the generally received opinion.[4]

But fornication with a widow, or with a woman who was not observing *'iddat* for a revocable divorce, or with an unmarried woman, does not, without any difference of opinion, prohibit her to him, and consequently he may lawfully marry her, however profligate she may be.

When a *muhrim* (person engaged in the performance of the *Hajj*) enters into a contract of marriage with a woman engaged in the same duty, knowing that it is not lawful for him to do so, she is for ever unlawful to him. But if he were not aware of the illegality, then, though that contract is vitiated, the woman herself is not prohibited to him (that is, he may lawfully enter into another contract with her).

---

1 Shara'ya, pp. 271, 272.

2 *Ibid*, pp. 272, 273.

3 *Ibid.*

4 *Ibid.*, p. 278, comp. the Tahrir-ul-Ahkam.

Equality.

As regards "equality" two conditions alone are insisted upon: (*i*) equality in respect of Islam, in other words, the general profession of the Islamic religion, and (*ii*) ability to support the wife.[1] And the democratic principle is carried so far that it is declared to be lawful for a free woman to marry a slave, for an Arab woman to marry a Persian, and even for a Hashimite woman to marry a man of another family, and *vice versa*.

When the *wali* of a woman marries her to a person who is not her equal,[2] she has a right to cancel the contract, though such contract would be binding upon her when entered into by herself.

Where a man has married a woman, and afterwards discovers that she had been previously guilty of fornication, he has no right to cancel the marriage, nor has he a claim against her guardian to refund the dower.

Guardianship in marriage.

Except a father and grandfather, no other relation nor the Judge has the power of contracting a minor in marriage. As regards an adult, neither the father nor the grandfather has any power. Should the father or grandfather refuse to marry an adult and discreet virgin girl to an equal, when desired by her to do so, she can contract herself even against their will.

An executor or executrix cannot act as a guardian in marriage, not even if the father had authorised him or her to do so, whether the (testator's) daughter be an infant or adult, and whether the father had or had not fixed a husband for his infant daughter. An executor, however, can contract in marriage a person who is of unsound mind, when it is for the latter's advantage.

Option of puberty.

When a person, other than the father or grandfather, contracts a minor, male or female, in marriage, its validity depends upon the ratification of the party for whom the contract is entered into; in other words, it is inoperative until it is distinctly ratified by the minor on attaining majority.

A woman adult and discreet cannot only marry of her own accord and authority, but appoint an agent to contract her in marriage and can herself act as an agent in another's marriage.

———

1 See ante.

2 *Ibid.*

CHAPTER X

TEMPORARY MARRIAGES

Temporary marriages—Akhbari doctrines.

Temporary marriages are regarded as lawful by the Akhbari Shiahs. This peculiar institution, analogues of which are not unknown among Western communities,[1] flourished among the Sabeans and Zoroastrians from early times, and seems to have continued in force among those people even after their conversion to Islam in spite of the prohibition of the Prophet.[2] Such marriages are known as *muta'a*, and are contracted for a fixed period of time,—as for a day, a month, or a year, or for any other specified period: The Sunnis and the M'utazilas regard such unions as *invalid*.

Declaration and acceptance are considered as essential in this kind of marriage also. But the forms of expression by which such an union may be contracted are given as follows:—

"The proper terms expressive of declaration are '*zawajtu-ka*', '*m'uttatu-ka*' ('I have united myself to thee') and '*ankahtu-ka*' ('I have married thee'); by any of these, declaration is effected, and by none other than any of these can the contract be made."

At the same time, it is declared to be abominable, though not actually prohibited, to marry in the *muta'a* form a virgin girl who has no father; and if one should do so, says the *Shara'ya*, he ought to refrain from connubial intercourse with her; the reason being that as such a marriage is to her prejudice, and she has had no paternal advice or guidance in the matter, she should not be subject to the degradation of a temporary union.

Specification of dower necessary.

The specification of dower is an essential condition to a contract in the *muta'a* form, and upon failure of this, the contract itself is void. In this respect, it differs from a permanent contract of marriage.

Period must be fixed.

The second essential condition is that the period for which the contract is made should be specifically fixed. If there be no mention of the period, *the contract would become permanent*.[3]

The extent of the period is left to the parties, but it is necessary that some limit should be distinctly specified, so as to

1 See Hepworth Dixon's New America.

2 See ante.

3 Shara'ya, pp. 280, 281.

guard against any extension or diminution. "Even if the time be shortened to any part of a day, the contract would be lawful, provided that its limit is distinctly known."[1]

After stating these general principles, the *Shara'ya* proceeds to lay down certain rules for the determination of these contracts.

(*a*) When the term and dower both have been mentioned, the contract is valid; but if there is a failure in respect of the dower, while the term is mentioned, the contract is void; but if there is a failure in respect of the time (while the dower is mentioned), the contract, though reckoned void as a *muta'a*, is valid as a permanent marriage.[2]

(*b*) Every condition stipulated for in this contract must be mentioned together with the declaration and acceptance, and no effect can be given to any stipulation previous to the contract unless the same be repeated at that time, nor to any condition made thereafter. As regards, however, the condition that has been mentioned in the contract, there is no necessity for its repetition after it.

(*c*) According to the generally received views, an adult and discreet female may contract herself in a *muta'a* marriage, and her *wali* would have no right to object, whether she be a virgin or not. But it is unlawful for a minor girl to marry except with the consent of her guardian, as it is abominable for a man to marry a fatherless virgin by the *muta'a* form.

No division in muta'a marriage.

(*d*) According to the generally received opinion, a woman so married *cannot be divorced*, but the parties become absolutely separated upon the expiration of the period. Nor is the woman subject to *l'aan*.[3]

Right of inheritance.

(*e*) A temporary contract of marriage creates no right of inheritance in either party. Whether an express stipulation that they should inherit from each other, or that only one of them should inherit from the other, creates such a right is a question on which the jurists are not agreed. According to the author of the *Shara'ya-ul-Islam*, and apparently also the author of the *Tahrir-ul-Ahkam*, a stipulation of this nature has no effect "according to the best report". Whilst another body of lawyers, among them the Shaikh, hold that when there is an express condition, the parties are entitled to inherit to each other.

1 Shara'ya, pp. 280, 281.

2 *Ibid*, p. 281.

3 See post.

Children legitimate.

The children born of such an union are, without difference of opinion, legitimate and inherit from their parents like the issue of a permanent contract.

(*f*) In this form of marriage the woman's probation extends only for two terms when consummation has taken place. The '*iddat* of a widow, however, is four months and ten days, but if she is pregnant it lasts until the delivery.

The *Tahrir-ul-Ahkam*, says that "a man may lawfully marry in the *muta'a* form wives above four, without limit, whether the women be free or slaves", though it adds that "the best opinion, however, is not to marry more than four."

If the man were to make to the woman a gift of the term (that is, to waive his right to her) before cohabitation, he would be liable for half the dower; but when consummation has taken place, she becomes entitled to the whole dower "on condition of her keeping the term (and adhering to him till its completion); but if it is not completed, the man is entitled to deduct a proportionate part of the dower".[1]

Maintenance.

The wife is not entitled to any maintenance under this form of marriage, unless it is expressly stipulated in the contract, but when there is a stipulation to that effect, she would be entitled to receive the maintenance during the whole term, even if the husband were to choose not to cohabit with her or, what is called, "to waive the term."

There are other points of difference between a *permanent* and a *temporary* contract of marriage. For example, when the parties are married by a *permanent* contract, the husband cannot refuse *procreation*. In a temporary contract, he is entitled to do so. In other words, what is called '*izl*[2] is allowed. "The practice of '*izl*", says the *shara'ya* "is lawful with a *muta'a* wife and is not dependant on her permission." If notwithstanding the '*izl* she bears a child, it is affiliated to the temporary husband; but if he should deny the paternity and allege that it is not born of his loins, "the denial is to be sustained apparently without any necessity for *l'aan*.[3]

The use of the word "apparently" shows that the lawyers are not agreed on the point and that the view is by no means certain.

---

1 Shara'ya, pp. 280, 281.

2 Extrahere ante emissionem seminis. In a permanent contract both according to the Sunnis and the Shiahs, there can be no 'izl, as being contrary to the purpose for which marriage is instituted, whereas these may be in this.

3 Shara'ya, p. 282.

"Gift of the term".

As already stated, "there is no divorce in this form of marriage";[1] in other words, the husband has no power to divorce the wife during the term fixed; the contract being for a stipulated period fixed by mutual consent comes to an end either by the efflux of the time so fixed or by the death of either of the parties. They may, however, dissolve the convenient relationship by mutual consent. This restriction on the power of divorce in marriages for stipulated periods seems to have proved irksome to some of the Akhbari legists, and thereupon they hit upon a device, the ingenuity of which is equalled by its injustice. "In order to effectuate a discharge or release (*ibra*) the *consent* of the debtor is not necessary; the wife in a *muta'a* marriage is only a debtor, the husband is the creditor, *ergo* the husband can 'give away' the term or any portion thereof without the wife's consent." So argued these learned legists, and this argument is to be found word for word in the *Sharh-ul-Lum'a*. If this argument be correct, a man might induce a woman, of whose person he cannot otherwise possess himself to enter into a *muta'a* marriage for a period of ninety-nine years, which is tantamount to a lifelong contract, and after satisfying his lust, might throw her off at any time he likes—by simply declaring that he has made "a gift of the term".

As I have already pointed out in the chapters on *Hiba*,[2] there is great difference of opinion between the Shiah lawyers on the question of acceptance in the case of "a gift of a debt".

The doctrine of the Mabsut.

The Shaikh,[3] the greatest of Shiah lawyers, has stated in the *Mabsut*—"When some person has a *mal* owing from another, and makes a *hiba* of the same to that other it is an *ibra* (release) by the word *hiba*. And whether for the validity of a release, the acceptance of the person released is requisite or not, there is difference of opinion. One body [of jurists] holds that, for the validity of an *ibra*, such acceptance is necessary; and so long as the person released does not accept it, the release is not valid; and when not accepted, the right remains intact. And this view is correct [lit. strong], in my opinion, for when one person has a right against another, to discharge it is to confer an obligation, but nobody can be compelled to accept an obligation, otherwise [the result will be] though he does not accept, he will be forced to accept. [For that reason also] in the case of a gift of a *dain* (debt) it is required that there should be acceptance; and without acceptance a *hiba* is not valid. Another body says that the *ibra* is valid whether the person who is liable accepts it or rejects it."

---

1 Shara'ya, p. 282; Mafatih; Irshad-ul-Azhan.

2 See Mahommedan Law, Vol. I, p. 117, where the Arabic passages are fully set out.

3 Shaikh Abu J'afar of Tus.

The Ghunia.

Similarly, the jurist, Abu Zahra, states in the *Ghunia,* that "if a person were to make a gift to another of what is due to him, that is a release by the word *hiba*; it is necessary, however, that the person from whom the debt is owing should consent to such discharge, for a discharge is conferring an obligation on the debtor, and there is no compulsion in the acceptance of a mere obligation."

The author of the *Shara'ya,* on the other hand expresses a different opinion.[1] He states that the gift of a debt to the debtor himself is valid and operates as a release, and "in release (*ibra*) acceptance (by the donee) is not a condition, according to the correct view." The "correct view" seems to be his own opinion. The author of the *Jawahir,* after giving the dicta from the *Mabsut,* the *Ghunia,* the *Sarair,* the *Intisar* and other works of high repute, both among the Usulis and Akhbaris, says that the opinion of the author of the *Shara'ya* refers only to cases where the obligation is one-sided; for example, where one person owes to another a sum of money, the creditor may release or discharge the debtor, and in order to effectuate such a discharge the acceptance of the donee (the debtor) is not a condition precedent. But when the creditor has also certain obligations to perform, his discharge of the debtor (without the debtor's consent) would not absolve him from the liabilities to which he is subject. For example, if *A* agrees to pay to *B* 500 dirhems, on the condition that *B* should supply him for five years with the fruit of his garden, unless the contract is put an end to by mutual consent, a release by *B* to *A*, in respect of the 500 dirhems, would not absolve *B* from the liability of supplying the fruit for the period agreed upon.

Again, suppose *A* contracts to serve *B* for five years on condition of receiving a monthly stipend of five dirhems, and *B* without the consent of *A*, and before the expiration of the period, declares that he has no need for the services of *A*, in such a case he would not be absolved from the liability of paying the stipend fixed upon for the full period.

Viewed in the light in which the author of the *Jawahir* puts it, the opinion of the author of the *Shara'ya* might possibly be considered to be little different from that of his great predecessors; for the Shaikh and his disciples only say that a discharge cannot be given effect to against the will of the obliger; he may accept it or reject it; his acquiescence is tantamount to acceptance.[2]

Gift of the term.

Even the Akhbari Mujtahid of Teheran, in his work called the *Sirat-un-Nijat* lays down that "though it is allowable [under the

1 Shara'ya, p. 242.

2 But so far as the weight to be attached to the two opinions is concerned there can be no question that the Mabsut is regarded as a work of the highest authority among the Shiahs.

dictum of the *Shara'ya*] to make a 'gift of the term', it is incumbent to obtain the consent of the wife (احوط قبول زوجه)".[1] And adds that in spite of the gift *every condition laid down in the contract must be strictly carried out.*

Kamar Kadar v. Ludden Sahiba.

One should have thought that having regard to this difference of opinion among Shiah lawyers, a British Indian Court would adopt the view most conformable to "equity, justice and good conscience." The doctrine of the *Sharh-ul-Lum'a*, however, has received judicial recognition by the High Court of Calcutta in the case of *Kamar Kadar* v. *Ludden Sahiba*[2]. The facts of this case were as follows:—The plaintiff, Kamar Kadar, married the defendant, a young unmarried woman of respectable parentage, by the *muta'a* form for a period of fifty years. A few weeks after the marriage he abandoned her, and, on her suing him for maintenance, alleged that he had married her for two months and a half only. This was found to be untrue, and he was ordered, under the provisions of the Criminal Procedure Code, to pay the maintenance. He then brought a suit to have it declared that the marriage relationship had been dissolved by his giving up the term, and that, consequently, he was not bound to maintain the woman. There was no allegation of infidelity or misconduct against her. The defendant pleaded that, under the law of her sect, the husband could not dissolve the union as alleged by him, of his own motion, and that even if he could do so, he was not absolved from his liability to maintain her, he having agreed to do so at the time of the marriage. After a varied fortune the case came up to the High Court of Calcutta, and the learned Judges there held that the *Mabsut* was an old work and could not possibly have been known to the parties, but that the *Shara'ya* was a later work and better known in India and, therefore, more binding. And they accordingly held, with the aid of the gloss of the *Sharh-ul-Lum'a*, that the husband, though he has no power of divorce, may still divorce his wife by giving up the term! *They did not decide the other question raised by the defendant, that the husband was not absolved from his liability to maintain her by virtue of the agreement entered into at the time of marriage.*

---

1 (احوط) Literally means 'superlatively precautionary'; in legal parlance it means 'incumbent'; see the Jawahir-ul-Kalam.

2 (1886) I L 14 Cal. 276.

CHAPTER XI

RIGHTS AND DUTIES OF THE MARRIED PARTIES

SECTION I

MAINTENANCE—ABSENT HUSBAND

Usually among the upper classes of Muhammedans the conditions relative to the wife's maintenance and residence are reduced to writing. But the husband's obligations are independent of any express contract; they spring from the *status* of marriage *validly* contracted.

Duties of the husband.

The husband is legally bound to maintain his wife and her domestic servants whether she and her servants belong to the Moslem Faith or not. "It is incumbent on the man to maintain his wife", says the *Fatawai Kazi Khan*, "whether she be Moslemah or non-Moslemah (*lit. zimmia*), poor or rich, whether there has been *copula* or not; whether grown-up [adult] or young, so that intercourse with her is possible."[1]

Shiah doctrines.

The Shara'ya enunciates the principle in similar terms:—"there is no difference in the right of a wife to maintenance whether she be a Moslemah or *Zimmia* (non-Moslemah), free or bound."[2] This obligation of the husband comes into existence from the moment the contract takes effect and the wife is subjected thereby to the marital control.[3] It continues in force during the union, and in certain cases for a time even after it is dissolved.

Meaning of nafkah.

"In the language of the Arabs", in other words, literally, "*nafkah* means what a man spends over his family". "In the language of the law, it signifies food, clothing and lodgment. This has been mentioned by Imam Mohammad . . . . The *nafkah* of a person becomes incumbent upon another from three causes; (*a*) from being a wife; (*b*) from being a relation; (*c*) from being a slave or servant.

---

1 Radd-ul-Muhtar, Vol. II, p. 1062; Fatawai 'Alamgiri, Vol. I, p. 732.

2 See Ante.

3 So I render the word Ihtebas (احتباس); see Fatawai Kazi Khan, Vol. I, p. 479; same under the Shiah Law.

How maintenance is to be regulated.

Karkhi has said that in fixing the amount of maintenance regard is to be paid to the condition of the husband and not to the position of the wife, and this is the *Zahir-ur-Rawayet* (*most approved doctrine*) and also the doctrine of Imam Shaf'ei. But Khassaf has said, and so it is stated in the *Hedaya*, that when the condition of the husband and wife are not equal, in other words, when one is rich and the other poor, a proper means should be adopted between the two; and on this is the *Fatwa*. And the *Hedaya* supports its view by the *hadis* in the *Sahih-ul-Bokhari* from 'Ayesha that on one occasion Hind, daughter of 'Otba, came and complained to the Prophet that her husband Abu Sofian was a miser, and did not support her and her child properly. The Prophet said, 'take what is necessary, but be moderate'."[1]

Shiah Law.

Under the Shiah Law the right to maintenance depends on two conditions, 1st, a permanent contract of marriage (*'akd-i-daim*), 2nd, a *tamkin-ul-kamil* which means such retirement (تخليه) between him and her as offers no impediment of place or time for conjugal relationship."[2]

"*Tamkin* being a necessary condition, the right does not arise in respect of a young girl (*saghira*) who is unfit for conjugal intercourse. But if the wife is adult and the husband a minor, *tamkin* [the ability of access] being established, she will be entitled to maintenance. Nor does her right drop in consequence of her illness or being afflicted with malformation of the generative organs obstructive to connubial intercourse or inability on his part to consummate the marriage."[3]

The maintenance of a wife has precedence over the maintenance of relatives (*akarib*).[4]

Hanafi Law.

The husband is bound to maintain his wife even if she be residing in her father's house, provided he has not required her to come to his own house, and can cohabit with her there.

---

1 Radd-ul-Muhtar, Vol. II, p. 1063.

2 Shara'ya, p. 304. The Tamkin-ul-kamil of the Shiah Law is therefore, analogous in some of its consequences to the Khilwat-us-sahih of the Hanafis.

It will be observed here that the author of the Shara'ya has involved himself in a contradiction. In the first place he states that there is no difference in the right of a wife to maintenance whether she be a Moslemah or non-Moslemah, that is, both are equally entitled to maintenance. Here he says, a permanent contract alone creates the right. In another place (see ante) he lays down that a (Shiah) Moslem can marry a non-Moslemah by a temporary contract only. This shows the weakness of the latter enunciation.

3 Shara'ya, pp. 304-5 ; the reason of the inability is specified in the original.

4 *Ibid*, p. 307, the word *akarib* means kinsfolk.

If he has called upon her to come and live with him, and she has refused without any valid or justifiable reason, such as the non-payment of prompt dower or illness, she is not entitled to maintenance while residing in her father's house.[1] But if she is ill in her father's house, and the husband wants to remove her to his house, and there is no risk or danger to her health in such removal, and she refuses, she will not be entitled to maintenance.

No maintenance due under an invalid marriage.

A man is not liable for the maintenance of a woman whom he has married by an illegal or invalid contract, or of one who has become unchaste.[2]

A wife cannot be compelled to go on a journey with her husband against her will, and the Kazi should not constrain her to accompany him. In case of refusal to go with the husband, she does not lose her right of maintenance, and would be entitled to it during the husband's absence.[3]

If the husband is away from home and deputes a stranger or a *ghair mahram*[4] to fetch her to him, she would be entitled to refuse to accompany the messenger.

But the right of the wife to maintenance is subject to the condition that she is not "refractory" or does not refuse to live with her husband without lawful cause.

Wife's refusal of cohabitation.

For example, a woman, who is living in her own house and would not allow the husband to "approach her", is not entitled to maintenance, unless she has asked him to take her to a house of his own, and he has either delayed or refused, and the woman has in consequence thereof prevented his "approaching" her.

A woman is not entitled to any maintenance if she has been imprisoned for any offence or has eloped with somebody or has been taken away forcibly by another person.

Respectable women not accustomed to do household work, such as grinding corn and cooking food, should not be constrained to perform such duties, "though it was usual for our Lady Fatima't-az-Zahra, who was the noblest (*afzal*) of women, to do such work, for that was the custom of Arabia."[5]

---

1 See Mohammed Ali *v.* Ghulam Fatima A I R 1935 Lah. 902. A husband is not bound to maintain the wife who refuses herself to him without a just cause or leaves his house merely on account of his having married a second wife.

Mst. Khatijan *v.* Abdulla A I R 1943 Sind 65 and A *v.* B 21 Bom. 77. In these cases it was held that the husband is not bound to maintain a wife who is disobedient to him. See also Aishan Bibi *v.* Sain P L D 1952 Lah. 460.

2 Radd-ul-Muhtar, Vol. II, p. 1065.

3 *Ibid.*

4 Ghair Mahram is a person before whom she does not appear unveiled; lit., a person between whom and the woman a union is absolutely interdicted.

5 Radd-ul-Muhtar, Vol. II. p. 1067.

Maintenance.

In fixing the amount of maintenance, the Kazi must pay regard to the position of the parties, the requirements of the wife and the dearness of provisions. And he may direct the payment to be made either daily, or by the month or by the year, as may be most convenient to the man, for a labourer earns by the day, and it may be convenient to him to pay daily. But in every case it must be in advance, though the husband may agree to pay, and the wife may agree to take, the maintenance in any way he chooses.[1]

Shiah doctrines.

The Shiah Law contains similar provisions. "The measure of maintenance, according to the standing rule, is regulated by the woman's requirements in the matter of food, condiments, clothing, residence, servants and articles for adjournment, subject [with due regard] to the custom of *her equals* among the people of her own town" . . . . .[2] "and even though she should be one who has not been accustomed to have a servant, yet in the case of illness she must be provided with one, from a regard to what is customary."[3]

Hanafi rules.

If the husband is possessed of means, in other words, is not impecunious or poor, the wife is entitled to a servant. The number of servants is dependant on the means of the husband and the position of the parties and their requirements. And if the woman belongs to the nobility, her personal servants' maintenance is obligatory on the husband. And on this is the *Fatwa*.[4]

The maintenance (*nafkah*) of a wife includes everything connected with her support and comfort, such as food, raiment, lodging, etc., and must be provided in accordance with the social position of the parties.[5]

The wife is not entitled merely to maintenance in the English sense of the word, but has a right to claim a habitation for her own exclusive use, to be provided consistently with the husband's means. It is incumbent on the husband to provide a separate apartment for his wife's habitation, to be solely and exclusively appropriated by her, because this is essentially necessary to her, and is, therefore her due, same as her maintenance, "and the word of God appoints her a dwelling-house as well as a subsistence."[6]

1 Radd-ul-Muhtar, Vol. II, p. 1069.

2 Shara'ya, p. 305.

3 *Ibid.*

4 Radd-ul-Muhtar, Vol. II, p. 1077.

5 *Ibid.*, p. 1062 ; Fatawai 'Alamgiri, Vol. I, p. 739 ; Fatawai Kazi Khan, Vol. I, p. 480, Ed. Cal. ; Hedaya, Vol. I, p. 392, 401.

6 Hedaya, Vol. I, p. 401.

According to the Shiah doctrines expounded in the *Shara'ya*[1] the woman has a right to demand a separate lodgment (*maskan*) without any companionship save that of her husband.

If the woman be apprehensive of the husband leaving the place without paying her maintenance, she would be entitled to apply to the Kazi to take security from him to pay the amount regularly.

A minor wife:—Hanafi and Shiah doctrines.

The Hanafis agree with the Shiahs in holding that if the wife be a minor (*saghira*) so that the marriage cannot be consummated, there is no legal obligation on the husband's part to maintain her.[2]

Shaf'ei doctrine.

With the Shaf'eis it makes no difference, in the obligation of the husband to maintain his wife, whether the wife be a minor or not.[3]

Nor is a husband, under the Hanafi and the Shiah Law, entitled to the custody of the person of a minor wife whom he is not *bound* to maintain.[4]

When husband minor and wife adult.

If the husband be a minor and the wife an adult, and the incapacity to complete or consummate the contract be solely on his part, she is entitled to maintenance.[5] If the minor has no property, the obligation of maintaining the wife devolves on his father with a right of recovery against him when he is in a position to repay the amount expended on his behalf. When both husband and wife are minors and cohabitation is impossible, there is no liability for maintenance.

It makes no difference in the husband's liability to maintain the wife, whether he be in health or suffering from illness, whether he be a prisoner of war or undergoing punishment, "justly or unjustly", for some crime, whether he be absent from home on pleasure or business, or gone on a pilgrimage, and whether he be rich or poor.[6] In fact, as long as the *status* of marriage subsists and the wife is subject to the marital power, she is entitled to

---

1 Shara'ya, p. 305.

2 Fatawai 'Alamgiri, Vol. I, p. 732 ; Kanz-ud-Dakaik ; Hedaya, Vol. I (Hamilton's), p. 394; Jam'a-ush-Shittat ; Radd-ul-Muhtar, Vol. II, p. 1064. If the girl, though under puberty, is capable of being a companion to her husband, she is entitled, says the Radd-ul-Muhtar, to maintenance.

3 Hedaya, Vol. I, p. 394 (Grady's Ed., p. 141).

4 In the matter of Khatija Bibi (1870), 5 B L R, O C, 557; Wazeer Ali *v.* Kaim Ali, 5 N W 196.

5 Hedaya, Vol. I, p. 395; Radd-ul-Muhtar, Vol. II, p. 1062; Fatawai Kazi Khan, Vol. II, p. 480; Jam'a-ush-Shittat.

6 Fatawai 'Alamgiri, Vol. I, p. 733.

maintenance from him. Nor does she lose her right by becoming afflicted with any disease after marriage.[1]

But when she becomes ill *before* she has taken up her abode in the conjugal domicile there is no obligation on the husband to provide for her maintenance.

A woman is also entitled to her maintenance, though refusing "herself" to her husband on the ground that he had not paid her prompt dower. And she has this right whether cohabitation has taken place or not.[2]

Powers of the Kazi.

Where the husband leaves the conjugal domicile without making any provision for the wife's support, and his whereabouts are known, the Judge has the power of decreeing maintenance against him on the wife's application. But where it is not possible to trace his whereabouts, so that he may be summoned to answer the complaint, the procedure for the enforcement of her right, according to the enunciations of both the Shiah and the Hanafi jurists, keeps in view the interests of both the husband and the wife.

When a man goes to the country, says the *Fatawai 'Alamgiri*[3] (quoting the *Kinia*), "leaving his wife in town, the Kazi may decree her maintenance against him, notwithstanding his absence, and it is not necessary for this purpose that he should be absent on a journey."[4]

This obviously refers to a case where the place of his abode is known and process can issue against him.

Desertion by the husband.

But where the husband has disappeared and it is not known where he is living, the position is somewhat complicated. The statements of the jurists with regard to such cases, properly analysed, resolve themselves into questions of procedure, subject to two main ideas, justice to the wife with due protection of the absent husband's interests.

Procedure.

"A woman goes to the Kazi and says 'I am so and so, daughter of so and so, and my husband so and so, son of so and so, has disappeared from me and has left no maintenance for me', and demands from the Kazi an order for her maintenance. If

1 Fatawai 'Alamgiri, Vol. II, p. 734; Radd-ul-Muhtar, Vol. II, p. 1062; Jam'aush-Shittat. The Radd-ul-Muhtar adds, "and it makes no difference in the liability of the husband even if the wife owing to some malformation is incapable of co-habitation", p. 1062.

2 Durr-ul-Mukhtar, p. 284; comp. Radd-ul-Muhtar, Vol. II, p. 1062.

See Mst. Mohammadi *v.* Jamiluddin P L D 1960 Kar. 663; Badruddin *v.* Aisha Begum 1957 A L I 300. In India if the husband has married another wife or keeps a mistress the wife may refuse to live with the husband and claim maintenance.

See Najmunnissa *v.* Sirajuddin A I R 1946 Pat. 467.

3 Fatawai 'Alamgiri, Vol. I, p. 737.

4 According to Fatawai Kazi Khan and the Muhit.

the absent [husband] has left present [available] property[1] in his house of the kind from which maintenance is (usually) paid,[2] the Kazi, on being satisfied that she is the wife of the absent person, may direct her to maintain herself out of such property in the customary manner, without extravagance or stint, after affirming her on oath that she had received no maintenance from the husband and that there was no cause which disentitled her to it such as disobedience (*nushuz*), and such like. And the Kazi shall [might] also take surety (*kafil*) from her."[3]

The reason for requiring a *kafil* from the woman is thus stated in the *Hedaya*:—"When the Kazi decrees a woman her maintenance out of the effects of her absent husband, it behoves him to take security from her for whatever she receives for the indemnity of the absentee, *as it is possible* that she may already have received her maintenance or that she may have been divorced and her '*iddat* be passed."[4]

This is not a rule of law but a simple matter of procedure for safeguarding the interests of the absent husband.

"If a man disappears, leaving property known to belong to him in the hands of another, the Kazi may decree the wife's maintenance out of the same . . . . . whether the property is held by him in trust (*amanat*), or as a debt (*dain*) or in partnership business (*muzaribat*). He [the Kazi] will, however, take surety from her and affirm her as before."[5]

The above *dictum* does not restrict the right of the wife to maintenance to any particular kind of property in "the hands of another."[6]

Right of maintenance when husband is absent.

In the *Fatawai Kazi Khan* the words are slightly different—"if the absent husband has left property in trust in the hands of a man, consisting of things of the kind used for maintenance, or debts owing from a [third] person, and the woman demands her maintenance out of the property held by the other in trust or from the debt, then if the depositary or the debtor admit it and of her being the wife, the Kazi shall make the order, etc." But if the debtor or the depositary were to deny the trust or the marriage, then according to Imam Zuffar "whose doctrine is adopted for the *fatawa* in the present day owing to people's

1 Property in substance not debt.

2 "Such as dirhems and dinars, and provisions and clothing."

3 *Ibid.*, p. 738, "according to Fatawai Kazi Khan, and this is correct according to the Muhit."

4 Comp. Hed. (Hamilton's paraphrase) Grady's Ed., p. 144.

5 "But the Kazi shall take surety from the wife and shall put her on her oath in view of the interests of the absent—Fatawai Kazi Khan, Vol. I, p. 496.

6 Fatawai 'Alamgiri, Vol. I, p. 738, after the Jowharat-un-Nayerreh.

needs", the Kazi shall receive evidence on behalf of the woman, and on being satisfied of her claim, shall make a decree for maintenance.[1]

The rule stated in the Durr-ul-Mukhtar.

"The people who are entitled to maintenance from the property of an absent person are the wife and the infant children. An adult son who is a cripple, and daughters whether adult or under age, are classed as *infant* children. The parents also have a claim, but not a brother or bondsman."

"They are entitled to maintenance from such articles as are ordinarily applied for that purpose . . . . . and from such property as has been left in the hands of a depositary, or a debt owing from another. And it should first be paid out of what is in deposit and then from the debt. If the depositary or debtor admit the relationship of the claimant, the Kazi shall make a decree for maintenance. Similarly, if the Kazi himself is aware of the relationship and of the deposit or debt. But if he knows of one fact and not the other, then he must take surety from the claimant and make them both take oath[2] for *ihtiat* (precaution). And this applies to all the 'takers' or maintenance save the infant child."[3] [That is, he should take an oath from them that they have no means of subsistence.]

"But when the depositary or debtor does not acknowledge the deposit or debt, or that the claimant is the absent man's wife, in that case . . . . . Zuffar (may the peace, etc.) has laid down that there should be a decree for maintenance [on her producing evidence of the facts in dispute]. And *Zuffar's doctrine is acted upon by the Kazi of the* [*present*] *day owing to the needs of mankind and the fatwa is thereon.*[4] The same rule applies when the woman seeks an order from the Kazi to borrow on the credit of the absent husband for her maintenance, and governs the claims of all persons entitled to maintenance."

"A decree made in such circumstances will only be operative as regards the woman's right to receive maintenance but will not be conclusive as to the fact of the marriage or to the establishment of the *nasab* of her children.[5] And this rule applies to a

1 Durr-ul-Mukhtar, p. 290; Radd-ul-Muhtar, Vol. II, p. 1098. "It is the duty of the Kazi", says the Hedaya, "to decree maintenance to her from necessity, even though the depositary or debtor may deny the debt or deposit, and the fact of her being the absentee's wife" see Grady's Ed., p. 145.

2 In the case of a wife, that the absentee had made no provision for her maintenance, or that she is not an irrevocably divorced woman, or that she is not a *nashiza*, *i.e.*, one who refuses without reason to take up her abode in the conjugal domicile, and is therefore disentitled to maintenance, or one who has cancelled her marriage, etc.

3 *Ibn-i-Kamal*, the author of the *Izah-ul-Islam*, is referred to here.

4 Durr-ul-Mukhtar, p. 290.

5 In other words, it will not preclude the absentee from proving that there was no marriage or that the children were not his.

claim of maintenance made by any other relative entitled to *nafka* such as a child or parent."

The *Durr-ul-Mukhtar* further states that "this is one of the six rules of Zuffar on which is the *fatwa*," *i.e.*, which has been acknowledged as authorities for passing decrees,[1] although in the *Sharh-ul-Kanz* and *Hamawi* the number of Zuffar's rules adopted for judicial decrees is said to be fifteen.

In all cases in which a Kazi may decree maintenance to a wife out of the property of her husband, she may lawfully take it herself out of the property "to such extent as may be justified by common usage without his order."[2] But where the property left by a husband, "in his own use or in deposit," is of a different nature to that from which a woman is entitled to take her maintenance, "according to all" it can neither be sold by herself nor by the Kazi on account of her maintenance.[3]

A missing person is in the position of one who is absent and the rules which are applicable to the latter apply to him.

Inability to maintain wife.

Inability to maintain a wife is no ground for separation under the Hanafi Law. A wife, therefore, under the Hanafi rules cannot obtain an order for separation either for desertion or inability or refusal to maintain her.

But the Kazi may direct her to raise her maintenance by borrowing on the husband's credit. But if she should disburse anything for her maintenance out of her own property after the decree of the Judge or a mutual agreement of the parties, she has a right of recourse against her husband. And so, also, when she contracts debt on account of it as against her husband, whether with or without the Judge's permission; except that when it is without his permission, she alone is responsible, and the creditor cannot have recourse against the husband, while if it is with the Judge's permission, she can transfer the responsibiiity to her husband so as to give the creditor a right of action against him.[4]

Desertion by the husband—Shaf'ei and Hanbali doctrines. Shaf'ei Kazi's decree binding on Hanafis.

Under the Shaf'ei and Hanbali system, inability on the part of the husband to maintain the wife, absence without any provision for her maintenance, desertion, cruelty and the like causes entitle a woman to apply for and obtain a separation from the Kazi. And though the Hanafi Law does not recognise this principle, it authorises the Hanafi Kazi to make over the

1 Durr-ul-Mukhtar, p. 290.

2 Fatawai 'Alamgiri, Vol. I, p. 739.

3 *Ibid.*

4 Fatawai 'Alamgiri, Vol. I, pp 739-40.

case to the Shaf'ei Kazi, whose decision would become imperative among the Hanafis and be given effect to by the Hanafi Kazis.

"According to Imam Shaf'ei, it is lawful (for the Kazi) to separate the husband and wife on account of the *iflas* of the husband (*i.e.*, his impecuniosity and consequent inability to pay her maintenance), as also from the injury to the wife if he be absent"; in other words, from injury resulting to the wife from desertion.

This is the text of the *Tanwir-ul-Absar*.

The comment of the *Radd-ul-Muhtar* paraphrased runs thus:—"Indeed, according to Imam Shaf'ei, when the husband is unable to discharge his obligation of maintaining the wife, the wife would be entitled to have the marriage cancelled. Similarly, if the husband has gone away and she cannot obtain any maintenance from him or it is difficult to do so, she would be entitled to obtain a cancellation of the marriage. This (doctrine) has been adopted by many of the Shaf'eis, but the reliable doctrine among them is, that so long as the woman is rich she would not be entitled to have her marriage cancelled, even though the husband has disappeared and no news can be obtained of him and it is difficult to get any maintenance from his property . . . . . But if the woman establishes that she has no means, nor has the husband left any with which she can support herself, she would be entitled to have the marriage cancelled . . . . . And the result of all this discussion is that, according to the Shafe'is, if the husband be present, and be unable to afford maintenance, it is lawful for the Kazi to cancel the marriage. So also if he has disappeared altogether, and also when he has gone away temporarily and she cannot obtain any maintenance from him or from his estate or can obtain it with great difficulty . . . . .'Our'[1] Mujtahids will give effect to first ground of cancellation but not to the second or the third."

"Imam Ahmed ibn Hanbal was asked, as is stated in the *Fatawai Kari-ul-Hedaya*, as to the case of a woman whose husband had disappeared or gone away and left no maintenance. He answered if the woman goes before the Kazi and asks him to cancel the marriage, it is lawful for him to do so even though the husband is absent. But if he be present, the Kazi must obtain proof that he does not maintain her or is unable to do so. And if the woman re-marries after observing her '*iddat*, it is lawful for her to marry another man."[2]

In the next it is added "that though the Hanafi Kazi may not give effect to the Shaf'ei doctrine he may delegate the task of deciding the matter to a Shaf'ei Kazi. And if there be no fear of collusion the separation will be effective."

---

1 The Hanafi Kazi's.

2 Radd-ul-Muhtar, Vol. II, p. 1080; Durr-ul-Mukhtar, p. 287.

The same principle is given in the *Sharh-i-Vikaya*:—

Shaf'ei rules in force among all Sunnis on the ground of equity.

"If the husband is unable to pay the wife's maintenance, they will not be separated, but she will be ordered to borrow on his credit and spend for her maintenance; and the husband will have to discharge all such debts. This is according to 'us' (Hanafis). According to Imam Shef'ei, the Kazi will separate the two, when the husband is unable to discharge the obligation in the usual way. And, therefore, to relieve the woman from oppression, the Kazi has the power to cancel the marriage. And 'our' masters, when they saw the necessity for the application of this rule for separation, and when they saw how difficult it is to discharge an unceasing want by incessant borrowing, and the truth being that such borrowing is difficult and such lender difficult to obtain, and the fact of the husband having means is imaginary, they [the masters] have, upon a liberal interpretation, held it commendable to depute a Shaf'ei Kazi to decide the case."[1]

The *Fatawai Kazi Khan* states the rule in the following terms:—"Inability [*viz.*, to provide for maintenance] does not create a right for separation; but Shaf'ei, on whom be peace, says that the woman is entitled in such a case to demand from the Kazi that he should effect a separation between them, and the separation (so) effected by the Kazi shall be a cancellation (*faskh*) of the marriage . . . . . "And this difference of opinion [between Abu Hanifa and Shaf'ei] exists [also] in the case of the inability of the husband to pay the prompt dower before cohabitation.[2] If the Kazi of the Shaf'ei school were to decree a separation [on either ground], his decree shall be given effect to, because the Shaf'ei Kazi has made a decree in a matter on which there is no text of the Koran, or *hadis* or *Ijma'a*, but in which the governing rule is deduced by *Ijtihad* [exercise of reasoning in the deduction of principles] and, therefore, his decree shall be given effect to according to all (*i.e.*, all the doctors) . . . . . . But if the husband is absent and the woman submits the question to the Kazi, and she establishes by proof (بينة) of witnesses that her absent husband is unable to maintain her and demands from the Kazi that he should effect a separation between them; then, if the Kazi is a Hanafi, we have stated what he ought to do; but if he be a Shaf'ei, and were to effect a separation between them, then the Jurists of Balkh have declared the decree shall be valid."

If the wife were to apply for a separation to the Hanafi Kazi, he cannot, according to the tenets of his school, make an order to that effect. But if he be authorised by his appointment to delegate his duties to another, he can direct a Shaf'ei Kazi

1 Now according to section 2 of the Dissolution of Muslim Marriages Act, 1939, a marriage of a Muslim woman of any sect is liable to dissolution on the grounds of failure to maintain her.

2 According to Abu Hanifa, the woman has no right after cohabitation to ask for separation on the ground of non-payment of the prompt dower though she has a right to refuse cohabitation.

"to try the case," otherwise he must refer the applicant to the Shaf'eite Kazi.[1] A decree of the Shaf'eite Kazi *properly* passed, would, as already stated, be given effect to by the Hanafi Kazi.

In Algeria, where the French, with commendable wisdom, have maintained intact the indigenous institutions, no difficulty arises. When a case of this kind arises among the Hanafis, the Hanafi Kazi refers the parties to the Shaf'ei Kazi, whose decision becomes binding. In India, [2]there is neither a Shaf'ei nor a Hanafi Kazi. The Civil Courts profess to exercise the powers vested in the Kazi, and it is to be presumed that they would act, in cases of marital disputes, in the manner indicated, that is, when the Hanafi Law is silent or refuses to give any relief, they would have recourse to the Shaf'ei doctrines.[3]

Shiah doctrines.

Under the Shiah Law the following procedure is pointed out in case of disputes between married parties:—

"In case of discord between the husband and wife, and an apprehension of an actual rupture, the Judge should appoint two umpires, one from among the relatives of the husband, and the other from among those of the wife, to decide as may be best in the case. He may, in his discretion, appoint both not belonging to the family of either, or he may appoint one from the family of one party, and the other a stranger to both. These persons should, according to the most authentic doctrine, be sent, not merely as agents, but with powers to decide hetween the parties as judges. If they agree as to measures of accommodation, they can give them effect without reference to the consent of the parties. Except that though the umpires should agree as to the necessity of a separation between them this cannot be effected without the husband's consent, if it is to be by a *talak* or divorce; or without the wife's agreeing to a compensation, if it is to be by *khula* or release."[4]

"When the umpires have been sent by the Judge, and the parties or either of them, refuse to appear before arbitrators, some [lawyers] are of opinion that judgment cannot be given as it would be against an absent person. But it were better to say that it can be given, for it is limited to what is for the good of the parties, and actual separation is made dependent on their own permission."

1 Fatawai Kazi Khan, Vol. I, p. 495, Sect. on Maintenance.

In most Sunni countries there are Kazis belonging to the different sects to adjudge cases arising among them.

2 Now Indo-Pakistan.

3 See section 2, Dissolution of Muslim Marriages Act, wherein the Shaf'ei and Maliki doctrines of dissolution of marriage have been adopted for all sects.

4 This evidently does not restrict the power of the arbitrators to a tafrik or separation, when no liability is cast on either side,

Whether an application can be made under the Civil Procedure Code[1] to file the arbitrators' award in Court and to obtain a judgment upon it has not been the subject of decision in the Indian tribunals. *Prima facie* there seems to be no reason against it.

According to the Shiah doctrines, when a person is missing but has left sufficient provision for his family and it is known that he is alive, or when the wife is maintained by his guardian or somebody acting on his behalf, in such a case the wife has no option, but is required to wait for his return or until she hears that he is dead.

Husband missing.

But when it is not known whether he is dead or alive, and the missing man has left no wherewithal for her maintenance, nor is there anybody to maintain her properly, she may, if she choose, apply to the Judge for permission to marry again. Upon receiving the application, the Judge should postpone the consideration of the matter for four years and institute an enquiry as to whether the husband is alive or dead. If the result of such enquiry be to prove that the husband is alive, the woman will be directed to wait, but it is incumbent on the sovereign to give her maintenance from the *Bait-ul-Mal* or public treasury. If, on the other hand, nothing can be heard of the husband, the Judge should direct her to observe for the missing man the *'iddat* of death, and on its completion, the woman will be at liberty to contract lawfully another marriage. Should the missing person then re-appear *before* the expiry of the *'iddat*, the marriage remains intact. But should he appear after she has completed her *'iddat* and married again, the second marriage will remain intact. And even if she has not married after the expiry of her *'iddat*, the first husband will have no rights against her, nor can he make her cohabit with him, but he may re-marry her.

The procedure indicated in the above passage is inapplicable, in its entirety, to Indian conditions. But it may be presumed that the Courts in India acting in accordance with the principles of equity, justice and good conscience, on the analogy of the Algerian cases decided in conformity with the Maliki doctrines which are similar to the Shiah rules, would, on proof of the husband's absence for four years without any provision for her maintenance, grant her permission to marry again on completing her 'iddat.

General doctrines.

When the husband is absent and has left immovable property either in the possession of his wife or of some other person on his behalf, the wife is not entitled to sell it for her support, though she may raise a temporary loan on it, which the husband will be bound to discharge provided the mortgage was created *bona fide* for her or her children's support, and did not go beyond the actual necessity of the case. Under such circumstances the

1 See now the Arbitration Act (X of 1940).

mortgagee will probably be bound to satisfy himself that the money advanced is legitimately applied to the support of the family of the absent husband.

Wife's refractoriness (nushuz). Abandonment of the conjugal domicile by the wife.

When the woman abandons the conjugal domicile without any valid reason, she is not entitled to maintenance.[1] Simple refractoriness, as has been popularly supposed, does not lead to a forfeiture of her right. If she were to refuse cohabitation or to obey the husband's wishes whilst living with him, she would not lose her right to her proper maintenance. But if she were to leave the house against his will without any valid reason, she would lose her right, but would recover it on her return to the conjugal domicile.[2]

What is a valid and sufficient reason for the wife to leave the husband's home is a matter for the discretion of the Judge. As a general principle and one which has been adopted and enforced by the Kazi's *makhamas* in Algeria, a wife who leaves her husband's house on account of his or his relations' continued ill-treatment of her does not come within the category of *nashizah* and continues entitled to her maintenance. Similarly, if the husband were to introduce a prostitute into the house or were to insist on the wife associating with common women, she would be justified in leaving his house and refusing to live with him.

A woman who is imprisoned for some offence or is undergoing incarceration in the civil jail for non-payment of a debt, or who goes on a voyage or pilgrimage without her husband's consent, has no right to claim any maintenance during her absence.[3] But should she be put in jail by the husband, she would not lose her right of maintenance.

Shiah doctrine.

Among the Shiahs, if she goes on an *obligatory* pilgrimage,[4] even without her husband's consent, she is nevertheless entitled to maintenance.

Hanafi rule.

The husband's liability to support the wife continues during the whole period of probation, if the separation has been caused by any conduct of his, or has taken place in exercise of a right possessed by her. The husband would not, however, be liable to support the wife during the *'iddat* if the separation is caused by her misconduct.[5]

---

1 Fatawai Kazi Khan, Vol. I, p. 733; Jam'a-ush-Shittat.

2 *Ibid*; Jam'a-ush-Shittat; Kitab-min la-Euhazzar-al-Fakih.

3 Fatawai 'Alamgiri, Vol. I, p. 734.

4 Hajj-ul-Farz.

5 Fatawai 'Alamgiri, Vol. I, p. 746; Fatawai Kazi Khan, Vol. I, p. 481; Jam'a-ush-Shittat.

"A woman undergoing the *'iddat*", says the *Fatawai 'Alamgiri* "on account of *talak*, is entitled to maintenance and lodging, whether the *talak* be revocable or irrevocable, and whether she be pregnant or not. The principle of this is, that when separation is induced by any cause proceeding from the husband, or by any cause proceeding from the wife in exercise of a right, or by any cause proceeding from a third party, the wife is entitled to maintenance during her *'iddat*. But if the separation is induced by any fault of the wife, she is not entitled to it. A *mala'inah*, separated by the proceeding of *l'aan*, is likewise entitled to maintenance and lodging. So also a woman separated by *khula* or by reason of the apostasy of her husband, or of his having been guilty of misconduct . . . . . So, also, the wife who has obtained a cancellation of her marriage on the ground of the impotency of her husband, and a young girl who avails herself of the option of puberty on arriving at the proper age, and a woman who after consummation has been separated from her husband for inequality.[1] But a woman who has apostatised, or who has been guilty of misconduct . . . . . . has no title to maintenance, unless the misconduct was against her will.[2] And she does not lose her right to lodging whatever be the cause of separation; because residence with her husband is in consequence of a right which he has over her, while maintenance is in consequence of a right which she has against him."[3]

Right of a talaked woman to maintenance,—Sunni doctrines.

It will be seen afterwards, that the Hanafi legists recognise a right in the husband to *talak* the wife, even though she may not be present and the proceeding may never come to her knowledge until sometime after. But they hold that in such a case the woman would be entitled to her full maintenance until she becomes aware of the *talak* and during the period of probation she has to observe thereon.[4]

If the woman be pregnant at the time of separation, her right remains intact until she is confined of the child.[5]

Shiah doctri nes.

Under the Shiah law it is only where the *talak* is revocable that the woman is entitled to "maintenance, clothing and residence" during the *'iddat* whether she be a Moslemah or non-Moslemah. Where the repudiation is irrevocable, she has no right to maintenance or lodging unless she is pregnant, when she is entitled to both until delivery.

1 Fatawai 'Alamgiri, Vol. I, p. 746; Fatawai Kazi Khan, Vol. I, p. 481; Jam'a-ush-Shittat.

2 *Ibid.*

3 See Mst. Mariam *v.* Qadir Bakhsh A I R 1929 Oudh 527; Azmatulla *v.* Imtiaz Begum P L D 1959 Lah. 167; *In re* : Mohammed Rahimullah A I R 1947 Mad. 61.

4 See Rashid Ahmad *v.* Anisa Khatoon A I R 1932 P C 25 ; Ahmad Qasim *v.* Khatun Bibi A I R 1933 Cal. 27.

5 See Jhanda *v.* Hussain Bibi A I R 1923 Lah. 949.

When cohabitation has taken place under a "semblance of right", the woman is bound to observe the *'iddat*; and according to the Shaikh,[1] she is entitled to maintenance during the period of her probation.

Hanafi Law—Widow has no right to maintenance.

Under the Hanafi law the widow has no right to maintenance whether she be pregnant or not. But not so a woman observing *'iddat* for a divorce.[2]

Under the Shiah Law also the widow has no right to maintenance. This principle has been affirmed by the Judicial Committee which has held that a Mahommedan widow has no right to maintenance out of her late husband's estate in addition to what she takes by inheritance or under his will.[3]

In the case of probation (*'iddat*) observed by a woman on the death of her husband,[4] the Sunnis calculate the period from the actual date of his disease. The Shiah rule is slightly different. The wife of a person who is present with him is to observe the *'iddat* from the actual time of his death or repudiation. But if the husband dies when he is away, her probation is calculated from the day on which the wife receives the news of the death, although she is not to re-marry until it is confirmed. Similarly, in the case of repudiation the *'iddat* becomes obligatory on the day the news is brought.[5]

Sunni doctrines.

The liability of the husband to maintain a pregnant wife whom he has divorced ceases at her confinement.[6]

Regarding the right of a pregnant widow, under the Shiah Law, there are two opinions—one affirming, the other denying her title.[7]

Under the laws in force in British India[8] the wife may sue for maintenance either in the Civil Court, or; in

---

1 Shaikh Abu J'afar of Tus the author of the Mabsut; see ante. The Shaikh is by far the most liberal-minded of Shiah lawyers. With regard to the question whether a woman in such a case is entitled to maintenance or not, the author of the Shara'ya says, "the point is one of difficulty" but does not suggest that there is a difference of opinion.

2 Fatawai 'Alamgiri, Vol. I, p. 745; Hedaya, Vol. I, p. 407.

The enunciation in the Koran, "such of you as shall die and leave wives ought to bequeath to them a year's maintenance", is regarded as a recommendation rather than a rule.

3 Aga Mahomed Jaffar Bindomin *v.* Koolsoom Bibi (1899) I L 25 Cal. 9; s. c., 1 C W N 449.

4 *i.e.*, four months and ten days—Fatawai 'Alamgiri, Vol. I, p. 715.

5 Shara'ya *in loco*.

6 Hedaya, Vol. I, p. 360.

7 The Shara'ya considers the latter opinion to be generally received.

8 Now Indo-Pakistan.

the absence of a special contract, apply for an order under s. 488 of the Code of Criminal Procedure (1898). Where the action is brought in the Civil Court, unless there is a special contract stipulating the amount, the wife is entitled to recover maintenance from date of decree but not to an order for *past* maintenance.[1]

Where the application is made to a Criminal Court, it can only order maintenance to the amount of fifty rupees[2] per month.

An order for maintenance, in the case of a divorce, ceases to have operation after the expiration of the woman's period of probation.[3]

According to the Shiahs, who recognise the lawfulness of temporary marriages, a *muta'a* wife is not entitled to maintenance unless it is fixed at the time of the contract.[4] But this special rule of the Shiah Law does not interfere with the statutory right to maintenance given by the Code of Criminal Procedure.[5]

SECTION II

CONJUGAL DOMICILE AND RESTITUTION OF CONJUGAL RIGHTS[6]

THE Mahommedan Law lays down distinctly, (*i*) that a wife is bound to live with her husband, and to follow him

---

1 Abdool Futeh Moulvie *v.* Zebunnissa Khatun (1881) I L 6 Cal. 31 s. c., 8 C L R 242.

But see Mohammed Haji *v.* Kalimabi 41 Mad. 211, where it has been held that according to Shaf'ei law the wife is entitled to past maintenance though there may be no agreement in respect thereof.

2 In Pakistan the amount has now been raised to rupees four hundred.

3 See Shah Abu Ilyas *v.* Ulfat Bibi (1896) I L 19 All. 50 and the cases referred to there.

4 See ante.

5 In the matter of the petition of Luddon Saheba; Luddon Saheba *v.* Kamar Kadar (1882) I L 8 Cal. 736; s. c., 11 C L R 237.

6 It may be remarked, by the way, that the Musulman Law on the subject of the conjugal domicile is very much in advance of the Jewish as well as the Roman Law. Under the Jewish Law, a woman who refused to follow her husband wherever he desired her to go, lost her right to her dower and the possessions which she herself brought from her parents' home, together with all rights which the law vested in her. Under the Roman Law, a wife followed the domicile of her husband without the smallest right to question his choice; and this principle has been imported into the modern English Law. The Code Napoleon provides (Art. 214) that "the woman is obliged to live with her husband and to follow him wherever he proposes to reside;" the consequence being that, however objectionable a place may be, the wife has no option in the matter. As will be seen from the text, the Mahommedan Law gives to the woman, in many cases, the right of questioning her husband's choice of the conjugal domicile.

Under the Code Napoleon, as under the Muhammedan Law, the woman who abandons the conjugal domicile temporarily, does not loss all the benefits of the contract of marriage (as is the case under the Jewish system), but simply her right to maintenance.

wherever he desires to go;[1] and (*ii*) that, on her refusing to do so without sufficient or valid reason, the Courts of Justice, on a suit for restitution of conjugal rights by the husband, would order her to live with her husband.

The wife cannot refuse to live with her husband on pretexts like the following:—

(1) That she wishes to live with her parents.

(2) That the domicile chosen by the husband is distant from the home of her father.

(3) That she does not wish to remain away from the place of her birth.

(4) That the climate of the place where the husband has established his domicile is likely to be injurious to her health.

(5) That she detests her husband.

(6) That the husband ill-treats her frequently (unless such ill-treatment is actually proved, which would justify the Kazi to grant a separation).[2]

Obligation not absolute.

The obligation of the woman, however, to live with her husband is not absolute. The law recognises circumstances which justify her refusal to live with him. For instance, if he has habitually ill-treated her, if he has deserted her for a long time, or if he has directed her to leave his house or even connived at her doing so, he cannot require her to re-enter the conjugal domicile or ask the assistance of a Court

---

1 Some jurists are inclined to hold that the wife may refuse to follow her husband into a country which is at war with the country of her domicile. This is the only meaning which can be attached to the dictum that she may refuse to go with him to the Dar-ul-Harb.

See Abdul *v*. Hussenbi (1904) 6 Bom. L R 728 ; Imam Ali *v*. Arfatunnissa 21 I C 87 and Fatima Bibi *v*. Noor Mohammed (1920) 1 Lah. 597. An ante-nuptial agreement giving choice to the wife to live with her parents after marriage being *ab initio* void is no answer to husband's suit for restitution of conjugal rights.

Meharally *v*. Shakerkhanoobai (1905) 7 Bom. L R 602. A post-nuptial agreement giving choice to the wife to leave the husband if she could not agree with him is void and no answer to sue for restitution of conjugal rights.

2 Most of these examples are taken from the cases decided by the Algerian Kazis and reported by Sautayra and de Manerville. But those who have any experience of Indian life will see at once that exactly similar pretexts are urged by the Indian Mussulman women among the lower classes when they refuse to live with their husbands.

See Mst. Bakht Bibi *v*. Qaim Din A I R 1934 Lah. 907. A decree for restitution of conjugal rights cannot be granted if the marriage though consummated was irregular one having been performed during *'iddat*.

of Justice[1] to compel her to live with him. The bad conduct or gross neglect of the husband is, under the Musulman Law, a good defence to a suit brought by him for restitution of conjugal rights.[2]

Stipulations entered into at time of marriage.

In the absence of any conduct on the husband's part justifying an apprehension that if the wife accompanied him to the place chosen by him for his residence she would be at his mercy and exposed to his violence, she is bound by law to accompany him wherever he goes. At the same time, the law recognises the validity of express stipulations entered into at the time of marriage, respecting the conjugal domicile. If it be agreed that the husband shall allow his wife to live always with her parents, he cannot afterwards force her to leave her father's house for his own. Such stipulation, in order to be practically carried into effect, must be *express* or entered in the deed of marriage, if any; a mere verbal understanding is not regarded as sufficient proof.

If the wife, however, were once to consent to leave the place of residence agreed upon at the time of marriage, she would be presumed to have waived the right acquired under the express stipulation, and to have adopted the domicile chosen by the husband. If a special place be indicated in the deed of marriage as the place where the husband should allow the wife to live, and it appears subsequently that it is not suited for the abode of a respectable woman, or that some injury was likely to accrue to the wife if she were to remain there, or that the wife's parents were not of good character the husband may compel the wife to remove from such place or from the house of such parents.

The husband may also insist upon his wife accompanying him from one place to another, if the change is occasioned by the requirements of his duty.

Every case in which the question of conjugal domicile is involved, depends upon its own special features, the general principle of the Musulman Law on the subject being the same as in other systems of law, *viz.*, that the wife is bound to reside with her husband, unless there is any valid reason to justify her refusal to do so. The sufficiency or validity of the

1 See Itwari *v.* Sm. Asghari A I R 1960 All. 684. In a suit for restitution of conjugal rights by a Muslim husband against his first wife after he has taken a second, the Court will refuse the relief if the circumstances reveal that in taking a second wife the husband has been guilty of such conduct as to make it inequitable to compel the first wife to live with him. Mulkan Bibi *v.* Mohammed Wazir Khan P L D 1959 Lah. 710. Where the plaintiff (husband) has married two wives, and has failed to prove that he has been treating both of them on equal footing, decree for restitution of conjugal rights will be refused.

2 See Buzloor Ruheem *v.* Shumsoon-nissa Begum, infra.

See Meharally *v.* Shekarkhamoobai (1905) 7 Bom. L R 602; Hussaini Begum *v.* Mohammed (1907) 29 All. 222; Hamid Hussain *v.* Kubra Begum I L R 40 All. 332; Genu Mea.. *v.* Begummah Bibi A I R 1933 Rang. 322 and Sofia Begum *v.* Zaheer Hasan A I R 1947 All. 16.

reason is a matter for the consideration of the Court, with the special regard to the place or country in which they reside.[1]

Suit for restitution of conjugal rights.

In the case of *Moonshee Buzloor Ruheem* v. *Shumsoonnissa Begum*[2] the Judicial Committee dealt in broad terms with the principles of the Mahommedan Law which regulate the relations between husband and wife, and its enunciations are so conformable with the spirit of the Islamic system that they deserve careful study. In substance it held that a suit for restitution of conjugal rights will lie in a Civil Court by a Mahommedan husband to enforce his marital rights; and that in such a suit he would be entitled to a decree for the return of the wife. But if there be cruelty to a degree rendering it unsafe for her to return to his dominion, or if there be a gross failure on his part to perform the obligations imposed on him by the marriage contract for the benefit of the wife, if properly proved, it would afford sufficient grounds for refusing the husband any relief in the suit.[3] In a suit for restitution of conjugal rights the Court is vested with the power to constrain the recalcitrant party to resume connubial relationship. Under the provisions of the Indian Civil Procedure Code, a decree in an action brought for that purpose may be enforced by attachment of the defaulter's property or by detention in the civil prison for a term not exceeding six months or both.[4]

If the action is brought by the husband, the wife is entitled to plead as a defence, besides habitual ill-treatment gross cruelty[5] or non-fulfilment of the conditions entered into at the time of marriage, *e.g.*, that she has not been paid her *exigible* or *prompt* dower,[6] or that she had rescinded the contract in the exercise of the "option of puberty."[7]

---

1 See Bai Jina *v*. Kharwa Jina (1907) I L 31 Bom. 366.

2 (1867) 11 Moo. I A 551; see also Husaini Begum *v*. Muhammad Rustam Ali Khan (1906) I L 29 All. 222.

3 See Abdul Kadir *v*. Salima (1886), I L 8 All. 149.

4 Rule 32, Order XXI, Act V of 1908. The Mahommedan Law also provides imprisonment for disobedience of the orders of the Court.

5 In the case Duler Koer *v*. Dwàrka Nath Misser (1905) I L 34 Cal. 971, the Calcutta High Court has held that when a husband introduces into the conjugal domicile a low caste woman as his mistress, to live with him as a member of the family and expels at her instance his wife and son from the house, his conduct amounts to cruelty within the meaning of the law as would justify the Court to refuse in his suit restitution of conjugal rights. The principle of that case would be applicable to Mahommedans.

Bai Jina *v*. Kharwa Jina (1907) 31 Bom. 366. The husband who has been expelled from the caste cannot be granted a decree for restitution of conjugal right.

6 See post.

7 See ante. See also Mst. Bhawan *v*. Gaman A I R 1934 Lah. 77 and Abdul Karim *v*. Amina Bibi A I R 1935 Bom. 308 : I L R 59 Bom. 426. The husband is not entitled to the decree of restitution of conjugal rights if the marriage took place during the minority of the wife and has been validly repudiated

See also Itwari *v*. Smt. Asghari A I R 1960 All. 684. In a suit for restitution of conjugal rights by the husband against the first wife after having married a second, it was held that the husband had been guilty of such conduct as to make it inequitable for the Court to compel the first wife to live with him and the relief was refused.

Suit for jactitation of marriage—Procedure.

The Mahommedan Law recognises suits for jactitation of marriage and provides a procedure for such cases. According to Abu Yusuf and Mohammed, if a woman make a claim against a man that he married her and he denies it, he shall be made to take an oath, the form of which is set out. According to Abu Hanifa, the trial would depend on *byyana* or proof adduced by the parties.[1] It is obvious that the rule of Abu Hanifa would commend itself to the British Indian[2] Courts, which clearly have jurisdiction to entertain a suit by a man to put to silence a woman who falsely claims to be his wife. In the case of *Mir Azmat Ali* v. *Mahmud-ul-nissa*[3] the Allahabad High Court pointed out that "the Court trying such a suit will of course take care before granting a plaintiff a decree, to see that it is strictly proved that the defendant did seriously allege that the disputed marriage had taken place, and that the plaintiff did not acquiesce in the claim or allegation of the defendant as to the disputed marriage; and further that in fact no marriage had taken place between the parties."

The Calcutta High Court has held that a suit between Mahommedans for restitution of conjugal rights is governed by Article 35 of Schedule II of the Indian Limitation Act, if at the time of the demand and refusal the wife or husband was of full age and sound mind; otherwise Article 120 would apply to the suit.[4]

SECTION III

MAINTENANCE OF CHILDREN; PARENTS AND OTHER RELATIONS

Pre-Islamic customs.

AMONG the pre-Islamic Arabs, no obligation existed on the part of either of the parents to maintain their children, nor was any relation bound to maintain another; on the contrary, we learn from history that, during that dark period of rapine, slaughter, and misery which immediately preceded the promulgation of the Islamic Laws in the Arabian peninsula, the birth of children imposed no obligations on the father. Female children, especially, were regarded as a misfortune, and were frequently buried alive to prevent their proving a burden to the tribe of their parents.

The Prophet's rules.

The Prophet of Islam strongly condemned this inhuman and unnatural practice, and declared the maintenance of children to

1 Fatawai Kazi Khan, Vol. I, p. 457.

2 Now Indo-Pakistan.

3 (1897) I L 20 All. 96.

4 Asirunnessa Khatun *v*. Buzloo Meah (1907) I L 34 Cal. 79.

be obligatory on the father; at the same time, he directed that where the parents were infirm and old and unable to support themselves, the children should provide for their support. He required the children to treat their fathers and mothers with respect and consideration; nor did he ever cease to repeat the words, which, according to MM. Perron and Sautayra, mark the great distinction between his legislation and all the ancient systems, that "a respectful and obedient child shall attain to heaven in the footsteps of its mother."

Primary obligation on the father.

In consequence of these precepts, the Musulman Civil Law imposes on parents the duty of maintaining their children and of educating them properly. This obligation rests naturally upon the father; and the *Hedaya* declares in explicit terms that "the maintenance of minor children, rests on their father, and no person can be his associate or partner in furnishing it" (that is, share the responsibility with him).[1]

In all cases concerning the maintenance of infant children consideration is chiefly to be paid to the interest of the children. So long as the father is able to maintain them, it is incumbent on him to do so, and debts incurred on their behalf by any person are recoverable from him.

A man who is able by his labour to procure sustenance for his family is bound to support them, although he may be in straitened circumstances. In case the father wilfully neglects and deserts his children, legitimate or illegitimate, and refuses to maintain them when he has the means, he is liable to punishment at the discretion of the Kazi. Under the Code of Criminal Procedure in force in India,[2] the Magistrate has the jurisdiction to order maintenance in the case of both legitimate and illegitimate children. When the children are illegitimate, the refusal of the mother to surrender them to the father would not justify the refusal of an order for their maintenance.[3]

Difference of faith or creed between father and child makes no difference in the obligation of the father to maintain the child.[4]

Hanafi rule.

Among the Hanafis, when the father is poor and the mother rich, the liability to maintain the infant children falls on her,

1 Hedaya, Vol. I, p. 408.

2 Now Indo-Pakistan.

3 Kariyadan *v.* Kayal Beeran (1885) I L 19 Mad. 461.

See Charan *v.* C. Mathur I L R 39 Mad. 957. The father's liability to maintain extends only to that child who is unable to maintain itself.

4 Fatawai 'Alamgiri, Vol. I, p. 750.

with an eventual right of recovery against her husband, even though the children may have a rich paternal grandfather.[1]

Shiah doctrine.

Among the Shiahs, if the father be poor, the liability rests primarily on the grandfather, if he have means, and not on the mother, even though she be rich.[2]

General doctrines.

When the father and mother are both poor, the grandfather possessed of means is liable to maintain his infant grandchildren, with a right to recover all money spent on them from the father. But if the latter be infirm, the grandfather would have no right of recovery against him for any debt incurred for the maintenance of the grandchildren.[3]

Maintenance of male children.

The obligation of maintaining the male children lasts until they arrive at puberty. After this, a father is not bound to maintain his male children, unless they are incapacitated from work through some disease or physical infirmity, or are engaged in study. When male children are strong enough to earn their own livelihood, though not actually adult, the father may set them to work for their own subsistence, or hire them out for wages.[4]

If the male children are actually able to work, but the employment found for them is unsuitable or improper for their rank in life, they would be placed on the same footing as children labouring under some infirmity. Ability to work must, in such cases, be considered with reference to the social position of the children, as well as the parents; so that a father occupying a respectable position, in which the children have been brought up delicately, must not hire them out for work which is degrading in its nature or associations.

When an adult son is lame, or paralytic, or is in any way a cripple, the obligation of maintaining him rests on the father; so also if he be insane.

Maintenance of female children.

A father is bound to maintain his female children until they are married, if they have no independent means of their own.[5]

1 Fatawai 'Alamgiri, Vol. I, p. 752.

2 Jam'a-ush-Shittat.

3 Fatawai 'Alamgiri, Vol. I, p. 753.

4 *Ibid.*, p. 753; Fatawai Kazi Khan, *in loco.*

5 See Mst. Sughra Begum *v.* Muhammad Din P L D 1957 Lah. 441.

He cannot hire them out for work or send them into service with any [male] person *not* within the prohibited degrees.

Marriage does not necessarily absolve the father from the obligation of maintaining his daughter.[1]

Should he contract a daughter in marriage to a man, concealing the fact that she was suffering from a disease which furnishes the husband with legal grounds for dissolving the marriage, he would be liable for her maintenance in case of the dissolution of the marriage.

Children possessed of private property are to be maintained out of it from the time they are weaned. Until then the father is bound to support and provide suitable attendance for them.[2]

Maintenance of children out of their earnings.

When a father maintains his children out of their earnings, it is his duty to be careful of the surplus and to make it over to them when they arrive at majority. If the father cannot discharge this duty, or if he be false to the trust reposed on him, the Judge should appoint some trust-worthy person to take care of the earnings of such children until they are of age to receive them.

A father is bound to maintain his son's wife when such son is young, or infirm, or engaged in study.[3]

Principle.

When a man is absent, but has left available property, the Judge may order maintenance out of the same for the following persons, *provided they are poor*, *viz.*, (*a*) the wife; (*b*) the male children, if young, or, if adult, unable to earn their own livelihood; (*c*) the female children whether young or adult (if unmarried); and (*d*) the parents.[4]

A woman may compound with her husband for the maintenance of her minor children, but if such composition prove prejudicial to their interests, it would not be binding on the mother. In the same way, if a woman, on separating from her husband, were to agree to take charge of the children of the union and

---

1 Hedaya, Vol. I, p. 410; Fatawai 'Alamgiri, Vol. I, p. 752; Radd-ul-Muhtar in loco; Jam'a-ush-Shittat; Jam'a-i-'Abbasi.

2 Fatawai 'Alamgiri, Vol. I, p. 753.

3 *Ibid*, p. 754.

4 *See* Pakrichi *v*. Kanhacha I L R 36 Mad. 385, where it has been held that after marriage a girl passes into her husband's family and the members of her natural family are not bound to maintain her even if she is divorced.

support them without requiring any assistance, and if she were to discover subsequently that she was unable to do so from poverty,[1] the law would compel the husband to support his children, in spite of the stipulation entered into at the time of separation.

A husband is not liable for the support of the children of his wife by a former husband, unless he has expressly agreed to do so at the time of the marriage.

When children have means, they are bound to maintain their parents if in straitened circumstances, and it makes no difference in their liability whether the parents are Moslems or non-Moslems.[2] Even should the parents be able to eke out a livelihood by manual labour, the children, if they have means, would not be absolved from the obligation of helping to maintain them.

Children's obligations to maintain their parents.

When the children are in straitened circumstances themselves, they are not bound to maintain their parents unless these are absolutely infirm and unable to obtain a livelihood even by manual labour. In such cases, the children are required to share their food with their weak and infirm father or mother, or with both.

Hanafi doctrines.

Under the Hanafi Law, a person is bound to maintain his grandparents, his infant male relations within the prohibited degrees if they are in poverty; all female relations within the same degrees, whether infants or adults, when they are in necessity; and also all adult male relations within the same degrees, if they are blind or disabled, and, at the same time, poor. But,

---

1 See Bayabai *v.* Esmail Ahmad I L R 1941 Bom. 643: A I R 1941 Bom. 369; Dinsab Kasimsab *v.* Muhammad Hussain A I R 1945 Bom. 390. A daughter who unjustifiably keeps away from her father's house, has no right to separate maintenance. Nor is the father bound to maintain the children to whose custody he is entitled if they are deliberately kept away from him.

Muhammad Shamsuddin *v.* Noor Jehan A I R 1955 Hyd. 144. A father who has divorced the child's mother is bound to maintain the child aged 9, although he has obtained a decree for guardianship but did not execute it.

Muhaidin Tharagnar *v.* Sainumba Ammal I L R 1941 Mad. 760: A I R 1941 Mad. 582; Umra Khan *v.* Sultana P L D 1954 Pesh. 13; Ghulam Fatima *v.* Muhammad Bashir P L D 1958 Lah. 596.

Mushaf Hussain Shah *v.* Hamida Begum P L D 1957 Lah. 220. As the father is the natural guardian of his children and as Shia law requires that a son aged more than 2 years should be in the custody of the father, there can be no neglect or refusal to maintain if the father is willing to maintain that child on the condition that it lives with him.

2 "It is incumbent", says the Hedaya (Vol. I, p. 411), "upon a man to provide maintenance for his father, mother, grandfather, and grandmother, if they should be in necessitous circumstances, although they be of a different religion . . . . but their poverty is a condition of the obligation."

with the exception of the grandparents, the support of these relations is only a *quasi*-legal obligation.[1]

In the case of wife, child, parents, and grandparents, difference of faith, according to the Hanafi doctrines, makes no difference in the obligation of maintenance, but it is otherwise in the case of other relations.[2] A rich Moslem is not bound to support his poor non-Moslem brother or uncle or cousin.

Principle—Shiah doctrines.

According to the Shiahs, the Shaf'eis and the Malikis, the support of any relation besides the children, the parents, and the wife, is a mere moral obligation.[3]

Parents.

Daughters as well as *sons* are liable for the maintenance of their poverty-stricken parents.[4]

When a mother is poor and the son is able to work for his livelihood, he is bound to support her according to his means, though he be in straitened circumstances himself.

Preferential liability for maintenance of child.

When a son is able to maintain one parent or grandparent only, the mother or the grandmother, as the case may be, has the preferential right. When a man has both parents and an infant child dependent on him, and has not the ability to support all of them, his child has the first claim on him.

When there are several persons on whom the liability of maintaining a particular individual devolves, the Hanafis hold that the liability should be apportioned according to the shares to which such persons would be entitled in the inheritance of the one whom they are required to support. For example, if a man who is poor have a son and a daughter, both possessed of sufficient competency, the son will have to contribute two-thirds of the maintenance and the daughter one-third.[5]

From the principle adopted by the Algerian Kazis and also from the cases given in the *Jam'a-ush-Shittat* it would appear that among the Shiahs and the Malikis, the more rational rule is followed of apportioning the liability according to the individual means of the parties. For example, if the daughter is rich and the son comparatively poor, the larger proportion of the maintenance devolves on her.

Kazi's power to modify his order.

When a particular sum is agreed upon between the person who is liable and the person to whom maintenance is due, or

1 Comp. Fatawai 'Alamgiri, Vol. I, p. 756.

2 *Ibid.*

3 Some of the Shiah jurists are in accord with the Hanafis in placing the grandparents in the same category as parents.

4 Fatawai 'Alamgiri, Vol. I, p. 755; Hedaya, Vol. I, p. 412; Jam'a-ush-Shittat; Mafatih.

5 Hedaya, Vol. I, p. 412; Fatawai 'Alamgiri, Vol. I, p. 752.

when the Judge has ordered a specific sum to be paid periodically, should a change occur in the circumstances of the parties, such change would justify a re-adjustment of the liability. If the liability has been fixed by an order of the Judge, it is in his discretion, upon a proof of a change in the circumstances of the parties to modify his order to suit the new requirements of the case.

If the person against whom an order is made fails to comply with it, satisfaction of the debt may be obtained either by an attachment and sale of his goods, or he may be imprisoned for contumacy.

Maintenance of wife and children.

A mere plea of poverty would not absolve an individual from the obligation of maintaining his wife or children. If the man be able to work for his livelihood, if he be not a cripple or so infirm that he cannot do anything to earn a sustenance, he is bound to provide for their maintenance.

CHAPTER XII

MAHR OR DOWER.—PROMPT AND DEFERRED DOWER.—WIDOW'S LIEN FOR DOWER[1]

SECTION I

GENERAL OBSERVATIONS

In order to constitute a valid marriage, the Mahommedan Law requires that there should always be a consideration moving from the husband in favour of the wife, for her sole and exclusive use and benefit. This consideration[2] is called *mahr* or *sadak*

1 Fatawai Kazi Khan, Vol. I, p. 425; Fatawai 'Alamgiri, Vol. I, pp. 426—460; Radd-ul-Muhtar; Kanz-ud-Dakaik; Hedaya, Vol. II, p. 58; Durr-ul-Mukhtar; Kitab-ul-Anwar; Jam'a-ush-Shittat; Shara'ya-ul-Islam; Mafatih; Irshad-ul-'Allamah; 1 Sautayra; D'Ohsson; Sice.

2 "Dower can be regarded as the consideration for connubial intercourse by way of analogy to price under the contract of sale" observed Mahmud, J., in Abdul Kadir *v.* Salima I L R 8 All. 149. "It is not the exchange or consideration, as understood in the technical sense in the Contract Act, given by the man to the woman for entering into the contract, but an effect of the contract imposed by the law on the husband as a token of respect for its subject, the woman. If dower were the bride price a post-nuptial agreement to pay dower would be void for want of consideration, but such an agreement is valid and enforceable." See also Mst. Fatima Bibi *v.* Lal Din A I R 1937 Lah. 345 and Jahuren Bibi *v.* Soleman Khan A I R 1934 Cal. 210.

In Nasiruddin Shah *v.* Amtul Mughni Begum A I R 1948 Lah. 135 I L R 1947 Lah. 565, it was observed that the husband's duty to pay dower flows from the tie of marriage similar to his duty of providing maintenance and raiment. And if the latter two cannot be regarded as consideration for marriage and are only given out of consideration and respect for the wife, equally is dower not to be regarded as its consideration as that term of art is understood in English language . . . . had it been so the omission to specify any dower would have affected the validity of marriage.

in legal treatises, and in common parlance *dain mahr* dower-debt.

The principle of ante-nuptial settlements is not peculiar to the Mahommedan Law. Sautayra thinks that the custom originated in ancient times with the payments which the husbands often made to their wives as a means of support, and as a protection against the arbitrary exercise of the power of divorce.

Jewish rules.

The Jewish Law insisted upon the specification of the total debt prior to the contract of marriage, and considered all marriages without a consideration as invalid; but among the Hebrews, the dower settled on the wife was never made over to her for her exclusive use and enjoyment; she acquired, in fact, no right over it until the marriage was dissolved, either by the death of the husband or by divorce, in which case the dower was made over to her, in order to enjoy or to dispose of, according to her own desire.[1]

Islamic legislation.

The Islamic legislation regarding the marriage-consideration differs in two important features from the rules prevalent among the Hebrews. In the first place it does not consider a marriage contracted without specification of dower, as invalid; when no dower is specified the law presumes a consideration in favour of the wife, which is estimated on a recognised basis. In the second place, the wife acquires an immediate right over the dower, or that portion of it which is "exigible" in its nature.

Donatio Propter nuptias.

The *mahr* of the Islamic system is similar in all its legal incidents to the *donatio propter nuptias* of the Romans. It is a settlement in favour of the wife made prior to the completion of the marriage-contract in consideration of marriage. There is, however, this essential difference between the Roman *donatio propter nuptias* and the *mahr* of the Musulmans, that whereas the former is purely voluntary on the part of the husband, the latter is absolutely obligatory. "*Mahr* or dower is so necessary", says the *Fatawai Kazi Khan*, "to the marriage, that if it were not mentioned at the time of the marriage, or in the contract, the law will presume it by virtue of the contract itself."[2]

A stipulation on the part of the woman before marriage to abandon all her right to dower is invalid and inoperative under the Mahommedan Law, and should such a stipulation have been entered into, the wife would, nevertheless, be entitled to the

---

1 Among the Athenians and the Romans the woman brought the dowry. The Code Napoleon (Art. 1540) attaches the same character to the French Dot. In England, any property the woman brings with her is popularly called her dowry. It is in fact analogous to the Jahaz or Jahez of the Mahommedans.

2 Fatawai Kazi Khan, Vol. I, p. 426; Fatawai 'Alamgiri, Vol. I, p. 428; Jam'a-ush-Shittat.

See Hamira Bibi *v.* Zubaida Bibi L R 43 I A 294: I L R 38 All. 581.

customary dower. She can, if she choose after marriage, discharge the husband from his liability for the dower-debt, or make over to him any property she may have received from him in satisfaction of his liability.

Malik has recommended to his followers the payment of the entire dower prior to the consummation of marriage, and the rule prescribed by him is practically followed in all those countries where his doctrines are in force.

Amount of dower.

The amount of dower or *mahr* varies in different countries; there is no fixed rule as to the maximum.[1] It depends on the social position of the parties and the conditions of society in which they live. The *Radd-ul-Muhtar* lays this down with considerable distinctness. "Whatever amount exceeding the minimum the man agrees to pay he will be liable therefor."[2]

The Shiah *Shara'ya* says: "There is no limit either to the maximum or the minimum of dower", it being a matter of contract between husband and wife; so long as the article given or assigned by way of dower possesses any definite value, the assignment is considered valid. There is no distinction so far as this principle is concerned between the Shiahs and the Sunnis. Both schools, however, regard excessive dower as improper[3] though[4] not absolutely illegal; but, as will be seen, this recommendation is totally disregarded by the Indian[5] Musulmans, for reasons which have been explained in the Introduction.[6]

Minimum dower.

The early Hanafi lawyers fixed ten *dirhems* (equal to about five shillings), as the minimum for dower. The Malikis, inhabiting a poorer and less populous country than that in which the early Hanafi lawyers flourished, considered even a smaller sum as permissible.

These minimums have become obsolete and it is now customary in different countries to fix the amount of dower entirely by a consideration of the circumstances of the husband and wife.

---

1 Mus'ab settled a dower of 500,000 dirhems on the grand-daughter of Abu Bakr. The Prophet did not enunciate any fixed rule as to the amount of dower. He expressly left it to custom and local usages; but as he appears to have settled 500 dirhems upon Maimuna, the Shiahs consider that amount to be the mahr-i-sunnat. The Radd-ul-Muhtar says the dower of "our Lady" Fatima was 400 dirhems.

2 Radd-ul-Muhtar, Vol. II, p. 511; see Omdutoonnissa *v.* Mirza Asad Ali, 1 Sel. R. 277 (19th May 1809).

3 Fatawai Kazi Khan *in loco.*

4 Wajeh-oon-nissa *v.* Mirza Hassan Ali, 1 Sel. R 206 (30th December 1808).

5 Now Indo-Pakistan.

6 See Mst. Sugra Bibi *v.* Masuma Bibi (1877), I L 2 All. 573.

In India,[1] for example, among the upper middle class, the amount of dower ranges from 4,000 rupees to 40,000 rupees. In Behar, the latter is, generally speaking, the customary dower; in Lower Bengal, there is no custom. Among the lower classes, the *mahr* varies from 50 rupees to 400 rupees. In princely families, the dower consists of several lakhs.

Excessive or extravagant dower contracted for minors.

Although there is no limit to the maximum dower, it must not be supposed that the Mahommedan Law does not keep in view those cases where the amount is exorbitant and is either beyond the means of the husband, or covers his entire property so as to exclude the rights of heirs. Where such a contract is entered into for a minor by his guardian, the husband's liability would be limited to the *mahr-i-misl* or the *customary dower* of the wife.

Extravagant dowers.

But where the husband is *sui juris* and himself enters into the contract, or it is entered into with his authority, the question assumes a different aspect. In India,[1] it is not unusual to enter large amounts in dower-deeds without any intention of paying or exacting payment of such amounts,—the real dower being settled either privately or left undetermined. The practice seems to have been general in Mahommedan countries, and was certainly in vogue in the seventeenth century, for the *Fatawai 'Alamgiri* devotes a special section to this subject.[2]

Often large sums are stipulated merely as a device to prevent, on the part of the husband, the capricious exercise of the power of divorce vested in him by the principal schools.[3] It is a wholesome method of maintaining the balance between husband and wife. But as the law is generally administered in British India, it often works great injustice on the children. For instance, when a man leaves children by a pre-deceased wife and a second wife on whom he has settled it,[4] either from vanity or pressure from her relatives as a device again divorce, a preposterous dower, which he never had an intention of paying, the British Indian Courts save in the Province of Oudh,[5] would enforce the contract in its entirety; thus, the widow

1 Now Indo-Pakistan.

2 Fatawai 'Alamgiri, Vol. I, p. 445, sect. 8, see post, p. 465.

3 Comp. Cases XXXV and XXXVII in Macnaghten's Precedents of Mahommedan Law.

4 See Chapter on Talak.

5 Mirza Sulleman Kadar *v.* Nawab Mehdi Begum Surreya Bahu (1893), I L 21 Cal. 135; s. c. L R. 20 I A 144; see also Mulkha Do Alum Nawab Tajdar Bahoo *v.* Mirza Jehan Kadr (1865), 11 M I A 252; s. c. 2 W R P C 55.

would get the whole estate of the deceased to the absolute exclusion of the children.[1]

Fictitious dowers.

Fictitious dowers are generally called *mahr-i-talji'i.* In Mahommedan countries the Kazi has the power of reducing excessive dowers. The same power is vested in the Civil Courts in Oude by section 5 of the Oudh Laws Act (XVIII of 1876), which declares that "where the amount of dower stipulated in any contract of marriage by a Mahommedan is excessive with reference to the means of the husband, the entire sum provided in the contract shall not be awarded in any suit by decree in favour of the plaintiff, or by allowing it by way of set-off, lien or otherwise to the defendant; but the amount of dower to be allowed by the Courts shall be reasonable with reference to the means of the husband and the *status* of the wife." And this rule is applicable whether the suit to enforce the contract is brought in the husband's lifetime or after his death.[2]

When no dower is fixed at the time of marriage, or has not been distinctly specified either before or after marriage, or has been intentionally or unintentionally left indeterminate, the woman becomes entitled to what is called the *mahr-i-misl*, "the dower of her equals", or the *customary* dower.

Customary dower.

The customary dower of a woman is regulated with reference to the social position of her father's family and her own personal

---

1 See Sughra Bibi *v.* Masuma Bibi I L R 2 All. 573. A Muhammedan widow was entitled to the whole of the dower which her deceased husband had on marriage agreed to give her, whatever it might amount to and whether or not her husband was comparatively poor when he married her or had not left assets sufficient to pay the dower debt.

In Collector of Muradabad *v.* Harbans Singh I L R 21 All. 17, the High Court granted a decree for a sum of one crore of rupees and 25,000 gold mohurs as the plaintiff's dower debt, though the effect was to deprive the son of the late husband of the plaintiff of all his property. The learned Judges fully realised the hardship resulting from the decree, and regretted that they had no power like the one under the Oudh Act 18 of 1876, to interfere but observed that they had no alternative but to pass a decree for the amount of the dower contracted for, however extravagant that amount might be. *See also* Sultan Begum *v.* Serajuddin Ahmad A I R 1936 Lah. 183: 161 I C 300; A. M. Muhammad Ibrahim *v.* Ma Ma A I R 1939 Rang. 28; 179 I C 47; Bano Begum *v.* Mir Aun Ali (1907) Bom. L R 188 and Basir Ali *v.* Hafiz 13 C W N 153: 4 I C 462.

2 The reasons which led the legislature to vest the Courts in Oudh with this power apply to the whole of India, and it is to be hoped that the Act will be extended to other provinces.

See the observations of the learned Judges in 21 All. 17 where they regretted that they did not possess power like the one given by the Oudh Act.

See also Abdur Rahman *v.* Inayati Bibi A I R 1931 Oudh 63: 130 I C 113 where the Oudh rule was applied; and Zakeri Begum *v.* Sakina Begum 19 I A 157: I L R 19 Cal. 689 where the Privy Council observed that the Oudh Act did not apply to a case where a Muslim residing outside Oudh married in Oudh a lady belonging to that Province.

qualifications, and also, as the author of the *Hedaya* points out, to the dowers that have been given to her female paternal relations, such as her consanguine sisters or paternal aunts, or the daughters, of her paternal uncles.

But, says the *Radd-ul-Muhtar*, it does not necessarily follow from the rule that the customary dower should be regulated with regard to the position of her father's family, that no attention should be paid to the mother's position.

In fixing the amount, other points besides the custom which prevails in the woman's paternal family must be taken into consideration. For example, if one sister marry a rich, and the other, a comparatively poor man, the dower of the one cannot be taken as a standard for the dower of the other. It is, therefore, laid down that, in order to find a proper test for the customary dower of a woman, "the *condition* of her husband in respect of wealth and lineage should be *like* that of the husband of the woman to whom *she* is compared."[1]

In the same way, a woman may be superior to all the female members of her father's family, in intellectual attainments or personal attractions, and accordingly her dower can hardly be regulated by the *mahr* of her less fortunately endowed female elations.[2]

Customary dower.

The customary dower or *mahr-ul-misl* varies, therefore, in amount according to the social position of the woman's family, the wealth of her husband, her own personal qualifications, the circumstances of the time, and the conditions of society surrounding her. No fixed rule can be laid down as to the amount of dower in any particular case. When, therefore, it is said that the dower of a woman, where no *mehr* is stipulated or specified at the time of marriage, should be the "dower of her equals", it is only intended to imply, that an approximation may be made by observing the custom which has prevailed in her father's family, provided she does not differ in intellectual capacity or personal attraction from the female relations with whom she is compared.[3]

---

1 Fatawai 'Alamgiri, Vol. I, p. 428; Radd-ul-Muhtar, Vol. II, p. 581.

In Hamira Bibi *v*. Zubaida Bibi 43 I A 294 : I L R 38 All. 581, their Lordships of the Privy Council observed: "Dower is an essential incident under the Musulman Law to the status of marriage, to such an extent is this so that when it is unspecified at the time the marriage is contracted the law declares that it must be adjudged on definite principles."

2 The Hedaya says: "In regulating the mahr-ul-misl of a woman, attention must be paid to her equality with the women from whose dowers the rule is to be taken, in point of age, beauty, fortune, understanding, and virtue, because the mahr varies according to any difference in all these circumstances, and, in like manner, it differs according to place of residence or time."—Hedaya, Vol. I, p. 148.

3 Radd-ul-Muhtar, Vol. II, pp. 581, 582.

Shiah doctrine similar.

The same rule respecting customary dower is in force among the Shiahs. "The *mahr-ul-misl* of a woman," says the *Irshad*, "is regulated by a regard to the nobility of her birth, the beauty of her person, and the custom of her female relations." To this the *Tahir-ul-Akham* and the *Jam'a-ush-Shittat* add that, "as there exist different customs in different places in respect of dower, in fixing the amount of the *mahr-ul-misl*, regard must be paid to the local customs, with special reference to the dowers of the women, who are the equals of the female in question, in knowledge, lineage, wealth, understanding and such like."[1]

Among the Shiahs, dowers are of three kinds, *viz.*, (*a*) the *mahr-i-sunnat*, or traditional dower; it refers to the amount of dower adopted by the Prophet, and is said to be 500 *dirhems*; (*b*) the *mahr-ul-misl*; and (*c*) the *mahr-ul-musamma*, the specified dower.

Some of the Shiah writers are of opinion that where no dower is settled at the time of marriage, and an approximation is made from the custom prevailing in the woman's family, the amount should not exceed the traditional 500 *dirhems*.

But this view has long been abandoned, and, nowadays, the same principles which regulate the approximation of the customary dower among the Sunnis are in force also among the Shiahs.

General principle.

When there is no example forthcoming for determining the *mahr-ul-misl*, the position of the father's family ought to be taken into consideration.. And it is allowable, may incumbent, on the Judge, in the absence of examples in the woman's family, to enquire into the custom among strangers occupying the same rank in life and living under the same circumstances—even in different cities. And when all the conditions are not similar, so much as are identical or analogous should be considered.[2]

Mahr-ul-misl is presumed only in those cases when the union is legal. Mere concubinage does not give rise to the presumption of dower.

Nujeemoodeen Ahmad v. Beebee Hosseinee.

The principles which regulate the determination of the *mahr-ul-misl* have been correctly enunciated by the Calcutta High Court in the case of *Nujmoodeen Ahmed* v. *Beebee Hosseinee*,[3] where the

1 Jam'a-ush-Shittat.

2 Radd-ul-Muhtar, Vol. II, pp. 583, 584.

3 (1865) 4 W R 110. The idea, however, that the very best description of oral evidence should be produced to support a claim for dower when no kabin-namah is forthcoming (7 W R 495, and 11 W R 65), is founded on a misconception. As I have pointed out in the test, in some places kabin-namahs are in vogue, in others not. And, therefore, in the latter class of cases, the claim can only be established by oral testimony, the character of which must depend on the circumstances of each particular case, and the nature of the evidence available,

learned Judges held in substance that a customary dower must be proved by showing a custom of the women of the wife's family to receive, rather than of the men of the husband's family to pay, a certain dower; the Mahommedan dower being the consideration paid by the bridegroom for the marriage, and, therefore, regulated by the position and conduct of the bride, especially as Mahommedan men often contract most unequal marriages, though the means and position of the bridegroom must not altogether be excluded from consideration.

As a rule, however, dowers are always settled before marriage; and in India, especially, no condition relating to it is left for future determination.

Principle—Marriage valid though dower not settled.

It has sometimes, been supposed that the validity of the marriage depends on the *constitution* of the dower, and that when there is no consideration for the contract of marriage, nor a settlement effected in favour of the wife, the marriage is invalid. The *Hedaya* and the *Fatawai Kazi Khan*, however, expressly declare that a marriage is valid, although there may not be any mention of dower at the time; "and", says the former authority, "a marriage is valid although no dower has been mentioned because literally *nikah* signifies a contract of union which is fully accomplished by the performance of the marital rites. Dower is obligatory as a mark of respect for the subject (*al-mahal*); therefore its mention is not essential to the validity of the marriage. For the like reason, a marriage is valid, although the man were to engage in the contract on the special condition that there should be no dower."[1] The dower specified at the time of the marriage can be increased subsequently.[2]

Similarly, the Shiah *Shara'ya* and the *Jam'a-ush-Shittat* declare that "the mention of dower is by no means a condition precedent to the validity of a contract of marriage, so that if a man were to marry a woman without any mention or specification of dower, or with the express stipulation that there shall be no dower, the contract will be valid and the law will award the woman the customary dower".[3]

SECTION II

PROMPT AND DEFERRED DOWER

Anything over which *dominion* or the right of property may be exercised, or anything which may be reduced into possession,

1 Hedaya, Vol. II, Bk. i.

2 See Jahuran Bibi *v.* Suleman Khan A I R 1934 Cal. 210: 149 I C 1150; Mst. Nasiban Bibi *v.* Mst. Iqbal Begum A I R 1935 Lah. 816: 160 I C 805; Chan Pir *v.* Fakar Shah A I R 1940 Lah. 104 : 189 I C 725 and Rukiyya Begum *v.* Radha Kishen A I R 1944 All. 214 : I L R 1944 All. 325.

3 Comp. the Mafatih, the Irshad-ul-'Allamah, and the Kitab-min-la Euhazzar-il-Fakih. In Kumarunnissa Bibi *v.* Hussaini Bibi (1881), I L R 3 All. 266, it was held that it was not necessary under the Muhammedan Law, that the dower should be agreed upon before marriage; it may be fixed afterwards. See Mst. Fatima *v.* Lal Din A I R 1937 Lah. 345.

See also Bashir Ahmad *v.* Zubaida I L R 1 Luck. 83 ; A I R 1926 Oudh. 186 and Mst. Amina Bibi *v.* Mohammad I L R 4 Luck. 343 : A I R 1929 Oudh. 520.

either *in proesenti* or *in futuro*, anything, in fact, which comes within the meaning of the word *mal*, and has a value, may according to the Hanafi doctrines, form the subject of dower.[1]

Munaf'a (profits accruing from land, investments business, industry, &c.), and debts owing to the husband from other people are proper subjects of dower. But if a free man were to marry on the stipulation that he would render his own services to his wife in lieu of dower, although the marriage would be valid, the woman would be entitled to her customary dower.[2]

Stipulation of service invalid.

The text of the *Tanwir-ul-Absar* is as follows:—"And if the husband be free and should marry either a free woman or a slave girl on condition of serving her for a year [in other words, a determinate period], the woman would be entitled to her *mahr-ul-misl.*"

The comment of the *Radd-ul-Muhtar*, on this passage, is as follows:—"If the husband should condition that he would serve the wife for a year, this, according to the two Sheikhs [Abu Hanifa and Abu Yusuf], would make the husband liable for the *mahr-ul-misl.* According to Imam Mohammed the woman would receive the value of the services." The author of the *Radd-ul-Muhtar* goes on to say that "here restriction is placed on the word 'service', for, should a man marry a woman on the condition that he would carry her load, or ride her animals, or cultivate her land and such like matters, which result in profits, for a determinate period by way of dower, such a condition is valid. For, all this is the profit of *mahr.*" According to the Hanafi doctrines, therefore, an assignment of insurance policies would form a valid *mahr*.

Among the Hanafis, if a man were to marry a woman, engaging to instruct her in religion, or to take her on a pilgrimage (in lieu of dower), the stipulation would be inoperative, and the woman would be entitled to the customary dower.[3] According to the primitive Hanafi notions, when a man married a woman on condition of instructing her in the Koran, he became liable for the *mahr-ul-misl*; but, according to the modern legists, the condition is valid.

Instruction in the Koran valid.

The author of the *Nahr-ur-Raik* states that it is lawful to receive remuneration for instructing in law or in the Koran, and that on this is the *Fatwa*, and that, consequently, it is lawful to make instruction in the Koran the subject of dower.[4]

---

1 Fatawai Kazi Khan, Vol. I, p. 425.

2 Fatawai 'Alamgiri, Vol. I, p. 426.

3 *Ibid.*

4 *Ibid.*, p. 427,

When something is assigned by way of dower which is not in existence at the time, either substantively, or as a creation of the law, such assignment is not valid. For example, if a man were to settle on his wife by way of *mahr* the future produce of certain trees or lands in his possession, it would be invalid, and the woman would have a right to the usual dower. But the assignment of a *chose in action,* or the sale-proceeds of something of which he is the proprietor, would constitute a lawful *mahr.*[1] The passages in the *Radd-ul-Muhtar* are distinct on this point.

The text of the *Tanwir-ul-Absar* is as follows:—"It is lawful for a man to assign for dower the ten dirhems which may be due to him from somebody else."

On this the comment runs thus:—"It is lawful for a man marrying a woman to fix for her dower anything which may be due to him from her, or which may be due to him from somebody else. . . . For example, if ten dirhems are due to him from Zaid, he may fix that for dower, and the woman would be entitled to get that amount either from the husband's debtor or from the husband. . . . If the debt is owing from the woman herself, it is on the footing of *'ain,* (a thing in specie).

"Similarly, if a man were to fix for dower a *manf'at* (profit), that also will be lawful; for example, residence in a house, or the right of riding on an animal, the right of cultivation, &c., but that the period thereof should be ascertained."[2]

Shiah and Shaf'ei doctrines.

Among the Shiahs and the Shaf'eis, however, a free man may assign to his wife his own services in lieu of dower.[3] Instruction in religion or art, an engagement to take the wife on a pilgrimage, the usufruct or property not in existence, contingent benefits, &c., may, according to the Shiah doctrine, form the valid subject of dower.[4]

Prompt and deferred dower.

As there is nothing in the Koran or in the traditions tending to show that the integral payment of the dower prior to consummation is obligatory in law, the later jurisconsults have held that a portion of the *mahr* should be considered payable at once or on demand, and the remainder on the dissolution of the contract, whether by divorce or the death of either of the parties.[5] The portion which is payable immediately is called the *mahr-i-mu'ajjal,*[6] "prompt" or "exigible"; and a wife can refuse to enter

---

1 Radd-ul-Muhtar, Vol. II, p. 517.

2 *Ibid.*, p. 540.

3 Hedaya, Vol. I, Bk. ii, chap. 3; Shara'ya, p. 290.

4 Jam'a-ush-Shittat.

5 See the case of Meer Meher Ally *v.* Amani (1869), 2 B L R, A C, p. 306; (s. c.) 11 W R 212.

6 (معجل)

the conjugal domicile until the payment of the prompt portion of the dower. The other portion is called *mahr-i-muwajjal*[1] "deferred dower", which does not become due until the dissolution of the contract. It is customary in India[2] to fix half the dower as prompt and the remaining moiety as deferred or "postponed:"[3] but the parties are entitled to make any other stipulation they choose. For example, they may allow the whole amount to remain unpaid until the death of either the husband or the wife. Generally speaking, among the Musulmans of India, the *deferred dower* is a penal sum, which is allowed to remain unpaid with the object of compelling the husband to fulfil the terms of the marriage-contract in their entirety.[4]

The late Sudder Dewani Adalut of Agra decided that when no specific portion of the dower was stipulated at the time of marriage to be exigible, the wife would be entitled only to one-third as such, and the remaining two-thirds would become due on the decease of the husband.[5] It does not appear from the report of that case, whether the decision proceeded upon the Shiah or the Hanafi doctrines.

Shiah doctrines.

Under the Shiah Law, where no time is specified for the payment of the dower, or where its nature is described only in general terms, and it is not mentioned in the contract of marriage how much is prompt and how much is deferred, the whole is considered prompt.[6]

Hanfi doctrine.

Under the Hanafi doctrines, each case will be decided on its own individual merits. "Where it has been explained how much of the dower is prompt", says the *'Alamgiri*, citing the *Fatawai Kazi Khan*,[6] "that much should be promptly paid. When this has not been done, regard should be had to the [qualifications of the] woman and the dower mentioned in the contract, with the object of determining how much of *such* dower should be considered prompt in the case of *such* woman; and the amount so

1 (مؤجل) From ajal (time) because time is given for its payment.

2 Now Indo-Pakistan.

3 The custom in India under the Emperor Aurungzeb was the same; for the Fatawai 'Alamgiri says "if half of the dower be prompt and the other half be deferred, as is customary in our cities, &c.

4 See Sultan Begum *v.* Sarajuddin A I R 1936 Lah. 183. Dower has important uses which affect the domestic life of the Muhammedans. The law giver of Islam was anxious to safeguard the wife against the arbitrary exercise of the right of divorce by the husband. If she survived her husband and his other heirs illtreated her, she could not be thrown into the street but would be able, apart from her legal share, to enforce against them her claim for dower which must be paid out of the heritage before the assets of the husband are distributed among the heirs. This is the keystone of the Muhammedan Law of dower in its purity.

5 Mariam-oon-Nissa Begum *v.* Imdadee Begum (1848) Morley's Dig. (New Ser.), 182.

6 Jam'a-ush-Shittat. In the case of Hussain Khan *v.* Sirdar Khan (1911) I L 35 Bom. 386 the Bombay High Court applied this rule to a Hanafi case. See however Nasiruddin Shah *v.* Amatul Mughni Begum A I R 1948 Lah. 135.

7 Fatawai 'Alamgiri, Vol. I, p. 448; Fatawai Kazi Khan, Vol. I, p. 426.

determined is to be *prompt* accordingly, without regard to the proportion of a fourth or a fifth, but what is customary is also to be considered. But when it is stipulated that the whole is to be *prompt*, the entire dower should be promptly paid without any regard to custom."

Similarly, it is laid down in the *Radd-ul-Muhtar* that "when nothing is mentioned as to what portion should be prompt and what portion deferred, regard must be had to *'urf* (custom), and on this is the *Fatwa*."[1]

And then the author adds that in Syria the custom is to make two-thirds *m'uajjal*.

Principle.

But the parties may stipulate that the whole should be deferred, and even if it should be deferred until death or divorce it would be lawful.

If the dower is deferred until the death of either party, and the husband dies, it becomes due on the expiration of the widow's *'iddat*.[2]

It is also lawful to stipulate that the husband should pay as much as he can at once, and the remainder at some fixed time after.

The decision of the Agra Sudder Court has been, to all intents and purposes, overruled by the Allahabad High Court. In the case of *Edun* v. *Mazhar Hussain*[3] and that of *Taufikunnissa* v. *Ghulam Kamber*,[4] the Allahabad High Court adopted and enforced the principle of law stated in the *Fatawai Kazi Khan*.[5]

In the first mentioned case, the plaintiff, Mazhar Hussain, sued his wife for restitution of conjugal rights. A dower of 5,000 rupees was settled at the time of marriage, but it was not stipulated how much of it should be "prompt", and how much "deferred". The wife refused to take up her abode in the conjugal domicile until the payment of the "prompt" portion of the dower. It was held, that in the absence of an express

---

1 Radd-ul-Muhtar, Vol. II. This principle seems to have been overlooked in the case of Bedar Bukht *v.* Mirza Khurrum Bukht (1879), 19 W R P C 315. See Nasiruddin Shah *v.* Amatul Mughni Begum A I R 1948 Lah. 135.

2 *ibid.*

3 (1879) I L 1 All. 483.

4 (1877) I L 1 All. 506; see also Fatima Bibi *v.* Sadruddin (1865) 2 Bom. H C R 291.

5 See Umda Begum *v.* Muhammadi Begum I L R 33 All. 291: 9 I C 200; Muhammad Subhan Ullah *v.* *Mst.* Saghirunnissa I L R 41 All. 562: A I R 1919 All. 280, Mst. Maimuna Begum *v.* Shafaat Ullah A I R 1931 All. 403: 131 I C 115; Mangat Rai *v.* Sakina Begum A I R 1934 All. 441; Muhammad Taqi Ahmed *v.* Farmoodi Begum A I R 1941 All. 181: I L R 1941 All. 326 and Bibi Rehana Khatun *v.* Iqtidaruddin Hasan A I R 1943 All. 184: I L R 1943 All. 295.

stipulation whether the whole dower was to be "deferred", the payment of a portion must be considered "prompt"; and the amount of such portion was to be determined with reference to custom, but when there was no custom it must be determined by the Court with reference to the *status* of the wife and the amount of the dower; and, as in the particular case in question, the wife had led an immoral life previous to her marriage with the plaintiff, the lower Court was held to have exercised its discretion soundly in holding that only one-fifth of the dower settled should, in her instance, be considered "prompt." The same rule was followed in the subsequent case of *Taufikunnissa* v. *Ghulam Kamber*.

The rule enunciated in *Mirza Bedar Bukht* v. *Mirza Khurram Bakht*[1] that where it is not specified what portion is prompt and what portion deferred, the whole dower is to be considered prompt, is applicable probably to cases arising among Shiahs. But it has been followed by the Madras High Court without consideration of the attendant circumstances.[2]

Shiah doctrine.

When no settlement has been made prior to marriage, the parties may, subsequently, come to terms respecting the amount. Such dower is called *mahr-i-tafwiz*; when the amount is settled by arbitrators or by the Judge (*Hakim-ush-Shar'a*), it is called *mahr-i-tahkim*.

Hanafi doctrines.

According to the Hanafi doctrines the wife becomes entitled to the dower, and if any property is contracted to be given in

---

1 19 W R 315.

But see Nasiruddin Shah *v*. Amtul Mughni Begum A I R 1948 Lah. 135 where it was held that in absence of any custom, the presumption is that it is half and half.

2 Masthan Saheb v. Assam Bibi (1899) I L 23 Mad. 371.

In Sheikh Muhammad Rowther *v*. Aiyesha Bibi I L R 1938 Mad. 609: A I R 1938 Mad. 107, the Madras High Court has followed its earlier decision on the basis of *stare decisis*.

In Nasiruddin Shah *v*. Amtul Mughmi Begum A I R 1948 Lah. 135: it has been observed "In the 8th century the author of Mukhtasir-ul-Waqayah expressed a different opinion while Qazi Khan differed from Isbijabi in the 6th century. From the 8th century onwards, the rule appears to have been laid down uniformly that urf or custom of a locality has to be looked at in deciding the question whether the whole or any portion of mahr was to be prompt. That this was considered to be the rule prevailing in India (now Indo-Pakistan sub-continent) at the time of Emperor Aurangzeb who was a great religious scholar himself and who must have taken care to select the large band of eminent scholars to complete the Fatawa, cannot be lost sight of. The ijma of the Muslim jurists during the last five centuries is thus clearly in favour of the view that *urf* or custom is to be a determining factor in deciding the amount of the dower which is in the absence of a specific agreement to be payable on the wife's demand."

lieu of dower, her right therein vests immediately, (*a*) on the consummation of the marriage; (*b*) on a "valid retirement" which among the Hanafis is considered equivalent to actual consummation; and (*c*) on the death of either the husband or the wife, before or after consummation.[1]

For example, if a husband consummate the marriage, the wife becomes entitled to the entire dower settled on her, and though she may realise only the "prompt" portion, she can make an assignment of the whole, as a specified debt against her husband. The same would be the case if, instead of consummation, there had been a "valid retirement" of the parties into the nuptial chamber.[2] Again, if the husband were to die, either before or after the consummation of the marriage, the wife would acquire an absolute right over the whole of her *mahr*; or, if she were to predecease him, her heirs would become entitled to the dower.

Principle—Shiah and Shaf'ei doctrines.

According to the Shiah and the Shaf'ei doctrines, *the wife's right to the entirety of the dower vests in her only when the marriage has been consummated*, or when either she or her husband has died before consummation and during the subsistence of the contract. According to these two schools, "retirement" without consummation does not entitle the wife to the *entirety* of the dower.

Principle—When a present must be made.

Under the Hanafi Law, when a separation takes place between husband and wife before consummation or "valid retirement" she is entitled to half the specified dower.[3] But when no dower has been specified at the time of marriage she is only entitled to a present, the amount of which depends upon the usages of the country. Even where the amount of the dower has been settled after marriage, she cannot claim a moiety of such dower, if the separation takes place before consummation, but is entitled to a present only.[4]

The Shiahs agree in the main with the Hanafis. They also hold, that if a separation takes place *before consummation*, the woman is entitled only to half her specified dower (*mahr-i-musamma*), but they differ from the Hanafis in holding that where a *mahr-i-tafwiz* or a *mahr-i-tahkim* has been settled on the wife

1 The Fatawai 'Alamgiri says "Dower is confirmed by one of three things, consummation, valid retirement, or the death of either husband or wife, and that whether the amount of dower be named or it be the mahr-ul-misl" : Vol. I, p. 428.

See Muhammad Zaman *v.* Naima Sultan P L D 1952 Pesh. 47.

2 See Omdat-oon-nissa *v.* Mirza Arsad Ali, supra.

3 Abdul Karim v. Mst. Fazilat-oon-nissa, 5 Sel. R 75 (15th Dec. 1830).

See Tajbi *v.* Nattar Sharif A I R 1940 Mad. 888 ; Muhammad Zaman *v.* Naima Sultan P L D 1952 Pesh. 47.

4 Hedaya 44-45; Baillie Vol. I, 96-97.

after marriage, and the husband separates from her before consummation, she is entitled to the moiety of such *mahr*, as in the case of the *mahr-i-musamma*.[1]

Principle—Hanafi rule.

Among the Hanafis, the husband is bound to make a present to a wife, from whom he separates before consummation of marriage, when no dower has been specified. But it is only when the husband furnishes the cause of separation that he is liable for a present. For example, when he has separated himself from the wife by a *talak*, he is under the obligation of making her a "present" (*mut'at*), if there has been no consummation or "valid retirement", and no dower has been specified before marriage. No present is due from him, however, when the cause proceeds from the wife. Were she to apostatise or commit adultery, or to cancel the marriage in exercise of her option of puberty or on the ground of inequality, she would have no right to a present.[2]

Shiah rule.

The same principle is in force among the Shiahs. "If the husband and the wife separate *before* consummation (*and there is no dower specified in the contract or settled afterwards*), the wife is entitled to a present which is to be regulated by the position and the means of the husband."[3] "No woman, however", says the *Shara'ya* "is entitled to a present, except one for whom no dower has been settled, and who has become separated from her husband before consummation."[4]

Shaf'ei doctrine.

Among the Shaf'eis, a present is incumbent on the husband in every case of separation.

When the right to the dower has once vested in the woman, it is not defeated or lost by any conduct on her part. For example, when the marriage has been consummated (according to the Sunnis as well as the Shiahs) or a "valid retirement" has taken place (according to the Hanafis), the woman's right to her dower is not lost by her subsequent apostasy or adultery; but it would be otherwise if the apostasy or misconduct occurred before the right vested in her. In such a case, the *entire* dower would fall to the ground.[5]

The right once vested is not lost, even if the woman were to murder her husband. Should she commit suicide or be killed by her husband, her right would pass to her heirs.[6]

---

1 Jam'a-ush-Shittat; Irshad-ul-'Allamah.

2 Fatawai 'Alamgiri, Vol. I, pp. 428, 429.

3 Jam'a-ush-Shittat.

4 Shara'ya, p. 292.

5 Fatawai 'Alamgiri, Vol. I, p. 447; Jam'a-ush-Shittat.

6 *Ibid.*

Principle—Dower in the case of an invalid marriage.

A woman is not entitled to any *mahr* or present under an invalid marriage judicially dissolved *before* consummation. Should consummation take place before the order is made, she would be entitled to her *mahr-ul-misl*, which must not, however, exceed the specified dower.[1]

It must be borne in mind also that in an invalid marriage, dower does not become due upon a "valid retirement" as in the case of a valid marriage.

Principle—Prompt dower when realisable.

The *prompt* portion of the *mahr* may be realised by the wife at any time before or after consummation;[2] the *deferred* portion remains unpaid until the dissolution of the contract or such other time as its payment may have been postponed to. There is no rule by which it necessarily follows that postponed or deferred dower becomes realisable only on the death of the husband, or if he happen to divorce the wife, on such divorce. The great difference between prompt and deferred dower is this; the portion of the dower specified in the contract as *prompt* is *payable* and *realisable* at once, and the wife can refuse all conjugal rights on the part of the husband until it is paid. As regards *postponed dower* it becomes payable only on the expiration of the period specified. If no period is fixed, it becomes payable on the dissolution of the contract.

But if there is no specification of how much is *prompt* and how much *deferred*, recourse must be had to the custom of the locality to determine the question.[3]

The *Mukhtasar-ul-Vikaya* says "if there is specification as to dower being *m'uajjal* or *muwajjal* it will be given effect to; if not, reference will be made to custom" (المتعارف). The same rule is laid down by Hamawi on the authority of the *bazazia*: "If it has not been specified in the contract what is *prompt*, regard will be paid to the [status of the] woman and the specified dower, with a view to determine how much of it was to be considered prompt for a woman like her [*i.e.*, of her position in life], and this should be determined according to *custom* ('*urf*) (بالعرف) and to the same extent should payment be directed (فيقضى)."

---

1 Radd-ul-Muhtar, Vol. II, pp. 573, 574; see ante.

2 See Rehana Khatun *v.* Iqtidaruddin A I R 1943 All. 184.

See also Mahadev Lal *v.* Bibi Muniran A I R 1933 Pat. 281 where it has been held that dower which is not paid at once may for that reason be described as deferred dower but if it is postponed until demanded by the wife, it is in law prompt dower.

In Manihar Bibi v. Rakha Singh A I R 1954 Manipur 1, it was held that deferred dower does not become prompt merely because the wife demands it.

3 See Nasiruddin Shah *v.* Amtul Mughni Begum A I R 1948 Lah. 135.

Hanafi doctrines.

The *Fatawai Kazi Khan* and the *Fatawai 'Alamgiri* give the rule in the same terms:—"if nothing is specified [how much is *prompt* or how much *deferred*] regard must be had to the woman and the dower named in the contract to determine how much of it should be *prompt* for such a woman out of such a dower, and should be treated as immediately demandable. It must not be considered to be one-fourth or one-fifth, but regard should be had to *custom*, for what is established by custom is also established by the *Shar'a* (the Law)."

There is another passage in the *Fatawai Kazi Khan* which is still more explicit:—"A man marries a woman for a thousand (*dirhems*) and the whole of it is said to be *deferred*, if the time [to which payment is postponed] is known, the postponment is valid; if not, it is not valid. And when postponment is not valid, the husband must be ordered to pay promptly that proportion which, by the custom of the people of the town [locality], is recognised as prompt, and the balance shall be realised from him after divorce or death, and the Kazi shall not compel the husband for the payment of the balance, nor shall he imprison him for same."

The *Sharh-i-Vikaya* explains that this is the rule adopted by the later jurists (المتاخرين).[1]

Shiah rule.

Actual possession is not necessary to enable the wife to exercise her rights over the portion deferred. Deferred dower, in fact, is *chose in action*; a woman can assign it to any one she chooses, and such person may recover the same, on its becoming due, from the husband or his estate. The *Shara'ya* says in explicit terms: "The dower becomes the property of the wife by the mere contract [when consummation has taken place], and she may deal with it in any way she likes, before she has obtained actual possession of the subject-matter."

General rule.

She can make a gift of the *mahr* either to her husband or to a stranger.

Ba'i mukasa.

In the former case, when she gives it to her husband, it answers as a discharge of his liability, or she may exchange it for any other property belonging to the husband. An exchange of property for dower is called a *Ba'i mukasa*.

---

1 The statement of the law by Macnaghten (Art. 22, Principles and Precedents), that when there is no specification the whole must be regarded as prompt is not correct. See also Umda Begum *v.* Muhammadi (1910) I L 33 All. 291.

General rule.

A wife, says the *Fatawai 'Alamgiri,* may make a gift of her dower to her husband, and none of her guardians, not even the father, has a right to object to her so doing.[1] She may exonerate her husband either from the payment of the whole debt or only from part of it. In order to be valid, the exoneration must be made while she is in good health and of sound mind. In India, when a woman is on a death-bed, she generally "forgives" her husband the unpaid dower-debt. Such "discharges" *in extremis* will probably be treated by the Courts as death-bed gifts.[2]

Shiah dectrine.

Under the Hanafi Law, a father cannot make any abatement in his daughter's dower in favour of the husband,[3] but under the Shiah Law, a father or grandfather may do so, and such abatement would be valid, unless there is reason to believe it was done fraudulently.[4] Under no circumstance, however, can either the father or grandfather discharge the husband of a minor daughter from the *entire debt.*[5]

Dower is only a debt like other liabilities of the husband, and has priority over legacies bequeathed by the testator and the rights of heirs. A partition of the estate cannot ordinarily take place until the dower-debt has been satisfied. But a partition of the estate before payment of the dower-debt does not invalidate the partition, the heirs take the shares subject to the rights of the widow for her *mahr.*

When the wife is alive she can recover the debt herself from the estate of her deceased husband. If she predeceases the husband, the heirs of the wife, including the husband, become entitled to her dower; and he is liable for the amount less his share.[6] They can sue him severally each for his or her share,

---

1 Fatawai 'Alamgiri, Vol. I, p. 446.

See Jynai Begum *v.* Umrav Begum I L R 32 Bom. 612 where it has been held that such remission even though without consideration is valid. See also Nasiruddin *v.* Amtul Mughni Begum A I R 1948 Lah. 135.

2 The Fatawai 'Alamgiri says: "It is necessary for a discharge to be valid that she should not be sick of death-illness at the time of giving her consent", Vol. I, p. 442. She must of course be sui juris (*i.e.* must have attained puberty although not majority under the Majority Act). See Qasim Hussain *v.* Kaniz A I R 1932 All. 649.

See Nurrunnessa *v.* Khaja Muhammad I L R 47 Cal. 537 and Hasnumiyya *v.* Halimunnissa A I R 1942 Bom. 128 where it has been held that the remission must have been made with free consent and that a remission made by a wife when she is in great mental distress on account of her husband's death is not one made with free consent, and is not binding on her.

See also Shah Bano *v.* Iftikhar Muhammad Khan P L D 1956 Kar. 363. Where a woman feels that the possible way to win or retain the affection of her husband is to remit the dower amount and forgoes her claim she is not a free agent and it would be inequitable to hold that she is bound by such remission of dower.

3 Fatawai 'Alamgiri, Vol. I, p. 446.

4 Jam'a-ush-Shittat.

5 Shara'ya, p. 295.

6 Ali Bukhsh Khan *v.* Kaeem Bibee, 1 Sel. R. 86 note (24th Aug. 1804).

but for a proper adjudication, all the heirs should be joined as parties to the action.[1]

In *Mubarak-un-nissa* v. *Mansab Hassan Khan*[2] it was provided in the deed of dower that the wife was to take possession of certain property in lieu of her dower, and enjoy the usufruct thereof, but in case she predeceased the husband it should revert to him and if he predeceased her, the property would become hers absolutely.

The husband having died before the wife, a question arose between the widow and his other heirs as to the effect of the deed of dower.

The High Court of Allahabad held that the agreement was neither a mortgage by conditional sale nor the special form of transaction known by the term *Mubahat*; but that it was a contract between the parties which was binding on their representatives.

In another case[3] the Allahabad High Court carried further the effect of an agreement between husband and wife. In this case a dispute between the parties was referred to arbitration with the result that an agreement was arrived at, confirmed subsequently by an award of the arbitrators that a certain property should be transferred in *praesanti* to the wife in lieu of her dower with a control to the husband over the application of the income. It was provided, however, that if she predeceased him, he should continue in possession during his life, but that if he died before her, she should become the owner and his heirs should have no right to interfere with her possession. On a question as to the effect of this agreement, the High Court held that the award was sufficient to transfer the property and that no further conveyance was necessary.

Lien of the widow for dower.

Under the Mahommedan Law, there is no hypothecation without seisin, and therefore a widow has no absolute lien over any *specific* property of her deceased husband so as to enable her to follow it, as in the case of a mortgage, into the hands of a *bona fide* purchaser for value. As stated already, the widow's claim for dower is only a debt against the husband's estate, and has priority over legacies and the rights of heirs.[4]

---

1 Mahammed Ishak *v.* Sheikh Akramal Haq (1907), 12 C W N 84. In this case one of the heirs was not made a party until more than three years from the death of the wife. The husband contended that the suit which was brought by another heir was barred. The High Court overruled the objection and decreed the claim.

2 (1911) I L 33 All. 421.

3 Muhammad Yakub Hussain *v.* Inayate Jan (1911) I L 33 All. 683.

4 Wahedunnissa *v.* Shubratun (1870) 6 B L R 54.

See Imperial Bank of Gaya *v.* Bibi Sayeedan A I R 1960 Pat. 132. The heirs of a deceased Muslim are not personally liable for the dower debt. Each heir is liable only to the extent of the share of the debt proportionate to his share of the estate.

But if she omits to put forward her claim for dower and assents to a person taking a legacy she cannot afterwards retract her assent.[1]

Ahmad Hussain v. Mst. Khadija.

When, however, she has obtained actual and lawful possession of the estate of her husband under a claim to hold it for her dower, she will be entitled to retain possession until the debt is satisfied, with the usual liability for account to the heirs.[2] In the case of *Ahmed Hussain* v. *Mussamat Khadija*, the Calcutta High Court held that even where the dower was unascertained, but the widows were in possession of their deceased husband's estate in satisfaction of their *mahr*, they had a lien over it as long as any portion of the dower remained unsatisfied.[3]

---

1 Reza Hossein *v.* Ifatoonnissa (1873) 24 W R 564.

2 Mussamat Beebee Bachun *v.* Sheikh Hamid Hussain (1871) 10 B L R P C 45; s. c., 14 M I A 398; see also Amanatunnissa *v.* Bashirunnissa (1894) I L 17 All. 77; Muhammad Karimullah Khan *v.* Amani Begum (1895) I L 17 All. 93.

See Tahir-un-nissa *v.* Nawab Hasan (1914) I L R 36 All. 558. A widow who has not obtained possession of her husband's estate in lieu of her dower, cannot exclude other heirs of her husband from possession. They are entitled to joint possession with her and if they claim such possession she is not entitled to say "I will now go into possession". Her only right is to retain possession of what she has before they obtained possession.

In Mst. Maina Bibi *v.* Chaudri Vakil Ahmed A I R 1925 P C 63: L R 52 I A 145 (a judgment of the Privy Council to which Syed Amir Ali himself was a party), it was observed that if a Muslim widow obtains possession of her husband's estate *peaceably* and *without force or fraud*, she is entitled to retain possession till her dower debt is paid.

According to Madras (Beeju Bee *v.* Syed Murtuja I L R 43 Mad. 214; Bombay (Hasnumiya Dadamiya *v.* Halimunnissa Hafizullah A I R 1942 Bom. 128 and a chain of Allahabad authorities (Ramzan Ali *v.* Asghari Begum I L R 32 All. 563, Mohammed Shoaib *v.* Zaib Jehan I L R 50 All. 423; Imtiaz Begum *v.* Abdul Karim I L R 53 All. 31; Zamin Ali *v.* Azizunnissa I L R 55 All. 139), all that is necessary for the widow to retain possession until her dower debt is paid is that she should obtain possession *not* by force or fraud. The consent of the heirs is not essential. If she has to depend upon consent of heirs that consent she will seldom get and the rule will become nugatory.

According to Calcutta (Sabur Bibi *v.* Ismail I L R 51 Cal. 124 dissenting from 38 Cal. 475), Patna (Mohammed Zubair *v.* Mst. Bibi Sahidan A I R 1942 Pat. 210) two earlier Allahabad decisions (Amanatunnissa *v.* Bashir-un Nissa I L R 17 All. 77, and Muhammad Karimulla *v.* Amani Begum I L R 17 All. 93) and the latest Allahabad case (Mst. Izhar Fatima Bibi *v.* Mst. Ansar Bibi A I R 1939 All. 348) the possession in order to be lawful must have been taken with the consent of the heirs of the deceased, express or implied.

According to Abdul Wahab Khan *v.* Mushtaq Ahmed A I R 1944 All. 68, if mutation was effected in favour of the widow after the death of her husband without any opposition whatsoever by the husband's heirs, that is enough under the Muhammedan Law to show that widow entered into possession lawfully, without any force or fraud.

3 (1868) 3 B L R A C 28 note: 10 W R 369.

See Abdus Sattar *v.* Mst. Agida Bibi A I R 1927 All. 319; Fahiman *v.* Bulaqi A I R 1935 Oudh 68; Jahuran Bibi *v.* Suleman Khan A I R 1934 Cal. 210. If a widow has been in possession of her husband's property during his lifetime, and continues in possession after his death, the presumption is that her possession has been lawfully obtained and is in lieu of dower.

[Foot-note continued on next page

If a widow, who has obtained possession of a property in lieu of dower, is dispossessed by the heir of her husband, such heir would take the property subject to her lien for dower.[1]

Widow's lien for dower.

Nor will a suit for ejectment lie against a widow in possession of her husband's estate for dower unless it is alleged that such dower has been satisfied, as a widow in possession of her husband's estate, under a claim of dower, has a lien upon it as against those

---

See Mirwahed Ali *v.* Rashid Beg A I R 1951 Bom. 22. Under such circumstances she need not assent or prove that she was in possession in lieu of her unpaid dower.

Jahuran Bibi *v.* Suleman Khan A I R 1934 Cal. 210. If the husband has been in possession during his life time and the widow takes possession after his death and falsely claims that her dower has been increased she has no right to retain the property.

Mst. Sampatia Bibi *v.* Mir Mahboob Ali A I R 1936 All. 528. Mere permissive possession of property does not entitle the widow to retain it in lieu of dower.

In Mst. Beebee Buchun *v.* Sh. Hamid Hussain 14 M I A 398, their Lordships of the Privy Council were pleased to observe: "Having obtained actual and lawful possession . . . . under a claim to hold them as lien for her dower . . . . . she is entitled to retain that possession until her dower is satisfied . . . . . It is not necessary to say whether this right is a lien in the strict sense of the term, although no doubt the right is so stated in a judgment of the High Court in the case of Ahmad Hussain *v.* Mst. Khadeja 10 W R 369. Whatever the right may be called, it appears to be founded on the power of the widow as a creditor for her dower to hold the property of her husband of which she has lawfully and without force or fraud obtained the possession until her debt is satisfied with the liability to account to those entitled to the property subject to the claim for the profits received."

In Hamira Bibi *v.* Zubaida Bibi L R 43 I A 294: I L R 38 All. 581, it was observed by the Privy Council "But the dower ranks as a debt, and the wife is entitled along with other creditors to have it satisfied on the death of the husband out of his estate. Her right however is no greater than an unsecured creditor except that if she lawfully, with the express or implied consent of the husband or his other heirs obtain possession of the whole or part of his estate to satisfy her claim with the rents . . . . accruing therefrom she is entitled to retain such possession until it is satisfied. This is called the widow's lien for dower of the Musulman law which has received recognition in the British Indian Courts and at this Board."

See Mst. Maina *v.* Chaudri Vakil Ahmed 52 I A 145: A I R 1925 P C 63. It was observed that the position of widow retaining her husband's property in lieu of dower was distinguishable from the case of a mortgagee in possession. In the case of a mortgage the mortgagee takes and retains possession under an agreement made between him and the mortgagor, while in the case of widow's lien for dower, neither the possession of the property nor the right to retain that possession when acquired is conferred upon the widow by the agreement or bounty of her deceased husband.

1 Umed Ally *v.* Safihan (1869) 3 B L R A C 175; Janee Khanum *v.* Amatool Fatima (1867) 8 W R 51; see also Woomatul Fatima Begum *v.* Mariamunnissa Khanum (1868) 9 W R 318. See also Musst. Umatul Mehdi *v.* Musst. Kulsoom (1907) 12 C W N 16.

See Majid Mian *v.* Bibi Sahib 40 Bom. 34: 30 I C 870.

entitled as heirs, and is entitled to possession as against them, till her claim of dower is satisfied.

In the case of *Azizullah Khan* v. *Ahmadullah Khan*,[1] the Allahabad High Court held that a Mahommedan widow, lawfully in possession of her husband's estate, occupied a position analogous to that of a mortgagee, and her possession could not be disturbed until her dower debt has been satisfied, and that after her death her heirs were entitled to succeed her in such possession, and if wrongfully deprived thereof, to maintain a suit for its recovery.

Ali Muhammad Khan v. Azizullah Khan.

But a widow in possession of her husband's estate pending payment of her dower is not entitled to alienate it either by sale or mortgage.[2] In the case of *Ali Muhammad Khan* v. *Azizullah*

---

1 (1885) I L 7 All. 353.

See Maina Bibi *v.* Chaudri Vakil Ahmed L R 52 I A 145: A I R 1925 P C 63. Her position is not that of a mortgagee for "in case of a mortgage the mortgagee takes and retains possession under an agreement or arrangement made between him and a mortgagor, but in the case of a Muhammedan widow who takes possession under a claim for her dower, neither the possession of property nor the right to retain that possession when acquired is conferred on the widow by the *agreement* or *bounty of her deceased husband.* The possession of the property being once peaceably and lawfully acquired, *the right of the widow to retain it till her dower debt is paid is conferred on her by the Muhammedan Law.*"

See Majid Mian *v.* Bibi Sahib I L R 40 Bom. 34; Cooverbai Nasarwanji *v.* Hyat Bi 45 Bom. L R 730. The widow's right arises only when possession is obtained. As was held in 43 I A 294, (301) she is only in the position of an unsecured creditor subject to this that she is entitled to *retain* the property *lawfully in her* possession. She has no right to sue for possession, if she never had it. *Prima facie* it would seem to follow that the widow's heirs, unless they follow her immediately into possession and are subsequently dispossessed, cannot sue to recover possession. So what is heritable would be merely the right to retain possession. The heirs cannot inherit more than what the widow herself had.

See Mashal Singh *v.* Ahmad Hussain I L R 50 All. 86: A I R 1927 All. 534. The lien of a Mohammedan widow over property on account of a dower debt only operates so long as she remains in possession of the property, on being deprived of possession she has a right, independently of her lien, to recover possession within 6 months under section 9, Specific Relief Act, 1877. The lien gives her no right or power to recover possession but only to retain possession.

See Abdul Wahab *v.* Mushtaq Ahmad Khan A I R 1944 All. 68. There is nothing in the provisions of section 9, Specific Relief Act which in any way militates against the principle that previous possession enjoyed peaceably by a Mohammedan widow in lieu of her dower debt or anybody else for a period short of the statutory period of 12 years entitle the person who has been in such possession to a decree for possession in a suit against the trespasser provided the suit is brought within 12 years of the date of dispossession. Since the right to retain possession by the Muhammedan widow in lieu of unpaid dower is heritable the heirs of the widow can institute a suit for possession against a trespasser under Art. 142, Limitation Act, 1908. If the suit be against the heirs of the husband, *i.e.*, the rightful owners of property it must be within 6 months.

2 Chuki Bibi *v.* Shamsunnissa Begum (1894) I L 17 All. 19.

Khan,[1] the Allahabad High Court held that a purchaser of a deceased husband's estate from a Mohammedan widow, in possession thereof pending payment of her dower, was not entitled to plead non-satisfaction of her dower debt to a claim by her husband's heirs for their share of his inheritance, as the widow's right to dower was personal to herself, and did not pass to a purchaser of the estate.

---

1 I L 6 All. 50. See also Ghufoorun Bibi *v.* Mustukedeh, 2 Agra 300; and Azeemun *v.* Asgar Ali 2 Agra Part II 167.

Both the above decisions have been overruled in Ali Bakhsh *v.* Allah Dad I L R 32 All. 551 wherein it was held that the right of a Muhammadan widow who has entered into possession of her husband's property peacefully and without fraud in lieu of her dower debt is a heritable right and her heirs are entitled to *remain* in possession until the debt is satisfied.

See Mohammed Shoab Khan *v.* Mst. Zaib Jehan 50 All. 423: A I R 1927 All. 850. The widow's right to retain possession is founded on her power as a creditor for her dower.

See Amir Hassan Khan *v.* Mohammed Nazir Hussain I L R 54 All. 499: A I R 1932 All. 345; Abdul Wahab *v.* Mushtaq Ahmed Khan A I R 1944 All. 68. No doubt the right of a Mohammedan widow to hold possession of her husband's property in lieu of her unpaid dower does not give the widow any title to the property but the right to hold possession is heritable and the heirs of the widow are entitled to inherit the right and to hold possession after the death of the widow.

In Ali Bakhsh *v.* Allah Dad I L R 32 All. 551; Amir Hassan *v.* Mohammed A I R 1932 All. 345; Abdulla *v.* Shams-ul Haq I L R 43 All. 127; Beeju Bibi *v.* Syed Murthija I L R 43 Mad. 214; Majid Mian *v.* Bibi Sahib I L R 40 Bom. 34; Ramija Bibi *v.* Sharifa Bibi A I R 1943 Mad. 561; Hussain *v.* Rahim Khan A I R 1954 Mys. 24 and Cooverbhai *v.* Hyat Bi 45 Bom. L R 730, it has been held that the widow's lien on her husband's property for unpaid dower debt is heritable and descends after her death on her heirs.

In Azizullah *v.* Ahmed I L R 7 All. 353 and Janbi Bibi *v.* Abbas Ali A I R 1941 Nag. 167, it has been held that the widow's right to hold possession is heritable as well as transferable.

In Sheikh Abdur Rahman *v.* Sheikh Wali Mohammad A I R 1923 Pat. 72, it was held that the widow's lien was not an interest in property which can be severed from the right to dower and transferred as a separate interest. It is a right to the possession of the property by the person entitled to be paid the dower as long as the debt is not discharged either by the income from the property or by payment by the heirs or others interested in discharging the debt. It certainly gives the widow right to possession and it may be assumed that *as long as she does not transfer her dower debt and that* debt remains undischarged, she may transfer for her lifetime possession of the property, the proceeds of which belong to her until the debt is paid off. *The possession of the transferee in such a case might be regarded as constructively her possession, and in this sense it would not be severed from the dower debt.*

In Mst. Bibi Maqbulunnissa *v.* Mst. Bibi Umatunnissa A I R 1923 Pat. 33, it was held that the right to hold the property as a security for the dower debt and to continue in possession thereof until the dower debt is satisfied, is both heritable and transferable.

In Maina Bibi *v.* Chaudri Vakil Ahmed A I R 1925 P C 63, their Lordships of the Privy Council doubted the power of the widow to transfer her dower debt or her lien on her husband's property and observed that by giving up the possession of the land, as in her deeds she alleges she has done, she has undoubtedly lost her right to hold the possession of them.

In Sh. Mohammed Zubair *v.* Mst. Bibi Sahidan A I R 1942 Pat. 210; Ram Prasad *v.* Bibi Khadijtul Kubra A I R 1944 Pat. 163; Abdus Samad *v.* Alimuddin A I R 1944 Pat. 174, and Zubair Ahmed *v.* Jai Nandan Prasad, A I R 1960 Pat. 147, the Patna High Court has expressly overruled its earlier

[Foot-note continued on next page

Widow's lien personal.

The lien which a Mohammedan widow has over the estate of her deceased husband for her unpaid dower is a purely personal one and does not descend to her heirs,[1] although the right to the dower itself passes to them by succession. It follows, therefore, that they cannot take possession of the husband's estate under the claim for dower.

The Madras High Court has taken a rather strained view of the widow's right to retain possession of the property in her hands in lieu of dower. It has held that where the husband had not specifically hypothecated his property for the dower-debt, the widow's possession gave her no right as against a purchaser in execution of a decree for sale passed on a mortgage executed by her husband.[2] Once the widow lawfully obtains possession in lieu of her dower, her position becomes that of a mortgagee in possession. It seems difficult to follow the reasoning by which her right is subordinated to that of a purchaser in execution of the decree of another mortgagee not in possession. It may make, however, a difference if the dower-debt was contracted after the mortgage in question.

Ameer-un-nissa v. Moradun-nissa.

In the case of *Ameerunnisa* v. *Moradunnisa*[3] it appeared that a Mohammedan, by a deed of dower, had charged the whole of his estate, with a certain sum payable on demand by his wedded wife, without, however, impignorating the estate; the dower was not demanded during the lifetime of the husband, but possession was taken of the property by the widow in satisfaction of her claim. In dismissing the suit by the brother of the deceased, the Judicial Committee made the following observations:—

"Lastly, there remains the question of the distribution and administration of the deceased's estate. No such relief is asked by the plaint. The claim made by the plaintiff is as sole heir against the defendants, charging them with collusion in keeping him out of possession. He does not claim in the alternative, that if the marriage of the respondent *Muradunnissa*, and the deed of dower are proved, then that he may have his share of the estate. It is possible it might have been competent to the Court below, in their discretion, to have entertained such a

---

decisions and held: "The dower debt of Mohammadan widow is not, properly speaking, a charge upon the property of her husband, the interest which she has in the property in her possession in lieu of dower debt is an interest restricted in its enjoyment to her personally within the meaning of section 6 (*a*) of the Transfer of Property Act, 1882 and as such is not capable of alienation.

Thus the position has once again veired round to the view expressed by Syed Amir Ali, that the right was personal and not transferable.

1 Hadi Ali *v*. Akbar Ali (1898) I L 20 All. 262; Muzaffar Ali Khan *v*. Parbati (1907) I L 29 All. 640.

2 Ameer Ammal *v*. Lankara Narayan Chetty (1901) I L 28 Mad. 658

3 (1885) 6 Moore's I A, p. 211.

question but it was a matter of discretion for the Judge of the *Sudder Dewany Adawlat*. Independently of this, *Moradunnissa* was in possession, by the consent of the local authorities, a possession very analogous to that of an executrix here. That fact, however, is not sufficient to decide the point of right, but the plaintiff has not asked for an account. Again, he has burthened the record with a number of unnecessary parties who ought not to have been there, and that would have created very considerable inconvenience in taking accounts. He has also excluded all the movable estate, and that portion of the immovable estate of which he himself obtained possession. We are of opinion, therefore, that the Judges before whom the case has been heard in India, took the right and convenient course in dismissing his suit, and leaving him to bring another suit to obtain an account; that, no doubt, was the effect of their decisions, though not in terms. Under these circumstances, their Lordships will add a recommendation in their humble report to Her Majesty, that the dismissal of the appeal be without prejudice to the appellant's right to bring a suit for an account and administration of the deceased's estate consistent with the establishment of the marriage and the deed of dower. Costs, if any, incurred in *India* by reason of the appeal, must be paid by the appellants."

And the report which was made thereon was as follows:—

"Their Lordships do agree humbly to report to your Majesty as their opinion that the judgment or decree of the *Sudder Dewany Adawlat* at *Agra* of the 21st of April 1846, ought to be affirmed, without prejudice to any suit which may be instituted for the recovery of the rights of the late appellant as one of the heirs of *Syud Moostefah* consistently with the establishment of the marriage of the respondent, *Moradunnissa*, and of the validity of the deed of dower alleged by her in the suit, both of which facts their Lordships consider to be proved in this case, and their Lordships direct that all costs, if any, incurred by the parties to the suit in *India* by reason of this appeal, be paid by the appellants."

Suit against the widow for ejectment.

In several cases, decided in the Sudder Court of the North-Western Provinces, it was held that when the widow, the defendant in a suit for ejectment, was found to be in possession of the property in suit in lieu of dower, and that the plaintiff was not entitled to sue for possession thereof until such claim for dower had been satisfied, it was unnecessary to determine the question of the amount of such dower; that a Mohammedan widow was entitled to a lien for whatever dower remained due to her, although there might be a dispute as to what was the amount actually due, and that the heir not being entitled to recover possession from the widow so long as any portion of the dower remained unsatisfied, nor to *mesne* profits, his proper course was to bring a suit for an account of what was due as dower, and to pray that on satisfaction of that amount he might be put into possession of his share of the estate.[1]

The mere fact that a widow is in possession of the property of her husband in lieu of dower does not preclude her from bringing a suit for the dower-debt against the heirs, although in such an action she would be bound to account for the rents and issues whilst the property was in her hands.[2]

The Judicial Committee have held that when a widow in possession of her husband's estate to obtain satisfaction of unpaid dower is called upon to account for rents and profits, she is entitled to claim interest at a reasonable rate upon her dower-debt.[3]

Limitation.

Limitation does not run against *deferred* dower until it has become due, either by the death of one of the parties or by divorce. The *prompt* or *exigible* dower, however, is a debt always due, and demandable during "the subsistence of the marriage, and certainly payable on demand." On a clear and unambiguous demand by the wife, for payment of dower and its refusal by the husband, it has been held by the Judicial Committee of the Privy Council that a cause of action accrues, against which limitation would began to run. When there has been no explicit demand on the wife's part, limitation will not affect her claim with reference to the *exigible* dower. The wife has an absolute option to demand the *mahr* during the lifetime of her husband, and to elect her own time for demanding it.[4]

---

1 Buland Khan *v.* Janee (1870) 2 N W 319; Ufzool Begum *v.* Ladlee Begum 2 N W 325; and Imdad Hossein *v.* Hosseinee Bakhsh (1869) 2 N W 327.

2 Ghulam Ali *v.* Saghir-un-nissa (1901) I L 23 All. 433.

3 Hamira Bibi *v.* Zubaida Bibi (1916) L R 43 I A 294.

See Woomatool Fatima *v.* Meerumunnissa (1868) 9 W R 318. Sahib Jan *v.* Ansaruddin I L R 38 Cal. 475 and Nawasi Begum *v* Dilafroz A I R 1926 All. 39.

See Shankar Dass *v.* Mehbub Jan A I R 1942 Pesh. 92. Awarding of is discretionary.

Ram Prasad *v.* Bibi Khodajatul Kubra A I R 1944 Pat. 163. The widow may agree to give up her right to compensation.

4 Khajurunnissa *v.* Saifullah Khan (1875) 15 B L R A C 306. See also Khijarannissa *v.* Risannissa (1870) 5 B L R 84, where the claim was held to be barred, and Mulleeka *v.* Jameela (1876) 11 B L R 375.

See Mohammed Taqi Khan *v.* Fermoodi Begum A I R 1941 All. 181. Where prompt dower has not been fixed, a demand and refusal is not a condition precedent for filing a suit for its recovery.

Mst. Amtul Rasul *v.* Karim Bakhsh A I R 1933 Pesh. 31. Limitation for prompt dower runs from the time when the dower is demanded and refused but both demand and refusal must be unambiguous.

Hamidulla Khan *v.* Najjo I L R 38 All. 568. Limitation for deferred dower does not run against the widow during the period she is in lawful possession of her husband's property in lieu of a claim for dower.

Mohammed Taqi *v.* Farmoodi Begum A I R 1941 All. 181; Mst. Pukhraj Begum *v.* Hidayat Ali A I R 1938 Pesh. 72. Consummation has not the effect of converting prompt dower into a deferred one, and a wife has the right to bring an action for prompt dower whenever it is demanded and refused, no matter whether before or after consummation.

If the widow was in possession of her husband's property as security for her dower, and was subsequently thrown out of possession, the cause of action in respect of the dower must be deemed to have arisen at the time when she was ejected.[1]

Shares of dower when received by the legal inheritors thereof cease to be dower, and become part of the recipient's estate.[2]

Articles 103-104, Schedule I, Act IX of 1908, provide the periods of limitation in the case of *exigible* (prompt) and deferred dower.

SECTION III

REFUSAL OF CONJUGAL RIGHTS

THE wife may refuse cohabitation or to take up her abode in the conjugal domicile without previous payment of the *prompt* dower.

The passage in the *Hedaya* bearing on this subject is as follows:—

Difference of opinion.

"The wife has the right to deny her person [to her husband or to go on a journey with him until she receive the dower. Her right in the consideration is the same as that of her husband in the object of the consideration [his conjugal rights over her person] as in sale. The husband has no power to prevent her from travelling or going out of his house and visiting her friends until he has paid the whole *exigible* dower, because the right of restraint is given to a person who has a right, and he has not the right to secure fulfilment before rendering fulfilment [himself]. And if the whole dower is *deferred*, it is not for her to deny her person because of her having waived her right by deferring it, as in sale. And in this matter Abu Yusuf holds the contrary opinion. And if the husband has cohabited with her, the same would be the answer according to Abu Hanifa [that is, she has the right to refuse conjugal relations until payment of the *prompt* dower]: but they, [the two Disciples], have said she has not the right [in such a case] to deny herself, and the difference of opinion exists [only where there has been cohabitation with her consent ;

---

1 Soorma Khatoon *v.* Altafoonnissa Khatoon (1863) 2 Hay. 210.

See Shah Bano Begum *v.* Iftikhar Mohammed Khan P L D 1956 Kar. 363. An unpaid dower is debt, and on the basis of the legal maxim the debtor must seek the creditor, the wife may bring a suit for payment of dower in a Court having jurisdiction at her place of residence.

2 Hosseinooddeen Chowdhry *v.* Tajunnissa Khatoon W R 1864, 199.

but if she was forced, or is an infant, or insane, her right of denying herself is not extinguished [by cohabitation] by *consensus*, [that is, all the doctors are agreed on it]."

The passage in the *Durr-ul-Mukhtar* on the same subject runs as follows:—"It is the wife's right to prevent the husband from connubial intercourse, and that which is implied therein, and from journeying with her, even though after connubial intercourse and 'retirement' to which she has consented, because all connubial intercourse has been contracted with her, and the rendering of some does not imperatively require the rendering of the rest. The right is for the purpose of obtaining what has been stated as *prompt* dower, whether wholly or partly. But she cannot do so if the payment of the dower is deferred to a future time, unless the period is manifestly indeterminate[1] . . . . . It is correct [lawful], however, by custom to defer [the payment of] the dower until death or divorce."

"According to the second [Abu Yusuf] if dower is deferred to a determinate time, the woman has a right to refuse cohabitation and on this is the *fatwa* according to *istehsan* [liberal interpretation]. And she is entitled according to the Imam [Abu Hanifa] to maintenance although preventing cohabitation [for the purpose of obtaining payment of her prompt dower]."[2]

In the *Fatawai Kazi Khan*, the law is stated thus:—"A woman surrenders herself to her husband before the payment of the dower, she then denies herself [to him] with a view to realise the dower. She has this right according to Abu Hanifa; but Abu Yusuf and Mohammed say that she has not the right of prohibiting him from connubial intercourse. And traditions differ from them in regard to her right to refuse journeying with him. And according to the opinion of Abu'l Kasim as-Saffar, it is her right that she may prevent him from taking her on a journey."[3]

Abu Hanifa's rule regarded as binding.

The *Fatawai 'Alamgiri* says:—In all places, wnen the husband has had connubial intercouse with his wife, or there has been "valid retirement" with her, the whole dower is confirmed, [that is, the wife becomes entitled to the dower in its entirety]. If she desires (resolves) to deny herself to him in order to secure fulfilment [*i.e.*, payment] of her *exigible* dower (*al-m 'uajjal*), it is her right to do so according to him [Imam Abu Hanifa]; but this is opposed to the opinions of the other two [Disciples]; and, similarly, the husband cannot prevent her from going out or travelling or going on a voluntary

---

1 *Jihalat-i-fahish* are the words used, which imply an uncertain contingency such as making payment dependent on the happening of an uncertain vent. In such case, the dower becomes immediately payable.

2 Durr-ul-Mukhtar, p. 208.

3 See Rahilan *v*. Sanaullah P L D 1959 Lah. 470. Prompt dower, as soon as it is demanded, becomes a debt, which the husband is liable to pay. The wife may refuse to live with the husband unless and until the prompt dower is paid.

pilgrimage, according to him [Abu Hanifa], except when she goes out for an indecent purpose. As to her right to all this before she has surrendered herself to him (قبل تسليم النفس) it is her right by *consensus* (بالا جماع). Similarly [she has the right] when the husband has had connubial intercourse with her, and the wife is a minor (*saghira*) or has been forced [to cohabitation] (مكره) or is insane. In such cases the father has a right to refuse her surrender until payment of the *prompt* dower. This is according to the *Inaya*. If the husband has cohabited or *retired* with her consent, [even] then she can refuse to go on a journey with him until payment of her whole dower according to the written engagement or the *prompt* part of it according to the custom of our country. This [view] is according to Abu Hanifa, but the other two [the Disciples] maintain that she has no such right; and the *Shaikh-ul-Imam*, the jurisconsult the pious Abu'l Kasim as-Saffar, was accustomed to decide according to the doctrine of Abu Hanifa about going on a journey but with regard to refusing herself, he used to decide according to the doctrine of the two Disciples, and some of our doctors have liberally adopted this."

The text of the *Tanwir-ul-Absar* on this point is as follows:—"The woman can refuse to accompany her husband on travel or to cohabit with him until payment of her *prompt* dower, even though the refusal takes place after there has been a 'valid retirement' or [previous] cohabitation with her consent . . . . ."

The comment of the author of the *Radd-ul-Muhtar* on this passage runs thus:—" . . . . Similarly, if he [the husband] has cohabited [with his wife] by force, or against her will, or if the woman is a minor or insane (*majnuna*), and after that the woman were to refuse to accompany him on travel she would he entitled to do so, and this is by *consensus*. But if cohabitation had taken place with her consent, and after that she refused cohabitation on account [of the non-payment] of the [*prompt*] dower, according to the two [the Disciples] she has no right to do so, and if she does, she would be called a *nashiza*, and would not be entitled to her maintenance, unless the refusal takes place in the husband's house, when she would be entitled to her maintenance."[1]

And again, "it is lawful for the wife", says the *Tanwir-ul-Absar* "to refuse cohabitation in order to exact payment of the dower or that portion of it which is payable immediately."[2]

On this passage the author of the *Radd-ul-Muhtar* comments as follows: " . . . If the husband has paid the [prompt] dower to the wife, but one *dirhem* is owing, for that even the woman can refuse cohabitation . . . Similarly, it is stated in the *Hindieh* [*Fatawai 'Alamgiri*] from the *Siraj-ul-Wahaj* and in the *Bahr-ur-Raik* from the *Muhit*. And if the woman has assigned the dower

1 Radd-ul-Muhtar, Vol. II, p. 587

2 See Nuruddin Ahmad *v*, Masuda Khanum P L D 1957 Dacca 242; Najmannissa *v*. Sirajuddin A I R 1946 Pat. 467. Where the wife has not been paid her prompt dower, she is entitled to stay away from her husband, and the husband is bound to maintain her. If he does not maintain her for a period of two years the wife is entitled to dissolution of her marriage on the ground of non-maintenance.

to somebody, she may refuse cohabitation until it has been delivered to her assignee, but not if the assignment has been made to the husband himself."

In the *Vikaya-ur-Rawaeh* of which the *Sharh-i-Vikaya* is the commentary, the law is stated thus:—"It is the right of the wife [*lit.* it belongs to her] to refuse cohabitation or to accompany the husband on a journey, and notwithstanding such refusal to obtain maintenance from him, although such refusal may take place after cohabitation or 'valid retirement' with her consent, so long as she does not receive her *mahr*, either the whole or such part as is specified as *mu'ajjal* (*prompt*) or which is customarily *prompt* for such woman, without consideration of whether it is a fourth or fifth unless it is specified."

The *Kanz-ud-Dakaik* gives the rules in the following words:—"and she [the wife] has the right of refusing cohabitation and being taken on a journey although cohabitation may already have taken place." The same doctrine is enunciated in explicit terms in the *Fatawai Hamadia*, the *Fatawai Mufti* and the *Badaya*.

These passages show clearly that the rule laid down by Abu Hanifa is recognised as law. None of the authorities support the proposition of the Disciples that the woman whose *prompt* dower remains unpaid, but who has once cohabited with her husband, may be compelled to cohabit against her will, if she refuses cohabitation in order to exact payment of such dower.

Eidan v. Mazhar Hossain.

This view was taken by the Allahabad High Court in the case of *Eidan* v. *Mazhar Hossain*,[1] where the Judges held that in a suit by the husband to enforce his conjugal rights, the wife was entitled to refuse to cohabit with him until he had paid her dower, and that she was not precluded from doing so by the mere fact of having consented to cohabit with him since the marriage.

Wilayat Husain v. Allah Rakhi.

In *Wilayat Husain* v. *Allah Rakhi*[2] also, the same Court pronounced that a Mohammedan husband could not, according to Mohammedan Law, maintain a suit against his wife for restitution of conjugal rights, even after such consummation with consent as is proved by cohabitation for five years, where the wife's dower is *prompt* and has not been paid.[3]

Nasarat Hussain v. Hamidan.

The same view was enunciated in *Nasarat Husain* v. *Hamidan*, where the learned Judges held that a woman belonging to the

1 (1877) I L 1 All. 483.

2 (1880) I L 2 All. 831; see also Sheikh Abdul Shukkoor *v.* Raheemoonnissa (1874) 6 N W P H C Rep. 94 ; Jaun Beebee *v.* Sheikh Munshee Beparee (1865) 3 W R 93.

3 See Nuruddin Ahmed *v.* Masuda Khatun P L D 1959 Dacca 242. The wife's right to prompt dower cannot be defeated on the ground that the husband has been denied the society of the wife.

Sunni sect married to a Shiah was entitled to the privileges secured to her married position by the law of her sect, and that she did not, by the mere fact of the marriage, become governed by the Shiah Law, and that, consequently, where a husband sued to recover his wife, the one being a Shiah and the other a Sunni, the wife's dower being *exigible* and not having been paid, the suit was not maintainable under the Sunni Law.[1]

Abdul Kadir v. Salima.

But in *Abdul Kadir* v. *Salima*[2] a Full Bench of the same Court took a totally different view of the law and enunciated propositions for some of which at least there is no authority in the Mahommedan Law.

They seem to have thought that the right of a wife to resist her husband so long as the dower remains unpaid was analogous to the lien of a vendor upon the goods sold while they remained in his possession, and so long as the price or any part of it was unpaid; and that her surrender to her husband resembled the delivery of the goods to the vendee; that the lien for unpaid dower ceased to exist after consummation, unless at such time the wife was a minor or insane or had been forced, in which case her father might refuse to surrender her until payment; and that it could not in any case be pleaded so as to defeat altogether the suit for restitution of conjugal rights, which is maintainable upon the refusal of either party to cohabit with the other; for, they added, it could only operate in modification of the decree for restitution by rendering its enforcement conditional upon payment of so much of the dower as may be regarded as *prompt*, in accordance with the principles recognised by Courts of Equity under the general category of compensation or lien, when pleaded by a defendant in resistance or modification of the plaintiff's claim. And they proceeded to lay down a general rule of interpretation, for which there is no authority that "in cases of difference of opinion amongst the jurisconsults, Imam Abu Hanifa and his two Disciples, Imam Abu Yusuf and Imam Mohammed, the opinion of the majority must be followed." As I have already shown, there is no such fixed rule as the learned Judges imagine, over and over again the opinion of only one is adopted for *Fatwas* or decrees.[3]

---

1 (1882) I L 4 All. 205.

2 (1886) I L 8 All. 149; the learned Judges adopted the judgment of Mahmood, J., who had already left the Court. It is clear from the judgment that it was based on the Hedaya for it contains no reference to the later authorities.

3 The late Moulvi Sami-ullah Khan, one of the most learned judicial officers in British India, has examined, in the case of Mussammats Rasulan and Zahooran *v.* Mirza Naimullah Beg (1891) the correctness of the propositions enunciated above. His judgment has been printed in the Indian Press (Allahabad). The learned Moulvi has cited authorities which amply warrant his proposition that the opinion of Abu Hanifa has greater authority than that of his disciples singly or together. In fact, as he points out, the disciples do not pretend to "oppose" Abu Hanifa; they profess to give expression to some opinion of his which he previously professed, and from which he subsequently resiled. That the opinion of Abu Hanifa supplies the governing principle is borne out by the Fatwa quoted in Macnaughten's Principles and Precedents, case xxi; see also the Manah-ul-Ghuffar.

It is respectfully submitted that this judgment proceeds on wrong analogies, and is founded on a total misconception of the rules which have already been set forth in detail and on which practically there is no difference among the later Jurists.

The case of *Abdul Kadir* v. *Salima*, which has revolutionised the practice of the Allahabad High Court, has since been followed by the Madras and Bombay High Courts.[1]

Shiah doctrine.

There are two opinions among the Shiahs, but the prevalent doctrine is that when a woman has once cohabited with her husband, she cannot subsequently refuse him conjugal rights on the ground of the non-payment of the *exigible mahr*[2] although she may sue him for the same.

Hanafi Law.

When the husband settles on the wife any property in exchange for the dower, or, to use the language of the *Fatawai 'Alamgiri*,

---

1 Kunti *v.* Moidin (1888) I L 11 Mad. 327; Bai Hansa *v.* Abdulla Mustafa (1905) I L 30 Bom. 122.

The case of Abdul Qadir *v.* Salima (1886) I L 8 All. 149, has become classical case on the point, and in spite of the scathing criticism of Syed Amir Ali and Maulvi Salimullah has been followed by the Punjab Chief Court in Mst. Sahib *v.* Rafiuddin 164 P R 1889 and Nawab Bibi *v.* Mohammed Dush 8 P L R 1918; the Madras High Court in Kunhi *v.* Moidin 11 Mad. 327; the Bombay High Court in Bai Hansa *v.* Abdulla I L R 30 Bom. 122; Bashiran Bi *v.* Abdul Wahab 188 I C 130; Chandra Bindo Kunda *v.* Sh. Allah Bux 58 I C 358; Nagpur Judicial Commissioners Court in Ramdayal *v.* Munna Lal A I R 1939 Nag. 186 and Najmunnissa *v.* Serajuddin A I R 1946 Pat. 467.

It has been dissented from only by the Oudh Chief Court in Wajid Ali Khan *v.* Sukhawat Ali Khan 15 I C 747: 15 P C 127 and a later Allahabad Bench in Anis Begum *v.* Mohammed Istifa Wali Khan I L R 55 All. 743, has followed Abdul Kadir's case on the basis of stare decisis.

In Mst. Rahim Jan *v.* Muhammed P L D 1955 Lah. 122, Kaikaus, J. (as His Lordship then was) has thoroughly examined Abdul Kadir's case in the light of original authorities, and later decisions, and although His Lordship did not agree with a number of points decided in the case, ultimately held, "I would explain that I am respectfully in entire agreement with the view of Mahmud, J. that rights arise at the time of marriage only, as in the case of specific performance of a reciprocal obligation may become a condition precedent. Just as in a suit for specific performance a plaintiff should be "able and willing" to perform his part of the contract so in the case for restitution of conjugal rights the husband has to pay the dower if he wants the restitution of conjugal rights. I would hold that even after consummation the wife retains the right to refuse the performance of marital obligation till the prompt dower is paid."

In the above authorities it has been held that if a suit for restitution of conjugal rights is brought by the husband, before sexual intercourse takes place, non-payment of the dower is a complete defence to the suit, which shall be dismissed outright. On the other hand, if the wife willingly consummates the marriage in spite of the non-payment of dower, the Court should not dismiss the suit but should pass a decree for restitution of conjugal rights in favour of the husband on the condition that it shall be executable only after the prompt dower has been paid to the wife as a condition precedent.

2 Shara'ya; Jam'a-ush-Shittat.

"sells her a chattel for her dower", she may, similarly, refuse cohabitation until such chattel or such property has been delivered to her.

When the property settled on the wife is lost before delivery, or a claim is established by a third person with reference to it, the husband is bound to give her a property of equal value. If the property settled be of inferior value than was alleged, the wife may, before consummation, insist on compensation or a change of the property. After the marriage has been consummated, she is supposed to have waived her right to compensation.

Transfer by the husband to the wife.

Under the Mahommedan Law, a wife is competent to deal with her husband; and, consequently, a transfer by the husband to the wife of any property belonging to him in lieu of her dower is valid and operative. And even if the husband be indebted at the time, or execution may have issued against him, at the instance of other creditors, the assignment would be valid, if she is not cognisant of any fraudulent intent on his part that the conveyance was to delay or defraud such creditors, or that he had no other property from which the debts may be satisfied.

Section 53 of the Transfer of Property Act [IV of 1882], which is borrowed from 13 Eliz., cap. 5, and 27 Eliz., cap. 4, avoids transfers when the transferor and transferee both act with a fraudulent intent. When the transferee takes in good faith for a not wholly incommensurate or a grossly inadequate consideration, the transfer is valid.[1]

A woman is entitled to assign her dower-debt to any one she likes, and the assignee, if authorised to that effect, is entitled to recover the same from the husband.

She can also appoint an agent to recover her dower-debt from the husband.

SECTION IV

MISCELLANEOUS PRINCIPLES CONCERNING DOWER

Pre-Islamic customs.

In pre-Islamic times it was an essential condition to the validity of a marriage, that the husband should settle on the wife a certain dower, which became her exclusive property. Such at least was the established custom, though, owing to the absence of an organised system of law or justice, the custom was often more honoured in the breach than in the observance.

1 See on this subject, Copis *v.* Middelton 2 Mad. 410; Middleton *v.* ollock 2 Ch. D 108; In re : Johnson, Golden *v.* Gillian 20 Ch. D 194; ayspool *v.* Collins 18 W R (Eng.) 730 ; Wood *v.* Dixie, 7 Q B 892; Kevan *v.* Crawford 6 Ch. D 29.

From contemporary records, it would appear that the Arab husbands, in spite of the qualified custom which prevailed among the tribes, frequently despoiled their wives, and turned them adrift on the world absolutely helpless and without means. These acts of injustice were expressly forbidden by the Koranic teachings. It was declared to the Arabs, "If you separate yourself from your wives, send them away with generosity; it is not permitted to you to appropriate the goods you have once given to them."[1]

The Jewish tribes settled in Arabia followed a different system. Among them, both the dower and the property which the wife brought with her remained in the hands of the husband until the dissolution of the contract.[2]

Dower may be increased after marriage.

The Musulman Law accepted in this matter the more liberal principle of the pre-Islamic Arab customs. Under the Islamic system there is no community of goods between husband and wife. She is absolute owner of her own property and of whatever the husband settles on her as dower. The terms of the settlement are agreed to before marriage, but when these have been omitted, they may be settled subsequently. The terms of the contract may be varied at any time during the continuance of the marriage by mutual consent. The wife has the power either to relinquish the whole dower-debt, or make an abatement in her husband's favour: whilst the husband, similarly, has the power of making additions to her settlement or dower.[3]

The amount of the dower, as already pointed out, is either settled by the contract of marriage or by custom, or, in the case of *tafwiz* or *tahkim*, by a subsequent agreement between the parties, or by an order of the Judge, or arbitrators.[4]

Specification of dower how effected.

When the dower has been specified in the deed of marriage and where the language of the document is precise and clear, no difficulty can possibly arise. When the terms are vague, obscure or contradictory, the Judge has to interpret them by a reference to the *presumed intention* of the parties, although the jurists have attempted to help in the elucidation of the subject by framing certain arbitrary rules for purposes of interpretation in such cases. For instance, Abu Yusuf says, that when a man is possessed of two things of unequal value, and settles upon his wife one of them, without sufficiently specifying which one is intended, the woman will be entitled to the article which is of the smaller value.[5] In the same way he holds that where a

1 Koran, chap. ii, v. 229.

2 Code Rabbinique, Ebn. Haezer, Vol. II, pp. 10, 88 and 154.

3 See Mst. Jahuran Bibi *v.* Suleman A I R 1934 Cal. 210; Mst. Fatima Bibi *v.* Lal Din A I R 1937 Lah. 345. Under the Mohammodan Law it is not necessary that the dower should be agreed upon before marriage, it may be fixed afterwards. So also where a certain sum is fixed at the time of the marriage, it may be increased afterwards or it may be subsequently remitted by the wife.

4 See Mst. Fatima Bibi *v.* Lal Din supra. Post-nuptial agreement for dower is binding on the husband as well as on persons guaranteeing its payment.

5 Hedaya, Vol. I, p. 139.

man settles on his wife a certain chattel the nature of which is described but not the value, she is entitled to a chattel of medium value.

With greater reason, Shaf'ei thinks that in such a case the customary dower should be accorded to the wife.[1]

When a man settles thirty *dinars* on his wife, and declares in the marriage-contract that ten *dinars* shall be considered *prompt*, and ten *deferred*, it has been held that twenty *dinars* shall be taken as the stipulated dower.

When the specific contract is admitted on both sides, little or no difficulty arises on the adjudication or adjustment of any question concerning dower arising either during the lifetime of the parties or after their decease. When, however, one of the parties denies the execution of the contract or alleges that it was obtained by force or fraud, or when it is stated that the contract entered into at the time of marriage has been modified or substituted by another, the question of dower becomes involved in difficulty, and it is necessary to consider the rules adopted by the Musulman jurists for the settlement of disputes in such cases regarding the *mahr*.

The rules which the Musulman jurists have laid down for the settlement of disputes relating to dower deal mainly with procedure.

The *Kifaya* says: "Disputes regarding the dower may take place [between the married parties themselves] in their lifetime, or between their heirs when both are dead, or, after the death of one of them, between his or her heirs and the survivor. When a dispute arises in the lifetime of the parties, it must be either before or after divorce; and in all cases, the dispute may relate either to the fact of any dower having been specified in the contract or to the amount of the specified dower."[2]

It then proceeds to give the underlying principle on which such questions should be decided. This principle may be summed up in a few words: whether the dispute is as to the amount of dower or to the fact of any dower being fixed, whether it takes place during the subsistence of the marriage or after separation by divorce, or on the death of one or both of the parties, the customary dower should be taken as the standard for the adjustment of the dower.

Although Abu Hanifa has said that when the dispute is between the heirs of the spouses (both being dead) [as to the amount of the dower] "the word should be with the heirs of the husband," the Disciples have "stated that the matter will be decided on the basis of the *mahr-ul-misl* as in their [the spouses'] lifetime and on this is the *fatwa*."[3]

Verbal contract for dower valid.

As stated before, it is not necessary that the contract of marriage should be reduced to writing. A verbal contract of

1 Hedaya, Vol. I, p. 141.

2 Kifaya, Vol. II, p. 86.

3 *Ibid.*, p. 209.

marriage and a verbal undertaking for dower are as valid in law as a written contract.

It is now customary, however, in most civilised Musulman communities, to reduce into writing, prior to the celebration of the marriage, the terms of the marriage-contract; the instances of "the disputes relating to dower", given by the older jurists, possess, therefore, less interest than in early times. They are not, however, entirely without value, for, even in India,[1] dower often depends upon a mere verbal stipulation between husband and wife.

When the contract of marriage is embodied in writing, which mentions specifically the amount of dower settled on the wife, the husband cannot disavow it and allege that he did not intend to make the settlement in question, unless he avers that the amount entered in the deed was fictitious and that the real dower was different.[2]

Dispute about dower.

When there is no written contract and "a dispute arises between the married parties at any time during their marriage regarding the amount of dower", the *mahr-ul-misl* of the woman must be taken as the standard by which the respective allegations of the husband and the wife are to be tested.

For example, if the wife were to allege that a sum of Rs. 500 was settled on her, and the husband were to say that Rs. 250 only was so fixed, it must be ascertained what the woman's customary dower would be. If it be not less than Rs. 500, the probability is that the allegation of the wife accorded with fact.[3]

The same principle would be adopted, in case the dispute arose subsequently to the death of one or both of the parties; that is, where it is impossible to ascertain what the exact dower is, the wife or her heirs, as the case may be, should be held entitled to the customary dower or *mahr-ul-misl*.[4]

This, however, refers to cases where no proof is obtainable on either side as to the amount of dower settled at the time of marriage. When a woman can establish presumptive grounds for coming to a different conclusion, and for holding that she is entitled to more than her *mahr-ul-misl*, she is not debarred from doing so.

The Court of Algiers enforced this principle in a case reported by M. Sautayra. A person died leaving three widows, two of whom established conclusively their right to dower. The third could offer no proof, but there was nothing to indicate that the amount of her dower was less than those of the two first wives.

1 Now Indo-Pakistan.

2 See post.

3 Kifaya, Vol. II, p. 87.

4 Fatawai 'Alamgiri, Vol. I, pp. 451, 452; Jam'a-ush-Shittat.

The Court held with the Kazi, who decided the case in the first instance, that she was entitled to the same *sadak* or dower as the others.

Principle—Fictitious dower—As-Sum'at.

Cases frequently occur where a moderate dower, in accordance with the means and *status* of the parties, is settled in private, but to give *eclat* to the marriage, and for purposes of "glorification", a large amount is mentioned in public and entered in the deed which is read out to the guests. This subject is treated in the *Fatawai 'Alamgiri* under the designation of *as-Sum'at.*[1]

As-sum'at (السمعة), according to the *Farhang*, means literally a public announcement of something with the object of self-glorification. "In the language of law" it means a dower announced to the public with the same object. The *Shara'ya-ul-Islam* briefly states the Shiah doctrine that in such cases the private arrangement will constitute the lawful dower.

Hanafi doctrines.

The *Fatawai 'Alamgiri* gives the Hanafi rules in some detail:

"If a man were to marry a woman for a certain *sadak* (dower) settled privately and announce a large amount in public (فى العلانية) the subject assumes two aspects: first when a dower is settled in private, and the parties then enter into the contract [of marriage] in public for a large amount; if the dower agreed to in public is of the same nature (*jins*) as that settled privately, the difference being only in respect of the one stated in public being more than the one settled in private, and the parties are agreed in its settlement [*viz.*, the private arrangement], or the man has called evidence to prove against her [the woman] or her guardian [if she be a minor] that the dower was that specified (المسمى) privately and the larger amount was *Sum'at* [for glorification], in that case the dower will be that which was settled in private. If, however, they differ as to the amount settled privately, and the man alleges that it was 1,000 [*dirhems*] and the woman denies that amount, her allegation will be accepted, and the dower will be that specified in the contract, unless the husband can adduce proof [of his allegation]."

Then, after stating the rule applicable to a case where the dower stated in public differs in kind from that settled in private, it goes on to say "when a man and a woman settle in private [a certain amount of] *dinars* as the dower, and then contract the marriage in public on condition that there shall be no dower to her, the *dinars* settled in private will be her dower; or if he were to marry her on condition that the *dinars* shall not constitute her dower, or if he were to marry her publicly observing silence as to

1 With a Zamma on the first syllable, and a fatha on the last.

the dower [without specification of dower]. In both these cases the marriage would be contracted at the *mahr-ul-misl* of the woman."

"The second aspect of the question (الوجه الثانى) when a contract is made in private for a smaller amount, and a larger amount is read out in public, if the parties are agreed as to what was settled in private, and [or][1] people are called to prove that what was stated in public was *Sum'at*, then the dower will be that stated at the private contract. But if no evidence be called as to the excess being *Sum'at* then, according to the *Sharh-i-Mukhtasar-ut-Tahtawi*, on the saying of Abu Hanifa and Mohammed (may etc.) the dower will be that stated in public . . . . And the Shaikh-ul-Islam (as-Sarakhsy) has stated that when a marriage is contracted in private on a thousand and something different to this announced in public and then arises a disagreement, and the husband says, 'what I acknowledged in public was *hazal* (a joke)', and the woman asserts that it was the fact, in such a case her statement will be accepted and the dower will be that mentioned publicly, *unless the husband adduces proof in support of his claim.*"

The *Kifaya* also is clear on the subject. It says—

"If one amount is fixed for dower in private and another announced in public, the dower fixed in private is the [real] dower,[2] although some have said (*Kila*) it is the public dower."[3]

This shows clearly that the Musulman Law recognises the validity of arrangements of this nature, regarding the private settlement as the real contract and treating the public declaration as nominal and fictitious.

The British Indian Courts in dealing with cases of exorbitant dower have lost sight of this principle, with the result that in many instances great injustice has been occasioned to the heirs of the husband.[4]

---

1 The (and) (و) would appear from the context to be a misprint for, (او) (or).

2 *Ibid*, p. 211.

3 The word (قيل) (kila) shows that no weight is attached to the latter statement.

4 See for example the cases in 1 S D A Rep., p. 279; and 2 S D A Rep. p. 199.

See also Mohammed Sultan Begum *v.* Sirajuddin Ahmad A I R 1936 Lah. 183 and Mohammed Ibrahim *v.* Ma Ma A I R 1939 Rang. 28. The mere fact that the amount stipulated is excessive or beyond the means of the husband is no defence to the wife's claim.

The burden of proof that the smaller amount settled in private was exigible would of course be on the party making the allegation of the fictitious nature of the dower.

In his outlines of Mohammedan Law (Ind. Edition) page 113, Mr. A. A. Fazie observes "An altogether different tendency is to be found in Utter Pardesh and also to some extent in Hyderabad Deccan, where the absurd rule appears to be that nobler the family, the higher the *mahar*, regardless of the husband's ability to pay or capacity to earn. In one case known to the writer a middle class man agreed to the sum of eleven lacs of ashrafis (or gold mohurs, originally 15—20 rupees each) as dower. This sum, even in these days of astronomical figures, would give serious case for anxiety to any young bridegroom."

Evidence Act, s. 92.

Section 92 of the Evidence Act does not touch the question. For an allegation that the real dower was different from that stated in public or recorded in the dower-deed would not mean a variation of the written contract; it would only amount to an assertion that the real contract was different. The *onus* of course will be on the person making the allegation.[1]

Shiah doctrine.

Under the Shiah doctrines the private arrangement will constitute the lawful dower. Of course, to have effect given to it, the arrangement must be properly proved.

Where a *wakil* or mandatory who accepts a commission to arrange a contract of marriage and to stipulate for a certain dower, exceeds his authority and fraudulently increases the dower, the husband would only be liable for it if he should be aware before he consummated the marriage that the *wakil* had exceeded his authority. If, before consummation, the woman knew of the fraud of the husband's agent, she would be entitled only to the sum for which the authority was actually given. If both parties were aware of the fraud, then the husband would be liable for the whole amount.

When it is alleged that the first contract has been modified by a subsequent one, the *onus* rests on the party making the allegation.

A woman is not entitled to any dower in the following cases, *provided the separation takes place before consummation*:—

(*a*) When two minors contract themselves in marriage without the consent of their guardians, and the marriage is cancelled at the instance of the latter.

(*b*) When a marriage contracted *for* minors is cancelled by them in exercise of their right of option.[2]

(*c*) When the marriage is cancelled by order of the Judge, for any cause which gives a right of option to the parties.[3]

---

1 In Mohammad Sultan Begum *v*. Sirajuddin A I R 1936 Lah. 183 which was a suit for dower, the plaintiff relied upon a kabin-nama in which the dower amount was mentioned but the defendant pleaded that the writing was a mere sham, that the amount mentioned therein was nominal and that no effect should be given to it.

Agha Haider, J., was of the view that oral evidence to prove such plea was not admissible under section 92 of the Evidence Act. Tek Chand, J. was however of the opinion that S. 92 was no bar as that section operates as a bar only when oral evidence is sought to be led to vary or modify the terms of an agreement, but that oral evidence was admissible to prove that the agreement in writing was not agreement at all and was only a sham and was not intended to be operative. The view of Mr. Justice Tek Chand which is in consonance with the view of Syed Amir Ali is, it is respectfully submitted, the correct view of law.

2 See the Durr-ul-Mukhtar, p. 270.

3 *Ibid.*

Marriage contracted in death-illness.

(*d*) When a man enters into a contract of marriage whilst labouring under an illness which comes within the meaning of death-illness, and dies from that illness before consummating the marriage.

(*e*) If the wife was suffering from some illness at the time of marriage which prevented consummation and eventually caused her death, her right to the dower would be transmitted to her heirs.

(*f*) But where a marriage is contracted by concealment from the husband or, if he be a minor, from his guardian, of the fact of the wife's illness there would be no right to dower; it is only where the man who contracts the marriage is aware that the woman is suffering from an illness which not only prevents cohabitation but also leads to death that he is liable to dower to the woman's heirs. Where, however, these facts are deliberately concealed from him, the element of fraud comes in and he is freed from the liability.

If a father were to contract his minor son in marriage for a certain dower, and the son were to die without leaving any property the father would be liable to the wife for such dower.[1]

Shaf'eite doctrine—addition to dower.

As we have already seen, the husband has the power of making an addition to the dower during the subsistence of the marriage,[2] just as the wife may make an abatement.[3] Among the Shaf,eis, such addition is regarded as a *gift*, and as under the Mahommedan Law no gift is valid without seisin, any addition made by the husband to the dower requires that delivery thereof should be made at the time to the wife.

Hanafi and Shiah doctrines.

Among the Hanafis and the Shiahs, the *addition* is not regarded in the light of a *gift* or *hiba*, and does not, therefore, require delivery of seisin, at the time the addition is made, to render it valid. "It is", says the *Hedaya*, "an alteration of the terms of the contract in a non-essential matter within the power of the parties, and, like an addition to the price in sale, becomes incorporated with the original dower."[4]

---

1 See the Durr-ul-Mukhtar, p. 270.

2 See Jahuran Bibi *v.* Suleman Khan A I R 1934 Cal. 210; Mst. Naseban Bibi *v.* Mst. Iqbal Begum A I R 1935 Lah. 816; Chan Pir *v.* Fakar Shah A I R 1940 Lah. 104; Ruqiyya Begum *v.* Radha Kishan A I R 1944 All. 214.

3 See Jyani Begum *v.* Umrao Begum I L R 32 Bom. 612; Nurunnessa *v.* Khaja Mahomed 47 Cal. 537; Hasnumiya Dadamiyah *v.* Halimunnissa Hafizullah A I R 1942 Bom. 128.

4 Hedaya, Vol. I, p. 127, and Hedaya, Vol. II, p. 485. Comp. the Durr-ul-Mukhtar.

When a separation takes place before consummation, the wife is not entitled to the benefit of any post-nuptial settlement or "additions made to dower after marriage".

The paraphernalia.

The *trousseaux* of a bride is provided by her father. How far he has a right to recover any money he has expended on it from the dower of his daughter, depends upon the customs prevalent in the community among whom the question arises. For example, in Algeria it has been held that the father is not bound to provide his daughter's *trousseaux*, and if he should do so, he may recoup himself from the dower which she receives on marriage. In India, the bride's father is bound to furnish her with a wedding outfit, unless he is in straitened circumstances, when the obligation rests with the husband. When a man advances a sum of money towards the *trousseaux* of his future wife,[1] it is obligatory on the father, if he be possessed of means, to do the same or contribute such an amount as is customary.[2] The *paraphernalia* or *dot* which a bride brings with her from her father's home is called *jahaz* (or *jahez*), and remains her absolute property and *peculium* over which the husband has no control. The marriage outfit provided by the bridegroom becomes, likewise, her exclusive property.[3]

The expenses of the marriage feast are defrayed by the bridegroom. The wife has to contribute nothing towards the support of the household.

Condition dehors legal right void.

A condition in the marriage-contract that the parties shall not inherit from each other or that the wife will not be entitled to maintenance is void.[4]

The property of husband and wife.

The property of the married parties is always distinct. Originally, and at the commencement of the married life, it is easy to distinguish which part of it belongs exclusively to the wife and which to the husband. Later, and after the husband and wife have lived together in one conjugal domicile, it becomes difficult to distinguish the property of the one from the property of the other. Should a dispute then arise between the parties, or after their decease, between their respective heirs, regarding the

---

1 This is called Dast-i-pyman.

2 Jam'a-ush-Shittat; Muhit. "The proper ratio of Jahaz", says the Fatawa "is that for every dinar of the dast-i-pyman there should be three or four dinars of the Jahaz."

3 See Mohammed Sadiq *v.* Fakhar Jehan A I R 1932 P C 13, Where a Muslim paid various sums of money from time to time to his wife, and there was no evidence that the payments were allocated to the dower debt, it was held that the payments could not be treated as having been made in satisfaction of the debt and that the wife was entitled to recover the full amount of her dower. The maxim *debitor non prosumitur donare* (the debtor is not presumed to give or make a gift) is not applicable between husband and wife.

4 Fatawai Kazi Khan.

household effects of the common domicile, then, in the absence of any direct proof, the presumption of law is that the "things which by custom appertain to women" will be considered as the wife's property, and those "which appertain to men" will be the husband's. The right to what is appropriate to *both* will be decided with reference to local usage or custom.[1]

According to the *Radd-ul-Muhtar*, a man may recover the value of the presents sent by him to the person whom he proposed to marry if the negotiations are broken off, and no marriage takes place ; though, according to the *Durr-ul-Mukhtar*, he can only recover such things as are still existing in specie.

If a father were to give article of *jahaz* to his daughter, he is not entitled to recover them or their price, and on this is the *Fatwa*.

If a father belongs to the class of people called *ashraf* (gentlefolk), his allegation that the things sent with the girl were only lent will not be accepted, the presumption in such families being that they form part of the *paraphernalia*.

In case of separation between husband and wife, every *paraphernal* article belongs to the woman.

CHAPTER XIII

DISSOLUTION OF THE MARRIAGE-CONTRACT.—PRE-ISLAMIC INSTITUTIONS.—TALAK.—DIFFERENCE AMONG THE SCHOOLS

SECTION I

GENERAL OBSERVATIONS

Power of divorce among the nations of antiquity.

AMONG all the nations of antiquity the power of divorce was regarded as a natural corollary to the marital right. Originally, this power was exclusively vested in the husband, and the wife was under no circumstance entitled to claim a divorce.

The progress of civilisation and the advancement of ideas led to a partial amelioration in the condition of women. They, too, acquired a qualified right of divorce, which they were never backward in exercising freely, until the facility with which marriages were contracted and dissolved under the Roman emperors passed into a by-word.

---

1 According to Abu Hanifa, whose views have been enforced in several cases by the Hanafi Kazis of Algiers, "everything which is regarded as having been necessary or useful to the household (tout ce qui est regard comme ayant ete necessaire ou utile au menage commun) belong to the survivor." Comp. the Fatawai Kazi Khan on this point.

Under the ancient Hebraic Law, a husband could divorce his wife for any cause which made her disagreeable to him, and there were few or no checks to his arbitrary and capricious use of this power.

Among the Athenians as well as the early Romans, the husband's right to repudiate the wife was as unrestricted as among the ancient Israelites.

In later times, amongst the Hebrews, the Shammaites, to some extent, modified the custom of divorce by imposing certain restrictions on its exercise, but the school of Hillel upheld the law in its primitive strictness.

At the time of the Prophet's appearance, the Hillelite doctrines were chiefly in force among the Jewish tribes of Arabia, and repudiations by the husbands were as common among them as among the pagan Arabs.

In some few exceptional cases, both among the Arabs and the Jews, the women of noble families would, before marriage, reserve to themselves the power of divorcing their husbands ; and when they exercised that power, they announced the separation by merely changing the position of their tents, which conveyed a sufficient intimation of the fact to the repudiated husbands.[1]

The reforms of Mohammed.

The reforms of Mohammed marked a new departure in the history of Eastern legislation. He restrained the power of divorce possessed by the husbands ; he gave to the women the right of obtaining a separation on reasonable grounds; and towards the end of his life he went so far as practically to forbid its exercise by the men without the intervention of arbiters or a judge. He pronounced "*talak* to be the most detestable before the Almighty God of all permitted things,[2]" for it prevented conjugal happiness and interfered with the proper bringing-up of children. The permission, therefore, in the Koran, though it gave a certain countenance to the old customs, has to be read with the light of the Lawgiver's own words. When it is borne in mind how intimately law and religion are connected in the Islamic system, it will be easy to understand the bearing of the words on the institution of divorce.

M'utazila doctrines.

Naturally, therefore, great divergence exists among the various schools regarding the exercise of the power of divorce by the husband of his own motion and without the intervention of the Judge. A large and influential body of jurists regard *talak* emanating from the husband as really prohibited except for necessity, such as the adultery of the wife.[3] Another section, consisting chiefly of the M'utazilas, consider *talak* as not

1 Perron, *Femmes* Arabes.

2 (الحلال الى الله عزو جل الطلاق) reported by Abu Daud; comp. Radd-ul-Muhtar, Vol. II, p. 682.

3 Comp. *ibid.*, p. 682.

permissible without the sanction of the judge administering the Musulman Law.

They consider that any such cause as may justify separation and remove *talak* from the category of being *forbidden* (ممنوع *mamn'u*), should be tested by an unbiassed judge ; and, in support of their doctrine, they refer to the words of the Prophet already quoted, and his direction that in case of dispute between the married parties, arbiters should be appointed for the settlement of their differences.

Hanafi, Shaf'ei, Maliki and Shiah doctrines.

The Hanafis, the Malikis, the Shaf'eis and the bulk of the Shiahs hold *talak* to be *permitted* (مباح *mubah*), though they regard the exercise of the power without any cause to be morally or religiously abominable.

The enunciation of the Radd-ul-Muhtar.

The *Radd-ul-Muhtar*, after stating the arguments against the proposition that *talak* is unlawful, proceeds to say: "No doubt, it is forbidden, but it becomes *mubah* for certain outside reason, and this is the meaning of those jurists who hold that it is really forbidden.[1] And its being *mubah* arises from the necessity of release [from the marital tie] in certain cases. Therefore, when there is no reason whatsoever, there is no necessity for release; and if *talak* is given without any reason, that is stupidity and ingratitude to God, and the giving of unnecessary and gratuitous trouble to the woman and her family and the children. . . . . . If there is no legal cause for *talak*, such as would render it *mubah*, then it must be considered unlawful ; for God says [in the Koran] that if your women are obedient to you, you must not seek separation from them."[2]

The author of the *Multeka* (Ibrahim Halebi) is more concise. He says : "The law gives to the man primarily the power of dissolving the marriage, if the wife, by her indocility or her bad character, renders the married life unhappy ; but in the absence of serious reasons, no Musulman can justify a divorce either in the eyes of religion or the law. If he abandon his wife or put her away from simple caprice, he draws upon himself the divine anger, for the curse of God,' said the Prophet, 'rests on him who repudiates his wife capriciously.' "[3]

Talak when permitted and when obligatory.

"*Talak* is permitted only when the wife by her conduct or her words does injury to the husband or happens to be impious." . . . . "And it is *wajib* (obligatory) when the husband cannot fulfil his duties, as when he is impotent or an eunuch."[4]

---

1 Kamal-ud-din ibn Himam is one of the jurists who holds it forbidden, but allowed only in cases of necessity.

2 Radd-ul-Muhtar, Vol. II, pp. 682, 683.

3 Comp. D,Ohsson, Vol. III, p. 79.

4 Radd-ul-Muhtar, Vol. II, p. 683.

Divorce in pre-Islamic times.

The pre-Islamic institution of divorce required no formula to make its operation valid, and as there was no check on the irresponsible power of the husband, a simple intimation from him to the effect that the tie was dissolved was considered sufficient.

Conditions necessary to the exercise of the power.

Even among the schools which recognise the validity of a divorce without the intervention of any judicial authority there are several conditions imposed on the exercise of the power by the husband, with the object of protecting the wife as much as possible from being thrown on the world at the mere caprice of the man. They also give to the wife the right of obtaining a dissolution of the contract under certain circumstances.[1]

Talak.

When the dissolution of the marriage-tie proceeds from the husband, it is called *talak*. Technically, the power of the husband is absolute ; but, virtually and in practice, it is restrained within definite bounds by the numerous formulae which are attached to its exercise.

Khula.

When it takes place at the instance of the wife, it is called *khula*.

Mubarat.

When it is by mutual consent, it is called *mubarat*.[2]

In all these cases according to the principal sects, no decree of the Judge is necessary to dissolve the union. The mere act of the parties is regarded as sufficient in law, provided all the conditions required for effecting a valid divorce are complied with.

There are other cases, however, in which the Judge is authorised to dissolve or cancel the union, on the application of either the husband or the wife.[3]

SECTION II

TALAK

Hanafi doctrines.

Two kinds of *talak* are recognised by the Hanafis, *viz*., (1), the *talak-us-sunnat*, and (2) the *talak-ul-bid'at* or *talak-ul-bad'ai*. The *talak-us-sunnat* is the divorce which is effected in accordance with the rules laid down in the traditions (the *sunnat*) handed down from the Prophet or his principal disciples. It is, in fact, the mode or procedure which seems to have been approved of by him at the beginning of his ministry, and is, consequently, regarded as the regular or proper and orthodox form of divorce.

1 See the Dissolution of Muslim Marriages Act, 1939 and the Muslim Family Laws Ordinance, 1961.

2 See Ghulam Sakina *v*. Umar Bakhsh P L D 1964 S C 456.

3 See Balqis Fatima *v*. Najmul lkram Qureshi P L D 1959 Lah. 566.

Talak-ul-bid'at.

The *talak-ul-bid'at,* as its name signifies, is the heretical or irregular mode of divorce, which was introduced in the second century of the Muhammedan era. It was then that the Omeyyade monarchs[1], finding that the checks imposed by the Prophet on the facility of repudiation interfered with the indulgence of their caprice, endeavoured to find an escape from the strictness of the law, and found in the pliability of the jurists a loophole to effect their purpose.

As a matter of fact, the capricious and irregular exercise of the power of divorce which was in the beginning left to the husbands was strongly disapproved of by the Prophet. It is reported that when once news was brought to him that one of his disciples had divorced his wife, pronouncing the three *talaks,* at one and the same time, the Prophet stood up in anger on his carpet and declared that the man was making a plaything of the words of God, and made him take back his wife.[2]

The Shiahs and the Malikis do not recognise the validity of the *talah-ul-bid'at,* whilst the Hanafi and the Shaf'eis agree in holding that a divorce is effective, if pronounced in the *bid'at* form, "though in its commission the man incurs a sin."

Talak-us-sunnat—the Ahsan form.

The *talak-us-sunnat* is either *ahsan* or *hasan—very proper* or simply *proper.* In the *talak-us-sunnat* pronounced in the *ahsan* form, the husband is required to submit to the following conditions, *viz*: (*a*), he must pronounce the formula of divorce *once, in a single sentence*; (*b*) he must do so when the woman is in a state of purity (*tahr*), and there is no bar to connubial intercourse, nor has there been any during that state and (*c*) he must abstain from the exercise of conjugal rights, after pronouncing the formula, for the space of three *tahrs.*[3] This latter clause is intended to demonstrate that the resolve, on the husband's part, to separate

---

1 See Mst. Ghulam Sakina *v.* Umar Bakhsh P L D 1964 S C 456.

See Amiruddin *v* Khatun Bibi I L R 39 All. 371 (the view of Syed Amir Ali relied upon). This ruling has been followed in Sh. Fazlur Rahman *v.* Mst. Aisha I L R 8 Pat. 690: A I R 1929 Pat. 81.

But according to an Hadeth quoted by M. Mohammed Ali in Manual of Hadeth page 2861 from Masnad of Imam Ahmad bin Hanbul 1; 34, the procedure during the time of the Holy Prophet, and the caliphate of Hazarat Abu Bakr, and the first 2 years of Hazarat Umar was that divorce uttered thrice was considered as one divorce. Then Umar said, "people had made haste in a matter in which that was moderation for them, so we may make it take effect with regard to them. So he made it take effect to them." The Holy Quran is hower quite clear on the point that such a divorce must be deemed to be a single divorce, making remarriage of the spouses without an intervening marriage of the wife with another man, perfectly valid.

In Pakistan, Talak-ul-Bid'at has been abolished. See the Muslim Family Laws Ordinance.

2 Radd-ul-Muhtar, Vol. II, p. 684.

See Manual of Hadeth, page 287, where the original Hadeth taken from Annisai Chap. 27 verse 6 is reported.

3 See Rashid Ahmad *v.* Anisa Khatoon A I R 1932 P C 25.

from the wife, is not a passing whim, but is the result of a settled determination. On the lapse of the term of three *tahrs*, the separation takes effect as an irrevocable divorce.

"It is proper and right to observe this form", says the *Radd-ul-Muhtar*, "for human nature (*nafs*) is apt to be misled and to lead astray the mind and to perceive faults which may not exist, and to commit mistakes of which one is certain to feel ashamed afterwards."[1]

Hasan form.

In the *hasan* form, the husband, is required to pronounce the formula three times during three successive *tahrs* namely three periods of purity of the wife. When the last formula is pronounced, the *talak* or divorce becomes irrevocable.[2]

These two forms alone, as stated before, are recognised by the Shiahs.[3]

Talak-ul-bid'at.

In the *talak-ul-bid'at*, the husband may pronounce the three formulae at one time, whether the wife be in a state of *tahr* or not. The separation then takes effect definitely after the woman has fulfilled her *'iddat* or period of probation.[4]

All these schools allow revocation; that is, a husband who has suddenly and under inexplicable circumstances pronounced the formula against his wife, may revoke any time before the three *tahrs* have expired. When the power of recantation is lost, the separation or *talak* becomes *bain*; whilst it continues, the *talak* is simply *raja'ai* or revocable.

Talak-ul-bain.

When a definite and complete separation (*talak-ul-bain*) has taken place, the parties so separated cannot re-marry without the formality of the woman marrying another man and being divorced from him, as mentioned before.[5]

Sautayra and Sedillot[6] agree with the Moslem jurists in thinking, that this rule was framed with the object of restraining the frequency of divorce in Arabia. Sedillot speaks of the condition as "a very wise one," as it rendered separation more rare, by imposing a check on its frequent practice among the Hebrews

---

1 Radd-ul-Muhtar, Vol. II, pp. 683, 684; Durr-ul-Mukhtar *in loco*.

2 Fatawai 'Alamgiri, Vol. I, p. 492.

See Rashid Ahmed *v*. Anisa Khatun A I R 1932 P C 25.

3 Shara'ya; Mafatih; Jam'a-ush-Shittat.

4 As to the validity of a talak-ul-bid'at see Furzund Hossein *v*. Tonu Bibi (1878) I L 4 Cal. 588; Hamid Ali *v*. Imtiazan (1878) I L 2 All. 71; and Ibrahim *v*. Syed Bibi (1888) I L 12 Mad. 63; In re Abdul Ali Ishmailji and his wife Husanbi (1883) I L 7 Bom. 180; Sarabai *v*. Rabiabai, infra.

5 See ante.

6 Sedillot, Hist. des Arabes, p. 85; comp. Syud Ahmad Khan's Ess iv, p. 14.

and the heathen Arabs of the Peninsula. Sautayra says that the check was intended to control a jealous, sensative, but half-cultured race by appealing to their sense of honour.[1]

Difference between the Sunni and Shiah rules.

As a general rule, the power of *talak* under the Sunni doctrines is larger than that under the Shiah Law. "Marriage" says the *Shara'ya* in its essence is an act of chastity established by the law, [*per se*] not admitting of dissolution; in order therefore, to remove the tie, it is necessary to adhere strictly to the formula (*sigheh*) prescribed for the purpose."[2]

The conditions which surround the power of *talak* under the Shiah Law, and limit its exercise, are accordingly stricter than under the Sunni Law.

Sunni doctrines.

According to the Sunni doctrines, *talak* may be effected by *express* terms (*sarih*), which leave no doubt as to the intention of the repudiator, or by the use of ambiguous or implicative expressions (*b'ilkinayeh*).[3]

The *Radd-ul-Muhtar* says that when expressions are used which are *sarih* or which are analogous thereto, the intention of *talak* is not necessary on the part of the husband. For example, if a man were to use the word *talak*, it would not be necessary to see whether he intended to divorce the wife.

---

1 Sultan Khuda Bandeh Uljaitu Khan's conversion to the Shiah doctrines is ascribed to his unwillingness to allow his wife, from whom he had separated in a fit of passion by an irregular divorce, to submit to the ordeal of a marriage with another. Certain rationalistic schools, notably that of the M'utazilas, think that the following passage of the Koran abrogates the condition laid down in the verse immediately preceding it : "When ye divorce women," says the passage referred to, "and the time for sending them away is come, either retain them with generosity or send them away with generosity; but retain them not by constraint so as to be unjust towards them."

2 Shara'ya p. 311.

3 Fatawai 'Alamgiri, Vol. I, p. 500; Fatawai Kazi Khan, Vol. II, p. 33; Radd-ul-Muhtar, Vol. II, p. 685.

See Amiruddin *v.* Khatun Bibi I L R 390 All. 371: 39 I C 513; Sh. Fazal-ur Rahman *v.* Mst Aisha I L R 8 Pat. 690: A I R 1929 Pat. 81; Rashid Ahmed *v.* Anisa Khatun A I R 1932 P C 25: I L R 59 I A 21; Lalan Bi *v.* Mohammad Ashfaq P L D 1951 Lah. 467. Talak in clear and manifest words is effective irrespective of intention.

Wajid Ali *v.* Jaffar Hussain A I R 1932 Oudh 34. The husband says "I give up all relations and would have no connection of any sort with you." There is no talak unless intention is proved.

Mohammed Irfan *v.* Mst. Mahando P L D 1952 Pesh. 55. (The Court must construe the words pronounced by the husband by looking more to the intention than the form. Where the husband in a quarrel with his brother declared that he would take a bottle of honey from his brother, and that if he did not do so his wives would be considered divorced, it was held that emphasis was on taking back the bottle of honey and therefore it did not constitute an effective divorce.

Shiah doctrines.

According to the Shiahs, repudiation pronounced "implicatively" or in ambiguous terms, does not take effect, whether there be intention on the part of the repudiator or not, nor does it take effect if it be made dependent upon or subjected to any condition.[1]

Besides the divergence existing between the Shiahs and the Hanafis regarding express and implied *talaks*, there is a marked difference between the two schools in respect of the *capacity* for repudiation. The Shiahs hold that, in order to pronounce a valid *talak*, the repudiator must not only be "adult and sane", but must act of his own free-will, and with the knowledge and comprehension of the nature of what he is doing.

The Sunnis, generally speaking, regard a repudiation pronounced by a person who is *sui juris* as valid in law, without requiring him to fulfil any other conditions.[2]

Section III

Capacity for Talak

Shiah doctrines.

Under the Shiah Law there are four conditions essential to the *capacity* of pronouncing a valid *talak*. It is required (*a*) that the husband should have attained majority; (*b*) that he should be sane and possessed of sound understanding; (*c*) that he should act of his own free will; and (*d*) that on his part, there should be a distinct intention to dissolve the marriage-tie.

Talak by a Minor.

A boy, who has not arrived at the age of puberty, is precluded from effecting a dissolution of the matrimonial contract, by pronouncing the *talak*; so also an insane person. There is, however, this difference between the case of a person who is a minor, and one who is disqualified by reason of insanity, that whereas the guardian of a minor husband has no authority to supply his ward's place in order to effect a valid repudiation, the guardian of a *confirmed* lunatic is authorised to do so. When the lunatic has no guardian, the Kazi or Judge can make a decree to dissolve the tie, the reason of this difference consists in the fact that the disability of age is temporary, whereas lunacy is usually permanent. The difficulty, therefore, which was felt under the English Law, in the case of *Baker* v. *Baker*,[2] where the husband being insane, a divorce was sought by his committee on the ground of the wife's adultery, cannot arise under the Shiah Law.

Repudiation under compulsion invalid—Shiah Law.

Repudiation pronounced under compulsion is invalid and ineffective under the Shiah Law. In order to invalidate a *talak* on the ground of its having been pronounced under compulsion, three conditions are requisite: (*a*) that the "compeller" is able to do what he threatens; (*b*) that there is a strong probability of the threat being carried into effect; (*c*) that the threat involves some

1 Jam'a-ush-Shittat; Shara'ya, p. 314.

2 49 L J, p. 49, affirmed 49 L J, p. 83; s. c. 6 P D 12.

imminent and serious danger to the "compelled" person himself or to some one near to him. "A trifling injury", says the *Shara'ya*, "is not sufficient to establish compulsion.'[1]

Shiah doctrines.

A repudiation obtained by fraud, or given under undue influence, is also invalid under the Shiah Law. Intention is a necessary element to the validity of all *talaks*. Where this essential condition is wanting, though the *talak* may be pronounced in *express* terms, yet it has no effect.[2] But even where there is actual intention, the repudiation must be formulated in *express* and *unequivocal* terms, or the entire proceeding would be invalid.

A *talak* pronounced by a person in a state of intoxication or by one labouring under a temporary stupor from the use of some narcotic, or any other cause, is likewise invalid. So also is the case of a *talak* given by mistake or inadvertence, in anger or in jest, or when the words have fallen whilst talking in sleep.[3]

Nor under the Shiah Law, is a *talak* pronounced in a paroxysm of anger during which all self-control is lost.

Hanafi doctrines.

Among the Hanafis, the power of repudiation belongs in principle to every husband who is adult and sane. This power is certainly greater in the Hanafi than in any other Sunni school.

According to the Hanafi doctrines, although an acknowledgment of a *talak*, *viz.*, an acknowledgment by a man that he had divorced his wife, extracted from him under compulsion, is ineffective,[4] a *talak* actually pronounced under compulsion is valid. "A *talak*", says the *'Alamgiri*, "pronounced by any husband who is of mature age (*baligh*) and possessed of understanding (*'akil*) is effective, whether he be free or a slave, willing or acting under compulsion;[5] and even though it were uttered in sport or jest, or inadvertently by a mere *slip of the tongue*."[6] But he must be awake at the time when he pronounces the *talak*.[7]

Whilst an acknowledgment extracted from the husband by compulsion [*ikrah*], whether embodied in writing or not, is ineffective, an acknowledgment of *talak* made in jest or falsely will take effect (*Kazan*) "judicially", though it will not have any force

1 Sha'a'ya; see the Jam'a-ush-Shittat and Irshad-ul-'Allamah.

2 Jam'a-ush-Shittat.

3 *Ibid*; Irshad-ul-'Allamah.

4 Fatawai 'Alamgiri, Vol. I, p. 499, after the Fatawai Kazi Khan.

5 *Ibid*, Vol. I, p. 497 (after the Jowharat-un-Nayyereh).
Ibrahim *v.* Enayat ur Rahman (1869) 4 Bom. L R A C 13.

6 *Ibid* (after the Muhit); Fatawai Kazi Khan.

See Syed Rashid Ahmed *v.* Anisa Khatun A I R 1932 P C 25; Muhammad Azam Khan *v.* Akhtiar-un-nissa P L D 1957 Lah. 195.

7 Radd-ul-Muhtar, Vol. II, p. 691. But see per contra. Muhammad Irfan *v.* Mst. Mahando P L D 1952 Pesh. 55.

inforo conscientioe; in other words, the man is bound to retract, but if he does not, the Kazi will give effect to it.[1]

Shaf'ei rule.

According to the Shaf'ei doctrine, a *talak* pronounced by a "person compelled" (المكره) is wholly ineffective.[2]

As regards the *talak* of a man who is intoxicated, there is great difference of opinion among the Sunnis.

Talak by a drunken man—Hanafi rule.

If a man is forcibly made drunk and in that state *talaks* his wife, according to the *Tuhfa*, such a *talak* will not take effect. And in the *Fath-ul-Kadir* "preference is given to this opinion." And this has been approved in the *Nahr-ul-Faik*, and "it is correct." So in the *Sharh-ul-Jam'a* the *Khanieh*,[3] *Tahtawi* and *Hashiat-ul-Madami*.

In Kahastani it is stated from Zahidi that, if a man be dead drunk and cannot distinguish between right and wrong, a *talak* pronounced by him will not be effective. Imam Shaf'ei also has declared that the *talak* of a drunken man is not valid. And this doctrine has been adopted by Tahawi and al-Karkhi, and in the *Tatar-Khanieh* it is stated "that the *Fatwa* is thereon." Mohammed Ibn a-Shahna has followed the same doctrine, which is also the view of Imam Zuffar.[4]

In the *Fatawai Kazi Khan*[5] the rules relating to a *talak* pronounced by a drunken man are thus stated—"so also[6] is effectual the *talak* of a man who has become intoxicated from taking wine (*khamar*) or *nabiz* [an extract from barley] although Karkhi and Tahawi have, following one opinion of Shaf'ei, held it is not." "[But] if he has been compelled[7] to take the wine, or has taken the wine under necessity (لضرورة) and has become intoxicated and then (*viz.*, in that condition) pronounced the *talak*, there is a difference on this point. And the correct view is that as the man is not liable to punishment [for drunkenness] the *talak* will not take effect, nor will any other dealing of his." "And it is reported from Imam Muhammed (on whom be peace) that if a man drinks of *nabiz* and it does not agree with him and the fumes thereof rise to his head and give him a headache and his understanding is lost thereby, and not from the drink, and he divorces his wife, the *talak* does not take effect." "Even if his understanding is lost from the drink or from being struck on the head, and he pronounces the *talak*, it will not be effective."

1 Radd-ul-Muhtar, Vol. II, p. 691.

2 Fatawai Kazi Khan.

3 *Ibid*.

4 Radd-Muhtar, Vol. II, p. 697.

5 Vol. II, p. 33.

6 Referring to a talak under compulsion.

7 (لوا كداه على شرب النحمد)

Talak by a drunken man.

"And if he takes a drink derived from grain[1] or fruit[2] or honey, and gives the *talak* or emancipates [his slave], there is a difference of opinion in respect thereto. The Jurist Abu J'afar (may, etc.) has declared that in such circumstances as the man is not liable to *hadd* [the specific punishment for drunkenness] so his dealings will be ineffective." "So, if a man has lost his understanding from taking *banj* (*bhang*) or the milk of the ass, his *talak* and emancipation will not have effect given to it."

The *Fatawai 'Alamgiri* gives the same principles from *Kazi Khan* and the *Tahzib*, but it adds another rule from the *Jawahir-ul-Akhlati*: "if a man gets drunk from *banj* (*bhang*, hemp)[3] and pronounces a *talak*, it will be effective, and he will be liable to punishment (*hadd*) *on account of the frequency of this act* (لفعلل) *among people* (بين الناس) *and on this is the Fatwa in our times.*"

The general principle deducible from these rules is that if the man is not liable to punishment, a *talak* pronounced by him is not valid.[4]

If a man were to take something lawful (*hallal*), such as the extract of honey or the juice of aniseed, etc., and become inebriated, or if he were to take anything unlawful like opium or wine as a medicine, or "for a necessary purpose", and should lose his consciousness thereby, and were, whilst in that condition, to pronounce a *talak*, it would not be effective.

Similarly, a *talak* pronounced by a man whilst in a state of intoxication from some liquor or drug administered against his will is not valid.

Shaf'ei doctrines.

Two opinions are reported from Shaf'ei. It is said that at first, he declared that the *talak* of a drunken man was not effective,[5] but afterwards he is said to have modified his view. Accordingly, his followers agree with the Hanafis in holding that a repudiation pronounced by a drunken man is effective subject to the limitations above stated.

1 Al-hubub.

2 Al-fawakih. The Fatawai 'Alamgiri says that Abu Hanifa and Abu Yusuf were of opinion that the divorce of a man who became intoxicated on fermented liquor obtained from grain or honey would not be effective. Imam Mohammed, however, differed from them, "and the Fatwa" is according to his doctrines; p. 498.

3 Just before this rule the contrary was stated from the Tahzib, showing clearly the change in the interpretation and application of the law according to the change of times and social conditions. This conception of the law is lost sight of in the British Indian Courts.

4 See Syed Rashid Ahmed *v.* Anisa Khatun A I R 1932 P C 25. If the husband pronounces talak in a state of voluntary intoxication or in order to satisfy his father or somebody else, the talak is valid.

5 Hedaya, Vol. I, p. 211; Fatawai Kazi Khan, Vol. II, p. 33.

Shiah and Maliki doctrines.

The Malikis, however, agree with the Shiahs in regarding such repudiations as absolutely invalid. The Maliki doctrine was laid down with great clearness and precision in a case decided by the Kazi of Tlemcen in Algeria, and reported by Sautayra. In that case, the wife applied for a divorce against her husband on the ground that he had pronounced a *talak-ul-bain* against her. The husband in defence stated that he was not aware of having pronounced a *talak*, as at the time of the alleged repudiation he was in a state of intoxication. The witnesses cited by the parties proved that the *talak* was actually pronounced, but that the husband was drunk at the time. The Kazi dismissed the wife's petition, holding that the *talak* was ineffective, as the man was in a state of inebriety when he uttered the formula constituting the basis of the charge.

Talak extorted under compulsion.—Hanafi doctrines.

There is a great divergence among the several Sunni schools with reference to a repudiation obtained or extorted from an individual by compulsion, or under the influence of threats. The Hanafis, as mentioned before, are of opinion that a *talak* pronounced under compulsion is as valid as one given voluntarily.

Shaf'ei and Shiah doctrines.

The Shaf'eis hold a diametrically opposite view. They agree with the Shiahs in considering that the husband who acts under the influence of threats of violence is not a free agent, and consequently his *talak* has no validity in law. Shaf'ei, the founder of the school, expressed this in terms which are given with some particularity in the *Hedaya*. He says: "That the *talak* of a man acting under compulsion is not effective, because a person who is *compelled* has no option, and no formal act of law is worthy of regard, unless it be voluntary ; contrary to the case of one speaking in jest, who, in mentioning divorce, acts from *option*, which is the cause of its validity."[1]

The answer of the Hanafi doctors to these pertinent remarks of one of the most rigid of all the Sunni jurists, is worthy of note. "Our doctors", says the author of the *Hedaya*, "allege that a person who is subjected to compulsion pronounces divorce under circumstances of complete competency [maturity of age and sanity of intellect], the result of which is that the divorce takes effect equally with that of a person who acts of his own free will. . . . . . The reason for holding this is that the man [who acts under compulsion] has the choice of two evils—one, the thing with which he is threatened or compelled, and the other, the divorce under compulsion; and viewing both, he makes a choice of that which appears to him the easiest, namely, divorce, and this proves that he has an option."[2]

Ibrahim Moola v. Enayat-ur-Rahman.

In the case of *Ibrahim Moolla* v. *Enayet-ur-Rahman*, the High Court of Calcutta held that the divorce of one "acting under

1 Hedaya, Vol. I, Bk. iv, ch. i, p. 149.

2 *Ibid.*

compulsion is effective."[1] The principle, however, enunciated in this judgment ought to be confined exclusively to the Hanafis.

Supposing a Hanafi, under the influence of threats and strong coercion, were to pronounce a *talak* against his wife, and on recovering his freedom of action, were to disavow the validity of his act, and in order to escape from the consequences of his act were to place himself under the Shaf'ei rules, there seems little doubt that he would be justified in doing so, and the repudiation he had pronounced would be invalidated.

Maliki doctrines.

The Malikis follow the same rule as the Shaf'eis. According to them, "the fear of punishment, the threat of death, violence, or imprisonment to the husband himself, or to anyone whom he holds dear, renders the repudiation ineffective."[2]

As regards the character of the compulsion which is held to invalidate a *talak* the Malikis and the Shaf'eis agree with the Shiahs in holding that it must be such as to influence the conduct or frame of mind of a reasonable man.

All the Sunni jurists agree that the repudiation of a boy under puberty, though possessed of understanding, is ineffective.[3]

If a youth under puberty were to *talak* his wife, or another person were to do so on his behalf, and he, on attaining majority, were to ratify what was done while he was a minor, such ratification would not make the divorce operative. In order to give effect to it, he must pronounce it *de novo*.[4]

Hanafi rules.

The *talak* of one who is insane or afflicted by pleurisy (*birsam*) or happens to be delirious or in a faint is invalid. So also, if a person were to pronounce a *talak* whilst asleep or unconscious (*madhush*) or lost in astonishment, no legal effect will be attached to it.[5]

Regarding a person suffering from paralysis or epilepsy, consideration must be paid to the length of time the disease has lasted and whether it has gone on increasing.[6]

If a lunatic, with lucid intervals, should pronounce a *talak*

---

1 (1869) 4 B L R, A C 13; (s. c.), 12 W R 46.

2 Kitab-ul-Anwar.

3 Fatawai 'Alamgiri, Vol. I, p. 498 (after the Fath-ul-Kadir); Kanz-ud-Dakaik.

4 *Ibid*; Durr-ul-Mukhtar, p. 223.

5 Fatawai 'Alamgiri, Vol. I, p. 498; Durr-ul-Mukhtar, p. 223; Radd-ul-Muhtar, Vol. II, p. 700.

6 See post.

whilst the fit is on him, it would be ineffective; but it would be valid if given in a lucid interval.[1]

Talak with an option.

Among the Sunnis, "a repudiation cannot be qualified by option." Thus, if a person were to say to his wife, "I have *talaked* you, but I reserve to myself an *option* for three days", the repudiation would be valid, but the option invalid. If a repudiation be pronounced conditionally, or be made dependent on the occurrence of a contingency not impossible in its nature, the condition is valid, the *talak* taking effect only when the condition is fulfilled.[2]

Shiah doctrines.

The Shiahs, on the other hand, regard all talaks to which an option or a condition is attached, as absolutely void.[3]

Talak in writing.

They do not allow a *talak* to be given in writing, nor in any language other than Arabic, when there is ability to pronounce the words necessary for a valid repudiation ; nor can a *talak* be effected among them by signs unless the husband be dumb.[4] A person who is dumb may give the repudiation in writing, but one who is able to speak is not allowed to do so. Even an absent husband cannot effect a valid *talak* in writing.[5] He must pronounce the words in the presence of the witnesses, and the fact of his doing so may be recorded in writing, which may be forwarded to the wife, or it may be intimated to her otherwise. The Sunnis, on the contrary, hold that "a *talak* may be effected by writing as well as words."[6]

---

1 Fatawai 'Alamgiri, Vol. I, p. 498; Durr-ul-Mukhtar, p. 223; Radd-ul-Muhtar, Vol. II, p. 700. All these refer to the Sunni doctrines.

See Bachchoo *v.* Bismillah A I R 1936 All. 387. The husband agreed to pay his wife maintenance within a specified time, and stipulated that in default the writing would operate as a divorce. It was held that on the husband's default, writing *ipso facto* took effect as a valid divorce.

2 See Ma Mi *v.* Kallandar Ammal A I R 1927 P C 15. A talak may be effected orally (that is by words spoken) or by a written document called talaknama. If the words are well understood, as implying divorce such as talak no proof of intention is required. If the words used are ambiguous, the intention of the user must be proved. It is not necessary that the repudiation should be pronounced in the presence of the wife or even addressed to her.

See Syed Rashid Ahmed *v.* Anisa Khatun A I R 1932 P C 25. Where the words of divorce addressed to the wife, though she was not present, were repeated three times by the husband as follows, "I divorce A for ever and render her haram for me", which clearly showed an intention to dissolve the marriage, and followed it by executing a deed of divorce, there can be no doubt that the method adopted was that of talak-ul-bid'dat.

3 Shara'ya.

4 Mafatih.

5 Shara'ya; Baillie's Imameea Law, p. 113.

6 Fatawai 'Alamgiri, Vol. I, p. 499.

Hanafi doctrines.

Writings, among the Hanafis, are said to be of two kinds, *viz.*, *marsumah* (customary) and *ghair-marsumah* (not customary). When repudiation is given by a writing of the description called customary, it is effective even when there is no real intention on the part of the husband to divorce the wife. But where the writing, though *marsumah*, is written so that it is not intelligible, or if it is written on something that cannot be deciphered, there will be no *talak*, even if he had the intention.[1] In the case of non-customary writings, if there be any ambiguity, the *talak* will not take effect; when there is no ambiguity and the meaning of the writer is "manifest", the repudiation is valid.[2]

General rule.

It is not necessary for the husband himself to pronounce the *talak* in the presence of the wife, but it is necessary that it should come to her knowledge.

If a *talak* is given by letter, it will take effect on the receipt of the letter by the wife. If the letter reaches her father and he tears it to pieces, there will be no *talak*, unless the father transacts all her business,—is, in fact, her agent, and resides in the same house with her. If the father should inform the wife of the receipt of the letter and deliver to her the torn pieces thereof, the *talak* will take effect only if the letter can be read and understood.[3]

A writing obtained from a husband by "beating and imprisonment", divorcing his wife is ineffective.[4]

Shiah doctrines.

Under the Shiah Law,[5] it is further necessary that there should be two *reliable* witnesses present at the time of repudiation to hear the words in which it is pronounced, or in the case of a

---

1 Radd-ul-Muhtar, Vol. II, p. 703.

See Lalan Bibi *v.* Mohammed Ashfaq P L D 1951 Lah. 467. The real difference in marsumah and ghair-marsumah forms is that in the former case the writing operates as a talak even though there is no intention to divorce but in the latter case it takes effect if the intention is manifest and not otherwise. But in neither case the validity of talak is dependent on the knowledge of the wife.

See also Sarabai *v.* Rabia Bai I L R 30 Bom. 537; Rasul Bakhsh *v.* Mst. Bholan I L R 13 Lah. 780: A I R 1932 Lah. 498; Ahmad Kasim *v.* Khatun Bibi A I R 1933 Cal. 27: I L R 59 Cal. 833; In re Raja Sahib I L R 44 Bom. 44: 54 I C 573; Mohammed Ishaq *v.* Mst. Sairan Bibi A I R 1936 Lah. 611: 163 I C 953.

2 Fatawai 'Alamgiri, Vol. I, p. 533; Fatawai Kazi Khan, Vol. II, p. 29.

3 Radd-ul-Muhtar, Vol. II, p. 703; Fatawai Kazi Khan, Vol. II, p. 35.

4 But see Mohammed Azam Khan *v.* Akhtur-un-nissa P L D 1957 Lah. 195.

5 The Shia Law in this respect is strictly in accord with the Holy Quran; see Chapter 65 Verse 2, according to which two witnesses are essential to the validity of a talak.

dumb individual, to see the writing or the signs in which it is expressed. Not only must the witnesses be present at the time, but they should understand the nature of the act and hear the distinct wording of the repudiation. If they be unable to testify to the exact character of the *talak*, or the words or signs used, it is invalid, although all other conditions may have been duly complied with.

It is a further condition under the Shiah doctrines that the witnesses should be present *together*. The Shiah Law is so strict in the matter of repudiation and throws so many obstacles in the way of a dissolution of marriage by this process, that it declares that, if one of the witnesses should be present at one stage and the other at another stage of the proceeding, the *talak* would not be valid. When they testify to the acknowledgment by the wife of a repudiation, it is not necessary that their testimony should be concordant, or relate to one and the same time, or "be given together." "Yet", says the *Shara'ya*, "if *one* should testify to the *fact* of repudiation and the *other* to the *acknowledgment* of it, their testimony would not be admissible."[1]

When a *talak* is pronounced in the presence of witnesses, it takes effect only when the appropriate words are employed. If a husband were to repudiate his wife first without witnesses and then in their presence, the former proceeding would count for nothing. The dissolution would come into effect only from the date of the second *talak* if valid'.

Sunni doctrines.

The Sunnis, on the contrary, do not require the presence of witnesses. So long as the repudiation comes to the knowledge of the wife, it is considered sufficient and valid in law.[2]

Sunni doctrines—the formulae.

For the purpose of effecting a *talak* they also allow the use of an infinite number of formulae—some obvious in their meaning,

---

1 Shara'ya, Vol. I, p. 316. Comp. the Jam'a-ush-Shittat.

2 In Aisha Bibi *v* Kadir Ibrahim I L R 33 Mad. 22, it was observed that according to Hanafi Law, it is not necessary that the talak or the words of repudiation should be addressed directly to the wife to constitute a valid divorce. It was further observed that the expressions mentioned in the 'Hedaya' as constituting express divorce are not exhaustive, but merely llustrative of the different forms in which the talak may be pronounced.

In Sarabai *v*. Rabia bai I L R 30 Bom. 537, it was held that a divorce in writing in cu tomary form showing express intention to divorce, effected irrevocable talak with effect from the date of writing even if not brought to the notice of the wife.

In Ahmad Kasim Mulla *v*. Khatun Bibi A I R 1933 Cal. 27 and in Lalan Bibi *v*. Mohammad Ashfaq P L D 1951 Lah. 467 it was held that the weight of authority is in favour of the view that the validity of *talak-ul bain* (irrevocable divorce) is not affected by the failure of the husband to communicate it to the wife.

others conveying the intention only implicatively.[1] The Shiahs recognise only two as effectuating a valid repudiation. The use of any other formulae, whether explicit or ambiguous, renders the proceeding void.

Furzund Hossain v. Tanu Bibi.

The author of the *Radd-ul-Muhtar*, following Hamawi in his *Sharh-ul-kanz*, lays down that in pronouncing the *talak* the man must address it to some particular person, otherwise it will not be valid. And this view was enunciated by the Calcutta High Court in the case of *Furzund Hossein* v. *Tanu Bibi*,[2] in which it was held that the mere pronounciation of the word *talak* three times, without its being addressed to any person, was not sufficient to constitute a valid divorce.[3]

As the principle contained in this decision is inherent in the Shiah doctrines, which insist that a *talak* in order to be effective should specify the particular person to whom it is addressed, the ruling would apply equally to Shiahs and Sunnis.[4]

Hanafi doctrines—a dumb person.

A dumb person may give *talak* by signs ; but if he is literate, a *talak* pronounced by him must be in writing. The *Radd-ul-Muhtar* says "this is the Shaf'ei doctrine, but most of our *ashabs* (masters) have adopted it."[5]

When the word *talak* or any of its customary synonyms is used, the separation would be effective, even should the man have no intention.[6]

Even if the words are mispronounced, for example, instead of pronouncing (طلاق) the man says (تلاک) it would be effective.[7]

And this idea of punishing the man for playing, as it were, with a double-edged instrument, is carried so far that it is laid down that if an ignorant man was taught the word *talak*, and he were to pronounce it against his wife without knowing its meaning, the *talak* would be effective "judicially", though not in the forum of conscience. But one lawyer, at least, takes a different view. Shaikh-ul-Ullama 'Uzjandi has held that the *talak* of such a person will not be effective, "that people may not be injured in their rights."[8] "This is stated in detail in the *Bazazia*."

---

1 For these formulae see Fatawai 'Alamgiri, Vol. I, pp 520—33; Fatawai Kazi Khan, Vol. II, pp. 2—33; Hedaya, Vol. I, pp. 147—50.

2 Supra.

3 Radd-ul-Muhtar, Vol. II, p. 685.

4 See foot note 2 on p. 446.

5 Radd-ul-Muhtar, Vol. II, p. 697.

6 *Ibid*, p. 704.

7 *Ibid*, p. 706.

8 *Ibid*, p. 709.

But where the words are mispronounced, and the husband were to say he pronounced the *talak* with the object of frightening the woman, and this is really so, the *talak* will not be effective.

And even if he were to pronounce the words rightly, but were to say that he used the words with the object of getting rid of his burden, the *talak* will not take effect.[1] Nor will there be any *talak* if he says 'thy *talak* is obligatory on me', or 'I am compelled to *talak* thee,' or 'God give thee *talak*', or 'I have bestowed on thee thy *talak*',[2] unless there is distinct intention.

So also if he were to spell out the word *talak*. But if he were to take an oath that his wife (so-and-so) should become *talaked* from him if he were to do a particular act, it would take effect if he did commit the act in question.

Expressions by which a talak may be effectuated.

A *talak* will take place if the man says, "I am forbidden (*haram*) to thee" or "thou art forbidden to me", or "I have released thee from being my wife", or "from thy marriage". But it will not be effective if he says, "I am free from thee", or "I am rid of thee."

If a woman were to say to her husband, "thou art not my husband", and he were to say, "yes, I am not, thou art not my wife", according to Abu Hanifa, a *talak* will ensue, if there was intention ; but, according to the Disciples, it will not be effective at all.[3]

Shiah doctrine.

According to the Shiahs, there will be no *talak* in any of the foregoing cases.

Waj Bibee v. Azmat Ali.

Neither school, with certain exceptions among the Usuli lawyers, requires the *talak* to be pronounced in the presence of the wife. Accordingly a *talak* pronounced in her absence is valid.[4] But so long as it does not come to her knowledge, she is entitled to maintenance.[5] In the case of *Waj Bibee* v. *Azmat Ali,*[6] the Calcutta High Court held that an instrument of divorce signed by the husband in the presence of, and given to, the wife's father was valid, notwithstanding that it was not signed in the presence of the wife.

---

1 Radd-ul-Muhtar, Vol, II, p. 708. See Muhammad Irfan *v.* Mst. Mahando P L D 1952 Pesh. 55.

2 Radd-ul-Muhtar, Vol. II, p. 714.

3 *Ibid*, p. 733.

4 See Ful Chand *v.* Nasib Ali Chowdhry (1909) I L 36 Cal. 184.

5 Zakhirat-ul-Maad, p. 747.

6 (1867) 8 W R 23.

In *Asha* v. *Kadir Ibrahim Rowther*[1] which also was a case under the Hanafi Law, the words constituting the *talak* were pronounced in the absence of the wife and addressed to her father. The High Court of Madras held they amounted to a valid *talak*. But the learned Judges in the course of their judgment entered into an elaborate discussion on the incidents of marriage and divorce under the Mahommedan Law, much of which was not required for the purposes of the decision, and is really *obiter*.

Under the Hanafi Law, the husband has the right to authorise any person to pronounce the *talak*. He may even give his wife the power to divorce herself from him according to the form prescribed by that law for divorce by the husband. This is called *tafwiz* or the *delegation of authority*.[2]

Badarun-nissa Bibee v. Mafiatulla.

In *Badarunnissa Bibee* v. *Mafiatulla*,[3] the Calcutta High Court held that, where a husband had entered into a private agreement with his wife, authorising her to divorce him upon his marrying a second wife during her life, and without her consent, the wife, on proof of her husband having married a second time without her consent, was entitled to a divorce.

Mohabuth Ally v. Mymonissa Hanfi.

This case, however, though not consistent with the decision in *Mohabuth Ally* v. *Mymonissa*,[4] seems in accord with the Hanafi Law.

Hamid Ally v. Imtiazan.

In the case of *Hamid Ali* v. *Imtiazan*,[5] a Sunni Mahommedan said to his wife, when she insisted against his wish on leaving his house and going to that of her father, that if she went she was his paternal uncle's daughter, meaning thereby that he would not regard her in any other relationship, and would not receive her back as his

---

1 (1909) I L 33 Mad. 22.

See Ma Mi *v.* Kallandar Ammal A I R 1927 P C 15: L R 54 I A 61; Ful Chand *v.* Nasib Ali I L R 36 Cal. 184: 1 I C 740; Syed Rashid Ahmed *v.* Anisa Khatun I L R 59 I A 21: A I R 1932 P C 25.

2 It is option of the husband to repudiate his wife by talak personally, or delegate the power of repudiation to a third or even to the wife herself. Baillie Vol. I, p. 238.

The position is the same in Shiah Law: Baillie, Vol. II, p. 109.

In Sayeeda Khanum *v.* Muhammed Sami P L D 1952 Lah. 113, it was observed that the power of delegation must be expressly given, and where the husband had agreed only to the appointment of mediators for the purpose of bringing about reconciliation between husband and wife in accordance with verse 35, Chapter IV of the Quran, the mediators in the absence of an express delegation of power by the husband in this behalf were not competent to effect a divorce between the parties.

3 (1871) 7 B L R 442; (s. c.) 15 W R 555; see also Poonoo Bibee *v.* Fyez Bukhsh (1874) 15 B L R App. 5; and Hamidulla *v.* Faizunnissa (1882) I L 8 Cal. 327 (s. c.); 10 C L R 291.

4 (1863) Marshall 361.

5 (1878) I L 2 All. 71.

wife. The High Court of Allahabad held that the expression used by the husband to the wife being used with intention constituted, under the Mahommedan Law, a divorce which became absolute if not revoked within the time allowed by that law ; and that the divorce having become absolute, the parties being Sunnis, the husband was not entitled to the custody of his infant daughter until she had attained the age of puberty.

But the learned Judges seem to have overlooked that a paternal uncle's daughter is not within the prohibited degrees.

Ashraf Ally v. Assad Ali.

In *Ashraf Ali* v. *Assad Ali*,[1] the Calcutta High Court held that where the husband gives the wife an option as to declaring herself repudiated, and she avails herself of it, the repudiation or divorce is binding on him ; and a discretion to repudiate when attached to a condition need not be limited to any particular period, but may be absolute as regards time. Such option is not lost by non-user where there is nothing in the contract between the parties obliging the wife to exercise the option directly a breach of the condition occurs. In the case of *Ayat-un-nissa* v. *Karam Ali*[2] some distinction has, on the authority of Wilson's Digest of Anglo-Mahommedan Law, been made between authority given at the time of marriage, and authority given after marriage. On principle however, there seems to be no difference.

As stated already, a *talak* pronounced in the absence of the woman is valid, but, until it comes to her knowledge, she is entitled to her maintenance.

Sherif Saib v. Usanbibi Ammal.

In the case of *Sherif Saib* v. *Usanbibi Ammal*,[3] the husband Sherif was sued by his wife for maintenance. The defendant pleaded that he had divorced the plaintiff on the 8th of January 1862. Both the lower Courts found upon the following facts that no divorce had taken place : Defendant went to Trichinopoly, leaving his wife at Tinnevelly. While at Trichinopoly he received letters from Tinnevelly, informing him that his wife was leading an immoral life. He, thereupon, went before the Town Kazi of Trichinopoly, made a written declaration in the shape of a letter to plaintiff to the effect that he had divorced her, and repeated the divorce three times successively before the Town Kazi of Trichinopoly. Defendant directed also that the letter of divorce should be sent to the plaintiff, but there was no evidence of her having received it.

---

1 (1871) 16 W R 260.

2 (1908) I L 36 Cal. 23.

See Sainuddin *v.* Latif-un-nissa Bibi I L R 46 Cal. 141. Ante-nuptial as well as post-nuptial delegation of divorce is valid. Such delegation is irrevocable, and need not be exercised the moment the event happens.

See Mohammad Yasin *v.* Mumtaz Begum A I R 1936 Lah. 716. Post-nuptial agreement delegating power to wife to pronounce talak is valid.

See however Imam Ali Patwari *v.* Arfatunnissa 1913 C W N 369 confirmed in 1916 Cal. 229.

3 (1871) 6 Mad. H C R 452.

The Madras High Court, on special appeal, held that a valid divorce had taken place, and that the compressing the expression of the intention into one sentence did not seem, on the authorities, to affect the legality of the repudiation, although some doctors consider the process immoral. But the learned Judges appear to have overlooked the right of the woman to receive maintenance until the *talak* came to her knowledge, and the rules on the subject in the *Fatawai 'Alamgiri* and the *Fatawai Kazi Khan*.[1]

In another case[2] a Mahommedan woman claimed a divorce from her husband on grounds which she failed to establish at the trial ; but the husband, at the suggestion of the Court, agreed to give her a *khula* on terms to be settled by a Kazi. The Madras High Court held that the action of the Court in not dismissing the suit, but proceeding to suggest a compromise by means of a *khula* divorce, was not illegal, and that a *khula* divorce is valid though granted under compulsion.

Jaun Bibee v. Beparee.

In *Jaun Bibee* v. *Beparee*,[3] the Calcutta High Court held that a charge of adultery by a Mahommedan against his wife does not operate as a divorce, though if false, it might be an item of ill-usage towards making up a sufficient answer to his claim for restitution of conjugal rights, and that ill-treatment by him and his second wife would justify the first wife in leaving him.

Bukhsh Ally v. Ameerun Bibee.

In the case of *Bukhsh Ally* v. *Ameerun Bibee*,[4] the Calcutta High Court was unable to express any opinion on the question whether the husband's statement that he had divorced his wife was sufficient proof of the fact. The dicta contained in the *Radd-ul-Muhtar* and other works of authority indicate that a mere statement on the husband's part that he had *talaked* his wife is not regarded as sufficient in law.

---

1 See Ful-Chand *v.* Nasib Ali I L R 36 Cal. 184. For the purpose of dower it is necessary that talak should come to the knowledge of the divorced wife.

Ma Mi *v.* Kallandar Ammal A I R 1927 P C 15; Syed Abdur Rashid *v.* Anisa Khatun A I R 1932 P C 25; Abdul Khader *v.* Azeena Bi A I R 1944 Mad. 227. The wife's right to maintenance continues till she is informed of the divorce.

Ahmad Qasim *v.* Khatun Bibi A I R 1933 Cal. 27; I L R 59 Cal. 833. If the divorce is not communicated to the wife until after the expiry of that period, she is entitled to maintenance till she is informed of the divorce.

Azmatullah *v.* Imtiaz Begum P L D 1959 Lah. 167. After divorce she is entitled to maintenance till she completes her 'iddat.

2 Vadake Vitil Ismal *v.* Odakel Beyakutti Umah (1881) I L 3 Mad. 347.

See Balqis Fatima *v.* Najmul Ikram Qureshi P L D 1959 Lah. 566. Khula can be granted even if the husband does not agree, if the Court is satisfied that the relations of the parties are so strained that they cannot live within the limits of Allah.

3 (1865) 3 W R 93. For the custom as to divorce among the Khoja Mahommedans of the Sunni sect, see *in re* Kasam Pirbhai and his wife Hirbai (1871) 8 Bom. Cr. 95.

4 (1864) 2 W R 208.

According to the Hanafis, a *talak* may be given to take effect at a future time even without the mention of any condition. It may also be suspended on or attached to a condition and made contingent on its occurrence. In the former case, repudiation takes effect immediately on the arrival of the time to which it may have been referred; in the latter, it takes effect on the occurrence of the event on which it has been made to depend. And revocable, as well as irrevocable, repudiations are susceptible of being referred to a time or made subject to a condition.

Legal effects of a Talak.

In the consideration of the question of *talak*, it is necessary to bear in mind the difference as to the legal effects which arise from the form in which the formulae are pronounced.[1] It has already been stated, that a *talak*, in view of the legal consequences arising from it, is either *bain* (complete or irrevocable), or *raj'ai* (incomplete or revocable). A *talak-ul-bain* involves a definitive dissolution of marriage, without reservation of the power of retractation. In the *talak-ur-raj'ai*, the husband has the option of resuming connubial intercourse. A *talak-ul-bain* takes effect immediately after the formulae are pronounced, under the following circumstances :—(*a*) when there has been no cohabitation; (*b*) when connubial intercourse is impossible by reason of tenderness of age on the part of the wife, or from old age ; (*c*) when the parties have dissolved the tie by mutual agreement.

Revocation.

The retractation or revocation in the case of a *talak-ur-raj'ai* is called *raj'at*.

If the *raj'at* is effected by words, the testimony of witnesses is admissible in evidence; if by act, the wife is to be believed on her affirmation. Every *talak-ur-raj'ai* becomes a *talak-ul-bain*, after the expiration of three of her terms or three months, during which the parties evince no intention of resuming cohabitation.

In both kinds of *talak*, both among the Sunnis and the Shiahs, it is necessary that at the time of the repudiation there should exist a valid marriage between the parties. With the Shiahs, it is further necessary that it should be a permanent contract of marriage (*nikah-ud-daim*). According to those Shiahs who recognise the validity of temporary contracts, there is no *talak* in such marriages.[2]

---

1 See Ghulam Mohyuddin *v.* Khizar Hussain I L R 10 Lah. 470: A I R 1929 Lah. 6. If the talaknama says, "I have divorced thee on 15th September, and the period of the third talak will expire on 15th November", the talak contemplated by the husband is a talak-ul-Hasan, and does not amount to a bain talak unless two more pronouncements were made.

2 See ante.

Generally, the initiative of the *talak* is left to the husband, but, as will be shown hereafter, the Judge can compel him, in a variety of cases, and for many specific causes, to dissolve the marriage-tie.

In a *talak-ur-raji'ai*, the Judge has a right to interfere if the husband acts against the spirit of the law.

In every case, where the *talak* is pronounced on the initiation of the husband, he has to render the wife an account of the administration of her estate during their marriage, and to make over to her all her property together with the ante-nuptial settlement or *mahr*. On failing to do so, he is liable to a suit for damages as well as for payment of the dower.

After the expiration of the period of probation in the case of a *talak-ur-raj'ai* as well as a *talak-ul-bain*, the woman has the right to contract a fresh marriage.

Section IV

Talak-ul-Mariz (Repudiation by the sick)

In many cases it may happen that the husband, lying in *extremis*,[1] or suffering from a disease which eventually caused his death, wants to exercise the power of *talak*, with a view of preventing his wife from succeeding to his estate. A person in this condition divorcing his wife is technically called a *farr*, an "evader" (of another's right). In order to obviate the mischief which might result from this unjust exercise of the power of *talak*, certain rules are laid down for such cases which require careful attention, as they mark a broad distinction between the Shiah and the Sunni schools.

Talak by a sick man.

"It is abominable and sinful", says the Shiah authority, "for a sick man (*mariz*) to repudiate his wife, yet if he should do so it is valid". The Sunni *Hedaya* is more concise. "A sick man may divorce his wife, though he be on his death-bed."

Among the Sunnis, when a man pronounces an *irrevocable talak in death-illness* and dies before the expiry of his wife's *'iddat*, she is entitled to take her share in his estate unless the *talak* was given at her request. But if he were to die *after* the expiration of her *'iddat*, her right would be lost.[2]

Shiah doctrine.

According to the Shiah doctrines, she has a right to inherit from him if he should die any time within a year from the date of the *talak*, whether it was revocable or irrevocable (*raj'ai*

1 See the Radd-ul-Muhtar, Vol. II, p. 855.

2 *Ibid* ; Fatawai 'Alamgiri, Vol. I, p. 638.

or *bain*), provided that in the meantime the woman did not marry any other person. If during this period, when the law, by its own operation, preserves, her right of inheritance, she contracted a second marriage, the right of succession to her first husband would be lost. Similarly, the woman would have no right to take a share in the estate of the husband if he should recover from the illness from which he was suffering when he pronounced the divorce, fall sick again and *then* die, unless the recovery, the relapse, and death all occur within the term of the woman's *'iddat for a revocable divorce.*

The reason of this rule is given by the Imam J'afar-as-Sadik; if the husband conceiving himself to be on death-bed were to attempt to deprive his wife of her inheritance, her right would be protected and secured by law as a punishment for his unjust attempt.

Hanafi Law.

The rule of the Sunni Law, as mentioned before, is different. Should a man who has pronounced a *talak-ul-bain* against his wife on his sick-bed, recover, but afterwards have a relapse and die within the term of the wife's probation, she would not inherit from him. If, however, the *talak* was only *raj'ai* and not definitive, she would retain her right of succession.[1]

Shiah doctrine.

Under the Shiah Law, if a person *in extremis* were to divorce his wife under a *revocable* or *raj'ai talak*, and she were to predecease him, *before* the expiration of her own *'iddat*, he would inherit from her; but if the *talak* were *bain*, or if he were to die *after* the probationary term, his heirs, would have no right of inheritance on the ground of his right.

Talak pronounced against a minor wife.

Reference having already been made to the invalidity of a *talak* pronounced by a minor or by his guardian on his behalf, attention must be directed to the effect on a minor woman of a *talak* pronounced against her by her legally qualified husband. Both schools insist that the formula or *sigheh*, by which the *talak* is pronounced, should in every case be understood by the wife. That being the rule it follows, that when she is of such tender age as to be unable to comprehend the legal consequences flowing from the act of repudiation, or does not possess discretion (*rushed*), a valid *talak* cannot be effected against her. The Shiah *Nail-ul-Maram* requires *'akl* (sound understanding) on both sides for the effectuation of a proper repudiation.

The *Radd-ul-Muhtar* states, however, that when a girl-wife is under the age of puberty, a *raj'ai talak* pronounced against her would become *bain* on the expiration of three months and not the usual three terms of purity.

1 Fatawai 'Alamgiri, Vol. I, pp. 638-639.

happens, your business will be in your hands for a month', she will have the power for a month after the event has happened.[1]

The option mentioned may be made conditional on his taking a second wife, or on his going from his place of residence without her permission, or on striking her without any legal cause.

But in all these cases, the condition must be fulfilled, literally and fully, before the power can be exercised. For example, if a man were to say to his wife, 'thy business will be in thy hands, if I go out of Bokhara', and he only goes to its suburbs, there is no option. In all cases of dispute, the husband's word (*kawl*) is to be preferred.

Mashiat is similar to the above forms of delegation; only it leaves the exercise of the power absolutely to the 'pleasure' or 'will' of the party to whom the power is delegated.

The authority to *talak* must be expressly delegated to a third party before he can *talak* the wife of another. A mere *mukhtar-'am* or general agent has no power.

Shiah doctrine.

Although under the Shiah doctrines, an option given to the wife has no effect, nor is a conditional *talak* valid, express authority may be reserved to the wife to dissolve the contract on breach of any of its stipulations.

---

1 See Hamidulla *v* Faizunnissa I L R 8 Cal. 327. A enters into an agreement before his marriage with B, that A should pay B Rs. 400 as her dower on demand, that he should not beat or illtreat her, that he should allow B to be taken to her father's house four times a year, and if he committed a breach of any of the conditions, B should have the power of divorcing herself from A. Some time after marriage, B divorces herself from A, alleging cruelty and non-payment of dower. A brings a suit for restitution of conjugal rights. The conditions of the contract being of a reasonable nature and not opposed to Muslim Law, the divorce is valid as a tafweez talak.

Moharram Ali *v*. Aisha Khatoon 19 C W N 1226: 31 I C 562; Sadiya Begum *v*. Atta Ullah A I R 1933 Lah. 885: 144 I C 497; Badrunnissa *v*. Mafittala (1871) 7 Beng. L R 442. An agreement between husband and wife by which the husband authorises the wife to divorce herself from him in the event of his marrying a second wife without her consent, is valid.

Marfat Ali Mirja *v*. Jabedannissa A I R 1941 Cal. 657. Such an agreement entered into by the guardians of minor spouses is valid and binding on the husband.

Ahmed Ali *v*. Sabha Khatun P L D 1952 Dacca 385. Where a Kabinnama gives the wife the power to divorce herself in case of non-maintenance for 2 years, she would be entitled to divorce herself only if she establishes her right to separate maintenance under Muslim Law.

Ayatunnissa Bibi *v*. Karam Ali I L R 36 Cal. 23. Where a power is given to wife by a marriage contract to divorce herself on her husband marrying again, she is not bound to exercise the option the very moment she hears the news of her husband's second marriage. The injury to her is a continuing wrong and she has a continuing right to exercise the power.

2 See Aziz *v*. Mst. Naro A I R 1955 H. P. 32. The mere happening of the event under which the wife would be entitled to exercise the option does not *ipso facto* dissolve the marriage. It shall be dissolved only if she exercises the option, and pronounces the divorce under the delegated powers.

Marriage being considered a holy institution, though it may be contracted, according to the Shiahs, without any witness, it cannot be dissolved unless in the presence of two male witnesses of "known probity", who hear the actual words.

SECTION V

MISCELLANEOUS PRINCIPLES

Revocation of a talak—Raj'at.

REVOCATION or *raj'at* is defined in the *Fatawai 'Alamgiri* to mean the expression of an intention on the part of the husband to continue the *status* of marriage whilst the wife is still in her *'iddat*.

When a man has *talaked* his wife by one or two revocable *talaks*, he may retain her whilst she is still in her probation.

Revocation.

Raj'at is of two kinds : *sunni*, that is in accordance with the *sunnat* (traditions), or *bad'ai* (irregular). When a man intimates his intention of revocation to the wife and calls on witnesses to attest the fact, it is said to be a *raj'at* in accordance with the *sunnat*. If he fails to give her any intimation of his intention, the *raj'at* is said to be *bad'ai.* But it is valid all the same. Any act tending to show that he has changed his mind would be tantamount to revocation; but the man is recommended to ask some person to attest the *raj'at*.

Raj'at is valid whether made in jest or under compulsion, but is ineffective if it is made subject to a condition.

When the parties are agreed as to the expiration of the *'iddat*, but differ as to the fact of *raj'at*, "the word" of the wife is said to be preferred. In other words, credence is to be attached to her statement that there was no resumption of cohabitation. If, however, the *'iddat* be still unexpired, preference is given to "the word" of the husband. If he should adduce proof after the *'iddat* that he had said, during her *'iddat*, "I have retained her" or "have resumed cohabitation" it would amount to a *raj'at*. Even his statement, 'I retained her during her probation', if assented to by the wife, would be a *raj'at*.

The right of *raj'at* ceases as soon as the three terms of a free woman are over.[1]

How the husband who has talaked a woman can remarry her—Hanafi doctrines.

"When a man has *talaked* his wife irrevocably without giving her three *talaks*", in other words, when he has given her a *talak*-

1 In the case of a bondswoman it is two terms.

al-bain in the *bad'ai* form and not according to the traditions, he is permitted to re-marry her during her *'iddat* or after its expiration. But when she has been *talaked* by three *talaks* given at the interval of each month or each term of purity during which no cohabitation had taken place, he is not allowed to re-marry her until she has been married to another man by a valid and operative contract, with whom she has cohabited and been either divorced from him or become his widow by his death.[1]

The first husband, who has *talaked* his wife, is permitted to enter into a fresh contract of marriage with her, upon her mere statement that after her *talak* by him she had been married to another man with whom she had cohabited, and from whom she had since separated by *talak* or death, and had completed her probation, *provided he (the first husband) believes her statement.*

But if the first marriage was invalid, the *talak* being unnecessary, the first husband is allowed to re-marry her without any second marriage.

In order to secure a separation from the *legaliser* the woman is recommended to marry him only on the condition of "having the business in her own hand" and to *talak* herself whenever she pleases.

'Iddat or probation.

Every woman married to a man by a lawful contract is bound, for the prevention of confusion of parentage, to observe a probation in the case of the dissolution of the marriage tie. But if the marriage is invalid and the parties have separated before *actual* consummation, there is no *'iddat*. But if consummation has taken place, the *'iddat* will be reckoned from the time of separation (*tafrik*).

There is no *'iddat* for fornication.

The *'iddat* of a free woman, Moslemah or *kitabia*, is three full terms, but of one who is too young or too old three months, counted by days; in other words, ninety days.

The period of probation when the husband dies after the talak—Hanafi doctrines.

In the case of a revocable *talak*, if the husband were to die after the divorce, the woman's *'iddat* would run from his death, whether the *talak* was given in health or in sickness. But if a *talak-al-bain* was given in health, and the woman does not inherit from him by reason thereof, the *'iddat* is not to be reckoned from

1 This seeond husband is called a legaliser. A murahik, an adolescent boy, is competent among the Hanafis, to be a legaliser, but not among the Shiahs.

The above view is no longer good law. In Syed Abdur Rashid *v.* Anisa Khatoon A I R 1932 P C 25, it has been held that talak-ul-bidd'at effects an irrevocable divorce, and the husband cannot validly remarry the woman llti she undergoes an intermediary marriage with a third person.

death. If he was ill at the time and the woman does inherit from him by reason thereof, *viz.*, owing to his having been ill and subsequently dying before the expiration, of the *iddat*, 'the period of probation is four months and ten days, during which there must be three of the usual terms : so that if these should not be completed during the period, the *'iddat* is to be carried on till their completion. When a young girl under puberty is *talaked*, and three months less one day have passed when she attains puberty, in such a case her *'iddat* will not be completed until the usual three terms have been completed. A man *talaks* his wife revocably, she keeps the *'iddat* for three terms but one day, when the husband dies; four months and ten days are now incumbent on her.

"When a divorced woman has kept her *'iddat* for one or two terms and they then cease, the *'iddat* is not completed until she despair of their return, whereupon she must commence a new by months."

The *'iddat* of *talak* commences from the *talak* and that of death from the death; so that if the events are not known until the period of the *'iddat* has actually passed, it is held to have expired. "And 'our' Shaikhs have decreed with respect to *talak* that it (*'iddat*) shall commence from the time of the acknowledgment (*ikrar*) to avoid the suspicion of collusion."

Shiah doctrines.

According to the Shiahs, *'iddat* is incumbent upon a woman, who is *talaked* or separated, only when there has been actual cohabitation, for *khilwat-us-sahih* is not recognised among them. *But a widow is bound to observe the probation in all cases whether there has been cohabitation or not.*

In the case of a pregnant woman *'iddat* lasts until delivery.

If after the expiration of her *'iddat* the woman remarries, and then it is suspected that she was pregnant, the *'iddat* is not invalidated. But if it turns out that she was actually pregnant from her husband, the second marriage is inoperative.

If a man were to *talak* his wife *revocably* and she is pregnant at the time, and the husband were to die during her *'iddat*, she must observe "the *'iddat* of death." But if the *talak* was *bain* she must only complete the *'iddat* of *talak* (already commenced).

When a married woman has become pregnant by adultery, and is then *talaked* by her husband, her *'iddat* would be three months, and not delivery.

The *'iddat* of death is the same as among the Hanafis, *viz.*, four months and ten days.

General doctrines.

When a woman's husband is away from home and she is informed by a trustworthy person that he has died and that he, the informant, was present at his funeral, in such a case, it is lawful for her to observe the *'iddat* and contract another marriage, even though some others may tell her that her (first) husband was alive, unless they mention a date subsequent to the time mentioned by the first informant as the date of his funeral. Similarly, if a man were to inform a woman whose husband was away that he was dead, whereupon she and the people of the house performed the usual ceremonies, and she, having kept her *'iddat*, inter-married with another person and cohabited with him, after which there came another man who informed her that her first husband was still alive, saying "I have seen him in such a city", the author of the *Bahr-ur-Raik* states that, in these circumstances, if the woman believed that first informant, the marriage between her and the second husband will not be nullified and they may both lawfully abide by it.

Recapitulation.

The divergence between the Shiah and Hanafi doctrines regarding the power of a husband to divorce the wife has been sufficiently indicated. It may be useful, however, to summarise the principal points of difference.

Shiah doctrines.

Under the Shiah Law to effectuate a valid *talak*, not only must the divorce be pronounced in the recognised words, but the man himself must fulfil certain conditions. He must be (*i*) adult; (*ii*) possessed of understanding and able to comprehend the nature of his act at the time of pronouncing the divorce; (*iii*) he must be a free agent acting of his own free will, and not under compulsion such as would overpower independent volition, and (*iv*) *there must be on his part distinct intention*. But even these are not sufficient, for it is essential that (*a*) the woman should be a *wife married by a permanent contract*, (*b*) that she should be in a state of purity at the time, and (*c*) that she should be distinctly indicated. Failure in any of these particulars makes the divorce ineffective.

Principle—Shiah rule.

Again, although a marriage may be contracted without witnesses it cannot be dissolved without the presence of two reliable persons ("of known probity"), to testify *together* to the fact of the divorce. Nor can it be effected in writing unless the man is dumb or unable to articulate the formula. Even a man who is absent from his wife cannot effect a *talak* in writing. He must pronounce in the presence of witnesses the *sigheh*, distinctly indicating the person against whom it is directed, and may then communicate the fact in writing to the wife.

Hanafi doctrines.

Under the Hanafi Law, witnesses are required for contracting a marriage but not for dissolving it; a divorce is effective even though given under compulsion, in jest or in anger. So long as the man is major and sane he must be presumed to know what he is doing and bear its consequences. Even the divorce of an intoxicated person is operative, unless the intoxicant was taken against his will or for a necessary purpose. Neither adherence to strict formula, nor regard for the wife's condition (*viz.*, whether she is in a state of purity or not) is necessary. Repudiations may be effected either in express words or by implication, either in writing which is customary or otherwise; only in the first, indication of intention is not required; in the second, intention must be shown.

Shiah doctrine.

A *talak* of a man suffering from an illness which eventually causes his death, although morally abominable under the Shiah Law, is legally effective. If it be a *revocable talak* which allows resumption of cohabitation any time before the expiration of the wife's *'iddat*, and she were to die during the period of probation, he would be entitled to a share in her inheritance, but not, if it were an *absolute* (*bain*) *talak* or she were to die after the completion of *her 'iddat*.

If the man, however, were to die from the illness under which he was labouring any time *within a year* from the *talak*, whether *revocable* or *absolute* (*bain*), she would have a right to a widow's interest in his estate, provided she did not, in the meantime, contract another marriage. Nor would she have a right of inheritance if the man recovered from his illness, fell ill again and then died, *unless she was still in her 'iddat* for a revocable divorce. Although a woman retains her right for a year even after the expiration of her *'iddat*, the man does not. So that if she were to die after the completion of her probation, he would have no right.

Shiah rule.

In case of a dispute between the wife divorced under such circumstances and the admitted heirs of the deceased husband as to his condition when he pronounced the *talak*, *viz.*, whether he was in health or ill from the malady which eventually caused his death, the Shiah Law throws on the woman the *onus* of proving that he was ill at the time, for if he was in health then, his subsequent illness would not affect the matter; and she would not inherit unless of course he died within her *'iddat*.

Hanafi doctrine.

There is no difference between the Shiahs and the Hanafis regarding the consequences of a *revocable* divorce pronounced by a sick man. Where a man divorces his wife by a revocable *talak*, whether in health or in sickness, with or without her consent, and he happens to die, says the *Fatawai 'Alamgiri*, before the expiration of her *'iddat*, she would have a right of inheritance to his estate. Similarly, if she were to die within that period, he would be entitled to inherit from her.

Difference between the Shiah and Hanafi doctrines.

With regard, however, to the effect of an absolute divorce pronounced by a man suffering from a mortal disease or *marz-ul-mout* ('illness of death') we notice a marked difference between the two schools. When a man in this condition divorces his wife, the Hanafi Law assumes that he does so with the object of depriving the wife of her right of inheritance. He is, therefore, called a *farr* or *evader*,[1] and as this is considered most reprehensible, the law throws its shield over the woman and protects her right from " evasion". It declares that in such a case if he were to die from that disease or any other cause *before* the expiry of her *'iddat*, she would be entitled to a share in his estate. But she would have no right if he *recovered* from the illness in the course of which he gave the *talak*, and died afterwards within the *'iddat*. She would also have no right if he died after the *'iddat* from the same illness or any other cause. Her right lasts only during the period of the *'iddat*. "The evader", however, would have no right in the inheritance of a wife whom he has irrevocably divorced if she were to die within the *'iddat*.[2]

The Shaf'eis deny the right of inheritance of either party in the case of a *talak bain* by a man stricken with a mortal illness. The Hanbalis continue her right until she remarries. Whilst according to Malik she does not lose it even though she may remarry several times.

Under the Hanafi Law, a woman, who is divorced by a sick man at her own request or in exercise of any power the law vests in her, has no right to inherit from him. But if she gives herself an absolute *talak* and the sick husband *allows* it, her right does not fall to the ground.

A Farr or evader.

As the right is dependent on the fact whether the malady of the divorcing husband was in the nature of a *marz-ul-mout*, it is necessary to analyse somewhat closely the Hanafi rules on the subject.

The Shiah jurists, it must have been noticed, lay down a definite limit of time within which the husband s death would give rise to the right. The Hanafi jurists have not adopted the time-limit; they, on the contrary, place stress on the mental condition of the man pronouncing the divorce. When a husband, who considers himself in imminent danger of death either from disease or any other cause, divorces his wife, it is evident that he does so with the intention of depriving her of her right in inheritance. The question then arises what are the circumstances which give rise to such an apprehension. In those days before the science of diagnosis had attained the perfection of modern times, it was only possible to indicate symptoms from which one might infer whether the disease was such as would give rise in the mind of the sufferer to the apprehension of death. All the tests that have been laid down are with this object.

---

1 Because it tries to "evade" the rights of his wife.

2 Radd-ul-Muhtar, Vol. II, p. 859.

A Farr.

The *Fatawai Kazi Khan* says "if a man has become so debilitated from sickness that he is bed-ridden and rendered incapable of managing his outside affairs, and the sickness is increasing day by day, then the right of the second party [the wife] attaches to his property, because the probability from his condition is death; and if the man in such a condition divorces his wife, he is declared to be a *farr* (or evader)." But a person who, though ill, is able to attend to his daily avocations, although the illness may eventually cause his death, is not regarded as one suffering from a mortal illness. Similarly, one struck with paralysis, or suffering from phthisis or palsy is accounted "sick" whilst the disease is on the increase; but when the "illness has lasted a long time" and is not becoming worse, the sufferer "is as one in health." Some lawyers have laid down that if a disease, however mortal, lasts for or over a year, it should not be regarded as such, because the man becomes so accustomed to it as to lose all apprehension as to his own condition. On the other hand, the *Fatawai 'Alamgiri* defines an "illness of death" to mean a malady which it is highly probable will terminate fatally whether, in the case of a man, it disables him or not from getting out of his house for necessary avocations, such as for instance if he is a *fakih* (jurist) from going to the mosque, or a merchant from going to his place of business; and in the case of a woman, whether it does or does not incapacitate her from pursuing her necessary avocations within doors.

The same test is given in the *Durr-ul-Mukhtar*. It says on the authority of the *Bazazia*, "when a person is in imminent fear of death whether from disease or any other cause, so that in the case of an illness the man is so broken [or weakened] by it as to be incapacitated from conducting his ordinary avocations outside his house; for example, a *fakih* from going to the mosque, a tradesman to his shop, a woman from attending to her indoor occupations", it is a mortal illness. And it adds from the *Mujtaba* that when the illness has become so severe as to make it permissible for the sufferer to offer his prayers without standing up [*lit.* in a sitting posture] it must be regarded as a fatal illness.

The law relating to *marz-ul-mout* or the "illness of death" has been discussed in a number of cases decided by the British Indian Courts. In *Hassarat Bibi* v. *Golam Jaffar*,[1] where the validity of a gift was impugned on the ground that it was made in death-illness, the High Court of Calcutta indicated the questions which require to be considered in determining whether the disease comes within the category of a *marz-ul-mout* illness; *viz*., (*i*) was the donor suffering at the time of the gift from a disease which was the immediate cause of his death; (*ii*) was the disease of such a nature or character as to induce in the person suffering the belief that death would be caused thereby, or to engender in him the apprehension of death; (*iii*) was the

1 (1898) 3 Cal. W N 57.

illness such as to incapacitate him from the pursuit of his ordinary avocations or standing up for prayers, a circumstance which might create in the mind of the sufferer an apprehension of death ; (*iv*) had the illness continued for such a length of time as to remove or lessen the apprehension of immediate fatality or to accustom the sufferer to the malady. And it was added, that "the limit of one year mentioned in the law-books does not, in our opinion, lay down any hard and fast rule regarding the character of the illness ; it only indicates that a continuance of the malady for that length of time may be regarded as taking it out of the category of a mortal illness."

The view expressed in this case was followed in *Fatima Bibee* v. *Ahmad Bakhsh*[1] where the learned Judges rightly observed that "whilst the lawyers have suggested that certain physical incapacities indicated dangerous illness, they did not lay down positively that these incapacities are conclusive."

In *Sarabai* v. *Rabiabai*[2] in which the question for determination was whether a *talak* pronounced by a deceased Hanafi Mahommedan deprived or not the divorced wife of her share in his inheritance, the learned Judge was of opinion that in order to establish *marz-ul-mout* there must be at least the following conditions :—"(*a*) proximate danger of death so that there is, as it is paraphrased, a preponderance (*ghaliba*) of *khauf* or apprehension, that is, at the given time death must be more probable than life: (*b*) there must be some degree of subjective apprehension of death in the mind of the sick person : (*c*) there must be some external indicia, chief among which I would place the inability to attend to ordinary avocations."

The last element, as already observed, is a mere test.

The views expressed in the above cases have been followed in *Rashid* v. *Sherbanoo*.[3]

It is not merely disease which may induce apprehension of death in a person. If a man advances to engage in actual fight with an enemy or is being led out to execution and in either situation divorces his wife, he is regarded as an "evader", and she does not lose her right of inheritance. Similarly, if he is on board a ship which is wrecked and if he finds himself on a plank in imminent risk of drowning, a *talak* pronounced by him does not destroy the wife's right. But when a divorce is given before

---

1 (1903) I L 31 Cal. 319.

2 (1906) I L 30 Bom. 537.

3 (1907) I L 31 Bom. 264.

See Shamshad Ali Shah *v*. Hasan Shah P L D 1964 S C 143. If a person was suffering from galloping tuberculosis and was therefore under apprehension of death when he made the gift, but was shot dead by someone or died of an accident or cholera or some other epidemic disease a short time after the gift (or divorce) there is no reason why the doctrine of *marzul mout* should not apply.

he has advanced from the ranks of a fighting force or when in prison though condemned to death, or before the ship is actually wrecked, the *talak* is effective—for in these situations there is still a hope of escape.[1]

Under the Hanafi Law in case of a dispute between the heirs of the deceased husband and the divorced wife as to his condition at the time *of the talak* the *onus* of establishing that it was given in *health* or in such conditions, that he would be regarded in law as being in health, is cast upon them.[2]

CHAPTER XIV

KHULA AND *MUBARAT*[3]

Previous to the Islamic legislation, the wives had no right to claim a dissolution of the marriage on any ground whatsoever. In special cases only the power of divorce was expressly reserved in their favour by contract. As a general rule, neither the Hebrews nor the pre-Islamic Arabs recognised the right of divorce for women. The Koran allowed them this privilege which had been denied to them by the primitive institutions of their country.

"When married parties disagree", says the *Fatawai 'Alamgiri*, following the *Hedaya* and the *Badaya*, "and are apprehensive that they cannot observe the bounds prescribed by the divine laws [that is, cannot perform the duties imposed on them by the conjugal relationship], the woman can release herself from the tie by giving up some property in return in consideration of which the husband is to give her a *khula*,[4] and when they have done this a *talak-ul-bain* would take place".[5]

The mode of procedure pointed out in the above passage is founded on the principle laid down in the Koran;[6] and whilst it has assumed only one form under the Sunni Law, under the Shiah it has taken two.

---

1 Fatawai Kazi Khan in loco; Durr-ul Mukhtar, Chapter on the Divorce by the Sick; Radd-ul-Muhtar, Vol. III, p. 855.

2 Fatawai 'Alamgiri, Vol. I, p. 641, citing the Zakhira.

3 Fatawai 'Alamgiri, Vol. I, p. 668; Fatawai Kazi Khan, Vol. II, p. 134; Kanz-ud-Dakaik; Shara'ya; Mafatih; Jam'a-ush-Shittat; Irshad-ul 'Allamah; D'Ohsson; Sice; Sautayra.

4 Lit. extinguishment; Radd-ul-Muhtar, Vol. II, p. 916.

5 Fatawai 'Alamgiri, Vol. I, p. 669.

6 Chap. ii, v. 229; chap. iv, v. 127.

See Ghulam Sakina *v.* Umar Bakhsh P L D 1964 S C 456 and Sayeeda Khanum *v.* Muhammad Sami P L D 1952 Lah. 113. In Khula the marriage is dissolved by an agreement between the parties for a consideration paid or to be paid by the wife to the husband, it being also a necessary condition that the desire for separation should come from the wife. Where the desire for separation is mutual the divorce is mubaraat.

When the wife, owing to her aversion to the husband, or her unwillingness to fulfil the conjugal duties, is desirous of obtaining a divorce, she may obtain a release from the marital contract by giving up either her settled dower, or some other property; such a divorce is consequently called *khula*. When a divorce is effected by mutual consent on account of mutual aversion, it is called *mubarat* which operates as a release and discharge on both sides.

The Sunnis place *mubarat* under the head of *khula*, but the Shiahs regard it as a distinct proceeding. The essential difference between *talak*, *khula*, and *mubarat*, has already been pointed out,[1] but it may be mentioned here that *khula* and *mubarat* take effect as an irrevocable divorce.

Capacity for khula—Shiah doctrines.

Under the Shiah Law, the four conditions necessary for the effectuation of a valid *talak* are also requisite for the performance of *khula*. The husband must be *baligh* (adult), sane (*'akil*), must be *mukhtar* (master of his own actions or a free agent), and should have the intention (*kasd*). "To effect a valid *khula*", says the *Shara'ya*, "the man must be adult in age, sane, free in choice, and it must be granted intentionally. No *khula* is valid if granted by a boy under puberty, with or without the permission of his guardian, or by one acting under compulsion, undue influence, or fraudulent representations." A *khula* is invalid when the grantor is in a state of intoxication, or deprived of self-control through a paroxysm of rage. The guardian of a *non compos mentis* may, however, enter into an agreement with the wife to dissolve the marriage-contract on her abandoning the dower. With reference to the woman herself, the same conditions are necessary as in the case of a *talak*.

In *khula* also, the Shiahs insist on the observance of particular forms. The formulae are required to be express in their significance and unconditional in their character. The words must be pronounced in the Arabic language (when there is ability to pronounce that language). If any *condition* be attached to the proceeding, it falls to the ground. After the expiration of the probationary term, a *khula* takes effect as a definitive divorce. A *khula* like a *talak* requires, under the Shiah Law, the presence of two witnesses of irreproachable character.

If a husband were to grant a *khula* to his wife, *while their disposition and tempers are still in harmony*, it would not be valid. "If the husband transgress his marriage-duties", says the *Nail-ul-Maram*, "the woman has the right of forcing him to accomplish those duties, or she can claim the intervention of the Judge." In case of habitual discord between husband and wife, an impartial woman, called *hakima*, is selected by the *Hakim-ush-shar'a* (Judge) to try and effect a reconciliation between them.

In some Moslem countries the Kazi has the right to proceed himself to effect the reconciliation.

---

1 See ante.

Shaf'ei and Hanafi doctrines.

Among the Shaf'eis and Hanafis, in countries where the Islamic law is in force, the Kazi in case of a disagreement between husband and wife, appoints two females, one on the woman's behalf, the other on the husband's, to arbitrate between them, and to endeavour to bring about a reconciliation. If the causes of dissension continue, or if the attempts to reconcile the parties prove unavailing, then they are allowed to dissolve their marriage by any of the procedures indicated above.

According to the M'utazila view all cases of this kind must be submitted to the Judge for a decision.[1]

Shiah rules.

Under the Shiah Law, the same formalities are required for *mubarat* as for *khula*. A *khula* obtained by the guardian of a woman or by her father is valid as a revocable divorce, but she is not bound to deliver the dower to her husband, unless she herself authorised the person, who obtained the divorce, to act for her. If she authorised him to act on her behalf, his powers would be limited within the scope of his authority; but if he acted without authority and the husband granted the *khula*, neither he nor the wife would be bound to pay back the dower. If the wife be a minor, and her guardian were to enter into an arrangement with her husband and obtain for her a *khula*, it would not be valid.

Hanafi doctrine.

The compensation, which the wife, in a proceeding of *khula*, makes to the husband is a means to an end, *viz.*, the dissolution of the marriage-tie by obtaining his consent. This is not, however, an essential condition, for divorce is validly effected when the consent of the parties to dissolve the relationship is given.

"Although the compensation agreed upon may not have been paid," says the *Hedaya*, "a *mubarat* (signified by a man saying to his wife, 'I am discharged from the marriage between you and me, and her consenting to it) is the same as a *khula* ; that is to say, in consequence of the declaration of both, every claim which each had upon the other drops, so far as those claims are connected with marriage."[2]

When the married parties have become divorced from each other by mutual consent, the proceeding effects a complete separation, even though the wife should fail to pay the compensation agreed upon, or to abandon the settled dower, and even though the husband should contend that on that account the *khula* was not valid.[3]

Shaf'ei and Maliki doctrines.

As a general rule, all women who can contract a valid marriage can initiate the proceeding of *khula* or *mubarat*. This rule is, however, subject to several exceptions. According to the

---

1 In Pakistan this view has been adopted by ptatute. See the Muslim Family Laws Ordinance, 1961.

2 Hedaya, Vol. I, p. 323; Fatawai 'Alamgiri, Vol. I, p. 669.

3 Munshe Bazlur Raheem *v.* Lateefutoonnissa 8 M I A 379 (397-398)

Malikis and the Shaf'eis, the adult female has a personal right; she alone can institute the proceeding and consent to give the *compensation* required, though she cannot always consent to her marriage or contract a valid marriage without the consent of her guardian or *wali*. The father can enter into an arrangement of *khula* on behalf of his daughter who is *sarira* (a minor) and on whom he has imposed the *status* of marriage. As she is subject to the *patria potestas*, the father can consent to a *khula* on her behalf and abandon a portion of her dower to obtain a dissolution of the contract. In the same way, the father of a boy who is a *sarir* (a minor), can consent to the *khula* on behalf of his son. The *wasi*, or the father's executor, can consent only when the powers of the father of the family are vested in him. The *sarira* herself cannot legally enter into *khula*, although the arrangement into which she enters is not necessarily, as far as the actual separation is concerned, invalid. Al-Karkhi is of opinion that when a minor wife has agreed to a separation on condition of abandoning her dower or of paying a compensation, the separation is valid, but the stipulation as to the dower or compensation is null and void ; and if she have made any payment, it must be restituted.

Hanafi rules.

The Hanafis accord to all adult females the exclusive right of entering into a *khula*. They make no distinction between a woman who has intellect and one who has not. As regards the *sarira*, they authorise the father or his executor to enter into a *khula* on her behalf. "If a father", says the *Hedaya*, "enter into a *khula* on behalf of his minor daughter for a certain compensation, engaging to hold himself personally responsible for its due payment, such *khula* is valid ; . . . . but if the father were to stipulate that it would be paid by her, then she has the power when she arrives at majority to accept or refuse the arrangement. According to the *Hadis* of the Prophet, a *khula* is dependent on the ratification of the woman."[1]

If the wife has been compelled by the ill-treatment of the husband to seek for a divorce, it is unlawful for him to take an indemnity. And if the man has forced the woman to accept the *khula*, a *talak* will take place without any liability to pay the indemnity.[2]

Among the Hanafis, the husband, if he be adult, may himself or by his *wakil* (authorised agent) consent to the *khula*, and by his guardian, if he be a minor.

---

1 Hedaya, Vol. I, Bk. iv, chap. 8.

2 See the Radd-ul-Muhtar, Vol. II, p. 928. If a khula is given and accepted, but the compensation is not mentioned the deferred dower, or any portion thereof remaining due, will be taken as such.

3 See Bilqis Fatima *v.* Najmul Ikram P L D 1959 Lah. 566. A wife is entitled to khula as of right on the restoration of what she had received in consideration of marriage, if the Judge apprehends that the parties will not be able to live amicably together or in the words of the Kuran they will not be able to keep within the limits of Allah. By deductions from passages in the Koran and Hadith it was held that incompatibility of temperament was itself a ground for the wife claiming khula divorce.

Marz-ul-mout.

A husband who is suffering from an illness which eventually causes his death, and which in the language of the law is called *death-illness* or *marz-ul-mout*, has the power of giving a valid consent ; but, as in the case of a *talak* pronounced in that condition, so also in that of a *khula* given under similar circumstances, the wife would not be divested absolutely of her heritable rights.

A woman can, whilst suffering from a fatal illness, enter into a *khula*; but, as in such cases there is a possibility of undue influence being exercised over her, the law declares that when a woman dies from an illness during which she has entered into a *khula*, any gift made by her in consideration of the *khula* shall be restored to her heirs.[1]

The consent to a *khula*, according to the Sunni doctrines, may be either conditional or unconditional. When it is simple and unconditional, it produces the effect of a complete and definitive separation like a *talak-ul-bain*. When the consent is conditional the separation does not take place until the condition is fulfilled.[2]

Shiah doctrines.

According to the Shiah Law, a *khula*, in order to be valid, must be absolutely unconditional.

According to the *Hedaya*, as well as the *Badaya*, consent given by the husband to a separation on condition of the wife abandoning the dower, or paying him a certain sum, or making over to him any property, does not entitle him to cancel the *khula* on her failing to fulfil the contract, but he may either sue her for the amount she agreed to pay him, or set off the same against any claim she may advance against him.[3]

When a wife sues her husband for her dower, alleging that he has given her a *talak*, and the husband in defence pleads that the wife entered into a *khula*, thereby abandoning her dower, the dispute resolves itself into a mere question of evidence, *viz*., whether or not it was at her instance that the separation took place, and whether or not she abandoned the dower in order to obtain a release from the marriage-tie. If there be no reliable evidence, the *Fatawai Kazi Khan* and the *Fatawai 'Alamgiri* say, "the word is hers, as to the dower, and his as to the maintenance," that is, she would be believed so far as her allegation is concerned that she did not abandon the dower, but the husband would not be bound to provide her maintenance during the *'iddat*.

---

1 Some authors hold that the husband is bound to restore such sum less the amount of his own share in the estate of the wife.

2 Fatawai Kazi Khan, Vol. II, p. 124; Durr-ul-Mukhtar. In a khula the husband has no option; the wife has. For example, if a khula is offered to the wife, she may take time to consider the matter; see the Radd-ul-Muhtar, Vol. II, p. 919.

3 Hedaya, Vol. I, p. 320; comp. Moonshee Bazul-ul-Raheem *v.* Luteefutoonnissa (1861) 8 Moo. I A 378.

Buzul-ul-Raheem v. Luteefutoonnissa.

In the case of *Moonshee Buzul-ul-Raheem* v. *Luteefutoonnissa,*[1] the Sudder Court held that the allegation of a *khula* on the part of the husband set up as a defence to the suit of the wife for dower on the ground of *talak*, is tantamount to a *talak*, if he fails to prove his allegation.

On appeal to the Judicial Committee, Lord Kingsdown, in a luminous judgment, after pointing out the substantial difference between *talak and khula*, affirmed the recognised principle of the Mahommedan Law, that when a divorce is given under the name of *khula* and the husband fails to prove that the wife gave her consent of her own free will or with due apprehension of its meaning, to the abandonment of her dower or property in the hands of the husband, the divorce would be effective, but not her agreement abandoning her dower. "The non-payment by the wife of the consideration for the divorce no more invalidates the divorce than in England the non-payment of the wife's marriage-portion invalidates the marriage."[2]

"When a husband asserts", says the *Mabsut*, "that he has entered into a *union* with his wife", that is, after agreeing to a discharge, "and the wife denies the same, the statement of the wife is to be credited, and a divorce takes place in consequence of the husband admitting a divorce".[3]

Shiah doctrine.

According to the Shiah Law, a *khula* requires to be pronounced in sacramental terms, the *sigheh* being as necessary in *khula* as in *talak*.

Sunni doctrine.

Among the Sunnis, no particular form of *sigheh* is needed, so long as the consent is formally expressed. They recognise one essential difference between *khula* and *talak* which it is important to bear in mind. In *talak*, the repudiation may be conveyed by the husband in any terms, implicatively or expressly; in *khula* though *kinayet* is allowed, the consent is required to be given in more definite language. For example, it is not sufficient for the husband to declare that he would not coerce his wife to remain with him if she would indemnify him; that he wished for the separation; that he would arrange with her relatives the matter of the separation, etc., because none of these expressions necessarily imply the intention of the parties to dissolve the contract. If the husband were to say that he was willing to dissolve the union if the wife wished it, or that he would do so at once if she gave up her dower and agreed to the terms, the *khula* would be valid, as in these cases the intention of the parties is sufficiently manifested. In the same way, if the woman were

1 Sevestre's Reports, p. 251.

2 Supra.

3 Fusul 'Imadia (Cal. Ed.), p. 481.

to say : "Give me a *khula* in exchange for my dower", and the man were to reply, "I do", a lawful dissolution of the marriage-tie would be effected and the dower would drop.

General rule—stipulation of indemnity.

Among all the schools, which recognise the power of the parties to a marriage-contract to dissolve it without the intervention of the Judge, the stipulation of an indemnity is a necessary condition to the validity of a *khula.* If the woman give in compensation something over which she has no right, the *khula*, under the Sunni Law, is not obligatory on the husband.[1]

Shiah doctrines.

Under the Shiah Law, the *khula* would be valid and the husband would be entitled to recover from his wife the value of the specific article which she had stipulated to give.[2]

As a general rule, everything which may be given in dower may serve as a compensation for *khula*. "Whatever is lawful for dower or is capable of being accepted as dower, may lawfully be given in exchange for *khula*."[3] The (Shiah) *Shara'ya* uses similar words. It says: "Whatever may be given for dower may validly be given as indemnity for *khula* and there is no limit to the same either in amount or quantity."[4]

The (Shiah) *Mafatih*, however, adds the following significant words to the dictim of the *Sharaya*:—"Anything that can validily be a dower, can validly be a compensation, whether it be a thing in existence or not—as suckling the child of the union, the mother's right of *hizanat*, her or her child's maintenance, etc."

Hanafi rules.

The Sunni jurisconsults, in their desire to afford the wife every facility for escaping from an irksome matrimonial tie, have prescribed the following rules on the subject of compensation for *khula*. It is declared:—

(1) That when a *khula* has been entered into, or has been granted in consideration of payment by the wife of things that are *haram* or unlawful under the Islamic Law, such as wine, pork, carrion, etc., the *khula* is valid, but the stipulation is void. In such cases, the *Fatawai 'Alamgiri* says: "A separation is established between the parties, but none of the *things* specified are obligatory

1 The woman can retract her consent to give the indemnity any time before the agreement is finally concluded; Radd-ul-Muhtar, Vol. II, p. 920. It is absolutely incumbent that the woman should understand the terms—*Ibid.*

2 The Shara'ya-ul-Islam says: "If a man should enter into a khula with his wife for a specific article which proves to be the property of another, it has been said that the khula is void; but it is better to hold that the khula is valid, and the man is entitled to the value of the specific article, or something similar to it, if it belong to the class of similars", p. 330.

3 Fatawai 'Alamgiri, Vol. I, p. 675; Hedaya, Vol. I, p. 318.

4 Shara'ya, p. 329.

on the wife, nor has she to restore any part of the dower;" the presumption of law being that when the husband, knowing that the articles were *haram*, agrees to accept them as indemnity, he cannot be supposed to have any intention to exact the exchange, and consequently is debarred from bringing forward a claim with respect to those articles, or demanding their value if they are destroyed by the public censor (*muhtasib*). In the same way, if the wife agree to give in compensation stolen property, known by the husband to be stolen, the separation would be valid, but the stipulation void, and the husband would have no right to proceed against the wife if the articles be restored to the rightful owner.

Shiah doctrine.

Under the Shiah Law, it is the same. "If the indemnity consist of things which cannot be legally possessed by the professors of Islam such as pork, etc., the *khula* is void, giving rise to the presumption of a divorce without indemnity if the *sigheh* of divorce or *talak* has been pronounced; but, if the *sigheh has not been* pronounced, the divorce would be absolutely null.[1]

Sunni doctrine.

(2) A *khula* may be entered into, under the Sunni Law, for things of an indeterminate value, such as the young of an animal not yet born.[2]

Shiah doctrine.

On this point there seems to be some divergence between the Shiah and the Sunni doctrines; for the *Shara'ya* says: When the indemnity consists of the young of an animal not yet born, the *khula* is not valid."[3] But several examples given in the *Jam'a-ush-Shittat* leave the matter involved in doubt.

General rule.

(3) The personal engagement of the wife to provide her own maintenance during her pregnancy, or to renounce her right of *hizanat* over her children, or to maintain them herself may, according to all the schools, form the subject of indemnity for *khula*.[4]

"If the indemnity", says the *Shara'ya*, "be the suckling of the husband's child it is valid, but the time during which it is to last must be distinctly specified; so also, if a man should give a *khula* for the child's maintenance, it would be valid."

An engagement by the wife to nourish the child for two years and also to maintain it afterwards for a limited period is valid; but if she only agrees to suckle it for two years or less, it would

1 Jam'a-ush-Shittat.
2 Durr-ul-Mukhtar.
3 Shara'ya, p. 329.
4 *Ibid*., p. 329; Fatawai Kazi Khan, Section on Khula.

not be a sufficient indemnity, as she is bound by law to suckle it for two years.

The indemnity is fixed by mutual agreement. The terms must be settled voluntarily on both sides. "If a man should *compel* his wife to take a *khula*, he would do what is unlawful; the separation would be valid, without any obligation on her part to any indemnity."

In early times, when the dower was invariably *prompt*, the indemnity for *khula* was also required to be paid immediately when the arrangement for the dissolution of the marriage-contract was entered into. At the present day, it is not considered necessary that the compensation should be paid when the *khula* is given, if a time for its payment is distinctly stated; it has even been held allowable on the part of the wife to agree to pay the amount upon her marriage with some other man.[1]

The parties who may arrange a khula.

Before proceeding further it may be as well to explain, who the parties are who may validly arrange a *khula* and agree to pay the indemnity required.

Hanafi doctrine.

In the first place, the woman herself; in the second, her relations, friends, and even strangers may, if authorized by her, demand a *khula* and enter into a composition with the husband. "Any person can", says the *Fatawai 'Alamgiri*, "if especially authorised by an adult woman, enter into an agreement with the husband on her behalf."[2]

It has already been shown what the powers of a father are in respect of an arrangement made by him for a minor daughter, and it remains only to mention the extent of his authority to act for an adult daughter. A father may, with the permission or authority of his adult daughter, enter into a *khula* for her, agreeing to abandon on her behalf the dower settled on her. If a *khula* is arranged without her consent at the time or subsequent sanction, and if the father has not become security for the compensation agreed upon, the transaction is not valid, and the *khula* is without effect. When the father has guaranteed the payment of the indemnity on his personal responsibility, then, unless the daughter subsequently ratifies what he has done and takes the payment upon herself, she is entitled to proceed against her husband for her dower, and he has a right against the father.[3]

---

1 Fatawai Kazi Khan, Section on Khula; Shara'ya, p. 331. "If a husband should grant a khula to his wife while their dispositions and tempers are still in harmony, the khula would not be valid."

2 Fatawai 'Alamgiri, Vol. I, p. 685.

3 *Ibid*, p. 686; a father has no authority to enter into a khula transaction for a minor son; if he does so, it is invalid; see also Baillie's Dig., p. 322, 2nd Ed.

Shiah doctrines.

Under the Shiah Law, the husband has no right to proceed against a *wakil* or the father, when the former has exceeded his authority, or the latter has acted without express authorisation from his daughter. In either case her right to dower remains intact, and the *khula* takes effect only as a single *talak* with option of revocation on the part of the husband.[1]

When a compensation or indemnity has been unlawfully received by the husband, he is bound to restore it.

When indemnity for khula unlawful.

An indemnity is unlawful (*a*) where the marriage is liable to be annulled for *initial* illegality; (*b*) where the marriage is annulled, in exercise of the right of option possessed by the wife; (*c*) where the husband has taken the initiative and given her a *talak*; and (*d*) where the wife has the right of demanding a separation from a Court of Justice.

Where a wife is forced by ill-treatment or otherwise coerced to agree to a *khula* and to the payment of a compensation, the arrangement will operate as a *talak* and the woman will be entitled to restitution of the compensation exacted from her.[2]

Difference between the Shiahs and Sunnis.

There is great difference between the Shiah and the Sunni schools regarding a *khula* taken by a woman under the influence of threats. Under the Shiah Law, when a man *forces* his wife to a composition with him for a *khula*, the separation takes effect only as *revocable* divorce without any obligation on her part to pay the compensation. Under the Sunni Law, however, it operates as a *definitive talak*.

Mubarat.

Mubarat (in law) signifies mutual discharge from the marriage-tie. Under the Sunni Law, when both the parties enter into a *mubarat*, all matrimonial rights which they possess against each other fall to the ground.[3]

The same conditions are required for the validity of a *mubarat* as in the case of *talak* or *khula*.

Shiah doctrines.

With the Shiahs, it is necessary that both parties should, *bona fide*, find the matrimonial relationship irksome in order to justify the parties entering into a *mubarat*. According to them *mubarat* is the mode of dissolving the marriage-tie which has become irksome to husband and wife by releasing any claim which

---

1 Shara'ya, pp. 329-333.
2 Fatawai 'Alamgiri, Vol. I, p. 649.
3 Hedaya, Vol. I, p. 323; Fatawai 'Alamgiri, Vol. I, p. 669.

one may have against the other. Viewed in this respect, there does not seem to be much difference between the doctrines of the two sects.

According to the Shiah Law, in *mubarat* also, the *sigheh* must be pronounced *expressly*. The *sigheh* of *mubarat* is (بارتيک علیٰ کذا) (وانت طلاق) "I have discharged you from the obligations of marriage for (such a sum), and you are separated (from me)." If the husband were simply to say, (بارتيک) without using the words (وانت طلاق) the entire proceeding would be invalid; whilst if he say, *anti talikun*, without using the expression about the "discharge", it would take effect as a *talak* and he would be liable for the dower. The *Shara'ya*, however, adds that when there is inability to use the Arabic language, or when the parties, are not cognisant of the technicalities of the law, attention must be paid to their intention. If it be clearly evident from their conduct and their words that "a mutual release" is intended, it would take effect as such, though the exact expressions may not have been used.[1]

General rule.

In all cases where the formalities have been duly complied with, the *sigheh* has been pronounced, established and proved, the proceeding is tantamount to a *talak-ul-bain*. It *definitively* dissolves the conjugal union, and the husband has thenceforward no power over his wife. "When the husband receives a compensation from the wife," says Al-Karkhi, "the divorce is *bain*, and even when it is without compensation and (consequently) *raj'ai* (reversible at the option of the husband), if during the wife's *'iddat* he were to accept from her a compensation, the separation would be equally *bain*."

Dispute between the parties.

In case of dispute between the husband and the wife regarding the *terms* of the composition for *khula* or *mubarat*, ordinarily "the word is with her", that is, her statement is to be preferred, and the *onus probandi* will primarily be cast upon the husband to prove the contrary.[2]

General rule.

When a wife admits obtaining a *khula* from her husband on condition of paying an indemnity, but alleges that she was forced to do so by her husband, the *onus* of proving the allegation of coercion rests on her.[3]

---

1 Shara'ya, p. 333.

2 Fatawai Kazi Khan, Vol. II, p. 124; Fatawai 'Alamgiri, Vol. I, p. 678. The technical differences drawn between different forms of speech, examples of which are given in the two Fatawas, may, for general purposes, be left out of consideration, for, with unimportant exceptions, when the fact of the divorce or separation is admitted, and the only dispute is as regards the terms, the onus is on the husband; but when the fact is disputed, *i.e.*, when the husband denies the divorce, the onus lies on the wife.

3 Fatawai Kazi Khan, Vol. II, p. 124.

When a *khula* has been entered into, and the terms of composition settled any addition made to the indemnity is void.

If a woman should enter into a *khula* on condition of maintaining the child of the union until it attains puberty, the *khula* would be valid if it be a female child, but not so if it be a son.

Sunni doctrine.

Should a woman authorise a *wakil* or an agent to enter into a *khula* with her husband for five hundred *dirhems* and the *wakil* were to exceed his authority and enter into a composition for one thousand, the *khula*, according to Al-Karkhi, would be valid, and the woman would be liable only for the sum which she authorised her agent to offer.[1]

Shiah rule.

A different rule, however, is in force among the Shiahs. "When a woman", says the *Shara'ya*, "appoints an agent to enter into a *khula* on her behalf without expressly defining his authority, the indemnity must not exceed her customary dower, *viz.*, the *mahr-ul-misl*. If a sum in excess of the amount of the dower is agreed upon, it is void, and the separation takes effect as a *talak-ur-raj'ai*, without the agent being held responsible."

The woman is entitled at any time before the *'iddat* to "reclaim" the indemnity, when the *khula* would change its character and become a *talak-ur-raj'ai*.

General rule—Maintenance.

A wife who has obtained a release from the marital tie by *khula* or *mubarat* is entitled to maintenance during her *'iddat*.[2]

CHAPTER XV

DISSOLUTION OF THE STATUS OF MARRIAGE BY A DECREE OF THE JUDGE.—FOR WHAT CAUSES.—L'AAN.—DIFFERENCE AMONG THE SCHOOLS

SECTION I

CRUELTY, ILL-TREATMENT AND DESERTION

ACCORDING to the Sunni and Shiah schools, when the married parties have no tangible cause of complaint against each other, but a mutual aversion due to incompatibility of temper, want of

1 This is under the Sunni Law.

2 Fatawai 'Alamgiri, Vol. I, p. 747.

sympathy, etc., they can dissolve the marriage-tie by mutual agreement.[1] When the husband is guilty of conduct which makes the matrimonial life intolerable to the wife, when he neglects to perform the duties which the law imposes on him as obligations resulting from marriage, or when he fails to fulfil the engagements voluntarily entered into at the time of the matrimonial contract, she has the right of preferring a complaint before the Kazi or Judge and demanding a divorce from the Court.

The Judge has the power of granting a divorce not only for habitual ill-treatment, for non-fulfilment of ante-nuptial engagements for insanity, but also for incurable impotency existing prior to marriage.

The power of the Kazi or Judge to pronounce a divorce is founded on the express words of the Prophet; "If a woman be prejudiced by a marriage, let it be broken off."[2] The Shiah *Bihar-ul-Anwar* also lays down that in case of *nushuz*[3] or *shekak*,[4] arbitrators may be appointed to settle the disputes, or the Judge may intervene; and if no settlement can be effected, the marriage ought to be dissolved.[5]

Principle—Desertion.

Divorce by act of justice, as mentioned before, may be claimed by the wife, whenever the husband neglects to perform his obligations. It may also be claimed when he refuses to fulfil the terms of the contract, or when he is unable to consummate the marriage. The legists have laid down several other grounds on which a wife may seek relief from a Court of Justice. For example if the man were to slander her or were to call her his mother or any other female relation within the prohibited degrees, or if he were to make a vow to abstain from her for four months which is called *ila*, she would be entitled to demand from the Judge a dissolution of the marriage-tie.

A wife is entitled to a divorce for the following, among other, reasons:—

(1) When the husband leaves her without any means of subsistence.

(2) When he deprives her of her raiment.

(3) When he forces her to beg for her living.

(4) When he allows her to suffer from starvation or want.

---

1 As already pointed out, the M'utazilas refuse to give to the parties to a marriage-contract, or to either of them, the power of dissolving the union without submitting their disagreement to the decision of the Judge; and they rely upon the words of the Prophet himself as showing the necessity of this course.

2 Sahih-ul-Bukhari.

3 Refusal to fulfil conjugal duties.

4 Violence, cruelty, disagreement, etc.

5 See Muslim Family Laws Ordinance, 1961.

(5) When he quits the conjugal domicile without making any provision on her behalf.

(6) When he persistently neglects to visit her.

(7) When he forces her to labour at work of a kind which is considered degrading to a woman in her position.

(8) When he does not provide her with a habitation.

(9) When he has several wives and does not treat them all equitably.

(10) When he treats her habitually in a cruel manner.

(11) When he is in the habit of beating her or threatening her with bodily injuries.[1]

These causes entitle a wife to claim a divorce, even where it appears that the means were resorted to with the object of forcing her to enter into a *khula*.

Hanafi doctrines—Neglect.

According to the Hanafis, mere inability to provide maintenance is not a sufficient ground for asking for a divorce. When the husband is possessed of means and is able to provide for the support of both himself and his wife, and wilfully refuses to do so and neglects her, then only can she apply for a divorce. The Kazi or Judge has the power of granting a divorce, when the refusal or neglect is wilful and unjustifiable. But if the husband be indigent and has neither the means to provide for her support nor ability to work, she cannot obtain a separation as a matter of right. Under the Shaf'ei Law inability to provide maintenance, wilful or otherwise, is a cause for which the Kazi may dissolve the marriage.[2] And, therefore, in order to avoid injustice, when a complaint is preferred by a Hanafi woman before a Hanafi Judge seeking separation on the ground of the husband's inability to maintain her, he refers the complainant to the Shaf'ei Kazi whose pronouncement becomes binding on the parties.

Ill-treatment.

The refusal to maintain, in order to entitle a woman to obtain a divorce, must be a continuing offence and must not refer to past conduct. When the husband expresses at the time of application his willingness to maintain the wife, and it appears to be *bona fide*, she is not entitled to a seperation, though the Kazi has a discretion in this case.

Arrears of maintenance are not due unless there is an order of the magistrate or Kazi fixing the amount, or the rate has been previously determined by private agreement between the parties. In these cases the wife may recover the arrears due by an action in the Civil Courts.

---

1 See section 2, Dissolution of Muslim Marriages Act, 1939.

2 Decrees are made among the Hanafis according to the Shaf'ei doctrine, see ante.

Principle.

If the husband has abandoned the conjugal domicile without making any provision for the support of the wife during his absence, or if he has left her absolutely without any means to support herself, the wife is entitled to apply to the Kazi for a divorce.

Desertion—Maintenance.

Upon receiving her application, the Judge is authorised to adjourn the case for thirty days, and to issue a notification for the appearance of the defaulting husband, or some person or persons on his behalf. Should an appearance be entered either by the husband or any other person acting on his behalf, the Kazi should direct an inquiry regarding the truth or falsity of any defence that might be urged. In default of such appearance, or on failure by the husband or his representatives to show that the wife has sufficient means with which to maintain herself the Kazi is authorized to make the order for a divorce.

Should the husband, however, have left any property either in the hands of the wife, or in trust, or in deposit, or invested in trade or partnership, the Judge has the power to order that the woman's maintenance should be provided from such property or from the income thereof.

The *onus* in all these cases lies, in the main, on the wife, to prove that she has been deserted and left without means.

The order for divorce is always made subject to the option of the wife. She may either continue subject to the conjugal rights, or accept a separation on the ground of desertion. If she were to accept a separation, it would take effect as a definitive divorce.

If the absent husband can himself, or through others, provide his wife with maintenance, she would not be entitled to a separation, unless his absence amounts to *desertion* within the meaning of the Mahommedan Law. The Mahommedan Law insists that cohabitation is a mutual obligation on the parties. If the husband were persistently to refuse to cohabit with his wife, this would amount to desertion.

If an offer should be made by the husband's father to maintain the wife, the same conditions regarding the amount and its mode of payment would apply, as in the case of the husband himself.[1]

Equality and justice being essential conditions in the treatment of wives, should a husband, who has more than one wife, neglect his duties towards any one of them, that one would be entitled to a separation in consequence of the neglect.

When a husband habitually uses vile expression towards his wife, it amounts to cruelty and forms a sufficient cause for divorce.[2] In the same way, if he accuses, her of having led an

1 See Satgunj *v.* Rahmat Dil A I R 1946 Sind 48. The maintenance contemplated is provision of food, raiment and lodging adequate for the wife taking into consideration the husband's station in life. Half-hearted and illusory attempts to provide maintenance is not maintenance contemplated by the Dissolution of Muslim Marriages Act, 1939.

2 See Begum Zohra Majid *v.* Mohammad Ishfaqul Majid P L D 1955 Sind 378.

immoral life previous to her marriage, she would be entitled to a separation. She is equally entitled to a separation, when he charges her with unfaithfulness to him and yet refuses to establish the accusation by a formal proceeding (*l'aan*).[1]

Principle—Cruelty, a ground for divorce.

The wife has a right to apply for and obtain a divorce when the husband habitually insults her parents or her relations, or leads an infamous life, or associates with woman of evil repute, or attempts to force her to lead an immoral life and to take up her abode with prostitutes, or introduces a concubine into the conjugal domicile, or threatens to kill the wife, or beats her, or disposes of her property, or makes her life miserable by cruelty of conduct, even when it does not amount to physical ill-treatment.[2]

A simple allegation of the wife, unsupported by independent testimony, is not sufficient in law to establish any of the charges above mentioned. When her statement is supported by the evidence of trustworthy witnesses or is corroborated by outward marks of cruelty, the Kazi has the power to grant her a separation.[3]

It is no defence to a claim for divorce on the ground of cruelty, that the cruelty was the result of the wife's own conduct. For example, if a man were to say that he beat the wife cruelly because she blasphemed the Mussulman religion, or because she was unfaithful to him, it would not be a sufficient defence in law.

Failure to carry out the stipulations of the marriage-contract.

A separation by decree of the Judge can take place, also, when the husband fails to carry out or to abide by the terms of the matrimonial contract. All the lawyers agree in holding, that when the husband recedes from his engagements, or refuses to act in conformity with them, the wife is entitled to a divorce. The conditions (*shurut*) or stipulations, which may be validly entered into at the time of marriage, have been already pointed out.[4]

Marriage-stipulation.

The most frequent of these conditions is, that the husband shall not take a second wife during the continuance of the first marriage. Should the husband, acting contrary to this express stipulation, contract a second union contemporaneously with the first, the first wife would be entitled to a divorce, and the husband would become liable for the whole of the deferred dower.[5]

The Kazi's Courts, which under the old regime dealt with matrimonial cases among Moslems, have, with many other useful

1 See Zafar Hussain *v.* Ummatur Rahman I L R 41 All. 278; Khatija Bi *v.* Umar Sahib I L R 52 Bom. 295: A I R 1928 Bom. 285.

2 See the Dissolution of Muslim Marriages Act, 1939.

3 See Khatija Bi *v.* Umar Sahib A I R 1928 Bom. 285.

4 See Chapter on Marriage.

5 These stipulations are common in India and act as a practical check on polygamy.

institutions, gradually disappeared in India. The difficulties which were formerly settled by a simple reference to the Kazi, without the employment of advocate or pleader, now pass without redress. To give an example, if a husband, at the time of his marriage made a stipulation with his wife that he would not contract a second union during her lifetime, and subsequently attempted to act contrary to the stipulation validly entered into, the Kazi had the power on the application of the prejudiced party to compel the husband to abide by his agreement or to dissolve the first marriage. Under present conditions, there is no machinery for affording the latter relief, though probably a wife may apply to the Civil Courts for, and obtain, an injunction to restrain the husband from infringing the terms of his contract with her.

Badarunnissa v. Mafiatulla.

In the case of *Badarunissa* v. *Mafiatulla*,[1] it was held that if the wife divorced herself under a stipulation of the character referred to, a suit on the part of the husband for restitution of conjugal rights would not lie.

Breach of stipulations.

The wife is entitled to a separation not only for non-fulfilment of anti-nuptial agreements, but also for breach of any stipulations which may have been entered into after marriage with the sanction of the Court between the husband and herself. For example, where the husband has bound himself before the judge not fo illtreat the wife or to provide her with separate maintenance, and he fails subsequently to abide by his engagement, the wife would have a right to ask for a separation.

The wife is not entitled to a divorce by a decree of the Court so long as she receives her maintenance on the husband's behalf and his whereabouts are known.

Would a wife be entitled to a divorce in a case where the husband's absence is involuntary ; for example, when he is in prison?

The answer to the question is furnished by an order of the Court of Algiers, dated the 19th of July 1865, which declared that, "under the Musulman Law, a wife of an individual detained in prison has not the right of obtaining a divorce by the mere fact of his imprisonment, if she receive during his enforced absence her proper maintenance."[2]

Shaf'ei rules.

'Ali Yezid al-Kazwini and 'Ali Abu'l Hussan, two Shaf'ei jurists, are of opinion that when the imprisonment last sover five years, the wife has the right of demanding a dissolution of her marriage and, after the necessary *'iddat*, of contracting a fresh union.[3]

---

1 Supra.

2 Sautayra, Vol. I, p. 265.

3 See the Dissolution of Muslim Marriages Act, 1939.

Shiah rules.

The Shiahs hold that in case of a husband's disappearance, a woman is entitled to re-marry after four years, if during that period no trace of him has been found. But the *Jama-ush-Shittat* adds that an order from the Court (the *Hakim-ush-Shar'a*) must be obtained before the second marriage is contracted.

Maliki rules.

The Malikis and Hanbalis agree with the Shiahs, but the Shaf'eis require that the woman should wait for her husband's return or re-appearance seven years, after the lapse of which period she is entitled to remarry by authority of a rescript or order from the Kazi.

Hanafi doctrines.

Abu Hanifa's doctrine is so startling that even the followers of his school are obliged to conform to the Maliki rule. He declares that a woman ought to wait one hundred and twenty years !

Abu Yusuf and Mohammed are no less unreasonable in their views; according to one, the term for waiting is ninety years; according to the other, seventy years.

Decree passed according to Maliki rule.

The Hanafi lawyers, in order to escape from the absurdity of the position into which the dicta of their masters lead them, invariably decide cases arising among their own sect according to the Maliki doctrine which laid down that when a husband is proved to have been a *mafkud-ul-khabar*[1] for the space of four years, and the woman has applied and obtained a rescript from the Kazi, she may lawfully contract a second union.[2]

The question naturally arises how should the parties act in British India[3] or even in Moslem feudatory states where no Kazis have been left to deal with matrimonial difficulties of this character. The Civil Courts have taken the place of Kazis. The woman whose husband has disappeared for more than four years cannot go to the Civil Court and ask for an authorisation or rescript to marry. Probably a sworn declaration by the wife before a Magistrate or some other constituted authority that her husband has disappeared for the period prescribed by the Maliki and Shiah law, and that no news has been received of him during that time, would be considered sufficient to bar further disputes, for the order of the Kazi is not necessary to give validity to the marriage, but simply to attest the *bona fides* of the wife and the new husband.[4]

---

1 See ante, Chapter IV.

2 This view has been adopted for all Muslims ; See the Dissolution of Muslim Marriages Act, 1939.

3 Now Indo-Pakistan.

4 See the Dissolution of Muslim Marriages Act, 1939.

SECTION II

L'aan

UNDER the Musulman Law, a charge of adultery preferred by a husband against his wife can only be established by the direct testimony of four witnesses to the fact. From the nature of the offence, however, the cases in which ocular and direct evidence is available are extremely rare. In order to obviate the evils which would necessarily result from a denial of all redress to the injured husband, in those instances where he is morally convinced of the guilt of his wife, but has no direct testimony to establish it, or when he alone is cognisant of the fact, the law has prescribed the proceeding by *l'aan*.

It must be added, however, that in prescribing the proceeding by *l'aan*, the law has in view not only the interests of the husband but also that of the wife.

Its reason.

A person who slanders another is liable to the *hadd-ul-kazf*, "the specific punishment for slander" under the Musulman Law. But when a man maligns his wife and accuses her of adultery, in the majority of cases he escapes the punishment usually inflicted for slander. In order, therefore, to subject the slanderer to some definite penalty for an unjustifiable accusation, as well as to enable the wife to clear her character by a public and solemn denial of the charge (*daf'a-ul-'aar*), it was provided that when a charge of adultery was made against a woman, the accuser and the accused were bound to proceed to the Kazi, and mutually take the sacramental oath prescribed by the law.

The disapprobation with which the proceeding of *l'aan* is regarded by Moslem jurists, is shown by the directions contained in the *Shara'ya* and the *Fatawai 'Alamgiri*. The *Shara'ya* says: "It is not lawful for a husband to accuse his wife on a mere supposition of guilt"; and the *Fatawa* directs that when the accuser and the accused appear before the Kazi, he should admonish them to abandon the proceeding. Should they persist, one in making the accusation and the other in insisting upon the charge being proved, then alone should the judge administer to them the sacramental oath prescribed, "invoking the curse of God" upon each other.[1]

Shiah doctrines.

Under the Shiah Law, it is only when the husband has no evidence to offer but his own, that he may proceed by *imprecation* against the wife.

Sunni rule.

Under the Sunni Law, he may even when he has corroborative testimony, institute the proceeding by *l'aan*.

---

1 Fatawai 'Alamgiri, Vol. I, p. 698; Fatawai Kazi Khan, Vol. II, p. 153; Durr-ul-Mukhtar; Shara'ya, pp. 348-349.

Object of the proceeding.

L'aan may be instituted by the husband with two objects,—either to establish a charge of adultery against his wife, or to disavow the parentage of a child born in wedlock, which, again, resolves itself into an accusation of unfaithfulness to the marriage-bed on the part of the wife. As the conditions requisite for the validity of the proceedings in the two cases are slightly different, it is as well to consider them separately. For instance, under the Shiah Law, *imprecations* can be mutually pronounced in the affirmation and denial of an accusation of adultery, *only when* the husband alleges that *he has had ocular demonstration of the fact but has no other proof of the fact.*[1] "It follows from this", says the *Shara'ya*, "that there can be no *l'aan* for a *charge of adultery* in the case of a blind man, though he may make an *imprecation* for the *disavowal* of a child."[2]

All the schools agree in requiring that the husband who institutes the proceeding by *l'aan* must be adult and sane. The Sunnis insist further that he should be a Musulman. The Shiah treatises do not expressly mention that Islam is a necessary qualification on the part of the husband, and the cases cited in the *Jam'a-ush-Shittat* leave it in doubt, whether a *zimmi* husband is qualified to take the *l'aan.* Judging by analogy, however, it would seem that non-Moslem subjects of a Shiah State would not be denied the power of instituting a proceeding by *l'aan,* if they were not proclaimed atheists.

Hanafi Law.

Under the Hanafi Law, "only those persons who are competent to give testimony in court are competent to take the *l'aan.*"[3] "So that", continues the *Fatawai 'Alamgiri,* "it cannot be taken by the married parties when either of them has or both have previously undergone the specific punishment for slander, or when one is an absolute slave, or an infidel, or dumb, or under puberty, or mad."[4] The blind and the deaf, however, are not precluded from taking the *l'aan.*

Among the Hanafis it is required further, that the wife should be a Moslemah of chaste character (*muhsina*). "When she is a person of loose character, or the parties have lived together only under a semblance of right", she is not entitled to claim the benefit of the proceeding by *l'aan.*

Shaf'ei doctrine.

The Shaf'eis and the Malikis agree with the Shiahs in allowing the dumb to take the oath of imprecation.[5] "The

1 Jam'a-ush-Shittat; Irshad-i-'Allamah; Shara'ya, pp. 346-347.

2 Shara'ya p. 347.

3 Fatawai 'Alamgiri, Vol. I, p. 698; Fatawai Kazi Khan, Chap. on L'aan.

4 *Ibid.*

5 Hedaya, Vol. I, p. 351; Shara'ya, p. 348; Kitab-ul-Anwar.

imprecation by the dumb is valid", says the *Shara'ya* "when their meaning can be ascertained by intelligible signs."

Disavowal of a child—Shiah rule.

The Shiahs agree with the Hanafis in requiring that the wife should be a person of irreproachable character, in order to validly take the *l'aan*. They, however, go further than the Hanafis in holding that she should be adult and sane and "free from deafness and blindness." In making Islam a condition on the part of the wife, they are in agreement with the Hanafis.

Hanafi rules.

Among the Hanafis, if a man were to slander his wife who is a non-Moslemah or a slave, he cannot be subjected to the formality of imprecation. Under the Shiah Law, "*l'aan* is established between a free man and a slave wife so that if he were to malign her he would be liable to *imprecation*."

Shaf'ei and Maliki doctrines.

The Shaf'eis and the Malikis agree with the Shiahs with reference to the latter principle. They make no difference between the free and the slave, in the exercise of the right of *l'aan*. Among them a *zimmia* or non-Moslemah occupies the same position in the eye of the law as a Moslem woman. They hold also differing from the Shiahs and the Hanafis that the mere fact of a woman being a person of questionable character ought not to debar her from taking the oath of imprecation, or exempt her husband from establishing formally the accusation he brings against her.

According to the Malikis and the Shaf'eis, when a non-Moslemah wife is charged with adultery, she is entitled to take the oath in the Church, if she be a Christian, and in the synagogue if a Hebrew.

Shiah Law.

Under the Shiah Law, when the husband is able to produce testimony, but declines to do so, he is not entitled to proceed by imprecation. When he swears that he actually saw the wife in the guilty act, but has no corroborative evidence the oath should be administered to him and to the wife respectively.

Hanafi rules.

If the husband refuse to take the oath, he would make himself liable to the punishment for slander. If the wife refuse to take the oath, the Kazi is authorised to dissolve the marriage by a formal decree issued under his hand and seal. "It is a condition of *l'aan* that the wife should demand

1 Jam'a-ush-Shittat; Shara'ya, p. 348.

it; and if the husband refuse to take the oath, the judge is empowered to imprison him until he submits or retracts, in which case he becomes liable to the punishment for slander. Similarly, if the woman prove contumacious, and refuse to take the oath, the Kazi has the power of sending her to prison until she takes the oath, or admits her guilt." These provisions of the Hanafi Law do not, however seem to be enforced by the Hanafi Kazis of Algeria, whose decisions alone furnish us with leading principles.

SECTION III

The Legal Consequences resulting from the Proceeding by Imprecation

WHEN both the parties have taken the oath in the prescribed form and the charge has been conclusively established, the Kazi must draw up an order of separation between the parties; and in accordance with such decree, the husband must divorce his wife. If he refuse to do so, the judge himself is to pronounce a divorce between them. The marriage, however, continues in existence, with all its concomitant rights, until the judge has made the order.[1]

All the schools agree in holding that a proceeding by *imprecation* can be validly effected only before the Kazi or Hakim, and that until he has made his order dissolving the marriage, it continues intact. There is a passage in the (Shiah) *Shara'ya* which leads to the inference, that if the parties were to appoint a private individual as arbitrator, his decision or award would have the same legal and binding effect as that of the authorised judge.[2]

Shiah doctrines.

The cases in the *Jam'a-ush-Shittat*, however, point to the conclusion, that the proceeding should be instituted in the *Murafai-Mujtahid-i-Shar'a* (in the Court of the *Mujtahid-i-Shar'a*, otherwise, the lawfully constituted judge).

Hanafi Law.

Under the Shaf'ei, the Maliki, and the Shiah doctrines, parties separated by an order of the judge in a proceeding by imprecation "are perpetually prohibited to each other,"[3] that is, they are debarred from re-marrying. Under the Hanafi Law, however, if the husband retracts the accusation[4] and undergoes the punishment for slander, or if it is found subsequently that, at the time of the proceeding, one or the

---

1 See Jaun Bibi *v.* Beparee (1865) 3 W R 93; Khatija Bi *v.* Umar Sahib A I R 1928 Bom. 285.

2 Shara'ya, p. 349.

3 Hedaya, Vol. I, p. 349; D'Ohsson, Vol. III, p. 112; Shara'ya, pp. 349-351; Kitab-ul-Anwar; Fatawai 'Alamgiri, Vol. I, p. 640.

4 See Mst. Fakhare Jehan *v.* Mohammad A I R 1929 Oudh 16; Abdul Aziz *v.* Mst. Bashiran P L D 1958 Lah. 59. Unconditional and sincere retraction is a good ground for not decreeing the suit.

See Khatijabi *v.* Umarsaheb A I R 1928 Bom. 285. There is no obligation on the Courts to give the husband an opportunity to retract the charge.

other of the two parties was labouring under some legal *disability* which would have invalidated the *l'aan*, or if either of them should apostatise and then return to Islam, they can contract a re-marriage.

Disavowal of a child.

The formalities required for a *l'aan* in order to constitute a valid disavowal of a child are the same as those observed when the charge is one of simple adultery, the only difference being that the formula is varied to suit the requirements of the case.

It must be added, however, that it is not necessary to comply with all the formalities of *l'aan* in order to obtain a valid dissolution of the marriage-tie on the ground of the wife's infidelity.

When a false accusation is preferred against a woman, and the husband is unable to establish the charge, the woman is entitled to claim a divorce from the Court.[1] Two cases are cited by Sautayra on this subject. In the first case Yehia bin Mohammed accused his wife of misconduct. She denied the charge, and cited him before the Kazi to establish it by formal evidence. On failure of the husband to do so, an order was made, at the instance of the wife, dissolving the marriage.

In the other case, which was decided by the Court of Algiers on the 13th of February 1871, the husband demanded a cancellation of the contract, on the ground that the wife had been guilty of immorality prior to her marriage. The wife denied his allegation and claimed a divorce. The husband failed to establish the accusation, and the Kazi accordingly pronounced a divorce in favour of the wife.[2]

SECTION IV

Talak-ul-Innin

Impotency as a Cause of Divorce

Principle—Impotency of the husband.

The right of the woman, under the Musulman Law, to a cancellation of the marriage on the ground of her husband's impotency is similar in all respects to her right under the English Law. The analogy, especially between the Shiah Law and the English Common Law, is close enough to deserve the attention of the student of comparative jurisprudence.

Shiah rules.

The wife is entitled to claim a divorce on the ground of her husband's impotency, if she was *unaware* of the infirmity

1 See Zafar Hussain *v.* Ummat ur Rahman I L R 41 All 278; Khateja Bi *v.* Umar Sahib A I R 1928 Bom. 285.

2 Comp. Bishop On the Law of Marriage and Divorce, Chap. xix.

prior to the marriage. If she accepted the husband with a knowledge of the fact that he was impotent and physically incompetent to consummate the marriage, she has no right to a divorce.

Similarly, if the infirmity supervened after consummation, the wife would have no right to ask for a divorce.[1]

Sunni doctrines—impotency versus hanc.

Under the Sunni Law, the wife is entitled to a dissolution of the marriage for what is called in English Law Impotency *versus hanc*. It makes no difference in her right to obtain an annulment of the marriage, whether the incapacity of the husband is *only especial* in her case, and whether he is able to have sexual intercourse with other woman or not.

Shiah doctrines.

There is considerable difference of opinion on this point among the Shiah jurists. One section agrees with the Sunni lawyers, whilst another holds that if the man be able to have intercourse with other women, but not with the wife in question, she has no right.

The wife's right to cancellation of the marriage on the ground of the husband's inability to consummate the contract is not destroyed by delay, and the woman, therefore, is no bound to exercise her right immediately on becoming aware of her husband's infirmity. Even if she, after becoming aware of his impotency, raised a question and then remained quiescent for a considerable time or slept in the same bed with him, her right would not be extinguished.[2]

General rule.

A claim for the dissolution of the marriage on the ground of impotency is to be preferred always before the Kazi or judge having jurisdiction in the matter (Kazi of the city or place).

A divorce granted by the *fatwa* of the *mullahs* is absolutely illegal and invalid. The *Jam'a-ush-shittat* says that no proceeding for divorce on the ground of physical incapacity is valid without recourse to the *muraf'a* (Court) of the *Hakim-ush-shar'a* (Judge).

Procedure upon the application of the wife for separation on the ground of the husband's impotency. General rule.[3]

When a woman, prefers a charge of impotency against her husband, the judge investigates the complaint and examines the parties. If the wife was, at the time of marriage, a virgin, a jury of matrons is empanelled to examine whether

1 Radd-ul-Muhtar, Vol. II, p. 977.

2 *Ibid*, p. 981; Fatawai 'Alamgiri, Vol. I, p. 700.

3 See the Dissolution of Muslim Marriages Act, 1939, section 2 (2).

she is *virgo intacta.* If her assertion be found to be true, the case is adjourned for a year commencing from the date of the order of adjournment if the husband be not a minor, or ailing from some temporary illness, or in a state of *ihram*, *i.e.*, performing the actual pilgrimage to Mecca. If he be a minor, the period for consummation should be fixed from his attaining puberty; if ill, when he becomes convalescent, and when a *muhrim*,[1] from after the pilgrimage.

If the husband should consummate the marriage in the interval, the wife's petition would be dismissed after the lapse of the period fixed by the judge. If he, however, fail in his marital obligations, the wife is entitled to a divorce. The period so fixed is the lunar year of 354 days. "And on this is the *Fatwa*."[2]

Delay on the part of the woman to apply again, or to bring the matter a second time before the Court, on the expiration of the period of adjournment, does not destroy her right. So long as there is no *copula*, her right remains intact; but cohabitation, though only once, would extinguish her right to obtain a cancellation on the ground of impotency.[3]

Under the Sunni Law, she would be entitled to her *full* dower in case there has been a *valid retirement* of the parties into the nuptial chamber. If there has been no such retirement, the Hanafis allow her only a moiety of her dower. The Shaf'eis, in every case, give her only half the dower.

When the woman herself is not *apta viro*, she is not entitled to a divorce. Similarly, if she was not a virgin at the time of marriage and the husband swears that he has had connubial intercourse with her, she has no right to a divorce.

Case of a mutilated husband.

A *majbub* or a person, whose genital organ is mutilated which prevents consummation of the marriage, stands on the same footing as an *'innin*, whose inability to consummate the contract arises from physical weakness. But in the case of a *majbub* the Kazi has not to grant any adjournment as in the case of an *'innin*, as in the latter case, it is possible the infirmity may be cured, whereas, in the other case, it is not. Nor is the Kazi to postpone the cancellation, though the husband be a minor, or ailing or *muhrim*, for connubial intercourse being impossible owing to the mutilation, any delay is wholly unnecessary if the woman is adult.[4]

Similarly, when the wife of an impotent person has herself a physical obstruction to generation, there is to be no adjournment.

1 A pilgrim who has adopted the ihram, the pilgrim's costume.

2 Radd-ul-Muhtar, Vol. II, p. 979.

3 *Ibid*; Fatawai Kazi Khan, chap. on Talak-ul-'innin.

4 Radd-ul-Muhtar, Vol. II, p. 980.

During the pendency of the proceedings the wife is not entitled to alimony, nor is the husband bound to pay her costs as under the English Law.[1]

If the woman be insane, her *wali* would be entitled to ask for a cancellation; or, if she has no natural *wali*, the Kazi should appoint a "plaintiff" for her, in other words, a guardian *ad litem.*[2]

Should a child be born to a woman who has been separated from her husband on the ground of impotency within ten months according to the modern rule[3] from the date of cancellation, the separation would "drop" provided she has not in the meantime married or cohabited with somebody else to whom the birth of the child may be ascribed.

Several jurists among them, Kazi Khan Shams-ul-Aimma Sarakhsi, and the authors of the *Khulasa* and the *Ghait-ul-Bayan*, "have for the sake of greater security (*ihtiat*)" held that "the period of adjournment [in the case of impotency] should be the solar year which exceeds the lunar by 11 days." But this opinion is weak." The other doctrine, according to the *Manah-ul-Ghuffar*, is more "trustworthy and approved, and the *fatwa* is thereon."[4] According to Kamal-ud-Din (*Mohakkik*) the difference has arisen, because "the Commander of the Faithful 'Omar may, etc., when he ordered a year for an impotent left it indefinite [*viz.*, did not say whether it was to be solar or lunar]. So some of the jurists have enlarged it for the sake of security."

If the year be fixed by date, as from the 15th of a particular month, the period will be reckoned by days and not months, and will consist of 360 days; so in the *Hashiat-ul-Madani.*[5]

The Sunnis and the Shiahs are generally agreed regarding the procedure to be observed in a case of impotency brought before the Court. According to the *Jam'a-ush-Shittat*, an order of the *Mujtahid-i-Shar'a*, who acts as Kazi in Shiah countries, is always necessary. With regard to the action after the judge has fixed the probationary period the *Shara'ya* says, "True in establishing impotency, a judge is required to fix the period allowed to the man in such cases to test his inability, yet at the expiration of the prescribed period, the woman can cancel the marriage by herself if no cohabitation has taken place in the interval."[6]

---

1 A *v.* B (1896) I L 21 Bom. 77.

2 Radd-ul Muhtar, Vol. II, p. 981.

3 According to the old legists the period was two years.

4 The Durr-ul-Mukhtar following the Hashiat-ul-Madani and the Manah-ul-Ghuffar.

5 Durr-ul-Mukhtar, chapter on Talak-ul-'Innin.

6 Shara'ya, p. 288.

Cancellation of marriage on the ground of one of the parties suffering from some virulent disease—Imam-Mahomed's doctrines.

Many Hanafi jurists, do not recognise the right of either party to have the marriage cancelled on the ground that the other was affected with insanity, or leprosy (*juzam* or *bars*). Nor do they give the husband the right to seek a cancellation of the contract if the wife is so malformed as to be unfit for connubial intercourse. Imam Mohammed, however, holds, says Kahastani,[1] that if the husband suffers from insanity or leprosy or any other incurable and pernicious disease which is injurious to the wife, she is entitled to apply for cancellation (*lit.* "she has the option").

Principle.

"The other three Imams, *viz.*, Malik, Shaf'ei and Ahmed ibn Hanbal differ [from the Hanafis]. They hold that if either party is suffering from any pernicious disease, the other has a right to be separated. Similarly has the husband the right to have the marriage cancelled if the wife be malformed. And if the Maliki, Shaf'ei or Hanbali Kazi were to make the order cancelling the union [in the case of a Hanafi] it would be valid.[2] In other words although the Hanafi school does not generally admit such a right, and the Hanafi Kazi, from conscientious motives, cannot grant relief in such cases, he can refer the Hanafi suitor to a Shaf'ei or Maliki Kazi, or appoint a deputy following the Shaf'ei or Maliki doctrines to try the case; and will give effect to their decree of cancellation.

Relief how accorded to a Hanafi suitor.

The Hanafi husband or wife can apply direct to the Maliki or Shaf'ei Kazi, who would decide according to the doctrines of his school. It is not incumbent on a Hanafi suitor to take his case before the Hanafi Kazi: as it is open to him to follow the tenets of any of the four Sunni Imams, it is open to him to take his case before a Kazi following the tenets of any of them. And the Shaf'ei or Maliki Kazi does not refuse jurisdiction because the suitor does not belong to his sect.

In Algeria, the French Government have retained the Kazis of all these schools. So there is absolutely no conscientious difficulty. In British India[3] all these are merged in the Civil Courts. It is presumed, therefore, on grounds of "equity, justice and good conscience", that if a wife, burdened with a leprous or insane husband, were to apply to the Civil Court for cancellation of her marriage it would adjudge the matter according to the Maliki or Shaf'ei principles (supported by the authority of Imam Mohammed of the Hanafi school), irrespective of the sect to which the parties belong.

---

1 The author of the Jam'a-'r-Ramuz; see the Hashiat-ul-Madani.

2 Durr-ul-Mukhtar, p. 268; Radd-ul-Muhtar, Vol II, p. 983; the Fath-ul-Kadir is referred to, but see also the Bahr-ur-Raik and the Hashiat-ul-Madani.

3 Now Indo-Pakistan.

CHAPTER XVI

THE STATUS OF INFANCY—PERSONAL EMANCIPATION—EMANCIPATION OF PROPERTY—INDIAN ACT IX OF 1875

Personal emancipation.

The disabilities under which minors labour are not peculiar to the Islamic Law. In most other systems, the attainment of majority carries with it the personal emancipation of the minors, and also vests in them the capacity of dealing with their property in any way they choose; but under the Musulman Law *personal* emancipation does not necessarily lead to an emancipation of property.

As a matter of fact, the Islamic system recognises two distinct periods of majority,—one of which has reference to the emancipation of the person of the minors from the *patria potestas*, and the other to the assumption by them of the management and direction of their property.

These two periods are designated as *bulughyet* and *rushd*, the age of puberty and the age of discretion.

Age of discretion.

Among the Hanafis and the Shiahs, puberty is presumed on the completion of the fifteenth year; among the Malikis on the completion of the eighteenth year. The Hanafis and the Shiahs generally consider *rushd* (discretion) and *buḷughyet* (puberty) to go together, and therefore the personal emancipation of minors, which occurs on their attaining puberty, carries with it the emancipation of their goods from the hands of their guardians. They then become entitled to take over the charge of their own property.

There are cases, however, in which a boy or a girl may have arrived at puberty and may yet not be sufficiently discreet (possessed of understanding) to assume the direction of his or her property. In such cases, the Mahommedan Law separates the two ages of majority, and whilst according to the minor personal emancipation from the right of *jabr*, takes care, in the minor's own interest, to retain the administration of his or her property in the hands of the legal guardian.

If a minor should not be discreet at the age of puberty, he or she is presumed to be so on the completion of the eighteenth year, unless there is any direct evidence to the contrary.

Two distinct periods of majority—The Indian Majority Act (IX of 1875).

The principle of two distinct, and yet concurrent periods of majority has been adopted in the Indian Majority Act (IX of 1875).

Section 2, cl. (*a*) of that Act declares "Nothing herein contained shall affect the capacity of any person to act in the following matters (namely) marriage, dower, divorce, and adoption." Section 3 provides that "subject as aforesaid" every minor who should not be a ward of Court, whether under Act VIII of 1890,[1] or the Court of Wards Act (B. C.), should be deemed to attain his or her majority on the completion of the eighteenth year, and "not before." But every minor of whose *person* or *property* a guardian "has been" or shall be appointed by a Court of Justice, and every minor under the jurisdiction of the Court of Wards "shall be deemed to have attained his majority when he or she shall have completed the age of twenty-one years and not before."

It will be seen, therefore, that so far as the principle of the Act is concerned, it is analogous to the principle of the Mahommedan Law in recognising two distinct periods of majority,—one for the emancipation of the person of the minor, the other for the emancipation of the property of such minor. Instead of leaving the age of *rushd*, when the management of the minor's property should be confided to him, in a variable condition, it has fixed in the case of all minors for whom a guardian has not been appointed by a Court of Justice or who are not under the jurisdiction of the Court of Wards, the age of eighteen as the age of discretion or majority.

In the case of those minors for whom a guardian has been appointed by a Court of Justice, it goes beyond the Musulman Law, and does not allow the emancipation of their property until they have completed the twenty-first year.

Right to impose the status of marriage on a minor.

So far, however, as the personal emancipation of minors is concerned, the Act leaves untouched the provisions of the Musulman Law. It has specially excepted from its operation the capacity of the Mahommedans "to act in the matters", to use the phraseology of the Statute, "of marriage, dower and divorce." The extension, therefore, of the age of minority by the Act does not extend the duration of the right of *jabr*.

The father's power to impose the *status* of marriage upon his minor children cannot be exercised, the Act notwithstanding, after the completion of their fifteenth year or on their arriving at puberty.

Similarly, they can, if Hanafis or Shiahs, enter into contracts of marriage without the consent of their guardians;[2] and if any contract of marriage be entered into on their behalf, it is dependent on their express ratification.

Difficulties apprehended under Act IX of 1875.

In the case of a minor contracted in marriage by a guardian other than the father or grandfather, a doubt arises as to whether

---

1 Which has taken the place of Act XL of 1858.

2 For the Maliki doctrine, see Chapter on the Right of Jabr.

he or she would be bound to exercise the *khyar-ul-bulugh* ("the option of puberty") on the completion of the fifteenth year, or whether the right would come into operation after the completion of the eighteenth year. It would appear from the wording of the Act, that as the provisions of the Mohammedan Law regarding the capacity of persons in matters of marriage, dower, and divorce are left intact, a minor so contracted in marriage may validly exercise the right of option on arriving at puberty. Should the right not be exercised then, it is difficult to suppose that it would fall to the ground, or that its not being exercised would be construed to imply acquiescence. As the Act declares that minority should extend in certain cases up to the eighteenth year, and in other cases up to the twenty-first, and as it nowhere says that a right acquired by any exceptional law, if not exercised immediately according to the requirements of that law, should drop, it may be assumed that no Court of Justice would debar a minor from exercising the *right of option* to cancel a contract of marriage entered into on his or her behalf, by any guardian other than the father or the grandfather, even though it may not be claimed or attempted to be enforced until the completion of the age of majority fixed by the Act.[1]

Provisions of the Musulman Law.

Under the Musulman Law, every individual upon attaining puberty is vested with the power or capacity of validly entering into *legal transactions* of every kind affecting his or her *status* as well as his or her property. The Act has postponed the capacity regarding any dealing with property, until after the age specified by the Legislature. But as it makes no exception in the case of contracts affecting *status* the result is that if a person on arriving at puberty were to enter into a contract of marriage and *make a settlement*, such a settlement would probably be held to be valid, as a necessary consequence of the marriage-contract. In the same way, the Statute leaving untouched the power of divorce under the Mahommedan Law if a Musulman husband, who was *sui juris* under the Musulman Law and a minor under the Act, were to exercise his power and divorce his wife, he would make himself legally liable for the dower, though the Act would protect him from incurring any liability which did not arise from any contract or breach of contract affecting *status*. These are some of the difficulties which are not unlikely to arise under the Indian Majority Act, owing to the exceptional clause referred to.

There are other difficulties to which attention may briefly be directed. The Statute, it will be remembered, applies to all persons domiciled in British India.[2] There are cases, however, in which a Musulman, native of Arabia, Persia, Afghanistan, or Turkey, may acquire a domicile in British India,[2] without expressly abandoning his original domicile. In such cases, it is almost impossible to ascertain, with any degree of certainty, whether the person in question has any definite intention of permanently residing in British India.[2] The Persian community in Calcutta

1 See the Dissolution of Muslim Marriages Act, 1939.

2 Now Indo-Pakistan.

furnish the best example of the difficulty suggested. Most of them have been settled in the Presidency-towns and the suburbs for several generations. They work and live and intermarry there; but none of them seems to have abandoned the intention of, some time or other, returning to their mother country. It is doubtful how the question of majority would be construed with reference to them. As yet there has arisen no case among them to enable the Courts to pronounce authoritatively whether they should be considered domiciled in British India or not. Probably when the matter actually comes before the Court, there will be little difficulty in deciding in the affirmative.

As the Malikis presume puberty only on the completion of the eighteenth year, there is less likelihood of conflict between their doctrines and the direct provisions of the Act, or the indirect conclusions or results which may spring from it. For example, in the case of a Maliki minor, for whom no guardian has been appointed by a Court of Justice, or who is not subject to the Court of Wards, the legal disability under the Act as well as the Maliki Law would expire simultaneously, and the minor in question would acquire the direction and management of his property together with his personal emancipation. If he be a ward of Court, the emanicipation of his property from tutelage would be deferred for three years. A Shiah or Hanafi minor, on the contrary, would not acquire the control of his property, in one case until three and in the other until six years after the attainment of majority under his own law.

CHAPTER XVII

GUARDIANSHIP OR TUTELAGE—ITS OBJECT AND SCOPE UNDER THE MAHOMMEDAN LAW—THE FATHER THE PRIMARY GUARDIAN—TESTAMENTARY GUARDIANS—INDIAN ACT IX OF 1880

Directions in the Koran for the conduct of guardians.

Guardianship or tutelage comprehends (*a*) the direction or care of the person of the infant, and this arises when the *hizanat* and the guardianship are vested in one and the same person; (*b*) a simple supervisory direction over the person of the infant, when the *hizanat* is vested in another person; and (*c*) the administration and care of the property of the minor.

In pre-Islamic times, the preservation and management of the goods of minors were confided to tutors or guardians taken from among the members of the family; but in the absence of all public authority to exercise a salutary control over them, cases of misappropriation and embezzlement were so frequent, as to necessitate the introduction in the Islamic legislation of most stringent rules for the protection of minors.

The Koran teems with denunciations against the gross malpractices frequent throughout the Penin sula at the time of the Prophet; and the rules contained in it furnish the foundation for the Musulman Law on the subject of guardians and wards. The following passages contain some of the rules bearing on the subject, and throw considerable light on the condition of morals in Arabia about the sixth and seventh century of the Christian era.

"Restore to the orphans", says the Koran, "when they come of age, their substance; do not substitute bad for good,[1] nor devour their substance by adding it to your own, for this is an enormous crime."[2]

Koranic rules.

It forbade the waste of the property of wards by their guardians,[3] and directed that the tutors may take a reasonable and moderate gratuity for their labour, but not more; "Let him who is rich abstain entirely from the orphan's estate, and let him who is poor take thereof according to what shall be reasonable."[4]

It further imposed on the guardians the duty of rendering accounts. "And when ye deliver unto your wards their property, call witnesses thereof in their presence. Surely, they who devour the possession of orphans unjustly shall swallow fire hereafter."[5]

It was also ordained that the Kazi should exercise a vigilant supervision over the guardians in the management of their wards' property.

In consequence of the fact that the principles which regulate the right of guardianship are based essentially on the express teachings of the Koran there is little room for divergence between the Shiahs and the Sunnis on this branch of Musulman jurisprudence.

Guardians are either *natural*, *testamentary*, or *appointed*.

Hanafi doctrine.

The first and primary natural guardian is the father. Among the Hanafis when the father is dead, the guardianship of his minor children devolves upon his executor. When he has died without appointing an executor, but his own father is alive, the tutelage of the minor children is allowed to the grandfather; when the grandfather also is dead, the guardianship devolves on *his* executor. Among the Shiahs if the grandfather is alive, he is entitled to the guardianship in preference to the

1 "That is, Take not what ye find of value among their effects to your own use and give them worse in its stead."—Baizawi.

2 Koran, chap. iv, v. 2.

3 Koran, chap. iv, v. 156.

4 Or, as Baizawi explains, "no more than what shall be sufficient recompense for the trouble of education and pupilage."—Chap. iv, v. 6.

5 Koran, chap. iv, v. 6.

father's executor. In default of the natural as well as the testamentary guardians, *viz.*, the father and his executor and the grandfather and his executor, the obligation of appointing a tutor or curator, for the preservation and management of the minor's property, rests on the Kazi or judge as the representative of the government or "Sultan". Among the Hanafis, if a person sufficiently qualified to undertake the guardianship of the minors, can be found among the male agnates of the deceased father, such person should be appointed by the Kazi in preference to a stranger, but no relative other than the father or grandfather has any right to interfere in any way with the property of a minor, unless appointed by the judge.[1]

Provisions of Act VIII of 1890.

The Guardians and Wards Act (VIII of 1890) gives to the Court the power of appointing anybody, but section 17[2] lays down rules which bring the provisions of the Act into line with those of the Musulman Law.

The father has, at all times, the amplest power to make by will such dispositions as he may think best relative to the guardianship of his minor children and the protection of their interests.

In order to be valid, however, the appointment of an executor or a testamentary guardian must be made by the father at a time when he is in full possession of his senses. If, at the time of making the appointment, he was in a state of imbecility, or had been for a long time unable to conduct his business owing to mental deficiency, the appointment would be invalid.

Similarly, in order to be valid in law, the appointment must be in favour of a person who is "adult and sane". If the guardian appointed by the father is a minor or a lunatic, the appointment is *ipso facto* void, and all acts committed by the minor guardian, before his removal by the judge, in exercise of the authority received from the testator, are inoperative in law.[3]

If the guardian becomes imbecile or insane after the appointment, the tutelage conferred by the father is voided and the right of appointing a guardian devolves on the Kazi.

Whether a minor who is appointed a guardian, and is not removed from his office by order of the judge, would validly exercise the rights of guardianship on attaining majority is a question on which there seems to prevail great divergence of views. Abu Hanifa replies in the negative. Abu Yusuf and Mohammed and the Western Imams hold a contrary opinion, and think that if the minor is not removed from the guardianship

1 Fatawai 'Alamgiri, Vol. VI, p. 223.
2 See ante.
3 Fatawai 'Alamgiri, Vol. VI, p. 214.

before attaining majority, the power granted by the testator re-vests in him on his becoming *sui juris.*[1] This opinion is in force among the Indian Hanafis.

A *Harbi*[2] (a non-Moslem native of any hostile country at war with a country of the testator) can under no circumstance be appointed the guardian of Moslem children, or the children of the non-Moslem subjects of a Mahommedan State.

A zimmi—Hanafi doctrine.

The position of a *zimmi*, or a non-Moslem, subject to the same sovereign as the testator, is different. Under the Hanafi Law, if a *zimmi*[3] is appointed a guardian, he can validly exercise his authority and the powers given to him by the deceased, until he is removed by the judge. It is in the discretion of the Kazi whether he should be removed or not, though it is recommended in the interests of the minor that he should be removed. All acts committed by him in exercise of his power are lawful, until the appointment is cancelled by the Kazi.[4]

Maliki and Shaf'ei rule.

Among the Malikis and the Shaf'eis, a *zimmi* may lawfully be appointed the guardian of the property of minors, though not as the guardian of their person.

Shiah doctrine.

Under the Shiah Law, the question is involved in some doubt. The *Jam'a-ush-Shittat* says in matters of guardianship a *zimmi* stands on the same footing as a *harbi*. Probably this may be construed to refer to the guardianship of the person of the infants.

But when the mother is the testamentary guardian, she may, though a non-Moslemah, validly exercise, according to all the schools, the rights of guardianship over the person as well as the property of the minors within the limits of the law. The Shiahs make an exception as to the right of *jabr*.

The appointment by the testator of his own slave as the guardian of his infant children is valid in law; but if the appointee be another person's slave, or if some of the testator's children be adult, the appointment is, in the first case, void, and in the other voidable, and liable to be annulled by the judge.

---

1 Fatawai 'Alamgiri, Vol. VI, p. 214.

2 Baillie translates this word as alien. As a matter of fact, the term signifies "a resident of the Dar-ul-Harb", as contradistinguished from the Dar-ul-Islam, in other words "an alien enemy." See Chap. II on the Conflict of Law.

3 Non-Moslem fellow subject.

4 Fatawai 'Alamgiri, Vol. VI, p. 214, Comp. Henry Imlach *v.* Zuhoorunnissa (1828) 4 Sel. R. 301; and Jahan Khan *v.* Mandley (1868) B L R S N 16; s. c. 19 W R 185.

The appointment of a "profligate".

The appointment of a "profligate", that is, a person who bears in the public walks of life, notoriously a bad character *from whom danger may be apprehended to the interest of the minor*, is invalid and liable to be set aside by the judge, both under the Shiah as well as the Hanafi Law. But all acts committed by such a person befere cancellation of his appointment are lawful if not contrary to the interests of the minor.[1] Subject to the foregoing conditions, the father can appoint at his discretion a man or a woman, a relative or a stranger, to be the guardian of his minor children. *His choice cannot be impugned, except on the ground that the tutor so appointed is acting prejudicially to the interest of the minors.*

When the Kazi has appointed a curator (or *mukaddam*) to take charge of the property of minors, and it subsequently appears that the father had confined the guardianship by his last will and testament to another person, the appointment made by the Kazi should be withdrawn and the father's choice upheld. ' If a judge not knowing that the deceased has appointed an executor, appoints another, the executor of the deceased is the lawful executor, and not the nominee of the judge."[2]

A verbal appointment of an executor, if supported by sufficient testimony, is valid in law.

A mother is not a natural guardian.

Mother's guardianship.

The extent of her powers has been discussed by the Judicial Committee in the case of *Imambandi* v. *Mustaddi*[3] and the principle governing her acts clearly explained. Unless she is appointed by the father as the guardian of his minor children's estate, or is so appointed by the judge she has no power to intermeddle with their immovable property (*akar*). All her dealings with *akar* are *ipso facto void*. But she may sell or pledge their goods and chattels for their maintenance. If they have no means of support excepting the *akar*, she must apply to the Court for sanction in order to deal with the property.

A mother, whether Moslemah or non-Moslemah, can be validly appointed executrix of the father, and when so appointed, is entitled to exercise the rights and powers which the law vests in testamentary guardians.

A testamentary guardian stands in *loco patris* in every matter relating to the welfare of the minors and the care and preservation of their property. In certain cases, and especially when the appointment of the *wasi* or executor is *general in its nature*, the father's or grandfather's executor may delegate the trust to his own *executor*.[4]

---

1 Jam'a-ush-Shittat; Fatawai 'Alamgiri, Vol. VI, p. 212.

2 Fatawai 'Alamgiri, Vol. VI, p. 213.

3 (1918) L R 45 I A 73; I L R 45 Cal. 787.

4 Fatawai 'Alamgiri, Vol. VI, p. 233; Jam'a-ush-Shittat.

The mother has no right to appoint a guardian for her minor children in respect of property received by them from their father. In the case of legitimate children, the power of appointing a tutor to take charge of their property belongs exclusively to the father; in the case of illegitimate children, to the Kazi or judge. But when the mother acts as the general executrix of the father, she may validly leave by will the charge of the children to her own executor. Or, when the property is her own which devolves on the children she has a right to make any disposition she chooses as to its curatorship during their minority.

Principle.

When, however, an executor has been appointed by the mother to take charge of her minor children, and also of movable and immovable property left by her, such executor has no power to sell anything that the minors may have inherited from their father, whether real or personal, or whether the property was involved in debt or not.

But he may lawfully dispose of, for the benefit of his wards, the *movable* property inherited by them from their mother, *but not the immovable property.*[1] If the estate left by her is involved in debt, and the debt is such as to absorb the whole estate he is authorised to sell the entire property, but not otherwise.[2]

When a guardian has been appointed by a Court of Justice, or there is a testamentary guardian, neither the mother nor any other relative has any right to interfere with the administration of the estate of the minor. She is at all times, however, entitled to institute a suit in her own name for the protection of the interests of her children. When, therefore, a guardian is dealing fraudulently with the property of the minors, or is embezzling or wasting their estate, she has a right to ask for the assistance of the judge to remove or restrain him.

Among the Hanafis if a person sufficiently qualified to undertake the guardianship of the minors can be found among the male agnates of the deceased father, such a person should be appointed by the Judge in preference to a stranger. If he considers the interests of the minors will be best promoted by the mother, he has the power to appoint her in preference to any of the deceased's agnates.

The Mahommadan Law carefully and jealously defines the powers and duties of guardians, natural, testamentary or appointed.

The powers of a guardian de jure.

A guardian *de jure* is authorised to sell the movable property of his ward for an *adequate* consideration, and invest the proceeds in a "profitable undertaking" for the benefit of the minor.

1 "Nor", adds the Fatawa, "lawfully buy anything but food (at-t'aam) and raiment (al-kiswat)."—Fatawai 'Alamgiri, Vol. VI, p. 223.

2 Fatawai 'Alamgiri, Vol. VI, p. 223.

Guardian's powers.

"A guardian may sell or purchase movables on account of his ward, either for an equivalent or at such a rate as to occasion an inconsiderable loss, but not at such a rate as to make the loss great and apparent, because the appointment of an executor being for the benefit of the orphan, he must avoid losses in as great a degree as possible; but with respect to an inconsiderable loss, as in the commerce of the word is often unavoidable, it is therefore allowed to him to incur it, as otherwise a door would be shut to the business of purchase and sale."[1] Similar opinions are expressed in the *Jam'a ush-Shittat* and the *Radd-ul-Muhtar*.

Inadequacy of consideration, which on the face of it bears the marks of fraud, or when the inadequacy is so *considerable* as to occasion serious injuries and detriment to the interests of the minor, or when it is the result of culpable negligence on the part of the guardian, will avoid any transaction entered into by him on behalf of the ward, and make him liable for its consequences. It remains, however, for the judge in his discretion to consider whether a consideration is adequate or not, or whether a particular transaction shall be held to be prejudicial to the interests of the ward or otherwise. If the transaction, though voidable has been entered into *bona fide* with due care and attention, the guardian would not be held responsible for any untoward consequences which may have resulted from it contrary to his expectation and forecast.

A guardian is allowed to borrow money for the *support and education* of his ward, even if he have to pledge the minor's property. All debts contracted *validly* and *bona fide* for that purpose form a charge on the minor's estate and have to be paid out of the same.

It is lawful for a guardian to trade on account of his ward, but in doing so he must be careful not to go beyond the bonds of *ordinary prudence* or to engage in transactions which he has reason to believe are hazardous in their nature.[2]

Restrictions on the powers of a guardian de jure.

A guardian is bound to keep his accounts separate from those of his ward, when the capital of both is engaged in the same trade or business.

A testamentary guardian, or a curator appointed by the Kazi, is not allowed to pledge the goods of his ward "into his own hands" on account of a debt due to himself, nor "into the hands of any person over whom he exercises control or parental authority; "for a guardian, being merely an *agent*, cannot of course have a double capacity in contracts."[3]

---

1 Hedaya, Vol. IV, p. 553.

2 This evidently means that a guardian may carry on a trade belonging to a minor.

3 Hedaya, Vol. IV, p. 214.

According to the *Hedaya*, a father *may pledge* the *movable* property of his minor child to himself for a debt due from the child to himself, or he may pledge it to another on account of a debt of his own, remaining, however, always liable for the value of the goods to the child.[1]

Limitations on the powers of a father acting as his child's guardian.

Other jurists seem to disagree with the author of the *Hedaya* in this latter view. According to them, the father stands in the same position as any other guardian; that is, it is not lawful either for him or for a tutor to pay off his own personal debts with the goods of the minor, or to pledge them on account of his debts.[2]

Some jurists think that it is lawful for the father to pledge the goods of his son for a debt jointly incurred by father and son. If, therefore, the pledged goods be lost, a father is bound "to compensate his son by the payment of a sum equivalent to his own share of the debt."

Abu Yusuf and several others have doubted the correctness of this view, holding that the father has no right to mix up his own property with that of his child, or to pledge the latter for a debt due from both, as "this is likely to lead to confusion."

Principle.

These principles have reference to movable property alone. With reference to the *real* or *immovable* property of the ward, the powers of guardians are more limited and circumscribed.

(*a*) A guardian *may not sell* his ward's real property "into his own hands" or into the hands of any one connected with him, under any circumstance.

(*b*) He may sell it to a stranger for double its value, or where it is to the *manifest* advantage of the ward.

(Section 31 of Act III of 1890 uses the words "evident advantage.")

Restrictions on the sale of immovable property.

(*c*) He may also sell it when there are some general provisions in the *wasiyet* (will) of the testator, which cannot be carried into effect without the sale of the property.

(*d*) When the property is required to be sold for the purpose of paying off the debts of the testator, which cannot be liquidated in any other way.

(*e*) When the income accruing from the estate is not sufficient to defray the expenditure incurred in its management and the payment of the *kharaj* (land-revenue).

(*f*) When it is in imminent danger of being destroyed or lost by decay.

1 Hedaya, Vol. IV, p. 215.

2 Durr-ul-Mukhtar, p. 846; Jam'a-ush-Shittat; Hedaya, Vol. IV, Bk. xlviii, chap. ii.

(*g*) When the minor has no other property, and the sale of it is *absolutely* necessary for his maintenance.

(*h*) When it is in the hands of a usurper, and the guardian has reason to fear there is no chance of restitution.[1]

In other words, even a guardian *de jure*, like the father or his executor, cannot sell the immovable property of the minor without absolute necessity or unless it is to the *manifest* or *evident* advantage of the minor.[2]

If the movable property of a minor is sold *bona fide* for an adequate consideration, with the object of investing the proceeds safely and for an increased income, its sale would be held valid upon a liberal construction of the law.[3]

The following cases decided by the Indian Courts in respect of the dealing of guardians in respect of the minor's property are now subject to the decision of the Judicial Committee in *Imanbandi* v. *Mutsaddi*.[4]

Bukshan v. Doolhin.

In the case of *Mussamat Bukshan* v. *Mussamat Doolhin*,[5] the Calcutta High Court held that, under the Mahommedan Law, a sale by a guardian of the property of a minor is permitted only in case of urgent necessity or clear advantage to the ward, and a purchaser from the guardian cannot defend his title on the ground of the *bona fides* of the transaction; nor could an elder brother stand in the position of such a guardian in respect of the property of his minor sisters.

Syedun v. Velayet Ali Khan.

In *Syedun* v. *Velayet Ali Khan*,[6] the same Court proceeded further and declared, what is in accordance with the Mahommedan Law, that in cases of sale made by the guardian of a Mahommedan ward, the question of legal necessity does not necessarily arise, though it may properly form an element for consideration when the conduct of a guardian is called in question. What the Mahommedan Law looks to is the benefit of the minor, and permits the guardian to dispose of movable property if it be for the benefit of the minor. In this particular case the sale was upheld, as it was to carry on an important litigation for the minor and was for his benefit.

---

1 Fatawai 'Alamgiri, Vol. VI, p. 222; Jam'a-ush-Shittat; Kitab-ul-Anwar; Durr-ul-Mukhtar, p. 846.

2 Comp. Hurbai *v.* Hiraji (1896) I L 20 Bom. 116; Thottoli *v.* Kunhammad I L R 34 Mad. 527.

See Bhawal *v.* Bajnath Partap Narain I L R 35 Cal. 320; Imambandi *v.* Mutsaddi L R 45 I A 73; Yeajuddin *v.* Rup Manjari Dasi A I R 1936 Cal. 326; Mohammad Abdur Rahman *v.* Muhammad Ibadul Ghani A I R 1937 Oudh 56.

3 Radd-ul-Muhtar; Jam'a sh-Shittat.

4 (1918) L R 45 I A 73.

5 (1869) 3 B L R A C p. 423; s. c. 12 W R p. 337. See also Ruttan *v.* Domee Khan N-W P H C R 1869 p. 21, where it was held that the brothers were not such guardians.

6 (1871) 17 W R 239.

Husaini Begum v. Zia-ul-nissa Begum.

In *Husaini Begum* v. *Zia-ul-nissa Begum,*[1] the Bombay High Court seems to have considerably stretched the point in order to sustain a transaction entered into by the elder brother of the minor with the sanction of an officer of Government. In this case, however, the ancestor had died heavily involved in debt, and the distressed condition of his heirs existed in a sufficient degree to justify the sale of the whole property of his heirs. But it was overlooked that the sanction to such a transaction could only be given by the judicial authority.

Bhutnath Dey v. Ahmed Hossain.

The Calcutta High Court, in the case of *Bhutnath Dey* v. *Ahmad Hossain,*[2] applied the law correctly in holding that a mortgage created by the adult co-heirs of certain Mahommedan minors in respect of their own shares, as well as those of the minors for the purpose of paying off the arrears of rent of a patni talook, did not bind the shares of the minors.

But the reservation made by the Court in deciding the question of law seems to be beside the point.

Hasan Ali v. Mehdi Hussain.

In the Allahabad High Court there has existed considerable divergence of opinion regarding sales by guardians. In *Hasan Ali* v. *Mehdi Hussain,*[3] the sale was upheld. In another case the sale, which was for the purpose of paying off an ancestral debt, was set aside, but subject to the minor paying a share of the debt proportionate to the share received by her in the inheritance of her father.[4]

Sitaram v. Amir Begum.

In *Sitaram* v. *Amir Begum,*[5] the Mahommedan Law was enunciated with considerable distinctness by Mahmood, J., who held the transaction entered into by a *de facto* guardian not binding on the minors.

Kali Dutt Jha v. Abdul Ali.[6]

In a case where disputes existed as to the title to revenue-paying land, of which part formed the minors' shares, and it was sold by their guardian for a *fair* price, and the sale had the result of ending the disputes and rendering the settlement of the remainder practicable, the validity of the transaction was maintained. It was also held that, although the sale-deed incorrectly stated the purpose of the sale, yet on the transaction being afterwards

1 (1882) I L 6 Bom. 467.
2 (1885) I L 1 Cal. 417.
3 (1877) I L 1 All. p. 533.
4 Hamir Singh *v.* Mussamat Zakia (1875) I L 1 All. p. 57.
5 (1886) I L 8 All. 324.

But see Imambandi *v.* Mutsaddi L R 45 I A 73: I L R 45 Cal. 878; Mata Din *v.* Ahmad Ali L R 39 I A 49: I L R 34 All. 213; Kannusami Chetty *v.* Rahimat Ammal A I R 1933 Mad. 806; Ramachandrayya *v.* Abdul Qadir 1948 Mad. 37; Relumal Kewalmal *v.* Hazur Bakhsh A I R 1947 Sind 179; Abdul Karim *v.* Mst. Muniran A I R 1954 Pat. 6; Kharag Narain *v.* Hamida Khatoon A I R 1955 Pat. 475; Ardhanari Mudaliar *v.* Abdul Rahiman (1956) 1 M L J 243, where it has been held that an alienation by a *de facto* guardian is not only voidable but void *ab initio*.

6 16 I A 96: I L R 16 Cal. 627.

impeached by the wards, it was open to the guardian to prove the real nature of the sale and to show that it was one beneficial to them.[1]

As a general rule, the powers of the testamentary guardian are subject to the same limitations and extend to the same degree as the powers of the testator.

Shiah Law.

The Shiah Law is in general accord with the Sunni Law regarding the powers of guardians. A few of the general principles stated in the *Mabsut* may usefully be inserted here:—

(1) The testamentary guardian or executor must be major, sane, professor of Islam and of good character.

(2) A minor cannot be appointed a guardian or executor by himself, but may validly be appointed with another. In the last case, he can act only on attaining majority.

(3) In the preceding case the adult tutor can act singly up to the majority of the minor guardian.

(4) A woman can be appointed an executrix or a testamentary guardian of minors.

(5) A *zimmi* cannot be appointed the guardian of Moslem children.

(6) The testamentary guardian cannot delegate the guardianship to his own executor, unless expressly authorised by the testator.

(7) If the grandfather is alive, the father cannot leave the guardianship of his minor children to an outsider, unless the grandfather is notoriously inimical to the interest of his grandchildren.

Act VIII of 1890.

The provisions of the Musulman Law relating to the appointment of guardians and their powers and duties must be read side by side with the provisions of Act VIII of 1890 (the Guardians and Wards Act) under which all matters relating to the appointment or declaration of a guardian in British India and all questions affecting his powers and responsibilities are to be dealt with.

Section 20 of the Act declares the fiduciary character of the guardian towards the ward, and impresses on his dealings with his ward's property the obligations which spring from that character.[2]

---

1 Kali Dutt Jha *v.* Abdul (1888) L R 16 I A 96 s. c. I L R 16 Cal. 627.

But it must be noted that in this case the guardian who held the immovable property of the minors was the father of the minors, and therefore their *de jure* guardian under Muslim Law.

See also Thottoli *v.* Kunhammad I L R 34 Mad. 527: 8 I C 1093; Muhammad Abdur Rahman Khan *v.* Mohammad Ibadul Ghazi Khan A I R 1937 Oudh 56: 165 I C 597; Basha *v.* Muthan 70 Mad. L W 706.

2 See Muhammad Abdur Rahman Khan *v.* Muhammad Ibadul Ghani A I R 1937 Oudh 56. Where a debt was incurred by a guardian on behalf of a minor and the minor soon after coming of age ratified this debt and acknowledged it in another deed executed by him, it was held that unless there be anything to show that the ratification was due to undue influence by the guardian no presumption of undue influence can be drawn and the ratification stands valid.

Sections 24, 25 and 26 lay down rules regarding the custody of the minor by one appointed under the Act as guardian of the person.

Sections 27 and 28 prescribe the duties and the limitations on the powers of guardians to deal with the property of their wards.

Section 30 declares the validity of transfers made by the guardians otherwise than with the sanction of the Court. And section 31 lays down the procedure for obtaining the sanction of the Court for a transfer by the guardian and the circumstances under which such permission may be granted.

Section 33 allows the guardian to apply for the advice or opinion of the Court in the management of the ward's property.

The powers, therefore, of a person appointed or declared to be guardian of the property of a ward are subject to the provisions of section 29 of the Act. Any disposal of immovable property by the guardians in contravention of sections 28 and 29 is declared by section 30 to be voidable at the instance of any other person affected thereby; the remedy is not confined to the minor.

Abbasi Begam v. Rajrup Koer.

In the case of *Abbasi Begum* v. *Rajrup Koer*,[1] it was decided by Ainslie and Macdonnell, JJ., that a guardian *de facto* who had not taken out a certificate under Act XL of 1858 had no larger powers than a guardian *de jure* duly appointed under it. In a latter case, however, a Full Bench of the Court have held a contrary view.[2] They have decided that it is only when a guardian takes out a certificate that his or her power becomes circumscribed within the limits imposed by section 18 of Act XL of 1858. In this view the position and powers, of a Muhammedan guardian, testamentary or natural, not appointed by the Court under the new Act, will be judged by the principles of the Mohammedan Law. But as the Musulman Law is extremely solicitous for the interests of minors there can be little doubt that in determining these questions in accordance with the principles of Musulman Law the Courts in India will be acting in conformity with the rule of equity.[3]

Thus, in all questions relating to the powers of a guardian, whether the father or any other person, the primary and essential matter for consideration is the *benefit* of the minor. The Calcutta High Court held[4] that although a mother is not the legal guardian of a minor's property, yet when she, acting as the *de facto* guardian, purports to deal with his property, the transaction, if it is for the *benefit* of the minor, ought to stand in the absence of fraud or any other element of that nature. The decision is clearly opposed to the Mahommedan Law. The provision of the

---

1 (1878) I L 4 Cal. p. 33.

2 Ram Chander Chuckerbutty *v.* Brojonath Mozumdar (1879) I L 4 Cal. 629.

3 Under the Muhammadan Law such a guardian would be merely a *de facto* guardian whose alienation would be void *ab initio*: see page 505, foot note 5.

4 Mofazzal Hosain *v.* Basid Sheikh (1907) I L 34 Cal. 36; Ram Churn Sanyal *v.* Anukul Chandra Achariya, *ibid.*, 65. As regards the position of a mother appointed as guardian *ad litem* to her minor children, see Muzaffar Ali Khan *v.* Parbati (1907) I L 29 All. 640. 648.

Mahommedan Law relative to a mother's right to the guardianship of her minor child's property was invoked to avoid a transaction which was manifestly to the advantage of the minor. Woodroffe, J., dealing with that contention, observed as follows:—"The law relating to guardians is one which exists for the benefit of the minors, and it would be both inconsistent and unjust to set up that law to defeat a transaction which in every respect fulfils its objects."[1]

Under the Mahommedan Law brothers have no authority to deal with a minor brother's or sister's property or to bind his or her estate except under the authority of an appointment by the Court or by virtue of appointment by the father as excutors of his will. An unauthorised guardian cannot clothe himself with legal power to alienate or charge a minor's property though he may assume responsibilities in relation thereto.[2]

Where a contract for the purchase of immovable property was made on behalf of a minor by his guardian, and it was attempted to be supported as being for his benefit, the Judicial Committee held that the guardian could not bind the minor's estate by such contract; and the minor could not obtain specific performance of such contract for want of mutuality.[3]

In the appointment also of guardians the primary matter for the consideration of the Court is the welfare of infants. In a dispute between the mother of certain minors and their paternal uncle regarding the guardianship of their property, the Allahabad High Court pointed out in distinct terms that under the Mahommadan Law, the paternal uncle has no legal right to such guardianship any more than the mother; the sole question therefore to be considered is whether it would be for the welfare of the minors to appoint their uncle as guardian rather than their mother. And upon a review of the circumstances the Court upheld the appointment of the mother, made by the District Judge.[4]

The husband of a girl is not entitled to the guardianship of her minor sister.[5]

When an application is made for the guardianship of an infant the applicant must reside within the jurisdiction of the Court in which he makes the application.[6]

---

1 See Imambandi *v.* Mutsaddi I L R 45 Cal. 878 (P C), where it has been held that the mother has no larger powers to deal with her minor child's property than any outsider or non-relative who happens to have charge for the time being of the minor.

2 Matadin *v.* Shaikh Ahmad Ali (1911) L R 39 I A 49; see also Abdul Khadir *v.* Chidumbaram Chattiyar (1908) I L 32 Mad. 276.

See Fateh Din *v.* Gurmukh Singh A I R 1929 Lah. 810 and Nizamuddin *v.* Anandi I L R 18 All. 373, where it has been held that an alienation by a brother or uncle is wholly void.

3 Mir Sarwar Jan *v.* Fakhrud-din Mahommed Chowdhury (1912) L R 39 I A 1; see also Fakhruddin *v.* Abdul Hussain (1910) I L 35 Bom. 217.

Venkatachalam Pillai *v.* Sethu Ram I L R 56 Mad. 433: A I R 1933 Mad. 322.

4 Akim Ullah Khan *v.* Abadi Begum (1906) I L 2 All. 10.

5 (1914) I L 36 All. 280.

6 *Ibid.*

APPENDICES

I—X

APPENDIX I

It may be of interest to practising lawyers and judicial officers to have an idea of the rites usually observed at a Musulman marriage in India[1].

Herklst gives in the "Qanoon-i-Islam" a description of the practice among the Mahommedans in Southern India; and Mrs. Meer Hassan Ali in her "Observations on the Musulmans of India" has given a long account of the ceremonies in vogue in Oudh and in the north generally. These may, however, be stated very briefly since the unfortunate abolition of the official *Kazi*,—a man learned in the law is usually selected for the purpose of officiating at a Musulman marriage and is called the *Kazi*. In Oudh among the Shiahs it is the duty of the *Mujtahid* who enters the fact of the solemnization in his register. The *Kazi's* first duty is to obtain the consent of the bride and of those acting on her behalf, or their formal consent to the terms of the contract which, generally speaking, are settled beforehand. After this is done he asks the bridegroom whether he is content, and on receiving his reply in the affirmative, proceeds to perform the service. In the first place, the bridegroom is seated with his face turned towards Macca and desired to repeat after the *Kazi* in Arabic the Creed and the Articles of Belief of the Musulman religion. The service then winds up with the prayer of praise (*dua-Kunut*). If the bridegroom be illiterate the *Kazi* explains the meaning in the vernacular. The *Kazi* then makes the bridegroom repeat after him in Arabic the formula or *sigha* of the marriage contract, and points out to him its signification. When this is finished the proxies of the bride and bridegroom are made to clasp their hands ; the *Kazi* then tells the former to say to the latter (naming her and her father), "Has through my agency in the presence of two witnesses, given her gracious consent to your marriage with her, and such a dower is settled upon her; do you consent to it?" The bridegroom replies "with my whole heart and soul to my marriage with this lady, as well as to the above-mentioned settlement made upon her, do I consent" repeating the "consent" three times.

After this the *Kazi* pronounces a benediction on the newly-married pair, saying "Oh! great God! Grant that mutual love may reign between this couple, as is existed between Adam and Eve, between Abraham and Sarah, between Moses and his wife Zippora, between our Lord and Master Mohammad and Khadija and the blessed 'Ali (the chosen) and Fatima-az-Zahra."

This concludes the religious ceremony. Custom, however, adds a little touch of poetry. The *Kazi* on the conclusion of the benediction blesses a piece of sugar-candy placed on a tray before him, puts half of it into the mouth of the bridegroom and delivers

---

1 Now Indo-Pakistan

the other half with a necklace of beads or pearls to the bridegroom's mother, or any other near relative, desiring her to convey it to the bride and to tell her that she must henceforth consider herself married to such a person, the son of such a one; that such a dower has been settled upon her ; and that she is to chew the sugar-candy as emblematic of the sweets of matrimony, and wear the necklace in token of her marriage.

Before the Kazi departs all the people assembled embrace each other whilst the same ceremony is repeated in the inner apartments.

APPENDIX II

The Mutazalas base their rule of monogamy on the express words of the Koran ; and their doctrine is clearly referred to in the *Radd-ul-Muhtar*. The Koran declares "you may marry one, two, three or four wives, provided you can deal with equity by them." The M'utazalas hold that "dealing with equity" is an essential condition to the legality of several contemporaneous contracts of marriage, that in fact it is a condition precedent to the valid exercise of the power; that equity under the Koranic rules implies equality in love and affection, and that such equality being impossible in the weakness of human nature, the Koranic permission amounts virtually to a prohibition. To this the *Radd-ul-Muhtar*, representing the Sunni legal conception, purports to reply in substance as follows: "It is contended by a section (meaning the M'utazalas) that "equity" (*adl*) includes in its meaning equality in love and affection, and that consequently a man may not marry more than one wife; but it is not so in our opinion; we hold that it means only equality in maintenance (*nafka*) and lodgment (*sukua*), and that, therefore, there is no such prohibition as they imagine."

APPENDIX III

The principle relating to the limitations under the Mahommedan Law on the powers of *de facto* guardians are now definitely settled by the decision of the Judicial Committee in the case of *Imambandi and others* v. *Sheikh Haji Mutasaddi and others.*[1] In that case a Mahommedan mother had conveyed her minor children's interest along with her own to the plaintiffs (respondents before the Board) for the purpose of litigation to establish her and their title to a share in the inheritance of their deceased father, her husband. The defendants who were the other heirs of the deceased had obtained possession of the whole property. The plaintiff under the conveyance from the mother, brought a suit to recover possession of the shares of the minors along with hers. Their Lordships after expressing concurrence with the Courts in India in their finding as to the validity of the minor's claim to inherit from the deceased, proceeded to deal with the question whether the plaintiffs had acquired a good title to the share of the infants under the conveyance executed by their mother. For the convenience of reference the judgment on this point is given here *in extenso.*

"The question how far, or under what circumstances, a mother's dealings with her minor child's property are binding on the infant has been frequently before the Courts in India. The decisions, however, are by no means uniform, and betray two varying tendencies: one set of decisions purports to give such dealings a qualified force; the other declares them wholly void and ineffective. In the former class of cases, the main test for determining the validity of the particular transaction has been the benefit resulting from it to the minor; in the latter, the admitted absence of authority or power on the part of the mother to alienate or encumber the minor's property."

"In this conflict of opinion their Lordships think it desirable that a definite rule should, if possible, be laid down ; and with this object they propose to review briefly the provisions and principles of the Mahommedan law, as they apprehend it, governing the subject."

"It is perfectly clear that under the Musulman law the mother is entitled only to the custody of the person of her minor child up to a certain age according to the sex of the child. But she is not the natural guardian; the father alone, or, if he be dead, his executor (under the Sunni law), is the legal guardian. The mother has no larger powers to deal with her minor child's property than any outsider or non-relative who happens to have charge for the time being of the infant. The term '*de facto* guardian' that has been applied to these persons is misleading: it connotes

---

1 I L R 45 I A, 73

the idea that people in charge of a child are by virtue of that fact invested with certain powers over the infant's property. This idea is quite erroneous; and the judgment of the Board in *Matadin* v. *Ahmed Ali* (L. R. 39, I. A., p. 49) clearly indicated it. There, an infant's share was sold by the elder brother, in whose charge the child was, along with his own share, to pay a joint ancestral debt. The vendee at the time of the sale was in possession of the whole property under a mortgage executed by the ancestor. On attaining majority the younger brother, ignoring the sale, brought a suit against the vendee-mortgagee for the redemption of his own share. The defence set up was that the sale by the infant's *de facto* guardian, made for a valid necessity, was binding on the infant. The lower Courts decreed the plaintiff's claim; on appeal to this Board the arguments proceeded on the same lines as in the present case, though in reverse order."

Lord Robson, in delivering the judgment of the Board, observed as follows :—

It is urged on behalf of the appellant that the elder brothers were *de facto* guardians of the respondent, and, as such, were entitled to sell his property, provided that the sale was in order to pay his debts and was therefore necessary in his interest. It is difficult to see how the situation of an unauthorised guardian is bettered by describing him as a '*de facto*' guardian. He may, by his *de facto* guardianship, assume important responsibilities in relation to the minor's property, but he cannot thereby cloth himself with legal power to sell it.

And he went on adding—

There has been much argument in this case in the Courts below, and before their Lordships, as to whether, according to Mahommedan law a sale by a *de facto* guardian, if made of necessity, or for the payment of an ancestral debt affecting the minor's property, and if beneficial to the minor, is altogether void or merly voidable. It is not necessary to decide that question in this case.

And he then proceeded to state the reasons why that was not considered necessary.

This latter passage in Lord Robson's judgment has created the impression that their Lordships' decision was confined to the special facts of that case and left open the general question regarding the validity of alienations by unauthorised guardians of the property of minors.

As already observed, in the absence of the father, under the Sunni law, the guardianship vests in his executor. If the father dies without appointing an executor (*wasi*) and his father is alive, the guardianship of his minor children devolves on their grandfather. Should he also be dead, and have left an executor, it vests in him. In default of these *de jure* guardians, the duty of appointing a guardian for the protection and preservation of the infants' property devolves on the Judge as the representative of the Sovereign. (Baillie's "Digest", ed. 1875, p. 689 ; Hamilton's *Hedaya*, Vol. IV, p. 555). No one else has any right or power to intermeddle with the property of a minor, except for certain specified purposes, the nature of which is clearly defined. But the powers of even the *de jure* guardians are confined within legal limits. For example, whilst an executor-guardian (*wasi*) may "sell or purchase movables on account of the orphan under his charge either for an equivalent or at such a rate as to occasion an inconsiderable loss", dealings with his immovable property are subjected to strict conditions (Baillie's "Digest", p. 687). The reason for the restrictions is thus given in the *Hedaya* (Vol. IV, p. 553) :—

"The ground of this" (the difference in the power of dealing with the two kinds of property) "is that the sale of movable property is a species of conservation, as articles of that description are liable to decay, and the price is much more easily preserved than the article itself. With respect, on the contrary, to immovable property, it is in a state of conservation in its own nature whence it is unlawful to sell it—unless, however, it be evident that it will otherwise perish or be lost, in which case the sale of it is allowed."

In fact, the Musulman law appears to draw a sharp distinction between movable and immovable property (*a'kar*) in respect of the powers of guardians, as will be seen from the following passage in Baillie's "Digest", p. 689 :

"With regard to the executor of a mother or brother,—when a mother has died leaving property and a minor son, and having appointed an executor, or a brother has died leaving property and a minor brother, and having appointed an executor, the executor may lawfully sell anything but *a'kar*[1] belonging to the estate of the deceased, but can neither sell the *a'kar*, nor lawfully buy anything for the minor but food and clothing, which are necessary for his preservation. The executor of a mother has no power to sell anything that a minor has inherited from his father, whether movable or immovable, and whether the property be involved in debt or free from it. But what he has inherited from herself when it is free from debts and legacies the executor may sell what is movable, but he cannot sell *a'kar*. If the estate is involved in debt or legacies, and the debt is such as to absorb the whole, he may sell the whole, the sale of *a'kar* coming within his power ; and if the debt does 'not absorb the whole, he may sell as much of it as is necessary to defray the debts, and as to his power to sell the surplus there is the same difference of opinion as has been stated above."

When the mother is the father's executrix, or is appointed by the Judge as guardian of the minors, she has all the powers of a

1 *A'kar* is immovable property, and includes houses, groves, orchards, &c.

de jure guardian. Without such derivative authority, if she assumes charge of their property of whatever description and purports to deal with it, she does so at her own risk, and her acts are like those of any other person who arrogates an authority which he does not legally possess. She may incur responsibilities, but can impose no obligations on the infant. This rule, however, is subject to certain exceptions provided for the protection of a minor child who has no *de jure* guardian. A fatherless child is designated in the law-books an "infant-orphan" (*yeteem saghir*). The *Hedaya* classifies the acts that may have to be done for an infant under three heads. It says—

"Acts in regard to infant-orphans are of three descriptions *viz.* :—(*i*) Acts of guardianship, such as contracting an infant in marriage, or selling or buying goods for him, a power which belongs solely to the *walee*, or natural guardian, whom the law has constituted the infant's substitute in those points; (*ii*) acts arising from the wants of an infant, such as buying or selling for him on occasions of need, or hiring a nurse for him, or the like, which power belongs to the maintainer of the infant, whether he be the brother, uncle, or (in the case of a foundling) the *mooltakit*,[1] or *taker-up*, or the mother, provided she be the maintainer of the infant; and as *these* are empowered with respect to such acts, the *walee*, or natural guardian, is also empowered with respect to them in a still superior degree; nor is it requisite, with respect to the *guardian*, that the infant be in his immediate protection; (*iii*) acts which are *purely advantageous*[2] to the infant, such as accepting presents or gifts, and keeping them for him, a power which may be exercised either by a *mooltakit*, a brother, or an uncle, and also by the infant himself provided he be possessed of discretion, the intention being only to open a door to the infants' receiving benefactions of an advantageous nature". (Vol. IV, p. 124, Bk. XLIV.)

The examples given under the second head indicate the class of cases in which the acts of an unauthorised person who happens to have charge of a child are held to be binding on the infant's property. They also help to explain and illustrate the extent of such "*de facto* guardian's" powers. The permissibility of these acts depends on the emergency which gives rise to the imperative necessity for incurring liabilities without which the life of the child or his perishable goods and chattels may run the risk of destruction. For instance, he may stand in immediate need of aliment, clothing, or nursing; these wants must be supplied forthwith. He may own "slaves" or live-stock : food and fodder must be immediately procured. And these imperative wants may recur from time to time. Under such circumstances power is given to the lawful guardian to incur debts or to raise money

---

1 A *mooltakit* is a person who undertakes to bring up a foundling or an orphan child.

2 In the original the words are *nafa' mahaz*, which mean "unmixed benefit".

on the pledge of the minor's goods and chattels (*mata*)[1] (*Majma'-ul-Anhar*, Vol. II, p. 571). And this power, in the absence of a *de jure* guardian, the law extends to the person who happens to have charge of the child and of the child's property, though not a constituted or authorised guardian.

There is no reference to the pledge or sale of immovable property (*a'kar*) as the power of dealing with that class of property is confined to the *de jure* guardians, and is treated in the *Fatawai 'Alamgiri* in a separate chapter (Baillie's "Mahommedan Law of Sale", Chapter XVI).

It is to be observed that under the third "description" of acts that may be needful for an infant, a person in charge of a child, although not a *de jure* guardian, may validly accept on behalf of his ward an unburdened bounty, it being an act "purely advantageous" to the child, to use the expression of the *Hedaya*.

The reasoning on which it is sought to give to persons who happen to have charge of the person and property of a child, and are, therefore, called "*de facto* guardians", the same powers as are possessed by *de jure* guardians is purely inferential. It proceeds on the analogy of a dealing by an outsider who purports to sell another's property without any authority from the real owner. Such a person in the Hanafi law is called a *fazuli*, or as Mr. Hamilton spells it, *fazoolee*, which expression is defined by Richardson to mean a person "busying himself in things not belonging to him, or acting without authority". With the effect of the acts of a *fazuli* their Lordships will deal presently. Before doing so, they wish to refer briefly to the state of the decisions in the Indian Courts.

The Calcutta High Court, in sustaining transactions entered into by *de facto* guardians, has proceeded mainly on consideration of necessity for and benefit to the infant. The other High Courts, generally speaking, have cut the Gordian knot by holding that all such dealings with a minor's property were void.

Their Lordships do not feel called upon to examine in detail either set of decisions. But the last case on the subject in the Madras High Court requires their careful and respectful consideration ; (*Ayderman Kutti* v. *Syed Ali*, I. L., 37 Mad. 514). In their judgment in this case the learned Judges have examined the law at considerable length, and their decision appears to divide itself into three broad propositions : *first*, that as regards the powers of guardians, *de jure* as well as *de facto*, the Mahommedan law recognises no distinction as to the nature or kind of property, *viz*., whether it is immovable or movable; *secondly*, that in substance the powers of an unauthorised person who has charge of an infant are co-extensive with those of a lawfully constituted guardian, except in so far that the acts of the former are subject to considerations of necessity or benefit to

1 Mr. Hamilton translates "*mata*" as meaning "personal chattels",

the infant ; and, *thirdly* (and this seems to form the essence of the judgment), that dealings by "a *de facto* guardian" are neither void nor voidable, but are "suspended" until the minor on attaining majority exercises his option of either ratifying the transaction or disavowing it.

With regard to the first of the above propositions, their Lordships have already indicated their views. In their opinion, the Musulman law, for obvious reasons, makes a distinction, and a sharp distinction, between "goods and chattels" (*mata*) and immovable property (*a'kar*) with regard to the powers of dealing by guardians.

The second proposition, speaking with respect, appears to their Lordships to lose sight of the fact that the acts of *de jure* guardians also are subject to the conditions of necessity for or benefit to the infant. So that upon the reasoning of the Madras judgment, the powers of "a *de facto* guardian" would, to all intents and purposes, be co-extensive with those of a *de jure* guardian. This conclusion would wipe out one of the most important safeguards provided by the Musulman law for the protection of the interests of infants. The learned Judges say that—

"The law as regards the effect of dealings with a minor's property by a *de facto* guardian otherwise than in a case of absolute necessity or clear advantage to the minor is but a corollary of the general rule relating to *salisly* [*sic*], a person professing to deal with another's property, but without having legal authority to do so, *i.e.*, by a *fazuli*, as he is technically called; such sales generally are treated as *mauquf*, or dependent."

Then, after referring to various authorities, they continue as follows :—

"The result of the above discussion is that, according to Mahommedan jurists, in cases of urgent and imperative necessity, such as those mentioned, the *de facto* guardian can alienate the property of the minor, no distinction being made between movable and immovable property."

It would have been an advantage to their Lordships if they had been placed in a position to judge for themselves, on the actual texts, the meaning of the Arabian text-writers and commentators. However, the *Hedaya* and the *Fatawai 'Alamgiri* are recognised as standard authorities in India on the Hanafi branch of the Sunni Law. Of the *Hedaya* there is a rendering in English made by Mr. Hamilton under the orders of Warren Hastings ; and a large part of the *Fatawai 'Alamgiri* has been paraphrased into English by Mr. Neil Baillie, which is commonly known as Baillie's "Digest" (Hanafia law). Both Mr. Hamilton and Mr. Neil Baillie in their renderings have, with the object of elucidation, occasionally added phrases which do not exist in the original, but on the whole the English versions of the *Hedaya* an of the *Fatawai 'Alamgiri* are valuable works on Mahommedan law.

The subject of sales by unauthorised persons is treated in the *Hedaya* in a separate section entitled "of Fazoolee Beea[1], or the sale of the property of another without his consent" (Book XVI, Vol. II, p. 508). It says :—

"If a person were to sell the property of another without his order the contract is complete, but it remains with the proprietor either to confirm or dissolve the sale as he pleases. Shaf'ei is of opinion that the contract, in their case, is not complete, because it has not issued from a lawful authority, for that is constituted only by property or permission, neither of which exist in this case."

It then proceeds to give the arguments of the Hanafi doctors in support of their view that the unauthorised contract is "complete". And then it adds :—

"If the proptietor should die, then the consent of the heirs is of no efficacy in the confirmation of the Fazoolee sale, in either case, that is, whether the price has been stipulated in *money* or in *goods*; because the contract rested entirely on the personal assent of the deceased."

In other words, the so-called sale remains wholly ineffective until it receives the "confirmation" of the owner, to whom alone belongs the power of "confirming" it. If he dies before he has "confirmed it", the transaction falls to the ground, as the right to adopt the *fazuli's* act does not pass to his heirs.

In the *Fatawai 'Alamgiri*[2] the subject is treated under the designation of "dependent sales" (Vol. III, p. 245 ; Baillie's "Mahommedon Law of Sale", pp. 218-219) :—

"When a person sells the property of another, the sale is suspended according to us [*i.e.*, the Hanafis], for the sanction or ratification of the proprietor ; and the existence of both the parties to the contract, and of the subject of sale, is a necessary condition to the validity of his sanction.

"If the owner should die before sanctioning the sale, sanction by his heir would not suffice to give it operation. Sanction by an owner himself renders a sale operative."

The word in the above passage translated as "suspended" is derived from the same root as the word that has been translated in the heading as "dependent", and in this connection really means "is dependent upon"; also the words "or ratification"

1 Correctly, Bai'.

2 The "Book on Sale" in the *Fatawai 'Alamgiri* has been rendered into English by Mr. Baillie under the name of the "Mahommedan Law of Sale".

have been introduced by Mr. Baillie by way of explanation. The word *Ijazat* in the original is rightly rendered into sanction.

The *Majma'-ul-Anhar* states the rule relating to a sale by a *fazuli* in similar terms; it says in substance that such a sale is "established" (takes effect) on the sanction of the *malik* (owner) subject to four conditions, which it specifies. And then it adds significantly that according to Shaf'ei (the founder of the second great Sunni school of law) all dealings by an unauthorised person are absolutely void (*batil*); Vol. II, p. 88.

In their Lordships' opinion, the Hanafi doctrine relating to a sale by an unauthorised person remaining dependent on the sanction of the owner refers to a case where such owner is *sui juris*, possessed of the capacity to give the necessary sanction and to make the transaction operative. They do not find any reference in these doctrines relating to *fazuli* sales, so far as they appear in the *Hedaya* or the *Fatawai 'Alamgiri*, to dealings with the property of minors by persons who happen to have charge of the infants and their property—in other words the "*de facto* guardians".

The Hanafi doctrine about *fazuli* sales appears clearly to be based on the analogy of an agent who acts in a particular matter without authority, but whose act is subsequently adopted or ratified by the principal which has the effect of validating it from its inception. The idea of agency in relation to an infant is as foreign, their Lordships conceive, to Musulman Law as to every other system.

In this connection it should be noted that whilst Chapter XII deals exclusively with the effect of "dependent sales", in Chapter XVI the rules relating to the powers of guardians are discussed at considerable length (Baillie's "Mahommedan Law of Sale", p. 243 ; *Fatawai 'Alamgiri*, Vol. III, p. 229). The following rule lays down the conditions governing sales by the executor (*i.e.*, the appointed guardian) of the immovable property of an infant :—

"And, according to modern decisions, the sale of immovable estate by an executor is lawful only in one of the three cases following : that is, where there is a purchaser willing to give double its value, or the sale is necessary to meet the minor's emergencies, or there are debts of the deceased, and no other means of paying them." (Baillie's "Mahommedan Law of Sale", p. 247 ; *Fatawai 'Alamgiri*, Vol. III, p. 233).

Having regard to the object in view, this dictum appears to their Lordships to apply to all forms of property which, like *a'kar* combine both security and permanency. But it does not exclude the discretion of the Judge to sanction any alteration of investment in the interests of the infant.

The following case affords a further illustration of the limitations on the powers of "*de facto* guardians" :—

"A woman after the death of her husband sells property that belonged to him, supposing herself to be his executrix, and her husband having left *minor* children; she after some time declares that she was not the executrix, her assertion, however, is not to be credited as against the purchaser, but the sale remains in suspense till her children arrive at puberty. If they should admit that she was the executrix, the sale by her is lawful; but if they deny the fact, the sale is void; and though the purchaser should have manured the purchased land, he has no recourse for reimbursement against the woman. What has been said is on the supposition that the woman sues for a cancellation of the sale, on the ground that she was not the executrix; but if the *minor* sue on that ground, his claim is to be heard." (Baillie p. 249; '*Alamgiri*, Vol. III, p. 234.)

The rest of the passage is immaterial for the purposes of this judgment.

The above case shows that even where the mother believes she is vested with authority as her husband's executrix, and in that belief purports to deal with the minor's property, a purchaser let into possession by her is liable to be ejected at the instance of the minor. Her own subsequent denial of authority does not affect the purchaser's position; but if the transaction is impugned by the rightful owner—*viz.*, the infant—the *onus* is on the vendee to establish the foundation of his title, that is, that his vendor possessed in fact the authority under which she purported to act.

A further rule, which is given in the "Book of Pledges" (Mortgages) (*Kitab-ur-Rahn*) of the *Fatawai 'Alamgiri*, which does not appear to have been translated by Mr. Baillie, is equally explicit. After stating the principle applicable to the powers of the father to pledge or mortgage his minor child's property, it goes on to say: "the mother: if she pledges (mortgages) the property of her infant child, it is not lawful, unless she be the executrix of the father] or be authorised therefor by the guardian of the minor; or the Judge should grant her permission to pledge the infant's property. Then it is lawful; and the right to possession and user is established in the *murtahin* (pledgee or mortgagee) without power of sale"; (*Fatawai 'Alamgiri*, Vol. V, p. 638).

It seems to their Lordships that the power to sell cannot be wider than the power to mortgage.

For the foregoing considerations their Lordships are of opinion that under the Mahommedan Law a person who has charge of the person or property of a minor without being his legal guardian, and who may, therefore, be conveniently called a "*de facto* guardian", has no power to convey to another any right or interest in immovable property which the transferee can enforce against the infant; nor can such transferee, if let into possession of the property under such unauthorised transfer, resist an action in ejectment on behalf of the infant as a trespasser. ᐟ follows that, being himself without title, he cannot seek to ɔver property in the possession of another equally without

APPENDIX IV

THE CHILD MARRIAGE RESTRAINT ACT, 1929

(XIX OF 1929)

[*1st October 1929*]

An Act to restrain the solemnisation of child marriages

Whereas it is expedient to restrain the solemnisation of child marriages; It is heredy enacted as follows :—

Short title, extent and commencement.

1. (1) This Act may be called the Child Marriage Restraint Act, 1929.

(2) It extends to the whole of Pakistan and applies to all citizens of Pakistan wherever they may be.

(3) It shall come into force on the 1st day of April 1930.

Definitions.

2. In this Act, unless there is anything repugnant in the subject or context,—

(a) "child" means a person who, if a male, is under eighteen years of age, and if a female, is under sixteen years of age;

(b) "child marriage" means a marriage to which either of the contracting parties is a child;

(c) "contracting party" to a marriage means either of the parties whose marriage is or is about to be thereby solemnised ;

(d) "minor" means a person of either sex who is under eighteen years of age;

(e) "Union Council" means the Union Council or the Town or Union Committee constituted under the Basic Democracies Order (P. O. No. 18 of 1959) within whose jurisdiction a child marriage is or is about to be solemnised.

3. [*Omitted by the Muslim Family Laws Ordinance, 1961 (VIII of 1961)*].

Punishment for male adult above eighteen years of age marrying a child.

4. Whoever, being a male above eighteen years of age, contracts a child marriage shall be punishable with simple imprisonment which may extend to one month, or with fine which may extend to one thousand rupees, or with both.

Punishment for solemnising a child marriage.

5. Whoever performs, conducts or directs any child marriage shall be punishable with simple imprisonment which may extend to one month, or with fine which may extend to one thousand rupees, or with both, unless he proves that he had reason to believe that the marriage was not a child marriage.

Punishment for parent or guardian concerned in a child marriage.

6.—(1) Where a minor contracts a child marriage, any person having charge of the minor, whether as parent or guardian or in any other capacity, lawful or unlawful, who does any act to promote the marriage or permits it to be solemnised, or negligently fails to prevent it from being solemnised, shall be punishable with simple imprisonment which may extend to one month, or with fine which may extend to one thousand rupees, or with both :

Provided that no woman shall be punishable with imprisonment.

(2) For the purposes of this section, it shall be presumed, unless and until the contrary is proved, that where a minor has contracted a child marriage, the person having charge of such minor has negligently failed to prevent the marriage from being solemnised.

Imprisonment not to be awarded for offences under section 3.

7.—Notwithstanding anything contained in section 25 of the General Clauses Act, 1897, or section 64 of the Pakistan Penal Code, a Court sentencing an offender under section 3 shall not be competent to direct that, in default of payment of the fine imposed, he shall undergo any term of imprisonment.

Jurisdiction under this Act.

8.—Notwithstanding anything contained in section 190 of the Code of Criminal Procedure, 1898, no Court other than that of a Magistrate of the first class shall take cognizance of, or try, any offence under this Act.

Mode of taking cognizance of offences.

9. No Court shall take cognizance of any offence under this Act except on a complaint made by the Union Council, or if there is no Union Council in the area, by such authority as the Provincial Government may in this behalf prescribe, and such cognizance shall in no case be taken after the expiry of one year from the date on which the offence is alleged to have been committed.

Preliminary inquiries into offences under this Act.

10. The Court taking cognizance of an offence under this Act shall, unless it dismisses the complaint under section 203 of the Code of Criminal Procedure, 1898, either itself make an inquiry under section 202 of that Code, or direct a Magistrate of the first class subordinate to it to make such inquiry.

11. [*Omitted by the Muslim Family Laws Ordinance, 1961* (*VIII of 1961*)].

Power to issue injunction prohibiting marriage in contravention of this Act.

12. (1) Notwithstanding anything to the contrary contained in this Act, the Court may, if satisfied from information laid before it through a complaint or otherwise that a child marriage in contravention of this Act has been arranged or is about to be solemnised, issue an injunction against any of the persons mentioned in sections 3, 4, 5 and 6 of this Act prohibiting such marriage.

(2) No injunction under subsection (1) shall be issued against any person unless the Court has previously given notice to such person, and has afforded him an opportunity to show cause against the issue of the injunction.

(3) The Court may either on its own motion or on the application of any person aggrieved, rescind or alter any order made under subsection (1).

(4) Where such an application is received, the Court shall afford the applicant an early opportunity of appearing before it either in person or by pleader ; and if the Court rejects the application wholly or in part, it shall record in writing its reasons for so doing.

(5) Whoever knowing that an injunction has been issued against him under subsection (1) of this section disobeys such injunction shall be punished with imprisonment of either description for a term which may extend to three months, or with fine which may extend to one thousand rupees, or with both :

Provided that no woman shall be punishable with imprisonment.

———

APPENDIX V

THE MUSLIM PERSONAL LAW (SHARIAT) APPLICATION ACT, 1937

(XXVI OF 1937)[1]

[*7th October 1937*]

An Act to make provision for the application of the Muslim Personal Law (Shariat) to Muslims in [2][the Provinces and the Capital of the Federation].

WHEREAS it is expedient to make provision for the application of the Muslim Personal Law (Shariat) to Muslims in [2][the Provinces and the Capital of the Federation]; It is hereby enacted as follows:—

Short title and extent.

1.—(1) This Act may be called the Muslim Personal Law (Shariat) Application Act, 1937.

(2) It extends to [3][all the Provinces and the Capital of the Federation] excluding the North-West Frontier Province.[4]

Application of Personal Law to Muslims.

2. Notwithstanding any custom or usage to the contrary, in all questions (save questions relating to agricultural land) regarding intestate succession, special property of females, including personal property inherited or obtained under contract or gift or any other provision of Personal Law, marriage, dissolution of marriage, including *talaq*, *ila*, *zihar*, *lian*, *khula* and *mubaraat*, maintenance, dower, guardianship, gifts, trusts and trust properties and *wakfs* (other than charities and charitable institutions and charitable and religious endowments) the rule of decision in cases where the parties are Muslims shall be the Muslim Personal Law (Shariat).

---

1 For Statement of Objects and Reasons, see Gazette of India, 1935, Pt. V, p. 136 ; and for Report of Select Committee, see *ibid.*, 1937, Pt. V, p. 235.

The Act has been applied to Baluchistan, see Gazette of India, 1938, Pt. I, p. 1371 ; and to the partially excluded areas of the Mymensingh district from the 20th January, 1944, see Bengal Government Notification No. 181-F, dated the 15th January, 1944. It has also been amended in its application to the Province of Sind by Sind Act XXII of 1950, ss. 2 and 3.

2 Subs. by the A.O. 1949, for "British India".

3 Subs. *ibid.*, for "the whole of British India".

4 For similar Law applicable to the N.-W.F.P., see the N.-W.F.P. Muslim Personal Law (Shariat) Application Act, 1935 (N.-W.F.P. 6 of 1935).

3.—(1) Any person who satisfies the prescribed authority— **Power to make a declaration.**

(a) that he is a Muslim, and

(b) that he is competent to contract within the meaning of section 11 of the Contract Act, 1872, and

(c) that he is a resident of [1][a Province], may by declaration in the prescribed form and filed before the prescribed authority declare that he desires to obtain the benefit of [2][the provisions of this section], and thereafter the provisions of section 2 shall apply to the declarant and all his minor children and their descendants as if in addition to the matters enumerated therein, adoption, wills and legacies were also specified.

(2) Where the prescribed authority refuses to accept a declaration under subsection (1), the person desiring to make the same may appeal to such officer as the Provincial Government may, by general or special order, appoint in this behalf, and such officer may, if he is satisfied that the appellant is entitled to make the declaration, order the prescribed authority to accept the same.

4.—(1) The Provincial Government may make rules to carry into effect the purposes of this Act. **Rule making power.**

(2) In particular and without prejudice to the generality of the foregoing powers, such rules may provide for all or any of the following matters, namely:—

(a) for prescribing the authority before whom and the form in which declarations under this Act shall be made;

(b) for prescribing the fees to be paid for the filing of declarations and for the attendance at private residences of any person in the discharge of his duties under this Act; and for prescribing the times at which such fees shall be payable and the manner in which they shall be levied.

(3) Rules made under the provisions of this section shall be published in the official Gazette and shall thereupon have effect as if enacted in this Act.

5. [Dissolution of marriage by Court in certain circumstances]. Repealed by the Dissolution of Muslim Marriages Act, 1939 (VIII of 1939), S. 6.

---

1 Subs. by the A.O. 1949, for "British India".

2 Subs. by the Muslim Personal Law (Shariat) Application (Amendment) Act, 1943 (16 of 1943), s. 2, for "this Act".

Repeals.

6.—[1][The undermentioned provisions] of the Acts and Regulations mentioned below shall be repealed in so far as they are inconsistent with the provisions of this Act, namely:—

(1) Section 26 of the Bombay Regulation IV of 1827;

[2][* * * * *]

[3][* * * * *]

[4][* * * * *]

(2) Section 5 of the Punjab Laws Act, 1872;

[4][* * * * *]

---

1 Subs. by the Muslim Personal Law (Shariat) Application (Amendment) Act, 1943 (16 of 1943), s. 3, for "Provisions"

2 Clause (2) omitted by the Federal Laws (Revisions and Declaration) Act, 1951 (26 of 1951), s. 3 and Second Schedule.

3 For the purpose of reviving the operation of s. 37 of the East Bengal Civil Courts Act, 1887 (12 of 1887), cl. (3) relating to that Act has been omitted by Act 16 of 1943.

4 Cls. (4), (6) and (7) rep. by the Federal Laws (Revisions and Declaration) Act, 1951 (26 of 1951), s. 3 and Second Schedule.

APPENDIX VI

THE DISSOLUTION OF MUSLIM MARRIAGES ACT, 1939

(VIII OF 1939)

[*17th March 1939*]

An Act to consolidate and clarify the provisions of Muslim law relating to suits for dissolution of marriage by women married under Muslim law and to remove doubts as to the effect of the renunciation of Islam by a married Muslim woman on her marriage tie.

Whereas it is expedient to consolidate and clarify the provisions of Muslim law relating to suits for dissolution of marriage by women married under Muslim law and to remove doubts as to the effect of the renunciation of Islam by a married Muslim woman on her marriage tie; It is hereby enacted as follows :—

Short title and extent.

1.—(1) This Act may be called the Dissolution of Muslim Marriages Act, 1939.

(2) It extends to all the Provinces and the Capital of the Federation.

Grounds for decree for dissolution of marriage.

2. A woman married under Muslim law shall be entitled to obtain a decree for the dissolution of her marriage on any one or more of the following grounds, namely :—

(i) that the whereabouts of the husband have not been known for a period of four years ;

(ii) that the husband has neglected or has failed to provide for her maintenance for a period of two years ;

(ii-a) that the husband has taken an additional wife in contravention of the provisions of the Muslim Family Laws Ordinance, 1961 ;

(iii) that the husband has been sentenced to imprisonment for a period of seven years or upwards ;

(iv) that the husband has failed to perform, without reasonable cause, his marital obligations for a period of three years ;

(v) that the husband was impotent at the time of the marriage and continues to be so ;

(vi) that the husband has been insane for a period of two years or is suffering from leprosy or a virulent venereal disease ;

(vii) that she, having been given in marriage by her father or other guardian before she attained the age of sixteen years, repudiated the marriage before attaining the age of eighteen years :

Provided that the marriage has not been consummated :

(viii) that the husband treats her with cruelty, that is to say,

(a) habitually assaults her or makes her life miserable by cruelty of conduct even if such conduct does not amount to physical ill-treatment, or

(b) associates with women of evil repute or leads an infamous life, or

(c) attempts to force her to lead an immoral life, or

(d) disposes of her property or prevents her exercising her legal rights over it, or

(e) obstructs her in the observance of her religious profession or practice, or

(f) if he has more wives than one, does not treat her equitably in accordance with the injunctions of the Quran ;

(ix) on any other ground which is recognised as valid for the dissolution of marriages under Muslim law :

Provided that—

(a) no decree shall be passed on ground (*iii*) until the sentence has become final ;

(b) a decree passed on ground (*i*) shall not take effect for a period of six months from the date of such decree, and if the husband appears either in person or through an authorised agent within that period and satisfies the Court that he is prepared to perform his conjugal duties, the Court shall set aside the said decree ; and

(c) before passing a decree on ground (*v*) the Court shall, on application by the husband, make an order requiring the husband to satisfy the Court within a period of one year from the date of such order that he has ceased to be impotent, and if the husband so satisfies the Court within such period, no decree shall be passed on the said ground.

3.—In a suit to which clause (*i*) of section 2 applies—

Notice to be served on heirs of the husband when the husband's whereabouts are not known.

(a) the names and addresses of the persons who would have been the heirs of the husband under Muslim law if he had died on the date of the filing of the plaint shall be stated in the plaint,

(b) notice of the suit shall be served on such persons, and

(c) such persons shall have the right to be heard in the suit :

Provided that paternal uncle and brother of the husband, if any, shall be cited as party even if he or they are not heirs.

Effect of conversion to another faith.

4. The renunciation of Islam by a married Muslim woman or her conversion to a faith other than Islam shall not by itself operate to dissolve her marriage :

Provided that after such renunciation, or conversion, the woman shall be entitled to obtain a decree for the dissolution of her marriage on any of the grounds mentioned in section 2 :

Provided further that the provisions of this section shall not apply to a woman converted to Islam from some other faith who re-embraces her former faith.

Rights to dower not to be affected.

5. Nothing contained in this Act shall affect any right which a married woman may have under Muslim law to her dower or any part thereof on the dissolution of her marriage.

(Repeal of section 5 of Act XXVI of 1937).

6. [Repealed by the Repealing and Amending Act, 1942 (XXV of 1942), section 2 and First Schedule.]

APPENDIX VII

THE MUSLIM FAMILY LAWS ORDINANCE, 1961

(VIII OF 1961)

[*2nd March 1961*].

An Ordinance to give effect to certain recommendations of the Commission on Marriage and Family Laws.

WHEREAS it is expedient to give effect to certain recommendations of the Commission on Marriage and Family Laws;

NOW, THEREFORE, in pursuance of the Proclamation of the seventh day of October 1958, and in exercise of all powers enabling him in that behalf, the President is pleased to make and promulgate the following Ordinance:—

Short title, extent, application and commencement.

1.—(1) This Ordinance may be called the Muslim Family Laws Ordinance, 1961.

(2) It extends to the whole of Pakistan, and applies to all Muslim citizens of Pakistan, wherever they may be.

(3) It shall come into force on such date[1] as the Central Government may, by notification in the official Gazette, appoint in this behalf.

Definitions.

2.—In this Ordinance, unless there is anything repugnant in the subject or context—

(a) "Arbitration Council" means a body consisting of the Chairman [2]* * * and a representative of each of the parties to a matter dealt with in this Ordinance [3][:]

[4][Provided that where any party fails to nominate a representative within the prescribed time, the body formed without such representative shall be the Arbitration Council;]

[5][(b) "Chairman" means the Chairman of the Union Council or a person appointed by the Central or a

---

1 *i.e.*, the 15th day of July, 1961, *see* Gazette of Pakistan, 1961, Extraordinary, page 1128 a.

2 The words "of the Union Council" omitted by the Muslim Family Laws (Amendment) Ordinance, 1961 (21 of 1961), s. 2.

3 Substituted *ibid.*, for semicolon.

4 Proviso, added *ibid.*

Substituted *ibid.*, for the original clause (*b*).

Provincial Government, or by an officer authorized in that behalf by any such Government, to discharge the functions of Chairman under this Ordinance:

Provided that where the Chairman of the Union Council is a non-Muslim, or he himself wishes to make an application to the Arbitration Council, or is, owing to illness or any other reason, unable to discharge the functions of Chairman, the Council shall elect one of its Muslim members as Chairman for the purposes of this Ordinance;]

(c) "prescribed" means prescribed by rules made under section 11;

(d) "Union Council" means the Union Council or the Town or Union Committee constituted under the Basic Democracies Order, 1959 (P. O. No. 18 of 1959), and [1][having in the matter jurisdiction as prescribed];

(e) "Ward" means a ward within a Union or Town as defined in the aforesaid Order.

Ordinance to override other laws, etc.

3.—(1) The provisions of this Ordinance shall have effect notwithstanding any law, custom or usage, and the registration of Muslim marriages shall take place only in accordance with those provisions.

(2) For the removal of doubt, it is hereby declared that the provisions of the Arbitration Act, 1940 (X of 1940), the Code of Civil Procedure, 1908 (Act V of 1908), and any other law regulating the procedure of Courts shall not apply to any Arbitration Council.

Succession.

4. In the event of the death of any son or daughter of the *propositus* before the opening of succession, the children of such son or daughter, if any, living at the time the succession opens, shall *per stirpes* receive a share equivalent to the share which such son or daughter, as the case may be, would have received if alive.

Registration of marriages.

5.—(1) Every marriage solemnized under Muslim Law shall be registered in accordance with the provisions of this Ordinance.

(2) For the purpose of registration of marriages under this Ordinance, the Union Council shall grant licences to one or more persons, to be called Nikah Registrars, but in no case shall more than one Nikah Registrar be licensed for any one Ward.

(3) Every marriage not solemnized by the Nikah Registrar shall, for the purpose of registration under this Ordinance, be reported to him by the person who has solemnized such marriage.

---

1 Substituted by the Muslim Family Laws (Amendment) Ordinance, 1961 (21 of 1961), s. 2, for "having jurisdiction in the area concerned".

(4) Whoever contravenes the provisions of subsection (3) shall be punishable with simple imprisonment for a term which may extend to three months, or with fine which may extend to one thousand rupees, or with both.

(5) The form of *nikahnama,* the registers to be maintained by Nikah Registrars, the records to be preserved by Union Councils, the manner in which marriages shall be registered and copies of *nikahnama* shall be supplied to the parties, and the fees to be charged therefor, shall be such as may be prescribed.

(6) Any person may, on payment of the prescribed fee, if any, inspect at the office of the Union Council the record preserved under subsection (5), or obtain a copy of any entry therein.

Polygamy.

6.—(1) No man, during the subsistence of an existing marriage, shall, except with the previous permission in writing of the Arbitration Council, contract another marriage, nor shall any such marriage contracted without such permission be registered under this Ordinance.

(2) An application for permission under subsection (1) shall be submitted to the Chairman in the prescribed manner, together with the prescribed fee, and shall state the reasons for the proposed marriage, and whether the consent of the existing wife or wives has been obtained thereto.

(3) On receipt of the application under subsection (2), the Chairman shall ask the applicant and his existing wife or wives each to nominate a representative, and the Arbitration Council so constituted may, if satisfied that the proposed marriage is necessary and just, grant, subject to such conditions, if any, as may be deemed fit, the permission applied for.

(4) In deciding the application the Arbitration Council shall record its reasons for the decision, and any party may, in the prescribed manner, within the prescribed period, and on payment of the prescribed fee, prefer an application for revision, in the case of West Pakistan, to the Collector and, in the case of East Pakistan, to the Sub-Divisional Officer concerned and his decision shall be final and shall not be called in question in any Court.

(5) Any man who contracts another marriage without the permission of the Arbitration Council shall–

(a) pay immediately the entire amount of the dower, whether prompt or deferred, due to the existing wife or wives, which amount, if not so paid, shall be recoverable as arrears of land revenue; and

(b) on conviction upon complaint be punishable with simple imprisonment which may extend to one year, or with fine which may extend to five thousand rupees, or with both.

7.—(1) Any man who wishes to divorce his wife shall, as soon as may be after the pronouncement of *talaq* in any form whatsoever, give the Chairman notice in writing of his having done so, and shall supply a copy thereof to the wife. Talaq.

(2) Whoever contravenes the provisions of subsection (1) shall be punishable with simple imprisonment for a term which may extend to one year or with fine which may extend to five thousand rupees or with both.

(3) Save as provided in subsection (5), a *talaq* unless revoked earlier, expressly or otherwise, shall not be effective until the expiration of ninety days from the day on which notice under subsection (1) is delivered to the Chairman.

(4) Within thirty days of the receipt of notice under subsection (1), the Chairman shall constitute an Arbitration Council for the purpose of bringing about a reconciliation between the parties, and the Arbitration Council shall take all steps necessary to bring about such reconciliation.

(5) If the wife be pregnant at the time *talaq* is pronounced, *talaq* shall not be effective until the period mentioned in subsection [1][(3)] or the pregnancy, whichever be later, ends.

(6) Nothing shall debar a wife whose marriage has been terminated by *talaq* effective under this section from re-marrying the same husband, without an intervening marriage with a third person, unless such termination is for the third time so effective.

8. Where the right to divorce has been duly delegated to the wife and she wishes to exercise that right, or where any of the parties to a marriage wishes to dissolve the marriage otherwise than by *talaq*, the provisions of section 7 shall, *mutatis mutandis* and so far as applicable, apply. Dissolution of marriage otherwise than by talaq.

9.—(1) If any husband fails to maintain his wife adequately, or where there are more wives than one, fails to maintain them equitably, the wife, or all or any of the wives, may in addition to seeking any other legal remedy available apply to the Chairman who shall constitute an Arbitration Council to determine the matter, and the Arbitration Council may issue a certificate specifying the amount which shall be paid as maintenance by the husband. Maintenance.

(2) A husband or wife may, in the prescribed manner, within the prescribed period, and on payment of the prescribed fee, prefer an application for revision of the certificate, in the case of West Pakistan, to the Collector and, in the case of East Pakistan, to the Sub-Divisional Officer concerned and his decision shall be final and shall not be called in question in any Court.

1 Substituted by the Muslim Family Laws (Second Amendment) Ordinance, 1961 (30 of 1961), S. 2 for "(2)".

(3) Any amount payable under subsection (1) or (2), if not paid in due time, shall be recoverable as arrears of land revenue.

Dower.

10. Where no details about the mode of payment of dower are specified in the *nikahnama*, or the marriage contract, the entire amount of the dower shall be presumed to be payable on demand.

Power to make rules.

11.—(1) The Provincial Government may make rules to carry into effect the purposes of this Ordinance.

(2) In making rules under this section, the Provincial Government may provide that a breach of any of the rules shall be punishable with simple imprisonment which may extend to one month, or with fine which may extend to two hundred rupees, or with both.

(3) Rules made under this section shall be published in the official Gazette, and shall thereupon have effect as if enacted in this Ordinance.

Amendment of Child Marriage Restraint Act, 1929 (XIX of 1929).

12. In the Child Marriage Restraint Act, 1929 (XIX of 1929),—

(1) in section 2,—

(a) in clause (*a*), for the word "fourteen" the word "sixteen" shall be substituted;

(b) in clause (*c*), the word "and" shall be omitted; and

(c) in clause (*d*), for the full-stop at the end a comma shall be substituted, and thereafter the following new clause (*e*) shall be added, namely:—

"(*e*) 'Union Council' means the Union Council or the Town or Union Committee constituted under the Basic Democracies Order, 1959 (P. O. No. 18 of 1959), within whose jurisdiction a child marriage is or is about to be solemnized.";

(2) section 3 shall be omitted;

(3) in section 4, for the words "twenty-one" the word "eighteen" shall be substituted;

(4) in section 9, after the words "under this Act", the words "except on a complaint made by the Union Council, or if there is no Union Council in the area, by such authority as the Provincial Government may in this behalf prescribe, and such cognizance shall in no case be taken" shall be inserted; and

(5) section 11 shall be omitted.

13. In the Dissolution of Muslim Marriages Act, 1939 (VIII of 1939), in section 2,— Amendment of the Dissolution of Muslim Marriages Act, 1939 (VIII of 1939).

(a) after clause (*ii*), the following new clause (*iia*) shall be inserted, namely:—

"(*iia*) that the husband has taken an additional wife in contravention of the provisions of the Muslim Family Laws Ordinance, 1961;"; and

(b) in clause (*vii*), for the word "fifteen" the word "sixteen" shall be substituted.

APPENDIX VIII

WEST PAKISTAN RULES UNDER THE MUSLIM FAMILY LAWS ORDINANCE, 1961

[*20th July 1961*].

No. Integ : 4-5/61.—In exercise of the powers conferred by section 11 of the Muslim Family Laws Ordinance, 1961 (VIII of 1961), the Governor of West Pakistan is pleased to make the following rules, namely :—

PRELIMINARY

1. These rules may be called the West Pakistan Rules under the Muslim Family Laws Ordinance, 1961.

2. In these rules, unless there is anything repugnant in the subject or context,—

(a) "Form" means a form appended to these rules ;

(b) "Ordinance" means the Muslim Family Laws Ordinance, 1961 (VIII of 1961) ;

(c) "Register" means a register of *nikahnamas* prescribed under rule 8 ; and

(d) "section" means a section of the Ordinance.

ARBITRATION COUNCIL

3. The Union Council which shall have jurisdiction in the matter for purposes of clause (*d*) of section 2, shall be as follows, namely :—

(a) in the case of an application for permission to contract another marriage under subsection (2) of section 6, it shall be the Union Council of the Union or Town in which the existing wife of the applicant, or where he has more wives than one, the wife with whom the applicant was married last, is residing at the time of his making the application ;

(b) in the case of a notice of *talaq* under subsection (1) of section 7, it shall be the Union Council of the Union or Town in which the wife in relation to whom *talaq* has been pronounced was residing at the time of the pronouncement of *talaq* ; and

(c) in the case of an application for maintenance under section 9, it shall be the Union Council of the Union or Town in which the wife is residing at the time of her making the application, and where application under that section is made by more than one wife, it shall be the Union Council of the Union or Town in which the wife who makes the application first is residing at the time of her making the application.

4. Where a non-Muslim has been elected as Chairman of a Union Council, the Council shall, as soon as may be, elect one of its Muslim members as Chairman for the purposes of the Ordinance, in the manner prescribed for the election of a Chairman of a Union Council.

5.—(1) All proceedings before an Arbitration Council shall be held *in camera*, unless the Chairman otherwise directs with the consent of all the parties.

(2) The Chairman shall conduct the proceedings of an Arbitration Council as expeditiously as possible.

(3) Subject to the provisions of sub-rule (4), such proceedings shall not be vitiated by reason of a vacancy in the Arbitration Council, whether on account of failure of any person to nominate a representative or otherwise.

(4) Where a vacancy arises otherwise than through failure to make a nomination, the Chairman shall require a fresh nomination.

(5) No party to proceedings before an Arbitration Council shall be a member of the Arbitration Council.

(6) All decisions of the Arbitration Council shall be taken by majority, and where no decision can be so taken, the decision of the Chairman shall be the decision of the Arbitration Council.

(7) A copy of the decision of the Arbitration Council, duly attested by the Chairman, shall be furnished free of cost to each of the parties to the proceedings.

6. (1) Within seven days of receiving an application under subsection (2) of section 6 or under subsection (1) of section 9, or a notice under subsection (1) of section 7, the Chairman shall, by order in writing, call upon each of the parties to nominate his or her representative, and each such party shall, within seven days of receiving the order, nominate in writing a representative and deliver the nomination to the Chairman or send it to him by registered post.

(2) Where a representative nominated by a party is, by reason of illness or otherwise, unable to attend the meetings of the Arbitration Council, or wilfully absents himself from such

meeting, or has lost the confidence of the party, the party may, with the previous permission in writing of the Chairman, revoke the nomination and make, within such time as the Chairman may allow, a fresh nomination.

(3) Where a fresh nomination is made under sub-rule (2), it shall not be necessary to commence the proceedings before the Arbitration Council *de novo*, unless the Chairman, for reasons to be recorded in writing, directs otherwise.

REGISTRATION OF MARRIAGES

7.—(1) Any person competent to solemnize a marriage under Muslim Law may apply to the Union Council for the grant of a licence to act as Nikah Registrar under section 5.

(2) If the Union Council, after making such enquiries as it may consider necessary, is satisfied that the applicant is a fit and proper person for the grant of a licence, it may, subject to the conditions specified therein, grant a licence to him in Form I.

(3) A licence granted under this rule shall be permanent and shall be revocable only for the contravention of any of the conditions of a licence granted under this rule.

(4) If any person to whom a licence has been granted under this rule contravenes any of the conditions of such licence, he shall be punishable with simple imprisonment for a term which may extend to one month, or with fine which may extend to two hundred rupees, or with both.

8.—(1) The Union Council shall, on payment of such cost as may be determined by the Provincial Government, supply to every Nikah Registrar a bound register of *nikahnamas* in Form II, and a seal bearing the inscription "The seal of the Nikhah Registrar of Ward *(*x*) . . . . (*y*) . . . . . ."

(2) Each register shall contain fifty leaves, consecutively numbered, each leaf having a *nikahnama*, in quadruplicate, and the number of leaves shall be certified by the Chairman.

(3) Notwithstanding the payment of cost under sub-rule (1), the register and the seal shall remain the property of the Union Council.

9.—(1) For the registration of a marriage registered under section 5, the Nikah Registrar shall be paid by the bridegroom or his representative a registration fee of two rupees, or when the dower exceeds two thousand rupees, a fee calculated at the rate of one rupee for every thousand or part of thousand rupees of such dower, subject to a maximum fee of twenty rupees.

---

*For (*x*) insert the name or number of the Ward, and for (*y*) insert name of the Union Council.

(2) Of the fees received under sub-rule (1), the Nikah Registrar shall retain for himself eighty per cent. and shall pay the remaining twenty per cent. to the Union Council.

(3) Where dower consists of property other than money, or partly of such property and partly of money, the valuation of the property shall, for purposes of fees under sub-rule (1), be the valuation as settled between the parties to the marriage.

10.—(1) The Nikah Registrar shall, in the case of a marriage solemnized by him, fill in Form II, in quardruplicate in the register, the persons, whose signatures are required in the Form, shall then sign, and the Nikah Registrar shall then affix his signature and seal thereto, and keep the original intact in the register.

(2) The duplicate and triplicate of the *nikahnama* filled in as aforesaid, shall be supplied to the bride and the bridegroom, respectively, on payment of fifty paisa each, and the quadruplicate shall be forwarded to the Union Council

(3) If any person required by this rule to sign the register refuses so to sign, he shall be punishable with simple imprisonment for a term which may extend to one month, or with fine which may extend to two hundred rupees, or with both.

11.—(1) Where a marriage is solemnized in Pakistan by a person other than the Nikah Registrar, such person shall fill in Form II, to be had loose on payment of such price as may be determined by the Provincial Government, the persons whose signatures are required in the Form shall then sign, and the person solemnizing the marriage shall then affix his signature to the Form and ensure delivery, as expeditiously as possible, of the same together with the registration fee to the Nikah Registrar of the Ward where the marriage is solemnized.

(2) If any person required by this rule to sign the Form refuses so to sign, he shall be punishable with simple imprisonment for a term which may extend to one month, or with fine which may extend to two hundred rupees, or with both.

12.—(1) In the case of a marriage solemnized outside Pakistan, by a person who is a citizen of Pakistan, such person shall ensure delivery of Form II, filled in, in accordance with the provisions of rule 11, together with the registration fee, to the consular officer of Pakistan in or for the country in which the marriage is solemnized, for onward transmission to the Nikah Registrar of the Ward of which the bride is a permanent resident, and in case the bride is not a citizen of Pakistan, the Nikah Registrar of the Ward of which the bridegroom is such resident.

(2) In the case of a marriage solemnized outside Pakistan by a person who is not a citizen of Pakistan, the bridegroom, and where only the bride is such citizen, the bride, shall for purposes of

filling in, as far as may be, Form II, be deemed to be the person who has solemnized the marriage under sub-rule (1).

13. On receipt of Form II under rule 11 or rule 12, the Nikah Registrar shall proceed in the manner provided in rule 10 as if the marriage had been solemnized by him :

Provided that, except where the marriage has been solemnized within his jurisdiction, it shall not be necessary for the Nikah Registrar to obtain the signatures of the necessary persons.

POLYGAMY

14. In considering whether another proposed marriage is just and necessary during the continuance of an existing marriage the Arbitration Council may, without prejudice to its general powers to consider what is just and necessary, have regard to such circumstances, as the following amongst others:—

Sterility, physical infirmity, physical unfitness for the conjugal relation, wilful avoidance of a decree for restitution of conjugal rights, or insanity on the part of an existing wife.

15. An application under subsection (1) of section 6 for permission to contract another marriage during the subsistence of an existing marriage shall be in writing, shall state whether the consent of the existing wife or wives has been obtained thereto, shall contain a brief statement of the grounds on which the new marriage is alleged to be just and necessary, shall bear the signature of the applicant, and shall be accompanied by a fee of one hundred rupees.

REVISION

16.—(1) An application for the revision of a decision of an Arbitration Council, under subsection (4) of section 6, or of a certificate under subsection (2) of section 9, shall be preferred within thirty days of the decision or of the issue of the certificate, as the case may be, and shall be accompanied by a fee of two rupees.

(2) The application shall be in writing, set out the grounds on which the applicant seeks to have the decision or the certificate revised, and shall bear the signature of the applicant.

RECORDS AND THEIR INSPECTION, ETC.

17. As soon as may be after the Arbitration Council has given its decision under rule 6, the record of the proceedings, before it in which such decision has been given shall be forwarded by the Chairman to the office of the Union Council, where it shall be preserved for a period of five years from the date of the decision.

18.—(1) The quadruplicate of the *nikahnama* forwarded by Nikah Registrar under sub-rule (2) of rule 10 shall be preserved in the office of the Union Council until such time as the register containing the originals is, on being completed, deposited by the Nikah Registrar in such office.

(2) The completed register so received shall be preserved permanently.

(3) In the office of the Union Council there shall be prepared and maintained an index of the contents of every register, and every entry in such index shall be made, so far as practicable, immediately after the Nikah Registrar has made an entry in the register.

(4) The aforesaid index shall contain the name, place of residence and father's name of each party to every marriage registered within the Union or Town, as the case may be, and the dates of the marriage and registration.

19.—(1) Subject to the previous payment of the fees prescribed in sub-rules (2) and (3), the index and the register shall, at all reasonable times, be open to inspection at the office of the Union Council by any person applying to inspect the same and copies of entries in the index and the register, duly signed and sealed by the Chairman, shall be given to all persons applying for such copies.

(2) The fee for the inspection of an index or register shall be fifty paisa.

(3) The fee for a certified copy of all or any of the entries relating to a marriage shall be—

(a) for those in an index ... Fifty paisa.

(b) for those in a register ... Two rupees.

(4) Fees payable under this rule shall be credited to the Union Council.

PAYMENT OF FEES

20. Except fees payable to the Nikah Registrar, which shall be paid in cash, all fees payable under these rules shall be paid in non-judicial stamps.

COMPLAINTS

21. No Court shall take cognizance of any offence under the Ordinance or these rules save on a complaint in writing by the Union Council, stating the facts constituting the offence.

FORM I

(*See Rule 7*)

Licence granted in pursuance of section 5 (2) of the Muslim Family Laws Ordinance (VIII of 1961)

In pursuance of subsection (2) of section 5 of the Muslim Family Laws Ordinance, 1961 (VIII of 1961), the *Union Council/ Union Committee/Town Committee of.................................. in the district of.....................hereby grants this.................... day of.....................19.....................to Mr........................ son of...................................resident of....................... this licence, subject to the conditions hereunder specified, to be from the said date the Nikah Registrar for the following *Ward/ Wards :—

(1) Ward........................

(2) Ward........................

(3) Ward........................

(4) Ward........................

Signature of the Chairman.

Seal

CONDITIONS

1. This licence is not transferable.

2. This licence is revocable for breach of any of the provisions of the Muslim Family Laws Ordinance, 1961 (VIII of 1961), or the rules made thereunder or of any condition of this licence.

3. The registers and seal supplied to the Nikah Registrar shall be returnable to the *Union Council/Union Committee/ Town Committee without refund of cost, when this licence expires or is revoked.

4. The Nikah Registrar shall not put the seal supplied to him to any improper use.

5. Such other conditions, if any, as may be specified by the Provincial Government.

---

*Strike out what is inapplicable.

APPENDIX IX

EAST PAKISTAN MUSLIM FAMILY LAWS RULES, 1961

[*11th July 1961*].

No. 658 Judl. IV/1A-2/61.—10th July 1961.—In exercise of the powers conferred by section 11 of the Muslim Family Laws Ordinance, 1961 (VIII of 1961), the Governor is pleased to make the following rules, namely :—

PRELIMINARY

1. These rules may be called the East Pakistan Muslim Family Laws Rules, 1961.

2. In these rules, unless there is anything repugnant in the subject or context,—

(a) "Form" means a form appended to these rules ;

(b) "Local area" means the area under the jurisdiction of a Union Council ,

(c) "Ordinance" means the Muslim Family Laws Ordinance, 1961 (VIII of 1961) ;

(d) "Section" means a section of the Ordinance ; and

(e) "Union Council" has the same meaning as defined in the Ordinance.

3. The Union Council which shall have jurisdiction in the matter for the purposes of clause (*d*) of section 2, shall be as follows, namely :—

(a) in the case of an application under subsection (2) of section 6, it shall be the Union Council of the Union or Town in which the existing wife, or where there are more wives than one, the wife with whom the applicant was married last, is residing at the time of his making the application ;

(b) in the case of a notice of *talaq* under subsection (1) of section 7, it shall be the Union Council of the Union or Town in which the wife in relation to whom *talaq* has been pronounced was residing at the time of the pronouncement of *talaq* ; and

(c) in the case of an application under section 9, it shall be the Union Council of the Union or Town in which the wife is residing at the time of her making the application, and where application under that section is made by more than one wife, it shall be the Union Council of the Union or Town in which the wife who makes the application first is residing at the time of her making the application.

4.—(1) Where a non-Muslim has been elected as Chairman of a Union Council, the Council shall, as soon as may be, elect one of its Muslim Members as Chairman for the purposes of the Ordinance.

(2) Any party to the proceedings before an Arbitration Council, who considers the Chairman to be interested in favour of the other party, may, with reasons to be recorded in writing, apply for the appointment of a different Chairman, to the Sub-divisional Officer, who on behalf of the Provincial Government may, if he thinks fit appoint any other member of that Council as Chairman for the purposes of the Ordinance. The Sub-divisional Officer shall stay the proceedings before the Arbitration Council until he has disposed of such application.

ARBITRATION COUNCILS

5.—(1) The Chairman shall conduct the proceedings of an Arbitration Council as expeditiously as possible.

(2) Such proceedings shall not be vitiated by reasons of a vacancy in the Arbitration Council, whether on account of failure of any person to nominate a representative or otherwise.

(3) Where a vacancy arises otherwise than through failure to make a nomination the Chairman shall require a fresh nomination.

(4) No party to proceedings before an Arbitration Council shall be a member of the Arbitration Council.

(5) All decisions of the Arbitration Council shall be taken by majority, and where no decision can be so taken, the decision of the Chairman shall be the decision of the Arbitration Council.

6.—(1) Within seven days of receiving an application under subsection (2) of section 6 or under subsection (1) of section 9, or a notice under subsection (1) of section 7, the Chairman shall, by order in writing, call upon each of the parties to nominate his or her representative, and each such party shall, within seven days of receiving the order, nominate in writing a representative and deliver the nomination to the Chairman or send it to him by registered post.

(2) Where a representative nominated by a party dies, or is, by reason of illness or otherwise, unable to attend the meetings of the Arbitration Council, or wilfully absents himself from such meetings, or has lost the confidence of the party, the party may, with the previous permission in writing of the Chairman, revoke

the nomination and make, within such time as the Chairman may allow, a fresh nomination.

(3) Where a fresh nomination is made under sub-rule (2), it shall not be necessary to commence the proceedings before the Arbitration Council *de novo* unless the Chairman, for reasons to be recorded in writing, directs otherwise.

REGISTRATION OF MARRIAGES

7.—(1) Any person, who is not below 25 years of age and who possesses sufficient acquaintance with the Arabic language and the Muslim Laws of Marriage and Divorce and who is of good character, may apply in writing to the Union Council for the grant of a licence to act as Nikah Registrar under section 5. Every such application shall be accompanied by two certificates that he possesses sufficient acquaintance with the Arabic language and the Muslim Laws of Marriage and Divorce, signed by two Muslim gentlemen of respectability and position, and two certificates of good character from persons of respectability and position, and shall contain the following particulars :—

(a) Name and usual signature of the applicant, date of application and address in full—

(b) Age of applicant—

(c) Profession or present employment of the applicant with present salary or pension, if any—

(d) Father's name, profession and address—

(e) Present family residence of the applicant—

(f) Whether the applicant has a masonry house for Office—

(g) If previously employed under Government, details of past service of the applicant ; and if ever dismissed from any post, particulars of the fact—

(h) Names and addresses of the persons from whom Certificates are obtained and attached to the application—

(i) Whether the applicant is acquainted with Arabic, Persian, Urdu, Bengali or English—

And

(j) Whether the applicant is acquainted with Muslim Laws and holds any certificate from any Government or Private Madrassah (stating its name).

(2) Every such application shall be considered at a meeting of the Union Council ; and if the Union Council, after making such

enquiries as it may consider necessary, is satisfied that the applicant is a fit and proper person for the grant of a licence, it may grant a licence to him in Form I, subject to the conditions specified therein. In granting a licence, the Union Council shall give preference to applicants having *Alim*, *Fazil* or Title Certificates from a recognised Madrassah :

Provided that, in the case of a person who at the time of the commencement of Ordinance was already exercising the powers of Muhammadan Registrar under the Bengal Muhammadan Marriages and Divorces Registration Act, 1876, the Chairman of all such Union Councils over which such Muhammadan Registrar was exercising such jurisdiction, may grant him licence to perform the duties of Nikah Registrar under the Ordinance within their respective Unions, if he so applies.

(3) A Nikah Registrar shall pursue his avocation, as such, from a fixed place within his jurisdiction easily accessible to the residents of the local area.

(4) Leave may be granted to the Nikah Registrars by the Chairman of the Union Council who may issue a temporary licence to a person having the requisite qualifications under sub-rule (1), only for the period of the absence on leave of the permanent incumbent :

Provided that, in the case of a Nikah Registrar who has been granted licence to act as Nikah Registrar by more than one Union Councils, leave may be granted to such Nikah Registrar by the Sub-divisional Officer concerned, or in his absence, by the Circle Officer.

(5) A licence granted under this rule shall be permanent and revocable only when the Nikah Registrar contravenes any of the conditions of the licence granted under this rule, or is found to be guilty of a breach of any of the provisions of the rule, or of any misconduct. The Union Council shall have the power to revoke the licence only after regular proceedings in this behalf. Any Nikah Registrar aggrieved by any such order of revocation may prefer an appeal to the Provincial Government within 30 days from the date of the order of revocation.

(6) If any Nikah Registrar to whom a licence has been granted contravenes any of the conditions of such licence, he shall be punishable with simple imprisonment for a term which may extend to one month, or with fine which may extend to two hundred rupees or with both :

Provided that no prosecution under the sub-rule shall be initiated except upon a complaint from the Chairman of the Union Council concerned.

8.—(1) The Union Council shall, on payment of such cost as may be determined by the Provincial Government, supply to every Nikah Registrar a bound register of *nikahnamas* in Form II, and a seal bearing the inscription "The seal of the Nikah Registrar of Ward............*(*x*)..........................in.........................**(*y*) ...."

(2) Each register shall contain fifty leaves, consecutively numbered, each leaf having a *nikahnama*, in quadruplicate, and the number of leaves shall be certified by the Chairman.

(3) Notwithstanding the payment of cost under sub-rule (1), the register and the real shall remain the property of the Union Council.

9.—(1) For the registration of a marriage registered under section 5, the Nikah Registrar shall be paid by the bridegroom or his representative a registration fee of two rupees, or when the dower exceeds two thousand rupees, a fee calculated at the rate of one rupee for every thousand or part of thousand rupees of such dower, subject to a maximum fee of twenty rupees.

(2) Of the fees received under sub-rule (1), the Nikah Registrar shall retain for himself eighty per cent. and shall pay the remaining twenty per cent. to the Union Council.

(3) Where dower consists of property other than money, or partly of such property and partly of money, the valuation of the property shall, for purposes of fees under sub-rule (1), be the valuation as settled between the parties to the marriage.

(4) An extra commission fee of Rs. 4 shall be payable to a Nikah Registrar, for himself for visiting any place other than his office for the registration of a marriage, in addition to a travelling allowance at the rate of 50 Paisa per mile for the distance actually travelled.

10.—(1) The Nikah Registrar shall, in the case of a marriage solemnized by him, fill in Form II, in quadruplicate, in the register, the persons whose signatures are required in the Form shall then sign, and the Nikah Registrar shall then affix his signature and seal thereto, and keep the original intact in the register :

Provided that in the case of an illiterate person his thumb-impression, and not any other mark, shall be taken, and his name shall be recorded at length by a person who shall also sign his name in attestation that the thumb-impression was affixed in his presence.

(2) The duplicate and triplicate of the *nikahnama* filled in as aforesaid, shall be supplied to the bride and the bridegroom respectively, on payment of fifty paisa each, and the quadruplicate shall be forwarded to the Union Council.

(3) If any person required by this rule to sign the register refuses so to sign, he shall be punishable with simple imprisonment

**For (x) insert the name or number of the Ward.

for a term which may extend to one month, or with fine which may extend to two hundred rupees, or with both.

11.—(1) Where a marriage is solemnized in Pakistan by a person other than the Nikah Registrar, such person shall fill in Form II, to be had loose on payment of such price as may be determined by the Provincial Government, the persons whose signatures are required in the Form shall then sign, and the person solemnizing the marriage shall then affix his signature to the Form and ensure delivery, as expeditiously as possible, of the same together with the registration fee to the Nikah Registrar of the Ward where the marriage is solemnized.

(2) If any person required by this rule to sign the register refuses so to sign, he shall be punishable with simple imprisonment for a term which may extend to one month, or with fine which may extend to two hundred rupees, or with both.

12.—(1) In the case of a marriage solemnized outside Pakistan by a person who is a citizen of Pakistan, such person shall ensure delivery of Form II, filled in, in accordance with the provisions of rule 10 to the consular officer of Pakistan in or for the country in which the marriage is solemnized, for onward transmission together with the registration fee to the Nikah Registrar of the Ward of which the bride is a permanent resident, and in case the bride is not a citizen of Pakistan, the Nikah Registrar of the Ward of which the bridegroom is such resident.

(2) In the case of a marriage solemnized outside Pakistan by a person who is not a citizen of Pakistan, the bridegroom, and where only the bride is such citizen, the bride, shall for purposes of filling in, as far as may be, Form II, be deemed to be the person who has solemnized the marriage under sub-rule (1).

13. On receipt of Form II under rule 11 or rule 12, the Nikah Registrar shall proceed in the manner provided in rule 10, as if the marriage had been solemnized by him :

Provided that, except where the marriage has been solemnized within his jurisdiction, it shall not be necessary for the Nikah Ragistrar to obtain the signatures of the necessary persons.

POLYGAMY

14. In considering whether another proposed marriage is just and necessary during the continuance of an existing marriage, the Arbitration Council may, without prejudice to its general powers to consider what is just and necessary, have regard to such circumstances, as the following amongst others :

Sterility, physical infirmity, physical unfitness for the conjugal relation, wilful avoidance of a decree for restitution of conjugal rights, or insanity,

on the part of an existing wife.

15. An application under subsection (1) of section 6 for permission to contract another marriage during the subsistence of an existing marriage shall be in writing, shall state whether the consent of the existing wife or wives has been obtained thereto, shall contain a brief statement of the grounds on which the new marriage is alleged to be just and necessary, shall bear the signature of the applicant, and shall be accompanied by a fee of twenty-five rupees.

REVISION

16.—(1) An application for the revision of decision of an Arbitration Council, under subsection (4) of section 6, or of a certificate under subsection (2) of section 9 shall be preferred within thirty days of the decision or of the issue of the certificate, as the case may be, and shall be accompanied by a fee of two rupees.

(2) The application shall be in writing, set out the grounds on which the applicant seeks to have the decision or the certificate revised, and shall bear the signature of the applicant.

PROCEEDINGS 'IN CAMERA'

17. All proceedings before an Arbitration Council shall be held *in camera* unless the Chairman otherwise directs.

RECORDS AND THEIR INSPECTION, ETC.

18.—(1) The quadruplicate *nikahnama* forwarded by the Nikah Registrar under sub-rule (2) of rule 10 shall be preserved in the office of the Union Council until such time as the register containing the originals is, on being completed, deposited by the Nikah Registrar in such office.

(2) The completed register so received shall be preserved permanently.

(3) In the office of the Union Council there shall be prepared and maintained an index of the contents of every register, and every entry in such index shall be made, so far as practicable, immediately after the Nikah Registrar has made an entry in the register.

(4) The aforesaid index shall contain the name, place of residence and father's name of each party to every marriage, and the dates of the marriage and registration.

(5) The Sub-divisional Officer or Circle Officer-in-charge of the local area shall inspect and audit the records and accounts of the Nikah Registrar from time to time in course of their visits.

19.—(1) Subject to the previous payment of the fees prescribed in sub-rules (2) and (3), the index and the register shall at all reasonable times, be open to inspection at the office of the Union Council by any person applying to inspect the same and copies of entries in the index and the register, duly signed and sealed by the Chairman, shall be given to all persons applying for such copies.

(2) The fee for the inspection of an index or register shall be fifty Paisa.

(3) The fee for a certified copy of all or any of the entries relating to a marriage shall be—

(a) for those in an index ... 50 Paisa.

(b) for those in a register ... Two rupees.

(4) Fees payable under this rule shall be credited to the Union Council.

PAYMENT OF FEES

20. All fees payable under these rules, except under rule 16, shall be paid in cash on obtaining proper receipt.

FORM I

(*See Rule 7*)

Licence granted in pursuance of section 5 (2) of the Muslim Family Laws Ordinance, 1961 (VIII of 1961)

In pursuance of subsection (2) of section 5 of the Muslim Family Laws Ordinance, 1961 (VIII of 1961), the *Union Council/ Union Committee/Town Committee of.................................
in the district of..
hereby grants this...............................day of........................
19..........................to Mr..
son of..resident of....................
......................................this licence to be from the said date the Nikah Registrar for the following *Ward/Wards :

(1) Ward...................

(2) Ward...................

(3) Ward...................

(4) Ward...................

....

Seal *Signature of the Chairman.*

CONDITIONS

1. This licence is not transferable.

*Strike out what is inapplicable.

2. This licence is revocable for breach of any of the provisions of the Muslim Family Laws Ordinance, 1961 (VIII of 1961), or the rules made thereunder or of any condition of this licence.

3. The registers and seal supplied to the Nikah Registrar shall be returnable to the Union Council, without refund of cost, when this licence expires or is revoked.

4. The Nikah Registrar shall not put the seal supplied to him to any improper use.

5. Such other conditions, if any, as may be specified by the Provincial Government.

FORM II

(*See Rules 8, 10, 11 and 12*)

Form of Nikahnama as prescribed by rule 8 of the East Pakistan Muslim Family Laws Rules, 1961

(1) Name of the Ward..................Town/Union.............. Tehsil/Thana.....................and District.................... in which the marriage took place.

(2) Name of the bridegroom and his father, with their respective residences :

....

(3) Age of the bridegroom.. ....

(4) The names of the bride and her father, with their respective residences :

....

(5) Whether the bride is a maiden, a widow or a divorcee...... ....

(6) Age of the bride.............................

(7) Name of Vakil, if any, appointed by the bride, his father's name and his residence :

....

(8) The names of the witnesses to the appointment of the bride's Vakil with their fathers' names, their residences and their relationship with the bride :

(1) ....

(2) ....

(9) Name of the Vakil, if any, appointed by the bridegroom, his father's name and his residence :

....

(10) The names of the witnesses to the appointment of the bridegroom's Vakil, with their father's names and their residences :

(1) ....

(2) ....

(11) Names of the witnesses to the marriage, their fathers' names and their residences :

(1) ....

(2) ....

(12) Date on which the marriage was contracted................

(13) Amount of dower :..................

(14) How much of the dower is *mu'ajjal* (prompt) and how much *mu'wajjal* (deffered)...

(15) Whether any portion of the dower was paid at the time of marriage, if so, how much :

....

(16) Whether any property was given in lieu of the whole or any portion of the dower with specification of the same and its valuation agreed to between the parties :

....

(17) Special conditions, if any :

....

(18) Whether the husband has delegated the power of divorce to the wife. If so, under what conditions :

....

(19) Whether the husband's right of divorce is in any way curtailed :

....

(20) Whether any document was drawn up at the time of marriage relating to dower, maintenance, etc. If so, contents thereof in brief :

....

(21) Whether the bridegroom has any existing wife, and, if so, whether he has secured the permission of the Arbitration

Council under the Muslim Family Laws Ordinance, 1961, to contract another marriage.

....

(22) Number and date of the communication conveying to the bridegroom the permission of the Arbitration Council to contract another marriage :

....

(23) Name and address of the person by whom the marriage was solemnized and his father.

....

(24) Date of registration of marriage..............................

(25) Registration fee paid :

Signature of the bridegroom or his Vakil :

....

Signature of the witness to be appointed of bridegroom's Vakil :

....

Signature of the bride :

....

Signature of the Vakil of the bride :

....

Signature of the witness to be appointed of the bride's Vakil :

....

Signatures of the witnesses to the marriage :

(1) ....

(2) ....

Signature of the person who solemnized the marriage :

....

....

Signature and seal of the Nikah Registrar :

....

Seal

APPENDIX X

THE WEST PAKISTAN MUSLIM PERSONAL LAW (SHARIAT) APPLICATION ACT, 1962

WEST PAKISTAN ACT V OF 1962[1]

[*31st December 1962*]

An Act to consolidate and amend the provisions for the application of Muslim Personal Law (Shariat) in the Province of West Pakistan.

Preamble.

WHEREAS it is expedient to consolidate and amend the provisions for the application of Muslim Personal Law (Shariat) in the Province of West Pakistan;

It is hereby enacted as follows:—

Short title and extent.

1.—(1) This Act may be called the West Pakistan Muslim Personal Law (Shariat) Application Act, 1962.

(2) It extends to the whole of the Province of West Pakistan except the Tribal Areas.

Application of the Muslim Personal Law.

2. Notwithstanding any custom or usage, in all questions regarding succession (whether testate or intestate), special property of females, betrothal, marriage, divorce, dower, adoption, guardianship, minority, legitimacy or bastardy, family relations, wills, legacies, gifts, religious usages or institutions, including *waqfs*, trusts and trust properties, the rule of decision, subject to the provisions of any enactment for the time being in force, shall be the Muslim Personal Law (Shariat) in cases where the parties are Muslims.

Termination of limited estates under Customary Law.

[2][3. The limited estates in respect of immovable property held by Muslim females under the Customary Law are hereby terminated:

Provided that nothing herein contained shall apply to any such estate saved by any enactment, repealed by this Act, and the estates so excepted shall continue to be governed by that enactment, notwithstanding its repeal by this Act.]

---

1 For Statement of Objects and Reasons; see Gazette of West Pakistan 1962, Extraordinary, pp. 4275-4276.

2 Subs. by the West Pakistan Ordinance No. XXXIX of 1963, s. 2, which should be deemed always to have been so substituted.

4. Where a will providing for more than one legatee succeeding to the testator's property one after the other is operative at the commencement of this Act, its further operation shall cease upon the death of the legatee-in-enjoyment.

Further operation of certain wills shall cease on the death of legatee-in-enjoyment.

5. The life estate terminated under section 3 or the property in respect of which the further operation of a will has ceased under section 4 shall devolve upon such persons as would have been entitled to succeed under the Muslim Personal Law (Shariat) upon the death of the last full owner or the testator as though he had died intestate; and if any such heir has died in the meantime, his share shall devolve in accordance with Shariat on such persons as would have succeeded him, if he had died immediately after the termination of the life estate or the death of the said legatee:

Devolution of property on the termination of life estate and certain wills.

Provided that the share to which a Muslim female holding limited estate under Customary Law would have been entitled under the Muslim Personal Law (Shariat) upon the death of the last full owner shall devolve on her.

6. Save as expressly provided by the provisions of sections 3, 4 and 5, this Act shall have no retrospective operation.

Sections 3, 4 and 5 only to be retrospective.

7.—(1) The following enactments are hereby repealed:—

Repeal and savings.

(a) The Punjab Limitation (Custom) Act, 1920;

(b) The Punjab Custom (Power to Contest) Act, 1920;

(c) The Muslim Personal Law (Shariat) Application Act, 1937, in its application to West Pakistan;

(d) The North-West Frontier Province Muslim Personal Law (Shariat) Application Act, 1935;

(e) The Punjab Muslim Personal Law (Shariat) Application Act, 1948;

(f) The Muslim Personal Law (Shariat) Application (Sind Amendment) Act, 1950;

(g) The Bahawalpur State Shariat (Muslim Personal Law) Application Act, 1951;

(h) The Khairpur State Muslim Female Inheritance (Removal of Customs) Act, 1952;

[1][(2) * * * *]

---

1 Omitted by the West Pakistan Act, XXVIII of 1964, s. 2.

INDEX

557—572

INDEX

ACKNOWLEDGMENT—
capacity to acknowledge, pp., 196, 197.
definition, conditions, and legal effect, pp. 195, 196.
effect of, not defeated by child's denial, p. 207
need not be expressed in the case of a child, p. 191.
of a child by a married woman, pp. 204, 205.
of other than filial relationship, pp. 205, 206.
of paternity produces all the effects of natural paternity, pp. 198, 199.
of a child affects other persons, p. 207,
establishes right of inheritance in the mother, pp. 191, 192.
of marriage, p. 260.
of *nasab* under the Shiah Law, p. 202.
of a child by a widow, p. 201.
of a wife, pp. 206.
of a husband, p. 208.
of *Talak*, p. 439.
Shiah rules, pp. 185, 202, 203, 205, 206, 209.
the effect of contradictory, as to legitimacy, p. 208.

ACTS—
IV of 1793, p. 16.
XI of 1793, p. 27.
V of 1843, p. 65.
XXI of 1850, pp. 14, 82, 233.
XL of 1858, pp. 236, 494.
XXVII of 1860, p. 37.
IX of 1861, p. 236.
XXI of 1866, p. 344.
XIV of 1869, p. 17.
I of 1872, p. 88.
IV of 1872, p. 17.
XV of 1872, p. 162.
III of 1873, p. 17.
IX of 1875, p. 210, 236, 493, 494.
XX of 1875, p. 17.
I of 1876, p. 258.
XVIII of 1876, p. 17.
IV of 1877, p. 17.
IX of 1880, p. 496.
V of 1881, pp. 35, 41.
XII of 1887, p. 16.
XI of 1887, p. 17.
VII of 1889, p. 42.
VIII of 1890, pp. 229, 236, 494, 498, 506.
V of 1908, p. 383.
IX of 1908, p. 416.
XXXIX of 1925, p. 42.
XXVI of 1937, p. 17.
VIII of 1939, pp. 220, 221, 333, 338, 342, 343, 350, 353, 374, 434, 479, 480, 481, 483, 489, 495.
X of 1940, p. 376.
VIII of 1961 (Ordinance), pp. 210, 434, 435, 478.
V of 1962, p. 17.
XXXIX of 1963 (Ordinance), p. 17.

AFFINITY—*See* MARRIAGE.
illicit connection amounts to, p. 248.
prohibitions on the ground of, p. 248.
Shiah rules, p. 355.

AGE—
of discretion, p. 245.

AHL-UL-ITIZAL—See M'UTAZALAS.

AKHBARIS—
doctrines of, p. 358.
marriage with a non-Moslemah, p. 252.
temporary marriages among, p. 358.

ALLEGIANCE—
difference of, affects succession when country different, p. 84.

APOSTASY—
a bar to the exercise of *hizanat*, p. 228.
effect of, on the status of marriage, pp. 344, 353.
no bar to succession under Act XXI of 1850, pp. 82, 83.
of the father, p. 215.
rules as to, under the Shiah Law, pp. 114, 115.
succession to property acquired after, pp. 82, 115, 116.

APOSTATE—
not entitled to the custody of a Moslem child, pp. 215, 228.
right of succession of an, pp. 82, 114.

'ASABAH—
'Asabah-be-nafsihi (Residuaries in their own right), p. 49.
'Asabat-un-Nasabiye (Residuaries by the tie of blood), p. 48.
'Asabat-us-Sababiye (Residuaries for special cause), p. 64.
by *wala*, p. 63.
different sections of, p, 49.
his right to guardianship, p. 228.
in another's right, p. 50.
Maliki and Shaf'ei rules, p. 89.
preference to propinquity, p. 52.
proprio jure, p. 49.
together with others, p. 50.

ASSETS—
of deceased, decree against, pp. 36, 37, 41.

ASUBAT—
established by *wala*, pp. 63, 64.
not recognised among the Shias, p. 94.
recognised among the Sunnis, p. 48.

AUL—
its meaning among the Sunnis, p. 69.
not recognised among Shias, pp. 69.
recognised by the Hanafis, p. 93.
when it takes place, p. 69.

BAIT-UL-MAL—
for the benefit of all the Mussulmans, p. 132.
foundlings supported from the, pp. 132, 238—239.
its four departments, p. 132.
revenues of, how spent, pp. 132—133.

BEQUESTS—
to be paid after discharge of debts, p. 35.

BORAHS—
how ruled, p. 123.

BROTHER—
consanguine, under Maliki Law, p. 91.
consanguine, succession under Hanafi Law, pp. 49, 51.
full, by whom excluded under Hanafi Law, p. 80.
full, a residuary under the Sunni Law, after lineal male ascendants and descendants, p. 49.
half, by the father, a residuary after full, p. 49.
with mother, his share, under Maliki Law, p. 49.
by whom excluded, under Maliki Law, pp. 89, 91.

BROTHER—(*concld.*)
by whom excluded, under Hanafi Law, p. 50.
under Shiah Law, excluded by all lineal descendants and immediate, ascendants, pp. 94, 104.
on the mother's side his share, p. 107.
with a sister on same side shares equally, p. 107.
brother's descendants prohibited in marriage, p. 248.
uterine, succession under Hanafi Law, p. 53.

CHILD—
a disavowed, pp. 52, 117, 193.
charge of—See *Hizanat*.
custody of, p. 222.
follows domicile of father, p. 138.
illegitimate does not succeed under Shiah Law, p. 177.
illegitimate, inherits under Sunni Law, from mother and maternal relations, p. 118.
its right to succession, pp. 49, 54, 94, 102.
like a child of imprecation, p. 53.
once acknowledged cannot be denied, pp. 176, 177, 200, 202.
of imprecation succeeds from mother and maternal relations, p. 118.
paternity of, born of an invalid union, pp. 170, 171, 180.
posthumous, inherits under what circumstances, pp. 70, 71.
under the Shiah Law, excludes from inheritance all other heirs excepting parents, pp. 72, 94, 95.

CLAIM—
to joint estate, p. 26.
to the custody of children, p. 222.
to the custody of foundlings, p. 239.

COMMON ACCIDENT—
persons perishing in a, pp. 71, 93.

COMPULSION—
in marriage invalidates contract, pp. 245, 323, 332, 343.
in *Talak* invalidates the divorce, Shiah rules, p. 438.
Sunni doctrine, p. 439.

CONDITIONS—
examples of lawful, pp. 277, 278.
illegal, p. 284.
of marriage, pp. 245, 284.
unlawful, pp. 280, 285.
unlawful, do not invalidate marriage, pp. 250, 285.
what are lawful, pp. 284, 287.

CONSANGUINITY—
disabilities to marriage springing from, pp. 247, 248.
rights of, Shiah rules, p. 98.

CONSENT—
by conduct, p. 275.
Hanafi rules, pp. 263, 265.
laughter in ridicule no consent, p. 272.
Maliki and Shaf'ei doctrines, p. 265.
may be express or implied, p. 271.
nature of, when proposal in writing, p. 276.
obtained by compulsion, p. 273.
of a woman *in extremis*, p. 272.
Shiah doctrines, p. 263.
smiling may amount to, p. 272.
the time it should be expressed, p. 275.
to marriage, p. 263.
when it should be express, pp. 271, 273.
when weeping may be construed to imply, p. 272.
when it need not be express, p. 275.

CONTINGENCY—
marriage must not depend on, p. 275.

CUSTODY OF CHILDREN—
belongs primarily to the mother, p. 223.
hizanat, how lost, pp. 229, 230.
mother's custody of a female child who is married, p. 236.
mother's custody of illegitimate children, p. 238.
of a foundling, p. 238.
no *ghair mahram* entitled to the custody of a female child, p. 227.
persons entitled to custody, pp. 226—228.
qualifications necessary for the *hazina*, p. 222.
removal of the child by the *hazina*, p. 233.
right to, how lost, p. 229.
the custody of a daughter, pp. 223, 225.
Hanafi doctrines, p. 223.
Maliki rule, p. 224.
the custody of a male child, Hanafi rules, pp. 224, 225, 227.
Hanafi rule, pp. 224, 227.
Shaf'ei doctrines, pp. 224, 227.
Shiah doctrines, pp. 225, 229.
the right of non-Moslem mother, pp. 228, 238.

CUSTOM—
ancient Arab, p. 42.
as to bride's paraphernalia, p. 431.
dehors the Mahommedan Law not recognised, p. 23.
immoral, p. 28.

DAR—
its meaning, p. 135.
ul-Aman, p. 135.
ul-Harb, pp 135, 348.
ul-ilm, p. 339.
ul-Islam, pp. 135, 345.

DAUGHTER—
children of, *Zav-il-Arham*, or distant kindred of the first-class, p. 53.
custody of a, p. 225.
examples of succession of daughters, p. 75.
excludes brothers and sisters of the deceased, pp. 95, 103.
her share, p. 99.
her descendant, prohibited in marriage, p. 248.
is made a residuary by a son, and takes half his share, p. 47.
Maliki and Shaf'ei Law, p. 92.
Shiah Law, included with their children in the first-class of heirs, p. 95
Sunni Law, her share, p. 47.
with son's son and son's daughter, pp. 47, 72.
with widow, mother and sister, pp. 71, 72.

DEATH-ILLNESS—
Khula in, p. 470.
marriage contracted in, p. 321
Talak in, p. 453.

DEBTS—
different kinds of, p. 35.
must be paid after funeral expenses, p. 35.

DECEPTION—See *Ghurur*.

DENIER—See *Kufr*.

DEVOLUTION—
of the right of inheritance, p. 36,

DISAVOWAL—

period for, p. 177.
among the Sunnis, pp. 178, 179.
among the Shiahs, p. 178.

DISPOSITION—

no limitation in power of, p. 20.
testamentary, p. 20.

DISSOLUTION—

of the marriage-contract—See *Talak*, *Khula*.

DISTANT KINDRED—

Imam Abu Yusuf's rule as to succession of, pp. 56—60.
Imam Mohammed's rule as to succession of pp. 55—58.
in the succession of, consideration paid to blood, p. 60.
Maliki Law, p. 91.
the right of, p. 53.
the four classes of Hanafi Law, pp. 53—56.

DIVORCE—

See *Talak*.

DOMICILE—

animus revertendi, p. 135.
capacity to contract marriage depends on the law of, p. 244
conjugal, p. 380.
effect of a change of, p. 158.
law of, p. 136.
lex loci rei situs, p. 137.
lex loci contractus, p. 139.
status depends on, p. 136.
stipulations regarding, p. 382.

DOUBLE INHERITANCE—See "*Vested Interest*".

DOWER—

amount of, pp. 392—395.
customary and specified, pp. 394, 395.
customary, p. 395.
dispute about, p. 425.
exchange of, for something else, p. 422.
fictitious or reputed, *as-sumaat*, pp. 426—428.
gift of, p. 407.
in what cases woman not entitled to, p. 428.
Islamic legislation relating to, pp. 380, 395.
marriage valid though—not settled, p. 397.
may be increased after marriage, p. 423.
moiety of, when wife entitled to, p. 403.
presents in lieu of, when made, pp. 404, 405.
prompt and deferred, pp. 399—410.
stipulation of service invalid, p. 398.
Shiah doctrines, pp. 399, 400.
Hanafi doctrines, p. 400.
in the case of invalid marriage, p. 405.
prompt, when realisable, p. 405.
lien of the widow, for, p. 408.
limitation against a claim for, p. 415.
wife may refuse to take up her abode in the conjugal domicile to enforce payment of the deferred, p. 416.
difference of opinion, discussed, pp. 416—421.
transfer by the husband to the wife for, p. 422.
verbal contract for, p. 424.
when vests on wife, p. 405.

EMANCIPATOR—
difference between Malikis, Shiahs and Hanafis, pp. 64, 65.
right of succession of, p. 64.

ENGLISH WOMAN—
marrying a Moslem, pp. 138, 139.

EQUALITY—
conditions of (Hanafi Law), pp. 326, 330.
when insisted upon, pp. 326, 327.
requisites of, p. 328.
right of veto possessed by the *wali* of an adult woman who marries herself to a man between whom and herself there is no, p. 330.
when the right of veto ceases, p. 331.
Kazi's power, p. 331.
Maliki and Shiah Law, p. 329.
in marriage, p. 326.

ESCHEATE—
no, under the Mahommedan Law, pp. 7, 132
See *Bait-ul-Mal*.

EXCLUSION FROM INHERITANCE—
examples of, pp. 80, 81.
partial and absolute, pp. 80, 81.
persons not liable to, p. 30.
total disqualification, p. 81.
under Shiah Law, absolute, pp. 81, 114, 117.
relative, p. 117.

EXCLUSION OF FEMALES BY CUSTOM—
effect on the rights of other heirs, p. 52.

FAMILY ARRANGEMENTS—
recognised in the Mahommedan Law, p. 22.

FARR—
person *in extremis* divorcing wife, pp. 453, 454, 470.

FATHER—
Maliki and Shaf'ei Law, p. 211.
Hanafi Law, p. 211.
right to guardianship (Hanafi doctrine), pp. 497, 498.
Shiah doctrines, p. 211.
the right of, p. 46.
among Hanafis, p. 46.
among Malikis, pp. 91, 92.
the right of the, among Shiahs, p. 98.
to establish *nasab*, pp. 169, 170.
to impose the status of marriage, pp. 209, 210.
to the custody of a child, pp. 220, 221, 224.

FEMALES—
rights of, p. 13.

FOSTERAGE—
disabilities springing from, p. 249.

FOUNDLINGS—
custody of, found near mosque, p. 240.
may be taken to places not prejudicial, p. 240.
religious obligation of supporting, p. 238.
the right to their custody, pp. 238, 239.
their support from the State, p. 238.
two persons claiming, preference to a Moslem, p. 239.

FRAUD—
may be a case for invalidating a marriage, pp. 321, 349.
Shiah doctrines, pp. 321, 349.
repudiation obtained by compulsion or, Maliki and Shiah doctrines, pp. 442, 443.
Sunni doctrines, pp. 321, 349.

FUNERAL—
expenses form first charge on the estate of a deceased, p. 35.

GESTATION—
period of, p. 170.
Hanafi doctrines, p. 170.
Maliki, Shaf'ei and Hanbali doctrines, p. 170.
Shiah rule, p. 171.
the origin of the Maliki rule, p. 170.
presumption of legitimacy founded on, pp. 169, 172.

GHURUR OR DECEPTION—
its meaning and effect, p. 183.
marriage under a *bona fide* mistake of fact, p. 183.
Shiah doctrines, p. 185.

GRANDFATHER—
distinction between true and false, p. 46.
rights of, under Shiah Law, pp. 46, 94.
right of guardianship, p. 488.
stands in the position of the father, when no father, p. 46.

GRANDMOTHER—
distinction between true and false, p. 46.
under Shiah Law, pp. 46, 94.

GUARDIANSHIP—
extent of the powers of guardians, pp. 501, 502.
for marriage, pp. 209, 222.
its object and scope under the Mahommedan Law, p. 496.
mother's, p. 500.
three classes of guardians, pp. 497, 498.
the father's right to, p. 498.
of the person, p. 497.
of property, p. 497.

HAJAB—See EXCLUSION.

HANAFIS—
capacity of witnesses to marriage among, p. 277.
conditions of marriage among, p. 277.
doctrine of acknowledgment among, p. 195.
equality in marriage among, p. 326.
Khilwat-us-Sahih (valid retirement) among, p. 289.
Khula among the, p. 472.
law relating to illegal and invalid marriages among, p. 303 *et seq.*
law of succession among, p. 44.
law relating to legitimacy among, p. 169 *et seq.*
legal disabilities to marriage among, p. 247.
maintenance of wife among, p. 370 *et seq.*
of children, pp. 385, 388.
of parents among, p. 388.
marriage how contracted among, p. 259.
option of puberty among, p. 332.
origin of, p. 11.
rights of a guardian among, p. 264.
Talak among the, pp. 439—440.
the custody of children among, p. 223 *et seq.*
the *patria potestas* among, pp. 214, 223.

HANBALIS—
origin of, p. 12.
doctrine about missing persons, p. 87.
about right of wife to maintenance, p. 372.
in force among Hanafis, pp. 372—374.

HEIRS—
classification of Hanafi Law, p. 44.
classification of, Shiah Law, p. 94.
general rule for distinguishing, pp. 29, 30.
See EXCLUSION.

HIZANAT—See CUSTODY OF CHILDREN.

HOMICIDE—
excludes from inheritance (Hanafi Law), p. 84.
Maliki Law, p. 85.
under Shiah Law, must be intentional, p. 116.

HUSBAND—
apostacy of, pp. 348, 349, 350.
its effect upon marriage, pp. 348, 349, 350.
impotency of, p. 488.
insanity of, p. 492.
liability of, p. 372.
for maintenance, pp. 372, 373, 374.
for dower, pp. 394, 395.
right of, to dissolve marriage, p. 431.
rights of, p. 66.
Hanafi Law, p. 66.
Shiah Law, p. 111.

IDDAT—
in an invalid marriage, p. 459.
in cases of *Talak*, p. 459.
of a free woman, p. 459.
of a pregnant woman, p. 460.
after *Talak*, p 459.
of death and *Talak*, p. 460.
why prescribed, pp. 70, 462.
widow's period of, pp. 70, 459.

IJMA'A-UL-UMMAT—
Its meaning, pp. 6, 7.

ILLEGITIMACY—
bar to succession, under the Shiah Law, p. 117.

IMAMATE——
disputes about the, p. 3.

IMAMIAS— p. 8.

IMPOTENCY—
ground for the cancellation of a marriage, p. 488.
Sunni doctrines, p. 489.
Shiah doctrines, p. 489.

INCREASE—See *Aul.*

INFANCY—
the status of, p. 493.
two distinct periods of, *Ibid.*
rules relating to personal emancipation, *Ibid.*

INFIDELITY—See *Kufr.*

INSANITY—

a ground for cancellation of marriage, p. 492.

ISLAM—

adoption of, by either of the married parties, p. 346.
its meaning, p. 82.
marriage between persons one of whom is a follower of, pp. 251, 252.

ISMAILIAS—

divided into two branches in India, p. 9.
their origin, p. 9.

ISNA 'ISHARIAS—p. 7.

JABR (*guardianship for marriage*)—

right of judge, pp. 212, 218.
right of, among the ancient Arabs, p. 209.
the Jews, p. 209.
emancipation from, p. 213.
executor has none, p. 218.
ends with puberty, p. 210.
Maliki and Shaf'ei doctrines, p. 211.
of insane persons, p. 218.
Hanafi doctrines, pp. 211, 215, 216, 217.
Shiah doctrines, pp. 211, 217, 320.
incompetency of father to exercise the right, pp. 215, 216.

JAHAZ—pp. 430, 492.

JOINTNESS—

no presumption of, among Mahommedans, p. 25.

KHILWAT-US-SAHIH (Valid Retirement)—p. 288.

conditions necessary to make, *real retirement*, Hanafi Law, p. 289.
Hanafi and Maliki doctrines, p. 289.
legal consequences resulting from, p. 290,
Shiah and Shaf'ei doctrines, p. 291.

KHOJAHS—

rules of succession among, p. 123.
subject to Hindu customs, pp. 123—124.

KHULA—

by a woman *in extremis*, p. 470.
capacity for, p. 467.
entered into, on behalf of a minor wife, pp. 469, 470.
extorted by coercion, p. 470.
for what consideration may be entered into, pp. 472—477.
its meaning and effect, p. 466.
Maliki rules, p. 468.
Shaf'ei and Hanafi doctrines, p. 469.
Shiah doctrines, p. 468.
when indemnity for, unlawful, p. 473.
when husband *in extremis*, p. 470.
who can consent to a, on behalf of a minor wife, p. 469.

KHYAR-UL-BULUGH—*See* OPTION OF PUBERTY.

KIYAS—
its signification, p. 6.

KUFR—
excludes from inheritance, pp. 82, 114.
its meaning, p. 82.

L'AAN—
its meaning, pp. 174, 484.
legal consequences resulting from the proceeding of, p. 487.
procedure of, p. 485.
Hanafi doctrine, p. 486.
Shaf'ei and Maliki doctrines, pp. 485, 486.
Shiah rule, pp. 484, 486.

LEGITIMACY—
acknowledgment of, p. 172.
children of temporary unions, Shiah doctrines, p. 358.
of the issue of invalid unions, p. 169, *et seq.*
presumption of, p. 172.
Shiah doctrines, p. 172.
status of (Sunni Law), p. 171.

MAFKUD-UL-KHABAR—
among Hanafis, p. 88.
among Malikis, pp. 87, 89.
declaration of the Kazi, p. 87.
Fatwa according to Malik, p. 87.
meaning of, pp. 86, 89.
presumption of death, p. 87.
Shiah doctrines about, p. 120.
the *Mafkud's* agent, p. 86.

MAINTENANCE—
Hanafi doctrines, pp. 365, 367.
of a minor wife, p. 365.
of children, p. 385.
of male children, p. 386.
of female children, p. 386.
of parents, pp. 387, 388.
of the wife, p. 360.
right of wife to, in case of desertion, p. 365.
right to when husband missing, p. 376.
when the woman abandons conjugal domicile, p. 377.
right of a divorced woman to, p. 378.
rules relating to, pp. 360, 361.
Shaf'ei and Hanbali doctrines, p. 368.
Shaf'ei rule adopted by the Hanafis, pp. 372, 373, 374.
Shiah rule, pp. 364, 365.
the Prophet's rules, p. 384.
when husband minor and wife adult, pp. 360. 365, 366.

MAJORITY—*See* INFANCY.

MALIKIS—
consent to marriage among, p. 264.
custody of children among, p. 224.
equality in marriage among, p. 328.
khula among, p. 468.
law of succession among, p. 89.
origin of, p. 11.
patria potestas among, p. 216.
talak among, p. 443.

MARRIAGE—

abjuration of Islam by a Moslem wife, pp. 349, 351.
absence of the *wali*, p. 267.
adoption of Islam by a married non-Moslem female, p. 346.
agency in, p. 283.
any expression conveying intention sufficient, p. 261.
as a civil institution, p. 241.
  capacity for, p. 244.
  legal disabilities, p. 247.
  prohibitions for consaguinity and affinity, pp. 248, 249.
  fosterage, p. 250.
  relative prohibitions, pp. 250, 251.
  intermarriages between Moslems and non-Moslems, pp. 139, 251.
  Sunni doctrines, p. 251.
  Usulis and M'utazalas, p. 252.
  Akhbari Shiahs, p. 252.
  marriage during pilgrimage, p. 255.
  marriage with a Hindoo woman, p. 252.
    with a non-Moslemah, p. 139.
    with a pregnant woman, pp. 253, 254, 318.
    Shaf'ei doctrines, p. 254.
    Shiah Law, pp. 254-255, 315, 317, 318, 319, 320, 321.
by a minor girl where there is no *wali* or Kazi, p. 266.
capacity of witnesses to, p. 279.
causes for which a, may be cancelled, Sunni doctrines, p. 340.
  Shiah Law, pp. 341, 342, 343.
conditional, invalid, p. 285.
conditions of, p. 283.
conditions of equality in, pp. 326, 330.
conditions opposed to public morality, p. 287.
consent to, obtained by fraud or force, pp. 321—322.
consent to, pp. 263—264.
contemporaneous, with two sisters, pp. 305, 309, 310.
contracted by different *walis* to different persons, p. 266.
contracted by two *walis* standing in the same degree of equality, p. 266.
contracted in a state of intoxication or *in extremis*, p. 321.
contracted in error (*shubh*), pp. 297, 298, 300.
dissolution of, p. 431.
  a marriage contracted by a woman *bona fide* after observance of '*iddat*, p. 459.
  by decree of Judge, p. 477.
  for what causes it may be granted, p. 477 *et seq.*
    desertion, p. 478.
    neglect, p. 479.
    ill-treatment, p. 479.
    impotency, p. 488.
    insanity, p. 492.
    failure to carry out anti-nuptial stipulations, pp. 481, 482.
distinction between an illegal and an invalid, p. 293 *et seq.*
effect of apostasy on the status of, pp. 348, 349.
equality in, p. 326.
examples of invalid, pp. 304, 313.
express consent when required, pp. 271, 273.
form of, p. 255.
girl married to two persons, first valid, p. 316.
Hanafi doctrines, p. 304.
Hanafi Law, right of veto on the Part of, *wali*, p. 330.
how celebrated, p. 258.
how contracted, Hanafi Law, p. 259.
if contracted in a foreign country according to foreign forms valid, p. 137.
in a state of *ihram*, p. 255.
legal effects of, p. 292.
limitations on father's powers to give minor child in, p. 324.
Maliki and Shiah doctrines, p. 329.

MARRIAGE—(*concld.*)
may be contracted by signs in the case of the dumb, p. 262.
number of witnesses, p. 282.
object, of, pp. 241, 242.
of a minor by a *wali* in a distant country, pp. 267, 268.
of a Moslemah with a non-Moslem, pp. 314.
ordained for the protection of society, p. 241.
period of probation in an invalid, p. 313.
presence of witnesses, Sunni Law, p. 255.
principles of the Shiah Law relating to, p. 354.
prohibited degrees, p. 355.
affinity, p. 355.
condition relating to temporary, under the Akhbari system, pp. 358—359.
gift of the term, p. 361.
difference between the jurists, p. 361 *et seq.*
words used to contract, pp. 260, 263.
proof of, p. 291.
proposal of, in writing, p. 276.
re-marriage with a woman separated by *l'aan*, p. 255.
re-marriage with a divorcee, p. 319.
Shiah doctrines, p. 256.
status of, p. 241.
temporary, pp. 284, 285, 358.
testimony to, p. 276.
to different persons by different *walis*, p. 266.
under Mussulman Law, pp. 137, 241 *et seq.*
Urfi and Sharai, p. 258.

MEMON—*See* KHOJAHS.

MENTAL DERANGEMENT—*See* INSANITY.

MINORS—
contracted in marriage by their guardians, pp. 74, 263, 265, 266, 325, 333 *et seq.*

MISREPRESENTATION—*See* FRAUD.

MISSING PERSON—See *Mafkud-ul-Khabar.*

MOAJJAL—See PROMPT DOWER.

MONOGAMY—
in Islam, pp. 144, 149, 150.

MOTHER—
her share with paternal half grand-uncles, p. 74.
her right to the custody of child, p. 223.
of guardianship, p. 500.

MOWAJJAL—See DEFERRED DOWER.

MUBARAT—
Difference between Sunnis and Shiahs, pp. 467, 468.
its meaning, p. 467.

MURTEDD—See APOSTATES.

MUSTAMIN—pp. 136, 347.

M'UTAZALAS—
marriage with a non-Moslemah among the, p. 252.
monogamy among the, p. 144.
origin of the, p. 8.
Talak among the, p. 432.

NASAB—See LEGITIMACY.

OPTION—
difference between the schools, p. 340.
of emancipation, p. 334.
of puberty, its meaning, pp. 334—336.
when it should be exercised—its legal effect, p. 337 *et seq*.

PARENTAGE—*See* LEGITIMACY.

PARTITION—
before payment of debts does not invalidate division of property, p. 35.

PATERNITY—*See* LEGITIMACY.

PATRIA POTESTAS—See *Wilayet-ul-Ijbar*.

PERSONS DYING TOGETHER IN A COMMON CLAMITY—
rule of succession, p. 71.

POLYGAMY—
not recognised among the M'utazalas, pp. 144, 149.
practically prohibited, pp. 149, 150.

PRIMOGENITURE—
rule of, partially recognised among the Ismailias and Shiahs, p. 103.

PROOF—*See* TESTIMONY.

PUBERTY—pp. 245, 246, 493.

RADD—
doctrine of, p. 66.

RAJ'AI—See *Talak*.

RAJ'AT IN *TALAK*—*See* REVOCATION.

REFUSAL OF CONJUGAL RIGHTS—
case-law, pp. 419—421.
doctrine of Abu Hanifa, p. 417.
when wife entitled to refuse, p. 416.

REGULATION—
VIII of 1827 (Bom.) p. 42.

RELIGION—
difference of, pp. 82—83.

RENUNCIATION—
of a vested right of inheritance, p. 31.
of an expectancy, p. 31.

REPRESENTATION—
principle of, not generally recognised among Mahommedans, p. 30.

REPUDIATION—See *Talak*.

RESIDUARIES—See *'Asabah*.

RETIREMENT—See *Khilwat-us-Sahih*.

RETURN—
doctrine of, p. 45.
to how many persons made, p. 45.
to the widow, Sunni rule, p. 45.
Shiah rule, p. 113.

REVOCATION—
how effected, p. 452.
its meaning, pp. 452, 456, 457.

SEMBLANCE OR ERROR—(*shubh*) in marriage,
three kinds of, p. 242.

SHAFE'IS—
Aul recognised among, p. 93.
origin of, p. 12.
patria potestas among the, p. 211.
rules of succession among the, p. 91.
rules relating to marriage with a pregnant woman among the, p. 253.
talak among the, p. 432.
the custody of children among the, p. 224.

SHARERS—See *Zav-il-Furuz*.

SHIAHS—
doctrine of acknowledgment among the, p. 202 *et seq*.
origin of, p. 9.
Status of legitimacy among the, p. 185 *et seq*.
subsections of, p. 7.
the law of succession among the, p. 93.
the custody of children among the, pp. 225, 229.
the law of marriage among the, p. 354 *et seq*.
of *Talak* among the, p. 438 *et seq*.

SISTER—pp. 46, 48, 51, 91, 101.

STEP-MOTHER—
has no right of inheritance, p. 74.

SLAVERY—
bar to succession, Sunni rule, p. 85.
Shiah rule, p. 117.

SUCCESSION—
ancient Arab customs, p. 42.
classification of heirs, p. 44.
of a woman divorced *in extremis*, pp. 74, 462 *et seq*.
different classes of heirs who take by, Shiah Law, p. 95.
distinction between Shiahs and Sunnis, p. 10.
Hanafi Law of, p. 44.
Jewish rules, p. 43.
law of, among the Shiahs, p. 93.
no right of, in *Mutaa* marriage unless specially agreed, p. 111.
of relations by consanguinity, Shiah Law, p. 98.
reforms of Mohammed, p. 43.
right of (consanguinous relations), p. 100.
of heirs of the first-class, p. 101.
second-class, p. 106.
third-class, p. 109.
rules relating to the, of husbands and wives, p. 111.
Shaf'ei and Maliki rules of, p. 89.
two causes giving right of, Shiah Law, p 93.

SUIT—
for restitution of conjugal rights, p. 383.
for jactitation of marriage, p. 384.

SUNNIS—
difference in form of prayer with the Shiahs, p. 20.
origin of, p. 5.

TADLIS—*See* FRAUD.

TAFWIZ IN DOWER—p. 402.
or delegation of power to the wife to *talak* herself, pp. 448, 455.

TALAK—
archaic rules, p. 431.
capacity for, p. 438.
compulsion in, pp. 438, 439, 440, 441, 442.
by a drunken man, pp. 440, 441.
by an insane person, p. 492.
in writing, p. 444.
expressions by which a, may be effectuated, p. 448.
in the absence of the wife, p. 448
by a man in *extremis*, pp. 453, 462, 463 *et seq*.
against a minor wife, p. 454.
delegation of the power of, p. 455.
different forms of delegation, pp. 455, 456, 457.
difference between the Sunnis and Shiahs, p. 437.
Mohammad's legislation, p. 432.
period of probation after, p. 459.
pre-Islamic customs, p. 431.
re-marriage after, p. 458.
retraction of, p. 457.
the M'utazala doctrine, p. 432.
the Hanafi doctrines, p. 433.
the *Talak-us-Sunnat*, p. 435.
the *Talak-ul-Bida't*, p. 435.

TEMPORARY MARRIAGES—
Akhbari doctrines, pp. 286, 358.
conditions in, pp. 359, 360.

TESTAMENTARY POWERS—
limitations on, p. 20.

TESTIMONY—
to marriage, p. 276.

USULIS—
a section of the Shiahs, p. 8.

UTERINE RELATIONS—See *Zav-il-Arham*.

VESTED INTERESTS—
its meaning, p. 68.
mode of division, pp. 68, 69.

WALA—
among the Hanafis, p. 63.
among the Shiahs, p. 96.
different kinds of, p. 64.
inheritance by, among the Shiahs, p. 95.
'l-Imam, pp. 95, 96.
meaning of, p 63.
ul-itk, pp. 63, 95.
ul-Mawalat, p. 64.
'z-zamin-ul-jarirah, pp. 95, 96.

WALAD-UL-MULA'INAH—
inherits from the mother among the Sunnis and Shiahs, pp. 50. 85, 117, 118

WALAD-UZ-ZINA—
definition of, p. 296.
inherits from the mother among the Sunnis, pp. 84-85.
not among Shiahs, pp. 85, 117.

WALI—pp. 258, 266 *et seq*, 330, 331.

WIDOW—
right of succession, under Sunni Law, pp. 47, 66.
Shiah Law, pp. 111, 112.
the *'iddat* of, pp. 458, 459.

WILAYET-UL-IJBAR—
absence of the nearer guardian, pp. 214, 228.
divergence among the schools, p. 210.
ends with puberty, p. 210.
Hanafi doctrines, pp. 214, 215.
its meaning and extent under the Mahommedan Law, p. 210.
near and remote guardians, pp. 214, 215.
Shiah doctrines, pp. 216, 221.
the powers of the Judge, p. 216.

WOMAN—
position of, among ancient Arabs, p. 42.
position of, pp. 14, 15.

ZAV-IL-ARHAM—
consideration paid to blood, p. 60.
rules of succession of, pp. 45, 54.

ZAV-IL-FURUZ—
their number, p. 45.

ZIMMI—
guardian of a Mahommedan, p. 499.

ZINA—
Shiah rules, p. 356.
Sunni rules, pp. 242, 295.